Contemporary Chinese Politics

CONTEMPORARY
CHINESE POLITICS:
AN INTRODUCTION

Second Edition

JAMES C.F. WANG

University of Hawaii at Hilo

Prentice-Hall, Inc., Englewood Cliffs, New Jersey 07632

Library of Congress Cataloging in Publication Data

WANG, JAMES C. F.
    Contemporary Chinese politics.

    Includes bibliographies and index.
    1. China—Politics and government—1976–
I. Title.
DS779.26.W365 1985   951.05   84–11779
ISBN   0–13–169996–2

Editorial/production supervision and
    interior design: Dee Josephson
Cover design: 20/20 Services, Inc.
Manufacturing buyer: Ron Chapman

© 1985, 1980 by Prentice-Hall, Inc., Englewood Cliffs, New Jersey 07632

Printed in the United States of America

10 9 8 7 6 5 4 3 2 1

ISBN 0-13-169996-2   01

Prentice-Hall International, Inc., *London*
Prentice-Hall of Australia Pty. Limited, *Sydney*
Editora Prentice-Hall do Brasil, Ltda., *Rio de Janeiro*
Prentice-Hall Canada Inc., *Toronto*
Prentice-Hall of India Private Limited, *New Delhi*
Prentice-Hall of Japan, Inc., *Tokyo*
Prentice-Hall of Southeast Asia Pte. Ltd., *Singapore*
Whitehall Books Limited, *Wellington, New Zealand*

To
Sally, my wife,
and children Sarah and Eric,
for their tolerance,
patience, and assistance

CONTENTS

PREFACE

This is the first revision of *Contemporary Chinese Politics,* published in 1980. The second edition adheres closely to the approach and organization of the first edition. I prefaced the first edition with the remark that it is necessary in an introductory textbook on Chinese contemporary politics to provide basic facts about China's fluid political institutions and processes so that undergraduates may understand fully the ever-changing Chinese political scene. In the short span of three years since the first edition was published, political events have moved forward at a rapid pace. During this period Hua Guofeng has lost power, and a collective leadership with Deng Xiaoping as its paramount leader has taken control. With changes in leadership have come new policies and interpretations. Thus, the textbook required updating. The reader will find new material and analysis in every chapter in the book.

Since considerable stress has been placed by the Chinese on modernization of agriculture, industry, science and technology, and national defense, Chapters 8 and 9 have been rearranged in order to provide a more meaningful presentation of current economic policies and analyses by the Chinese themselves as well as by Western observers. New material has been added in these two chapters on the mixture of market economy and centralized planning, the responsibility (profit) system in agriculture and industry, the system of private enterprise without capitalism, the state of education at all levels, the role of science and technology, the youth problem, and the treatment of intellectuals. In Chapter 1 I have added new material on the trial of the radicals; the reasons for Hua Guofeng's rise and fall from power; and the collective leadership of Deng Xiaoping, Hu Yaobang, and Zhao Ziyang. Also added to Chapter 1 is an analysis of the Chinese assessment of the turbulent Cultural Revolution. Chapter 2 discusses in detail the reevaluation of Mao and his role in history by the party under Deng's control. Additions in Chapter 3 focus on organizational changes in the Chinese Communist Party brought on by the 1982 party charter, and the problem of party discipline. Changes in Chapter 4 center on the 1982 state constitution (the fourth since 1954), the structure of the central government, the criminal and civil codes and procedures, and the problem of cadre corruption and competence.

The problem of Tibet has been included in Chapter 5 to illustrate China's changing policy toward ethnic national minorities. New material in Chapter 6 centers on the military reform measures introduced by Deng and the continued problem of dissent within the military as regards the reforms. The section on military modernization has been updated to include the latest facts and analyses. The reader will find in Chapter 7 a fuller discussion of the 1978–79 "Democracy Wall" movement and its tragic end. In the last chapter, new material includes discussions of current Sino-Soviet negotiations for rapprochement, the strategic importance of the Soviet invasion of Afghanistan on the Sino-Soviet border dispute, the sweet and sour state of Sino-American relations and the troublesome arms sale to Taiwan, and a reexamination of the "strategic consideration" in United States-China relations.

The second edition contains the same features found in the first edition. The source material cited in the notes to each chapter contains rich and up-to-date references, so that the reader can explore specific topics in depth. Charts, tables, and maps have been updated and are included to provide illustration and detail. The appendixes contain the texts of some significant recent documents, for easy reference. A guide to romanization of the Chinese pinyin system used in the text, with notation of the old Wade-Gile system, has been preserved as a unique teaching aid.

The preparation of this revision would not have been possible without the help of a number of persons. Many colleagues have made useful comments and suggestions. To all of them I owe a debt of gratitude. I owe particularly profound gratitude to Professor Andrew Nathan, East Asian Institute, Columbia University, for his valuable comments and suggestions in the text. Once again, I must acknowledge my great indebtedness to China scholars and observers whose works are cited in this edition. I especially want to thank my colleague and close friend Professor Louis P. Warsh, at this university, for his painstaking reading of both the first edition and this revision for style and editorial corrections; and my wife Sally, for her editorial assistance and critique. I am also grateful to the University of Hawaii at Hilo for reducing my teaching load during the spring semester of 1983 so that I might work on the revision. Lastly, Stan Wakefield, editor of political science at Prentice-Hall, has been instrumental in the development of this project. Without his leadership, this book would not have been possible. I would also like to express my thanks to the reviewers of the second edition: Parris H. Chang, Pennsylvania State University; John Moon, University of Texas; Andrew J. Nathan, Columbia University. Joe Murray has also given both support and encouragement since the project's inception. My appreciation is also extended to Dee A. Josephson of Prentice-Hall for her skillful and methodical editing of the final draft. Of course, any errors, omissions, or misinterpretations in this book are solely my responsibility.

JAMES C. F. WANG
University of Hawaii at Hilo

Romanization of Chinese Names of Persons and Places*

CHINESE PHONETIC ALPHABET, OR THE PINYIN SYSTEM

How to Pronounce

Following is a Chinese phonetic alphabet table showing alphabet pronunciation, with approximate English equivalents. Spelling in the Wade system is in parentheses for reference.

"a"   (a), a vowel, as in *far*

"b"   (p), a consonant, as in *be*

"c"   (ts), a consonant, as "ts" in *its;* and

"ch" (ch), a consonant, as "ch" in *church,* strongly aspirated

"d"   (t), a consonant, as in *do*

"e"   (e), a vowel, as "er" in *her,* the "r" being silent; but "ie," a diphthong, as in *yes* and "ei," a diphthong, as in *way*

"f"   (f), a consonant, as in *foot*

"g"   (k), a consonant, as in *go*

"h"   (h), a consonant, as in *her,* strongly aspirated

"i"   (i), a vowel, two pronunciations:

*Based on official version published in *Beijing Review,* 1 (January 5, 1979), 18–20. A specific rule requires that the traditional spelling of historical places and persons such as Confucius and Sun Yat-sen need not be changed.

           1) as in *eat*

           2) as in *sir* in syllables beginning with the consonants *c, ch, r, s, sh, z,* and *zh*

"j"   (ch), a consonant, as in *jeep*

"k" (k), a consonant, as in *kind,* strongly aspirated

"l"   (l), a consonant, as in *land*

"m" (m), a consonant, as in *me*

"n" (n), a consonant, as in *no*

"o" (o), a vowel, as "aw" in *law*

"p" (p), a consonant, as in *par,* strongly aspirated

"q" (ch), a consonant, as "ch" in *cheek*

"r"   (j), a consonant, pronounced as "r" but not rolled, or like "z" in *azure*

"s"   (s, ss, sz), a consonant, as in *sister;* and

"sh" (sh), a consonant, as "sh" in *shore*

"t"   (t), a consonant, as in *top,* strongly aspirated

"u" (u), a vowel, as in *too,* also as in the French "u" in *tu* or the German umlauted "ü" in *Müenchen*

"v" (v), is used only to produce foreign and national minority words, and local dialects

"w" (w), used as a semivowel in syllables beginning with "u" when not preceded by consonants, pronounced as in *want*

"x" (hs), a consonant, as "sh" in *she*

"y" used as a semivowel in syllables beginning with "i" or "u" when not preceded by consonants, pronounced as in *yet*

"z" (ts, tz), a consonant, as in *zero;* and

"zh" (ch), a consonant, as "j" in "*jump*"

Spelling of Chinese Names of Persons

In accordance with the Chinese phonetic alphabet, the late Chairman Mao Tsetung's name will be spelled "Mao Zedong"; the late Premier Chou En-lai's name will be "Zhou Enlai"; and the late Chairman of the Standing Committee of the National People's Congress, Chu Teh, will be "Zhu De."

Following are names of party leaders of China, romanized according to the Chinese phonetic alphabet. The old spelling is in parentheses for reference.

Chairman of the Central Committee of the Chinese Communist Party:
    Hua Guofeng (Hua Kuo-feng)

Vice-Chairmen of the Party Central Committee:
    Ye Jianying (Yeh Chien-ying)
    Deng Xiaoping (Teng Hsiao-ping)
    Li Xiannian (Li Hsien-nien)
    Chen Yun (Chen Yun)
    Wang Dongxing (Wang Tung-hsing)

Members of the Political Bureau of the Party Central Committee:
    Hua Guofeng (Hua Kuo-feng)

(The following are listed in the order of the number of strokes in their sur-
names.)

Wang Zhen (Wang Chen)
Wei Guoqing (Wei Kuo-ching)
Ulanhu (Ulanfu)
Fang Yi (Fang Yi)
Deng Xiaoping (Teng Hsiao-ping)
Deng Yingchao (Teng Ying-chao)
Ye Jianying (Yeh Chien-ying)
Liu Bocheng (Liu Po-cheng)
Xu Shiyou (Hsu Shih-yu)
Ji Dengkui (Chi Teng-kuei)
Su Zhenhua (Su Chen-hua)
Li Xiannian (Li Hsien-nien)
Li Desheng (Li Teh-sheng)
Wu De (Wu Teh)
Yu Qiuli (Yu Chiu-li)
Wang Dongxing (Wang Tung-hsing)
Zhang Tingfa (Chang Ting-fa)
Chen Yun (Chen Yun)
Chen Yonggui (Chen Yung-Kuei)
Chen Xilian (Chen Hsi-lien)
Hu Yaobang (Hu Yao-pang)
Geng Biao (Keng Piao)
Nie Rongzhen (Nieh Jung-chen)
Ni Zhifu (Ni Chih-fu)
Xu Xianqian (Hsu Hsiang-chien)
Peng Chong (Pen Chung)

(The following are listed in the order of the number of strokes in their sur-
names.)

Alternate Members of the Political Bureau of the Party Central Committee:
Chen Muhua (Chen Mu-hua)
Zhao Ziyang (Chao Tsu-yang)
Seypidin (Saifudin)

Spelling of Chinese Place Names

Names of well-known places in China are listed as follows. The old spelling is in parentheses for reference.

Municipalities directly under the central authorities:
Beijing (Peking)
Shanghai (Shanghai)
Tianjin (Tientsin)

Provinces, autonomous regions for minority nationalities, and some well-known cities and other places:

Anhui (Anhwei) Province
  Hefei (Hofei)
  Bengbu (Pengpu)
Fujian (Fukien) Province
  Fuzhou (Foochow)
  Xiamen (Amoy)
Gansu (Kansu) Province
  Lanzhou (Lanchow)
Guangdong (Kwangtung) Province
  Guangzhou (Kwangchow)
  Shantou (Swatow)
Guangxi Zhuang (Kwangsi Chuang) Autonomous Region
  Nanning (Nanning)
  Guilin (Kweilin)
Guizhou (Kweichow) Province
  Guiyang (Kweiyang)
  Zunyi (Tsunyi)
Hebei (Hopei) Province
  Shijiazhuang (Shihchiachuang)
  Tangshan (Tangshan)
Heilongjiang (Heilungkiang) Province
  Harbin (Harbin)
  Daquing Oilfield (Taching Oilfield)
  Qiqihar (Chichihar)
Henan (Honan) Province
  Zhengzhou (Chengchow)
  Luoyang (Loyang)
  Kaifeng (Kaifeng)
Hubei (Hupeh) Province
  Wuhan (Wuhan)
Hunan (Hunan) Province
  Changsha (Changsha)
Jiangsu (Kiangsu) Province
  Nanjing (Nanking)
  Suzhou (Soochow)
  Wuxi (Wuhsi)
Jiangxi (Kiangsi) Province
  Nanchang (Nanchang)
  Jiujiang (Chiuchiang)
Jilin (Kirin) Province
  Changchun (Changchun)
Liaoning (Liaoning) Province
  Shenyang (Shenyang)
  Anshan (Anshan)
  Luda (Luta)
Nei Monggol (Inner Mongolia) Autonomous Region
  Hohhot (Huhehot)
  Baotou (Paotou)

Ningxia Hui (Ningsia Hui) Autonomous Region
   Yinchuan (Yinchuan)
Qinghai (Chinghai) Province
   Xining (Sining)
Shaanxi (Shensi) Province
   Xian (Sian)
   Yanan (Yenan)
Shandong (Shantung) Province
   Jinan (Tsinan)
   Qingdao (Tsingtao)
   Yantai (Yentai)
Shanxi (Shansi) Province
   Taiyuan (Taiyuan)
   Dazhai (Tachai)
Sichuan (Szechuan) Province
   Chengdu (Chengtu)
   Chongqing (Chungking)
Taiwan (Taiwan) Province
   Taibei (Taipei)
Xinjiang Uygur (Sinkiang Uighur) Autonomous Region
   Urumqi (Urumchi)
Xizang (Tibet) Autonomous Region
   Lhasa (Lhasa)
Yunnan (Yunnan) Province
   Kunming (Kunming)
   Dali (Tali)
Zhejiang (Chekiang) Province
   Hangzhou (Hangchow)

Abbreviations

APC	Agricultural Producers' Cooperatives
CCP	Chinese Communist Party
Comintern	Communist Third International
CPPCC	Chinese People's Political Consultative Conference
CYL	Communist Youth League
MAC	Military Affairs Committee
NCNA	New China News Agency
NPC	National People's Congress
PLA	People's Liberation Army

CONTEMPORARY
CHINESE POLITICS

Introduction: The Chinese Revolution in Historical Perspective

TRADITIONAL CHINESE
POLITICAL SYSTEM

To understand contemporary China, we must first look at some historical background and at the traditional political system that existed prior to the revolution of 1911. The traditional Chinese political system was based upon a predominantly agrarian society. It was administered by an officialdom of scholars and was controlled, theoretically, by an authoritarian emperor. Although the Chinese empire was centralized, there was a great deal of regional and local autonomy. In the following pages we will examine some of the major characteristics of the traditional Chinese political system: the emperor, Confucian ideology, the gentry-officialdom, and the nature of local autonomy.

The Emperor: Mandate
of Heaven and Dynastic Cycle

The Chinese emperor ruled with unlimited power over his subjects. His legitimacy and power to rule the vast empire derived from the belief that he was the "Son of Heaven" with a mandate to rule on earth. The mandate of heaven was legitimate as long as the emperor ruled in a righteous way and maintained harmony within the Chinese society and between the society and nature. A corollary to the mandate of heaven theory was the right to rebel if the emperor failed to maintain harmony. It was, therefore, an unwritten constitution providing for rebellion as a means of deposing an intolerable imperial ruler—but rebellion was legitimate only if it succeeded.

Rebellions in Chinese history fall into two general patterns: peasant uprisings with religious overtones, and military insurrections. The peasant uprisings, such as the Taiping Rebellion of 1850, while at times widespread, only once led directly to the founding of a new imperial dynasty. The Ming Dynasty, which succeeded that of the Mongols in the fourteenth century, was founded by a laborer.[1] Peasant unrest and rebellions did, however, contribute indirectly to new dynasties by further weakening declining reigns and providing evidence of the loss of the mandate of heaven. These new dynasties, with the exception of the Ming, were founded either through a takeover by a powerful Chinese military figure, who had exploited peasant discontent and obtained the support of the scholars, or by foreign invasion.

While dynastic changes were effected through rebellion or invasion, the form and substance of government remained essentially unchanged. Each new emperor accepted the Confucian ideology, claiming the mandate of heaven for himself by virtue of success. He governed the empire through an established bureaucratic machinery administered by career officials. Each ruler was dependent upon these officials to administer the vast, populous empire. Dynasties rose and fell, but officialdom remained intact. Each of the twenty-four historic dynasties followed a common pattern of development, the dynastic cycle. At the beginning of a new dynasty, a period of national unity under virtuous and benevolent rule flourished and usually was accompanied by intellectual excitement and ferment; then midway in the cycle, there emerged a period of mediocre rule, accompanied by signs of corruption and unrest. Finally, natural disasters occurred for which the ruler was unable to provide workable remedies, and a successful rebellion or invasion was mounted. A new dynasty was born, and the cycle repeated itself.[2]

Confucian Ideology

Confucianism, which permeated traditional Chinese society, was basically conservative and establishment-oriented. The central concepts stressed the need to achieve harmony in society through moral conduct in all relationships. The mandate of heaven implied explicit adherence to the Confucian theory of "government by goodness."[3] This code of proper behavior for the emperor and all government officials was prescribed in detail in the writings of Confucius and his disciples. Officials were recruited on the basis of competitive examinations designed to test mastery of the Confucian classics. It was assumed that once the Confucian ethic was mastered and internalized by the scholar-officials, a just and benevolent government would result. Since the government was administered by those who possessed the required ethics and code of conduct, there was really little need for either the promulgation of laws or the formal structuring of government institutions.

As the officially sanctioned political ideology, Confucianism conditioned and controlled the minds of the rulers and the ruled alike; it became the undisputed "orthodox doctrine of the imperial state."[4] It was perpetuated by the scholars as the basic foundation for the education of young men of means. Traditional Confucian ideology made its greatest impact on the wealthy elite. It left an "ideological vacuum" among the peasantry—the bulk of the population then, as now—who were more concerned with the burden of taxes and the hardship of life than with theories of government.[5] In later chapters we will discuss in detail how the Chinese Communist Party purposefully molded the minds of the Chinese people to conform to a different, but equally orthodox, political ideology. It is sufficient to note here the central role of political ideology in both imperial and communist Chinese systems.

The Gentry-Officialdom

Under the imperial system, the government officials—the mandarins—dominated the political and economic life of China. The mandarins were those individuals who held office by virtue of imperial degrees obtained by passing the civil service examinations. They came almost solely from a wealthy landholding class with resources to provide extended education for their sons. Because of the status and the power of the office, the mandarin officials were able to acquire fortunes in landholdings for themselves and their families. They constituted the small, privileged upper class of the Chinese agrarian society. Under the imperial civil service for the Manchu Dynasty—the last dynasty before the revolution of 1911—these officials were estimated to total not more than 40,000, or one one-hundredth of 1 percent of the population.[6] The officials of the imperial civil service wielded complete and arbitrary power over their subjects, the vast majority of whom were peasants living in the countryside. A typical magistrate for a Chinese county, according to one study, was responsible for the lives and well-being of about a quarter of a million subjects.[7] The magistrate, therefore, had to seek the cooperation and support of the large landholders to administer the county on behalf of the emperor and the central administration in Beijing. This administrative setup illustrates the gulf that existed between the educated elite and the illiterate peasants and indicates the hierarchical structure of Chinese imperial rule.

The Chinese bureaucracy was classified into ranks and grades, each with a special set of privileges and a compensation scale. A voluminous flow of official documents and memoranda moved up and down the hierarchical ladder. At each level of the hierarchy, a certain prescribed form and literary style had to be observed—a multiplication of bureaucratic jargon. To control the huge bureaucracy, the emperor designated special censors at the various levels of government to report on the conduct of public officials. The provincial governor or the top man in a branch of the central bureaucracy in Beijing could become a bottleneck in the policy initiation and implementation process. At the lowest level of administration—the Chinese county—all important decisions affecting the community were made by the elites with the blessing of the magistrate. These decisions often disregarded, or were contrary to, the wishes of the earthbound peasants, who constituted the majority. Arbitrary decision making, unresponsive to the uneducated masses in the villages, remains to this day a basic problem in the relationship between the leaders and the led in China. In traditional Chinese politics, as in modern China, the elites or officials exercised control over the mass of peasants.

Local Autonomy

While the Chinese imperial government was centralized at the court in Beijing and was hierarchical in structure, the system did permit some degree of autonomy at the local level, provided that this did not interfere with the absolute authority of the emperor. A magistrate for a county, the lowest administrative unit in traditional China, could not possibly carry out his duties without working with and through the "local power structure."[8] While this power structure was headed by the large landowners, it also included merchants, artisans, and other persons of wealth and power in the community. As a convenient administrative arrangement, these groups were permitted by the magistrate to manage their own affairs within their own established confines. The magistrate naturally reserved the right to intervene if he deemed it necessary. Under this pragmatic arrangement, spokesmen for special interest groups in the community, such as the clans, the merchants' guilds, and the secret societies, often articulated their views and positions before the magistrate by informal and unofficial means, but never by overt pressure. It was considered an unforgivable sin for officials to organize themselves into factions which advocated competing interests of groups in the community. But articulation of group interests often was carried out by officials within the bureaucratic framework.[9] Thus, there was keen competition and maneuvering by officials, within the bureaucratic setup, to gain favorable decisions on a particular matter. In all instances politics of this sort was conducted in secrecy and was influenced by the personal ties which competing officials might have with the local power structure, by their own rank within the bureaucratic hierarchy, and by their finesse in these maneuverings.

THE CHINESE REVOLUTION, 1911–37

Long before the Manchu Dynasty reached its lowest ebb, reform efforts were made to prevent further decay. Reformers basically sought remedial measures to abolish an inefficient and corrupt bureaucracy. They attempted to strengthen the imperial government's capability to meet unrest and rebellion in the countryside, the source of China's manpower, food supply, and government revenues. Unrest and rebellion were triggered by the demands of an increased population on the limited supplies the land could produce and by the perennial occurrence of drought, flood, and famine. Confidence in the Manchu Dynasty's ability to govern received a severe blow in 1842, when European governments forced open the closed doors of China with unequal treaties that provided for special territorial concessions to foreigners for trade and missionary activities. Reformers then sought to strengthen the old Chinese empire by making changes in such traditional institutions as the examination system and the military establishment. The optimism of the reformers was dashed when China received her greatest humiliation—defeat by Japan in 1895. This defeat convinced some that reform alone could not possibly save the empire, and it gave rise to the idea that a revolution might be necessary to overthrow the traditional imperial system.

Revolution of 1911

One leader who advocated revolutionary change was Dr. Sun Yatsen. In 1894 he founded a small secret society among overseas Chinese for the purpose of overthrowing the decaying Manchu dynasty. As a revolutionary with a price on his head, much of the time Sun was forced to operate and organize abroad. After many years of hard work in Southeast Asia, Japan, and Hawaii, Sun's movement took hold among educated young Chinese abroad. In 1905, 400 of Sun's followers gathered in Japan to form the first viable revolutionary movement, the Tung Meng Hui.[10] The members took a solemn oath to bring down the alien Manchu empire and to replace it with a Chinese republic. Ten different attempts were organized and financed by the group, headquartered variously in Tokyo and Hanoi, to strike down the vulnerable Manchu rule by assassinating imperial officials. As these revolutionary attempts failed, one by one, and more revolutionaries lost their lives, the movement became demoralized and ran low on funds. On October 10, 1911, an eleventh attempt was made. It resulted in a successful uprising by discontented and dissatisfied provincial officials, merchants, and imperial army commanders. The Manchu emperor abdicated, and shortly thereafter the Chinese imperial dynastic system was ended.

While Dr. Sun's revolutionary movement, comprised largely of students, youths, and overseas Chinese, gave impetus and momentum to the revolution, it was not the force which brought down the empire. It was the new imperial army, headed by Yuan Shihkai, that forced the abdication. Under an agreement with Dr. Sun, who had little bargaining power, Yuan Shihkai assumed the power of the government immediately after the abdication and stayed on to become the first president of the Chinese republic. The new republic floundered from the start. Very few Chinese had any real understanding of Western democracy. All the Chinese political traditions and institutions were designed for imperial rule and, therefore, were ill suited for constitutional democracy. Yuan Shihkai increasingly disregarded the constitution, and finally attempted to establish himself as emperor. The Chinese nation disintegrated as the new government proved incapable of commanding allegiance from the people in the midst of mounting domestic problems and the constant meddling in Chinese internal affairs by European powers and Japan. Yuan's death in 1916 marked the final collapse of the central government's effective authority.[11]

Warlordism and the Nationalist Revolution

The disintegration of the Chinese nation led to the emergence of a warlord period, which prevailed for two decades, from 1916 to 1936. At Yuan's death some of his officers—and others with sufficient power—seized control of various regions. These territories were controlled by the warlords, who maintained private armies manned with conscripted peasants, to protect and extend their provincial domains. Even Sun Yatsen and his followers had to seek refuge under the protection of the warlord in Canton. Sun's revolutionary program now called for the eventual establishment of constitutional government in three stages: (1) unification of the nation through elimination of warlordism by military force and termination of foreign intervention in China; (2) a period of political tutelage to prepare the people for democratic government; and (3) the enactment of a constitution by the people. Neither the European powers nor the warlords paid any attention to the disillusioned Dr. Sun, who was now desperate for a way to save China from further disintegration.

The political turmoil in China provided the impetus for an intellectual awakening. In 1919 this intellectual ferment culminated in the May Fourth Movement. It was instigated by high school and university students and their teachers who were searching for a model on which to build a new China. The May Fourth Movement led to reform in the written Chinese language, from the archaic classical style to use of the vernacular, or everyday spoken form.

It also introduced the study of Western science, technology, and political ideologies, including Marxism. The movement was closely tied in with demonstrations by university students against foreign intervention in Chinese affairs and against warlordism. These activities gave impetus to a new nationalistic and patriotic feeling emerging among the general population.

It was in this atmosphere—one of anger, humiliation, and disillusionment—that the Nationalist revolution took place. In 1922 Dr. Sun was forced to flee Canton for Shanghai in order to escape from the southern warlord. While in Shanghai, he was contacted by an agent of the Communist Third International (Comintern), who offered to assist the Chinese revolutionary movement by providing Soviet personnel. Sun accepted the offer and signed an agreement which reorganized his hitherto ineffective political party as a Chinese counterpart of the Soviet Union's communist party. Sun's party became the Nationalist Party (the Nationalists), the Guomindang, and formed an alliance with the newly formed Chinese Communist Party. Another agreement provided limited support in terms of arms and military training in the Soviet Union for members of Sun's revolutionary army. Although Dr. Sun died in 1925, a military expedition was launched in 1926 to unify China by defeating the warlords. News of the expedition both unified the people with nationalistic feelings and aroused the populace against foreign imperialism.

The expedition was launched under an uneasy alliance between Sun's followers, who were receiving financial backing from merchants in coastal cities and from large landowners in the countryside, and the members of the Chinese Communist Party, controlled by the Comintern. By March 1927 the new Nationalist government was dominated by the left-wing elements of the Guomindang and the communists with headquarters in Wuhan in central China. When the expedition gained control of eastern China on its push north, Chiang Kaishek, commander of the revolutionary armies and successor to Sun Yatsen, decided to end the internal schism between the left and the right by first eliminating members of the Chinese Communist Party within the revolutionary movement. In April 1927 a lightning strike massacred communists in the cities under Chiang's control. This surprise blow, known as the "Shanghai Massacre," was so effective that it practically decimated the communist ranks. Chiang also expelled Soviet advisers from China. He then established the Nationalist government in Nanjing, and this was recognized by most nations as the legitimate government of China in the 1940s. The remaining Chinese communists sought refuge in the mountainous regions in central China after 1930.

China Under the Nationalists: 1927–37

During the decade of Guomindang rule, from 1927 to 1937, modest progress was made in many areas of modernization, initiated by the Nationalists under the leadership of Chiang Kaishek and his Western-trained advisers and administrators. For the first time, China had a modern governmental structure. As soon as major provincial warlords were eliminated or coopted into the system, the transportation and industrial facilities were improved and expanded in the area. Earnest attempts were made to expand elementary school education and to provide political indoctrination for the young. Most important from Chiang's point of view was the building of a more efficient and dedicated modern army for a host of purposes—including the eventual elimination of warlords and of communist guerrillas in mountainous areas of central China, as well as protection of China's borders from foreign attack.

There were glaring negative features in the Nationalist balance sheet. First, no real efforts were made to provide progressive economic and social programs to improve the lot of the people. Land reform measures were few. Second, the regime alienated the intellectuals by its repressive measures against them in the guise of purging any elements of communist influence from their ranks. Third, enormous expenditures from the national treasury were devoted to the "extermination" of the Chinese communists operating in remote mountain regions. The Nationalists steadfastly refused to seek a nonmilitary solution to the problem of insurrection by the communists. Nor were they willing to seek consultation with other political groups, let alone share political power with other elements of society. The Guomindang's modest accomplishments in nation building were soon obliterated by its obsession to eliminate all opposition.

Time was not on the side of the Nationalists. In 1931, when they had achieved some measure of national unification and modernization in the midst of waging encirclement campaigns against the communist guerrilla forces, Japanese militarists annexed resource-rich Manchuria and made advances into northern China, inside the Great Wall. The Nationalist regime faced a hard choice in allocating its limited resources between the Japanese aggressors and the communist insurgents. In the early 1930s, Chiang's strategy was to rapidly annihilate the communist guerrilla forces and then turn to face the Japanese. However, rising public sentiment, expressed in frequent demonstrations, demanded that the regime prevent further territorial losses to the Japanese. In December 1936 Chiang was forced to join in a united front with the Chinese communists to fight the Japanese.

THE ORIGIN AND RISE OF THE CHINESE COMMUNIST MOVEMENT

Although Marxism was introduced in China about the time of World War I, this ideology, which called for revolution by an urban proletariat under mature capitalism, elicited little attention. Fabian socialism—progressive and social change through gradual constitutional means, developed in England in 1884—became the most popular liberal ideology from the West. For example, Dr. Sun's program incorporated socialist planks, including nationalization of land, a welfare state, and a planned economy. Interest in Marxism suddenly flowered among Chinese intellectuals after the 1917 Bolshevik Revolution in Russia. They saw in Lenin's revolution a relevant solution to China's political and economic problems. The keen interest in Bolshevism also reflected disillusionment with Western democracy as a model for Chinese development. In addition, it expressed Chinese bitterness over the imperialist activities of the Western democracies in China.

The early Chinese Marxists and the founders of the Chinese Communist Party were leading intellectuals in the Beijing National University (Beita). In 1918 Li Dazhao, the university's head librarian, formed a Marxist study group to which many young students, including a library assistant named Mao Zedong, were attracted. These young students were more interested in learning how to make a revolution than in theorizing about Marxism. With some urging from Comintern agents, the Chinese Communist Party (CCP) was formed on July 1, 1921. The group of thirteen intellectuals and revolutionaries, representing a total of fifty-seven members, were called together by Chen Duxiu, who became the first secretary general. Meetings for the first two party congresses were held secretly in the French concession in Shanghai to prevent harassment from the police. This was the very modest beginning of the party and the movement that took root in later years.

The CCP and the Comintern

For the first six years of the CCP's existence, 1921–27, the movement was under the control and direction of the Third International, or the Comintern. The Comintern was formed in 1919 at the insistence of Lenin, who wanted a new international organization, controlled by Moscow, to provide direction for all proletariat parties and to promote anti-imperialist revolutions throughout the world. Moscow directed and controlled the CCP and its leadership through Soviet Comintern agents who came to China with financial aid and military materiel. The leadership of the CCP before 1934, with few exceptions, was in the hands of the "returned Chinese Bolsheviks," trained for party work in Moscow under the sponsorship of the Comintern.

The Comintern's doctrine insisted that revolutions in colonial areas be based on industrial workers. Its strategy called for the participation of non-proletariat elements, such as the bourgeoisie, in a united front alliance to lead national revolutions. The manifestos adopted by four consecutive CCP congresses, from 1922 to 1925, echoed the Comintern line, calling for a revolutionary alliance with the landlord-merchant-based Guomindang, Dr. Sun's Nationalist Party. This Comintern strategy, which limited the communist base to urban industrial workers and called for individual communists to join the Guomindang under a united front, enhanced the CCP's growth as a viable political party during its early years.

By 1927 the united front alliance had become unworkable. Chiang Kaishek's power as commander in chief and head of the Guomindang was threatened by leftist elements in control of the revolutionary government, which was supported by the communists. As pointed out earlier, Chiang decided to purge the communists from his organization and to set up a rival government in Nanjing. Not long after, the leftist-dominated Wuhan government also turned on the communists when it became known that the Comintern, acting under direct orders from Stalin, instructed the CCP to eliminate the landlord elements and militarists in order to transform the alliance into a new revolutionary force. The result was a bloody mass execution of the communists who were caught.

Instead of admitting the mistake of his China policy, Stalin blamed the CCP leaders for their failure to prepare the workers in Wuhan for action.[12] Partly as a rebuttal to criticism raised by Leon Trotsky, Stalin ordered the Comintern agents in China to plan a series of armed insurrections. He hoped that quick victories would silence critics of his unsuccessful united front policy.[13] On August 1, 1927, now celebrated as the founding day of the People's Liberation Army, Zhou Enlai and Zhu De led a mutiny of communist troops within the Guomindang forces in Nanchang in central China. After occupying the city briefly, the communists were forced to seek refuge as guerrillas in the hills of eastern Guangdong province. The CCP also authorized a number of "Autumn Harvest Uprisings" in the fall of 1927 in central and southern China. One of these was led by Mao Zedong in his home province of Hunan. These uprisings were ill-fated misadventures which ended in defeat and brought heavy losses to the already decimated CCP ranks. When Mao and his group sought refuge in the mountain stronghold of Jinggangshan on the Hunan-Jiangxi border in central China, he repudiated the Comintern-inspired strategy. As a reprimand, Mao briefly lost his membership on the Politburo, the executive and policy-making body of the party.

After the rupture of the united front between the CCP and the Guomindang, the Chinese communist movement fragmented into two areas of operation: one in the cities, as an underground movement, with close links to the Comintern; the other in rural areas, as experimental soviets, operating almost autonomously and feuding constantly with the Comintern advisers. By the end of 1930, the party had been driven out of the cities, and only pockets of guerrilla bands operated in remote mountain regions of central and southern China and northern Shaanxi. The plight of the CCP was evidenced by the fact that its Central Committee had to operate underground in Shanghai's foreign concessions, and the Sixth Party Congress had to meet in Moscow in 1928. The leadership of the party was still in the hands of the returned Bolsheviks, who adhered to the Comintern policies. In a last attempt to recapture an urban base for a proletarian revolution in the summer of 1930, the CCP leadership, under Li Lisan, launched an attack from rural bases with the objective of capturing a number of cities on the Changjiang (Yangtse) River. Like previous Comintern-instigated misadventures, this one also ended in failure, with the small bases in rural mountain regions under blockade by Chiang

Kaishek's forces. The Chinese communists' future at this juncture seemed bleak.

The Rise of Mao Zedong
and Military Communism

The future of the Chinese communist movement hinged on the survival of the small pockets of experimental soviets in the remote rural areas, mostly in central and southern China. The CCP's decision, in the fall of 1931, to establish a Chinese Soviet Republic—which would unite the scattered bases—was both a political necessity and an admission that a revolution based on an urban proletariat was no longer possible in China. Thus, by 1931, when the CCP's Central Committee moved from urban Shanghai to the rural Jiangxi soviet, a decade-long quarrel within the Chinese communist movement—regarding the theoretical correctness of a revolutionary strategy based on the peasants—officially ended. The foremost proponent of a peasant base was the leader of the Jiangxi soviet, Mao Zedong. Mao had developed a strategy for victory during the six years he operated the Jiangxi guerrilla base. Besides the need for a highly disciplined united party, Mao's strategy contained three indispensable ingredients: (1) the development of a strong and mobile peasant-based Red Army for a protracted armed struggle; (2) the selection of a strategic terrain for military operations; and (3) the establishment of a self-sufficient economic base in the Red Army-controlled soviet areas to provide personnel and supplies for the armed struggle.[14] Mao believed that a highly disciplined party could only be built by a recruitment policy that would draw in the tough and dedicated guerrilla soldiers of the Red Army, who were predominantly poor peasants. The party became "militarized" as Mao began to build a new base for revolution.[15]

The Guomindang intensified its attack against the guerrilla base in its fifth and most extensive military campaign, which included an effective blockade that deprived the guerrilla base of outside supplies, particularly salt. By 1934 the guerrilla base had to be abandoned. The communists broke out of the Guomindang encirclement and moved the surviving forces, numbering not more than 150,000, westward and then north to the Great Wall. This was the legendary Long March of more than 6,000 miles over treacherous terrain of high mountains and rivers, amidst ambushes from warlords, Guomindang troops, and hostile minorities.[16] In October 1935, after almost a year's march, the greatly reduced forces of about 20,000 survivors arrived in Yanan in the northwestern province of Shaanxi and established a new base for guerrilla operations. By this time, the stormy Politburo meeting—held at Zunyi in southwest Guizhou Province in January 1935—had selected Mao as the undisputed leader of the CCP, including the cells operating mainly in industrial centers such as Shanghai and Wuhan. This marked the end of Comintern dominance and the beginning of Mao's supremacy as the CCP's political and military leader. This supremacy lasted until his death in 1976, forty years later.

Expansion of Communism
Under Mao, and Final Victory

When Chiang Kaishek learned that the communists had established a base in Yanan, he sent his crack troops to Shaanxi. The Guomindang force included soldiers that had been driven from Manchuria by the Japanese army in 1931. The Manchurian troops showed signs of low morale and a reluctance to fight the communists. This was largely due to effective political propaganda by the communists, which stressed the urgent need for a united front against Japan. In an effort to step up the offensive, Chiang Kaishek went to Xian in Shaanxi to direct the campaign personally. The mutinous Manchurian troops seized Chiang as a hostage in order to force him to agree to a united front policy. The Chinese communists by then had established contact with the Manchurian troops. Both Mao Zedong and Zhou Enlai served as mediators for the release of Chiang Kaishek under an agreement for a united front to fight the Japanese. This was the Xian Agreement, which temporarily terminated the civil war and marked the beginning of a second alliance between the CCP and the Guomindang.

When Japan attacked northern China in the summer of 1937, the Red Army was slowly brought into action under the united front agreement. The cessation of the civil war gave the CCP the needed respite to expand its base of operations and to strengthen its military forces for the eventual showdown with the Guomindang.[17] As China suffered repeated military defeats by the Japanese, the CCP-controlled Red Army expanded its guerrilla operations behind enemy lines. Party membership grew rapidly from a little over 20,000 at the end of the Long March in 1935, to over 800,000 in 1939, and to about 1.2 million at the end of the war in 1945. Of this enlarged party membership, perhaps a million were party members of the "military supply system," peasants and patriotic students who served the Red Army without salary but under strict military discipline.[18] They were the backbone of the leadership, not only for the communist guerrilla forces but also for the militarized border-region governments established in the areas under Red Army control. In each of these border regions, experiments in mild land reform and self-government by popular election were introduced. It was during this period that many of the practices and experiences became revolutionary traditions which persist today under the overall label "Yanan spirit."

When the Japanese surrendered in 1945, open clashes occurred between the Guomindang and the communist forces in many parts of China. China was once again engulfed in civil war, but this time the communists were in a much stronger position in terms of discipline, numerical strength, and the will to combat—not to mention the support of the intellectuals and a large segment of the rural population. The policy of President Truman of the United States was to bring the parties together for a political settlement. A series of cease-fire agreements were reached under American supervision. The mediation efforts by General Marshall for the United States soon deteriorated. Neither side had any intention of observing the truce and settling the future of China by political means. As the strength and morale of the Guomindang forces ebbed, the People's Liberation Army won victories over the Nationalist troops, equipped and supplied by the United States. By the summer and fall of 1948, the People's Liberation Army had overrun Manchuria and most of northern China. Guomindang forces were surrendering in divisional strength. With captured American military hardware, a large-scale military offensive was launched by the communists in the spring of 1949 against the remaining Guomindang forces in central and southern China. Although the Nationalists did not flee to the island of Taiwan until December 1949, the communists convened the People's Political Consultative Conference on October 1, to establish a new People's Republic of China in Beijing. At last the Chinese communist movement, which began as a Marxist study group, had seized power in China. A new search now began to find a suitable model to follow in building an industrially powerful China.

CHINA'S SEARCH
FOR A DEVELOPMENT MODEL

After almost eight years of war with Japan and four years of civil war, the initial years of the new republic were preoccupied with the immediate problems of consolidation and reconstruction. In the beginning, the CCP formed a coalition government, applying the tenets first formulated by Mao Zedong in his "New Democracy" (1940) and "On Coalition Government" (1945).[19] In this pragmatic way, twenty-three other political groups were permitted a partial share of political authority. The central government in Beijing proliferated with ministries on economic affairs. More than 55 percent of the top national administrative posts were reserved for leaders of the CCP; the remainder were distributed among experienced and talented liberal noncommunist intellectuals. During these early years, the new regime also relied heavily on the regional pattern of government to superintend the provinces. The regional government was in turn bolstered by the military field armies which had conquered and had remained in these regions after the civil war.

The enormous task of reconstruction called first of all for a solution to the problem of mounting inflation. During the last few months of the Nationalist regime, prices had risen 85,000 times.[20] Inflation abated somewhat when the new regime came to power, but with huge budget deficits from increased governmental expenditures, it still remained a serious problem. By a variety of fiscal and monetary devices, including the central control of local taxes, and the measuring of prices and wages in terms of commodity units, prices were finally stabilized by the summer of 1950.

Private industry and commerce, while restricted, were rehabilitated and developed along with the socialistic national economy. National ministries of economic production saw to it that the privately owned industries obtained needed raw materials to make their products and that they received orders from private or state-owned enterprises for these goods and services. Rapid economic recovery was made, and by 1952 production had reached China's peak pre-1949 levels. This rapid recovery was attributable to the policy of gradualism in nationalization, with no outright confiscation of private industry. Privately owned industries were eventually transformed into joint state and private enterprises and finally into completely state-owned operations through the "buying-off" policy, under which former owners of private enterprises were paid interest on their shares at a rate fixed by the state.[21]

Land Reform: Transformation of the Countryside

The most important program enacted by the new regime from 1950 to 1953 was agrarian reform. Land redistribution, a basic plank in the CCP program, had been carried out in the early soviet phase in the Jiangxi border areas, and later in the northwest, with varying degrees of intensity. In 1949, when the CCP took over the country, some 500 million people were living in the rural villages. The land tenure system was such that "half the cultivated land was owned by less than one-tenth of the farm population, while two-thirds of the population owned less than one-fifth."[22] This serious problem of uneven land distribution was further aggravated by the large number of landless tenants who had to pay exorbitant annual rents, as high as 60 percent of their production. The 1950 Agrarian Reform Law was basically a mild reform measure which permitted rich peasants to retain their land and property (Article 6), and landlords to retain the land for their own use (Article 10). The later harsh treatment of landlords, which accompanied the implementation of land redistribution through the "struggle meetings" and the "people's tribunals" to settle accounts by the peasants, was attributable to the speedy implementation needed to prevent "foot dragging" by cadres and activists assigned to do the job and by the peasants themselves.[23] The Korean War also generated some fear on the part of the peasants of the possible return of the Nationalists.[24] Land redistribution was completed in 1952, when 113 million acres—plus draft animals and farm implements—were distributed to over 300 million landless peasants.[25]

It soon became obvious that land redistribution was only a step toward collectivizing the countryside. The millions of new landowning peasants realized very quickly that their small plots of land were too small to produce enough even to feed their own families. The individual peasants simply did not have the means to acquire modern tools, much less to build irrigation projects. Having committed themselves to the party's cause by participating in land redistribution, the peasants had to accept the party's new appeal for mutual aid teams and for the pooling together of draft animals, implements, and shared labor. In 1953–54, the mutual aid teams gave way to larger and more complicated cooperative ventures, the mandatory agricultural producers' cooperatives (APCs). An agricultural producers' cooperative was, in essence, a unified management system of farm production. The individual peasants pooled their land, draft animals, implements, and houses in return for shares in the enterprise. Detailed accounting was kept, and after deductions were made for expenses incurred and taxes to be paid, income was distributed to the members on the basis of their contributions, stated in terms of shares. While the movement was voluntary, the party conducted massive campaigns to persuade and sometimes to coerce peasants to join the APCs. Although an overwhelming majority of the peasants had joined the cooperatives by 1957, official accounts showed resistance to the program. In some parts of the country, peasants deliberately consumed what they produced to avoid forceful delivery to government purchasing agencies.[26]

The APCs enabled the peasants to better utilize resources and labor. During the slack seasons, surplus labor could be mobilized easily to carry on small-scale irrigation works, such as making ditches, ponds, and dams. Combined surplus labor could reclaim land through irrigation and reforestation. The APCs certainly allowed the peasants to realize greater savings and investment. Even more important was the sharing of the risks of crop failure. Individual peasants no longer had to face the possibility of bankruptcy if crops failed. But there were also many problems inherent in the APCs: Many peasants were too poor to contribute funds to the cooperatives; there was a lack of qualified technical personnel such as accountants among the illiterate peasantry to provide efficient management; and peasants were frequently unhappy when centralized purchasing and marketing operations were imposed on the cooperatives by the state, leading to intensified animosity toward the party, and a reluctance to cooperate.[27]

The First Five-Year Plan, 1953–57, and the Soviet Model

By 1953 the regime had completed the immediate tasks of rehabilitating the war-torn economy and consolidating their control over the nation. With the end of the Korean War, the regime was confident enough to embark on a rapid industrialization program. The approach selected was the Stalinist strategy of long-term centralized planning, a proven socialistic model which had enabled the Soviet Union to emerge from World War II as the second most powerful nation in the world. For ideological reasons it was the only logical strategy comprehensible to the Chinese communists at the time, particularly in view of the emerging bipolarization of the world into Soviet and Western orbits. The pragmatic Chinese were aware of the benefits of Soviet aid, in terms of both financial credit and technical assistance, which would be forthcoming to promote this model.[28]

Fundamental to the Stalinist model was the rapid buildup in the heavy industry sector through the concentrated allocation of investment into capital goods industries. The model also called for highly centralized decision making at the top to determine targets and quotas to be fulfilled by the various economic sectors.[29] In many ways, this strategy required basic structural change in the agricultural sector, from which the bulk of savings for investment must come. The introduction of agricultural producers' cooperatives was needed in order to accumulate savings through increased agricultural production and controlled consumption. The First Five-Year Plan allocated 58 percent of the 20-billion-dollar investment fund to capital goods for heavy industries.[30] The bulk of these investment funds was financed by the Chinese themselves. The Soviet Union made considerable contributions in the form of technical assistance; construction; and equipment for 154 modern industrial plants which were paid for by the Chinese; and the training of Chinese technicians. In June 1960, when Soviet-trained Chinese technicians numbered about 10,000, Soviet aid was suddenly withdrawn. By 1957, when the First Five-Year Plan was completed, an annual growth rate of 8 percent had been added to China's economic growth,[31] an impressive achievement by any standard. In addition, the First Five-Year Plan made a lasting investment in education (130,000 engineers graduated) and public health (control of such communicable diseases as cholera and typhoid, which formerly had plagued the Chinese people).[32]

The First Five-Year Plan also had a number of drawbacks. First, the plan was rather costly when one considers that the bulk of the 20 billion dollars in investments came from the Chinese. Second, the plan required large forced savings from the agricultural sector. Third, the Stalinist model placed undue concentration of investment in such heavy industries as steel, at the expense not only of agriculture but also of light and consumer goods industries. Fourth, the model required a high degree of centralization and the development of an elaborate bureaucratic structure to implement, control, and check the plan according to fixed targets and quotas. Fifth, since planning and implementation of the model emphasized the roles of technocrats, engineers, and plant managers, it thus neglected the need to involve politically the millions of uneducated and tradition-oriented peasants to the rapid construction of an industrial socialistic state. After an agonizing reappraisal of the First Five-Year Plan, Mao and his followers launched the Great Leap Forward in an attempt to obtain a faster rate of growth and to develop a socialist economic model more suited to China's conditions and needs.

The Great Leap Forward and Communization Program, 1958-59

Under the Great Leap Forward, the regime mobilized the creative enthusiasm of the Chinese masses for economic growth and industrialization in the same way it had mobilized them for the communist revolution.[33] The Great Leap would substitute China's most plentiful resource, manpower, for capital goods, in the same way it had successfully substituted committed men for modern weapons during the guerrilla and civil war days. The unemployed were to be put to work, and the employed were to work much harder, under military discipline, so that China could make the gigantic leap required to become an industrial power through the widespread use of labor-intensive, small-scale production. The emphasis was placed on the techniques of mass mobilization.

The program called for use of "dual technology." The Chinese economy at the end of the First Five-Year Plan consisted of a mixture of modern sectors (capital-intensive and large-scale) and traditional sectors (labor-intensive and small-scale). These two types of economic sectors in a typical developing country (like China) are more or less independent of each other. In the modern sectors, goods produced are mostly exported to earn foreign exchange to pay for the imported machines. In the traditional sectors, small-scale industries in villages are self-sufficient, providing virtually all their own consumptive and productive needs. Under the Great Leap strategy, the modern sector would not need to supply capital goods for the traditional sector, but the traditional sector would increase its flow of food and raw materials to build up the industrial sector. This was the meaning of the Chinese slogans so familiar during the Great Leap period: "walking on two legs" and "self-reliance in the simultaneous development of industry and agriculture." Land was to be reclaimed, and irrigation systems were to be built by the peasants, using simple tools at their disposal. Rural communities were to build "backyard furnaces" to produce enough pig iron to allow China to surpass Great Britain in steel production. Other popular small-scale projects were electric power generators and chemical fertilizer plants.

Conceptually, the Great Leap model was not only rational but had some economic validity.[34] However, there were unrealistic expectations and overzealous implementation of the program. In an effort to fulfill the required quotas, workers often sacrificed quality for quantity. Quality also suffered from a lack of technical knowledge among the peasants. Some statistics on increased production were based on exaggeration and fabrication. Millions of tons of pig iron, much substandard and all a long way from being steel, were produced by backyard furnaces. Pig iron accumulated along railways, which could not possibly handle its movement, causing a serious bottleneck in the entire transport system.[35]

The merging of cooperatives into people's communes was an integral part of the Great Leap Forward program. The communes were, in essence, a device to collectivize agricultural production on a scale much larger than that of the cooperatives. Unlike the APC, the commune became a local government, performing a multiplicity of functions in agriculture, industry, education, social welfare, public health, public works, and military defense. The peasants turned over to the collective entity their ownership in land, tools, draft animals, houses, and shares in the cooperatives. They then became members of a commune, of which they claimed collective ownership. In return, they were to receive five guarantees: food, clothing, housing, medical care, and education. During the early stage of commune development (1958), communal kitchens were installed to free more women for production. In some extreme cases, men and women lived in segregated communal dormitories, with their children in communal nurseries. The people's communes were hailed with great fanfare as the ideal collective life described by classical Marxism: "From each according to his ability and to each according to his needs."

By the spring of 1959, there were 26,000 communes. Although there was no uniform size, an average commune consisted of about 2,000 households, or about 10,000 peasants. Within each commune peasants were organized into production brigades and production teams, the basic unit of the commune. This radical experiment encountered a host of problems. For instance, the peasants could not adjust to communal kitchens and dormitories. The discipline imposed by the cadres, those selected for leadership positions, for long hours of work at a feverish pace, sapped the peasants' energy and enthusiasm. Without their tiny private plots for vegetables to supplement their meager diet, the peasants' general health declined. Initially, the peasants were neither willing nor able to make decisions under the commune setup, which required their participation. Their inexperience in the management of complex productive activities also made them reluctant to assume responsibilities. In 1959 some corrective measures were implemented: Private garden plots were permitted, forced communal living were halted, and commune members were given adequate time for rest and recreation.

The numerous problems implicit in the Great Leap and communization, accompanied by the natural disasters of flood and drought, should have doomed the program. In 1958, when the Great Leap and commune programs were launched, there was a good harvest. In 1959 heavy floods and drought laid waste almost half the cultivatable land. Then, in 1960, floods, drought, and pests ravaged millions of acres. To make matters worse, the Soviets withdrew all their technicians and advisers from China in June 1960 because of a disagreement over development strategy. The drastic reduction in agricultural production stalled the drive for rapid development of industry. Famine occurred and rationing was imposed in the communes. There were large purchases of grain from abroad. China's experience was typical of an agricultural setback in developing nations: Scarce foreign exchange had to be diverted from capital goods to food imports. A new policy had to be adopted to give first priority to a minimally sufficient food supply rather than to industrialization.

Post–Great Leap: Leadership Dissension and Economic Recovery

The failure of the Great Leap brought to a head growing division within the Chinese leadership, not only over development strategy but also over the ideological implications of the strategy. This division is frequently referred to as the "red" (politics) versus "expert" (technology) controversy. Mao later made a self-criticism for the errors committed in the Great Leap. Mao's most outspoken critic was Marshal Peng Dehuai, the defense minister and a Politburo member.[36] Peng's criticism focused on three effects of the Great Leap: (1) the damage to the long-term economic development of China, which must rely on technical proficiency rather than on sheer mobilization of the masses; (2) rejection of the Soviet development model, which caused a deterioration in Sino-Soviet relations; and (3) the obvious decline in morale and efficiency he had observed in his inspection of the armed forces. Marshal Peng's central concern seemed to be that China needed a modern army, which must rest on the development of heavy industries and technical skills to produce and operate advanced weapons, including nuclear weapons. Peng delivered his criticisms at an enlarged meeting of the Politburo in Lushan in July and August of 1959. Red Guard pamphlets, circulated later during the Cultural Revolution, revealed that Mao admitted some mistakes in the implementation of the Great Leap; but in the main, he vigorously defended his role and the policies associated with the program. He demanded a showdown at a subsequent enlarged meeting of the Central Committee, and won. After these Lushan meetings, Marshal Peng was purged. Mao later was criticized for the purge of Peng. As planned before the Lushan meetings, Mao stepped down as the President of the People's Republic and handed the powerful position over to Liu Shaoqi, a leading party theoretician and able administrator.[37]

The policies initiated by Liu Shaoqi reversed and corrected the Great Leap programs. It should be noted that before Liu assumed office, the Central Committee and its Politburo, in close consultation with the party's provincial secretaries, had already made a number of recommendations to correct the mistakes of the Great Leap. Some of these measures are given here as background to the policy dissension that came into full bloom during the Cultural Revolution. First, Liu called for a reintroduction of material incentives, such as private plots and free markets, to spur agricultural production. Second, he issued directives to those who managed state enterprises to pay strict attention to profits and losses: All enterprises must be managed and evaluated in terms of efficiency. Third, Liu insisted that technical "expertise" must command ideological "redness": Managers must have more authority in their plants than the ideologues. Fourth, he declared a relaxation of centralized planning by giving local units more freedom in setting their production quotas and targets. Fifth, he demanded that basic-level cadres observe strict discipline and report accurate statistics. Sixth, Liu introduced measures to reorganize the party by placing more emphasis on party discipline and institutional control mechanisms; these measures helped him consolidate his power and place his supporters in key positions.

The economic recovery soon took shape under Liu Shaoqi's direction.[38] Agricultural development was now the top economic priority. With the introduction of material incentives and a good harvest in 1962, economic conditions improved in the countryside. With hard work and an end to constant ideological and political interference, many of the industrial projects were completed and new ones were initiated, despite the withdrawal of Soviet technical assistance. The new economic policy continued to encourage the development of medium- and small-sized industries in the countryside, such as farm equipment factories and rural electrification plants. In order to reduce China's dependence on Soviet imports, self-reliance was stressed by encouraging technological innovation and exploration for such new resources as petroleum, found in Daqing. By 1964 Premier Zhou Enlai announced that the recovery was complete, and a Third Five-Year Plan was ready for implementation in 1966. The Chinese had learned that with some realistic adjustment to suit Chinese conditions, a centralized, planned economy, based on the Stalinist model, worked for China.

The Socialist Education
Campaign, 1962–65

The Socialist Education Campaign was the prelude to the Cultural Revolution.[39] It was a campaign of ideological education and of rectification of cadre behavior (which requires honest, hard-working leadership qualities). The main theme of the campaign was class struggle, a theme for which Mao fought hard when he resumed an active political role in the party at the tenth session of the Eighth Central Committee in 1962. Mao and other top leaders had become alarmed at reports of widespread corruption among the rural cadres. They feared that the free markets and private vegetable plots were fostering the growth of economic individualism, which posed a serious threat to the collective economy. The Socialist Education Movement consisted of three interrelated mass campaigns: (1) an educational campaign to assist the formation of poor and lower-middle peasant associations in order to prevent the rise of a class of well-to-do middle peasants; (2) a rectification campaign aimed at eliminating the corrupt practices of rural cadres, such as embezzlement, large wedding parties, and misuse of public property; and (3) a purification movement for the nation—with the People's Liberation Army (PLA) heroes as models—which stressed the virtues of self-sacrifice, the collective good, and endurance of hardship.

There was a great deal of controversy with respect to the directives and guidelines issued by the Central Committee. Mao's original instructions, the "earlier ten points," were altered by the Central Secretariat on instructions from Liu Shaoqi and Deng Xiaoping, who were then responsible for the day-to-day operation of the party. There were debates and quarrels among the top leaders, primarily between Mao and Liu, on methods of investigating corrupt cadres in rural communes.[40] Mao advocated open investigation in the communes by work teams of top cadres from the center; Liu wanted in-depth investigation by covert infiltration among the peasants, both to gather true information and to ferret out the corrupt cadres.[41] There was also divergence between Mao and Liu in terms of the party's role and its leaders in the Socialist Education Movement. Mao intended it to be a mass education movement. Liu wanted a party-controlled rectification operation, with emphasis on corrective and remedial measures, in accordance with established norms within the party organization.

The entire Socialist Education Movement was carried out under a cloud of uncertainty and contradictory instructions. The local cadres, most of them recruited after land reform in the early 1950s, had developed strategies for survival; they knew how to play the game and how to protect themselves against outside investigations by work teams dispatched from far away Beijing or from provincial capitals. If necessary, these bureaucratized cadres would withhold information or intimidate poor peasants. By 1965 most of the Socialist Education Movement had ended in failure, mainly because of disagreements over its implementation.

Only the campaign to emulate PLA heroes was a success. It began in the military, where the soldiers were required to form small groups to systematically study Mao's writings, particularly three essays on self-sacrifice and self-negation, written for the cadres during the Yanan days. Exemplary PLA companies were formed to demonstrate their living application of the thought of Mao. This ideological education campaign within the PLA was personally supervised by the new defense minister, Lin Biao. With the campaign's success in the military, a nationwide movement to emulate the PLA was launched.

The battle lines for the Cultural Revolution were now clearly drawn. Although the party apparatus under Liu Shaoqi and Deng Xiaoping had shown its disdain for Mao's mass mobilization approach (seeing it as disruptive to the routine operation of the party and government), the PLA, under Lin Biao, had not only embraced Mao's style but applied Mao's teachings to their activities. Mao now saw that the cadres who monopolized the party apparatus, and the career-oriented status seekers, had become resistant to change and were reluctant to accept the new socialist values. The party could no longer be considered an effective instrument for the revolutionary change Mao so desired.

THE CULTURAL REVOLUTION AND THE LIN BIAO AFFAIR

Before describing the events of the Cultural Revolution, let us look briefly at some of the issues underlying this great upheaval. If we survey the voluminous literature about the Cultural Revolution, we find several basic themes which serve to explain the causes of the upheaval.[42] One popular view depicted the Cultural Revolution as an "ideological crusade" aimed at preventing gradual erosion of the revolutionary spirit fostered by the early guerrilla experience of reliance on the masses, and egalitarianism. Closely related to this was the idea that a thorough rectification campaign had to be waged in order to halt further growth of bureaucratic tendencies within the party and government. Another approach contended that as the regime moved toward further development, its leaders inevitably would reach a point where resolution of policy differences regarding strategy and priority would become more difficult. Prolonged dissension among the top leadership generally resulted in a power struggle between contending groups, with each jockeying for position and eventual vindication of its views. Thus, policy differences and power struggles among a divided leadership became intertwined. In addition, the contest for power among the top leadership in China probably was intensified by the question of who would succeed Mao as leader of the party.

There is some evidence that the launching of the Cultural Revolution coincided with deterioration of Sino-Soviet relations and the escalation of the Vietnam War by the United States. Some scholars contend that the Soviet Union's offer to China in 1965 of a joint action to counteract United States' escalation in Vietnam served as the catalyst that triggered the policy debate among China's top leaders.[43]

Events of the Cultural Revolution

The Cultural Revolution was officially launched on August 8, 1966, when the eleventh session of the Eighth Central Committee approved a sixteen-point guideline for conducting a thorough revolution. The revolution was to be concerned not only with the economic base (the socialist collectivized economy) but also with the superstructures (education, the arts, literature, and institutional arrangements).

Some nine or ten months before the Central Committee approved the guidelines, the battle had actually begun with a controversy over the political implications of a play by a historian and playwright, Wu Han. Wu Han, who was also deputy mayor of Beijing, and his superior, Peng Zhen, mayor of Beijing and a member of the Politburo, were politically allied with Liu Shaoqi. The play, *Hai Rui's Dismissal from Office,* was a historical allegory about a Ming official's final vindication after dismissal from office. Mao and his supporters charged that the purpose of the play was to vindicate Marshal Peng Dehaui, who had been purged for his 1959 criticism of Mao and the Great Leap program. When a lengthy critique of the play by Yao Wenyuan, a radical writer from Shanghai and a supporter of Mao, was refused publication in the party press, Lin Biao had it published in the PLA paper, the *Liberation Army Daily.* This action forced publication in the leading party paper, the *People's Daily,* for nationwide circulation. At first the party leaders refused to admit the political implication in the play, saying it was a purely academic matter. After Mao's supporters intensified their attack, Liu Shaoqi and Peng Zhen appointed a team to investigate the matter. The team's final report, known as the "February Outline Report," written under the direct supervision of Peng Zhen and subsequently approved by the Politburo under the acting leadership of Liu Shaoqi, called for toleration of ideas within the party, less stress on the class struggle in academic and literary fields, and a rectification campaign against the radical left. Mao rebuked the "February Report" and asked for mass criticism of art and literature.

The literary debate was followed by mass criticism, which led to purges of top party and military leaders. The purged party leaders included Beijing municipal party committee members Peng Zhen and Wu Han. General Lo Ruiqing, the chief of staff for the PLA, was also purged because of his advocacy of military professionalism and his reluctance to implement the Socialist Education Movement in the army. The attack then spread to the party committees in China's two leading universities, Beita and Qinghua. The university students organized themselves as Red Guards, Mao's "revolutionary successors."[44]

Some high school and university students throughout China formed their own Red Guard groups to investigate cadres' behavior and attitudes.[45] This gave the students an opportunity not only to air their grievances against school officials and teachers but also to vent their frustrations with the system's inability to absorb the large number of graduating youths into appropriate jobs and to provide advancement opportunities.[46] By the autumn of 1966, the Red Guard movement had grown to such proportions that normal schooling had to be abandoned. Mass criticism, led by Red Guards against the party leaders and their apparatus, became an everyday occurrence. Party leaders were dragged out into the street for failing to provide the answers the students wanted to hear. To counter the roaming Red Guards organized by university students, party leaders in many localities formed their own Red Guards. This was a period of chaos and violence as factional Red Guard groups feuded endlessly with each other. All functions of the party and some activities of government came to a standstill. The only organization that was intact was the military. The Red Guard movement was supported by the radical leaders loyal to Mao and was fueled by access to confidential information about the leaders and their policy differences. From this movement the tabloid Red Guard wall posters became a major source of insight for the outside world into the policy debates. The Central Committee and its secretariat had by now ceased to function. In its place a Central Cultural Revolution Group—dominated by the radicals, with shifting membership—now served as the party's most authoritative spokespersons, with direct lines of communication to Mao.[47]

To outside observers China in January and February 1967 was a gigantic spectacle of big-character posters, slogans, and endless processions and meetings in the sea of banners and portraits of Mao. Factionalized Red Guard groups openly employed physical force in their frequent skirmishes against each other all over China after the party machinery had been effectively paralyzed. The established party authorities, in some cases with the active support of the local PLA commands, mounted their counterattack against the radical Red Guards, which resulted in more bloodshed. This chaos and violence reached such alarming proportions that the only alternative left was to call in the military to restore order and to prevent any more violence. The PLA was ordered by Mao to intervene in this domestic turmoil in January 1967. The main tasks of the military were to fill the power vacuum created by the dismantled party and government organizations in the provinces, to supervise economic production, and to prevent violence by the rampaging Red Guards. The PLA was also to provide ideological training in universities and schools and thereby to exercise control over the students after their return to campus. Military control commissions, a device that had been employed for control and consolidation of the country in the early 1950s, reappeared in order to provide supervision and control in industries and many other institutions of the party and government. By the end of 1967, the military effectively controlled China and began rather uneasily to govern.[48]

Once in control, the military intervened in provincial politics to establish provincial revolutionary committees—a new power structure to temporarily replace the provincial party committees. The provincial revolutionary committees were made up of representatives of the PLA commands, the Red Guards as a mass organization, and the repentant veteran cadres—the "three-way alliance." With the inception of the revolutionary committees, the military became the real power. The success of the revolutionary committees was dependent upon the PLA's active intervention on behalf of Mao's supporters in Beijing. Order was gradually restored in the provinces as new revolutionary committees were formed to operate as party committees, purged and cleansed of "revisionist" tendencies, at least for the moment.

The convening of the Ninth Party Congress in Beijing in April 1969 signaled the end of the Cultural Revolution and the reestablishment of the party structure. The party congress, dominated by Lin Biao and his military supporters, sanctioned "a revolutionary seizure of power," as described by Edgar Snow.[49] Unity, proclaimed by Lin Biao, was the major, but short-lived, theme of the Ninth Party Congress.

Effects of the Cultural Revolution

Although the effects of the Cultural Revolution on the Chinese political system will be discussed in later chapters, it may be helpful to outline here some of the long-term effects the upheaval had on the Chinese political scene.

One direct and far-reaching effect of the Cultural Revolution was the change it brought about in the relationship between the power center in Beijing and the provinces. Beginning in 1969 there was a steady increase in the representation of provinces at the central decision-making level, as evidenced by the number of provincial party secretaries elected to the party's Central Committee (see Table 5.1 in Chapter 5). Second, the political prominence of the military at both the central and provincial levels was more apparent during and immediately after the Cultural Revolution. The increase of provincial and military authorities in decision making, both at the center and in the provinces, benefited the more pragmatic veteran administrators (who had been allies of the regional and provincial military powers) in their conflict with the more radicalized party ideologues. This rise in political influence by the provincial leaders, many of whom had their power base in the military establishment, certainly must be attributed to the military intervention in the Cultural Revolution.[50] Third, the greatest impact of the Cultural Revolution was on education.[51] As we shall see in later chapters, not only were curriculum content and teaching methods reorganized, but educational opportunities were opened up for those of rural, nonelite background. However, abolition of the examination system for university entrance and for measuring competence at the higher education level contributed to low academic quality in students and, in the long run, impeded the country's advanced scientific and technological development and research. Fourth, the Cultural Revolution's stress on decentralization in decision making and on mass participation in economic development programs called attention to the evils of bureaucratization, so common in all planned economic systems. To some analysts, participation in economic decision making contributed to both more institutional responsiveness and more institutional accountability to the masses.[52]

What final assessment can one make regarding the Cultural Revolution? In its official evaluation in 1981, the Chinese Communist Party admitted that the launching of the upheaval[53] by Mao was a serious mistake, in that it was responsible for "the most severe setback" and "the heaviest losses suffered by the party."[54] Party general secretary Hu Yaobang called the decade between 1966 and 1976 an economic, cultural, and educational "catastrophe" for China.[55] Perhaps the gravest indictment that can be leveled against the Cultural Revolution is that great human suffering was caused by the radicals' witch-hunting escapades and the breakdown of regular party authority.[56] Prior to the trial of "the Gang of Four," the Chinese media published reports of one episode after another of the maltreatment and persecution of cadres and intellectuals.

No one knows exactly how many party members and intellectuals were persecuted and tortured by the Red Guards and radicals. In many cases it was sufficient merely for the accused to be labeled "rightist" or "counterrevolutionary." The denounced and their relatives were subjected to beatings, imprisonment, loss of jobs, and banishment to rural areas to do menial labor. During the 1981 trial of the Gang of Four, it was revealed that 729,511 people had been persecuted, including a number of high-ranking party and state officials. Of that group, about 34,000 died.[57] Other official figures indicated that political persecution was even more widespread. In 1978 more than 100,000 victims of false accusations and persecution were rehabilitated and exonerated.[58] In 1980 some 13,000 overseas Chinese were found to have been wrongly accused of "crimes against the state."[59] At the same time, Deng Xiaoping was personally convinced that as many as 2.9 million people had been victims of persecution during the decade of the Cultural Revolution.[60]

There seems to be no question that the Cultural Revolution was not only a gross policy error in the name of ideological purity but was also a dark page in the CCP's history. In his interview with Oriana Fallaci, Deng Xiaoping emphasized that it actually had been a civil war which decimated the ranks of the experienced veteran cadres.[61] Further, a large percentage of China's intellectuals—educators, scholars, teachers, and scientists—were uprooted from their institutions, with their talents wasted in menial work in the countryside. Finally, the Cultural Revolution failed to produce any long-term fundamental institutional changes. Most of the institutional changes actually accomplished were either abandoned or have undergone drastic alterations.

The Lin Biao Affair, 1969–73

In a rare occurrence in the regime's history, a complete and nationwide halt of all civilian and military flights was ordered by the central government of the People's Republic of China for three days, from September 11-13,

1971—an unprecedented event in terms of its intensity and duration. The halt was accompanied by sudden orders canceling all furloughs for the People's Liberation Army, which were monitored by the Japanese. A week later the British Foreign Office was advised by its charge d'affaires in Beijing that the annual October 1 National Day parade and reception were to be canceled. There were reports of unusual troop movements and of an army alert throughout China.[62] The ubiquitous Premier Zhou and the familiar top military leaders were conspicuously absent from public view and became inaccessible to foreign visitors. As the unresolved Chinese mystery deepened, the outside world could only speculate as to what was happening inside China.

Then, on September 30, as the Chinese kept their silence, the Soviet news agency Tass reported from Moscow that a Chinese air force jet plane had crashed on September 13 at Unden Khan, west of Ulan Bator, the capital of the Mongolian People's Republic. The Mongolian government accused the Chinese of violating its air space and demanded an explanation. The crashed air force plane contained, Tass reported, nine charred bodies with firearms, documents, and equipment identified as belonging to the Chinese air force.

For ten months, from September 1971 to June 1972, the outside world continued to be confused, speculating on links between the plane crash in Mongolia and the probable downfall of Lin Biao and his lieutenants in the military hierarchy. Then, in 1972,[63] in separate meetings with Prime Minister Bandaranaike of Ceylon in June and Foreign Minister Schumann of France in July, Chairman Mao revealed that Lin Biao was killed in a plane crash while fleeing from China after his unsuccessful attempt to assassinate the chairman in an aborted coup d'etat. Simultaneously, statements were issued by the Chinese embassy in Algiers and by Wang Hairong, an assistant foreign minister and Mao's niece, confirming Lin Biao's death in a plane crash and the reason for the flight abroad. Subsequently, Premier Zhou, in an interview with visiting members of the American Society of Newspaper Editors and Publishers, elaborated further on the manner in which Lin Biao had met his death.[64]

Although semiofficial revelation to foreign visitors by Mao and Zhou about Lin Biao's death had solved the ten-month mystery for the outside world, the reasons for Lin's demise remained a puzzle. It must be noted here that these semiofficial revelations were made primarily for external consumption. Internally, an intensive rectification campaign had begun in September 1971, which involved study, discussion, and criticism based upon official documents and directives about the Lin Biao affair. The debate and intensive criticism which engaged all the cadres of the party and government culminated in the secret convocation of the Tenth National Congress of the Chinese Communist Party in August 1973. It was then that the death of Lin Biao was officially announced, along with a list of his crimes of conspiracy against the party.

It is rather instructive to read Premier Zhou Enlai's political report to the secretly convened Tenth National Congress of the CCP in August 1973. An important portion of Zhou Enlai's political report dealt with Lin Biao's "antiparty" activities. Zhou dated Lin's disagreement with the leadership to the Second Plenum of the party's Ninth Central Committee in August 1970.

Premier Zhou's report revealed only in general terms the abortive military coup engineered by Lin Biao, and confirmed officially the flight that resulted in Lin's death on September 13, 1971. Zhou's report gave neither clues as to how Lin Biao attempted to assassinate Chairman Mao nor any details about the military's attempted coup. What the political report to the party congress presented was an official version of Lin Biao's death and his antiparty conspiracy. The report also indicated that the rectification campaign, launched soon after Lin's demise, emphasized not only the correct revolutionary line but also the proper work style, particularly for the PLA. In language which was couched in general theoretical and ideological terms, Zhou indicted Lin Biao for being an "ultrarightist" and a "conspirator" who had attempted to "split" the unity of the party.

While Premier Zhou gave no details in his report to the party congress on Lin Biao's abortive coup, he nevertheless admitted that "the course of the struggle to smash the Lin Biao anti-party clique and the crimes of the clique are already known to the whole party, army, and people." What this implied was the intense discussion, criticism, and rectification campaign that had been waged inside China, leading up to the convocation of the Tenth Party Congress.

In addition to the purge which followed the demise of Lin Biao, the Politburo of the CCP appointed a top-level investigation committee on the Lin Biao affair. A series of documents were said to have been issued by the Central Committee on the findings of the investigation—these were considered internal reading material for the cadres in conducting the rectification campaign against Lin Biao and his followers.[65] One document, dated January 13, 1972, contained an outline of the "571 Engineering Project," the military coup plan of Lin Biao's group, as evidence of the conspiracy against the party. The document also contained an excerpt of a confession, by a Lin Biao coconspirator on the execution of the plan.

Much more revealing information about the inner struggle among the top leaders, particularly between the chairman and his designated successor Lin Biao, was contained in another document. This was a summary of, or notes on, Mao's talk with provincial military and party cadres during his inspection trip to the interior, conducted from mid-August to mid-September 1971, on the eve of the Lin Biao's alleged assassination attempt. Mao presumably made the trip in order to use his personal charisma to rally the support of military and party leaders in his struggle with Lin.

This particular document revealed in Mao's own words his view of the power struggle and of the disagreement over the issues of leadership direction and the loyalty and command of the army. While the account of Lin's death summarized above has been questioned, Mao and Lin Biao disagreed on a number of issues. (An account by Yao Ming-le called the official version of Lin's death, presented at the 1981 trial of the Gang of Four, a coverup and concluded that Lin was killed on orders from Mao.)[66] Mao and Lin's major disagreements centered on the following issues: the need for collective leadership after Mao, the dominance of the military in the party and the government with the resultant erosion of party authority, the failure by the military to expedite Mao's orders, and preferential appointments of Lin Biao's protégés to important positions at the expense of experienced veteran cadres. Confrontations over these issues evidently took place at party gatherings in March 1970.

A detailed discussion of the rise of military power in Chinese politics since the Cultural Revolution, and its implication in the Lin Biao affair, will be found in Chapter 6. What needs to be pointed out here is that expansion of the military's political role was the basis of top leadership's disagreement and conflict. The purge of a large number of senior military officers, and the attempts to restore party control over the military, became the focal concerns of the post–Lin Biao collective leadership of Premier Zhou and the radicals who survived the onslaught of the army during the Cultural Revolution. This new coalition of forces (factions), although accepted by the Tenth Party Congress, proved to be temporary and illusory. The contest for power between the forces behind Premier Zhou and the radicals, led by Mao's wife Jiang Qing, eventually culminated in the Tian An Men Square incident after Zhou Enlai's death in January 1976 and in the arrest of the radical leaders in October of that year, a month after Mao's death.

In the spring of 1981, Lin Biao was put on trial figuratively, along with the radical leaders led by Jiang Qing, for plotting against Mao's life and for an attempted military coup d'etat.[67] A dozen or so top-ranking military officers closely associated with Lin Biao were sentenced to long-term imprisonment.[68] The elimination of the radicals ushered in not only a new leader to succeed Mao but also a new era of moderation and pragmatism. It is this period we must now examine.

THE "GANG OF FOUR" AND THE TRIAL[69]

The top radical leaders, later known as the "Gang of Four," included Jiang Qing, Zhang Chunqiao, Yao Wenyuan, and Wang Hongwen. Jiang Qing, Mao's wife, had been a member of the Central Committee's Cultural Revolution Group, which directed the Red Guards and the upheaval, and a vice-chair person of the Cultural Revolution Committee in the PLA under Lin Biao. Zhang Chunqiao and Yao Wenyuan were active in the Shanghai Municipal Party Committee and had used Shanghai as a bastion for Mao's counterattacks against Liu Shaoqi's forces during the Cultural Revolution. It was Yao who wrote the first critique of the play *Hai Rui's Dismissal from Office*, which served as the first salvo against Liu Shaoqi at the beginning of the Cultural Revolution. Both Yao and Zhang, along with Jiang Qing, subsequently became key members of the Central Committee's Cultural Revolution Group. Wang Hongwen was a young leader of the Shanghai Congress of Revolutionary Workers Rebels, a workers' group which supported the radical activities in Shanghai during the Cultural Revolution.

The radicals were a minority group within the party and advocated continuous class struggle under the dictatorship of the proletariat. Their greatest strength came from activists and young university students. As a group, the radicals had little institutional support within the society. Their survival after the Cultural Revolution was dependent upon two factors: personal support from Chairman Mao and their fragile alliances, first with Lin Biao and then with Zhou Enlai's forces. The fact that they served as Mao's spokespersons on ideological matters during and after the Cultural Revolution gave the radicals an aura of strength. While Mao remained mentally alert, few dared to oppose his views openly for fear of incurring Mao's wrath. The radicals' control over the mass media and over the fields of art, literature, and drama added to their strength. Hua Guofeng later charged that they had "spread a host of revisionist fallacies" and that "metaphysics" ran wild and "idealism went rampant." The radicals' base of operation was limited to a few urban centers, primarily the municipalities under the direct administration of the central government: Beijing, Shanghai, and Tianjin. Their activities were mainly concentrated in the trade union federations in these cities.

Realizing their weakness in case of a showdown, the radicals helped build an urban militia in an attempt to secure a countervailing force to the PLA. The urban militia, which was organized and controlled by the various trade union federations and municipal party committees allied with the radicals, appeared to be a potentially powerful political instrument for the radical elements within the party.[70]

During and after the Cultural Revolution, the top radical leaders acquired influence and position in the party. The Ninth Party Congress in 1969 elected all four radical leaders members of the Central Committee. Zhang Chunqiao, as first secretary of the party's Shanghai Municipal Committee, was also elected to the Politburo. With the demise of Lin Biao, the four leaders were elected to the Politburo of the Tenth Central Committee in August 1973. In addition, Wang was said to have been Mao's personal choice for vice chairman of the party, the post previously held by Lin Biao.

When the much delayed Fourth National People's Congress, China's equivalent to parliament, convened in January 1975, it presented an appearance of surface unity. However, behind the scenes, the radicals, led by Jiang Qing, jockeyed for power against the moderates, who supported Premier Zhou Enlai. At first Zhou made some compromises with the radicals. Zhang Chunqiao was made a vice-premier and a director of the PLA's General Political Department, responsible for the political and ideological education of the troops. But at Zhou's insistence, Deng Xiaoping was brought back and rehabilitated as a vice-premier and as the chief of staff for the PLA. Deng, considered a chief villain by the radicals, had been purged along with Liu Shaoqi during the Cultural Revolution. Zhou, in failing health, wanted Deng, who was a capable and trusted colleague, to provide the needed leadership and experience in the central government.

The Fourth National People's Congress was dominated by Zhou and his party and government veterans. Zhou made it very clear at the session that in order to speed up development and modernization of the economy, it was necessary to make changes, including implementing wage differentials to spur production, placing decision making in factories into the hands of plant managers and experts, and emphasizing scientific research through the upgrading of university education. Zhou even invoked one of Mao's statements on the need for a technical revolution and for borrowing scientific and technical know-how from abroad.[71] These changes were viewed by the radicals as reversing the gains of the Cultural Revolution.

The radicals' offensives soon converged on the individual who they considered most vulnerable in the Zhou Enlai group, the rehabilitated Deng Xiaoping, who had been designated by Zhou to implement the economic acceleration and modernization. As Zhou became increasingly incapacitated by cancer (and was hospitalized most of the time in 1975), the attacks against him and Deng intensified in the radical-controlled media. The radicals were very much concerned about who would take over the premiership in the event of Zhou's death. Wang Hongwen was said to have been dispatched on several occasions to see Chairman Mao, to persuade him to designate either Zhang Chunqiao or Jiang Qing to succeed Zhou.[72] Their aim was to at least prevent Deng Xiaoping from assuming the premiership in case Zhou should die in office. In the radicals' eyes, Deng was the "capitalist roader" who had long advocated that hard work, not politics in command, was what really mattered: "Never mind about the color of the cat as long as it catches mice." In January 1976 Zhou Enlai died. There was a genuine outpouring of affection and respect by the masses for Zhou. But as soon as the nation had paid final tribute to the leader, the battle for succession began in earnest. Wall posters in the streets of Beijing demanded that Deng Xiaoping be purged again for his efforts to restore "bourgeois rights." The campaign of vilification against Deng culminated in April in the Tian An Men incident.

The entire incident at Tian An Men Square was a large, spontaneous demonstration during the traditional festival in honor of the dead. The crowd, reportedly more than 100,000 at its height, was angered by the removal of flower wreaths placed in the square to honor the late Premier Zhou. The demonstrators created disturbances and damaged property belonging to the public security units stationed at public buildings on the square. The incident was a spontaneous show of support for the late premier's policies on material development and incentives. It could also be considered a show of support for Deng Xiaoping, who was a major target for attack by the radical leaders. Toward the end of the demonstration, the radicals entered this round-of-power contest by dispatching some units of the urban militia, presumably to quell the riots. By all accounts, this show of strength by the urban militia was rather feeble and unimpressive.[73]

While the urban militia did not prevent the mass riot at Tian An Men, an estimated 3,000 to 4,000 demonstrators were arrested by the public security forces with the assistance of the urban militia.[74] Among those arrested were workers, cadres, and intellectuals.[75] The CCP subsequently declared the demonstration "a revolutionary mass action against the radicals."[76]

The radicals used the incident for their own purposes. They labeled the disorderly conduct of the demonstrators in support of Zhou and Deng as "counterrevolutionary" and blamed Deng for instigating the incident. The radicals at this time had the support of Mao and enough Politburo members to have Deng dismissed from all positions of power and, thereby, to remove him as a candidate to succeed Zhou Enlai for the premiership. The spontaneous outburst of the huge crowd in the Tian An Men Square incident demonstrated the radicals' alienation from the masses. The radicals, nevertheless, won the first round of the succession struggle by removing Deng Xiaoping from the seat of power for the second time. The compromise choice of Hua Guofeng as first vice chairman of the CCP, a newly designated position, and as acting premier may have been made personally by Mao, who surely by then had realized the danger of a split within the top echelons of the party. While Mao lived, he somehow kept the factions in balance—even, at times, tipping the balance slightly in favor of his radical disciples.

The campaign to criticize Deng Xiaoping sputtered forward, without arousing any genuine mass support or enthusiasm, from April through July, ending in August when a series of a major earthquakes shook the Beijing area. The ancient Chinese saying that unusual natural phenomena generally precede some earthshaking event seemed prophetic: Chairman Mao died on September 9, 1976, at the age of eighty-two. While the nation again mourned the loss of a great leader, political maneuvering for the succession contest reached its peak. At first the open dispute revolved around Mao's will. The radicals claimed that the will called for the gains and values of the Cultural Revolution to be upheld by Mao's successors. The moderates, now a close alliance of party, government, and veteran military cadres, claimed that Mao had designated in writing that Hua Guofeng be named his successor: "With you in charge, I am at ease."[77] These were merely skirmishes of the pen. The real combat took place from the end of September to the first week of October at Politburo meetings, which included some heated debates. Reportedly, the radical leaders proposed that Jiang Qing be named the new party chairperson, and Zhang Chunqiao the new premier. It has also since been reported that the radical leaders mapped out a military coup to be staged in Shanghai as a last resort in the contest for power.[78]

The final decision of the Central Committee on October 7 was firm and direct: Hua Guofeng was to succeed Mao as chairman of the party, and all opposition to this decision had to be silenced. Almost simultaneously, the four radical leaders were placed under arrest by the special security force no. 8341, directly under the supervision of the Central Committee and the Politburo and under the personal command of Politburo member Wang Dongxing. Swiftly, regular PLA units, all under the command of Politburo members, moved into Beijing, Shanghai, and other cities to disarm the urban militia. The PLA placed these cities under temporary military control to prevent any disturbances. By October 24 Hua's successful move against the radicals was complete, and an estimated 1 million Chinese gathered in Tian An Men Square to cheer a new leader and to celebrate the dawn of a new era for China.

The Gang of Four, along with twelve other principal defendants (all former ranking military officers closely associated with Lin Biao), were tried during November and December 1980 under the recently enacted criminal code. The trial was open to selected observers and was televised as a spectacular to demonstrate the need for a return to law and order. The pragmatic leaders hoped that by using the legal process, rather than summary execution, public confidence and respect for socialist legality would be restored. Nonetheless the staging of the trial by the pragmatic leaders served to vindicate the position they took during the Cultural Revolution.

The new leadership also wanted to tie the Gang of Four to Lin Biao's attempted assassination of Mao and the abortive coup d'etat, even though each faction had its own goals. This linkage was designed to achieve two objectives. First, it attempted to protect Mao's reputation and to downplay his close relationship with the radicals on trial. Second, the strategy was also intended to shield Hua Guofeng. An agreement reportedly was worked out to delete any reference to Hua's association with the radicals—particularly his role in suppressing the 1976 Tian An Men demonstration.[79]

The radical leaders and the former top military brass under Lin Biao were convicted for persecuting veteran party leaders, for plotting to assassinate Mao, and for organizing a secret armed rebellion. All but two of the defendants received sentences varying from sixteen to twenty years in prison. Jiang Qing and Zhang Chunqiao were sentenced to death, with a two-year stay of execution.[80] In January 1983 the Supreme People's Court ruled that since both Jiang and Zhang had shown "sufficient repentance" and "had not resisted reform in a flagrant way" during the two-year reprieve period, the execution would not be carried out in 1983.

The trial of the radical leaders seems to have been successful not only in repudiating the Cultural Revolution but also in meting out punishment through the judicial process. The trial represented a victory for the pragmatic leaders who were themselves victims of the Cultural Revolution. However, for cynics inside and outside of China, the trial was just another episode in the grand tradition of Beijing opera.

The Rise and Fall of Hua Guofeng, 1976–81[81]

Prior to Zhou's death, the world knew very little about the man who would emerge as chairman of the party, premier, and chief of the military complex in China. His rise to one of the most powerful positions in the world was not really very spectacular. Let us look briefly at his background from the information now available to us.

Hua was born in 1920 to a peasant family in the northwestern province of Shanxi. He joined the communist guerrillas in his home province at a young age, and by 1947, at the age of twenty-seven, was a young party secretary for a county and a leader of a local guerrilla band with considerable experience in making explosives. In 1949 he moved with the PLA forces to Hunan, where he remained as a local and provincial party leader until 1971. During this period Hua, who is now a widower, raised four children.

In 1952 Hua was appointed party secretary for Xiang-tan Special District, which included Mao's birthplace, Shaoshan. In this post Hua supervised the planning and construction of a memorial hall, which was formally dedicated to Mao in 1955. By 1959 Hua had carved out an impressive administrative record in Hunan in a number of posts in diverse functional areas, giving him a wealth of knowledge about party and government affairs. These areas included agriculture, education, cultural affairs, water conservation, finance, and trade. Each new position was a promotion in responsibility, if not always in grade.

When Mao visited his birthplace in June 1959, for the first time in thirty-seven years, he was impressed with the memorial and beautification of the village, and undoubtedly mentioned this to Hua when they met. Then, during the summer, Hua participated in the Lushan Conference, where Mao was being criticized for the Great Leap and the commune programs. Hua, as a leading figure in the Hunan provincial government, wrote at least two investigative reports supporting the communes and defending the Great Leap. Reportedly, because of his staunch defense of Mao at Lushan, Hua was appointed to the position of provincial party secretary for Hunan on Mao's recommendation.[82]

In rising to the position of provincial party secretary, Hua had to be adept at coping with intraparty conflicts. On the major questions of cooperatives, communes, and the purge of Peng Dehuai, Hua supported Mao's policies. He also supported the Great Leap Forward program in Hunan but cautioned against excesses. He was one of the few provincial bosses who survived the Cultural Revolution and emerged intact to lead the formation of one of the first provincial revolutionary committees in China. Hua was also involved at the provincial level in preventing military supporters of Lin Biao from exerting influence in provincial affairs in 1969 and 1970. Hua by then had been elected by the Ninth party Congress to full membership on the Central Committee.

By 1971 Hua's political activities had extended beyond Hunan. Either because of his personal contacts with Mao or the impression he had made on such key central leaders as Ye Jianying and Li Xiannian, Hua was called to Beijing to direct the staff office of the State Council. In that capacity Hua was one of the top aides to Premier Zhou. Hua's stay in Beijing was short; he returned to Hunan in the summer of 1971 to resume his duties as the provincial party chief. His experience in serving directly under Zhou Enlai in the State Council was most likely an important factor in his being asked to chair the State Council in April 1976 and, hence, his subsequent selection as head of the party.[83]

Nineteen seventy-one was the turbulent year in which the Lin Biao affair surfaced. The Politburo established a special committee to investigate Lin Biao's alleged attempted coup. Hua was appointed to the investigation committee, along with six senior Politburo members. Apparently, Hua, who was noted for his investigative skills, did a good job on the committee, which indicted Lin Biao for antiparty crimes. Perhaps as a reward for Hua's work in the Lin Biao investigation and also perhaps as a recognition of the need to promote talented provincial leaders to the center, Hua was elected to the all-powerful Politburo in August 1973. He was soon brought into the State Council in 1974, in a position of considerable importance and power, as the minister for public security, the nation's chief law enforcer.

For Mao Zedong and the radicals, Hua was, nevertheless, a compromise choice in January 1976, when Premier Zhou died. The other choice, Deng Xiaoping, was a bitter pill to swallow. The selection of Hua as acting premier immediately after Zhou's death might be considered Mao's way of keeping the contending groups in balance. The compromise became the only possible choice when the Tian An Men Square demonstration occurred in April. After that incident Hua Guofeng must have sensed that his political future rested in a coalition of party and government administrators and the military. As a shrewd leader who had engaged in and survived many power contests as a provincial party secretary, Hua must have realized by the spring of 1976 that the radicals had neither the popular support for their revolutionary causes nor the institutional base for the power contest, particularly in view of the poor showing by the urban militia at Tian An Men. He marked his time until the appropriate moment arrived to deal a mortal blow to the radicals at the urging and with the support of the military.

Hua's position became precarious in 1978, when his role in the Tian An Men demonstration was questioned at inner party meetings. By the fall of 1980, Hua was forced to relinquish his premiership. In 1981 the Politburo, now under Deng's control, demanded that Hua make self-criticism about his past errors and step down from his party chairmanship as well. Hua was said to have balked at admitting that he had made any mistakes in launching the 1978 modernization program; he was then criticized as being overambitious and unrealistic. He was also criticized by Hu Yaobang for refusing to accept the new ideological line of "seeking truth from fact."[84] When the Twelfth Party Congress met in September 1982, Hua was barely able to get elected to membership on the Central Committee; by then he had lost all other top party and governmental positions.

Why had Hua's fortunes fallen so rapidly after his spectacular rise to power immediately after Mao's death? The reasons were many and complex. The following are some of the most relevant factors that contributed to his downfall.[85] First, Hua was elevated to the national political scene on the assumption that he had the requisite administrative ability, as shown by his work at the local and provincial level. This proved to have been a gross miscalculation on the part of his mentors, the late Zhou Enlai and Ye Jianying. Hua's background was essentially that of a rural guerrilla, and his education was limited—to say the least. His provincial administrative training was inadequate to prepare him for the enormous tasks of administering China's complex economic and industrial system. By all accounts his performance was inadequate, or at best "highly undistinguished" and "unimpressive", according to one China expert. Second, when it came to political infighting and maneuvering at the center of power, Hua was no match for seasoned players like Deng Xiaoping or Chen Yun. During his four years in power (from 1976 to 1980), Hua not only was unable to consolidate power under his leadership but was challenged and outmaneuvered at every turn by Deng's forces. The coalition on which Hua relied was made up largely of the few remaining followers of Mao, the "Whatever" faction, which proclaimed that whatever Mao said must be implemented. They suffered a severe blow at a December 1978 top-level work conference, when a number of Deng's supporters were placed on the Politburo to outvote them. A year later, in February 1980, the four key "Whatever" leaders were removed from the Politburo, leaving Hua with no viable means of support in the political contest. Third, as the trial of the Gang of Four was about to begin, Hua's position and involvement with the radicals became difficult to defend. The April 1976 Tian An Men demonstration, which resulted in Deng's purge, was suppressed by the public security forces, China's national police—then headed by Hua. Following the arrest of the radicals, Hua openly espoused the line that whatever Mao said must be carried out. This ran counter to the pragmatic views of the reformers, led by Deng, who called for a reevaluation of Mao and his mistakes. Fourth, Hua cultivated a "personality cult." After Mao's death Hua allowed his own picture to be placed alongside that of Mao. A casual visitor to China during 1978 and 1979 could not help noticing the widespread display of Hua's picture in factories, offices, schools, and workers' homes. This practice of "personality cult" definitely tarnished Hua's image as a new leader in post-Mao China. It also provided ammunition for the pragmatic leaders to attack Hua for adhering to Mao's "feudal practice." Fifth, as the economists and technocrats at the top reviewed the modernization plan launched in 1978 under Hua's leadership, and as China experienced many financial and managerial problems, Hua was blamed for errors in the 1978 modernization plan and for making unrealistic projections reminiscent of the Great Leap in 1958.

COLLECTIVE LEADERSHIP OF DENG XIAOPING, HU YAOBANG, AND ZHAO ZIYANG

According to official sources, China is now under the collective leadership of three key leaders: Deng Xiaoping, Hu Yaobang, and Zhao Ziyang. This triumvirate controls the three main pillars of the Chinese political system: the military, the party, and the government. Some analysts think that the triumvirate is a facade to disguise the fact that Deng Xiaoping really is the paramount leader: They see power in China during the early 1980s becoming consolidated under the control of Deng. The pragmatic reform measures introduced since 1978 might be called Dengism. The recent publication of the selective works of Deng lend credence to this view. Let us take a brief look at these three key leaders.

Deng Xiaoping: Architect
of the Power Transition

In 1979 Americans had a chance to observe at first hand China's new strongman, Deng Xiaoping, when he visited the United States at the invitation of President Carter. For eight days Deng traveled from Washington to Atlanta, Houston, and Seattle, accompanied by members of Congress and the Carter cabinet. He was interviewed by the press at each stop; he mingled with the crowd in Atlanta; and he donned a ten-gallon hat at a Texas rodeo. His tour included visits to the space technology complex and oil-drilling-machine plants in Houston, and the Boeing plant in Seattle.

What type of person is China's paramount leader, and what are his views? Although a dedicated communist and Leninist, Deng has never been dogmatic. When China was experiencing economic recovery during the early 1960s following the disastrous Great Leap, Deng said, "It makes no difference if a cat is black or white—so long as it catches the mice." In 1975 he expressed his disdain for a requirement that everyone spend long hours after work studying correct political thought. He called the practice "social oppression." A pragmatist, Deng has advocated the line of profit-in-command, rather than Mao's dictum of politics-in-command.

Deng was born in Sichuan province in 1904. He was an early organizer for the Chinese communist movement when both he and the late Zhou Enlai were students in France under a work-study program.[86] Before returning to China in 1927 to work in an underground party cell in Shanghai, Deng studied briefly in Moscow. He joined Mao's guerrilla movement during the early 1930s and took part in the Long March. His rise in the party hierarchy was rapid, and by 1955 Deng was elected to the powerful Politburo and held the position of general secretary to the party. He remained the party's general secretary until 1966, when he was purged by the radicals during the Cultural Revolution.[87] In 1974 he returned to power at the request of the then ailing Zhou Enlai and Mao to introduce reforms that would enable China to modernize its industry, agriculture, sciences, and military defense. When the Tian An Men riot erupted in 1976, Deng was again purged. Following the arrest of the Gang of Four, Deng was once more returned to power to oversee China's modernization program as a deputy premier and vice-chairman of the party.[88] The twice-purged Deng realized that to fulfill his task as chief architect of modernization, he must consolidate his power by replacing the remnants of Mao's followers with his own people.[89]

Political maneuvers among the top leaders in China were factional and did not necessarily follow ideological lines. The factions were based on personal relationships and associations. Several China scholars have studied factionalism in Chinese politics.[90] For instance, Parris Chang comments on the emergence of two major coalitions, or groupings, among top leaders since the arrest of the Gang of Four in 1976.[91] One coalition, the "Whatever" group, consisted of Politburo members who were Mao loyalists and who collaborated with the Gang of Four during the Cultural Revolution. Included in the "Whatever" coalition was the so-called "petroleum" or "oil" faction, a group of veteran economists and technocrats who directed the economy. Hua Guofeng became the "Whatever" coalition's symbolic leader. The pragmatists of the second coalition, led by Deng, consisted mainly of Politburo members who were veteran party leaders and northern military leaders. Most of the Deng group had been victims of purges during the Cultural Revolution. Allied with the Deng pragmatists were (1) the Chen Yun economic planners, (2) elder statesmen (Ye Jianying), and (3) so-called "independents."

Another commentator, Dorothy Fontana, has constructed a factional model utilizing the familiar radical-left, left-of-center, and political-right spectrum.[92] She believes that the radical left was made up of the Gang of Four and the "Whatever" group, joined earlier by the Lin Biao supporters. The left-of-center faction included the Long March military leaders and the "oil", or "petroleum" group of central economic administrators. The political-right faction included the late Zhou Enlai, the purged party victims of the Cultural Revolution, such as Deng, and the southern military leaders who later split with the Deng group.

In 1978 Deng Xiaoping began taking steps to consolidate his power and control over the party. A campaign was first launched against party officials who had collaborated with the Gang of Four and were now supporters of the "Whatever" faction. The campaign soon focused on the Politburo members who were led by Hua Guofeng and Wang Dongxing and who opposed Deng's reform policies. Hua's group appealed for reconciliation with those who had made serious mistakes during and after the Cultural Revolution. Marshal Ye, Hua's mentor on the Politburo, intervened by calling for "stability and unity" in order to mitigate the leadership purge that was about to begin and perhaps save something for those Politburo members who were known to have collaborated with the Gang of Four in the past.

At the Third Plenum of the Eleventh Central Committee (December 1978), Deng made some important gains as well as some concessions. The most important gain was the designation of Deng's protégé, Hu Yaobang, as the CCP general secretary to supervise the daily administration of the party affairs in an effort to dilute Chairman Hua's power. Deng gained another victory when the Central Committee agreed to elect four of his supporters as additional members of the Politburo. Those named were Chen Yun, Deng Yingchao (widow of Zhou Enlai), Hu Yaobang, and Wang Zhen. Chen Yun's elevation to Politburo membership was owed primarily to his reputation as a realistic economic planner. Chen was also made a vice-chairman of the Politburo's Standing Committee as a way of obtaining the support of the "independents," of whom he was a leading spokesperson. In addition, nine veteran party officials purged during the Cultural Revolution were elected as additional Central Committee members.

The party's declaration at the Third Plenum that the 1976 Tian An Men demonstration was an "entirely revolutionary mass movement" must be viewed as a personal vindication for Deng.[93] It was also a blow to those Politburo members who, sooner or later, would have to make self-criticism about their role in support of the Gang of Four in that riot which caused Deng's second purge. Finally, after some heated discussion, the party adopted Deng's view that practice was to be the sole criterion for testing truth, and that things did not have to be done according to books or to "ossified thinking." This was a direct refutation of the "Whatever" faction's stand. Deng was not yet strong enough to demand the immediate ouster of his opponents still sitting on the Politburo. Actually, Deng had to agree to shelve for the time being any further discussion on the sensitive, divisive issue of assessing Mao's role in the Cultural Revolution.

During 1979 Deng made little headway in instituting organizational reforms because of resistance from his adversaries. However, he prevailed upon the party at its Fourth Plenum in September 1979 to add twelve new members to the Central Committee. These new members included veteran leaders Peng Zhen, Po Yibo, and Yang Shangkun. Deng was also able to install Peng Zhen and Zhao Ziyang as alternate members of the Politburo and thus further improve his numerical strength on that body.

In February 1980 Deng's final move came at the party's Fifth Plenum. Key Deng supporters Hu Yaobang and Zhao Ziyang were elevated to membership on the Politburo's Standing Committee, the apex of the apex in decision making in the party hierarchy.[94] Their elevation was preceded by the removal of four Politburo members (Wang Dongxing, Ji Dengkui, Wu De, and Chen Xilian) who were held to be collaborators of the Gang of Four and critics of Deng's policies. While Hua Guofeng remained as the nominal party chairman, his power and influence by this time were those of a mere figurehead. For it was at the Fifth Plenum that the Central Secretariat was reestablished to manage and oversee the day-to-day work of the party, presided over by Hu Yaobang, the general secretary. By September Hua also had been replaced as premier of the State Council by Zhao Ziyang at a session of the NPC. Having removed his critics from the Politburo, Deng now was in a firmer position to issue a party communiqué calling for the implementation of the modernization program. By the end of 1980, he controlled the party, government, and military. But the new era in Chinese politics was not ushered in until some time later in September 1982, when the Twelfth Party Congress was convened under the complete control and domination of China's paramount leader, Deng Xiaoping, and his supporters.

Hu Yaobang: The Pragmatic
Party Boss[95]

The diminutive Hu Yaobang is a cool and courageous individual, as well as an effective party organizer. When the Red Guards dragged him in front of the Young Communist League headquarters in 1966, they shaved his head and wrapped him in a wooden chain. He was beaten repeatedly and daily; he was verbally abused in public. Hu remained composed and told the shouting Red Guards that he had committed no wrong. Following this ordeal, he was banished to the countryside for almost three years, and then was placed under house arrest for another five years. Hu survived the ordeal to emerge as one of the most powerful leaders in post-Mao China—the general secretary of the Chinese Communist Party.

Hu's strong character was shaped by years of guerrilla activity, which began at the age of thirteen in his home province of Hunan. From 1929 to 1934, he worked in guerrilla bases as a youth organizer. Then, in 1934, he joined the Long March—a qualification none of the other, younger leaders in the post-Mao era can claim. Following the era of the Long March, Hu developed a firm association with Deng, the political commissar for the eighteenth army corps, which later—in the 1940s—merged with other military units to become the Second Field Army. When Deng was elevated to work at the party center in Beijing in 1952, his protégé, Hu, joined him as general secretary of the Young Communist Youth League until both were purged in 1966. When Deng was reinstated in 1977, Hu rejoined him to oversee reforms in science and technology, preparing a number of key policy studies for China's modernization program. Like Deng, Hu was purged again in 1976.

After Deng returned to power in 1977, he made sure that Hu was appointed director of the party's organization department, which was responsible for party cadres' assignments and removals. In 1978 Hu took over the party's other important post, director for the propaganda department, to help Deng Xiaoping launch the new party line of "seeking truth from facts." Shortly thereafter, Hu became the party's general secretary, a job that provides daily direction and administration of party affairs. This move, in essence, eroded Hua Guofeng's role as the party's nominal head. When Hua was removed from his party position in June 1981, Hu temporarily became the party chairman. In September 1982, when that position was abolished, Hu was officially installed as the party's general secretary.

The major items on Hu Yaobang's agenda, at least for the foreseeable future, are (1) the restoration of party prestige, (2) the rebuilding of the party with a better workstyle, and (3) the placement of younger and more competent personnel in party leadership positions. Hu stressed these rebuilding priorities in both his maiden speech as the head of the party in June 1981 and in his keynote address to the Twelfth Party Congress in September 1982.[96] In his speeches Hu urged an end to the practice of one-person rule—"What one person says, goes." He also called for strict adherence to the Leninist principles of collective leadership and democratic centralism. He demanded urgent party reform so that party leadership at all levels would be in the hands of those who were "younger in average age, better educated, and more professionally competent." He spoke of restoring party discipline and correcting the "flabbiness" and "paralysis" in party organizations by 1986. Hu maintained that party unity, discipline, and work style were the essential ingredients for the success of China's modernization.[97]

To ensure his control over the party organization, Hu Yaobang entrusted a number of his own close supporters and associates with pivotal positions in the party. His single most important strength seems to come from middle-level leaders in the party and government, many of whom were members and cadres of the Young Communist League when Hu was its general secretary. Contrary to some reports, Hu Yaobang is not a stranger to the military. His early work as a young political commissar under Deng Xiaoping with the Second Field Army provided extensive contacts within the military. Only time will tell whether these associations can, in the long run, enable Hu to control the military after Deng Xiaoping is gone.

Zhao Ziyang: Top Bureaucrat and Economic Innovator[98]

By Western standards, the job of the premier of China's central government, the State Council, is about the lowest-paid position in the world. While the president of the United States receives a salary of about $200,000 a year, the Chinese premier receives the U.S. equivalent of $3,800, a figure which is below the poverty line in the United States. Yet the Chinese premier may have one of the toughest governing tasks in the world: the job of improving the living conditions in a country the size of the United States with a population of over 1 billion.

Zhao Ziyang rose to the position of premier not as a Deng protégé but through promotion to various positions in local and provincial administration. After serving as a party secretary for a small district in Hunan province during the 1940s, Zhao was transferred to the south in the early 1950s to work on land reform programs in Guangdong. Under the tutelage of a powerful party regional overlord, Tao Zhu, he became an expert in rural affairs and was promoted to sub-bureau chief for the party's regional organization in southern China. In 1962 Tao elevated Zhao to the second in command for the provincial party committee. In 1966 both Tao and Zhao were purged. Like Hu Yaobang, Zhao Ziyang suffered physical abuse at the hands of the Red Guards in 1966. In fact, Zhao went through numerous "struggle sessions," perhaps as many as 200 by one account, over the two-year period from 1967–68.[99] He was paraded through the streets of Guangzhou wearing a dunce cap and was put on a stand in a sports stadium in front of 40,000 spectators. He spent the years 1967–71 in a Mao thought study group, and was then banished to work as a basic-level cadre in Inner Mongolia in 1971. Shortly afterward, Zhao became a party secretary in the Inner Mongolian autonomous region, a post he held until 1974, when he was released and returned to his position as provincial party secretary for Guangdong. In 1976 Zhao was appointed first secretary for the populous Sichuan province in western China. In Sichuan he initiated a number of innovative economic reforms that caught the attention of the pragmatists, who were eager to implement the modernization programs.

When Zhao arrived in Sichuan, the province was in the midst of economic disaster, with factories either closed or idle. Although a rich province, Sichuan's agricultural output was very low. Zhao made many inspection trips to the factories and communes and dispatched work teams to find out why the output was low. Finally, he introduced "baogan daohu" ("fixing output for each household under contract"). This policy, to be discussed in Chapter

8, has since become a basic agricultural policy throughout China. As an incentive scheme to boost rural production, it places responsibility on individual peasants to manage their farms as they like, so long as they meet their share of the state quota; the peasants could grow anything for themselves or for sale at the free markets Zhao introduced. Zhao also allowed for sideline production on private plots.

To boost industrial production, Zhao allowed each enterprise to manage its own production on the basis of profit and loss. Bonuses and merit rewards were initiated as material incentives for factory workers who wanted to earn them.

After the introduction of these innovative programs, Sichuan's agricultural and industrial production increased by as much as 50 percent across the board. Zhao became a nationally known figure for his bold experiments. In September 1980 Zhao Ziyang was chosen to become China's new premier.

NOTES

1. Charles P. Fitzgerald, *Revolution in China* (New York: Holt, Rinehart & Winston, 1952), pp. 12–16.

2. John King Fairbank, *The United States and China,* 3rd ed. (Cambridge, Mass.: Harvard University Press, 1971), pp. 90–95.

3. Fairbank, *The United States and China,* p. 55.

4. Fitzgerald, *Revolution in China,* p. 23.

5. Kung-chuan Hsiao, *Rural China: Imperial Control in the Nineteenth Century* (Seattle, Wash.: University of Washington Press, 1960), pp. 253–54.

6. Fairbank, *The United States and China,* pp. 20–34.

7. Ibid., p. 103.

8. Ibid., and James Townsend, *Politics in China* (Boston: Little, Brown and Co., 1974), pp. 35–36.

9. Townsend, *Politics in China,* p. 37.

10. Fairbank, *The United States and China,* p. 191.

11. Fitzgerald, *Revolution in China,* p. 38; and Fairbank, *The United States and China,* pp. 197–98.

12. For a detailed account of the events in 1927, see Franklin Houn, *A Short History of Chinese Communism* (Englewood Cliffs, N.J.: Prentice-Hall, 1967), pp. 21–33.

13. Ibid., pp. 35–38.

14. Hsiung, *Ideology and Practice: The Evolution of Chinese Communism* (New York: Praeger Publishers, 1970), pp. 61–62. See also Edgar Snow, *Red Star Over China* (New York: Grove Press, 1961).

15. John M. H. Lindbeck, "Transformation in the Chinese Communist Party," in *Soviet and Chinese Communist: Similarities and Differences,* ed. Donald Treadgold (Seattle: University of Washington Press, 1967), p. 76; and Stuart Schram, "Mao Tse-tung and the Chinese Political Equilibrium," *Government and Opposition,* vol. 4, no. 1 (Winter 1969), 141–42.

16. Hsiung, *Ideology and Practice,* pp. 45–46; and Dick Wilson, *The Long March 1935: The Epic of Chinese Communism's Survival* (New York: Avon Books, First Discus Printing, 1973). Also see Edward E. Rice, *Mao's Way* (Berkeley, Calif.: University of California Press, 1972), pp. 83–88.

17. Hsiung, *Ideology and Practice,* pp. 52–53; and Fairbank, *The United States and China,* pp. 269–70.

18. John Lindbeck, "Transformation in the Chinese Communist Party," p. 76.

19. See *The Selected Works of Mao Tse-tung* (Peking: Foreign Language Press, 1967), II, 339–84; III, 205–70.

20. Fairbank, *The United States and China,* p. 313.

21. Houn, *A Short History of Chinese Communism,* pp. 173–77.

22. E. Stuart Kirby, "Agrarian Problems and Peasantry," in *Communist China, 1949–1969: A Twenty Year Appraisal,* eds. Frank N. Trager and William Henderson (New York: New York University Press, 1970), p. 160.

23. Ezra Vogel, "Land Reform in Kwangtung 1951–1953: Central Control and Localism," *The China Quarterly,* 38 (April–June 1969), 27–62.

24. Ibid., pp. 27–62.

25. Houn, *A Short History of Chinese Communism,* p. 159.

26. Ibid., p. 164; and Kirby, "Agrarian Problems and Peasantry," p. 162.

27. See the official documents dealing with the debate over the cooperatives. The texts of these documents are in Robert R. Bowie and John K. Fairbank, *Communist China, 1955–1959: Policy Documents With Analysis* (Cambridge, Mass.: Harvard University Press, 1965), pp. 92–126.

28. Discussion on the First Five-Year Plan was based on the following sources: Alexander Eckstein, *China's Economic Revolution* (London and New York: Cambridge University Press, 1977), pp. 31–66; E. L. Wheelwright and Bruce McFarlane, *The Chinese Road to Socialism: Economics of the Cultural Revolution* (New York: Monthly Review Press, 1970), pp. 31–65; and Houn, *A Short History of Communist China,* pp. 177–85.

29. Houn, *A Short History of Chinese Communism,* pp. 178–79; Wheelwright and McFarlane, *The Chinese Road to Socialism,* p. 35.

30. Houn, *A Short History of Chinese Communism,* pp. 178–79.

31. Ibid., pp. 178–79.

32. Wheelwright and McFarlane, *The Chinese Road to Socialism,* p. 36.

33. Discussion in this section on the Great Leap program is based on these sources: Houn, *A Short History of Chinese Communism,* pp. 181–82; Fairbank, *The United States and China,* pp. 369–75; Eckstein, *China's Economic Revolution,* pp. 54–65; Roderick MacFarquhar, *The Origin of the Cultural Revolution: The Contradictions among the People, 1956–1957* (New York: Columbia University Press, 1974), pp. 57–74; Hsiung, *Ideology and Practice,* pp. 185–99.

34. Eckstein, *China's Economic Revolution,* p. 59.

35. Byung-joon Ahn, *Chinese Politics and the Cultural Revolution: Dynamics of Policy Processes* (Seattle, Wash. and London: University of Washington Press, 1976), pp. 31–47.

36. *The Case of Peng Teh-huai* (Hong Kong: Union Research Institute, 1968); and J. D. Simmons, "Peng Teh-huai: A Chronological Re-examination," *The China Quarterly,* 37 (January-March 1968), 120–38.

37. There are many accounts of the Lushan decision. The latest is in Ahn, *Chinese Politics and the Cultural Revolution,* pp. 38–44.

38. The brief survey here is based on Eckstein, *China's Economic Revolution,* pp. 202–205, and on Houn, *A Short History of Chinese Communism,* pp. 182–85. Also see Ahn, *Chinese Politics and the Cultural Revolution,* pp. 48–86, for a more detailed account of the recovery for the period 1962–65.

39. Discussion on the socialist education campaign is drawn from these sources: Hsiung, *Ideology and Practice,* pp. 200–16; Richard Baum and Frederick C. Teiwes, *Ssu-Ch'ing: The Socialist Educational Movement of 1962–1966* (Berkeley, Calif.: Center for Chinese Studies, University of California, 1968); Ahn, *Chinese Politics and the Cultural Revolution,* pp. 89–122; Philip Bridgham, "Mao's 'Cultural Revolution': Origin and Development," *The China Quarterly,* 29 (January–March 1967), 1–35; Richard Baum and Frederick Teiwes, "Liu Shao-chi and the Cadres Question," *Asian Survey,* vol. viii, no. 4 (April 1968), 323–45; and Richard Baum, *Prelude to Revolution: Mao, the Party and the Peasant Question, 1962–1966* (New York: Columbia University Press, 1975).

40. C. S. Chen, ed., *Rural People's Communes in Lien-chiang,* trans. Charles P. Ridley (Stanford, Calif.: Hoover Institution, 1969); Baum and Teiwes, "Liu Shao-chi and the Cadres Question"; and Ahn, *Chinese Politics and the Cultural Revolution,* pp. 99–108. Also see Hsiung, *Ideology and Practice,* pp. 206–208.

41. Ahn, *Chinese Politics and the Cultural Revolution,* p. 103; and for an insight into the interpersonal behavior of the cadres, see Michel Oksenberg, "The Institutionalization of the Chinese Communist Revolution: The Ladder of Success on the Eve of the Cultural Revolution," *The China Quarterly,* 36 (October–December 1968), 61–92.

42. For a bibliography on the subject, see James C. F. Wang, *The Cultural Revolution in China: An Annotated Bibliography* (New York and London: Garland Publishing, Inc., 1976).

43. See Donald Zagoria, *Vietnam Triangle: Moscow, Peking, Hanoi* (New York: Pegasus, 1967); Uri Ra'amam, "Peking's Foreign Policy 'Debate,' 1965–1966," in *China's Policies in Asia and America's Alternatives,* ed. Tang Tsou (Chicago: University of Chicago Press, 1968), pp. 23–71; Robert Scalapino, "The Cultural Revolution and Chinese Foreign Policy," in *The Cultural Revolution: 1967 in Review* (Ann Arbor, Mich.: Michigan Papers in Michigan Studies No. 2, Center for Chinese Studies, University of Michigan, 1968), pp. 1–15.

44. For an account of the struggle at these two universities during the Cultural Revolution, see Victor Nee, *The Cultural Revolution at Peking University* (New York: Monthly Review Press, 1969); and William Hinton, *Hundred Day War: The Cultural Revolution at Tsinghua* (New York and London: Monthly Review Press, 1972).

45. See Gordon Bennett and Ronald N. Montaperto, *Red Guard: The Political Biography of Dai Hsiao-ai* (New York: Anchor Books, Doubleday, 1972).

46. See Michel Oksenberg, "China: Forcing the Revolution to a New Stage," *Asian Survey,* vol. vii, no. 1 (January 1967), 1–15; and John Israel, "The Red Guards in Historical Perspective: Continuity and Change in Chinese Youth Movement," *The China Quarterly,* 30 (April–June 1967), 1–32.

47. See Lowell Dittmer, "The Cultural Revolution and the Fall of Liu Shao-chi," *Current Scene,* vol. xi, no. 1 (January 1973), 1–13; Israel, "The Red Guards in Historical Perspective: Continuity and Change in the Chinese Youth Movement," 1–32.

48. Philip Bridgham, "Mao's Cultural Revolution in 1967: The Struggle to Seize Power," *The China Quarterly,* 34 (April–June 1968), 6–36; Ellis Joffe, "The Chinese Army in the Cultural Revolution: The Politics of Intervention," *The Current Scene,* vol. ii, no. 18 (December 7, 1970), 1–25; William Whitson, *The Chinese Communist High Command: A History of Military Politics, 1927–69* (New York: Holt, Rinehart & Winston, 1971); Jean Esmein, *The Chinese Cultural Revolution* (Garden City, N.Y.: Anchor Books, Doubleday, 1973); Stanley Karnow, *Mao and China: From Revolution to Revolution* (New York: Viking, 1972), pp. 276–316.

49. Edgar Snow, "Mao and the New Mandate," *The World Today,* vol. 25, no. 7 (July 1969), 290.

50. Parris H. Chang, "Regional Military Power: The Aftermath of the Cultural Revolution," *Asian Survey,* vol. xii, no. 12 (December 1972), 999–1013, and "The Revolutionary Committee and the Party in the Aftermath of the Cultural Revolution," *Current Scene,* vol. viii, no. 8 (April 15, 1970), 1–10.

51. "Recent Development in Chinese Education," *Current Scene,* vol. x, no. 1 (July 1972), 1–6.

52. See Richard M. Pfeffer, "Serving the People and Continuing the Revolution," *The China Quarterly,* 52 (October–December 1972), 620–53.

53. "On Questions of Party History-Resolution on Certain Questions in the History of Our Party Since the Founding of the People's Republic of China," (adopted by the Sixth Plenary Session of the Eleventh Central Committee of the CPC on June 27, 1981), *Beijing Review,* 27 (July 6, 1981), 20.

54. Ibid.

55. Summary of an interview with the visiting editor of the Greek Communist Party, reported in *Ta Kung Pao Weekly Supplement* (Hong Kong), December 8, 1980, p. 3.

56. For a series of articles assessing the impact of the Cultural Revolution, see *Asian Survey,* vol. xii, no. 12 (December 1972). Also see Maurice Meisner, *Mao's China: A History of the People's Republic* (New York: The Free Press, 1977), pp. 340–59; and David Bonavia, "The Fate of the 'New Born Things' of China's Cultural Revolution," *Pacific Affairs,* vol. 51, no. 2 (Summer 1981), 177–94. Also see William Hinton, *Shenfan: The Cultural Revolution in a Chinese Village* (New York: Random House, 1983).

57. *A Great Trial in Chinese History* (New York: Pergamon Press, 1981), pp. 20–21.

58. Jiang Hua, president of the Supreme People's Court, recently reported that 326,000 people framed or falsely imprisoned had been exonerated after investigation by the court. See Michael Weisskopf, "China Reports End of Trials," Washington Post Service, as reprinted in *Honolulu Advertiser,* January 28, 1983, p. A–18.

59. *People's Daily,* July 16, 1980, p. 1.

60. Fox Butterfield, *China: Alive in the Bitter Sea* (New York: Times Books, 1982), p. 349.

61. "Cleaning Up Mao's Feudal Mistakes," *The Guardian,* September 21, 1980, p. 16.

62. *The New York Times,* September 23, 1971, sec. 1, pp. 1, 6.

63. *The New York Times,* July 28, 1972, sec. 1, p. 1.

64. *The New York Times,* July 29, 1972, sec. 1, p. 1; and *The New York Times,* October 12, 1972, sec. 1, p. 1.

65. For the texts of these internal documents, see Y. M. Kau, *The Lin Piao Affair, Power Politics and Military Coup* (White Plains, N.Y.: International Arts and Sciences Press, 1975), and also *The New York Times,* July 23, 1972, sec. 1, pp. 1, 6.

66. See Yao Ming-le, *The Conspiracy and Death of Lin Biao,* (New York: Alfred A. Knopf, 1983). Also see review of the book by Orville Schell, "A Chinese Puzzle Missing Some Pieces," *The New York Times Book Review,* May 15, 1983, p. 3; Richard Bernstein, "New Book Says Mao Ordered Lin Biao Killed," *The New York Times,* May 1, 1983, p. 13; Jay Mathews, "China Puzzle: Real Horror, Red Herring?" *Los Angeles Times Book Review,* May 15, 1983, p. 3; and "Was Lin Biao Murdered?" *Time Magazine,* May 16, 1983, p. 55.

67. *A Great Trail in Chinese History,* pp. 18–25.

68. Ibid., pp. 232–33. Also see "Lin Biao's Abortive Counter-Revolutionary Coup D'etat," *Beijing Review,* 51 (December 22, 1980), 19–28.

69. Suggested readings about the downfall of the Gang of Four include Jurgen Domes, "China in 1976: Tremors of Transition," *Asian Survey,* vol. xiii, no. 1 (January 1977), 1–17; Peter R. Moody, Jr., "The Fall of the Gang of Four: Background Notes on the Chinese Counter-revolution," *Asian Survey,* vol. xvii, no. 8 (August 1977), 711–23; Jurgen Domes, "The 'Gang of Four' and Hua Kuo-feng: Analysis of Political Events in 1975–76," *The China Quarterly,* 71 (September 1977), 473–97; James C. F. Wang, "The Urban Militia as a Political Instrument in the Power Contest in China in 1976," *Asian Survey,* vol. xviii, no. 6 (June 1978), 541–59; and Andres D. Onate, "Hua Kuo-feng and the Arrest of 'Gang of Four,' " *The China Quarterly,* 75 (September 1978), 540–65. For coverage of the trial by the Chinese press, see "Written Judgment of the Special Court Under the Supreme People's Court of the PRC," *Beijing Review,* 5 (February 2, 1981), 13–28; "Trial of Lin Biao and Jiang Qing Cliques—Major Points of the Indictment," *Beijing Review,* 47 (November 24, 1980), 12–17; "Trial of Lin-Jiang Cliques: Indictment of the Special Procuratorate," *Beijing Review,* 48 (December 1, 1980), 9–28. For Chinese people's impressions of the trial, see Butterfield, *China: Alive in the Bitter Sea,* pp. 357–61; Richard Bernstein, *From the Center of the Earth: The Search for the Truth About China* (Boston and Toronto: Little, Brown and Co., 1982), pp. 107–8; Frank Ching, "Mao's Widow Finally Finds Her Place in the Spot Light," *The Asian Wall Street Journal Weekly,* December 22, 1980, p. 6.

70. Wang, "The Urban Militia in China," p. 550.

71. Chou En-lai, "Report on the Work of the Government," *Peking Review,* 4 (January 24, 1975), 24.

72. "The Crux of 'Gang of Four's' Crimes to Usurp Party and State Power," *Peking Review,* 2 (January 7, 1977), 30.

73. Wang, "Urban Militia in China," pp. 552–53.

74. For an eyewitness account, see Roger Garside, *Coming Alive: China After Mao* (New York: McGraw-Hill Book Co., 1981), pp. 114–41. For the current status of those who were still under detention, see *Ming Pao* (Hong Kong), April 9, 1981, p. 1.

75. *Beijing Review,* 46 (November 17, 1978), 13.

76. "Communiqué of the Third Plenary Session of the Eleventh Central Committee," *Beijing Review,* 52 (December 29, 1978) 14. Also see "Carry Forward the Revolutionary Tian An Men Spirit," editorial of *Renmin Ribao,* reprinted in *Beijing Review,* 15 (April 13, 1979), 9–13; *Ming Pao* (Hong Kong), April 8 and 9, 1981, p. 1; Garside, *Coming Alive: China After Mao,* pp. 114–41; *Beijing Review,* 46 to 48 (November 17–December 1, 1978).

77. See "Chairman Mao Will Live For Ever in Our Hearts," *Peking Review,* 39 (September 24, 1976), 35; and "Comrade Wu Teh's Speech at the Celebration Rally in the Capitol," *Peking Review,* 44 (October 29, 1976), 12.

78. Wang, "Urban Militia in China," pp. 555–58.

79. See Lowell Dittmer, "China in 1981: Reform, Readjustment, Rectification," *Asian Survey,* xxii, 5 (January 1982), 33–34. Also see Ching, "Mao's Widow Finally Finds Her Place in the Spot Light," *The Asian Wall Street Journal Weekly,* December 22, 1980, p. 6; and David Bonavia, "Exit Jiang Left With Hua Not Far Behind," *Far Eastern Economic Review* (January 2, 1981), 12.

80. *A Great Trial in Chinese History,* pp. 232–34.

81. Michel Oksenberg and Sai-cheung Yeung, "Hua Kuo-feng's Pre-Cultural Revolution Hunan Years, 1949–66: The Making of a Political Generalist," *The China Quarterly,* 69 (March

1977), 3–53; "Hua Kuo-feng," *Issues and Studies,* vol. xii, no. 3 (March 1976), 80–88; Jen Hua, "Comrade Hua Kuo-feng in Hunan," *Peking Review,* 9 (February 25, 1977), 5–11; and "Comrade Hua Kuo-feng in The Years of War," *Peking Review,* 15 (August 8, 1977), 9–12.

82. Jen Hua, "Comrade Hua Kuo-feng in Hunan," p. 6.

83. Hua's experience at local and national levels were the points mentioned in Ye Jianying's endorsement of Hua for party chairmanship. See "Report on the Revision of the Party Constitution," *Peking Review,* 36 (September 2, 1977), p. 24.

84. Chang, "The Last Stand of Deng's Revolution," *Journal of Northeast Asian Studies,* i (June 2, 1982), 5, 12; Lo Bing, "What's Deng Xiaoping's Plan," Zhengming (Hong Kong), 47, September 1981, p. 8; and Yu Ting, "Hu Yaobang and Hu Xiomu's Criticism of Hua Guofeng," *Zhengming* (Hong Kong), 61 (November 1981), p. 13.

85. For analyses of Hua Guofeng's problems, see Parris Chang, "Chinese Politics: Deng's Turbulent Quest," *Problems of Communism,* xxx (January–February 1981) 1–21, and "The Last Stand of Deng's Revolution," pp. 3–19; Lowell Dittmer, "China in 1980: Modernization and Its Discontents," *Asian Survey,* vol. xxi, no. 1, (January 1981), 36–42, and "China in 1981: Reform, Readjustment, Rectification," pp. 33–35, 42–43; Xu Sangu, "Starting with Hua Guofeng's Resignation of Premiership," *Perspective* (Hong Kong), 557, September 16, 1980, 4–6; Frank Ching, "Central Committee Said to Plan Consideration of Hua's Resignation Soon," *The Asian Wall Street Journal Weekly,* December 29, 1980, p. 2; Yen Qing, "What Happened to Hua Guofeng," *Ming Pao* (Hong Kong) January 22, 23, and 24, 1981; Dorothy Grouse Fontana, "Background to the Fall of Hua Guofeng," *Asian Survey,* vol. xxii, no. 3, (March 1983), 237–60; "Hua Guofeng's Political Fate," *Issues and Studies,* vol. xviii, no. 2 (February 1981), 4–6; "The Two Whatevers and Discussions on Criteria for Truth," *Beijing Review,* 44 (November 2, 1981), 24–25, 28; "Document of the CCP's Central Committee, Chung-fa, 1981, No. 23," *Issues and Studies,* vol. xcii, no. 12 (December 1981) 71–78.

86. See Nora Wang, "Deng Xiaoping: The Years in France," *The China Quarterly,* 92 (December 1982), 698–705.

87. Deng once told Oriana Fallaci that he was purged for the first time in 1932 for lending his support to Mao in the inner party struggle against the Moscow-trained returned Chinese group led at that time by Wang Ming. See "Deng: Cleaning Up Mao's Feudal Mistakes," p. 16.

88. Chang, "The Last Stand of Deng's Revolution," pp. 5–6. Also see Michael Ng-Quinn, "Deng Xiaoping's Political Reform and Political Order," *Asian Survey,* vol. xxii, no. 12 (December 1982), 1187–1205.

89. See Chang, "Chinese Politics: Deng's Turbulent Quest," and "The Last of Deng's Revolution"; "A Speech at the Enlarged Meeting of the Politburo of the Central Committee" in *Issues and Studies,* vol. xvii, no. 3 (March 1981), 81–103; "Important Speech by Deng Xiaoping to the 1980 December 25 Central Work Conference" printed in *Ming Pao* (Hong Kong), May 3–8, 1981; and "Text of Deng Xiaoping's Speech at the Great Hall of People on January 16, 1980," *Ming Pao* (Hong Kong), March 2–4, 1980. Also see Suzanne Pepper, "Can the House that Deng Built Endure," *The Asian Wall Street Journal Weekly,* August 10, 1981, p. 10; Fox Butterfield, "The Pragmatists Take China's Helm," *New York Times Magazine,* December 28, 1980, pp. 22–31; and Lowell Dittmer, "China in 1980: Modernization and Its Discontents," pp. 31–42, and "China in 1981," pp. 33–45.

90. For a more detailed study of factionalism in China, see Lucian Pye, *The Dynamics of Factions and Consensus in Chinese Politics: A Model and Some Propositions* (Santa Monica, Cal.: The Rand Corporation, July 1980). Also see Dorothy Grouse Fontana, "Background to the Fall of Hua Guofeng," pp. 237–60, and Richard D. Nethercut, "Leadership in China: Rivalry, Reform, and Renewal," *Problems of Communism,* xxxiii (March–April 1983) 30–32.

91. Chang, "The Last Stand of Deng's Revolution."

92. Fontana, "Background to the Fall of Hua Guofeng."

93. "Communiqué of the Third Plenary Session of the Eleventh Central Committee of the CCP."

94. Christopher Wren, "Deng Opens Drive on His Leftist Foes," *The New York Times,* October 3, 1982, p. 3. Also see Frank Ching, "Chinese Party Shuffle Bolsters Deng As Pragmatists Gain Over Ideologues," *Asian Wall Street Journal Weekly,* July 13, 1981, p. 7.

95. For biographical information about Hu Yaobang, see Shu-shin Wang, "Hu Yaobang: New Chairman of the Chinese Communist Party," *Asian Survey,* vol. xxii, no. 9 (September 1982), 801–22; Bai Dang-jar, "Hu Yaobang Dares to Create a New Situation," *Perspective,* 562 (December 1, 1980), 9–10, and "Rise and Fall of Hu Yaobang," *Perspective,* 545 (March 1980),

4–5; By Song Yu, "A Scene From the Past Yields Hope for China," *The New York Times,* August 8, 1981, p. 21; Takashi Oka, "Chinese Chairman Hu," *Christian Science Monitor,* July 2, 1981, p. 7; *China Trade Report,* October 1982, p. 6. Also see Parris H. Chang, "Interview With Hu Yaobang," *Problems of Communism,* xxxii (November–December 1983) 67–70.

96. See "Hu Yaobang's Speech," *Beijing Review,* 28 (July 13, 1981), 19–24; and "Create a New Situation in All Fields of Socialist Modernization," *Beijing Review,* 37 (September 1, 1982), 33–40.

97. "Hu Yaobang's Speech," pp. 19–24.

98. Biographical sketch about Zhao Ziyang is culled from the following: Paul L. Montgomery, "China's Premier," New York Times Service, as reprinted in *Honolulu Star-Bulletin,* September 9, 1980, A–17; Frank Ching, "China's Premier Is Upbeat About Economy," *The Asian Wall Street Journal Weekly,* December 7, 1981, pp. 1, 23; David Bonavia, "In Economy, Learn From Sichuan," *Far Eastern Economic Review* (November 21, 1980), 30–31; Linda Mathews, "From Dunce Cap to Premiership," Los Angeles Times Service, as reprinted in *Honolulu Advertiser,* September 8, 1980, A–4; Chen Yungsheng, "Chao Tsu-yang: His Rise to Premiership," *Issues and Studies,* vol. xvi, no. 12 (December 1980), 25–37; Qing Hua, "Zhao Ziyang, Deng Xiaoping's Second in Command," *Ming Pao* (Hong Kong) (April 1980), 22–24; *Perspective* (Hong Kong), 545, 553, and 557, 1980.

99. *Perspective,* 553 (July 16, 1980), 4.

The Chinese Communist Ideology:

Marxism-Leninism, Mao's Thought, and De-Maoization

Let us begin by defining the term *ideology*. It may be defined as the manner in which an individual or a group thinks. Ideology is a set of political values, feelings, and ideas which guides individuals to act or behave in a certain manner for the purpose of achieving a particular goal. It has been said that the success of the Chinese communist movement rests on two basic elements: an effective set of organizations, guided by a set of clearly stated principles.[1] Schurmann differentiates among ideologies in terms of the consequences the ideas may generate. If an idea leads to the formulation of a policy or an action, it is a "practical" ideology; but if an idea is employed for the sole purpose of molding the thinking of the individual, it is a "pure" ideology.[2] Pure ideology is a set of theories; practical ideology is based on experiences and practices. The Chinese make a clear distinction between these two sets of ideologies in their political communication. To the Chinese, the ideas of Karl Marx and of Lenin are pure ideology which has universal application. In the Chinese language, pure ideology is called *lilun* or *chuyi,* and practical ideology is *suxiang.*

The Chinese communist ideology consists of three basic elements: (1) the influence of the Chinese revolution, particularly the intellectual ferment of the May Fourth Movement; (2) the ideas of Marxism-Leninism; and (3) the thought of Mao Zedong. Let us keep in mind that while the thought of Mao constitutes a major portion of the Chinese communist ideology, it is by no means the only element. In the sections that follow, we shall briefly discuss the origin and the nature of the main elements of Chinese communist ideology today.

THE MAY FOURTH MOVEMENT

As was pointed out in Chapter 1, there was very little interest in Marxism among the Chinese intellectuals before 1917. The rapid rise in the study of Marxism was brought about by the 1917 Bolshevik revolution and by the appeal of Lenin's thesis on anti-imperialism. The anti-imperialist plank struck a responsive chord among the Chinese intellectuals, who were already committed to saving China from imperialism through a nationalist revolution. The early founders of the Chinese Communist Party—people like Li Dazhao and Chen Duxiu—were exponents of anti-imperialism and a "new culture" for a modern China. Many of the ideas which were translated into concrete programs after the establishment of the People's Republic in 1949 had their roots in the May Fourth Movement. The May Fourth Movement was a reaction by intellectuals to the imperialist West and its economic system of exploitation. It represented the search for ways to develop a modern Chinese nation. Programs of the May Fourth Movement included reform of both the written language and the educational system; introduction of scientific methods; and exploration of political ideologies, including Marxism. It was a populist appeal to the innate goodness of the common people, particularly the earthbound peasants whose well-being had been always neglected by the intellectual urban elite. Many of the movement's young students went into the countryside to work with the peasants. The ideas from the May Fourth Movement have been continuous threads running through modern Chinese revolutions, including the communist revolution.[3] (The May Fourth Movement's major themes of democracy and science were given new life in 1978–79 both by the dissidents at the Democracy Wall and by the modernization program.[4])

MARXISM-LENINISM

The theoretical foundation of the Chinese communist ideology is Marxism-Leninism. It is the guiding principle for both the party and the state. It is pure theory with universal application. Let us examine briefly the essential features of Marxism.

The first key Marxist concept is historical materialism. Karl Marx began with the assertion that the character of any society is determined by the manner or the mode of production by which people make their living. The mode of production determines social structure and political order; it also determines social ideas and customs. Therefore, to change the minds of people, it is necessary to change the mode of production or the economic system. This, Marx said, is the universal truth and the "evolutionary law of human history." Every human society has at its foundation an economic base, the mode of production which produces goods and services to support human life. This economic basis, in turn, is supported by superstructures of culture, law, courts, and governmental institutions.

Having asserted that materialism determines the nature of society, Marx described how human history evolves in a predictable pattern. This is dialectical materialism. For this, Marx borrowed the dialectical development of history from the German philosopher Hegel. Hegel proposed that every idea or thesis, once started, goes too far and becomes exaggerated or false. When this inevitably happens, the thesis is met with an opposing idea, the antithesis. These two opposing ideas clash, and out of the conflict comes the synthesis, an entirely new idea which contains the essential truths of both opposing ideas. Soon this synthesis becomes a thesis, and the process of change continues, ad infinitum. Marx used Hegelian dialectics to predict that a communist society would inevitably result from this historical development after society had passed through certain stages: first, the primitive communal society, with no class differentiation; then the slave society, with the concept of ownership and with caste status separating the slaves and the masters; next, feudal society, with pronounced class distinction between the lord and his serfs; and the fourth stage of development, the capitalistic society, with the owners of the means of production pitted against the impoverished workers who lead a meager existence suffering exploitation by the capitalists. Marx predicted that this struggle between the capitalists and the working class would result in a communist society where there would be no class distinctions. The economy would be operated under Marx's dictum: "From each according to his ability, to each according to his need." Finally, the state, with its coercive instruments, would no longer be needed and would wither away.

Marx believed that the course of human history must pass through these stages; but before the arrival of the communist stage, there must be intense class struggle. In fact, Marx maintained that human history is a history of class warfare. As long as property or the means of production is owned by private individuals for the purpose of exploiting the work of others, there will always be a struggle between the two classes. It is an unfair struggle, since all the superstructures of society—laws, police, courts, and other political institutions—support the property-owning class. The property-owning class has all the privileges, sanctioned by social customs and mores. Marx argued that this situation cannot endure long; the working class has no alternative except to forcefully overthrow the existing social order. He concludes the Communist Manifesto with a call for revolution: "Workers of the world unite, you have nothing to lose but your chains."

It is not the purpose of this section to engage in a critique of Marxism. However, we need to keep in mind that two basic responses to this doctrine have developed under different sets of circumstances, in answer to the appalling conditions of the early industrialization Marx criticized. One was the evolution of social democracy in the West, which brought changes through constitutional reform and progressive social legislation. The other was the Russian Bolshevik Revolution, which brought change through violent revolution.

Lenin made two basic modifications to Marxism. One was his treatise on imperialism, published in 1916. Marx had predicted that a forceful but spontaneous workers' revolution would descend upon the capitalistic European societies, such as England, France, and Germany. But for over seventy years, no revolution by the working class occurred in continental Europe. When the revolution came, it came to Russia, an industrially backward country. Even more significant was the fact that the lot of workers in the advanced capitalist countries had improved through progressive social legislation. How could the disciples of Marx explain this phenomenon? Lenin answered this question in his treatise, *Imperialism*. Lenin argued that capitalism had broken away from the cycle of contradiction as prescribed by Marx in his dialectical materialism theory. Capitalism had expanded and grown by seeking new sources of raw materials abroad, in undeveloped parts of the world, and by setting up factories with cheap labor in colonies, which in turn became the ready markets for the manufactured goods. Lenin rationalized the situation by claiming that the capitalist nations had developed a monopoly which accumulated enormous profits from the backward areas of the world and then rewarded labor at home with better wages and working conditions from these profits. By making concessions to labor at home, the capitalists were able to maintain the status quo, preventing a workers' revolution. Therefore, the imperialists' exploitation of the backward areas of the world had sustained capitalism. Capitalism would not collapse as long as colonial power and monopolistic capitalism could successfully exploit the backward areas of Russia, China, India, and Africa. From this analysis Lenin thought that the first blow of the revolution must be dealt to the weakest part in the system, the colonial complex in Asia and Africa. The Bolshevik Revolution and Lenin's treatise on imperialism made sense to the Chinese intellectuals, who were frustrated by their previous effort in revolution making. Now there was a meaningful and emotional link between nationalism on one hand and anti-imperialism on the other.

Lenin's second major modification of Marxism was in regard to organization for the revolution, which Marx had not discussed beyond saying that it would be spontaneous. In *What's To Be Done?* Lenin outlined his strategy for the working class to achieve and to maintain political power. His first key principle was that a revolutionary party was needed, led by a highly disciplined and dedicated corps of professional revolutionaries, to serve as the vanguard of the proletariat. Lenin insisted on professionalism and self-discipline in this vanguard. Another key organizational principle was the doctrine of "democratic centralism." This calls for centralized decision making, with free discussion at the policy formulation level. Once a decision is made at the top, however, all must abide by it without dissent. Lenin insisted on strict discipline within a "single unified party." The Leninist organizational model is hierarchical and pyramidal, with the supreme power vested in the hands of a few at the apex. At the base of the pyramid is the level of primary organizations—units or cells. Between the base and the apex are a myriad of intermediary organizations (see Chapter 3).

A few remarks on the current state of Marxism-Leninism in China after Mao may be in order. First, there is rising doubt about the validity of Marxism- Leninism among the young. American journalists stationed in China have reported an increasing lack of interest among China's youth in the compulsory study of Marxism.[5] Reportedly, a survey taken at Fudan University in Shanghai revealed that only 30 percent of the students polled believed in communism.[6] Disillusionment about communism and the dissidents' campaign for democracy and human rights prompted Deng Xiaoping in 1979 to insist that the party adopt some basic guidelines within which criticism about the communist system could be tolerated. These guidelines directed that no one should speak against the socialist road, the dictatorship of the proletariat, the leadership of the party, Marxism-Leninism, and Mao's thought.[7] Presumably, these guidelines were intended to put a stop to the rising tide of dissent against communism.

In 1979 propaganda efforts were mounted to reiterate the applicability of Marxism-Leninism and to reinterpret its meaning in the light of the aberration of the Cultural Revolution and the liberal reforms introduced in the economic system. In July 1981, in his maiden speech as the new party chief, Hu Yaobang called Marxism the "crystallization of scientific thinking" and theory verified in practice. Hu then cautioned that Marxism was only a guide to action; as a theory it should neither be looked upon as a "rigid dogma to be followed unthinkingly" nor viewed as comprising "all the truth in the unending course of human history.''[8] In answer to those who advocated the abandonment of socialism in China, numerous theoretical studies were published in the media to justify the socialist nature of Chinese society. For instance, in a theoretical essay, the vice-president of the CCP's party school stated that socialism is basically public ownership of the means of production and the principle of "to each according to his work."[9] These two fundamental principles are the only way to judge the socialist nature of a society, and China—the theoreticians now argued—had completed the transfer of agriculture, handicrafts, industry, and commerce to public ownership.[10] The Chinese leaders seemed to argue that the concepts of Marxism-Leninism must go through stages of modification as dictated by new concrete conditions.[11] Now that China is a socialist society in accordance with Marxism, Hu Yaobang stressed, all Marxists must make sure that "it does not become divorced from social life and does not stagnate, wither or ossify; they must enrich it with fresh revolutionary experiences so that it will remain full of vitality."[12] The new party chief urged that the application of Marxism-Leninism be integrated with the "concrete practice of China's realities."[13]

We must now turn to a discussion about the thought of Mao Zedong.

THE THOUGHT OF MAO ZEDONG

Mao Zedong, The Man

> Wind and thunder are stirring.
> Flags and banners are flying
> Wherever men live.
> Thirty-eight years are fled
> With a mere snap of the fingers
> We can clasp the moon in the Ninth Heaven
> And seize turtles deep down in the Five Seas;
> We'll return amid triumphant song and laughter.
> Nothing is hard in this world
> If you dare to scale the heights.[14]

This is the second stanza of a poem written by Mao in May 1965 when he revisited Jinggangshan, the mountain retreat where he had gathered the remnants of the defeated and disillusioned urban revolutionaries in 1927 before reorganizing them into a fighting guerrilla force. This poem shows a familiar image of Mao: a man with infinite faith in the ability of human beings to accomplish any task, no matter how difficult. Mao Zedong was a much more complex person than has commonly been portrayed. In this section we will look at Mao, the man, by focusing on his background.

Mao was born in 1893 to a middle-class, not poor, peasant family in the village of Shaoshan, Hunan Province, in central China. He was brought up in a traditional Chinese family environment, where the father exercised almost dictatorial power over the family. Mao usually submitted to his father's wishes, but on occasion he rebelled. As a boy he learned the value of hard labor by helping his father on the farm. His primary school curriculum centered on recitation of the Confucian classics, but he enjoyed reading popular romantic literature depicting heroic adventures, peasant rebellions, and the contests of empires. At the time of the 1911 revolution, Mao was eighteen, a fledgling youth, not too sure of what was happening to China. His social awakening did not begin until he went to the provincial capital of Changsha for his secondary education in 1912. In Changsha he learned from the newspapers about the various revolutionary activities of Sun Yatsen and others. Excited by these events, Mao wrote his first wall poster, already a popular medium for expressing political opinions. Following local uprisings in Changsha and Wuhan, he joined the revolutionary army. Military life with its regimentation and authoritarianism did not suit young Mao, who was alert and impatient with the world around him. For some months after his short sojourn in the army, Mao toyed with the idea of becoming a lawyer. Finally, in 1918, at the age of twenty-five, he settled for a teaching career and obtained a degree from a teacher training school. Stuart Schram, an authoritative biographer of Mao, views the five years in teacher training school as an important landmark in the shaping of Mao's future.[15] The greatest and perhaps most successful role that Mao played was as a teacher to his people: He showed them how to learn by themselves and how to learn together.[16] In later years schoolmates described the Mao of this period as a loner, but a well-behaved person.[17]

The most important change that occurred in Mao's life was the move from his native province of Hunan to Beijing, the center of political and intellectual ferment. Toward the end of the first World War, Mao went to Beijing with some thirty fellow Hunanese as members of a society to study new ideas. Through his former teacher in Changsha, Mao obtained a menial job as a librarian's assistant at Beijing National University to support himself. Although he shared a room with seven other students from Hunan, Mao was lonely. As a means of meeting people, he joined the Marxist Study Group, organized by Li Dazhao, founder of the Chinese communist movement. As Mao later admitted to Edgar Snow, at that time he was rather confused by the new ideas proliferating like mushrooms at Beijing National University, and he leaned toward anarchism while "looking for a road."[18] Before becoming a Marxist in the summer of 1920, Mao had read only three Chinese translations of major works on Marxism: *The Communist Manifesto* by Marx, *Class Struggle* by Kautsky, and *History of Socialism* by Kirkupp. A year later Mao was a delegate to the founding of the Chinese Communist Party in Shanghai. From 1921 until 1927, he was an obedient Chinese communist, following the orders of the Comintern. From 1927 to 1935, he began to shape a different movement, with reliance on the peasantry as a base. Mao's rise to leadership of the Chinese Communist Party, and his maintenance of that position until his death in 1976, are discussed in Chapter 1 and in other parts of this book.

As Lucian Pye has pointed out, Mao must be seen at various times and under various conditions.[19] In his youth he was a loner and exhibited signs of "aloofness and solitariness."[20] When he went into the field as an organizer among the workers and peasants, Mao not only dressed but acted like them. As Mao gained power and grew as a leader, he was distinghished as a "man of decisive action, great energy, and increasing aloofness."[21] He developed his maturity as a student of Marxism-Leninism and as a theoretician of guerrilla warfare during the Yanan years of 1935 to 1940, when he wrote and lectured to the soldiers and cadres. He was then looked upon by his followers as a scholar, a teacher, and a man of wisdom, an image that remained with him long after the establishment of the People's Republic in 1949. This image of a scholar and of a man with answers to problems became veiled with an aura of mysticism and magic—the image of a charismatic leader. But the private Mao remained a Chinese scholar, reading books and reports or writing poetry in the traditional style. As many foreigners who interviewed him testified, he was a good conversationalist and was remarkably well informed. Interestingly, he engaged in philosophic conversations about the existence of a god or gods with the late Edgar Snow.[22] Mao personally seemed to have detested the campaigns to build an image of him as a god or an emperor, to be worshipped by the people. The epithet that Mao preferred was that of a "great teacher."[23] There is really no appropriate epithet to describe so complex a man as Mao. The recent attempt to measure Mao in the scale of history has produced a number of themes on major areas of Mao's public life: philosopher, Marxist, theorist, political leader, soldier, teacher, economist, patriot, statesman, and innovator.[24] Mao's contribution to the development of the Chinese communist ideology is truly enormous. The following discussion represents only some of the salient aspects of his thought.

Before examining Mao's thought, the importance of the Yanan years (from 1935 to 1945) in the development of Mao's thinking must be stressed. About half the articles in the first four volumes of the *Selected Works of Mao Tse-tung* were written during this period. Mao, as leader of the communist movement, was under great pressure in 1939 and 1940 to develop ideas and to provide leadership not only for the communists but also for all Chinese who would listen.[25] The fifth volume of Mao's collective works, covering the period 1949–57, was published in April 1977. It was edited mainly under the direction of Hua Guofeng and Wang Dongxing, leaders of the "Whatever" faction. Apparently, the new pragmatic leaders felt that it was sufficiently radical to merit reediting.

Peasantry as the Base
for Revolution

In 1927 Mao reported on his investigation of the peasant movement in Hunan province. In the report Mao made a strong appeal to the party, then dominated by the Comintern, to exploit discontent in the countryside and to organize peasant associations as a vanguard for the revolution.[26] Mao noted that poor peasants had been fighting the landlords and feudal rule and that the countryside was on the verge of an agrarian revolution. Mao urged that "a revolutionary tidal wave" must be generated in the countryside to mobilize the masses and to "weld them into this great force" for revolution.

The thrust of Mao's guerrilla efforts in the 1930s and 1940s was the mobilization and welding of the peasants into a formidable revolutionary force for the CCP in its quest for eventual control of the nation. This concept and practice of mobilizing the peasantry as a revolutionary base has created some controversy among scholars as to whether Mao was a heretic or an original thinker and contributor to communist theory.[27] We may attribute the origin of the idea not to Mao but to Lenin, who recognized the potential of the Russian peasants as a revolutionary force in 1905. We may also say that Mao probably was influenced by Li Dazhao, who saw the peasantry as a possible base for the revolution. The importance of Mao's contribution, as some scholars have noted, was the timing. Mao was the first orthodox Marxist-Leninist to advocate using the peasantry as a major rather than a secondary force, and he made his appeal at the time when the CCP leadership had committed the party to relying on the urban proletariat.[28] With the benefit of hindsight, we might argue that reliance on the peasants was not a conceptual contribution but rather the only practical revolutionary strategy that could be effective. Practical ideas based on experience were the keynote of Mao's practical ideology.

Mass Line and Populism

At the heart of Mao's political philosophy is the concept of "from the masses, to the masses," commonly known as the mass line. Briefly stated, the concept of mass line specifies that a party policy is good only if the ideas of that policy come originally from the masses—the peasants and the workers—and only if the interests and wishes of the people are taken into account and incorporated into the policy. The implementation of a policy, no matter how good it is, must have the wholehearted support of the masses. The mass line concept is applied in several stages to achieve the enthusiastic support of the masses for its implementation. These stages have been described by John W. Lewis as "perception, summarization, authorization, and implementation."[29] First, the party cadres list the "scattered and unsystematic" views of the masses. Second, the cadres study these ideas and put them into systematic and summary form in their reports to higher authorities. Third, the higher authorities make comments or give instructions based on these systematic ideas and return them to the masses. During this stage political education or propaganda is carried on by the cadres among the masses, not only to explain the ideas but also to test their correctness. Finally, when the masses have embraced the ideas as their own, the ideas are translated into concrete action.[30] According to Mao, this is not the end; the proper application of mass line must repeat the process several times "so that each time these ideas emerge with greater correctness and become more vital and meaningful."[31]

The mass line concept, formulated during the Jiangxi soviet days of the 1930s, was an effective method for securing the support of the masses. The application of the mass line required that both the leaders and the masses go through an educational process, learning from and supporting each other. It provided for a continuous dialogue between the leaders and the led. In going through the various stages of the mass line process, the masses were given ample opportunity to participate in the decision-making process, and the leaders were able to obtain popular commitment for policies and programs.

While Mao had immense respect for the virtues of the masses, this did not mean that there were no limits to what the masses could do. The Red Guards' demonstrations and big-character posters during the Cultural Revolution were applications of the mass line.[32] As we saw in Chapter 1, however, when the fighting between the various factions of Red Guards reached a state of anarchy, Mao did not hesitate to call in the army to restore order in the tradition of Lenin's democratic centralism. Stuart Schram writes that Mao, who clearly opposed unrestricted mass rule, prevented the Shanghai radicals from organizing leaderless people's committees.[33] Within limits, the concept of mass line does provide a monitoring device on the bureaucratic elite and their tendency to rule the inarticulate masses by party and governmental sanction.[34]

Mass line is considered Mao's theoretical contribution to populism.[35] At the root of this concept is the assertion that simple people—peasants and workers—possess virtue and wisdom. Mao again seems to agree with Li Dazhao, who once said that one becomes more humanistic as one gets closer to the soil. The methods of mass campaigns and small study groups, developed for applying the mass line, have been what Townsend terms "the primary institutions of Mao's populism."[36]

Closely associated with the mass line is Mao's belief in the intellectual tradition of voluntarism: Human will and determination will, in the end, remove all obstacles in making a better world. To Mao, it was this human will—diligence, hard work, and self-reliance—which must be inculcated into the minds of China's impoverished masses, whose potential had been inhibited by centuries of ignorance and superstition. Before and particularly during the Cultural Revolution, repeated references were made to Mao's favorite folk tale about a foolish old man who was able to move mountains through faith and perseverance. The tale, or parable, conveys the idea that it is necessary to rely on one's own strength and to have faith in one's own ability to accomplish revolutionary tasks in building a new society.[37]

Theory and Practice

"We should not study the words of Marxism-Leninism, but study their standpoint and approach in viewing problems and solving them," Mao wrote in a theoretical essay in 1943.[38] He warned that too much reliance on purely abstract ideas or theory yields nothing but dogmatism, for theory is of no value if it does not involve practice. For Mao, the process of cognition involved more than merely what one observes and conceptualizes from observations. There was a third element—action or practice for the purpose of making changes in the material world. Knowledge cannot be separated from practice, since it begins with our experience. For example, Mao wrote that Marxism as a theory did not experience imperialism, and therefore, it was good only up to a point. When Lenin, who had perceived and experienced imperialism, added imperialism to the body of Marxist theory, it became meaningful to the Chinese situation. Theory must be subject to modification as changes occur and as new experiences enter into the situation. Marxism, according to Mao, must take into account both the historic experience and the characteristics of China in order to discover solutions to that country's problems. If one compares Mao's essay on practice with the writings of American pragmatists, such as John Dewey and William James, one will find many interesting parallels. As John Bryan Starr has noted, the philosophy of American pragmatists suggested not only that we discover the world around us but that we "know how to remake it."[39]

An example of the application of theory and practice can be seen in Chinese education during the 1950s and the Cultural Revolution, when students split their time between study and work in rural areas. Another example was revealed in Mao's attitude toward student participation in the Cultural Revolution. He would fondly tell the millions of students that they were the "revolutionary successors" and that the only way they could learn about revolution was to dare to make revolution in the streets. Perhaps the most important point to remember about Mao's treatise on practice is that Mao thought that we can discover knowledge and truth only through practice, which must become an integral part of theory, or conceptual knowledge. This conceptual knowledge will be changed by additional experiences and practices. If knowledge comes from practice, as Mao argued, then practice means action, or at the very least, an orientation toward action.

Contradiction

Mao's theory of contradiction begins with the assertion that society has always been full of contradictions: life-death, sun-moon, darkness-lightness, black-white, individual-collective, and red-expert. It is from the juxtaposition of these contradictions that changes can take place in society. Change takes place because there is a tendency for one aspect of the contradiction "to transfer itself to the position of its opposite" through some type of a struggle between the two opposites. Adhering to Marxist theory, Mao said that all conflicts are class conflicts between social groups: prior to socialism, peasants versus landlords; now, proletariat versus bourgeoisie. The origin of this theory, sometimes known as the "law of unity of opposites," can be traced to Hegelian dialectics and Marxian dialectical materialism. As others have noted, Mao probably was also influenced by the traditional Chinese concept of opposites, yin and yang.[40] The idea that conflict and change are normal was certainly revolutionary. As was said in Chapter 1, the traditional Chinese society, under Confucianism, had been told to strive for harmony and to maintain the status quo. The theory of contradictions is considered by many to be the core of the thought of Mao Zedong.

Mao felt that the interplay of contradictions would continue even though society had advanced into the higher level of socialism. In 1957 Mao said that none of the socialist countries, including China and the Soviet Union, could transcend the contradictions of social classes by forgetting the class struggle. In an essay entitled "On the Correct Handling of Contradictions Among the People,"[41] Mao advanced the idea that class struggle would continue for an indefinite period of time. It would no longer be in regard to the contradictions between "friends" and "enemies" but rather would apply to those between proletarian and bourgeois thinking and behavior. In 1957 Mao explained that there are two types of contradictions: "antagonistic contradiction" between ourselves and the enemy; and "nonantagonistic contradiction" among working people, between peasants and workers, or between cadres and the masses. The nonantagonistic contradictions are essentially matters of ideological and political right and wrong. Since there are two different types of contradictions, Mao proposed two different methods of resolving these conflicts. For antagonistic contradictions, the proletariat dictatorship must suppress the reactionary elements in society; but for the nonantagonistic contradictions among the people, a continuous process of struggle and criticism must be employed to "raise the level of consciousness" and to correct erroneous thinking and behavior of the people. It is through this continuous process of struggle and criticism that unity can be achieved. The key objective of struggle and criticism is to proletarianize the behavior and thinking of the individual, no matter what economic background he or she may possess. It is the "proletarian consciousness" which is important in the final determination of one's class status.[42] Mao defined several major nonantagonistic contradictions or problems which the Chinese must resolve: (1) those between heavy industry and agriculture; (2) those between central and local authorities; (3) those between urban and rural; (4) those between national minorities and the Han peoples over pluralism or radical assimilation.[43]

Mao made it clear that there were bound to be conflicts and struggles to resolve issues within the party:

> Opposition and struggle between different ideas constantly occur within the Party, reflecting contradictions between the classes and between the old and new in society. If in the Party there were no contradictions and no ideological struggles to solve them, the life of the Party would come to an end.[44]

The intraparty disputes, which have beset the party since the 1930s, usually are to be resolved by rectification campaigns; but when the contradictions within the party are so severe that they cause a serious "cleavage of opinion" among the members of Politburo, the contradictions must be resolved by some type of mass campaign.

The Cultural Revolution has been viewed both as a rectification campaign and as a mass campaign for class struggle to resolve the contradictions between the proletariat and the bourgeoisie. It was called a "Cultural Revolution" because, according to both Marx and Mao, the construction of a total socialist society demands transformation in the superstructure of culture, customs, and habits to eliminate the contradictions between proletarian collectivism and bourgeois individualism.[45]

Most Americans tend to be very skeptical about the utility of Mao's theory on contradictions, treating it as a piece of incomprehensible diatribe. It is very difficult for our highly technological and analytical minds to understand why, for instance, the workers and staff in a blast furnace attribute their higher output to simply studying the dialectics on contradiction. Still, the theory of contradiction was said to have helped the peasants and workers develop "a habit of analysis." Take for instance the case of the blast furnace. The workers and staff sat down and analyzed why the conventional way of increasing the temperature of the furnace brought about an increase in output only up to a certain level. By altering the structure of the layers of the furnace through analysis, they were able to control the flow of coal gas and to realize a greater yield after the standard level of pressure had been applied.[46] Another example is of peasants who have just been thrust into a position of leadership in their village and are daily confronted by a host of conflict-of-interest situations for which they must provide resolution. By studying the theory of contradiction, they are able to carry on some analyses of their own and to feel more confident in providing resolution to the conflicts.[47] Second, the theory of contradiction is useful, as pointed out by Schurmann, in a struggle-and-criticism session, where the deviant individual's erroneous thinking is brought into sharp focus to facilitate correction through thought reform.[48] Finally, the theory on contradiction, by focusing on the law of unity of opposites, compels those involved in a conflict situation to agree on the proper means for resolving the conflict. Schurmann describes how discussion of a controversial issue at the Politburo level first produces two opposite sets of opinions and then results in the adoption of one set of opinions as a majority view and the other set as a minority view. Before a decision is reached, however, there must be what Schurmann calls the "juxtaposition" or polarization of opinion as a logical consequence of the application of the theory of contradiction.[49]

Permanent Revolution[50]

The ideas about change and struggle contained in Mao's essays on practice and contradictions logically lead to his concept of a permanent, or continuous, revolution: If society is rampant with contradictions, then "ceaseless change and upheaval" must be the normal condition to enable the society to reach a higher level of proletarian consciousness. The continuous class struggle is therefore necessary to create the "new socialist man."

Mao emphasized that his concept of the permanent revolution was different from Leon Trotsky's, a point which Khrushchev seemed to have missed. In 1959 Khrushchev compared the two concepts, labeling Mao's concept of a permanent revolution as a mixture of anarchism, Trotskyism, and adventurism. One essential difference was that Trotsky was merely concerned about "the transition from the democratic to the socialistic stage of the revolution," while Mao was concerned about "a separate stage of social transformation" during which the revolutionary environment must be maintained to eliminate all bourgeois influences and tendencies and to rebuild the superstructures.[51] Another difference was that Trotsky and Stalin would permit a new class of technocrats to emerge in order to establish the new economic base. Mao, on the other hand, argued that a new economic base does not necessarily bring about a new superstructure; class struggle must continue from the beginning to the end when the society is undergoing transformation. Mao believed that "politics must take command so that the elites understand the correct ideological line." The contradictions must be solved by continuous struggle or revolution. Mao would insist: "We must destroy the old basis for unity, pass through a struggle, and unite on a new basis." Viewed from this perspective, both the Socialist Education Movement and the Cultural Revolution were important examples of the theory of permanent revolution. At the heart of Mao's theory of permanent revolution is the thesis that even after the establishment of a new economic base, both individuals and institutions can acquire bourgeois tendencies and thus change the color of the revolution.

In light of the events since Mao's death and the pragmatic leaders' quest for political and economic reform, how have the basic tenets of Mao's thought come to be viewed in China? To what extent has there been modification of Mao's thought?

First, efforts were made by pragmatic leaders to demolish the myth that Mao was the only contributor to the thought of Mao. The party's assessment of its history clearly stated that Mao's thought was "a summary of the experiences that have been confirmed in the practice of the Chinese revolution." In other words, it was the product of "collective wisdom," since "many outstanding leaders of our party made important contributions to the formulation and development of Mao Zedong Thought."[52] The new leaders took the position that Mao's thought had been contaminated by the erroneous "ultra-Left" ideas of the radicals. The 1981 party assessment maintained that Mao's thought must continue to play the guiding role in China's revolution; it should not be discarded "just because Comrade Mao Zedong made mistakes in his later years."[53] The party document went on to point out that "it is likewise entirely wrong to adopt a dogmatic attitude toward the sayings of Mao Zedong, to regard whatever he said as the immutable truth which must be mechanically applied everywhere, and to be unwilling to admit honestly that he made mistakes in his later years."[54]

Second, major modifications have been made with regard to Mao's concepts and ideas of class struggle, continued revolution, and contradiction.[55] The Cultural Revolution, the party now said, conformed neither to Marxism-Leninism nor to Chinese reality: "They represent an entirely erroneous appraisal of the prevailing class relations."[56] The actual targets of the upheaval were not "revisionist" or "capitalist" but instead were Marxist and socialist principles.[57] The 1981 party document declared that "class struggle no longer constitutes the principal contradiction after the exploiters have been eliminated as classes in socialist society."[58] While there would be class struggles in the future, they would differ in terms of scale, targets, and methods. Large-scale class struggle, such as that of the Cultural Revolution, which stressed the overthrow of one class against another, was no longer to be tolerated.[59] The targets for future class struggle would be counterrevolutionaries; enemy agents; criminals who engage in economic crimes such as bribery, embezzlement, and profiteering; and the remnants of the Gang of Four.[60] Since class struggle was no longer the principal contradiction in Chinese society, "tempestuous mass movement" was no longer the appropriate method to be employed. Instead, legal procedures embodied in the state constitution and party rules ought to be prescribed as the proper way for handling different types of contradictions in society.[61] Thus, the theory of contradiction must be discarded because it is not only wrong but "runs counter to Marxism-Leninism and Chinese conditions."[62]

The party's assessment went on to say that labeling party leaders as "capitalist roaders" failed to distinguish the people from the enemy.[63] The reinterpretation then invoked Mao by saying that class struggle between antagonistic classes was eliminated when landlords and rich peasants were eliminated in the 1950s. Moreover, to differentiate among classes according to people's political attitudes, as the radicals had done in the Cultural Revolution, was fallacious because "it is impossible to make scientific judgment of class by using people's thinking as a yardstick."[64] The principal contradiction, it argued, was no longer between the proletariat and the bourgeoisie but between the need of the people for more and better material well-being and the present low level of economic development.[65] Since the downfall of the radicals, certain "social contradictions" had surfaced: for example, the craving for Western-type individual freedom and decadent lifestyle versus the socialist system and the people's interest.[66] The method for resolving these new "social contradictions" should be that of criticism, not of physical struggle.

MAO'S LEGACY
AND DE-MAOIZATION

Something unusual has happened in China: The present leadership has moved to deemphasize the "personality cult" of Mao. On July 1, 1978, the fifty-eighth anniversary of the founding of the Chinese Communist Party, the major mass media published the text of Chairman Mao's 1962 talk to some 7,000 cadres at an enlarged central work conference.[67] What was so significant about the publication of the talk was that it was at that 1962 gathering that Mao admitted he had made serious mistakes and should be criticized for the ill-fated Great Leap programs. Mao admitted frankly that he knew very little about "economic construction" or about industry and commerce. Some of the policies of the Great Leap, Mao confessed, had been mistakes on his part, and he took full responsibility for them. There were many other small signs or signals of the downgrading of some of Mao's teachings: For instance, the *People's Daily* stopped carrying Mao's quotations on the front page.

But there is also continued veneration for Mao as a great leader. One need only look at the thousands of people who have filed silently into the memorial hall in the Tian An Men Square in Beijing every day since it opened in 1977 to realize the profound affection the people had for Mao. None of China's new leaders ever makes a speech without quoting a line or two from Mao, either to illustrate or to justify his or her own position. In the post-Mao era, as well as in those periods when he was alive and active, Mao Zedong has been a unifying symbol for the Chinese. More than any other leader in modern China, Mao has left an enormous legacy for his people.

The thinking of Mao Zedong was very complex, as we have pointed out. His ideas had their roots in the Chinese intellectual tradition, particularly in the May Fourth Movement, in the Marxist-Leninist tradition, and in the revolutionary experiences of the Chinese Communist Party. Yet Mao's populist approach, contained in the concept of mass line, was distinct and went beyond Marx, Lenin, and the Chinese tradition. The vision that the semiliterate peasants and workers—collectively, the masses—could be the source of ideas and inspiration for the leaders was truly revolutionary. The application of this core concept enabled the CCP to secure popular support from the period of guerrilla operations in the 1930s and 1940s through the land reform and communization movements in the 1950s and 1960s. The failure of the Great Leap and the questions raised about the results of the Cultural Revolution make it appear doubtful that Mao's concept has been realized. Yet in spite of the dampening effect of the Great Leap and the Cultural Revolution, Mao's prescription for a proper relationship between the leaders and the led in the mass line formula remain a fundamental work style for the Chinese leaders. The state constitution of 1982 and the party charter of 1982 enshrine this Maoist vision of relying on the masses for inspiration, support, and implementation of policies and programs. It is the mass line as an ideological concept which has give the Chinese their national identity.[68]

Mao's practical ideology also has functioned as a guide, if not as a basis, on which individuals in Chinese society shape their attitudes and regulate their behavior. These ideas serve as a set of preferred societal values on which actions and thoughts are gauged. Mao's philosophical ideas and teachings, such as human will and determination, self-sacrifice, and service to the people, have become an integral part of today's value system, governing behavior. To many Americans and to some of Mao's own colleagues, the idea of a permanent revolution and of ceaseless change may be too unsettling, bordering on anarchy; but in Mao's vision, the revolution is like a pair of straw sandals which have no definite pattern but rather "shape themselves in the making." Stuart Schram's tribute to Mao is worth quoting: "Mao has left the sandal of the Chinese revolution unfinished, but it has already begun to take shape, and for a long time to come it can scarcely fail to bear his stamp."[69]

Ideology alone could not have had such a great impact on China. In the final analysis, it took a man like Mao, with exceptional skill and acumen as a political leader, to translate ideas into concrete actions and to make people do over a long period of time what the leader wanted. No other Chinese leader in modern times was involved directly in so many important issues over such a long period of time as was Mao Zedong.[70]

It has been fashionable since Mao's death and since the arrest of the radical leaders in October 1976 to detect signs of the deemphasis of Mao's ideology and of the programs he supported during the Cultural Revolution. The newly coined word *de-Maoization* has come into vogue.[71] There is even some debunking of "Maoism," which has been termed a "myth"—too abstract to be understood.[72] However, we must use caution in assessing Mao's ideas and programs. First, the function of a political ideology is to serve a unifying purpose, and the thought of Mao, perhaps more than anything else, has done just that. Mao's ideas have given the Chinese people the hope that they can do something about their lives using their own initiative and hard work. The accomplishments of the Chinese during the past forty years in finding solutions to some of the most pressing and difficult problems of humankind cannot be dissociated from Mao's ideology and the organizations he established for translating these ideas into concrete programs. Second, because of the enormity of these human problems for so large a populace—who for centuries lived in stagnation, inertia, and pessimism—Mao's ideas offered the message that the people must constantly experiment, think afresh, and be willing to take risks.

Mao, however, has been subjected to intensive criticism since 1978. One of the first such criticisms appeared in the publication of a speech made by Zhou Enlai to the First All-China Youth Congress in 1949, in which Zhou warned the youth not to look upon Mao as a demigod.[73] Zhou related a story about how unhappy Mao was when he learned that a school textbook had said that he had been opposed to superstition when he was a boy of ten. On the contrary, Zhou explained, Mao believed in gods when he was a little boy and "prayed to Buddha for help" at one time when his mother became ill.[74] Zhou's message to the youth in 1949 was twofold: They should not regard Mao as an infallible leader, and they should seek truth from facts. It is this blind worship of Mao which, in time, will be deemphasized or eliminated altogether. Truth, including Mao's thought, as the leaders now insist, must eventually be tested by practice—this is the major theme in China's policy of moderation.

After a lengthy debate at the Third Plenary Session of the Eleventh Central Committee meeting (December 18–22, 1978), China's new leadership agreed that the time had come for the people to "emancipate their thinking, dedicate themselves to the study of new circumstances, things, and questions, and uphold the principle of seeking truth from facts."[75] While paying tribute to Mao's "outstanding leadership," the party's Central Committee nevertheless found that Mao had made mistakes: "It would not be Marxist to demand that a revolutionary leader be free of all shortcomings and errors."[76] This was the beginning of the drive to deemphasize Mao and to dispel the myth of his infallibility, which had been built up over the years by the radicals. Anti-Mao posters appeared in Beijing in late 1978 and early 1979, along with the party's admission of "erroneous" action in the Tian An Men Square incident in April 1976 and its reexamination of the events of the Cultural Revolution. In December 1978 the Central Commitee exonerated and rehabiliated a host of top leaders purged in 1959 and during the Cultural Revolution for opposing Mao or his policies, including Peng Dehuai, Peng Zhen, Bo Yibo, and Tao Zhu. Deng Xiaoping, who repeatedly endured Mao's wrath, has been quoted as saying that Mao was perhaps "seventy percent correct and thirty percent wrong."[77]

The Central Committee's final assessment of Mao came at its June 1981 session, when it approved the report on the party history.[78] The document represented a culmination of intensive discussion and debate about Mao's role in the party. The report was initiated by the pragmatic leaders under Deng Xiaoping. It may be instructive for us to find out how these leaders evaluated Mao Zedong and what they considered to be Mao's mistakes.

First, an agonizing attempt had been made by the pragmatic leaders to distinguish between Mao as a leader and the body of ideas collectively known as the thought of Mao Zedong. Deng Xiaoping repeatedly emphasized that Mao's contribution to the Chinese communist revolution could not possibly be "obliterated" and that "the Chinese people will always cherish his memory."[79] In the party document, Mao's thought was considered "a correct theory" and "a body of correct principles and a summary of practical experience."[80] It went on to point out that it would be wrong to deny its guiding role in the Chinese revolution "just because Comarade Mao Zedong made mistakes in his later years."[81]

One may ask why they insisted on such a distinction. One possible reason may be that this was a necessary political compromise to placate opposition within the party and the army. The army in particular still found it difficult to denounce Mao's leadership after years of religious adherence to his ideology.[82] Chinese leaders now argued that Mao made a "tremendous contribution" to the formation of his thought. But that did not imply that "every word Mao uttered and every article he wrote, much less his personal mistakes, belong to the Mao Zedong Thought."[83] It was obvious that the party was not prepared to completely denounce Mao, as Khrushchev had denounced Stalin in 1956. Chinese theoreticians and propagandists adhered to the line that "under no circumstance should one confuse a leader's mistakes with the scientific ideological system named after him or describe the mistakes as a component part of the scientific system."[84] To either abandon Mao's thought[85] or reject Mao's correct ideas would "lead China along a dangerous path, bring a great loss to us and court disaster."[86] During the top leaders' debate in 1978, the venerable Marshal Ye emphasized that "we cannot negate entirely Mao Zedong Thought." Ye expressed the fear that if the party lost its theoretical and ideological base, China would regress to its position prior to 1949.[87]

What mistakes had Mao committed in his later years? The party's official assessment identified five major political errors that were largely attributed to Mao.

First, the 1957 "rightist" rectification campaign launched after the "hundred flowers bloom" movement was misdirected. Instead of criticizing "a handful of bourgeois rightists," the class struggle was extended in scope and intensity so that it eventually engulfed a substantial segment of the population. The intellectuals particularly were branded unfairly as "rightists," and were purged. Some leaders now in power admitted that Mao was not the only one responsible for the large-scale purge of the intellectuals in 1957; other senior party officials supported the ill-considered policy at the time.[88]

Second, Mao was responsible for mistakes committed in the 1958 Great Leap Forward and the commune programs. He was blamed for the "Leftist" errors in promoting "excessive targets" and issuing "arbitrary decisions." The party assessment charged that Mao violated his own practice by initiating the Great Leap and the commune programs without thorough investigation, study, and experimentation. He was criticized for "smugness" and "arrogance" and charged with being impatient—looking for "quick results" and ignoring economic realities. One senior party leader extended the blame to the entire Central Committee that had endorsed the Great Leap decision in 1958.[89] While the party assessment noted that Mao had made self-criticism in 1962 for his mistakes in the 1958 Great Leap, this did not exonerate him from the error.

Third, Mao erred in forcing the Eighth Central Committee in 1959 to launch a vicious campaign to discredit and vilify a number of senior party leaders, including Marshal Peng Dehui, the defense minister at the time, for disagreeing with Mao over the Great Leap policies. Mao was condemned for launching a struggle within the top party leadership which "gravely undermined inner party democracy" at all levels.[90] Fourth, Mao was blamed for widening the erroneous policy of class struggle and mistakenly applying the theory of contradiction in another mass campaign, the Socialist Education Campaign, in 1963. Here Mao was blamed for insisting that the contradiction between the proletariat and the bourgeoisie was the main contradiction and for proclaiming that the bourgeoisie class continued to exist under socialism. The 1963 Socialist Education Campaign focused on party leaders who had taken "the capitalist road." Mao, the party assessment in 1981 pointed out, had contradicted himself—treating contradiction among the people as contradiction with the enemy. The 1963 mass campaign unjustly purged a large number of party cadres and plunged China once again into confusion and chaos.

Finally, according to the party assessment, the greatest mistake Mao made was the Great Proletarian Cultural Revolution in 1966. The new pragmatic leaders viewed this upheaval as an extreme expansion of Mao's "ultra-Left" ideas of class struggle and continued revolution.[91] The party declared that the theses of the Cultural Revolution were not only erroneous but inconsistent with Mao's thought; for these ideas misinterpreted the class relations that existed in China at that time. The very things the Cultural Revolution denounced were, in fact, Marxist and socialist principles. To insist on continued revolution, Deng now pointed out, was to make a "wrong judgment of the Chinese reality." The gravest of all Mao's mistakes, in Deng's view, was the attack launched during the Cultural Revolution on veteran party leaders with years of dedicated revolutionary service and administrative experience.[92] Deng revealed that Mao himself admitted a year or two before his death that the Cultural Revolution had been wrong because it had resulted in the "decimation" of experienced cadres through purge and physical abuse and, in effect, had constituted a nationwide "civil war."[93]

The party's assessment charged that in the Cultural Revolution—where "one class overthrows the other"—Mao had violated his own mass line principle. The upheaval was "divorced both from the party organization and from the masses."[94] It involved masses but was "devoid of mass support" because, the new leaders now argued, it was launched by Mao personally with the knowledge that "the majority of the people were opposed to the 'ultra-Left' ideas."[95] The party assessment concluded that the Cultural Revolution was initiated by one leader, Mao, who labored under "misapprehension" and was taken advantage of by the radicals. The final result of the Cultural Revolution was "catastrophe to the party, the state and the whole people."[96]

The new leaders also made remarks about Mao as a leader and about his personal character. Deng Xiaoping found Mao's "patriarchal behavior" to be a major shortcoming, an "unhealthy style of work": "He acted as a patriarch. He never wanted to know the ideas of others, no matter how right they could be; he never wanted to hear opinions different from his."[97] Associated with this behavior was Mao's "smugness" about his early success, which led to his "overindulgence" of ultra-Left ideas in his later years. He became "overconfident" and "arrogant."[98] He also was accused of "feudal practice," a disparaging remark used by Deng to describe Mao as a leader and as a person. To Deng, the manner in which Mao chose Lin Biao as his successor in 1969 clearly illustrated Mao's feudal practice—he behaved as though he were the emperor who could pass on the reign to his chosen successor.

Perhaps the most damaging condemnation of Mao was for his promotion of the "personality cult" that viewed him as a demigod and treated his thought as "infinite and boundless."[99] The party assessment concluded that Mao had gradually isolated himself from the masses and the party. He had "acted more and more arbitrarily and subjectively, and increasingly put himself above the Central Committee of the party." Thus, he had become less "democratic."[100] With Mao's image reduced to that of a Marxist mortal, Hu Yaobang, the party's new general secretary, declared at the 1982 party congress that "personality cult" must henceforth be forbidden.[101] Further, the new leaders abolished the practice of life-long tenure for leaders.[102]

In effect, what the Chinese said in their reevaluation was that there were really two Mao Zedongs: a good Mao and a bad Mao. The serious mistakes of his later years must be renounced; but his thought, ideas, and practice—as reinterpreted and modified by the pragmatists now in power—must be preserved and enshrined. Was this a true and accurate assessment of Mao, or was it some sort of "convoluted logic"?[103] Can we really separate the man from his ideas? Was the Mao of the Great Leap and the Cultural Revolution really different from the Mao that existed before 1957? Was Mao more innovative and less arrogant before 1957? Can we really say in the same breath that Mao violated his own principles and practices but was also "the spiritual asset of the party"? It may also be argued that Mao had always been an innovator who preferred an "alternative model of development for China."[104] Perhaps the Great Leap and the Cultural Revolution were actually symbols of Mao's constant search for a new lifestyle.[105]

Certainly, the process of assessing Mao is by no means complete. We have not exhausted our study of Mao the man nor of his role in Chinese history.[106] Nevertheless, the reevaluation of Mao has yielded and will continue to yield important facts—as well as varied perspectives—on his role in the Chinese revolution and his legacy to the people.

NOTES

1. Franz Schurmann, *Ideology and Organization in Communist China* (Berkeley, Calif.: University of California Press, 1966).

2. Ibid., pp. 21–22.

3. See Lawrence Sullivan and Richard H. Solomon, "The Formation of Chinese Ideology in the May Fourth Era: A Content Analysis of Hsin ch'ing Nien," in *Ideology and Politics in Contemporary China,* ed. Chalmers Johnson (Seattle and London: University of Washington Press, 1973), pp. 117–60. Also see "Chairman Hua Guofeng on May 4th Movement," *Beijing Review,* 19 (May 11, 1979), 9–11.

4. "May 4th Movement Commemorated," *Beijing Review,* 20 (May 18, 1981), 5–6.

5. Butterfield, *China: Alive in the Bitter Sea,* pp. 300, 417; and Richard Bernstein, *From the Center of the Earth,* pp. 104–5.

6. Bernstein, *From the Center of the Earth,* p. 104.

7. "Recognize Correctly the Situation and Policy by Upholding the Four Guidelines," *Hongqi,* 5 (March 1, 1981), 2–11; "Overcoming Two Erroneous Trends of Thought," *Beijing Review,* 24 (June 8, 1979), 3.

8. "Hu Yaobang's Speech," *Beijing Review,* 28 (July 13, 1981), 20.

9. Feng Wenbin, "Following the Party Line Laid Down by the Third Plenum, Resolutely March Forward on the Socialist Road," *Hongqi,* 10 (May 16, 1981), 2–12. Also see *Beijing Review,* 23, 25, and 26 (June 8, 22, and 29, 1981).

10. "Nature of Chinese Society," *Beijing Review,* 23 (June 8, 1981), 22.

11. Ibid., pp. 7–8.

12. "Hu Yaobang's Speech," p. 20.

13. Ibid., p. 20.

14. Mao-Tse-tung, "Ching Kanshan Revisited," *Peking Review,* 1 (January 2, 1976), 5.

15. Stuart Schram, *Mao Tse-tung* (London: Penguin, 1970), p. 36.

16. See Enrica Collotti Pischel, "The Teacher," in *Mao Tse-tung in the Scale of History,* ed. Dick Wilson (London: Cambridge University Press, 1977), pp. 144–73.

17. Lucian Pye, *Mao-Tse-tung, the Man in the Leader* (New York: Basic Books, 1976), pp. 20–21.

18. Snow, *Red Star Over China,* p. 151.

19. *Pye, Mao Tse-tung, the Man in the Leader,* pp. 17–38.

20. Ibid., pp. 17–38.

21. Ibid., p. 23.

22. Edgar Snow, *The Long Revolution* (New York: Vintage Books, 1973), pp. 170–71.

23. Snow, *The Long Revolution,* p. 169.

24. Dick Wilson, ed., *Mao Tse-tung in the Scale of History.*

25. Hsiung, *Ideology and Practice: The Evolution of Chinese Communism,* p. 67.

26. Mao Tse-tung, "Report on an Investigation of the Peasant Movement in Hunan," in *Selected Works of Mao Tse-tung* (Peking: Foreign Language Press, 1967), vol. i, pp. 23–59.

27. Benjamin I. Schwartz, *Communism and China: Ideology in Flux* (Cambridge, Mass.: Harvard University Press, 1968), p. 41; Hsiung, *Ideology and Practice,* pp. 61–62; and Chester

C. Tan, *Chinese Political Thought in the Twentieth Century* (Garden City, N.Y.: Doubleday, 1971), pp. 345–46.

28. Hsiung, *Ideology and Practice*, pp. 61–62; and Conrad Brandt, Benjamin Schwartz, and John Fairbank, *A Documentary History of Chinese Communism* (New York: Atheneum, 1966), pp. 80–93.

29. John W. Lewis, *Leadership in Communist China* (Ithaca, N.Y.: Cornell University Press, 1963), p. 72.

30. Mao Tse-tung, "Some Questions Concerning Methods of Leadership," in *Selected Works of Mao Tse-tung* (Peking: Foreign Language Press, 1967), vol. iii, pp. 117–22.

31. Ibid., p. 113.

32. See Lowell Dittmer, "Mass Line and Mass Criticism in China: An Analysis of the Fall of Liu Shao-chi," *Asian Survey*, vol. xiii, no. 8, (August 1973), 772–92.

33. Schram, "The Marxist," in *Mao Tse-tung in the Scale of History*, p. 48. Also in Lewis, *Leadership in Communist China*, p. 79.

34. Lewis, *Leadership in Communist China*, pp. 84–86.

35. James R. Townsend, "Chinese Populism and the Legacy of Mao Tse-tung," *Asian Survey*, vol. xviii, no. 11 (November 1977), 1006–11.

36. Ibid., p. 1009.

37. See James C. F. Wang, "Values of the Cultural Revolution," in the *Journal of Communication*, vol. 27, no. 3 (Summer 1977), 41–46. Also see Maurice Meisner, "Utopian Goals and Ascetic Values in Chinese Communist Ideology," *Journal of Asian Studies* vol. 28, no. 1 (November 1968), 101–10.

38. Mao Tse-tung, "On Practice," *Selected Works of Mao Tse-tung* (Peking: Foreign Language Press, 1967), vol. i, pp. 295–309.

39. Starr, *Ideology and Culture: An Introduction to the Dialectic of Contemporary Chinese Politics* (New York: Harper and Row, 1973), p. 30.

40. Hsiung, *Ideology and Practice*, pp. 102–3; Pye, *Mao-Tse-tung: the Man in the Leader*, p. 45; Schram, "The Marxist," in *Mao Tse-tung in the Scale of History*, p. 60.

41. *Selected Works of Mao Tse-tung* (Peking: Foreign Language Press, 1977), vol. v, pp. 384–421.

42. Starr, *Ideology and Culture*, p. 128.

43. Mao Tse-tung, "On the Ten Major Relationships, April 25, 1956," *Peking Review*, 1 (January 1, 1977), 10–25.

44. Mao Tse-tung, "On Contradiction," in *Selected Works of Mao Tse-tung* (Peking: Foreign Language Press, 1967), vol. i, p. 317.

45. William Hinton, *Turning Point in China: An Essay on the Cultural Revolution* (New York: Monthly Review Press, 1972).

46. Shih Kang, "Dialectics in Blast Furnaces," *Peking Review*, 41 (October 12, 1973), 19–20.

47. The illustration is given by Gray and Cavendish, *Chinese Communist in Crisis* (New York and London: Holt, Rinehart & Winston, 1968), pp. 59–60.

48. Schurmann, *Ideology and Organization*, p. 54.

49. Ibid., p. 55.

50. "Talks at the Chengtu Conference, March 1958" in Stuart Schram, ed., *Chairman Mao Talks to the People, Talks and Letters, 1956–1971* (New York: The Pantheon Asia Library, 1974), p. 108. For further insights into the concept, see Stuart Schram's two articles, "Mao Tse-tung and the Theory of Permanent Revolution," *The China Quarterly*, 46 (April–June 1971), 221–44, and "The Marxist," *Mao Tse-tung in the Scale of History*, pp. 56–62. Also, see John Bryan Starr, "Conceptual Foundations of Mao Tse-tung's Theory of Continuous Revolution," *Asian Survey*, vol. xi, no. 6 (June 1971), 610–28.

51. Starr, "Conceptual Foundations of Mao Tse-tung's Theory of Continuous Revolution," p. 612.

52. "On Questions of Party History," p. 29.

53. "How to Define Mao Zedong Thought," *Beijing Review*, 1 (January 7, 1980), 5–6. Also see Deng Xiaoping's interview with Oriana Fallaci, *The Guardian Weekly*, September 21, 1980, p. 17.

54. "On Questions of Party History," p. 35.

55. Ibid. On the matter of class struggle, see the following issues of *Beijing Review:* 7 (February 18, 1980), 6; 20 (May 19, 1980), 24; 22 (June 2, 1980), 24; 34 (August 24, 1981), 3; 44

(November 2, 1981), 20; 17 (April 26, 1982), 3; 33 (August 16, 1982), 17; 49 (December 6, 1982), 16.

56. "On Questions of Party History," p. 21.

57. Ibid.

58. Ibid., p. 37.

59. See editorial of the *People's Daily,* November 6, 1982, p. 1; and Xi Xuan, "Why Should a Theory Be Discarded," *Beijing Review,* 44 (November 2, 1981), 20.

60. *People's Daily,* November 6, 1982, p. 1.

61. "Communiqué of the Third Plenary Session of the Eleventh Central Committee, Adopted on December 22, 1978," Peking Review, 52 (December 29, 1978), 19.

62. Ibid., p. 11; and *Beijing Review,* 7 (December 18, 1980), 6.

63. "Why Should a Theory be Discarded," p. 20.

64. Ibid., pp. 21–22.

65. "Current Class Struggle," *Beijing Review,* 17 (April 26, 1982), 3.

66. Ibid.

67. Mao Tse-tung, "Talk at an Enlarged Working Conference Convened by the Central Committee of the CCP," *Peking Review,* 27 (July 7, 1978), 6–22. The version has been, however, included in translation form in Schram, *Chairman Mao Talks to the People,* pp. 158–87.

68. Townsend, "Chinese Populism and the Legacy of Mao Tse-tung," p. 1011.

69. Schram, "The Marxist," in *Mao Tse-tung in the Scale of History,* p. 69.

70. Mike Oksenberg, "Mao's Policy Commitments, 1921–1976," *Problems of Communism,* vol. xxv, no. 6 (November-December 1976), 19–26. Also see his article "The Political Leader," in *Mao Tse-tung in the Scale of History,* pp. 88–98.

71. Fox Butterfield, "China Disputes Legacy of Mao More Directly," *The New York Times,* May 17, 1978, pp. 1–2; Linda Mathews, " 'Demaoization' Extends to People's Daily," Los Angeles Times Service, reprinted in *Honolulu Advertiser,* January 13, 1978, E–15; and David Bonavia, "Dismantling Parts of Maoism—But Not Mao," *Far Eastern Economic Review,* October 7, 1977, 39–41.

72. Simon Leys, *Chinese Shadows* (Middlesex, England: Penguin, 1978).

73. Chou En-lai, "Learn from Mao Tse-tung," *Peking Review,* 43 (October 27, 1978), 7.

74. Ibid., p. 8.

75. Communiqué of the Third Plenary Session of the Eleventh Central Committee of the Communist Party of China, pp. 14–15.

76. Ibid., p. 15.

77. *Ming Pao* (Hong Kong) November 30, 1978, p. 1.

78. "On Questions of Party History," pp. 8–39.

79. Deng Xiaoping's interview with Oriana Fallaci in "Deng: Cleaning Up Mao's Feudal Mistakes," p. 16.

80. "On Questions of Party History," p. 29.

81. Ibid., p. 35.

82. See Dittmer, "China in 1981: Reform, Readjustment, and Rectification," pp. 34, 42.

83. "Differentiations Are Necessary," *Beijing Review,* 38 (September 21, 1982), 17.

84. "On Questions of Party History," p. 35; and "Differentiations Are Necessary," p. 17.

85. Huang Kecheng, "How to Assess Chairman Mao and Mao Zedong Thought," *Beijing Review,* 17 (April 17, 1981), 22.

86. Ibid.

87. See text of document entitled "Senior Cadres' Appraisal of Mao Zedong," in *Issues and Studies,* vol. xvi, no. 5 (May 1980), 77.

88. Huang Kecheng "How to Assess Chairman Mao and Mao Zedong Thought." Also see "Deng: Cleaning Up Mao's Feudal Mistakes," p. 17.

89. Huang Kecheng, "How to Assess Chairman Mao and Mao Zedong Thought."

90. "On Questions of Party History," p. 19.

91. Huang Kechang, "How to Assess Chairman Mao and Mao Zedong Thought," p. 21; and "Deng: Cleaning Up Mao's Feudal Mistakes," p. 16.

92. "Deng: Cleaning Up Mao's Feudal Mistakes," p. 16.

93. Ibid., p. 16.

94. "Had 'Cultural Revolution' Mass Support?" *Beijing Review,* 47 (November 23, 1981), 20–21.

95. "On Questions of Party History," p. 22.

96. Ibid.

97. "Deng: Cleaning Up Mao's Feudal Mistakes," pp. 7, 18.

98. "On Questions of Party History," pp. 19, 25. Also see "Hu Yaobang's Speech," p. 12.

99. "The Correct Concept of Individual Role in History," *People's Daily,* July 4, 1980, p. 1. Also see "On Questions of Party History," p. 25.

100. "On Questions of Party History," p. 25.

101. Ibid.

102. *People's Daily,* August 14, 1981, p. 1.

103. Krishna P. Gupta, "Mao's Uncertain Legacy," *Problems of Communism,* xxxi (January–February 1982), 45.

104. Gupta, "Mao's Uncertain Legacy," p. 50.

105. Ibid.

106. For some of the current scholarship on Mao, see Ross Terrill, *Mao: A Biography* (New York: Harper and Row, 1980); Dick Wilson, *The People's Emperor Mao: A Biography of Mao Tse-tung* (New York: Doubleday, 1980); Maurice Meisner, "Most of Maoism's Gone, But Mao's Shadow Isn't," *Sunday New York Times,* July 5, 1981, E–15; Raymond F. Wylie, *The Emergence of Maoism* (Stanford, Calif.: Stanford University Press, 1980).

The Basic

Political Organization:

The Chinese

Communist Party

The Chinese Communist Party (CCP) is the source of all political power and has the exclusive right to legitimize and control all other political organizations. The Chinese Communist Party alone determines the social, economic, and political goals for the society. The attainment of these goals is pursued through careful recruitment of its members and their placement in party organs which supervise and control all other institutions and groups in the society. All other institutions in China are controlled by the elites, who are themselves leaders of the party hierarchy.

HIERARCHICAL STRUCTURE OF THE PARTY

One of the most salient characteristics of the party as an organization is that it is hierarchical, pyramidal, and centralist in nature. A simplified representation of the structure of the CCP is shown in Figure 3.1. The pyramidal structure of the CCP has four main levels of organizations: (1) the central organizations; (2) the provincial and autonomous regional organizations; (3) the xian (county) or district organizations; and (4) the basic and primary organizations—party branches in schools, factories, and communes.

FIGURE 3.1:   Simplified Model of CCP Organizational Pyramid

Source: Modified version of Joseph L. LaPalombara, Politics Within Nations *(Englewood Cliffs, N.J.: Prentice-Hall, 1974), p. 527. By permission of publisher.*

CENTRAL-LEVEL PARTY ORGANIZATION

In this section the central level of the party organization will be discussed in some detail.

National Party Congress

In conformity with the tradition of a Leninist party, the CCP vests its supreme authority, at least nominally, in the National Party Congress. During its sixty-three year history, only twelve National Party Congresses have convened. The 1969, 1973, and 1977 party constitutions all stipulated that a congress must meet every five years. The two longest intervals between congresses were eleven years and thirteen years, between the Seventh Congress in 1945 and the Eighth Congress in 1956, and between the Eighth Congress and the Ninth Congress in 1969. The party constitutions of 1956, 1969, 1973, 1977, and 1982 contain a proviso, an escape clause, which states that "under special circumstances, it [the National Party Congress] may be convened before its due date or postponed" by the Central Committee. The 1982 party constitution also stipulated that the party congress may be convened if more than one-third of provincial party organizations so request. Since the party congress generally meets in a perfunctory manner to approve policy changes recommended by the Central Committee, generally its sessions have been short, a week or two in duration.

We do not know how the delegates are chosen. The procedures for selection are generally determined by the Central Committee. Presumably, delegates are selected at the provincial and district levels to reflect the "constellation of power" at the central level. It is also possible for the power at the center to engage in slate making. The process of packing the congress at the various levels of the party organization to represent factionalized leaders also may be in operation. Wang Hongwen, a radical leader from Shanghai who was subsequently arrested, had been accused of pressuring his close supporters to run for the position of delegate for the Tenth Party Congress.[1] However, it was revealed in 1968 by Xie Fuzhi, the minister for public security, that delegates to the Second through the Seventh Party Congress had been appointed.[2] The Central Committee instructed that the delegates to the 1982 party congress be elected "by secret ballot after full consultation at party congresses" at every level of the party structure. For the first time, the instructions stipulated that "the number of candidates shall be greater than the number of delegates to be elected."[3] This was an attempt to democratize the party's election process. In addition, the Central Committee urged election to the party congress of experts in economics, science, and technology, and of women and minorities.

The sheer size of the party congress—1,545 delegates for the Twelfth Congress (1982) and 1,510 for the Eleventh Congress (1977)—makes too unwieldly a body to be truly deliberative. However, the party congress does have certain basic functions to perform. Generally speaking, each session of the party congress has three standard items which constitute the entire agenda: a political report by the party chairperson or the latter's designee, a report on the revision of the party constitution, and the election of the Central Committee and its Standing Committee.

In 1980 some modification was made to the party congress agenda. The Central Committee in its February 1982 resolution set five agenda items:[4] report of the Central Committee, report by the party's discipline inspection commission, revision of the party constitution, outline of the long-term economic development plan, and election of a new Central Committee and Politburo.

A major task of the National Party Congress is to select the new Central Committee. Selection perhaps is not the proper term to describe the actual process involved: A preliminary list of those to become members of the Central Committee is usually drawn up by the key leaders in the hierarchy, and then the list is presented to the party congress for formal ratification. For instance, the draft list for members of the Eighth Central Committee (1956) was prepared by Liu Shaoqi supporters—Peng Zhen and An Ziwen.[5] At the Twelfth Party Congress (1982), delegates were given colored computer cards listing the names of all nominees for the Central Committee and for Central Advisory Commission membership. It was reported that during the balloting delegates in 1982 were permitted to delete any names on the list, as was the practice of the Seventh Party Congress (1945). Another feature introduced at the 1982 party congress, presumably a measure designed to democratize the party, gave delegates the right to "write up" names not on the nominations list.[6] It has been suggested that an appeal by Deng Xiaoping and Hu Yaobang for party unity allowed the demoted Hua Guofeng to retain one last vestige of power, his seat on the Central Committee.[7] The membership of the Central Committee elected in 1982 clearly reflects the power lineup within the party. Omissions from the powerful Central Committee membership are indicative of power shifts or simply of a reduction of influence within the party's hierarchy.

In the preparation of the party constitution to be ratified by the party congress, inputs are made by all party organizations. We now know that, at Mao's insistence beginning in 1967, party organizations at levels below the Central Committee participated in revision of the constitution.[8] Both the 1969 and 1973 party constitutions involved participation and discussion by party cadres at all levels before the final version was enacted by the delegates to these congresses. Wang Hongwen gave a detailed account of the revision process for the party constitution adopted in 1973 by the Tenth Party Congress.[9]

The party constitution adopted by the 1982 party congress was said to have been initiated by Deng Xiaoping, Hu Yaobang, and Hu Qiaomu, a key member of the Central Secretariat before he was elevated to the Politburo, and a former president of the Chinese Academy of Sciences. Hu Qiaomu and Peng Zhen presided over the drafting of the 1982 party constitution. The draft was circulated for discussion and comment at the Fifth Plenum of the Eleventh

Central Committee in February.[10] After further revision by the Politburo and the Central Secretariat, it was sent to all levels of the party apparatus for discussion. While the 1977 party constitution was influenced by the remnants of the Left led by Hua Guofeng and Wang Dongxing, the 1982 party constitution represented the influence and power of Deng Xiaoping. The preparation of the 1982 party constitution actually was carried out in the winter of 1979 by the leaders associated with Deng. It went through four drafts before being introduced at the last session of the Eleventh Central Committee for adoption. The 1982 party constitution was as lengthy and detailed as the 1956 party constitution.

Some students of Chinese politics have pointed out that in addition to the important tasks of ratification of the party constitution and election of the Central Committee, the party congress accepts and reviews political reports from party leaders.[11] Reports presented at the National Party Congress have been published, and one can infer policy shifts and program emphasis from them. Since the Central Committee debates are never published except for occasional communiqués summarizing policy formulations and personnel changes, reports of the National Party Congress provide a unique source of information about the issues and programs of concern to the party. For example, on September 1, 1982, the political report delivered by Hu Yaobang (the party's new general secretary) to the Twelfth Party Congress outlined the party's long-term strategy for quadrupling China's industrial and agricultural production through science and technology. The lengthy report called for the attainment of a higher level of social democracy for the people. While declaring that class struggle no longer constituted the principal contradiction, Hu nevertheless called for struggle against those who deliberately disrupted economic stability and debased the actual moral life of the people. Hu proposed that the following steps be taken in order to revitalize the party: The restoration of inner party discipline, the placement of younger and more competent cadres in leadership positions, and the reregistration of party members (designed to ferret out remnants of the radical Left), to be completed by 1986.[12]

Finally, there has always been a great deal of fanfare and publicity focused on the party congress. This is more than mere public relations work by the party. The convocation of the congress serves as a rallying point for the party members and for the populace in general. It creates a feeling of participation in the important decisions of the party among the delegates themselves, many of whom come from very humble backgrounds and remote regions of China. It instills in them the "sense of commitment" to and unity with their leaders and the party.[13] In 1982, for the first time, television programs focused on the proceedings of the 1982 party congress. Provincial and local stations broadcast many features about the party, including new songs composed for the occasion.

In view of the limited duration and agenda of the party congress, the question arises as to how preparations for it are made. Technically, the outgoing Central Committee is responsible for preparing the forthcoming congress. In practice, however, the Politburo or the Standing Committee of the

Politburo prepares the agenda and designates members to draft the political reports and work on the new party constitution under its supervision. We know, for instance, that the original draft of Lin Biao's political report to the Ninth Party Congress was rejected by the Central Committee or Chairman Mao.[14] Evidently, the final report, as read by Lin Biao to the delegates at the 1969 party congress, was drafted "under Chairman Mao's guidance." We probably can assume that political reports from the Seventh Party Congress (1945), to the Tenth Party Congress (1973), received personal approval from Mao. There have been admissions of hasty preparation for the proceedings of the party congress. Mrs. Liu Shaoqi (Wang Guangmei) admitted, under Red Guard interrogation during the Cultural Revolution, that "everything was done in a hurry" in preparation for the Eighth Party Congress (1956).[15]

Evidently, this was not the case when preparations for the 1982 party congress were initiated in the winter of 1979. The agenda for the 1982 party congress was not approved until February 1980 at the Central Committee's sixth plenary session.[16] The date for convening the party congress was not set by the Politburo until the spring of 1982, a delay of more than two years—but yet within the five-year interval prescribed by the previous 1977 constitution. There were several reasons for the long delay in convening the party congress: (1) Deng needed time to consolidate his power by first installing Hu Yaobang and Zhao Ziyang in key party and governmental positions; (2) the vestiges of the "Whatever" faction had to be removed from the center of power; and (3) the issue of how to assess Mao needed to be decided before delegate selection to the new party congress could take place. Thus, disunity and disagreement had to be minimized or eliminated. In short, Deng Xiaoping needed time to arrange matters so that his control over delegate selection would be assured.

Central Committee

The party constitution vests in the Central Committee the supreme power to govern party affairs and to enact party policies when the party congress is not in session. The large size of the Central Committee makes it an unwieldly body for policy making. Although the Central Committee as a collective body rarely initiates party policy, it must approve or endorse policies, programs, and major changes in membership in leading central organs. Thus, with a few exceptions, the Central Committee usually holds annual plenary sessions, either with its own full membership and alternate membership in attendance, or with non-Central Committee members as well in enlarged sessions. The few deviations from the norm occurred during the Korean War (1950–53), during the turbulent period prior to the Cultural Revolution (1962–66), and during the Lin Biao affair (1971–73). These regularized plenums of the Central Committee are the forums through which party and state policies and programs are discussed and ratified. On at least two occasions—the October 1955 plenum (enlarged), and the August 1959 plenum (enlarged)—the Central Committee became the "ultimate" body in deciding which agricultural policies were to be implemented. This occurred as a result of dissension among top leaders of the party.[17]

There has been a steady increase in the size of the Central Committee. The first session of the Eighth Party Congress (1956) expanded the full membership of the Central Committee from 44 to 97; the Ninth Party Congress (1969) almost doubled the size to a cumbersome 170; the Eleventh Party Congress (August 1977) elected 201 full and 132 alternate members to the Central Committee, for a total of 333; the Twelfth Party Congress (1982) elected 210 full and 138 alternate members, making the size (348 members) of the Twelfth Central Committee the largest to date. There are several reasons why the membership of the Central Committee has increased to its present enormous proportions. First, increased membership in the Central Committee reflects the phenomenal growth of the party membership as a whole since the Cultural Revolution, from approximately 17 million in 1961, to over 28 million at the time of the Tenth Party Congress in August 1973, to 39 million when the Twelfth Party Congress convened in the fall of 1982. Second, as in the Soviet Union, membership in the Central Committee has been used as a reward for loyal service to the party and to the government. Preeminent scholars and scientists have been elevated to Central Committee membership. Third, the Ninth and Tenth Party Congresses expanded Central Committee membership in order to make it reflect the post–Cultural Revolution party leadership recruitment policy—increased representation by workers and peasants who have rendered significant political service to the party. As shown in Table 3.1, of the full members elected to the Ninth Central Committee in April 1969, 32 (19 percent) were from mass organizations representing workers and peasants. This representation increased to 58, or 30 percent, in the Tenth Central Committee in August 1973. But the representation for mass organizations—the source of support for the radical wing of the party—was reduced to 32, or 16 percent, in the Eleventh Central Committee full membership in August 1977. Veteran cadre representation increased slightly by about 1 percent in the Tenth Central Committee, but their representation in the full membership of the Eleventh Central Committee leaped to 107, or 53 percent of the total—clear evidence of the veteran cadres' dominance in the party after the purge of the radicals in 1976. While PLA representation in the full membership of the Tenth Central Committee declined 11 percent from the Ninth Central Committee (from 43 to 32 percent), its representation in the Eleventh Central Committee full membership remained almost the same, at 31.8 percent. The combined representation of the PLA and the veteran cadres in the Eleventh Central Committee full membership was over 84 percent. A fourth reason for membership expansion in the Central Committee is related to increased female representation at the Ninth and Tenth Central Committees. There were 23, or 8.2 percent, female members on the Ninth Central Committee. This representation was increased to 41, or 12.8 percent, on the Tenth Central Committee . However, female representation was reduced to 38, or 11.4 percent in the membership of the Eleventh Central Committee.

There has been a marked continuity in the membership of the Central

TABLE 3.1 Groups Represented By Members of 9th–11th Central Committees

Group Represented	9th Full	Central Committee Alternate	Total	10th Full	Central Committee Alternate	Total	11th Full	Central Committee Alternate	Total
					Number				
PLA	74	49	123	63	37	100	62	41	103
Veteran Cadres	59	20	79	71	20	91	107	28	135
Mass Organizations	32	23	55	58	49	107	32	63	95
Unknown	5	17	22	3	18	21	—	—	—
	170	109	279	195	124	319	201	132	333
					Percent				
PLA	43%	45%	44%	32%	30%	31%	31.8%	31%	31%
Veteran Cadres	35	18	28	36	16	29	53	21	41
Mass Organizations	19	20	20	30	40	34	16	48	29
Unknown	3	16	8	2	15	7	—	—	—
Total[a]	100%	100%	100%	100%	100%	100%	100%	100%	100%

[a] Totals may not equal 100% due to rounding

Sources:
Ninth Central Committee: Figures are based on the published list in Hongqi (Red Flag), 5 (May 1, 1969), 49–50.
Tenth Central Committee: Figures are based on the published list in Hongqi (Red Flag), 9 (September 3, 1973), 32–35.
Eleventh Central Committee: Figures are based on the published list in Remin Ribao (People's Daily), August 21, 1977, p. 3.

Committee in recent years. For instance, the Tenth Party Congress in 1973 failed to reelect only 39 of the 170 full members of the Ninth Central Committee to the new Tenth Central Committee—all of them were supporters of Lin Biao. The Eleventh Party Congress in 1977 reelected 111 of the 195 full members of the Tenth Central Committee to the new Eleventh Central Committee, which had a full membership of 201. In other words, close to half the Eleventh Central Committee full membership was carried over from the old Tenth Central Committee elected in 1973. Those not reelected to the Eleventh Central Committee were apparently the supporters of the Gang of Four. The Eleventh Central Committee had a preponderant representation of the old veterans of the party, government, and the military. The average age of both full and alternate members of the Eleventh Central Committee was over sixty-five.[18] For the 1982 Twelfth Central Committee, however, 210, or 60.6 percent, of the 348 full and alternate members were new. There was an even larger percentage of new faces in the alternate membership category: 114, or about 83 percent, of a total of 138 alternate members. Six of the 138 alternate members of the Twelfth Central Committee were members of the "Whatever" faction, demoted from full to alternate membership.[19] About two-thirds of the 210 newly elected full Central Committee members were under sixty years of age. However, only about 40 percent of the total membership were under sixty years of age. There was a sharp increase in the category of professional and technically trained cadres elected to the 1982 Central Committee: 59, or 17 percent, as compared to 9, or less than 3 percent, who served on the Eleventh Central Committee (1977).[20]

The Politburo and Its Standing Committee

The principle of Lenin's democratic centralism calls for decision-making power for the party to be vested in a small number of key leaders who occupy positions at the apex of the power structure, the Political Bureau (Politburo). The formal language in the party constitution does not reveal the actual power of this top command for the CCP. The party constitutions of 1969, 1973, 1977, and 1982 simply stipulate that the Politburo shall be elected by the Central Committee in full session and shall act in its behalf when the Central Committee is not in session. The day-to-day work of the Politburo is carried out by its Standing Committee, the apex of the pyramidal structure of the party.[21] In essence, it is the Politburo and its Standing Committee which possess "boundless" power over the general policies of the party and all important matters of the regime that affect the government organs.[22] It is the Politburo which selects top personnel to direct the vast apparatus of the party, the government, and the military.

The Politburo holds frequent meetings; discussion is said to be frank and unrestrained. It has been compared to a corporate board of directors.[23] Decisions of the Politburo are generally reached by consensus after thorough discussion of the available alternatives.

When the party took power in 1949, the CCP Politburo consisted of eleven members, and its operation very closely resembled that of Lenin's inner circle of key leaders who made all the important decisions for the Soviet party, government, and state.[24] By 1956 the CCP Politburo membership had increased to seventeen full and six alternate members, paralleling the enlargement of the party congress and the Central Committee. With fluctuations—as a result of deaths and purges—its membership rose to over twenty full members in later years. The Eleventh Party Congress in 1977 elected a twenty-six-member Politburo, which was expanded to thirty in 1978. The Twelfth Party Congress (1982) elected twenty-eight members to the Politburo: twenty-five full and three alternate members. As we have seen with the party congress and the Central Committee, enlargement reflected a shift in function. The 1956 party constitution introduced the concept of the "apex of the apex": the formation of the Standing Committee of the Politburo, which became the top ruling clique. The membership of the Standing Committee has varied from five to nine. The 1982 party congress elected a six-member Standing Committee. In many instances the Standing Committee makes decisions without even consulting the Politburo.[25]

The dynamics of decision making, involving key leaders and cadres of the party and government, will be discussed in Chapter 4. It should be noted here, however, that prior to the Cultural Revolution, the decision-making process was institutionalized to a large extent by the frequent use of work conferences under the sponsorship of the Politburo or the Central Committee.[26] Since the purge of the radical leaders in October 1976, this institutionalized device for policy formulation has been revived, so that at least several dozen national conferences have been convened to develop national policies on various matters, including modernizing agriculture and industry, national defense, and science and technology.

According to the party constitution, the Central Committee elects members to the Politburo and its Standing Committee, but between 1935–75 the actual selection rested in the hands of Chairman Mao. In fact, the determination of which Central Committee members were to sit on the powerful Politburo had been termed Mao's "personal prerogative."[27] Franklin Houn points out that Mao followed a general set of guidelines in his selection of candidates to Politburo membership: seniority in the party, contributions made to Mao's own rise to power, and loyalty and usefulness to Mao and to the party.[28] To what extent Hua Guofeng had a decisive role in the selection of the twenty-six-member Politburo for the Eleventh Central Committee (1977) is difficult to determine. But sixteen of the members were reelected from the previous Politburo membership, and the ten newly elected members all had backgrounds of long service in the party, government, and military bureaucracy. Thus, administrative experience may be an important factor in Politburo membership selection.

Of the twenty-eight members of the Politburo elected in 1982, nine were new faces. The new members were recognized as capable party and government administrators; a majority of them, at one time or another, were associated with either Deng Xiaoping or Hu Yaobang. However, it should be pointed out that the Politburo elected in 1982 can best be described as a "gerontocracy," with the average age of its members being over seventy-two. Five members were over eighty years old. The average age for members of the Politburo's six-member Standing Committee, the apex of the apex in decision making, was seventy-four. The two youngest Standing Committee members (Hu Yaobang and Zhao Ziyang) were in their mid-sixties. Three were in their late seventies (Deng Xiaoping, Li Xiannian, and Chen Yun), and one was over eighty-five (Ye Jiangying). (Presumably, the four septuagenarians on the Standing Committee will eventually make way for those in their sixties to move up the ladder.)

Other Principal Organs
of the Central Committee

The Central Committee and its Politburo are serviced by a host of centralized organs, responsible for executing party policies and managing party affairs. Some of this machinery deals with the routine matters of party organization, propaganda, and united front work. However, three principal central party organs need to be briefly mentioned here: the Central Secretariat, the Military Affairs Commission, and the Central Commission for Discipline Inspection.

The Central Secretariat, as it existed from 1956–66, was the administrative and staff agency that supervised the party's numerous functional departments, paralleling the functional ministries of the central government. The total number of these central party functional departments may once have reached more than eighteen. Membership of the Central Secretariat was not fixed; it ranged from six or seven to ten or eleven top-ranking Central Committee members. For over a decade, the Central Secretariat was under the control of Deng Xiaoping, who served as its general secretary. Deng and the members of the Central Secretariat used the machinery to make or influence many important party decisions without even consulting Mao, the chairman of the party.[29] In the aftermath of the Cultural Revolution, the Central Secretariat, as a formal unit, was abandoned, probably at the insistence of Mao, who felt that it had overstepped its authority. From then until 1977 or 1978, the administrative functions of the party secretariat were absorbed by the General Office for the Politburo, headed by Politburo member Wang Dongxing. In the winter of 1978, Wang was replaced by Yao Yilin. At the same time, a newly elected Politburo member, Hu Yaobang, a trusted protégé of Deng Xiaoping, was appointed secretary-general of the Central Secretariat, which has been reestablished in its pre-Cultural Revolution form.

The reinstitution of a general secretariat and the abolition of the post of party chairperson must be viewed as an obvious rejection of Mao's practice of "overconcentration of personal power" in the party. The daily work of the party or of the Central Committee was now to be supervised by the Central Secretariat headed by Hu Yaobang, who in turn was assisted by eleven other members (one died in January 1983), four of whom were concurrently members of the Politburo. The 1982 party constitution makes it clear that the daily work of the Central Committee is to be carried out by the Central Secretariat under the overall direction of the Politburo and its Standing Committee. Article 21 of the 1982 party constitution stipulates that the general secretary must be a member of the Standing Committee of the Politburo and that it is his or her responsibility to convene its meetings. One must recall that the Cultural Revolution and its aftermath had disrupted almost completely the work of the party secretariat; its daily responsibilities were taken over by two other organs: the Central Office of the Politburo and the Cultural Revolution Committee (both were controlled and staffed by the radicals and the Lin Biao group). The reestablishment of the Central Secretariat with its general secretary represented a distinct party reform demanded by the pragmatic leaders in the post-Mao era.

The Central Secretariat now consists of seven major departments:[30] organization, propaganda, united front work, liaison office with the fraternal parties abroad, publication office of the *Red Flag* and the *People's Daily*, a policy research office, and an office of party schools. We now know that the Central Secretariat meets twice a week behind the red walls of Zhongnanhai, a part of the former imperial palace and now both party headquarters and the seat of the central government, the State Council. Members of the Central Secretariat, elected by the National Party Congress, can initiate and formulate policies on anything they wish. The Central Secretariat has invited leaders in industry, commerce, agriculture, science, and education to Zhongnanhai to brief its members on current developments or problems. In addition, it processes a large volume of mail received from party cells and branches, as well as from the public.

Although the Military Affairs Commission (MAC) is a subunit of the Central Committee of the CCP, it reports directly to the Politburo and its Standing Committee. The MAC supervises the administration of the armed forces and makes policies in national defense. The MAC directly controls the General Political Department (GPD), the party's political agent within the PLA, which is in theory a branch of the Ministry of Defense but in practice operates independently of it. The General Political Department is responsible for the political education of the troops and publishes the *Liberation Army Daily*, the military's own daily newspaper.

The basic function of the MAC has been its exclusive responsibility in directing the party's military activities, including the power to appoint and remove military personnel. As a subunit of the Central Committee, with responsibility for strategy and tactics of the Chinese army, it can be traced back to the guerrilla days of the early 1930s.[31] After the 1935 Zunyi Conference, Mao assumed the chair of the Revolutionary Military Committee, the predecessor of the present MAC. By that time the committee had assumed the responsibilities of educating the troops in political matters and of approving the party's political commissars assigned to the various armies. The MAC operates through a standing committee; the members of that committee regularly conduct inspection trips to the thirteen regional military commands and submit reports directly to the Politburo. Throughout the years the MAC has held periodic special work conferences for military leaders from all regions and provinces on military and political-ideological topics. New policies and directives are explained at these conferences to ensure proper implementation. From around 1954 on, the MAC has also been responsible for conducting numerous political training schools for army officers. Ralph Powell points out that MAC supervision of the PLA is extensive and diverse, covering even the most routine matters.[32]

A longstanding practice, instituted by Mao, was to have the party chairperson automatically serve as the chairperson for the Military Affairs Commission. That practice was abandoned by the 1982 party constitution, which stipulates only that the chairperson of the MAC must be a member of the Standing Committee of the Politburo (see Article 21 in Appendix B). In 1978 Deng Xiaoping assumed the chairmanship of the MAC, assisted by a permanent vice-chairman, Yang Shangkun, a trusted Deng associate. The three military marshals—Ye Jiangying, Xu Xiangqian, and Nie Rongzhen—served as nominal vice-chairmen of the commission by tradition.

Although no official list of MAC members has been published, two general guidelines seem to determine its composition: (1) Members include most of the senior military figures, particularly the PLA marshals; and (2) members usually reflect the composition of the Politburo. The size of the MAC ranges from at least ten members to perhaps nineteen or twenty. Traditionally, the first vice-chair of MAC concurrently serves as the minister of defense. By 1982 that tradition, too, was abandoned. The current defense minister, Zhang Aiping, age seventy-two, was elevated from the position of deputy chief of staff in the military's senior command. Zhang was not, at the time of his appointment as defense chief, a vice-chairman of the MAC. The chief of staff for the PLA is usually a member of the Standing Committee of the MAC. There is also an interlocking membership situation existing among the MAC, the Politburo, and the Central Committee. The high degree of interlocking membership between the MAC and the Politburo is such that at least nine members of the Politburo elected by the Eleventh Central Committee (August 1977) have been members of the MAC. Similarly, at least ten members of the Politburo elected in 1982 had been members of the MAC, including Deng and Yang Shangkun.

The true functions of the Central Commission for Discipline Inspection have not been spelled out anywhere, not even in the informative party constitution of 1956, which gave the hierarchical structure of the original Control Commission. However, based on recent revelations, the reestablished party control mechanism seems to have the following main functions: (1) maintenance of party morality and discipline; (2) control over the performance of party organizations; and (3) investigation of breaches of party discipline.[33]

As the party's internal rectification campaigns became more numerous and intensified in the late 1950s and 1960s, the Control Commission at all levels became more active in conducting investigations. This was particularly true on the eve of the Cultural Revolution, when a disunited party at the center caused confusion about the direction of party policies for the lower-level organizations. By the time the Cultural Revolution was in full swing in 1966, the entire party control mechanism simply fell apart. The end result was the abolition of the old Control Commission by the Ninth Party Congress. Both the 1969 and 1973 party constitutions directed that the masses, not the party control machinery, must provide overall supervision and control over matters of party discipline and the correctness of party policy or line. At least three forms of mass supervision over party discipline and unity were provided: (1) direct contact between the party cadres and the masses when investigation was required; (2) mass criticisms when policy was being implemented; and (3) mass participation in the management of party affairs through their representation in the revolutionary committee.

The party constitution of 1977 created a new control device—the Central Commission for Discipline Inspection—to strengthen party discipline and internal party democracy in the aftermath of the abusive practices instituted during the Cultural Revolution by the recently purged radical leaders. The new commission for party discipline is charged with the task of enforcing party rules and regulations, as well as with the development of sound party style, including the inculcation of all the requisite party virtues. In 1978 the Third Plenary Session of the Eleventh Central Committee elected the first hundred-member Central Commission for Discipline Inspection, headed by veteran party administrator Chen Yun.[34] Prior to the Cultural Revolution, the sixty-member Control Commission operated through a standing committee of nine or ten members.[35] The standing committee for the newly formed Central Commission for Discipline Inspection consists of twenty-four party veterans, all purged or mistreated during the Cultural Revolution. In their first report, published in March 1979, the party's inspection commission urged that any false charges, wrong punishments, and frame-ups leveled against any party members be corrected and the victims rehabilitated. Thus, a first step was taken to tighten the slackened party discipline and to restore internal party democracy.

The Central Commission for Discipline Inspection was given considerable power and jurisdiction by the 1982 party constitution to monitor party rules and regulations; it reports directly to the Central Committee on violations of party discipline and on the implementation of party policies and decisions. An elaborate system of local commissions for inspecting party discipline was also established at the various party levels. The commission and its subsidiary bodies were now also made responsible for providing education among party members about party discipline and work style.

The Central Commission for Discipline Inspection is authorized to receive appeals and complaints from any party members and cadres who can prove that they were framed and charged by the radicals with false evidence. Xinhua News Agency reported in September 1979 that there were 150,000 letters of appeals addressed to the commission between December 1978 and August 1979.[36] Lower-level investigation of inner party discipline and breach of party rules from seventeen provinces, municipalities (Shanghai and Beijing), and autonomous regions processed 3.8 million cases of appeals and complaints.[37] The statistics provide us with some idea as to the number of verdicts reversed from 1979 to 1980.[38] The officially published statistics also seem to indicate the widespread ferreting out from the party ranks of those who evidently blindly followed the orders of the radicals during the decade of the Cultural Revolution. In one province, Fujian, the commission's investigation resulted in 1,560 cases of expulsion from party membership for violating party discipline.[39] The pingfan (reinstatement and exoneration) campaign was followed in January 1981 by another inner party review, ostensibly of all 38 million party members, but in actuality aimed at the rapid expulsion of the undesirables among the 15 million who became party members during the Cultural Revolution.[40] This inner party membership cleansing campaign was preceded by the commission's investigation and expulsion posthumously of two leading party veterans of the Cultural Revolution: Kang Sheng, Politburo member and close advisor of Mao, and Xie Fuzhi, another Politburo member and public security minister at the height of the Cultural Revolution. They were charged with participating in the plots of the Gang of Four to "usurp the supreme leadership of the party" and other grave crimes.[41]

If correct party style is a matter of life and death for the Central party, to use the words of Chen Yun (the first secretary for the Commission for Discipline Inspection), then some serious efforts must be made to rebuild the party on the basis of discipline and rules that will regulate and govern the behavior of party members. From this perspective, the guidelines for inner party political life must be considered a major accomplishment of the commission. Upon recommendation of the commission, the Central Committee in March 1980 adopted a set of twelve guidelines, or guiding principles, for inner party political life.[42] These general guidelines reflect the abuses, anarchism, and laxity in party discipline that prevailed during the Cultural Revolution. Collectively, these guidelines tell us clearly what happened to the party when Mao permitted radical ideologues to seize the party machinery and disrupt inner party life. These rules may be read as a catalog of indictments against Mao's personal arbitrary rule and the ills of the party. For instance, one of the guidelines is to uphold the collective leadership of the party, not individual, arbitrary decision making. On important issues the guidelines now provide for collective discussion by the rank and file of the party and for decision making by the party committee. The fostering of a "personality cult" is now strictly prohibited: There may be no celebration of leaders' birthdays, no gifts, and no congratulatory messages. Henceforth, no memorial hall shall be erected for any living person, nor shall a street, place, or school be named after a party leader.

The new inner party political life guidelines demand tolerance for dissenting views at the discussion stage of policy making. No punishment is to be given for erroneous statements by a party member—so long as these dissenting opinions do not advocate factional activities or divulge party and state secrets. It is a criminal act to organize secret groups within the party. Party members are to speak the truth and to be honest in words and deeds. There shall be no abridgment of a party member's right to participate in meetings or to criticize any party organization or individual at party meetings. All party committees are to hold regular meetings and elections. Erroneous tendencies and evil deeds such as graft, embezzlement, factionalism, anarchism, extreme individualism, bureaucraticism, and special privileges are to be opposed at all times. In inner party struggles, a correct attitude must be adopted toward those who make mistakes, but "it is prohibited to wage ruthless struggle against those erring party members." Everyone is equal within the party and before party rules and regulations. No party member is permitted to show favoritism toward family or relatives. Finally, all party members must be reviewed and rewarded in accordance with their ability and competence. Hu Yaobang, the new party general secretary, argued that life-long tenure in a leadership position should be abolished, and that emphasis should be placed on promoting those capable party cadres who are in their prime.

Preliminary review of the work of the Central Commission for Discipline Inspection indicates clearly that the CCP has revived the pre-1956 concept of a central party organ to serve as a "party court" or "ecclesiastical court," for governing not only party discipline but also the inner party political life. It has also performed the task of "judicial review"—overruling a previous Central Committee decision by declaring a decision on Liu Shaoqi to be "unconstitutional" in accordance with party rules and discipline. As a kind of party court, the commission has also cleared the names of millions of party members and cadres who were unjustly accused of wrongdoing during the Cultural Revolution.

The commission may have been given another role when it was assigned the task of drafting the document on guidelines for inner party political life and shepherding its passage through the Central Committee: that of serving as a central organ for supervising the implementation of the guidelines. The commission is encountering difficulties and resistance among party members and cadres as regards this new role. A proper attitude toward good work style and party life, notwithstanding the promulgation of the guidelines, is still lacking.

Another new central-level body established by the 1982 party constitution is the Central Advisory Commission, designed to serve as "political assistance and consultant to the Central Committee" (see Article 22 of the 1982 constitution in Appendix B). Membership on the commission is limited to party elders with at least forty years of party service. This is mainly a device to permit party elders to vacate their long-held positions so as to provide some upward mobility for younger members. Also, the Central Advisory Commission is intended to do away with the tradition of providing life tenure for top leaders in the party. As consultants, commission members may attend plenary meetings of the Central Committee without a vote. The Advisory Commission's vice-chairperson is also permitted to attend Politburo meetings ex-officio, if necessary. The Advisory Commission can make recommendations to the Central Committee, at least on paper, on party policy formulation or on tasks assigned by the Central Committee. Initially, the commission had 172 members and was presided over by Deng Xiaoping. Roughly 50 members, or over one-third of the membership of the Eleventh Central Committee, were forced to become Advisory Commission members. The Advisory Commission also included elderly senior military officers and provincial and local party chiefs. A vast majority of the Advisory Commission members were over seventy years of age. Some were under seventy but evidently were forced to join the group because of their past political mistakes—former Politburo members Wu De, Chen Xilian, and Xu Shiyou were forced to retire from the Politburo when Deng Xiaoping consolidated his power.

There was some inconsistency in making elderly veterans retire and join the Advisory Commission. Marshal Ye, now over eighty-five, apparently either refused to join the commission or was urged by Deng to remain on the Politburo. Despite rhetoric to the contrary, the thorny problem of longevity in office and life tenure in the party have still not been completely resolved at the top level of the party structure.

REGIONAL PARTY ORGANS AND FUNCTIONS

Administratively speaking, China is governed, as it always has been, by provinces, the most immediate and important subunit below the central level. The party organization below the Central Committee level is the provincial party apparatus in each of the twenty-one provinces and the five autonomous regions and three municipalities (Beijing, Shanghai, and Tianjin), administered directly by the central government. From 1949 to 1954, and again from 1960 to 1966, the party established an intermediate layer of organs to supervise the provincial party affairs on behalf of the Central Committee. These were the six regional bureaus for the northeast, north, east, central south, northwest, and southwest, as shown in Figure 3.2.

The party regional bureaus were formed in 1949 to parallel the regional administrative bureaus for the central government. The party constitution of 1956, in formally establishing the regional bureaus, said little about their functions except that they were to serve as a linkage between the party, centered in Beijing, and the vast regional areas administered traditionally as provinces. The operation of the party's regional bureaus from 1949 to 1954 showed that the regional party secretaries and the functional departments of these bureaus had enormous power over provincial party affairs. In fact, it was mainly the growth of the regional bureaus' power—which posed a threat to the center—that led to the abolition of the regional bureaus in 1954, following the purge of Gao Gang and Rao Xuzhi. Gao Gang, the party secretary for the Northeast Bureau, had exercised a considerable amount of independence in supervising the party activities of the three provinces bordering the Soviet Union. Gao, who was also a member of the Politburo and a vice-chair of the central government, was charged by the Central Committee with creating an "indepen-

FIGURE 3.2:   Regional Bureaus of the CCP Central Committee

Source: Li Shih-fei, "The Party's Middleman: The Role of Regional Bureaus in the Chinese Communist Party," Current Scene: Developments in Mainland China, *vol. iii, no. 25 (August 15, 1965), 15.*

dent kingdom'' for the northeast. Both Gao Gang and Rao Xuzhi, as spokesmen for the vital regions of China's northeastern and eastern provinces, had attacked Mao's collectivization and agricultural and economic policies and had challenged the leadership of both Liu Shaoqi and Zhou Enlai; this brought on the combined wrath of the top leaders in the party's hierarchy.[43] The purge of these two ''regionally based'' party leaders in 1954 strengthened the position of the ''centrally based'' leaders, Liu and Zhou, and resulted in a ''high degree of centralization'' of control in Beijing.[44]

The six regional bureaus were reestablished in 1960, presumably to provide better coordination and supervision by the party over economic recovery activities in the provinces in the aftermath of the Great Leap. The new regional bureaus of the Central Committee, which existed until the Cultural Revolution, maintained a close relationship with the thirteen regional military commands: In most cases regional bureau secretaries concurrently served as political commissars for the military commands, and military commanders frequently concurrently served as the party's regional bureau secretaries.[45] This relationship became a major obstacle in implementing the directives from the center during the Cultural Revolution. Regional bureau leaders and provincial party leaders defied orders issued from Beijing and maintained their own local policies. For instance, before he was finally purged, Li Jingquan, the first secretary of the Southwest Bureau and the political commissar for the Chengdu Military Region, defiantly spoke against the Cultural Revolution by saying, "Give prominence to politics? No, we should give prominence to fertilizer. Fertilizer can solve problems."[46] Li had refused to receive emissaries from Beijing and had tried very hard to protect his party leaders from attacks by the students.[47] The purge meted out by the students and the radicals to the regional bureaus' secretaries was so complete that by 1968 the structure itself once again was abandoned. The party constitutions of 1969 and 1973 made no reference to the regional bureaus. They had begun as the intermediate link between the center and the far-flung provinces; but they became "mountain-strongholds" or "independent kingdoms" occasionally obstructing the will of the center.

However, the concept of economic regions with local autonomy seems to have been revived in order to coordinate and effectively implement the various economic programs launched in the 1978 modernization drive.

PROVINCIAL PARTY ORGANS AND FUNCTIONS

Theoretically speaking, provincial party committees derive their power from the party congresses at the provincial level. The party constitution of 1956, adopted by the Eighth Party Congress, called for the convening of provincial party congresses once a year (Article 38). The 1969, 1973, and 1977 party constitutions mandated that party congresses at the provincial level and below meet every three years. The 1982 party constitution (Article 24, see Appendix B), mandates that party congresses at the provincial level and in autonomous regions, in municipalities under the central government, and in cities with districts be held once every five years. County- and city-level (without districts) congresses are to be held at least once every three years. Each provincial party committee is generally run by a standing committee consisting of the first secretary and a number of subordinate secretaries within the hierarchy of the provincial party structure.

The provincial party committee is responsible for supervision and provides direction over five basic areas: organization and control of the party; economic activities in agriculture, industry, finance and trade; capital construction; mobilization of women and youth; and research for policy development. Initially, the provincial party committees played a subordinate role in supervising provincial economic development. This was more pronounced during the period of high centralization of the First Five-Year Plan (1953–56), when the national functional ministries had a great deal of authority and control over the provincial party activities. During and after the Great Leap Forward (1957–59), there was a period of decentralization; the provincial party committees were given greater responsibility and more power in managing economic activities in the provinces. In many respects the provincial party committees behaved as though they were "underdeveloped nations" in bidding for resources to develop economic and productive activities.[48]

Since the provincial party committees and their subordinate primary party organs within the provinces are responsible for implementing party policies, they hold a unique position within the party structure. The first secretary of the provincial party committee wields an enormous amount of power. Provincial party secretaries, as pointed out by one study, on occasion have deliberately refused to carry out directives from the center.[49] This power is reflected in and enhanced by the provincial party secretaries' participation in central party affairs (see Chapter 5).

PRIMARY PARTY ORGANS AND FUNCTIONS

Below the provincial party committees are the primary units at the county level and below. They are the "fighting bastions" (to use the phraseology in the 1982 party constitution) for carrying out the party policies and line. It is here that the party makes its immediate contact with the rest of the society. Like the provincial party structure, all basic units of the party are headed by a party secretary, who in turn is guided by a party committee. Party units at the primary level never contest policies and programs imposed from above. However honest and vigorous discussion often prevails at these lower-level party meetings.

The lowest level of party organization, the so-called primary party units or cells, are party branches formed in "factories, shops, schools, city neighborhoods, people's communes, cooperatives, farms, townships, towns, companies of the People's Liberation Army and other basic units, where there are three or more full party members," in accordance with Article 30 of the 1982 party constitution. While there are no official figures on the total number of party branches at the lowest level, one source estimated the total number in 1982 at 2.5 million.[50] It is at this level that the organizational functions of the party are carried out: membership recruitment, political and ideological education about the party line, exercise of party discipline, and maintenance of "close ties with the masses." It is generally the party branch in a given enterprise, commune, or office which provides leadership, supervision, and guidance in party affairs. Like the first secretaries in the higher party organizations, the party branch secretary exercises overall leadership. In addition, a party branch secretary also serves as a "friend, counselor, and guardian of all the people under his [or her] jurisdiction."[51] Popular literature and drama often depict the party branch secretary as one who is always fearless, fair, firm, and devoted to the welfare of his or her people in the unit.

Party branches operate somewhat differently in rural and urban areas. The party committee in a commune is the leading organizational unit, providing leadership, supervision, and management of all political and economic activities in the countryside. This function and power was shared with the revolutionary committee representing the masses before they were abolished in the 1980s. But as party discipline slackened, and as opportunities arose for persons with special privileges to use their office for personal gain, it was not uncommon to find the corrupt practices of party secretaries exposed. There were also a number of cases of commandism and incompetence found within the ranks of party secretaries.[52] The party committee at the basic level directs party organizational work and is responsible for general policy. It also controls the assignment of personnel at the local level.

A few words must be said about the Cultural Revolution's impact on the party. The upheaval was more than a power struggle and a purge of such top leaders as Liu Shaoqi, Deng Xiaoping, and Peng Zhen—a key Politburo member and former mayor of Beijing. Certainly, a primary objective of the upheaval was to shake up the party machine because of its increasing bureaucracy and routinization. There were also extensive purges of party personnel at the middle and lower levels for their lack of understanding of the mass line in their work with the people. One result of the Cultural Revolution was structural reform, the formation of revolutionary committees at the party's central, provincial, and primary levels as a temporary substitute for the party machine. What was novel about the experiment was the introduction of the masses from outside the party into these revolutionary committees. For the duration of the Cultural Revolution and thereafter, they performed the functions of the party and government.[53] Party and government administrative structures were also reduced under the slogan of "simplified administration."

How fundamental and lasting have these structural changes been? Events in China since Mao's death, and the subsequent purge of the radical Gang of Four in 1976, gave indication of a restoration of the basic structures which existed prior to the Cultural Revolution. The Twelfth Party Congress (1982) reemphasized many of the familiar practices and structures of the party that had operated quite effectively prior to the Cultural Revolution. An example of this is the institution of the Central Commission for Discipline Inspection at all levels of the party in order to maintain and strengthen inner party discipline.[54]

After a considerable period of confused jurisdiction, the revolutionary committees were legalized in the 1978 state constitution to become executive organs of local government. As will be pointed out in Chapter 4, the revolutionary committee system, a legacy of the Cultural Revolution, was abolished as the 1982 state constitution was being drafted. At the grassroots level, party branches and cells now function as the party's primary organizations.

We can summarize by saying that the party was highly institutionalized from the 1950s to the early 1960s. This was interrupted during the turbulent years 1966 to 1976 by the Cultural Revolution. The process of reinstitutionalization now appears to be accelerating under the leadership of Hu Yaobang and Deng Xiaoping. This process can be expected to lead to a period of stability and moderation, for China is again under the leadership and control of professionally oriented, veteran party administrators.

RECRUITMENT OF PARTY MEMBERS

When the Eleventh Party Congress convened in August 1977, almost a year after the downfall of the Gang of Four, it was announced that the party had a membership of more than 35 million. In his speech Ye Jianying pointed out that 7 million of the 35 million party members had been recruited since the last party congress in 1973 and about one-half of the total party membership had been recruited since the Cultural Revolution.[55] He admitted that there was a serious problem in party organization and discipline, which resulted from the rapid recruitment of so many party members by the Gang of Four. The old soldier, now a vice-chairperson of the party, bluntly indicated that the radicals had recruited a large number of new party members in accordance with their own standards. What Ye was demanding was tighter requirements for party membership. What he failed to mention was that the Chinese Communist Party (see Table 3.2) membership had been steadily increasing since

TABLE 3.2   **CCP Membership Growth Pattern**

Party Congress	Year	Number of Members
1st Congress	1921	57
2nd Congress	1922	123
3rd Congress	1923	432
4th Congress	1925	950
5th Congress	1927	57,967
6th Congress	1928	40,000
7th Congress	1945	1,211,128
8th Congress	1956	10,734,384
	1961	17,000,000
9th Congress	1969	20,000,000
10th Congress	1973	28,000,000
11th Congress	1977	35,000,000
12th Congress	1982	39,650,000

Sources: Figures from 1921 to 1961 are based on John W. Lewis, Leadership in Communist China *(Ithaca, N.Y.: Cornell University Press, 1963), pp. 108–20.*

The 1969 party membership figure is an estimate calculated on the basis of about 40 percent increase in 1973 over 1969 given by Jurgen Domes, "A Rift in the New Course," Far Eastern Economic Review *(October 1, 1973), 3.*

The 1973 total and membership figure is taken from Zhou Enlai's "Report to the Tenth National Congress of the CCP," Beijing Review, *35–36 (September 7, 1973), 18.*

The 1977 party membership figure is based on Ye Jianying, "Report on the Revision of the Party Constitution to the Eleventh Party Congress, August 13–18, 1977," Beijing Review, *36 (September 2, 1977), 36. The 1982 figure was based on* Beijing Review, *36 (September 6, 1982), 6. Also see New China News Agency release of August 18, 1982, as printed in* Ming Pao *(Hong Kong), August 21, 1982, p. 1, and* The New York Times, *September 6, 1982, A-2.*

the party came to power in 1949, and that the party had not always insisted on ideological purity and correctness as the most important criterion for membership. Let us now discuss the factors which contributed to the expansion of party membership.

Factors in Party Membership Expansion

Several general remarks may be made with respect to the growth of the CCP membership. First, for the period from 1920 to 1927, from the party's First Congress to its Fifth Congress, members of the party were primarily urban intellectuals, intermixed with some members of the proletariat from coastal cities and from mines in the inland provinces. When the Sixth Party Congress convened in 1928, most of its members had been driven underground by the Nationalists. There was a significant reduction in membership, by as much as 17,900, between the Fifth Party Congress in 1927 and the Sixth Party Congress in 1928. This reduction can be attributed to the slaughter by the Nationalists in the 1927 coup and to the subsequent defections.

Second, from the Sixth Congress in 1928 to the Seventh Congress in 1945, the primary membership recruitment shifted from intellectuals to peasants, who became the mainstay of the guerrilla armies. In fact, beginning in 1939, the CCP, under the firm leadership of Mao, undertook to militarize the party membership. The 1.2 million members reached by the Seventh Congress in 1945, at the termination of the war with Japan, largely operated under the appropriate description "military communism." Party members essentially were recruited from the famed Eighth Route and from the New Fourth Armies. The late John Lindbeck noted the profound impact of the recruitment pattern on the character building of the party membership:

> The result of the militarization policy was that dedication, fighting spirit, and responsiveness to discipline and orders became the hallmark of Communist Party members, as well as the harsher virtues of a soldier—ruthlessness, toughness, and a will to override and subdue other people. They held the guns out of which Mao's political power and everything else grew. By the time the party had conquered China, the bulk of its membership was made up of triumphant warriors.[56]

Lindbeck also pointed out that the militarization of the party membership created many problems which have continued to beset Chinese party politics. These problems—concerning the army as a special political power and as an independent interest group—will be discussed in later chapters. What we need to point out here is that the army has always been the model emulated by the CCP in organizational disciplinary matters.

Third, the period from 1945 to 1956, or from the Seventh to the Eighth Party Congress, represented the most rapid growth period in the party's history: from a little over 1.2 million members to just under 11 million members, or approximately an 886 percent increase. The years 1955–56 saw another sudden rise in membership recruitment, followed by the temporary lull and then a gigantic rise in 1956–57, when party organizational work was intensified in all rural areas of China. This was the period preceding the Great Leap Forward, launched in 1958. Although party recruitment took some great strides quantitively—by 1961, some 90 percent of the 17 million party members had been recruited after 1949,—the ideological purity of the new party recruits was questionable.

Fourth, during the period from the Eighth Party Congress in 1956 to 1961, recruitment of party members became institutionalized to ensure that party members possessed both ideological redness and technical expertise. Membership expansion during 1954 and in 1956–57 was designed to recruit personnel needed to direct and manage the nation's extensive political and economic activities. The rapid recruitment of those who possessed the needed technical skill resulted in a shift in the recruitment pattern of new party members in terms of social background. This trend is clearly discernible in the limited data available, presented in Table 3.3. From 1956 to 1957, only the "intellectuals" gained in relative representation in party membership, rising from 11.7 percent to 14.8 percent and accounting for over 31 percent of all new recruits. All other groups declined in relative representation. While peasants still made up a clear majority of new party members, their representation was well below their proportion of the total population. Conversely, the intellectuals were vastly overrepresented.

Following this changed pattern of recruitment, the party cadre system was institutionalized to make it more attractive to intellectuals who were being coopted into the party. By 1955 a rank system for cadres' work assignments had been instituted, based on the acquisition of technical skills. In addition, a salary scale system was promulgated, along with the rank system for cadres. Recruitment and promotion rules were also instituted in the late 1950s. Recent studies point out the bureaucratization of the party. One study concludes that by 1965 China was no longer a revolutionary society because, by initial contact with the political system and a careful selection of education and occupation,

TABLE 3.3   Background of Party Members, 1956 and 1957

	Numbers			Percent of Total		
	1956	1957	Increase 1956–57	1956	1957	Increase 1956–57
		(Thousands)			(Percent)	
Workers	1,503	1,740	237	14.0	13.7	11.9
Peasants	7,417	8,500	1,083	69.1	66.8	54.5
Intellectuals	1,256	1,880	624	11.7	14.8	31.4
Others	558	600	42	5.2	4.7	2.1
Total	10,734	12,720	1,986	100.0	100.0	100.0

Source: Modified version of Franz Schurmann, Ideology and Organization in Communist China *(Berkeley, Calif.: University of California Press, 1966), p. 132. By permission of publisher.*

a careerist could very well predict the outcome of his or her life.[57] Another study points out that one inevitable result of the institutionalization of the party in the late 1950s and the 1960s was bureaucratization, which stressed order, discipline, and routine as organizational virtues.[58] While no detailed official statistics on party membership have been released since 1961, when membership stood at 17 million, the general level of party membership has been indicated, as shown in Table 3.2. During the Cultural Revolution, aggregate membership remained at around 17 million, virtually unchanged from 1961. Membership for 1969 was approximately 20 million, a net increase of only 3 million from 1961. However, after 1969 party membership resumed its rapid rise, with the addition of 8 million members from 1969 to 1973, when the total stood at 28 million, and the addition of 7 million from 1973 to 1977, when the total stood at 35 million. This means, as Marshal Ye has indicated, that over half the 35 million party members in 1977 were recruited after the Cultural Revolution.[59] For the four-year period from 1978 to 1982, another 4 million new members were added, for a grand total of 39 million. The rate of increase from 1978 to 1982 was not as large as that between 1973 and 1977, when 7 million new members were admitted, or between 1969 and 1973, when 8 million new members were added.

Without detailed data, we cannot be sure of the background of the new members recruited since the Cultural Revolution. However, fragmentary official figures showing the characteristics and social composition of new party members have been reported.[60] The party membership for the Beijing municipality may be used here as an illustration. From the Cultural Revolution to 1973, some 60,000 new members were added to the party membership roster for Beijing. Of these, about 75 percent were "workers, former poor and lower-middle peasants or children of such families," and just under 5 percent were "revolutionary intellectuals working in the fields of culture, health, science and education." The overwhelming majority of these new Beijing municipality party members were under thirty-five years of age, and women constituted 25 percent of the total.

Another important element in the recruitment pattern following the Cultural Revolution was the effort made to recruit members of the minority groups in the autonomous regions. Apparently, 143,000 new members from minority nationalities were admitted to party membership from 1969 to 1973. Although we do not have comprehensive official statistics for the entire CCP membership from 1961 to 1976, we may surmise, based on fragmentary data, that the new membership recruitment pattern placed greater emphasis on (1) industrial workers of urban areas (2) women, (3) minority nationalities, and (4) youths. Since 1978 there has been a sharp increase in recruitment of party members from among intellectuals, particularly scientists and persons with technical knowledge, who in the past had been discriminated against either for being politically unreliable or for having complex social backgrounds. If the above conclusion is correct, and I believe it is not too far off target, then the CCP has greatly broadened its base, regardless of the shifting recruitment requirements.

Membership Requirements:
Changing Emphasis

There is a marked difference between the party constitutions of the Eighth Congress (1956) and, those of the subsequent congresses (1969, 1973, 1977, and 1982) with regard to eligibility for party membership. The 1956 constitution stipulated no class basis or origin for party membership: It was open to "all Chinese citizens" who qualified. The party constitutions approved in 1969 by the Ninth Party Congress, at the end of the Cultural Revolution, and the ones adopted by the Tenth and Eleventh Party Congresses in 1973 and 1977, required that only those who are "workers, poor peasants, or lower-middle peasants" were eligible to become members of the CCP. In addition, PLA soldiers and "other revolutionary elements" might also be eligible for membership. The 1982 party constitution is less restrictive, providing that any worker, peasant, member of the armed forces, and—more significantly— intellectual may be eligible for party membership (see Article 1 in Appendix B). All recent party constitutions—1973, 1977, and 1982—prescribed four steps through which an applicant for party membership must be scrutinized: (1) recommendation by two party members, after filing the application individually; (2) examination of the application by a party branch which solicits opinions about the applicant from both inside and outside the party; (3) acceptance of the application by the party branch at its general membership meeting; and (4) approval of the party branch's acceptance of membership by the next higher party committee. It has been a frequent practice, dating back to the late 1940s, for an applicant to be admitted to party membership solely upon the recommendation of top party leaders.[61]

All party members were obligated by both the 1969 and 1973 party constitutions to live up to the five requirements that Chairman Mao advanced for worthy revolutionary successors: to conscientiously study the works of Marx, Lenin, and Mao; to always serve the collective interests of the people and never work for private gain; to strive for united front work; to consult the masses; and to be willing to engage in criticism and self-criticism. The 1977 party constitution added three more requirements: never to engage in factional activities to split the party, to observe party discipline, and always to perform well tasks assigned by the party and to set examples as a vanguard. The added demands were designed to strengthen the standards for recruitment of party members and to tighten admission policy, in order to avoid the "crash admittance" program allegedly practiced by the purged radical leaders. In his report on the need to tighten requirements for party members, Marshal Ye said in 1977: "In recent years the "gang of four" set their own standards for party membership and practical "crash admittance" and as a result some political speculators and bad types have sneaked into the party."[62] The fact that the provisions for "purification of the ranks" and strict party discipline, as well as for tightening admission standards, were written into the 1977 and 1982 party constitutions illustrated the importance of the recruitment process to the party leaders and their awareness that the pattern of recruitment has great influence on the character of the party.

The 1982 constitutional requirements for party membership are almost identical to the provisions of the 1977 party constitution. However, the 1982 version stresses in Article 3 the responsibilities of party members to work "selflessly" and "absolutely never to use public office for personal gains or benefits." This provision certainly expresses the party's concern for the outbreak of widespread corruption among party members in recent years.

Party recruitment in the 1980s was still beset with problems, despite the crackdown on "crash admittance," widely practiced during the Cultural Revolution and immediately afterwards. Two of these problems were how to weed out unfit or unqualified party members, and how to upgrade party members' professionalism and competence as China moved toward modernization. In a speech to a conference of party cadres in January 1980, Deng Xiaoping stressed the fact that too many party members were simply unqualified.[63] He deplored their preoccupation with acquiring special privileges, instead of serving the people.

Although no attempts have been made to implicate all those party members admitted during the Cultural Revolution, about 15.6 million (40 percent of the total membership of 39 million) have evidently been selected as targets for rectification.[64] Hu Yaobang told the 1982 party congress that beginning in mid-1983, for a period of three years until 1986, concerted efforts would be made to weed out undesirable and unqualified party members. The method to be used for the housecleaning would be reregistration of all party members. The requirements for membership stated in the new party constitution would be applied against party members who had been "rabble-rousers" during the Cultural Revolution or who had practiced factionalism or instigated armed violence. Hu Yaobang indicated that "those who failed to meet the requirements for membership after education shall be expelled from the party or asked to withdraw from it."[65] Also targeted for expulsion from party membership were those who had committed economic crimes, such as bribery, embezzlement, or smuggling. The number targeted for expulsion by 1986 has been estimated at as high as 2 million.[66]

Upgrading the competence and professionalism of party members is a much harder task to accomplish. Since a majority of government leaders are party members, the problem centers on the educational level of the party cadres. The 1982 party constitution contains a special chapter on party cadres. Article 34 states that party cadres (leaders) must possess both political integrity and professional competence. But the fact remains that perhaps as many as 50 percent of the 18 million state cadres have a minimal education, equivalent to an American junior high school level.[67] It is probably lower among cadres at the party's basic organizational level in the countryside. Even at the party's central and provincial organizational levels, there is a dire need for trained and skilled administrators and managers. Some efforts have been made to upgrade party cadres' professional competence. Cadres younger than forty with only a junior middle school education (the equivalent of an American eighth-grade education) have been sent to specialized party schools for three years on a rotation basis.[68] The ultimate goal in upgrading party cadres is to provide leaders at every level of the party who are "revolutionized, youthful, intellectualized, and expert."[69] The task is enormous, considering the sheer number of party cadres who are undereducated and in need of professional training.

NOTES

1. *Renmin Ribao,* March 1, 1977; and *Ming Pao* (Hong Kong), March 3, 1977, p. 3.

2. *Survey of Chinese Mainland Press,* 4097 (January 11, 1968), 1–4.

3. "Resolution On the Convening of the Twelfth Party Congress," *Beijing Review,* 10 (March 10, 1980), 11.

4. Ibid.

5. Roderick MacFarquhar, *The Origins of the Cultural Revolution, Vol. 1: Contradictions Among the People, 1957–1967* (New York: Columbia University Press, 1974), p. 144.

6. Lo Bing, "Inside View of the Elections at the Twelfth Party Congress," *Zhengming* (Hong Kong), 60 (October 1982), 7.

7. Lo Bing, "Inside View of the Elections at the Twelfth Party Congress," p. 8. Also see Lowell Dittmer, "The Twelfth Congress of the Communist Party of China," *The China Quarterly,* 93 (March 1983), 114.

8. Lin Piao, "Report to the Ninth National Congress of the CCP," *Peking Review,* 18 (April 30, 1969), 16–35.

9. Wang Hung-wen, "Report on the Revision of the Party Constitution," *Peking Review,* 35–36 (September 7, 1973), 29–33.

10. "Communiqué of the Fifth Plenary Session of the Eleventh Central Committee of the CCP," p. 8. Also see Dittmer, "The Twelfth Congress of the Communist Party of China," pp. 112–13.

11. William Brugger, "The Ninth National Congress of the CCP," *The World Today,* vol. 25, no. 7 (July 1969), 297–305; Roderick MacFarquhar, "China After the 10th Congress," *The World Today,* vol. 29, no. 12 (December 1973), 514–26; Richard Wich, "The Tenth Party Congress: The Power Structure and the Succession Question," *The China Quarterly,* 58 (April–May 1974), 231–48.

12. "Creating a New Situation in All Fields of Socialist Modernization", 11–40.

13. Houn, *A Short History of Chinese Communism,* p. 87.

14. For text of Chou En-lai's political report to the Tenth Party Congress, see *Peking Review,* 35–36 (September 3, 1973), 17–21.

15. Roderick MacFarquhar, *The Origins of the Cultural Revolution,* p. 101.

16. "Resolution on the Convening of the Twelfth Party Congress," p. 11.

17. Parris Chang, *Power and Policy in China* (University Park, Penna. and London: The Pennsylvania State University Press, 1974), p. 184.

18. See Jill Lai, "The Power Structure After China's Tenth Party Congress," *Far Eastern Economic Review* (October 1, 1973), 5. Her calculation for the Tenth Central Committee member's average age was 65, and since close to half of the Eleventh Central Committee members are carried over from the Tenth, the average for the Eleventh is probably from 65 to 68. Also see Jurgen Domes, "China in 1977: Reversal of Verdict," *Asian Survey,* vol. xviii, no. 1 (January 1978), 7.

19. "Twelfth Party Congress Closes," *Beijing Review,* 38 (September 20, 1982), 4. Also see *Ta Kung Pao Weekly Supplement* (Hong Kong), September 16, 1982, p. 2.

20. "Twelfth Party Congress Closes," p. 4. Also see Hong-Yung Lee, "China's 12th Central Committee: Rehabilitated Cadres and Technocrats," *Asian Survey,* xxiii, 6 (June 1983), 673–91.

21. "Constitution of the Communist Party of China, Adopted by the Eleventh National Congress on August 18, 1977," in *Peking Review,* 36 (September 2, 1977), 21–22.

22. Houn, *A Short History of Chinese Communism.* p. 89.

23. "Board of Directors, China, Inc.," *Far Eastern Economic Review* (September 2, 1977), 9.

24. Robert J. Osborn, *The Evolution of Soviet Politics* (New York: The Dorsey Press, 1974), pp. 213–14.

25. Houn, *A Short History of Chinese Communism,* p. 93.

26. Chang, *Power and Policy in China,* p. 184.

27. Houn, *A Short History of Chinese Communism,* p. 91–92.

28. Ibid., p. 89.

29. "Talk at the Report Meeting, 24 October 1966," in *Chairman Mao Talks to the People,* pp. 266–67.

30. "The Central Committee's Secretariat and Its Work," *Beijing Review,* 19 (May 11, 1981), 21.

31. Gittings' notes on the formation of this organ in 1931 by the First All-China Soviet Congress; see John Gittings, *The Role of the Chinese Red Army* (London: Oxford University Press, 1967), pp. 263–65.

32. Ralph Powell, "Politico-Military Relationships in Communist China," External Research Staff, Bureau of Intelligence and Research, Department of State, October 1963.

33. Yeh Chien-ying, "Report on the Revision of the Party Constitution," *Peking Review,* 36 (September 2, 1977), 32.

34. Yeh Chien-ying, "Report on the Revision of the Party Constitution"; and "Communiqué of the Third Plenary Session of the Eleventh Central Committee," *Peking Review,* 52 (December 29, 1978), 6, 16.

35. John W. Lewis, *Leadership in Communist China,* p. 134.

36. *Ming Pao* (Hong Kong), September 2, 1979, p. 3.

37. Ibid.

38. See *Renmin Ribao* editorial, "Earnestly Strengthening Party's Discipline Investigation Work," March 25, 1978, p. 1.

39. Ibid.

40. *Renmin Ribao,* December 5, 1980, p. 1; and *Min Pao Daily* (Hong Kong), December 17, 1980, p. 1.

41. "Chinese Communist Party Expels Kang Sheng and Xie Fuzhi," *Beijing Review,* 45 (November 10, 1980), 3.

42. English translation of the text can be found in "Guiding Principles for Inner Party Political Life," *Beijing Review,* 15 (April 14, 1980), 11–19. For the original text see *Hongqi,* 6 (March 16, 1980), 2–11.

43. Jurgen Domes, "Party Politics and the Cultural Revolution," p. 65.

44. Chang, *Power and Politics in China,* pp. 48–49.

45. Li Shih-fei, "The Party's Middlemen: The Role of Regional Bureaus in the Chinese Communist Party," *Current Scene: Development in Mainland China,* vol. iii, no. 25 (August 15, 1965), 6.

46. See Thomas Jay Mathews, "The Cultural Revolution in Szechwan," in *The Cultural Revolution in the Provinces,* East Asian Monographs No. 42 (Cambridge: Harvard University Press, 1971), pp. 106–10.

47. Ibid.

48. Schurmann, *Ideology and Organizations,* p. 210.

49. Chang, "Provincial Party Leaders Strategies for Survival During the Cultural Revolution," in *Elites in the People's Republic of China,* ed. Robert A. Scalapino (Seattle, Wash. and London: University of Washington Press, 1972), pp. 501–39.

50. "Decision of the Central Committee of the CCP on Party Consolidation's," *Beijing Review,* 42 (October 17, 1983), vi.

51. Houn, *A Short History of Chinese Communism,* p. 106.

52. *People's Daily,* June 27, 1982, p. 1.

53. See Gordon Bennett, "China's Continuing Revolution: Will It Be Permanent?" *Asian Survey,* vol. x, no. 1 (January 1970), 2–17; Parris H. Chang, "The Revolutionary Committee in China—Two Case Studies: Heilungkiang and Honan," *Current Scene,* vol. vi, no. 9 (June 1, 1968), 1–37; Jurgen Domes, "The Role of the Military in the Formation of Revolutionary Committees, 1967-68," *The China Quarterly,* 44 (October–December 1970), 112–45; Garbel Feurtado, "The Formation of Provincial Revolutionary Committees, 1966–68; Heilungkiang and Hopei," *Asian Survey,* vol. xii, no. 12 (December 1972), 1014–31.

54. Yeh Chien-ying, "Report on the Revision of the Party Constitution," p. 32.

55. Ibid., p. 36.

56. John Lindbeck, "Transformation in the Chinese Communist Party," p. 76.

57. Ezra Vogel, "From Revolutionary to Semi-Bureaucrat: The 'Regularization' of

Cadres," *The China Quarterly,* 29 (January–March 1967), 36–40; Michel Oksenberg, "Institutionalization of the Chinese Communist Revolution: The Ladder of Success on the Eve of the Cultural Revolution," *The China Quarterly,* 36 (October–December 1968), 61–92.

58. Charles Neuhauser, "The Chinese Communist Party in the 1960s: Prelude to the Cultural Revolution," *The China Quarterly,* 32 (October–December 1967), 3–36.

59. See Yeh Chien-ying, "Report on the Revision of the Party Constitution," p. 36.

60. New Party Members—A Dynamic Force," *Peking Review,* 27 (July 6, 1973), 6–7; "Millions of New Cadres Maturing," *Peking Review,* 52 (December 1973), 3; "Commemorating the 10th Anniversary of the CPC Central Committee's May 16 'Circular,'" *Peking Review,* 21 (May 21, 1976), 3.

61. Red Guard interrogation of Wang Guangmei, wife of Liu Shaoqi, revealed the practice of admission to party membership by recommendation by top party leaders. See Chao Tsung, *An Account of the Great Proletarian Cultural Revolution,* vol. ii (Hong Kong: Union Research Institute, 1974), pp. 836–39.

62. Yeh Chien-yien, "Report on the Revision of the Party Constitution," p. 36.

63. "Important Talk by Deng Xiaoping," *Ming Pao* (Hong Kong), March 5, 1980, p. 1.

64. Song Renqiong, "Use the New Party Constitution to Educate New Members," *Hongqi* (*Red Flag*), 24 (December 16, 1982), 15.

65. "Create a New Situation in All Fields of Socialist Modernization," p. 38.

66. *Ming Pao* (Hong Kong), October 7, 1982, p. 1. Also see Dittmer, "The Twelfth Congress of the CCP," p. 120.

67. *People's Daily,* September 25, 1981, p. 1.

68. *Ming Pao* (Hong Kong), October 16, 19, and 20, 1982. Also see Song Renqiong, "Building the Revolutionized, Youthful, Intellectualized and Specialized Cadres Forces," *Hongqi* (*Red Flag*), 19 (October 1, 1982), 14.

69. Song Renqiong, "Building the Revolutionized, Youthful, Intellectualized and Specialized Cadres Forces," p. 14.

The Government and the Party: Interlocking Structure and Decision Making

4

In this chapter we shall examine the structure of the Chinese central government by focusing on the central government complex. Subjects to be discussed include constitutions, the National People's Congress (NPC), the State Council and its multifarious agencies, the legal system, and the cadre system. Before we take up these topics, two general comments must be made about the Chinese national government. First, as discussed in the previous chapter, the Chinese Communist Party controls and directs the complex system of government machinery. It is through the agencies of the government that the policies and programs approved by the party are implemented. The CCP closely monitors how the government executes its directives. Second, the People's Republic of China is a unitary state. In a federated system, such as that of the United States or the Soviet Union, certain governmental powers and responsibilities are reserved for local governments. Under a unitary system, all powers theoretically are vested in the central government and must be specifically delegated to local governments by the central authority. This centralization of power in the national government has led to perennial debate in China over the degree and nature of power to be allocated to local governments. The governments in the provinces and local units generate constant pressure for decentralization by seeking to increase their discretional power over such local affairs as finances and allocation of resources. The subject of provincial and local politics and government will be discussed in detail in Chapter 5.

POLITICAL CONSULTATION
AND CONSTITUTION MAKING

The CCP first participated in constitution making with the Guomindang in January 1946 under the cease-fire agreements mediated by General Marshall. The various political parties participated in the Political Consultative Conference, which resolved to draft a revised version of the 1935 Guomindang constitution and to establish a constitutional government with an elected national assembly. These plans were shattered by the eruption of full-scale civil war.

In 1948, with victory in sight, the CCP Politburo passed a resolution calling for a united front of all parties and groups, and for a new political consultative conference to form a coalition government and to establish a people's congress.[1] The new Chinese People's Political Consultative Conference (CPPCC) convened in Beijing in September 1949, with Mao presiding over the 662 delegates from more than 20 political parties and mass groups. This national conference established the People's Republic of China and promulgated the Common Program and the Organic Law. On October 1, 1949, Mao proclaimed the new government by raising the now familiar red flag with one large gold star beside four small ones, symbolic of the dominant CCP and the four classes of people—peasants, petty bourgeoisie, owners of enterprises, and workers. The Common Program and the Organic Law became a provisional constitution for the People's Republic until the new regime could consolidate its power. The Common Program was a set of guiding principles for the affairs of state, couched in moderate language acceptable to all the cooperating parties. The Organic Law prescribed the power and structure of the national government.

From 1949 until 1954, the People's Republic operated under two specific organs established to exercise the power of the central government. One was the fifty-six-member Central Government Council, the executive organ of the CPPCC, chaired by Mao. The Central Government Council assumed a supervisory function with power to enact laws and to make appointments. The second was the Government Administrative Council, headed by Premier Zhou Enlai. The Government Administrative Council was charged with the daily administration of the central government and operated through a multitude of functionally specific ministries. A majority of these ministries were concerned with economic and financial affairs.

With the formation of these two governmental organs as the interim de facto central government, the People's Political Consultative Conference faded rapidly into the background as an instrument for political consultation. Nevertheless, the CPPCC still exists, primarily to carry on united front work in support of CCP policies, often serving as a liaison between the CCP and minor political parties. The CPPCC was given the responsibility of rehabilitating the 293 war criminals, mostly civil war Guomindang army officers, who were released from prison under the 1975 special amnesty.[2] In early 1978 the mass media gave prominent coverage to CPPCC participation in preliminary discussions with delegates to the Fifth National People's Congress, in regard to the revised constitution.[3] This renewed political consultative role for the CPPCC is ironic in view of charges that the Gang of Four deliberately sabotaged the normal functions of political consultation.[4]

The Common Program provided for nationwide general elections to elect representatives to a national congress, which was to draft and enact a constitution. For a variety of reasons, this process did not begin until 1953. First, time was needed for the regime to consolidate its control over the vast territory and population. We must remember that the land reform program was not completed until 1953, about the time the Korean War reached a stalemate. Second, time was needed to reorganize local governmental units. During the initial years of the republic, from 1949 to 1951, provincial and local government functions were generally carried out by the army through the Military Control Commission, a type of military rule. Gradually, military rule was replaced in rural areas by people's congresses with limited authority for conducting local governmental affairs under close supervision of the local CCP. Third, the regime had to prepare and lay the groundwork for an elaborate election law that would demonstrate to the world that China's first national election was a legitimate exercise of the people's will.

The Election Law, enacted in March 1953 by the Central People's Government Council on behalf of the CPPCC, called for universal suffrage for persons eighteen years old or older, except for those classified as counterrevolutionaries or those otherwise deprived by law of their right to vote. Voters participated directly only at the lowest basic level, in the selection of representatives to people's congresses for the village or local unit. The representatives to the local people's congress then elected representatives to the provincial people's congress, who then elected representatives to the 1,226-member First National People's Congress. This indirect election system, which has continued to be used for electing National People's Congresses, will be discussed further in Chapter 7.

The 1954 Constitution[5]

A great deal of effort went into the 1954 constitution presented to the First National People's Congress for enactment. The initial draft was prepared by a committee of the party's Central Committee, with considerable input from Mao. Reportedly, the constitution's draft was submitted to some 8,000 individuals for comment, and was circulated to over 150 million people for discussion before it was completed.[6] This process took over twenty-one months. The constitution was lengthy, with 106 articles detailing the general principles of government, the structure of the national and local governments, and the fundamental rights and duties of citizens.

The constitution created a "People's Democratic Dictatorship," which was to practice democratic centralism. The National People's Congress (NPC) was designated the highest organ of state power and the only legislative power for the state. The NPC was to elect a chairperson and vice-chairperson for the People's Republic of China. Since the NPC was to meet only once a year, its standing committee was designated the "permanent body" of the NPC. The executive functions of the government were to be carried out by the State Council, the Central People's Government, headed by a premier and vice-premiers appointed by the NPC. Provisions were also made for local people's congresses and councils, as well as for organs of self-government for the autonomous areas. The local governments will be discussed in Chapter 5. The judicial functions were to be exercised by a Supreme People's Court, local people's courts, and special people's courts.

The 1954 constitution was modeled on the Soviet constitution of 1936 and, therefore, was representative of "socialist legality," a phrase denoting the legal responsibility of the dictatorial state to its citizens. The constitution stated:

> . . . the fundamental tasks of the state are, step by step, to bring about the socialist industrialization of the country and, step by step, to accomplish the socialist transformation of agriculture, handicrafts, industry, and commerce.

The planned economy, with its gradual transition to socialism, would allow for the "gradual abolition of systems of exploitation." While the constitution sought to protect the ownership of ordinary peasants' land and artisans' means of production as well as other property, such as savings and houses, it called for the restriction and gradual elimination of rich peasants and industrialists.

Work was exhorted as a "matter of honor" and was to be carried out with enthusiasm and creativity.

The constitution provided a list of fundamental rights and freedoms for citizens: the right to vote and to have due process of law; and the freedoms of speech and press, assembly, association, procession, demonstration, religion, privacy, residence and change of residence, scientific research, and artistic creativity. Economic rights included the right to work and to rest from work; the right to education; the right to receive assistance in old age, illness, and disability; and finally, the right to bring complaints against any person working in organs of the state. The first duties listed were to uphold the constitution and the law, to maintain discipline at work, to keep public order, and to respect social ethics. Others included respecting public property, paying taxes, and defending the homeland.

The basic principles of the 1954 constitution were incorporated in the revised constitutions of 1975, 1978, and 1982. Changes made in these revisions reflected a growing political climate of maturity and consolidation.

The 1975 Constitution[7]

The 1975 constitution was submitted to the NPC for the party's Central Committee by Zhang Chunqiao, the radical leader from Shanghai who was later arrested as one of the Gang of Four. Apparently, constitutional revision had been prepared as early as 1970, with Lin Biao as a key drafter, but the revisions were not acceptable to Chairman Mao. The NPC, which had not met since 1965, was postponed until after the Lin Biao affair. It finally convened in secret in January 1975 under the supervision of Zhou Enlai. Zhang explained that a new constitution was needed to reflect the transition to socialism, the gains of the Cultural Revolution, and the defeat of Liu Shaoqi and Lin Biao.[8]

According to Zhang, with the consolidation of power completed after the demise of Lin Biao, the constitution, which was streamlined and shortened to only thirty articles, no longer needed to be so specific nor to play down the role of the CCP. Article 2 of the 1975 constitution stated:

> The Communist Party of China is the core of leadership of the whole Chinese People. The working class exercises leadership over the state through its vanguard, the Communist Party of China.
>
> Marxism-Leninism-Mao Zedong Thought is the theoretical basis guiding the thinking of our nation.

The role of the CCP was made more specific in Article 16: "The National People's Congress is the highest organ of state power under the leadership of the Communist Party of China." The list of functions and powers of the NPC were condensed and abridged. In addition, the position of chairperson of the republic was abolished, thus eliminating the most powerful position in the government, which might be used as a base for power contention with the party chairperson. Mao had chaired the republic as well as the party and had used the position to his advantage. For instance, he convened at least fifteen supreme state conferences as chairman of the republic, bypassing the established party channels of consultation to obtain support for his views on crucial policy matters. Soon after the Great Leap, Mao relinquished, as planned, the leading position in the republic at the 1959 NPC session in favor of Liu Shaoqi. Liu, who was the vice-chairman of the party, used the position to acquire considerable power in the central government and the party. Liu's successful use of this position contributed to Mao's antagonism toward him and his corps of senior cadres. As discussed in Chapter 1, the question of who should head the republic may have been one of the contentious issues between Mao and Lin Biao. Certainly, Mao—who remained party chairman until his death—had no desire to return to the pre-Cultural Revolution conditions of "two chairmen" competing for power. The crucial role of the army was also recognized by designating the chairperson of the CCP, rather than the chairperson of the republic, as commander of the armed forces as required in the 1954 version. In his report Zhang Chunqiao explained that these changes were to help strengthen the party's centralized leadership over the structure of the state.[9] At the local level, the constitution recognized the revolutionary committees as the "permanent organs of the local people's congresses and at the same time the local people's governments at various levels."

With the socialist transition complete, as explained by Zhang, the constitution of 1975 called for carrying on the three great revolutionary movements of class struggle, the struggle for production, and scientific experiment, using self-reliance as the main mode of operation. The document affirmed the right of ownership by the whole people and socialist collective ownership by working people. While restricted nonagricultural individual labor was allowed, the individual laborers were to be "guided on the road of socialist collectivization, step by step." The people's communes were recognized as the legitimate form of land ownership, but members were given permission to farm small plots, engage in limited household sideline production, and keep a small amount of livestock. Article 9 described the work-play relationship: " 'He who does not work, neither shall he eat' and 'from each according to his ability, to each according to his work.' "

Accomplishments of the Cultural Revolution were incorporated into the 1975 constitution: The goals were to "put proletarian politics in command, combat bureaucracy, maintain close ties with the people." Culture, education, literature, art, physical education, health work, and scientific endeavors must all serve proletarian politics. Encouragement and specific rights, such as the right to debate and to put up large-character posters in order to carry on the revolution were given.

In 1975 the rights of citizens were condensed from the 1954 constitution, with a few deletions. The rights to residence and change of residence were eliminated, in view of the programs to send people to the countryside for manual labor. Also, the rights of scientific research and artistic creativity were eliminated, since these were to serve proletarian politics. The duties to maintain discipline at work, to maintain public order, and to respect social ethics were eliminated in the 1975 constitution. The right to strike was added.

The 1978 Constitution[10]

The draft of the 1978 constitution was prepared by a committee composed of all twenty-six members of the party's Politburo, with repeated consultation with "the broad masses both inside and outside of the party." After adoption by the party's Central Committee, Marshal Ye Jianying, a vice-chairperson of the party and a powerful supporter of Hua, introduced the sixty articles of the revised constitution to the Fifth NPC in February 1978. Among the reasons given by Ye for a new constitution were the need to eliminate any vestige of influence of the Gang of Four, to facilitate implementation of the decision of the Eleventh Party Congress to accelerate development of China's economy by moderating and liberalizing cultural and educational policies, and to return to an orderly state of affairs after more than a decade of turmoil.[11]

The constitution states the general task for the new period of development:

> To persevere in continuing the revolution under the dictatorship of the proletariat; to carry forward the three great revolutionary movements of class struggle—the struggle for production and scientific experiment, and to make China a great powerful socialist country with modern agriculture, industry, national defense, and science and technology, by the end of the century.

While the CCP was still included as the "core leadership of the whole Chinese people," there was no mention of the NPC being under the leadership of the CCP. In addition, the functions and powers of the NPC were again listed separately. For the first time, NPC delegates were to be elected "by secret ballot after democratic consultation." The idea of moderation in politics is summed up as follows:

> We should endeavor to create . . . a political situation in which there are both centralism and democracy, both discipline and freedom, both unity of will and personal ease of mind and liveliness.

Much attention was given in the 1978 constitution to developing education, science, and technology. While cultural undertakings must continue to serve socialism, the arts and sciences were to be promoted by "letting a hundred flowers blossom and a hundred schools of thought contend."

In the 1978 constitution, there were admonitions not only against undermining the economy, as in 1975, but also against disrupting the economy. Wage incentives and professional competency were specifically sanctioned. While the right to strike remained, provisions in the 1954 constitution were reintroduced: to preserve labor discipline, to keep public order, and to respect social ethics. The constitution of 1978 recognized the state's duty to protect the environment.

The 1982 Constitution[12]

The 1982 constitution is China's fourth state constitution. The 1978 constitution was said to have become obsolete, in that it "no longer conforms to present realities or needs of the life of the state."[13] The 1978 constitution had been drafted when the "Whatever" group still commanded some influence in Chinese politics; it had to be revised to reflect the thinking of the new leaders under Deng and Hu Yaobang. We must remember that in China the state constitution has never been regarded as a sacred document meant to be permanent and inviolable.

We are told that the 1982 constitution was the product of more than two years of work by the Committee for Revision of the Constitution, which was established in September 1980 by the Fifth NPC. The revised draft of this constitution was circulated within party and government circles for debate and discussion. Reportedly, 7.3 million speakers commented on the draft constitution at millions of meetings held across the nation. The review produced over a million suggestions for revision.[14] The final version of the draft was adopted by the Fifth NPC at its session on December 4, 1982. The Sixth NPC, which met in June 1983, was elected, organized, and conducted under the provisions of the 1982 constitution.

One major change in the 1982 constitution was deletion of lavish praise of Mao and of reference to the Cultural Revolution in the preamble. In its place the new constitution affirms adherence to the four fundamental principles of socialism, the people's dictatorship, Marxism-Leninism and Mao Zedong Thought, and the leadership of the CCP.

Articles 79–81 provide for the election of a president of the republic—a position the 1975 and 1978 constitutions failed to provide presumably in deference to Mao's long opposition to Liu Shaoqi, the president under the 1954 constitution who subsequently was purged in 1966 and died while under house arrest. Another new feature was the establishment of the State Military Council to provide direction for the armed forces (see Articles 93–94 in Appendix A). As will be discussed in Chapter 5, the 1982 constitution restricts the role of rural people's communes to economic management in rural areas; they no longer have responsibilities in local government and administration.

A provision in the 1982 constitution that aroused a flurry of speculation was Article 31, which authorizes the NPC to establish "special administrative regions." To many, this provision opened the way for the return of Hong Kong, Macao, or even Taiwan to China as "special administrative regions." The 1982 constitution represents a step backward from the viewpoint of individual rights. The rights to strike and to "speak out freely, air their views fully, hold great debates, and write big-character posters" were deleted from the text. In fact, the right to speak out freely and to hold big-character posters had been stricken from the 1978 constitution soon after a ban was imposed on the Democracy Wall movement in March 1979. These rights, known to the Chinese as "sida" or "four big freedoms," were abolished by a resolution of the NPC in December 1980 after party leaders complained about the abuse of these rights by the dissidents during the 1978–79 Democracy Wall movement.

NATIONAL PEOPLE'S CONGRESS

The NPC is the highest government organ and has constitutional duties similar to those of many parliamentary bodies in other nations. It is empowered to amend the constitution, to make laws, and to supervise their enforcement. Upon recommendation of the President of the People's Republic, the NPC designates, and may remove, the premier and other members of the State Council and can elect the president of the Supreme People's Court and the Chief Procurator of the Supreme People's Procuratorate. These structural relationships are reflected in Figure 4.1.

Since 1954 five National People's Congresses have been convened, as shown in Table 4.1. The first three congresses, which then were elected for four-years terms rather than the present five-year terms, met annually from 1954 through 1964. After 1964 the regular annual meetings were interrupted first by the Cultural Revolution and then by the Lin Biao affair. The Third NPC was not replaced by the Fourth NPC until 1975. After the Fourth NPC promulgated the 1975 constitution, the work of the congress was again interrupted by the radicals' attack on the Zhou Enlai–dominated government. In accordance with the election law adopted by the Fifth NPC in December 1982, the Sixth NPC, convened in June 1983, had a ratio of one deputy, or delegate, for every 1.04 million people in rural areas, and one for every 130,000 people

TABLE 4.1   The National People's Congress, 1954–1978

NPC	Year Convened	Number of Delegates	Chief of State	Constitution Promulgated
1st	1954	1,226	Mao Zedong	Constitution of 1954
2nd	1959	1,226	Liu Shaoqi	
3rd	1964 (Dec.) 1965 (Jan.)	3,040	Liu Shaoqi	
4th	1975	2,885	—	Revised, 1975
5th	1978	3,459	—	Revised, 1978
6th	1983	2,978	Li Xiannian*	Revised, 1982

Elected by the Sixth NPC on June 18, 1983.

Source: Delegate number is based on "Brief Notes About the People's Congresses," in Renmin Ribao, *February 27, 1978, p. 2. For delegates to the Sixth NPC, see "Sixth NPC Meets in Beijing,"* Beijing Review, *24 (June 13, 1983), 5.*

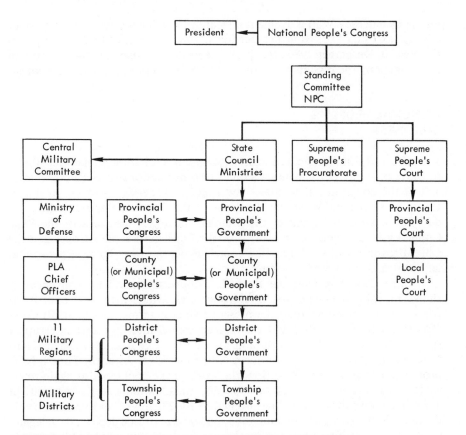

FIGURE 4.1:   Governmental Structure of People's Republic of China (1982 Constitution)

Source: A modified version based on Kim and Ziring, An Introduction to Asian Politics (*Englewood Cliffs, N.J.: Prentice-Hall, 1977), p. 74. By permission of publisher.*

in the urban areas. Sparsely populated provinces and autonomous regions, however, were entitled to no less than fifteen deputies each. The Sixth NPC, dominated by Deng Xiaoping and his reform-minded supporters, seemed to have achieved some degree of stability under a moderate and pragmatic program.

The size of the NPC increased markedly from 1,226 members in 1954 to 3,459 members in 1978. It then declined to 2,978 in 1983. Apparently, the size of the NPC has been expanded to broaden the representation and to allow greater participation in the government. The Fifth NPC had the following class or occupational representation: workers, 26.7 percent; intellectuals, 24 percent; peasants, 20.6 percent; and soldiers, 14.4 percent. Among these groups, women constituted 21 percent, and minorities accounted for 10 percent.[15] The Sixth NPC has the following occupational representation among its delegates: workers and peasants, 26.6 percent; intellectuals, 23.5 percent;

cadres, 21.4 percent; democratic parties, 18.2 percent; soldiers, 9 percent; and overseas Chinese, 1.3 percent.[16]

In drafting the 1982 constitution, the question was raised as to whether the size of the NPC should be reduced to a more manageable level. The suggestion evidently was rejected on the grounds that it was necessary to have "every class, every social strata, every nationality, every locality, and every field of work" represented. The size of the 1983 NPC—2,978 deputies—remained cumbersome.

The enormous size of the NPC raises the question of whether this institution was ever intended to be a genuinely deliberative body. The argument can be made that if the NPC was intended to be a "rubber stamp" for the CCP, then it might as well be very large and representative. However, the NPC cannot be totally dismissed as a rubber stamp. Under the leadership of Liu Shaoqi, the NPC at times did scrutinize proposals on economic development programs before giving its approval. On at least one occasion, at the 1957 session, NPC delegates attacked Mao in relation to the antirightist campaign and the party's meddling in the affairs of a Shanghai unversity.[17] Delegates to the third session of the Fifth NPC (September 1980) demanded information from officials of the Ministry of Petroleum Industry about the 1979 capsizing of the offshore oil rig Bohai No. 2, which cost more than seventy lives. The disaster was the result of many years of management neglect and disregard for safety measures in offshore oil drilling.[18] However, the fact remains that generally the NPC enacts legislation of importance only after the CCP has made its wishes known within the party hierarchy.

A session of the NPC generally meets for a period of about two weeks. During that period only a handful of full plenary meetings are convened to discuss and approve reports of the central government. Delegates or deputies are divided into groups, according to regions, which meet constantly throughout the two-week period when the NPC is in session. It is at these group meetings that one can find occasional spirited discussions on matters of national concern. It is there that the delegates can exercise their oversight functions by submitting motions or inquiries on the performance of the various administrative bodies in the central government. At these sessions vice-ministers representing the central government usually are present on the floor either to answer questions or to provide information about governmental affairs. It was reported that at the December 1981 session of the Fifth NPC, a total of 2,318 motions on a variety of concerns were submitted. However, a majority of these motions were tabled after investigation by an ad hoc committee.[19] The ad hoc committee served as a clearinghouse, referring these motions to the various governmental agencies concerned for comment.[20]

When the NPC is not in session, its Standing Committee serves as the executive body to act on behalf of the congress. (The second session of the Fifth NPC in June 1979 approved a constitutional change which required the establishment of standing committees for people's congresses at and above the county level. The provision remained intact in the 1982 constitution.) While the Standing Committee is elected by the NPC, it is this committee which has the power to conduct elections of the deputies of the NPC and to convene the NPC sessions. Since the NPC meets once a year at most, the Standing Committee controls a great deal of that body's powers. The 1954 constitution provided for as many as sixty-five members on the Standing Committee. In recent times it has had about twenty members drawn from the chairperson, numerous vice-chairpersons, and the secretary-general for the NPC. The Standing Committee of the Fifth NPC had a membership of 175. The Sixth NPC's Standing Committee, elected in 1983, had a membership of 133. Since neither the 1975 nor the 1978 constitutions provided for a chief of state, the functions of the chief of state were placed in the hands of the Standing Committee in a collective leadership role. In practice, the chairperson of that committee assumed many of the ceremonial functions of the chief of state. In 1978 the venerable Ye Jianying, a powerful member of the party's Politburo, was elected chairman of the Standing Committee. Ye stepped down in March 1983 because of his advanced age and poor health. The Sixth NPC in June 1983 elected Peng Zhen chairman of the Standing Committee. The powers of the Standing Committee under the 1978 constitution were curtailed somewhat in comparison with the 1954 constitution. (Article 13 of the 1954 constitution gave the NPC's Standing Committee the power to declare decrees and policies of the State Council unconstitutional.) Article 67(8) of the 1982 constitution (see Appendix A) grants the Standing Committee the power to change and annul inappropriate decisions adopted by provincial and local governments. Theoretically, under the 1982 constitution, the Standing Committee can also restrain the State Council, the executive and administrative arm of the central government. Also Article 67(1) of the 1982 constitution authorizes the Standing Committee of the NPC to interpret the constitution.

The 1982 constitution gives the Standing Committee the power to enforce martial law in the event of domestic disturbance. Article 67(20) (see Appendix A) states that the NPC's Standing Committee can declare martial law either for the country as a whole or for a particular province, autonomous region, or municipality directly under the central government. Hypothetically, measures for suppression of domestic disturbance can now be constitutionally instituted and enforced.

Also, the 1982 constitution gives the Standing Committee the powers and functions normally possessed by the NPC itself, to serve as an interim national congress when the NPC is not in session. The Standing Committee now supervises a new system of parliamentary committees on nationalities, law, finance and economics, public health, education, foreign affairs, overseas Chinese, and any other areas deemed necessary (Article 70, Appendix A). As an interim NPC, the Standing Committee can enact and amend decrees and laws in civil and criminal affairs, including those affecting the structure of the central government. It can annul any administrative regulations and decisions of the central government, and it has the power to interpret the constitution. In order that the Standing Committee be an independent body, its members are not permitted to hold posts in any branch of the central government concurrently.

THE STATE COUNCIL

The State Council, the nation's highest executive organ, administers the government through functional ministries and commissions, as indicated in Table 4.2. The constitution stipulates that the State Council be comprised of a premier, vice-premiers, and heads of national ministries and commissions. The State Council may also include others, such as vice-ministers. The membership of the State Council has ranged from a low of thirty to over one hundred members. As the government expanded over the years, the number of ministries and commissions expanded to a peak of forty-nine just prior to the Cultural Revolution. Administrative reduction and simplification, major aims of the Cultural Revolution, were instituted by the Fourth NPC in 1975, when the number of ministries and commissions was reduced to twenty-nine. With the downfall of the Gang of Four and the launching of an extensive moderization program, some of the old ministries reappeared under the Fifth NPC, such as the state planning and science and technological commissions. The constitutionally mandated membership of the State Council, appointed by the Fifth and Sixth NPCs, are presented in Table 4.2.

To streamline the ministerial structure within the State Council, the total number of ministries and commissions was reduced, from ninety-eight to forty-one, mainly through the merging of functions and staff. The staff personnel in the State Council were reduced from 49,000 to 32,000.[21] The new State Economic Commission was the product of a merger of at least six separate ministries and commissions: agriculture, machine building, energy, building material, standards, and patents. The new Ministry of Electronics Industry was the result of a merger of the old Fourth Ministry of Machine Building, the National Bureau of Radio and Television, and the State Computer Administration. The new Ministry of Foreign Economic Relations and Trade, headed by Madame Chen Muhua—an alternate Politburo member—is an amalgamation of three former state agencies dealing with foreign economic relations, foreign investment, and export and import administration.

Since the full State Council is too large for effective decision making, in

TABLE 4.2   Composition of the State Council

	State Council Ministers Appointed by	
	Fifth NPC (1978–82)	Sixth NPC (1983)
Premier	1	1
Vice-Premiers	13	4
Ministers and Vice-Ministers	505	167
Secretary-General	1	1
Total	520	173

Source: Peng Zhen, "Explanations on the Draft of the Revised Constitution of the PRC," Beijing Review, 19 (May 10, 1982), 3.

practice this role has been assumed by an inner cabinet of the premier and his vice-premiers.[22] In 1982–83 the inner cabinet consisted of a premier, four vice-premiers, ten State Council senior counselors, and a secretary-general for the Office of the State Council. The personnel of the State Council has remained relatively stable over the years. During the Cultural Revolution this body suffered much less than the party apparatus, largely due to the leadership of Zhou Enlai, who was premier from 1949 until his death in 1976. Zhou stayed away from the debates during the initial stage of the revolution but joined Mao and Lin Biao when he realized their faction would emerge dominant. For Zhou's support, concessions were made for the State Council, including exemption from participation in the upheaval by scientists and technicians. As Thomas Robinson points out, Zhou was Mao and Lin's "chief problem solver, troubleshooter, negotiator, organizer, administrator, guide-advisor to revolutionary groups, and local enforcer of Central Committee policy."[23] It has been estimated that between one-half and two-thirds of the 366 ministers, vice-ministers, commissioners, and vice-commissioners kept their posts during the turbulent period from 1966–68.[24] Another reason for the stability of the State Council, whose members represented a concentration of administrative and technical expertise, was the need for production to continue unimpeded. The ability of the State Council to issue directives, often jointly with the party's leading committees, is evidence that central civil bureaucracy was quite institutionalized and functionally effective in spite of the turmoil during the Cultural Revolution.

Doak Barnett has described the State Council aptly as the "command headquarters" for a network of bureaus and agencies staffed by cadres who administer and coordinate the government's programs at the provincial and local levels.[25] The degree of centralization of authority has fluctuated over the regime's history. During the First Five-Year Plan, from 1953 to 1957, the ministries had enormous power over the provincial authorities in terms of quota fulfillment, allocation of resources, and management of such enterprises as factories and mines. The increasing complexity of coordinating the economy and the gravitation of power to the individual ministries, the "ministerial autarky," led to numerous problems and a continuing debate over centralization versus decentralization.[26] In 1957, during the Great Leap, decentralization was instituted by giving the provinces authority to administer and coordinate consumer-goods-oriented industries. The decentralization of the Great Leap hampered central planning and resulted in inefficiency. Following the failure of the Great Leap, a modified version of centralization was adopted until the Cultural Revolution ushered in another period of decentralization.[27] With the reestablishment of planning operations and the emphasis on research and development under the Sixth Five-Year Plan (1981–85), approved by the Fifth NPC in December 1982, the pendulum once again has swung back to more centralization. In his report to the Fifth NPC, Premier Zhao Ziyang indicated that to execute the Sixth Five-Year Plan, it was necessary for the State Planning Commission to exercise strict control over the volume of total investment in fixed assets. Investments in capital construction were to be placed under the control of the Bank of Construction of China.[28] Most ministries under the State Council are concerned with economic affairs; a minority deal with matters such as defense, foreign relations, public security, civil and minority affairs, education, and public health. The ministries on economic matters can be grouped into the categories shown in Table 4.3.

Several new features were added to the State Council by the 1982 constitution. First, a group of ten senior administrators were designated as advisors to the State Council. These senior advisors were retired veteran administrators such as Bo Yibo, age seventy-five, who had been a vice-premier and minister for machine building, and Geng Biao, age seventy-four, former Politburo member and defense minister. Second, tenure for the premiership was now limited to two consecutive five-year terms. Finally, the 1982 constitution mandated the establishment within the State Council of an independent audit agency, under the supervision of the premier, for the purpose of auditing the revenues and expenditures of the various ministries both at the central and provincial levels. The power of audit may eventually become an effective instrument in monitoring and checking the vast Chinese bureaucracy.[29] A ma-

TABLE 4.3   Ministries on the Economic Functions of the State Council, 1982–83

Planning	Economic/Finance	Special Industries
State Planning Commission	State Economic Commission	Machine Building[a]
Scientific/Technological Commission	Urban and Rural Construction	Nuclear[b]
Statistical Commission	Foreign Economic Relations and Trade	Aviation[c]
Restructuring Economic System	Agriculture	Electronics[d]
Family Planning	Forestry	Ordnance[e]
	Railways	Space[f]
	Communications	Power
	Post and Telecommunications	Metallurgical
	Finance	Water Power
	People's Bank	Coal
	Commerce	Chemical
		Petroleum
		Textile
		Light
		Geology and Minerals

[a] Formerly the First Ministry of Machine Building

[b] Formerly the Second Ministry of Machine Building

[c] Formerly the Third Ministry of Machine Building

[d] Formerly the Fourth Ministry of Machine Building

[e] Formerly the Fifth Ministry of Machine Building

[f] Formerly the Seventh Ministry of Machine Building (The former Sixth Ministry of Machine Building was abrogated).

Sources: "Explanations on the Draft of the Revised Constitution of the PRC," Beijing Review, 19 (May 10, 1982), 4; and China Trade Report, June 1982, p. 12.

jority of the twenty-three new ministers and vice-ministers appointed in 1982 were in their fifties and early sixties, slightly younger than their predecessors.

INTERLOCKING STRUCTURE
OF THE GOVERNMENT AND PARTY

To students who are familiar with Western constitutions, it is often a surprise to read in the Chinese constitution the stipulation that the party is "the core of leadership of the whole Chinese people," and that "the working class exercises leadership over the state through its vanguard, the Communist Party of China." This, of course, means that the governmental institutions in China exist to serve the party.

The Chinese Communist Party controls and directs the machinery of state through an interlocking system of party personnel and a structure parallel to that of the state government. Fewer high party leaders held high government positions concurrently in 1982–83 than at any previous time. The 1977–78 period represented a heightened state of interlocking between the party and government hierarchy. The best example was Hua Guofeng, who was chairman of the CCP, premier of the central government, and chairman of the party's Military Affairs Commission. Of the thirteen vice-premiers of the State Council elected by the Fifth NPC in 1978, nine were members of the powerful CCP Politburo, and all were members of the CCP Central Committee elected in 1977. Of the thirty-six ministers in charge of the various governmental agencies, twenty-nine, or 81 percent, were members of the Central Committee. All major economic ministries, including economic planning, capital construction, research and development, foreign trade, and heavy and light industries, were in the hands of ministers who were members of either the Politburo or the Central Committee. In fact, the party's highest policy-making body, the Politburo, is functionally organized to parallel the government ministries, with members specializing in the various governmental activities. In each state bureaucracy, there is always the presence of the party cell of leading CCP members who provide direction for the state organ. The party has always been able to exercise its control in a state bureaucracy by supervising its personnel. Thus, the state structure and the party are not truly parallel entities, since they interlock from top to bottom.

The party control over the state bureaucracy has been the subject of much discussion among scholars. Too often students of Chinese politics look at the bureaucracy under the State Council as if it were an independent power base competing with the party. The fact that all the forty-five ministers approved by the Sixth NPC are members of the CCP's Central Committee demonstrates that the State Council is not only interlocked with the party but is controlled by it. Conflicts that do occur are not primarily between the government and the party but rather are intraparty conflicts between high-ranking party members.

Interlocking Relationships
of the Politburo Members

The interlocking relationships of the members of the Politburo, the highest decision-making body of the party, not only demonstrate how the party exercises its control over the central government but also give an indication of possible areas of specialty and of power bases for the top elites who are members of the Politburo. Table 4.4 lists the members of the Politburo elected by the Twelfth Party Congress in 1982 by their affiliation with either the military, the central government administration, or an ethnic minority.

The interlocking system in 1982–83 was not so widespread. For example, Hu Yaobang, the party's general secretary, held no high government position. However, the premier and his two vice-premiers for the State Council (Wan Li and Yao Yilin) were also members of the Politburo. Politburo members were also in charge of major governmental ministries: state planning, restruc-

TABLE 4.4   Politburo Members Elected in 1982 by Their Affiliation with the Military, Central Government Administration, or Ethnic Minority

		1. Hu Yaobang	
Standing	2. Ye Jianying	4. Deng Xiaoping	6. Chen Yun
Committee of	3. Li Xiannian	5. Zhao Ziyang	
Politburo:			

Professional Military Background	Veteran Administrators	Ethnic Minority
7. Li Desheng	14. Wan Li[b]	27. Wei Guoqing (Zhuang)
8. Nie Rongzhen	15. Xi Zhongxun[b]	28. Ulanhu (Mongolian)
9. Xu Xiangqian	16. Fang Yi	
10. Yang Dezhi[b]	17. Deng Yingchao[c]	
11. Zhang Tingfa	18. Yang Shangkun[b]	
12. Wang Zhen	19. Yu Qiuli	
13. Qin Jiwei[ab]	20. Sung Renqiong[b]	
	21. Hu Qiaomu[b]	
	22. Ni Zhifu	
	23. Peng Zhen	
	24. Liao Chengzhi[bd]	
	25. Yao Yilin[ab]	
	26. Chen Muhua[ac]	

[a] *Elected as alternate members of the Politburo*

[b] *Newly elected for the first time to the Politburo*

[c] *Female*

[d] *Deceased (June 10, 1983)*

Source: "First Plenum of Central Committee," Beijing Review, 38 (September 20, 1982), 5–6;
"New Members of CPC Central Leading Organs," Beijing Review, 38 (September 20, 1982),
22–24; Ming Pao (Hong Kong), September 11, 1982, p. 1; and Issues and Studies, vol. xviii, no. 11
(November 1982), 25–62.

turing the economic system, science and technology, and foreign trade. A majority of the state ministers and vice-ministers were members of the party's Central Committee elected in September 1982. The Standing Committee of the Fifth NPC was under the control of the Politburo. Yang Shangkun, a newly elected Politburo member, served concurrently as the general secretary and vice-chairperson of the NPC Standing Committee. Yang also held the position of permanent vice-chairperson for the Military Affairs Commission, headed by Deng Xiaoping. Another new Politburo member, Xi Zhongxun, served concurrently as a vice-chairman of the NPC's Standing Committee and director of its legislative affairs. Hu Qiaomu, yet another newly elected Politburo member, was a key member in the drafting of the 1982 state constitution. Peng Zhen, the Politburo member who helped to draft both the 1978 and 1982 state constitutions, also served as one of the 1982 NPC vice-chairmen, along with four other Politburo members. We may conclude by saying that the NPC was under the control of these four Politburo members: Yang Shangkun, Xi Zhongxun, Peng Zhen, and Hu Qiaomu. It must be remembered that it is the NPC and its Standing Committee that provide direction and supervision for the central government through the State Council.

Some attempts have been made recently to separate the work of the party and government. These changes seem to indicate a desire that the party curb its interference in governmental operations.[30] However, these changes may not mean very much, since the preamble to the 1982 party constitution still maintains that the party must exercise overall political, ideological, and organizational leadership. Often in the past, this very exercise of party leadership led to the virtual takeover of normal governmental functions by the party.

THE CHINESE LEGAL SYSTEM AND LAW ENFORCEMENT

We begin this section on the Chinese legal system with two case studies: one, a criminal case of deviance; the other, a civil case of divorce. The purpose of these case illustrations is to enable those who are not familiar with the Chinese concept of law to have some understanding of how it works and why. Outsiders looking in at Chinese legal institutions and proceedings may get the impression that either the Chinese legal system today is nonexistent or there is no need for law at all, since there are few—if any—criminals in their society. Both of these impressions are, of course, misconceptions. The Chinese legal system is quite different from that in the West, and the manner in which deviance and disputes are handled has been shaped to a large extent by China's own revolutionary experiences of past decades, as well as by the communist political ideology.

In the criminal case,[31] a worker had stolen about $250 worth of material and equipment from his factory. A colleague and neighbor reported his deviant behavior to the factory revolutionary committee, which referred the matter to the public security unit. An investigation was made by a procurator, who—in accordance with Chinese legal practice—served as both prosecuting attorney and public defender. The procurator then presented a dossier of the case to an intermediate court. The court ordered an open trial to be held in the factory so that other factory workers could participate in the proceedings. At the trial the judge, with the help of two community-elected lay assessors, examined the charges and the evidence as presented by the procurator. A trade union leader who personally knew the defendant testified about the defendant's good character and appealed for leniency. After the defendant made a confession about his crime, the judge solicited the opinion of the masses, the workers in the factory. The consensus of the masses in attendance at the trial was that the defendant was a good worker but that his crime must be punished. Upon the suggestion of the masses, the judge sentenced the defendant to two years of labor in the factory under the supervision of his fellow workers.

The civil case[32] is a divorce case. While divorce cases are not frequent, they represent 60 percent of all civil cases in China. The case came to trial in a lower court after reconciliation attempts had been made, first by the committee that handles misdemeanors, then by the procurator, and finally by the judge's department. The hearings were held in a store front and included a judge, two lay assessors, and a procurator. The judge heard arguments from both the husband and the wife, and then retired for an hour with the two assessors to reach a decision. The verdict was that a final reconciliation attempt was to be made over forty-eight hours, and that a divorce would be granted if this last effort failed.

The Chinese legal system utilizes two basic approaches: one, the formal set of structures and procedures seen in the two cases summarized above; the other, a set of what Professor Jerome Cohen calls "extrajudicial" structures and practices, which generally emphasize continuous education on acceptable social norms, peer pressure dynamics, and persuasion to correct deviant behavior. These two approaches, or "models," interact and coexist within the Chinese legal system.[33] From 1954 to 1956, the formalized legal structures and procedures were dominant. From the Great Leap in 1958 through the Cultural Revolution, the extrajudicial structures and practices increased in importance. Following the convocation of the Fifth NPC and the promulgation of the 1978 constitution, there has been a reversion to more formalized structures and procedures, including the revising of civil and criminal codes by a group of experts headed by Peng Zhen, a former Politburo member purged during the Cultural Revolution but now rehabilitated.[34]

The Courts: Formal Structure and Functions

The 1982 constitution provides that judicial authority for the state be exercised by three judicial organs: the people's courts, the people's procuratorates, and the public security bureaus. The Supreme People's Court is responsibile and accountable to the NPC and its Standing Committee. It supervises the administration of justice of the local people's courts and the special people's courts. The local people's courts operate at the provincial, county, and district levels. The local people's courts at the higher levels supervise the administration of justice of the people's courts at lower levels. The local people's courts are responsible and accountable to the local people's congresses at the various levels of local government. Article 125 of the 1982 constitution stipulates that all cases handled by the people's courts must be open and that the accused has the right to a defense.

When legal reforms were introduced in 1978, 3,100 local people's courts were established at four levels: basic people's courts at the district and county level, intermediate people's courts at the municipal level, higher people's courts at the provincial and autonomous region level, and the Supreme People's Court at the national level. Each of the basic people's courts has a civil and criminal division presided over by a judge. An economic division has been added at the intermediate and higher levels to help process cases that involve economics and finance.

Alongside the court system is a parallel system of people's procuratorates, headed by the Supreme People's Procuratorate, which is responsible to the NPC and supervises the local procuratorates at the various levels. The system of procuracy is rooted both in Chinese imperial practices and in the Napoleonic civil code, which was used in part by the Soviets and many other continental European nations in their legal systems.[35] As was mentioned earlier, the procurator serves as both prosecuting attorney and public defender during a trial. The procurator is also responsible for monitoring and reviewing the government organs, including the courts, to provide a legal check on the civil bureaucracy.[36] Further, the procuratorate is responsible for authorizing the arrests of criminals and counterrevolutionaries. In other words, the procuratorate examines charges brought by the public security bureau (the police) and decides whether to bring the case before a court for trial.

The 1954 constitution provided for independence, under the law, of the courts and procuratorates. These provisions were eliminated by both the 1975 and 1978 constitutions. The period between 1954 and 1957 witnessed the strong development of judicial independence. Judges frequently made their own decisions, disregarding the views and wishes of the party in important cases. This independence elicited much criticism from the party and resulted in increased tension between the courts and the party.[37] Coupled with the development of judicial independence was a movement to develop legal professionalism and expertise. Law schools were established, and offices of "people's lawyers" were formed in cities to provide legal aid to citizens. In 1957 the party countered judicial independence with a two-pronged attack: First, it purged or transferred to other branches of government those court cadres who advocated strengthening judicial independence and professionalism; and second, it introduced many of the extrajudicial institutions and practices for handling cases, in order to bypass the formal court system. In addition, in 1959 the functions of the local procuratorates were merged into the party's political and legal departments at the local levels. Thus, for all practical purposes, local procuratorates disappeared during the Cultural Revolution, and the Supreme People's Procuratorate existed in name only.[38] As mentioned earlier, the 1982 constitution restored the 1954 constitutional provision concerning judicial integrity. Article 126 declares that all China's courts shall exercise judicial power independently without interference from "administrative organs, public organizations or individuals." To what extent this provision will be applied in practice remains to be seen.[39]

The New Criminal and Civil Procedures

To restore law and order after the Cultural Revolution, a set of criminal and civil procedures were drafted in 1978. The astonishing fact was that since its founding in 1949, the People's Republic had had no criminal code. At its second session in July 1979, the Fifth NPC adopted the first criminal code and procedure, which came into effect in January 1980. The code contained some 192 articles in eight major areas. These covered offenses concerning counterrevolutionary activity, public security, socialist economic order, rights of citizens, property, public order, marriage and the family, and malfeasance. Principal penalties for offenses included public surveillance, detention, fixed term of imprisonment, and death. The death sentence was reserved for adults who committed the most heinous crimes; and an exception was made for pregnant women. Productive labor and reeducation were to be stressed for detainees and prisoners.[40]

Although the new criminal code represented China's effort to develop "a more predictable and equitable" criminal justice system,[41] the inclusion of "counterrevolutionary" activity as a criminal offense was reminiscent of the Cultural Revolution. The code defined the term *counterrevolutionary* so that an "overt act"—not merely a thought a person might have at a given moment against the socialist system—must be involved. It must be pointed out that a large number of those placed under detention during the Cultural Revolution were accused of committing "counterrevolutionary" offenses under a law enacted in 1951 which remains in force today.[42]

In summary, the Chinese criminal procedure now calls for presentment of charges by the public security bureau after an investigation has been made. The procuratorate must then examine the charges and evidence submitted by the police; and if it determines that a criminal offense has indeed been committed, it approves the arrest. Before a trial is held, the procuratorate must file an indictment against the accused. All trials must be open to the public, except when a case deals with state secrets, private lives of persons, or a minor below the age of eighteen.[43] A trial must be presided over by a judge, assisted by two assessors. Together they must render a decision on the accused, who now can be defended by a court-appointed lawyer.

The civil procedure, which came into effect in October 1982, permits persons to bring a suit to a people's court in a dispute regarding infringement of rights. The court must then conduct an investigation and gather evidence on the suit. Once the court has decided when and where a trial on the civil case will take place, litigants in the case may gather facts and witnesses for the trial. The new civil procedure stresses mediation for solving disputes rather than a formal court trial. Because of increased contact and investment with foreigners, a section in the civil procedure deals with cases involving disputes with foreigners (persons, enterprises, or organizations). In these civil disputes, the court must apply the Chinese law, as well as treaties and international conventions. When there is a difference between the Chinese law and a treaty, the treaty must prevail. Foreigners may engage Chinese lawyers to file a suit or to defend themselves in a contractual dispute. The new civil procedure also provides for arbitration to settle disputes arising from contractual arrangements between China and foreign corporations.[44]

In both the criminal and civil procedures, provisions are made for the services of lawyers. For instance, Article 26 of the criminal code states that the accused not only has the right to defend himself or herself but also can obtain legal counsel from a lawyer or from citizens recommended by a people's organization in which the accused works or has close relatives. The court must assign a lawyer for the accused if he or she has none (Article 27).

A lawyer's position in China is very different from that in the West. In the first place, lawyers in China are organized to practice law collectively. They must work for state-supported legal advisory offices that assign them cases; they cannot engage in private practice. They are, in fact, "state legal workers," semiprofessional at best. The role of these legal advisors is rather limited; they are not advocates or adversaries in the Western sense. They act, when requested, as legal advisors to governmental units, state economic enterprises, and people's communes on property disputes or contract disagreements with foreign firms. They also dispense legal information to the public. In the streets of Guangzhou (Canton), lawyers set up street corner stands to answer questions on rent disputes, property inheritance, and domestic quarrels.[45] Their role is not to protect their clients but merely to advise them as to what the law says. In fact, their first duty is "to safeguard the interests of the state."[46]

Lawyers' organizations known as "legal advisors' offices" existed prior to 1957 in many cities. These legal service organizations—which then numbered approximately 800, with about 2,500 full-time lawyers—disappeared in 1957 and were not revived until 1979, when the Fifth NPC enacted regulations for lawyers' services.[47] In 1979 there were 5,500 full-time and 1,300 part-time paid lawyers in some 1,500 law advisory offices in twenty-five provinces.[48] In 1983 there were about 8,000 lawyers in China, about one lawyer for every 300,000 people. This compares with 350,000 lawyers in (the much less populated) United States. In 1981 the capital city of Beijing had only 56 lawyers for a population of 8 million.[49] The shortage of legal services has become more acute as the role of lawyers has expanded with the new criminal and civil codes and as economic activities have proliferated. The Ministry of Justice plans to augment the number of legal service personnel to include one lawyer for every 10,000 persons in the cities, and one for every 50,000 peasants in the rural areas, by 1985.[50] Thus, China must train as many as 200,000 qualified legal personnel by the next decade. The rate at which universities turn out law graduates certainly has not been adequate. Peida, the Beijing National University, produced only between eighty to one hundred law graduates a year over the past several years.[51] Some provinces have resorted to short-term professional training on legal affairs to provide the needed personnel.[52]

Informal Practices and Community Mediation

The party cadres who came from a guerrilla background had acquired a set of legal experiences which relied heavily on the use of reeducation, persuasion, and social group pressure. As Victor Li has pointed out, the informal handling of deviance by guerrillas had its roots in traditional China.[53] Except for very serious cases, the traditional settlement of a dispute was one of informality, compromise, and facesaving for everyone involved. Disputes were settled largely by mediation of elders in a family, clan, or village, with consultation all around. In China today we see similar mediation roles assigned to organizations, such as street or neighborhood committees, in settlement of disputes or in cases concerning deviant behavior. For instance, if a person steals a bicycle, the family is notified, and the family elders impose minor disciplinary action. If the person refuses to admit his or her wrongdoing or refuses to accept the sanction from the family, the neighborhood committee becomes involved. The leaders of the neighborhood committee then guide a group of neighbors in attempts to reeducate the offender. If the person is a first-time offender and confesses to the wrongdoing, the action is usually forgiven, and the individual is given a chance to amend his or her behavior under the supervision of the group. If the person repeats the deviant act, the public security unit is called in. The public security, or police, do not jail the individual but instead attempt reeducation. Only the incorrigibles are incarcerated in labor reform camps.[54] In a more serious criminal case, such as the one illustrated at the beginning of this section, the judicial proceedings are informal and emphasize mass participation in reaching a verdict. In fact, the illustration points out that the judge's sentence was handed out after the view of the masses—the fellow workers in the factory of the defendant—had been solicited.

A large percentage of both civil and criminal cases are settled in China by this type of informal method, without going through a court trial. In 1980 China institutionalized the informal method of mediation for settlement of disputes as an important feature in the new civil code and procedure. Mediation as a method for dispute settlement can now be conducted by a people's court or by people's mediation committees. The mediation committee is comparable to the neighborhood justice system found in many American cities. As of 1982 there were about 1 million people's mediation committees, which are basically grassroots mass organizations. The primary role of the committees is "to mediate between the two parties by persuasion and education on a voluntary basis."[55] The process operates on the premise that conflicts or disputes are usually quarrels in a family or between neighbors, and that such conflicts can be settled most speedily and equitably by those who live within the community and act as mediators. These grassroots mass organizations exist within production brigades in communes, within neighborhoods in cities, and even in some workshops and units of industrial enterprises. As of 1982 close to 6 million mediators had been elected at the various basic levels with the responsibility of settling civil and minor criminal cases on the spot.[56] It has been reported that in 1980 alone the mediators handled over 6 million cases.[57] In Beijing 81 percent of the civil cases reportedly ended in court mediation.[58] One Western source recently estimated that up to 90 percent of all civil and minor criminal cases have been handled by the mediation committees.[59]

Public Security Bureau: Law Enforcement

The public security bureau performs all the police tasks in China (national, provincial, and local) and is responsible for maintaining law and order. The operation of public security is headed by a national Ministry of Public Security Affairs and has local branches in cities, towns, and villages. Its responsbilities include surveillance of the movements of citizens and foreigners and the investigation of all criminal cases. Since 1957 it has been empowered to pronounce sentence in criminal cases, including internment in labor reform camps under its control. The power of the public security bureau to sentence is another major type of extrajudicial practice, instituted in 1957 to bypass the courts. Local public security personnel are usually all members of the party or of the Communist Youth League.[60] At times public security offices have even been operated as organizations of the local party apparatus. Because of close ties with the party, the public security bureaus usually reflect the view of the party leaders in control.

Just prior to the Cultural Revolution, the procuratorate functions were carried out by the public security units. During the upheaval the attacks by Red Guards on the party frequently focused on the public security bureaus, disrupting—if not paralyzing—their functions. When the People's Liberation Army intervened in January 1967, the functions of the public security bureaus were placed under military control. During this period it became a common practice for the PLA to perform police work: arresting criminals, stopping riots, supervising prisons and labor reform camps, and even directing traffic.[61] In January 1982 the PLA's internal security units were transferred back to the Ministry of Public Security to serve as their own armed police units. This was done in an attempt to strengthen provincial and local public security power and to safeguard people's life and property.[62] The various provincial and local headquarters of the armed police were subject to the command and direction of the party units within the Ministry of Public Security. The 1975 constitution again placed the procuratorate functions and powers in the local public security units. That constitution also prescribed that citizens could be arrested either by a decision of the courts or "by sanction of the public security organ." The constitution of 1978 restored to the people's procuratorate the sanction of arrest of criminal offenders, but assigned the duty of arrest to the public security unit. This fine distinction may not mean very much, since at the local levels, both the public security units and the procuratorate operate from the same administrative office of the party. In June 1979 the second session of the Fifth NPC enacted the new organic laws for the courts as well as a criminal procedure which delineated the relationship between public security organs and the courts as follows: The public security organ is responsible for investigation of crimes and detention of criminals; the procuratorate has the power of approving arrests and prosecuting criminal cases; the people's court is to try cases.

The restoration of the procuratorate and the enunciation of citizens' fundamental rights and duties in the 1978 constitution seemed to have provided a new framework of law and justice in post-Mao China. A campaign for human rights and equal justice for all was launched soon after the promulgation of the 1978 constitution; reached its height in the winter of 1978, just prior to the convening of the Third Plenary Session of the Eleventh Central Committee. Meanwhile, the Central Committee reevaluated the events of the Cultural Revolution and corrected erroneous decisions with respect to the purge of a number of top leaders. Special articles in mass media, and wall posters in Beijing, focused on human rights and injustices to those who had been arbitrarily arrested and mistreated from the days of the Cultural Revolution to the time of the arrest of the Gang of Four. A special group of legal specialists was formed to undertake the major task of codifying and revising some thirty codes and regulations, including criminal and civil justice procedures, as mentioned earlier. The release and rehabilitation of over 100,000 "right deviationists" (a convenient label used by the radicals for those who were tagged as such in the antirightist campaign of 1957, for having attacked the party during the Hundred Flowers Movement), demonstrate the new leadership's intention to observe and enforce "socialist legality and democracy." The many exposés appearing in the mass media in 1978 and 1979 pointed out clearly how widespread were the abuses sanctioned and practiced by the radicals in arbitrarily arresting and detaining cadres and masses alike. From this campaign for law and justice came the approval of regulations governing the arrest and detention of persons. The specific prohibitions contained in the new law on arrest and detention, promulgated by the second session of the Fifth NPC in June 1979, give us some idea of the state of lawlessness that had existed in China for some time. The new law provides that no person shall be arrested without a specific decision of a people's court or the approval of the procuratorate. Within three days of detention or arrest, the police (Public Security Bureau) must submit the evidence to the procuratorate or make formal charges for the detention. The new law requires that interrogation of the detainee must commence within twenty-four hours of the arrest and that persons detained must be released immediately if there is no evidence against them.

Notification must be made within twenty-four hours to the kin of the person under arrest.

The public security bureau maintains correctional labor camps for those who have committed serious crimes, including political ones. The public security units are also involved in criminal reform through education and hard labor for the incarcerated. For instance, minor criminals in the city of Beijing are sent to reformatories by decision of the Beijing municipal government's reformatory committee, headed by a deputy major, who is assisted by a deputy director of the city's public security bureau.[63] Public security bureaus are also actively involved in the campaign to apprehend persons who engage in the "economic crimes" of smuggling, profiteering, and bribery.

In June 1983 the Sixth NPC approved a new Ministry of State Security, modeled on the Soviet Union's Committee on National Security, commonly known as the KGB. This national security agency was established because of the expressed need to protect the state security and to strengthen China's counterespionage work. Premier Zhao reported to the NPC that the new ministry was to combine the work of the public security units, the people's armed police force, border guards, and counterintelligence organs. Apparently, China wanted to intensify its domestic surveillance to prevent "leaks" of "state secrets," particularly to foreigners. In a number of cases, party cadres with overseas connections were sentenced to prison for writing articles for Hong Kong journals under pseudonyms. In at least one case, an American scholar conducting research in China was expelled for allegedly obtaining "state secrets." (Chinese classify information on routine matters as confidential, or secret). With the establishment of the new national security ministry, it is possible that in the future we may see, in addition to the vast social control mechanisms already present in Chinese society, the growth of a monstrous security bureaucracy staffed by secret agents who spy on both Chinese and foreigners.

There are three compelling reasons for what the Chinese term "new beginnings" in restoring and strengthening the legal system, particularly in providing some protection for the cadres and the masses against arbitrary arrest and detention. One is the new regime's desire to create some order out of the anarchical conditions created and fostered by the radicals. Hu Yaobang told the 1982 party congress that there must be a close link between socialist democracy and the legal system "so that socialist democracy is institutionalized and codified into laws."[64] In addition to order and stability, which are necessary conditions for China's modernization, an atmosphere free from fear of arbitrary arrest and detention must be created so that China's intellectuals can dare to think, explore, and make innovations. Finally, if it is to be successful in efforts to encourage foreign trade and investment, China must demonstrate that it has a creditable legal system and that Chinese justice is workable and predictable.

The legal reforms introduced by the pragmatic leaders represent an attempt to establish a creditable legal system in order to restore the people's respect for law after more than a decade of lawlessness. However, there is still some doubt about the new regime's willingness to observe the legal procedures formulated in the criminal code enacted by the NPC in 1979. Mass executions conducted by the police throughout China in August and September 1983 have created a chilling effect on China's legal reforms and raised serious question about human rights. For a period of two months in 1983 more than 600 executions were carried out in twenty cities in China in an attempt to crack down on the rising wave of crimes, such as murder, rape, and robbery. Moreover, the police extended its dragnet to ensnare as many as 50,000 criminals and then banished them to labor camps in remote regions of Xingjiang and Qinghai. In these mass arrests and executions, no pretense was made to apply the new criminal code procedure. This flagrant disregard of the criminal code procedure indicates to the rest of the world that perhaps China has a long way to go toward the establishment of a creditable legal system.

THE CHINESE TOP ELITE
AND THE CADRE SYSTEM

In this section we shall first discuss the characteristics of China's top elite, the members of the Politburo, in terms of their socioeconomic background. A discussion of the development of the Chinese bureaucracy, the cadre system, will follow.

Profile of the Chinese Top
Political Elite

Considerable data has been compiled by scholars in the West on the elites of China, particularly on members of the Eighth and Ninth Central Committees and their Politburos.[65] One of the most comprehensive studies of the Eighth and Ninth Central Committees found that the members were largely from China's interior and rural areas, that they generally had received less formal education than most modern elites, that they were predominantly administrative cadres of a generalist type, and that they were were mostly past their middle years.[66]

Table 4.5 presents a frequency tabulation of characteristics of the twenty-eight members of the Politburo elected by the Twelfth Party Congress in 1982. Over 71 percent of the members were over seventy, and the average age was about seventy-four. Only 25 percent of Politburo members elected in 1982 were considered young—above sixty years of age. Two women—Deng Yingchao and Chen Muhua—were elected to this top policy-making body in 1982. Over 67 percent of the members came from the provinces in central, north, and eastern China.

The summary of primary occupational background and institutional affiliation reveals that the largest group, almost 40 percent, was still from a dominantly military background. However, only five of the twenty-eight Politburo members were active military commanders. The second largest groups, almost 18 percent each, were top administrators in the central government and leaders in scientific/technological ministries. These two categories combined,

TABLE 4.5   Characteristics of the Chinese Top Elite Politburo Members Elected by the Twelfth Party Congress, 1982

	Number	Percentage of Total
Age		
80 and over	6	21.4
70s	14	50.0
60s	7	25.0
50s	1	3.6
40s	—	—
	28 Average: 74	
Sex		
Male	26	92.9
Female	2	7.1
	28	
Nationality		
Chinese	26	92.9
National Minorities	2	7.1
	28	
Geographic Origin		
Central	11	39.3
East	4	14.3
North	4	14.3
Northeast	1	3.6
Northwest	—	—
South	2	7.1
Southwest	5	17.8
Tokyo	1	3.6
	28	
Occupational Background		
Provincial	4	14.3
Central Party Apparatus/ State Apparatus	5	17.8
Military/Public Security	11	39.3
Economic Specialists/Scientific Academic/Intellectual	5	17.8
Workers	1	3.6
Peasants	—	—
Mass Organizations	2	7.1
	28	

Source: Compilation is based on the following: Donald Klein and Anne B. Clark, Biographic Dictionary of Chinese Communism, 1921–1965, *vols. i & ii (Cambridge, Mass.: Harvard University Press, 1971);* Who's Who In Communist China *(Hong Kong: Union Research Institute, 1970);* Ming Pao Daily *(Hong Kong), September 11, 1982, p. 1;* Ta Kung Pao Weekly Supplement *(Hong Kong), September 16, 1982, p. 3; and* China Trade Report, *July 1982, pp. 12–13.*

totaling 85 percent, represent important decision makers who hold critical central administrative positions in the party and government. Very few active provincial party secretaries were elected to the Politburo in 1982. Two came from minority nationality background—both Wei Guoqing (Zhuang) and Ulanhu (Mongol) had been party veterans with strong provincial ties.

No one can really predict the future cohesiveness of the top elite elected to Politburo membership in 1982: The top decision makers have always been beset with factionalism.[67] Lucian Pye postulates that the dynamics of Chinese politics is a continous tension that exists among the top elite between the need for consensus and the need for "particularistic relationships" which tend to produce factions.[68] Generational differences, geographic affinity, institutional affiliation, degree of power, and personal association with "in-groups" are the factors that contribute to factionalism, according to Pye. Both Lucian Pye and Parris Chang point out that Chinese factionalism is neither ideologically oriented nor policy oriented. Rather, it is the elite's personal relationships or ties with each other that serve as "the glue" cementing the factions together.[69] Parris Chang developed a Chinese leadership factional scheme to show the dominance of the Deng group in coalition with the groups associated with the "Elder Statesmen" group of septuagenarians.[70] As pointed out in Chapter 1, by 1982 Deng Xiaoping and his close associates had emerged as the dominant faction in Chinese politics. Key members of the Deng faction—Hu Yaobang, Zhao Ziyang, and Wang Li, who were still in their mid-sixties—had now become the first-line decision makers.

The Development of the Chinese Bureaucracy: the Cadre System

A government's policies and programs are generally carried out by the functionaries who staff the administrative agencies. In the noncommunist world, we call these people bureaucrats, the "vast impenetrable and well-paid" corps of paper shufflers.[71] The Chinese call these bureaucrats "cadres" or "ganbu" which title denotes leadership skill and capability in an organizational setup. Thus, we may refer to Zhou Enlai, Hu Yaobang, or Deng Xiaoping as the party and central government's leading cadres. The intermediate layer of bureaucrats is the middle-level cadres; and those on the bottom layer, who must deal directly with the masses, are the basic-level cadres.

It should be kept in mind that not every cadre is a party member, nor is every party member a cadre. In short, cadres are the functionaries who staff the various party and government bureaucracies and who have authority to conduct party or government business. When we use the term elite in discussing Chinese politics, we are generally referring to the cadres at various levels.

On the basis of their employment, the cadres are divided into three general broad categories: state, local, and military. Each group has its own salary classification system with ranks and grades, similar to civil service systems in noncommunist countries. Urban state cadres have a system with twenty-four grades, while local cadres have twenty-six grades. Local cadres at the commune level or below are paid directly by the organizations they work for. This ranking system is also associated with status, privileges, and the degree of upward mobility in the career ladder. A cadre's rank, particularly at the state level, is determined not necessarily by length of service or seniority but frequently by educational background, expertise, or technical competence. Those cadres who have served the party since the days of the Long March and the war against Japan naturally command more prestige than those who joined after the liberation in 1949. During the Cultural Revolution, the term *veteran cadres* was widely used to denote cadres who had acquired administrative experience in managing party and government affairs prior to the Cultural Revolution.

It is difficult to obtain precise figures for the total number of state, local, and military cadres in China today. We know that in 1958 there were about 8 million state cadres, or one state leader for every eighty persons in China. If we use the ratio of 1:80 as a basis for a rough estimate, the total number of state cadres may now be over 20 million,[72] This figure does not include the millions of cadres at the local level and in the military, and it includes only some of the 35 million party members, many of whom are cadres. The leadership nucleus in China may well total between 50 and 60 million cadres. This is the Chinese elite that must provide leadership for the masses.

Development of the Cadre System

In the early days, when the Chinese communist movement was engaged in guerrilla activities, the vast majority of the cadres were basic level. They were the link between the party and the masses, the go-betweens in the execution of party directives. They were expected, then as now, to conscientiously apply the principle "from the masses, to the masses" and to always be attentive and responsive to the wishes of the masses. Most of these basic-level cadres were peasants with experience mainly in managing governmental affairs of a rural nature. Because of the guerrilla operation, it was necessary to require all cadres to be dedicated party members and to adhere strictly to the party principle of democratic centralism. In implementing policies, these cadres supervised the tasks called for by the policies. They were required, from time to time, to conduct investigations into the results of programs and to make reports to the party. The ideal cadre during the guerrilla days was also a combat leader who lived among the masses and exemplified the traits of modesty and prudence.

After the communist takeover in 1949, a new type of cadre was needed to manage the complex social and economic affairs of the vast nation. This required persons with administrative skills and experience not possessed by the cadres who came from the rural environment and guerrilla background. A massive infusion of both party members and government cadres took place from 1949 into the early 1950s. As a stopgap measure, party membership and loyalty were no longer required for the government cadres. Instead, education, technical skill, and experience became the prerequistes for cadre rank. The cadres from the guerrilla experience were placed in special training programs to prepare them for work in complex governmental agencies. By 1953 about 59 percent of the 2.7-million cadre force were graduates of either regular or people's universities; the remaining 41 percent had attended special training courses to prepare for their work in various government agencies.[73]

The transformation of cadres from revolutionary leaders, engaged in guerrilla welfare, to government bureaucrats, concerned largely with paper work, became formally institutionalized in 1955, when the State Council promulgated a rank classification system for the cadres.[74] Rank within the system was based on acquisition of technical skills and on when the cadre had joined the revolution. As the need for manpower in government service grew, a salary system with a promotional ladder was also established to attract career-oriented young people.[75] It has been said that by this time a cadre could predict with some accuracy future promotions and status.[76] These developments in the bureaucracy presented a host of problems for a society dedicated both to egalitarian principles and to modernization, with its concomitant requirement for specialization and expertise, which could only be administered in a complex hierarchical structure. In an effort to maintain the egalitarian society and to correct various abuses, the regime developed three major strategies aside from the use of persuasion through education and the dispatch of special work teams to correct specific local abuses. These strategies were rectification campaigns, the xiafang movement, and May Seventh Cadre Schools.

Rectification Campaigns

Rectification campaigns have been used to correct deviant behavior of both party and government cadres. The campaigns generally have involved education, reform, and purge. These campaigns have been undertaken periodically to strengthen the cadres' discipline, to raise their political and ideological awareness, and to combat corruption and inefficient work performance.[77]

The first rectification campaign, conducted by Mao from 1942 to 1944, following his selection as party chairperson, was designed to remove lingering opposition to his strategy for revolution. This was followed by the 1950 rectification campaign, aimed at correcting deviant attitudes among party cadres at all levels. The party cadres were criticized for "commandism," or issuing orders without proper consultation with the masses; tendencies of bureaucraticism, including excessive paper shuffling; distrusting the masses; and lack of direction and coordination in their work. The campaign was also an attempt to resolve differences between cadres from the guerrilla days and those recruited after 1949, which had created friction and tensions within the party. The 1950 campaign required the cadres to study systematically selected key party documents, to analyze China's situation, and to participate in self-criticism during small group discussions. These two campaigns were followed by at least six more rectification campaigns, including the Socialist Education Campaign in 1963, prior to the Cultural Revolution. As Teiwes has pointed out, the measures used in these successive rectification campaigns ranged from educational persuasion, to reduction of rank and pay, to punishment by purge or even death.[78]

Despite these rectification campaigns, on the eve of the Cultural Revolution, the cadres—as bureaucrats and administrators—were committed more to efficiency and orderly completion of tasks than to revolutionary enthusiasm and vision.[79] As careerists, the cadres as a whole had established political power, comfortable income, and security as life goals.[80] There were particular problems which included difficulties in actual implementation of the mass line principle, deviant behavior, acquisition of special privileges, declining morale, and increased tensions.[81] The Cultural Revolution can be considered both a gigantic rectification campaign and a mass campaign aimed to a large extent at these bureaucratic problems. The numerous rectification campaigns have created fear and uncertainty among the cadres and have led to administrative chaos and waste in the management of government activities.

The Xiafang, or "Downward Transfer" Movement and the May Seventh Cadre Schools

The temporary transfer of party cadres down to a lower-level assignment or to a rural village or factory was introduced in the 1940s. Originally, the primary purpose of the movement was to reduce bureaucratic machinery and to strengthen the basic-level leadership. The system of temporary downward transfer of party and government cadres became institutionalized in 1957, when the movement's primary purpose shifted to the "education and reform of cadres through labor." From 1961 to 1963, as many as 20 million education cadres, a large number with technical skills, were sent to work in villages with the peasants.[82] The movement was intensified during the Cultural Revolution, when it became fashionable for cadres to opt for downward transfer to rural villages and communes. The major objective then was twofold: (1) to combat the cadres' bureaucratic tendencies through physical labor in the fields, alongside the peasants; and (2) to develop the mass line by enabling the cadres to understand the masses' problems and aspirations through living and working among them. The program resulted in a marked change in the cadres' attitudes toward the masses. Interestingly, the manual labor also improved the participating cadres' health.[83] While the downward transfer of skilled cadres must be considered an underemployment of resources, the xiafang movement represents an innovative technique to check the perennial problem of elitism in China. However, one must also point out that when the concept is carried to its extreme, as it was during the Cultural Revolution, human resources are wasted. Further, doubts and disillusionment arise about a system which sanctions such widespread waste.

One of the devices that came out of the Cultural Revolution was the May

Seventh cadres schools for the reeducation and rehabilitation of incorrect attitudes and ideological thoughts. Thousands of these cadre schools were formed under a directive—issued by Mao on May 7, 1966—that emphasized the need to reeducate and to rusticate cadres for ideological remolding. The schools' curriculum consisted of manual labor, including working in the fields with commune production teams, performing duties required to run the school, and theoretical studies of works by Mao, Marx, and Lenin. Life at the May Seventh cadres schools was initially spartan, and provisions for daily living had to be obtained by the participants through their own labor. A cadre was usually sent to a school for three, six, or twelve months. Occasionally their stay was for more than a year. Some Westerners and Chinese considered these schools innovative because they provided the opportunity to engage in both physical exercise and ideological study, all aimed at curbing tendencies toward bureaucratic elitism.[84] To many Chinese who endured the ordeal at the May Seventh cadre schools it was simply a waste of time.

Trends in the Cadre System

Over the past decade and a half, life for a cadre as an intermediary was not easy. The cadre was not able to please either those at the top of the party nor the masses at the bottom. Since all decisions were subject to criticism from many directions, frequently the wisest choice was to make no decision at all. The cadres who came from the intellectual class but who possessed technical expertise were subject to special abuse as China's privileged "new class."[85] To redeem themselves, cadres opted for physical labor in the countryside, putting aside their professional development, at least temporarily.

The pendulum has now swung back to the moderation of the mid-1950s, when China's economic development demanded the rapid recruitment of capable, skilled persons as cadres to manage the nation's complex economic activities. The attacks against the new "bourgeois right" of elites and intellectuals were silenced with the downfall of the radical Gang of Four. Recently, deliberate attempts have been made to reform the cadre system. One key reform measure has been to place leadership positions in the hands of cadres who are "staunch revolutionaries, younger in age, better educated, and technically competent."[86] Hu Yaobang has called for greater emphasis on cadre utilization and promotion according to education and skills: "We must work strenuously to strengthen the education and training of cadres in order to prepare personnel needed for socialist modernization."[87] To implement this directive, a rotation system for further education and training has been instituted for government cadres whose educational attainment is below the secondary level. But the task of upgrading cadres' competence seems formidable indeed when one considers the fact that a large number of cadres both at the center and in the provinces have only the equivalent of a primary school education.[88]

Closely related to the upgrading of cadres' competence is the problem of upward mobility for the middle-aged cadres. About 2 million of the 20 million cadres working for the Central Committee and the State Council are considered veteran cadres, having been recruited before 1949.[89] These veteran cadres, now advanced in age, still cling to their posts in the party and government. A retirement system has been instituted to provide turnover in personnel. During 1981 and 1982, there were massive resignations of older cadres. In one machine-building industry ministry, the 13 vice-ministers and 269 cadres resigned or retired at the bureau level.[90] In 1981 some 20,000 aged cadres retired in one province.[91]

There are two other serious problems in the Chinese cadre system. One is corruption, and the other is bureaucratism. Corruption is not a new problem, but since 1978 its scope and intensity have reached an unprecedented level. The mass media have been saturated with exposés of so-called "economic crimes" committed by cadres at all levels. Premier Zhao Ziyang has called these corrupt practices "obnoxious," citing lavish dinner parties with presents to the bosses, influence peddling for personal gain, and graft.

The use of bribery or favoritism to get scarce goods or to get things done by way of "back-door" dealings have been common practices.[92] The offspring of higher party and government cadres in Hong Kong have often served as "connections" for foreign merchants who desire to establish contacts for trade with China.[93] Also widespread is the practice of gift giving and wining and dining by cadres who do business with each other—Beijing municipal authorities have imposed a new prohibition against such practices.[94] In April 1982 the party Central Committee, the State Council, and the NPC Standing Committee enacted an order which demanded life sentences or death by execution for those cadres who were involved in graft or similar corrupt practices.[95] The party's theoretical journal, the *Red Flag*, called economic crimes such as embezzlement of public funds and smuggling new elements in the class struggle.[96] The number of economic crimes committed by the offspring of senior cadres also has been on the rise; one senior army officer agreed that his son should be punished for graft in an illegal timber sale scheme.[97] The extent of cadre corruption may be seen from a report made by Premier Zhao. It revealed that over a nine-month period, 136,000 economic crimes were committed by party and government cadres.[98]

Since 1980 bureaucratic practices have been under constant attack in China. One manifestation of bureaucratism is inertia and the inability to make decisions. This foot dragging is more evident at the middle and lower levels of the party organization and government structure. Deng Yingchao, a member of the Commission for Discipline Inspection, made a lengthy speech at one of the commission's forums charging that a few cadres have adopted bureaucratic work style and have created a bad image for the party.[99] She characterized the bureaucratic work style as follows: "When there is a problem, they suppress it: when it is not possible to suppress it, they push the problem aside; when it cannot be pushed aside, they then procrastinate."[100] Foreign businessmen stationed in China have given vivid pictures of the cadres' bureaucratic work style.[101] Deng Xiaoping charged that cadres seemed to be devoted to rules and regulations and to exhibit obstinacy, timidity, and an air of infallibility; they spent an enormous amount of time reading the interminable flow of documents and directives.[102]

Cadres are a special class in Chinese society. Like their counterparts in the Soviet Union, they enjoy special privileges. The acquisition of these special privileges sets them apart from the masses. The problem of special privileges and material comfort for party and government cadres can best be seen by Chen Yun's talk at a high-level work conference:

> For transportation, we travel by car and do not have to walk; for housing, we have luxurious Western style buildings . . . Who among you comrades present here does not have an air conditioner, a washing machine, and a refrigerator in your house? Take the TV set for example, please raise your hand if the one in your house is not imported from some foreign country.[103]

High cadres and members of their families not only have access to goods and services not available to ordinary citizens but also have access to foreign magazines and movies. Chen Yun also indicated that the children of higher cadres were the first ones to go abroad to study once the door was opened to the West in 1977. As a special privileged class, party and government cadres have been reluctant to give up any of these special prerogatives.

At first the campaign against official corruption and the extravagant lifestyle of high party and government cadres seemed to coincide with Deng's attempt to oust the "Whatever" faction within the Politburo. However, subsequent campaign efforts indicated a genuine desire on the part of the leaders to make the party more creditable.[104] The general public has maintained its usual skepticism about the party and the government's ability to eventually correct such undesirable bureaucratic behavior.

NOTES

1. See Houn, *A Short History of Chinese Communism,* pp. 72–73; and Chou Erh-fu, "The CPPCC: Consulting on Affairs of State," *China Reconstructs,* vol. xxvii, no. 8 (August 1978), 3–4.

2. "Granting Special Amnesty to and Releasing All War Criminals in Custody," *Peking Review,* 12 (March 21, 1975), 11–12; and Chou Erh-fu, "The CPPCC," p. 5.

3. For a summary of activities in English, see *Peking Review,* 9 (March 3, 1978), 4–5.

4. Chou Erh-fu, "The CPPCC," p. 5.

5. For text of 1954 constitution, see Theodore H. E. Chen, *The Chinese Communist Regime* (New York: Praeger, 1967), pp. 75–92.

6. Houn, *A Short History of Chinese Communism,* p. 138.

7. For the text of 1975 constitution, see *Peking Review,* 4 (January 24, 1975), 17.

8. Chang Chun-chiao, "Report on the Revision of the Constitution," *Peking Review,* 4 (February 24, 1975), 15–16.

9. Ibid.

10. "The Constitution of the PRC," *Beijing Review,* 11 (March 17, 1978), 5–14.

11. Yeh Chien-Ying, "On the Revision of the Constitution," *Peking Review,* 11 (March 17, 1978), 15–16.

12. See Appendix A for the text of the 1982 constitution. Also see Byron Weng, "Some

Key Aspects of the 1982 Draft Constitution of the People's Republic of China," *The China Quarterly,* 91 (September 1982), 492–506.

13. "Report on the Draft of the Revised Constitution of the People's Republic of China," *Beijing Review,* 50 (December 13, 1982), 9.

14. *Ta Kung Pao Weekly Supplement,* June 3, 1982, p. 10.

15. *Renmin Ribao,* February 26, 1978, p. 1. Also see "China's Structure of State Power," *Beijing Review,* 20 (May 18, 1979), 19.

16. See "Deputies to the Sixth NPC On June 6," *Beijing Review,* 22 (May 30, 1983), 5.

17. See MacFarquhar, *The Origins of the Cultural Revolution,* pp. 273–78.

18. "Investigating the Causes of Oil Rig Accident," *Beijing Review,* 31 (August 4, 1980), 7.

19. Peng Zehn, "Explanations on the Draft of the Revised Constitution of the PRC," *Beijing Review,* 19 (May 10, 1982), 24.

20. Ibid., p. 3; and *China Trade Report,* June 1982, p. 12. Also see Dorothy J. Sollinger, "The Fifth NPC and the Process of Policy-making: Reform, Readjustment, and the Opposition," *Asian Survey,* vol. xxii, no. 12 (December 1982), 1239–76.

21. "The Present Economic Situation and the Principles for Future Economic Construction," *Beijing Review,* 51 (December 21, 1981), 4. Also see *Ta Kung Pao Weekly Supplement,* December 17, 1981, pp. 1, 4.

22. Donald Klein, "The State Council and the Cultural Revolution," *The China Quarterly,* 35 (July–September 1968), 78–95.

23. "Chou En-lai and the Cultural Revolution in China," *The Cultural Revolution in China* (Berkeley: University of California Press, 1971), p. 279.

24. Klein, "The State Council," p. 81.

25. See Doak Barnett, *Cadres, Bureaucracy, and Political Power in Communist China* (New York: Columbia University Press, 1967), pp. 3–17.

26. Chang, *Power and Politics in China,* p. 50.

27. Ibid., pp. 63–64, 106–108; also see Barnett, *Uncertain Passage,* pp. 136–43.

28. "Report on the Sixth Five-Year Plan," p. 24.

29. Weng, "Some Key Aspects of the 1982 Draft Constitution of the PRC".

30. "Reforming the Political Structure," *Beijing Review,* 4 (January 26, 1981), 18.

31. Franklin P. Lamb, "An Interview with Chinese Legal Officials," *The China Quarterly,* 66 (June 1976), 323–37.

32. Frank Pestana, "Law in the People's Republic of China," *Asian Studies Occasional Report,* no. 1 (Arizona State University, June 1975).

33. J. Cohen, "The Party and the Courts: 1949–1959," *The China Quarterly,* 38 (April–June 1969), 131–40. Discussion of "models" in the Chinese approach to the legal system is based on Victor Li's article "The Role of Law in Communist China," *The China Quarterly,* 44 (October–December 1970), 72–110.

34. See "Socialist Legal System Must Not Be Played Around With," *Peking Review,* 24 (June 16, 1978), 28; and "Discussion on Strengthening China's Legal System," *Peking Review,* 45 (November 10, 1978), 5–6. Also see "Speeding the Work of Law-making," *Peking Review,* 9 (March 2, 1979), 3.

35. Pestana, "Law in the PRC," p. 2. Also see Li, "The Role of Law," p. 78; and George Ginsburgs and Authur Stahnake, "The People's Procuratorate in Communist China: The Institution Ascendant, 1954–1957," *The China Quarterly,* 34 (April–June 1968), 82–132.

36. Ginsburgs and Stahnake, "The People's Procuratorate in Communist China," pp. 90–91.

37. For an account of these tensions and criticisms, see Cohen, "The Party and the Courts: 1949–1959," pp. 131–40.

38. Gerd Ruge, "An Interview with Chinese Legal Officials," *The China Quarterly,* 61 (March 1975), 118–26. Also see Lamb, pp. 324–25.

39. "China's Criminal Law and Law of Criminal Procedure," *Beijing Review,* 23 (June 9, 1980), 17–26.

40. For more information about China's criminal code and procedure, see *Beijing Review,* 33 (August 17, 1979), 16–27; *Beijing Review,* 23 (June 9, 1980), 17–26; *Beijing Review,* 44 (November 3, 1980), 17–28; Hungdah Chiu, "China's New Legal System," *Current History,* 459 (September 1980), 29–32; Fox Butterfield, "China's New Criminal Code," New York Times Service, as reprinted in *Honolulu Star-Bulletin,* July 20, 1979, A-19; Takashi Oka, "China's Pen-

chant for a Penal Code," *Christian Science Monitor,* September 3, 1980, p. 3; and Stanley B. Lubman, "Emerging Functions of Normal Legal Institutions in China's Modernization," *China Under the Four Modernizations, Part 2: Selected Papers,* Joint Economic Committee, Congress of the United States (Washington D.C.: Government Printing Office, December 30, 1982), pp. 235–85.

41. "Hungdah Chiu, "China's New Legal System," p. 32.

42. Ibid., p. 31.

43. Ronald C. Keith, "Transcript of Discussion with Wu Daying and Zhang Zhonglin Concerning Legal Change and Civil Rights," *The China Quarterly,* 81 (March 1981), 115.

44. Cheng Yanling, "China's Law of Civil Procedure," *Beijing Review,* 33 (August 16, 1982), 20–23.

45. *Ming Pao* (Hong Kong), January 6, 1983, p. 3.

46. HeBian, "China's Lawyers," *Beijing Review,* 23 (June 7, 1982), 14.

47. Li Yun Chang, "The Role of Chinese Lawyers," *Beijing Review,* 46 (November 17, 1980), 24. Also see Lubman, "Emerging Functions of Formal Legal Institutions," pp. 251–54.

48. Li Yun Chang, "The Role of Chinese Lawyers," p. 9.

49. *China Trade Report,* March 1981, p. 6.

50. "The Need for more Lawyers," *Beijing Review,* 49 (December 8, 1980), 3.

51. *Christian Science Monitor,* February 10, 1983, p. 11. Also see *The New York Times,* December 5, 1982, p. 22.

52. *Ming Pao* (Hong Kong), February 7, 1983, p. 3.

53. Li, "The Role of Law," p. 92.

54. Martin King Whyte, "Corrective Labor Camps in China," *Asian Survey,* vol. xiii, no. 3 (March 11, 1973), 253–69.

55. Chen Yanling, "China's Law of Civil Procedure," p. 21.

56. "The Xiebeijiao Neighborhood Mediation Committee," *Beijing Review,* 47 (November 23, 1981), 24–28.

57. "Mediation Committees," *Beijing Review,* 41 (October 12, 1981), 8–9; and "China's System of Community Mediation," *Beijing Review,* Also see Lubman, "Emerging Functions of Formal Legal Institutions," pp. 257–59.

58. Chen Yanling, "China's Law of Civil Procedure," p. 21.

59. *The New York Times,* December 5, 1982, p. 22.

60. Barnett, *Cadres, Bureaucracy, and Political Power in Communist China,* p. 227; and Ralph Powell and Chong-kun Yoon, "Public Security and the PLA," in *Asian Survey,* vol. xii, no. 12 (December 1972), 1082–1100.

61. Barnett, *Cadres, Bureaucracy, and Political Power in Communist China,* p. 227; and Powell and Yoon, "Public Security and the PLA," pp. 1082–1100.

62. *Ming Pao* (Hong Kong), July 31, 1981, p. 1.

63. "Reforming Criminals: Interviewing Deputy Director of Public Security Bureau," *Beijing Review,* 8 (February 23, 1981), 24.

64. "Creating a New Situation in All Fields of Socialist Modernization," p. 27.

65. See Robert A. Scalapino, ed., *Elites in the People's Republic of China.*

66. Robert A. Scalapino, "The Transition in Chinese Party Leadership: A Comparison of Eighth and Ninth Central Committees," in *Elites in the People's Republic of China,* pp. 67–148.

67. On the subject of factionalism in Chinese politics, see Lucian W. Pye, *The Dynamics of Factions and Consensus in Chinese Politics* (Santa Monica: Rand Corporation, 1980); Parris H. Chang, "Deng's Turbulent Quest," *Problems of Communism,* xxx (January-February, 1981), 1–21; and "The Last Stand of Deng's Revolution," *Journal of Northeast Asian Studies,* vol. 1, no. 2 (June 1982), 3–20.

68. Pye, *The Dynamics of Factions and Consensus in Chinese Politics,* pp. 5–6.

69. Ibid., p. 6.

70. Chang, "Deng's Turbulent Quest," p. 8.

71. Robert Sherrill, *Governing America: An Introduction* (New York: Harcourt Brace Jovanovich, Inc., 1978), p. 412.

72. See Hong-Yung Lee, "Deng Xiaoping's Reform of the Chinese Bureaucracy," *Journal of Northeast Asian Studies,* vol. 1, no. 2 (June 1982), 21–35. The ratio for the number of people per cadre has been estimated by Lee as 1:50 for a total of 18 million state cadres.

73. See Vogel, "From Revolutionary to Semi-Bureaucrat," p. 45.

74. Ibid.

75. Oksenberg, "The Institutionalization of the Chinese Communist Revolution," pp. 61–92.

76. Ibid.

77. For a fuller discussion of the rectification campaigns, see Frederick C. Teiwes, "Rectification Campaigns and Purges in Communist China, 1950–61," unpublished doctoral dissertation, Columbia University, 1971, in University Microfilms, Ann Arbor, Michigan. Also see S. J. Noumoff, "China's Cultural Revolution as a Rectification Movement," *Pacific Affairs,* vol. xi, nos. 3 and 4 (Fall and Winter 1967–68), 221–33.

78. Teiwes, "Rectification Campaigns and Purges in Communist China," pp. 150–61.

79. Vogel, "From Revolutionary to Semi-Bureaucrat."

80. Oksenberg, "The Institutionalization of the Chinese Communist Revolution."

81. See Richard Baum, *Prelude to Revolution: Mao, the Party, and the Peasant Question, 1962–66* (New York and London: Columbia University Press, 1975); and Richard Baum and Frederick Teiwes, "Liu Shao-chi and the Cadres Question," *Asian Survey,* vol. viii, no. 4 (April 1968), 323–45.

82. See Jan S. Prybyla, "Hsia-fang: The Economics and Politics of Rustication in China," *Pacific Affairs,* vol. 48, no. 2 (Summer 1975), 153. Also see Paul E. Ivory and William R. Lanely, "Rustication, Demography Change, and Development in Shanghai," *Asian Survey,* vol. xvii, no. 5 (May 1977), 440–55.

83. Notes of conversation with cadres in Peking during my visit in 1973.

84. See James C. F. Wang, "The May Seventh Cadre School for Eastern Peking," *The China Quarterly,* 63 (September 1975), 522–27.

85. *Ming Pao* (Hong Kong), July 7, 1981, p. 1.

86. "Create a New Situation in All Fields of Socialist Modernization," p. 36.

87. Ibid.

88. Peng Zhen, "Report on Work of NPC Standing Committee," *Beijing Review,* 39 (September 29, 1980), 24–25.

89. "Reforming the Cadres System," *Beijing Review,* 9 (March 1, 1982), 3.

90. "Veteran Cadres Retire," *Beijing Review,* 7 (February 15, 1982), 5.

91. Ibid.

92. See editorial of *Renmin Ribao,* August 7, 1980.

93. *Ming Pao,* (Hong Kong), August 14, 1981, p. 3.

94. *Ming Pao,* (Hong Kong), August 18, 1981, p. 1.

95. "Economic Criminals Surrender," *Beijing Review,* 17 (April 19, 1982), 7–8.

96. "Decision on Combating Economic Crimes," *Beijing Review,* 17 (April 26, 1982), 7; and *Hongqi,* 4 (February 16, 1982), 8.

97. "Senior Cadres Support Sentences on Their Criminal Sons," *Beijing Review,* 20 (May 17, 1982), 5.

98. *Ming Pao* (Hong Kong), December 4, 1982, p. 1.

99. *Ming Pao,* (Hong Kong), April 6, 1980, p. 3.

100. Ibid. Translation is by this author.

101. Butterfield, *China: Alive in the Bitter Sea,* pp. 217, 288; and Richard Bernstein, *From the Center of the Earth,* pp. 104, 131, 134, 136–137, and 140 for anecdotes to illustrate how Chinese bureaucracy works.

102. "A Speech at the Enlarged Meeting of the Politburo, August 18, 1980," in *Issues and Studies,* vol. xxiii, no. 3 (March 1981), 88; also see *Ming Pao* (Hong Kong), February 14, 1982, p. 3.

103. For text of Chen Yun's speech at the CCP Central Committee Work Conference, see *Issues and Studies,* vol. xvi, no. 4 (April 1980), 82.

104. Deng Xiaoping, "A Speech at the Enlarged Meeting of the Politburo of the Central Committee, August 31, 1980," *Issues and Studies,* vol. xvii, no. 3 (March 1981), 88. Also see *Ming Pao* (Hong Kong), February 14, 1982, p. 3.

Provincial and Local Government and Provincial Politics

OVERVIEW OF PROVINCIAL
AND LOCAL GOVERNMENT

The government of China is administered through twenty-one provinces, five autonomous regions, and three municipalities—Beijing, Shanghai, and Tianjin. The five autonomous regions of Inner Mongolia, Ningxia, Xinjiang, Guangxi, and Xizang are located on China's borders with neighboring countries and are inhabited by minority groups.

The constitution of 1982 specifies three layers of local political power: provinces and autonomous regions, cities and counties, and townships. The source of constitutional power at these levels is the people's congress. We must keep in mind that deputies to the provincial people's congresses are elected indirectly. The 1982 constitution states that the deputies to the provincial people's congresses are to be elected by people's congresses at the next lower level. Eligible voters at the lower level of government (in this case, the counties and townships) elect directly deputies to their own people's congresses. The electoral law now provides that election for the county people's congress is carried out by dividing the county into electoral districts, each of which elects delegates to the county people's congress. A simple chart of the provincial and local government is shown in Figure 5.1. Deputies to the provincial congress are elected for a five-year term; deputies to the township and county congresses are elected for three-year terms.

It would be wrong to assume that the people's congresses at the various local levels are legislative bodies. However, Article 99 of the 1982 constitution authorizes the local people's congresses to "adopt and issue resolutions." These bodies have six main responsibilities: (1) to enact local statutes according to local conditions (authorized by the Organic Law of Local People's Congresses and Local Government in July 1979); (2) to ensure the observance and implementation of the state constitution, the statutes, and administrative rules; (3) to approve plans for economic development and budgets at the county level and above; (4) to elect or recall governors, mayors, and chiefs for the counties and townships; (5) to elect and recall judges and procurators; and (6) to maintain public order.

Theoretically, the deputies are not subject to the influence of local party committees—a political reform imposed under the 1982 constitution. In 1982 Peng Zhen reported that the organs at the grassroots level must be strengthened in order to serve as the basic organization of state power: "These organs must really be in the hands of the people, elected, supervised and removed by them."[1] The party, the pragmatic leaders now maintained, neither replace the government nor give orders to organs of government.[2]

A word must be said here about the revolutionary committee, a product of the Cultural Revolution. It will be recalled from Chapter 1 that the revolutionary committee was originally established as a temporary organ to replace the regular party structure dismantled by the Cultural Revolution; thereafter it remained a grassroots organization through which the masses could participate directly in making decisions at the basic level. With the reestablishment

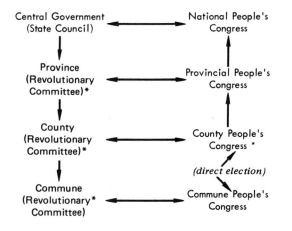

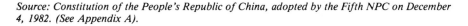

FIGURE 5.1: Provincial and Local Government Structure

Source: Constitution of the People's Republic of China, adopted by the Fifth NPC on December 4, 1982. (See Appendix A).

of the party structure in the early 1970s, many of the functions of the regular party were duplicated by the revolutionary committees. Then, when the Gang of Four was arrested in the fall of 1976, the status of the revolutionary committees at the basic level became rather unclear. Visitors to China during 1977 and the first few months of 1978 observed little evidence of their existence in factories and communes. Before the Fifth National People's Congress convened, there was even talk about abolishing the revolutionary committees. This confusion and uncertainty about the status of the revolutionary committees was clarified when the Fifth National People's Congress approved a constitutional revision which provided that the revolutionary committees at the local levels were to become executive organs of the local people's congresses and "local organs of state administration" (Article 37, 1978 constitution). They were to perform administrative work at their respective levels and areas under the overall direction of the State Council. Thus, the revolutionary committees, an important legacy of the Cultural Revolution, became governmental administrative units at the local levels. Furthermore, the revolutionary committees under the 1978 constitution were empowered to appoint and remove the personnel of the people's courts and procuratorates. The local party committees were responsible only for decisions concerning the general line and principles of the party. Despite this constitutional delineation of responsibility for the revolutionary committees at the provincial and local levels, confusion remained over which organ should make what decisions. A large part of this confusion stemmed from the appointment of individuals to hold concurrent, parallel positions on both the party and revolutionary committees. It had become a standard practice, for instance, to have the party secretaries at the various local levels hold the chairperson or vice-chairperson of the revolutionary committees as well. We need to bear in mind, however, that the original rationale for the formation of the revolutionary committee was to ensure some participation and representation by the masses on matters of strictly local concern. The revolutionary committees at the local level also afforded young cadres an opportunity to acquire leadership skills. After 1973 a deliberate effort was made to have both veteran and younger cadres in leadership positions.

In June 1979 the Fifth NPC at its second session abolished the revolutionary committees as administrative organs for local government. They were replaced by the people's governments at all levels.[3] This action removed one of the last vestiges of the Cultural Revolution. The rationale for abolishing the revolutionary committees was that they no longer could meet the needs of socialist modernization and that their elimination would "strengthen democracy and the legal system."[4] With the abolition of the revolutionary committees, the positions and titles of governor (for the provinces), mayor (for the cities and counties), and chief (for the townships) were restored.[5] These changes regarding local people's congresses and governments were incorporated into the 1982 constitution (see Section V, Articles 95–110, in Appendix A).

ISSUES IN PROVINCIAL POLITICS

Chinese provincial politics is a very complex subject. Three interrelated issues that have dominated provincial politics in China are discussed below.

Regionalism, Provincialism, Localism

We have noted that China is a unitary state with political power concentrated at the central government level, and that throughout China's long history there were many incidents where centrifugal forces pulled away from the center because of geographical and sectional interests. The warlord period of 1916–26 epitomizes this aspect of regional separation in recent history. Another general characteristic of Chinese politics has been the trend toward local initiative and self-government. In this section we will briefly examine the development of regionalism in provincial politics.

The terms *provincialism, regionalism,* and *localism,* have been used to describe the problems of regions versus the center, or the central authority in Beijing. These terms are used here somwhat interchangeably because they all denote the centrifugal force constantly at play in Chinese politics. Regionalism has been defined as "the phenomenon whereby distinct groups, living in discrete territorial enclaves within larger political communities, exert pressures for recognition of their differences."[6]

The presence of regional forces that tend to pull away from the center in Chinese politics may be accounted for, to a large extent, by China's vast size and by the various cultures represented in her different geographic areas. It is common to speak of China as divided geographically into the north, south, central, east, west, and the Asian portions of Inner Mongolia, Xinjiang, and Xizang.[7] Each of these regions may be considered an entity dominated by features of climate, drainage systems, soil composition, or dialect variations. A visitor who enters China by train from Hong Kong will notice the subtropical climate of southern China which permits the harvest of two rice crops each year. The rugged hills and mountains of the south tend to foster a variety of dialects among the inhabitants. A visitor arriving at Beijing in the north sees an entirely different China in terms of climate, which is temperate and thus cold in the winter, and soil formation, which is the dry powdery loess of the Huanghe (Yellow) River basin. Wheat, millet, and cotton are the main crops grown in the north and northeast. Central and east China are watered by the Changjiang (Yangtse) River, whose vast plains permit the cultivation of rice and other crops that support a large population. The mountainous west and southwest is sparsely populated, except for the fertile valley of Sichuan, one of the richest but most difficult provinces to govern because of its geographic isolation and its relative economic self-sufficiency. These geographic and topographic variations are primary factors that have contributed to the feelings of sectional independence.

Centralization vs. Decentralization

In a continuous search for an appropriate administrative formula, China has alternated between an emphasis on decentralization and centralization since 1949. When the communists took over in 1949, the provincial and local governments were built upon the base of the guerrilla army and governments, which by their very nature operated with a great deal of autonomy in implementing government policies and programs. These new governments were staffed largely by local residents, both for convenience and to avoid accusations of a takeover by outsiders. To aid the central government's administration in Beijing and the coordination of the provinces, the six regional districts (shown in Figure 3.2) were established. Each region was governed by both a military and an administrative committee. A corps of veteran party military leaders headed these committees with considerable authority and flexibility. A good deal of local autonomy was permitted under this regional arrangement while the regime consolidated its rule. The communists had neither the administrative personnel nor the experience to mount a tight central administration over the vast population and area. Under these conditions the ever-present local tendencies exerted themselves, frequently resulting in political factions at the local level.[8] Local officials often manipulated party officials at the regional level.

The conflict between the central and regional power structures came to a head with the introduction of the First Five-Year Plan. Centralized planning—with allocated resources, production quotas, forced savings, and formation of the voluntary agricultural producers' cooperatives (APCs)—required strong central control. Gao Gang, chairperson of the Manchurian Military and Administrative Committee as well as the area's party chief, was purged for opposing the APCs and for disagreeing with the party over allocation of investment funds for Manchuria. Similarly, Rao Xuzhi, chairperson of the East China Military and Administrative Committee and party chief, was purged for demanding a slower-paced introduction of the APCs into his area. It was alleged that both powerful regional leaders had attempted to solicit support from the military stationed in their respective areas. The six regional government bureaus and the six party bureaus were abolished following these purges.[9] The 1954 constitution specifically stipulated that China was to have a single form of government, with headquarters in Beijing. Under the constitution the provincial authorities were the agents of the central government, with limited power to implement and execute the plans and directives from the center.

The years 1953 to 1957 turned out to be a period of overcentralization, with excessive control over the provinces by the central authority in Beijing, particularly by those central functional ministries that proliferated under the First Five-Year Plan. All economic enterprises were placed under the direct control and management of the central ministries. Regulatory control devices were promulgated at the center, and all important decisions had to be made in Beijing. Even the acquisition of fixed property worth about one hundred dollars needed specific permission from the central ministry concerned.[10] This frequently resulted in delay and frustration in decision making. Even worse, the centralization of decision making resulted in ministerial "autarky." A ministry became an independent economic system that tightly controlled the supply of materials and the allocation of resources under its jurisdiction. Instead of regional, independent fiefdoms, there were centralized, ministerial, independent kingdoms which interfered with provincial and local administration, drew up ill-conceived plans, and made repeated revisions of the plans. This resulted in the neglect of priorities and the waste of raw materials.[11]

At the end of the First Five-Year Plan, the Chinese leaders made an agonizing reappraisal of their experience with the Stalinist model of development. In advocating the return to decentralization, Mao spoke out openly for the extension of power in the regions. In his 1956 speech on the ten major relations or contradictions, Mao criticized the central functional ministries' habit of issuing orders directly to their counterparts at the provincial and municipal levels without even consulting the State Council and the party's Central Committee. He pointed out that local interests must be given due consideration if the central authority is to be respected and strengthened at the provincial and local levels.[12]

While Mao was genuinely concerned about the excess of centralization and the loss of local and provincial initiative, he may have been motivated also by purely political considerations. Centralism had placed tremendous power in the centralized ministries and with the members of the State Council, who, from time to time, challenged Mao's policies and who were opposed to rapid collectivization. By advocating the return of power to the provinces, Mao would receive support from the provincially based political forces, which could serve as a counterweight in a showdown with the top party-government officials at the center.[13] Mao's view on the return to decentralization was evidently accepted by the party leadership: In the fall of 1956, it met to endorse the Second Five-Year Plan, which provided for local initiative and administration that would be appropriate to local needs and interests.

The Great Leap of 1958 marked the beginning of real efforts at decentralization. Under the decentralization policy, the provincial and local authorities were granted a variety of powers in the administration and management of economic enterprises. Control of enterprises in consumer goods industries was transferred from the Ministry of Light Industry to provincial authorities. While certain basic industries of economic importance, such as oil refining and mining, were still controlled by the central ministries, the provincial authorities were given some say in their operations. In the area of finances, the provincial and local governments gained considerable power. Under the decentralization plan of 1957, provincial and local authorities were granted their own sources of revenues from profits of local enterprises and taxes, freeing them from complete dependence on central government grants for their budgets. The provincial authorities were to retain 20 percent of the profits from the enterprises transferred to the local authorities and a share of local taxes on commodities, commercial transactions, and agriculture. The provinces were even allowed to levy new taxes and to issue bonds, as long as the methods were approved by the center. Even more important for the initiative and growth of the provinces, local authorities were allowed to rearrange or adjust production targets within the framework of the targets of the overall state plan.[14] Thus, in the latter part of the 1950s, the top leaders, including Mao, recognized that the provinces had a definite role to play in the top-level decision-making process. By 1956 Mao had formulated a set of guidelines to be applied in the debates over central versus local issues. A key provision of these guidelines was Mao's insistence that the center must consult the provinces: "It is the practice of the Central Committee of the Party to consult the local authorities; it never hastily issues orders without prior consultation."[15]

A direct consequence of the 1957 decentralization under the Great Leap was the emergence of the provinces as independent entities. The provinces behaved as though they were little "underdeveloped nations"; each wanted to build its own self-sufficient industrial complex.[16] The inevitable result of the weakened centralized ministerial supervision over economic activities in the provinces was the rapid growth of localism, with provincial leaders acquiring an economic power base that challenged the center on policies and programs. In addition to being the agents of the party at the center, the provincial party secretaries also became spokespersons for the particular interests of their own provinces.

With the failure of the Great Leap in 1959, the Central Committee enacted a recentralization program to strengthen the leadership of the center over the provincial leaders. In 1961 the regional bureaus were reestablished to supervise the provinces and to control their tendencies to become "subnational administrations."[17] These regional bureaus also were mandated to supervise the rectification campaign launched by the Liu Shaoqi group to purge the radicalized provincial party leaders who supported the Great Leap program.[18] The recentralization in the early 1960s did not return the center-local relationship to the pre-1957 status of overcentralization. Many of the powers granted to the provincial and local authorities during the Great Leap remained intact. However, the crucial functions of economic planning and coordination were largely returned to the central authority.[19] Provincial politics remained a very important force during the early 1960s. During the period from the end of the Great Leap in 1961 to the eve of the Cultural Revolution in 1966, the provincial leaders were active participants at regularized central work conferences—a form of enlarged meetings of the Politburo or the Central Committee. These meetings also included selected party leaders who were not members of the highest decision-making body.

There has been reduced tension in provincial-center relations since 1978. During the initial period of economic readjustment (1979–80), to be discussed in Chapter 8, the provinces were given considerable autonomy in foreign trade matters. Provinces were encouraged to expand their foreign trade by obtaining from Beijing the right to import from or export to foreign countries directly. It was common for trading corporations to be formed at the provincial level to participate in foreign trade. A number of provinces, Guangdong and Fujian in particular, were designated as special economic zones (SEZs) for foreign trade and were encouraged to enter into joint investment ventures with foreign concerns. This policy led to a scramble to export provincial products in many inland localities. Decentralization also gave rise to price cutting, bureaucratic game playing, and overlapping of responsibilities between and among provincial and local enterprises. Finally, the central authorities in Beijing had to revert to the policy of "balancing decentralization with unified planning,"[20] meaning more centralized control over provincial activities.

Tensions in Provincial-Center Relations

On the eve of the Cultural Revolution, the new center-provincial relationship showed signs of uneasiness as dissension within the top leadership deepened. Two major areas of tension were the allocation of resources and the types of economic activities to be carried on in the various provinces. For example, the party leader in the southern province of Guangdong was accused of promoting the development of a complete industrial complex for his province rather than concentrating on the development of light industries as dictated by the center.[21] On occasion, particular local conditions were used by provincial leaders as justification for resisting certain economic programs initiated by the center. Ganshu province used its backwardness as justification for not embarking on a rapid program of economic development.[22]

The degree of provincial autonomy or independence from the center varied, according to the province's share of China's total industrial and agricultural resources and the stature of the provincial leaders in the hierarchy of the party and the central government. Thus, provinces of the northeast, the massive industrial base in Manchuria, and the provinces of eastern and central China, with their commanding share of the resources, were in a better bargaining position when it came to allocation and distribution of these resources. For example, the southwestern province of Sichuan traditionally has been known as a difficult province for the center to govern because of its rich resources and its remoteness from Beijing. Li Qingchuan, the party leader in Sichuan before the Cultural Revolution, was an old revolutionary veteran with close supporters at the center. He was also the party secretary for the southwest region before the Cultural Revolution. He enjoyed considerable autonomy and independence in governing the province of Sichuan and the southwest region.[23] Ulanhu, a powerful member of the Politburo at the beginning of the Cultural Revolution who had long governed the affairs of Inner Mongolia, could be described as an overlord for the autonomous region. Ulanhu not only identified himself with, but banked on, local nationalism to provide local resistance to orders from the center during the Cultural Revolution.[24] Prior to their purges during the Cultural Revolution, both Li Qingchuan and Ulanhu had been brought into the decision-making process at the Central Committee level. After 1978 many provinces formed their own independent shipping services to Hong Kong, Japan, and Southeast Asia in order to avoid domestic transportation bottlenecks. One province in southwest China offered preferential tax incentives in order to attract contracts from foreign investors for exploration of the province's hydroelectric power resources and ore mines.[25] Provincial autonomy was also reflected in the language, messages, and issues articulated in political communications between the center at Beijing and the provinces.[26]

Provincial Representation at the Center

The turmoil of the Cultural Revolution created the need for an extensive "cooperative and consultative style of policy making" between the provinces and the center, to restore order as well as to reduce the tensions.[27] The cooperative role played by the provincial leaders during the Cultural Revolution had enhanced their position in relation to the center. By the time the Ninth Central Committee was formed in 1969, a significant percentage of provincial party secretaries had been elected to that body.

As Table 5.1 shows, the provincial leaders' link with the center was strengthened further by their increased representation as full members on the Eleventh (1977) Central Committee—from 36 percent to 43 percent. When Hua Guofeng was the new party chief and premier of the central government, he sought a balance in the relationship between the provinces and the center. He cautioned about the tendency of the central departments and ministries to hamper local initiatives, but at the same time warned against the tendency of

TABLE 5.1　Provincial and Municipal Party Secretaries Serving On the Tenth Through Twelfth Central Committees

Position in Provincial/Municipal Party Committees	Central Committee					
	Full Members			Alternate Members		
	10th (195)	11th (201)	12th (210)	10th (124)	11th (132)	12th (138)
Provincial First Secretaries	22	24	42	7	0	0
Lesser Provincial Secretaries	49	62	30	22	31	46
Total Provincial Secretaries	71	86	72	29	31	46
Provincial Secretaries Percent of Total	36%	43%	34%	23%	23%	33%

Source: Beijing Review, *14 (April 4, 1969), 9,* Beijing Review, *35, and 36 (September 7, 1973), 9–10; and* Beijing Review, *35 (August 26, 1977), 14–16. Figures for the Twelfth Central Committee are culled from* Issues and Studies, *vol. xviii, no. 11 (November 1982), 26–45.*

the provinces and regions to "attend only to their own individual interests to the neglect of the unified state plan."[28]

The power of provincial representatives on the Twelfth Central Committee (1982) decreased. While the number of provincial secretaries serving as alternate members rose 10 percent (from thirty-one to forty-six) the number serving as full members declined 9 percent (from eighty-six to seventy-two). The actual number of provincial representatives remained essentially the same, but more members were relegated to alternate membership. The decline of provincial party secretaries serving as full Central Committee members perhaps can be explained by the larger percentage of central party–governmental administrators, technical specialists, and academicians, who comprised 46 percent of the total full membership of the Central Committee elected in 1982. However, it should be noted that the provincial party secretaries and governors represented the single largest group on the Twelfth Central Committee.

LOCAL GOVERNMENTS IN CHINA

The County Government[29]

Below the province is the administrative unit called the county, or xien. There are approximately 2,000 counties in China; each has a population of about half a million or less. The people's government is elected by the people's congress and supervised by the standing committee at the county level, which administers a host of local government activities. First, the county government exercises control over the personnel assignments for the entire county. In this manner the party manages to keep an eye on all the cadres working for the various units of county government. It is at the seat of the county that a people's court hears and handles serious cases of deviance. It is at the county level that we find the procuratorate operating when serious crimes are to be prosecuted. It is also at the county level that the public security bureau maintains a station for the surveillance of the county populace and for arresting criminals and counterrevolutionaries. Militia activities and relations with the regular PLA are handled at the county level.

The Township as a Local Government Unit[30]

The lowest level of government used to be the commune. In China there are about 75,000 communes, varying in number of households and the total acreage under production. Each commune is organized into production brigades and teams.

A typical production team has from 100 to 200 members and is subdivided into work groups. The work groups are led by team cadres, who are seldom members of the party. The team members elect a committee to conduct the team's affairs. Frequently, group leaders are placed on the nomination slate and elected to the committee. We should note that the slate of candidates for the committee election must be approved by the party cell. The team serves as the basic accounting unit on the commune. Team committee members are assigned specific jobs, such as treasurer, accountant, work-points recorder, or security officer. The most important are the accountant and work-points recorder, who must keep detailed books on expenditures and income and on team members' earned work points, respectively. The work points usually range from zero to ten, with an able-bodied adult earning between eight and nine points per unit of time worked. The number of work points earned by a team member for a unit of time worked is determined at the beginning of each year by a meeting of all team members. Each member makes a claim to this worth. This claim is evaluated by the assembled team members and a decision is reached on the points to be earned for each member for the coming year.

An average production brigade consists of five or six production teams—over 1,000 people. Each production brigade has an elected people's congress, whose main responsibility is to elect a brigade chief and a revolutionary committee to assist the chief in administering the brigade's daily affairs. Frequently, the brigade chief is also chairperson of the revolutionary committee as well as the party secretary. The revolutionary committee and its staff are responsible for managing economic and financial affairs, including planning, budgeting, record keeping, and accounting. The committee is also in charge of providing social welfare, and medical and educational services. Brigades with the use of agricultural machinery also maintain repair service units. In a number of communes visited by the author, a small-scale research and development unit was attached to the brigade's revolutionary committee.

From 1958 until 1982, the commune officially served two functions: It was the grassroots government below the county level, and the collective economic management unit. This combination of government administrative and economic management functions created a number of problems.[31] Many of the problems stemmed from the overconcentration of decision-making powers in the hands of a few commune leaders. Particularly troublesome was the interference of the commune, in its role as governmental administrator, in the activities of the production teams. Zhao Ziyang's experiments with local government in three counties in Sichuan province indicated that the separation of government administration from economic management in communes improved both economic activity and "the peoples' democratic life."[32] Specifically, the new local structure for the rural areas permitted a greater degree of independent management of the rural economy. Formerly, the cadres at the commune centers held too many positions; it was practically impossible for them to devote much of their limited energy to economic activities. Too often these commune cadres had to spend most of their time supervising governmental affairs—such as planning, finances, and taxation for the communes—with insufficient time left to supervise production. In addition, there was a pressing need for a separate and more effective local government organization to discharge responsibilities in the areas of dispute mediation, public security maintenance, tax collection, and welfare distribution in rural areas.

The 1982 constitution reestablished the township government that existed before 1958 as the local grassroots government and limited the commune system to the status of an economic management unit. Under the new local government arrangement, the township people's congress elects the township people's government. Administration of law, education, public health, and family planning are the exclusive responsibilities of the township people's government. As of January 1983, sixty-nine counties in thirteen provinces, including the municipality of Beijing, have instituted experiments to transfer the local governmental functions from the communes to the townships.

Local Government
in the Urban Areas

There are two types of municipalities in China. One type includes the important urban centers—Beijing, Shanghai, and Tianjin—administered directly by the central government. The other type includes subdivisions of the provincial governments.

The municipal government of a city like Beijing or Guangzhou is administered by the municipal people's government, elected by the municipal people's congress. As a municipal government, the people's government for the city must supervise a large number of functional departments or bureaus dealing with law and order, finance, trade, economic enterprises, and industries located within the city limits. We also find in these cities subdivisions of state organs, such as the people's court, the procuratorate, and the public security bureau for social control and law and order. Because of the size of some of the larger municipalities, the administration of the municipal government is subdivided into districts. The municipality of Beijing, with a total population of more than 7 million, is divided into ten districts as administrative subunits. Each district has a district people's congress, which elects a district people's government as the executive organ for district affairs.

Within each district of a city are numerous neighborhood committees, which are—in the words of the 1982 constitution—"mass organizations of self-management at the grassroots level" (Article III, Appendix A). More than 1,794 neighborhood committees in Beijing city serve as arms of district government within the city. Each neighborhood committee has a staff of trained cadres whose work is to mobilize and provide political education for the residents in the area. Generally, a neighborhood committee has 2,500 to 3,000 residents.

The neighborhood committees perform a variety of functions, including organizing workers, teachers, and students in the neighborhood for political study and work; organizing and managing small factories in the neighborhood; providing social welfare services, such as nurseries and dining halls, to supplement those provided by the cities; and administering health, educational, and cultural programs. They also perform surveillance activities in cooperation with the public security units in the area.[33]

Neighborhood committees are the self-governing units organized and staffed voluntarily by the residents. A typical neighborhood committee has about twenty families, or approximately one hundred persons. It is generally headed by an elderly or retired woman, and it can deal with any matter of concern to the residents. It is common in the cities to find that a neighborhood committee is linked to a city hospital for family planning or birth control: The neighborhood committee disseminates information about the need for family planning. Meetings of all residents decide how to allocate the allowable births and who may have them.

ETHNIC POLITICS: AUTONOMOUS REGIONS AND NATIONAL MINORITIES

One of the interesting things about China is that it too has a minority problem. Like many of China's policies on major political, economic, and social matters, policies toward ethnic minorities also were subject to the periodic pendulum swings of the past two decades. This section will discuss the development of China's policies on national minorities and the reasons for policy changes, the status of autonomous regions, and minority group representation in party and government.

First, a few essential facts about China's national minorities are in order. There are about 67 million people in China who are considered to be national minorities. The largest of the fifty-five minority groups are the Zhuangs (13.3 million), Hui or Chinese Muslims (7.2 million), Uygur (5.9 million), Yi (5.4 million), Tibetans (3.8 million), Miao (5.0 million), Manchus (4.3 million), Mongols (3.4 million), Bouyei (2.1 million), and Koreans (1.7 million).[34] Although these minority groups—the non-Han people—total only 67 million, or 7 percent of China's population, they inhabit almost 60 percent of China's territory, covering sixteen different provinces. In two autonomous regions, Xizang and Inner Mongolia, the minority people constitute the majority. An extremely important element in understanding China's policies toward minorities is that over 90 percent of China's border areas with neighboring countries are inhabited by these minority people. When we discuss the border dispute between China and the Soviet Union, we inevitably are reminded that the disputed areas are inhabited by the Manchus, Mongolians, Uygurs, Kazakh, and Koreans. China's relations with Laos, Cambodia, and Vietnam bring to mind the minority people of Zhuang, Yi, Miao, and Bouyei in the autonomous region of Guangxi and provinces of Yunnan, and Guizhou. The border dispute between India and China involves the Tibetans living in Chinese territory in Xizang, Sichuan, and Qinghai. Changes in China's minority policies in recent years have been influenced to a large extent by concern for the security of her border areas.[35]

When the Chinese People's Republic was established in October 1949, the regime followed a policy which can best be described as one of gradualism and pluralism. Primarily for the purpose of a united front to consolidate control of the nation immediately after the civil war, minority customs and habits were tolerated in regions inhabited by minorities. Compromises were made to include as political leaders prominent minority elites of feudal origin in the newly formed autonomous areas for the minority nationalities. At the same time, modern transportation and communication networks were constructed to link the autonomous regions with the adjacent centers of political and economic power populated by the Chinese. The nomadic Mongols in pastoral areas were exempt from the application of land reform measures. The concept and practices of class struggle, so prevalent in other parts of China, were purposefully muted when applied to minority regions. However, no serious attempts were made to assimilate the national minorities into the main throes of the revolutionary movement in other parts of China.

The period of the Great Leap ushered in a rapid change in policies toward the national minorities. From 1956 to 1968, the policy shifted from gradualism and pluralism to one of radical assimilation. For the first time, the Chinese spoken language was introduced in the minority areas. Training of minority cadres was intensified. More important, socialist reforms such as cooperatives and communization were introduced. The campaign against the rightists was also extended in the minority areas, aimed at those who advocated local nationalism. These policies of assimilation resulted in tension and violent clashes in the early 1960s between the Hans (Chinese) and the minority groups, particularly in Xizang and Xinjiang. It was precisely because of these disturbances in the minority areas that the assimilation programs were relaxed in the mid-1960s, prior to the Cultural Revolution. Radicalized communization programs in certain minority areas were disbanded. The slowdown did not last long. The Cultural Revolution brought back the radical line of assimilation for minority groups. Many prominent minority leaders in the border areas were subject to purges and vilification by the Red Guards, who were encouraged by the radicals. Ulanhu, of Inner Mongolia; Li Qingchuan, of Xizang; and Wang Enmao, of Xinjiang, were purged by the time the Cultural Revolution ran its full course (1966–68).[36] But the Sino-Soviet border dispute, according to Lucian Pye, made the Chinese realize the necessity of winning over the minority groups for reasons of national security.[37] The policy of assimilation was again modified to provide for diversity. In addition to having minority nationalities learn Chinese, the Chinese cadres were asked to learn the minority languages. Minority customs, dress, music, and dance were encouraged as expressions of ethnic diversity. It was within this policy of pluralism and diversity in the post-Cultural Revolution era that we began to see an increase in the representation of China's minority groups in party and government organs.

Both the constitution of 1954 and its revisions in 1978 and 1982 provided identical detailed provisions for self-government in autonomous regions, in marked contrast to the brevity of such provisions in the 1975 constitution. This can be interpreted as a return to the policy of pluralism and gradualism. The people's congresses, as local organs of self-government for the autonomous regions, can make specific regulations in light of the special characteristics of the national minorities in these areas. This concept of diversity and pluralism was not mentioned in the 1975 constitution. In addition, the 1954, 1978, and 1982 constitutions mandated that local organs of self-government in these minority areas employ their own ethnic language in the performance of their duties. This represents a marked departure from past policies of assimilation, which urged the use of the Chinese language, both written and spoken, as the official medium of communication.

There has been increased recognition of minority groups in both the party and the government. Special efforts evidently were made to recruit new party members from the minority regions. We have figures which show that from 1964 to 1973, over 140,000 new members from the minority areas were admitted into the party.[38] There is no precise breakdown of party membership distribution over the various autonomous regions, but there appears to have been a steady increase in party membership. Three minority leaders (Wei Guoqing, a Zhuang; Seypidin, an Uygur; and Ulanhu, a Mongol) were elected to the presidium of the Eleventh Party Congress, and thirteen minority representatives were elected to the Eleventh Central Committee (seven full and six alternate members). Thirteen national minority leaders representing eight national minority groups were elected to full membership of the Twelfth Central Committee in 1982. Sixteen other minority leaders were elected to alternate membership. National minority leaders have held key government positions in various autonomous regions. For example, the chairpersons of the standing committees of the people's congresses for the autonomous regions of Xinjiang, Tibet, Guangxi, and Ningxia were leading cadres of national minorities.[39] At the national level, Ulanhu, a Mongol, was elected to the vice-presidency of the republic in June 1983. Similarly, the Fifth National People's Congress, which promulgated the 1978 constitution, had 11 percent of its deputies drawn from the fifty-five national minority groups. At least four of the minority leaders (Wei Guoqing, Ulanhu, Seypidin, and Ngapo Ngawang-jigme) were elected as vice-chairpersons of the congress. Thus, after more than two decades of policy vacillation in search of an appropriate formula for dealing with the minority groups in the border areas, China seems to have found a solution which stresses the preservation of the cultural diversity of the 67 million national minority peoples and at the same time opens up channels for minority participation in decision making at the highest levels in the Chinese political process.

In recent years a great amount of world attention has been focused on Tibet as one of China's most troubled autonomous regions.[40] In 1980 Hu Yaobang, the party chief, and Wan Li, a member of the party's Central Secretariat, made an inspection tour of Tibet. Then, in the summer of 1982, the Chinese announced that 11,000 Chinese (Han) cadres would be withdrawn gradually from Tibet to permit the native Tibetans to take over and manage their own affairs. The immediate objective of this new self-government policy for Tibet was to replace more than two-thirds of Tibet's governmental functionaries with native Tibetans by 1983.[41] Ngapo Ngawang-jigme, chairman of the Tibetan Autonomous Regional government, indicated that more than 12,000 Tibetans were being trained to take over the administration of Tibetan affairs from the Chinese cadres.[42] As of 1981 there were 29,400 Tibetan cadres in the autonomous regional government, comprising 54 percent of the total.[43] Other changes for Tibet included the abrogation of certain regulations imposed on the region that were deemed unsuitable to Tibetan conditions. In addition, farm and animal products were to be exempt from taxation for two years. More state funds were to be allocated for Tibet to improve the economy and living conditions in the region.[44]

The policy changes in Tibet must be viewed in the context of China's continuing attempt to persuade the Dalai Lama to return to Lhasa after more than fourteen years of exile in India.[45] The Dalai Lama, the religious and political leader of the traditional Tibetan theocracy, escaped to India after Chinese troops marched into Tibet in 1959 to put down a rebellion. Since his escape, the Dalai Lama has been joined by over 100,000 Tibetan refugees who refused to live under Chinese rule. The Dalai Lama's exile and his continuing criticism of Chinese misrule in Tibet has been an embarrassment for Beijing. Since 1978 the Chinese official position has been to relax its control over Tibet with the hope that the Dalai Lama might be persuaded to return. However, his holiness has shrewdly used the Chinese desire to seek reconciliation, manipulating it as a bargaining chip to obtain concessions for his people. He has remained abroad to speak out against Chinese rule in Tibet and has delivered lectures in numerous countries to arouse world opinion in favor of Tibetan causes.[46] In 1982 a three-member delegation was dispatched by the Dalai Lama to Beijing, after the 1980 visit by the Dalai Lama's sister, to negotiate possible terms for reconciliation with China's new leaders. So far no tangible progress has been made in these negotiations. The Dalai Lama was reported to have proposed (1) that Tibet should not be treated as an autonomous region but should be given a special status with complete autonomy; and (2) that a larger Tibet should be created to include Tibetans now living in southeast China.[47] The Chinese did not accept these proposals, and the impasse continued. In the meantime, the Chinese have made further concessions by allowing pilgrimages to the lamaseries and the use of the Tibetan language in schools. Lately, the Dalai Lama told Western reporters that he would like to pay a visit to Tibet by 1985.[48]

Let us conclude this discussion by returning to the theme expressed at the beginning of this section: China's policy toward its national minorities has been to a large extent dictated by the strategic considerations vis-à-vis her relations with neighboring countries. China's policy toward Tibet must be viewed in the context of its strategic importance in China's relations with the Soviet Union and India.[49]

NOTES

1. "Explanations on the Draft of the Revised Constitution of the PRC," 25–26.

2. Feng Wenbin, "Reforming the Political Structure," *Beijing Review,* 4 (January 26, 1981), 18.

3. Hua Guofeng, "Report on the Work of the Government," 23–24. Also see "Amendments to the Constitution," *Beijing Review,* 28 (July 13, 1979), 10.

4. "Amendments to the Constitution," p. 10.

5. Peng Zhen, "Explanations on Seven Laws," *Beijing Review,* 28 (July 13, 1979), 9.

6. See Dorothy J. Solinger, *Regional Government and Political Integration in Southwest China, 1949–1954: A Case Study* (Berkeley: University of California Press, 1977), p. vii. Also see "Politics in Yunnan Province in the Decade of Disorder: Elite Factional Strategies and Central-Local Relations, 1967–1980," *The China Quarterly,* 92 (December 1982), 628–62.

7. George Cressey, *Asia's Lands and Peoples* (New York: McGraw-Hill, 1951), pp. 96–165.

8. Schurmann, *Ideology and Organization,* p. 214.

9. For an account of the purge of Gao and Rao, see Jurgen Domes, "Party Politics and the Cultural Revolution," pp. 64–65; Edward E. Rice, *Mao's Way* (Berkeley, Calif.: University of California Press, 1972), pp. 130–32; Albert Ravenholt, "Feud Among the Red Mandarins," American University Field Service, East Asia Series, (February 1954); Chang, *Power and Policy in China,* pp. 47–48; Jurgen Domes, *The Internal Politics of China* (New York: Holt, Rinehart & Winston, 1973), pp. 24–25.

10. Chang, *Power and Policy in China,* p. 50.

11. Chang, *Power and Policy in China,* p. 51; and Audrey Donnithorne, *China's Economic System* (London: Allen and Unwin, 1967), p. 460.

12. The text of "On the Ten Major Relations" is to be found in *Peking Review,* 1 (January 1, 1977), 16, and *Selected Works of Mao Tse-tung,* vol. v (Peking: Foreign Language Press, 1977), p. 293.

13. Chang, *Power and Policy in China,* pp. 52–53.

14. For a detailed discussion on the powers granted to the provinces, see Chang, *Power and Policy in China,* pp. 55–61; and Victor C. Falkenheim, "Decentralization Revisited: A Maoist Perspective," *Current Scene,* vol. xvi, no. 1 (January 1978), 1–5.

15. "On the Ten Major Relations," in *Selected Works of Mao Tse-tung,* vol. v, p. 293.

16. Schurmann, *Ideology and Organization,* p. 210.

17. Ibid.

18. See Chang, *Power and Policy in China,* pp. 129–30.

19. Ibid., pp. 144–45.

20. *China Trade Report,* March 1981, p. 8.

21. See Frederick C. Teiwes, "Provincial Politics in China: Themes and Variations," in

John Lindbeck, ed., *Management of a Revolutionary Society* (Seattle, Wash.: University of Washington Press, 1971), pp. 126–27.

22. Ibid.

23. See Thomas Jay Mathews, "The Cultural Revolution in Szechwan," in *The Cultural Revolution in the Provinces* (Cambridge, Mass.: Harvard University Press, 1971), pp. 94–146.

24. See Paul Hyer and William Heaton, "The Cultural Revolution in Inner Mongolia," *The China Quarterly*, 36 (October–December 1968), 114–28.

25. Vigor Keung Fang, "Chinese Region Offers Lures to Foreign Investors," *Asian Wall Street Journal Weekly*, December 21, 1981, p. 6.

26. Lewis M. Stern, "Politics Without Consensus: Center-Province Relations and Political Communication in China, January 1976–January 1977," *Asian Survey*, vol. xix, no. 3 (March 1979), 260–80.

27. Falkenheim, "Decentralization Revisited: A Maoist Perspective," p. 7.

28. Hua Kuo-feng, "Unite and Strive to Build a Modern, Powerful Socialist Country!" *Peking Review*, 10 (March 10, 1978), 25.

29. Information on the local government structure and functions is based on Barnett, *Cadres, Bureaucracy, and Political Power in Communist China;* Chu Li and Tien Chien-yun, *Inside a People's Commune* (Peking: Foreign Language Press, 1975); personal notes of my visits to China in 1972–73 and 1978; and "Our Neighborhood Revolutionary Committee," *China Reconstructs*, vol. xxii, no. 8 (August 1973), 2–3.

30. Barnett, *Cadres, Bureaucracy, and Political Power in Communist China;* Li and Chien-yun, *Inside a People's Commune;* personal notes of my visits to China; and "Our Neighborhood Revolutionary Committee."

31. "Important Changes in the System of People's Communes," *Beijing Review*, 29 (April 19, 1982), 13–15.

32. Ibid; and 13–15 "Reestablishment of Township Experimented in Sichuan," *Ta Kung Pao Weekly Supplement* (Hong Kong), June 17, 1982, p. 2.

33. "Our Neighborhood Revolutionary Committee," p. 3; "City Dwellers and the Neighborhood Committee," *Beijing Review*, 44 (November 3, 1980), 19–25; and John Roderick, "Kumming Housewife Helps Govern China," reprinted in *Honolulu Star Bulletin*, October 29, 1981, p. 8.

34. Figures here are based on *Beijing Review*, 21 (May 23, 1983), 19–20. Also see "China's Minority Peoples," *Beijing Review*, 6 (February 9, 1979), 17–21. The State Council in June 1979 recognized the Jinuo people, numbering over 10,000 in Yunnan province in the southwest, as the 55th national minority. See *Beijing Review*, 25 (June 22, 1979), 5–6.

35. Lucian W. Pye, "China: Ethnic Minorities and National Security," *Current Scene: Developments in the People's Republic of China*, vol. xiv, no. 12 (December 1976), 7–10.

36. For an account of the change of policies toward the minority groups from 1957–69, see Dreyer, *China's Forty Millions* (Cambridge, Mass.: Harvard University Press, 1976), pp. 140–259; "China's Quest for a Socialist Solution," *Problems of Communism*, xxiv (September–October 1975), 49–62: Pye, "China: Ethnic Minorities," pp. 5–11; and Hung-mao Tien, "Sinicization of National Minorities in China," *Current Scene*, vol. xii, no. 11 (November 1974), 1–14.

37. Pye, "China: Ethnic Minorities," pp. 9–10.

38. "New Party Members—A Dynamic Force," *Peking Review*, 27 (July 6, 1973), 6–7.

39. "Minority Leader Cadres in Various Provinces and Autonomous Regions," *Beijing Review*, 10 (March 10, 1980), 23.

40. For recent news about Tibet, see the following issues of the *Beijing Review:* 40 (October 4, 1982), 5–7; 46 (November 15, 1982), 3–4; 47 (November 22, 1982), 15–18; 48 (November 29, 1982), 14–17; 49 (December 6, 1982), 21–24; 50 (December 13, 1982), 28–29; and 51 (December 20, 1982), 37–38.

41. "New Principles for Building up Tibet," *Beijing Review*, 24 (June 16, 1980), 3.

42. "Latest Development in Tibet," *Beijing Review*, 25 (June 21, 1982), 19.

43. "Tibet: An Inside View II," *Beijing Review*, 48 (November 29, 1982), 14.

44. "New Economic Policy for Tibet," *Beijing Review*, 27 (July 7, 1980), 4; and Ngapoi Jigme, "Great Historical Changes in Tibet," *Beijing Review*, 22 (June 1, 1981), 17–19.

45. "Situation in Tibet," *Beijing Review*, 31 (August 2, 1982), 6. Also see Harrison E. Salisbury, "Return of Dalai Lama to Tibet is Expected Soon," *The New York Times*, August 31, 1980, p. 11; Liu Heung Shing, "China Pulling Officials from Tibet," Associated Press, reprinted in *Honolulu Star-Bulletin*, August 12, 1982, C-5; and David Chen, "Dalai Lama Team

Plans Visit to Tibet,'' *South China Morning Post* (Hong Kong), April 24, 1982, p. 1; Christopher S. Wren, ''Chinese Trying to Undo Damage in Tibet,'' *The New York Times,* May 31, 1983, A-1, A-8.

46. This was made very clear to the author in a rare luncheon with the Dalai Lama when he came to Hawaii to dedicate a Tibetan temple in Woods Valley on October 28, 1980.

47. ''Policy Towards Dalai Lama,'' *Beijing Review,* 46 (November 15, 1982), 3.

48. See Michael Ross, ''Tibet's Dalai Lama Ponders Return,'' United Press International, as reprinted in *Honolulu Advertiser,* August 18, 1983, A-19.

49. See Dawa Norbu, ''Strategic Development in Tibet: Implications for Its Neighbors,'' *Asian Survey,* vol. xix, no. 3 (March 1979), 245-59.

The Military's Role

in Chinese Politics

Chinese politics has been complicated by the participation of the military establishment at both the central and the provincial levels. In fact, following the Cultural Revolution, the military assumed the dominant political role in the local levels of government. In this chapter we shall examine first the structure of the PLA, focusing on the regional and provincial military commands as important factors in China's provincial politics; and second, the military's political role, with particular emphasis on the Cultural Revolution and its aftermath.

ORGANIZATION OF THE PEOPLE'S LIBERATION ARMY

The 1975 and 1978 constitutions stipulated that the chairperson of the CCP was to be commander in chief of the armed forces and that this individual would control the military through the CCP's Military Affairs Committee. The 1982 constitution provided a new Central Military Commission—responsible only to the National People's Congress—to direct the country's armed forces (see Articles 93–94 in Appendix A). This was a significant departure from the past in that the Chinese armed forces had always been under the control of the party. The 1982 constitution seemed to say that the armed forces now belonged to the nation, even though the party continued to exercise its leadership over the military.[1] The respective jurisdictions of the party's Military Affairs Commission and the new state Central Military Commission, however, are not clear. Politburo member Hu Qiaomu explained to the New China News Agency that there would be no parallel central military commissions.[2] At the Sixth NPC (June 1983), Deng Xiaoping was elected chairperson of the new Central Military Commission; he concurrently chaired the party's Military Affairs Commission. In effect, he became China's supreme commander for the armed forces. The minister of defense, who operates under the State Council and the premier, is the administrative head of the PLA. Under the defense minister is the chief of staff for the PLA General Headquarters in Beijing, who is responsible for the execution and coordination of combat operations of all the services and commands. The PLA General Headquarters has a general logistics and procurement service. The party exercises its ideological and political control over the armed forces through the General Political Department. The GPD, as it is called, is responsible for the party cells within the PLA and propaganda, education, and cultural activities of the troops. Under the General Staff Office, the various service arms, such as the air force, naval headquarters, engineer corps, railway corps, armored command, and artillery, maintain their central headquarters for supervision of the armed forces.

At the regional level, the approximately 3.5 million troops are organized under the thirteen military regions, twenty-three provincial military districts, and nine garrison commands for principal population centers (see Table 6.1). Elements of the PLA are assigned to these regions and districts on an almost

TABLE 6.1   Force Structure of the Chinese People's
            Liberation Army, 1978–79

Ground Forces
   115 infantry divisions
   11 armored divisions
   3 airborne divisions
   40 artillery divisions
   16 railway and construction divisions
   150 independent regiments
Naval Forces
   68 "Whiskey"- and "Romeo"-class submarines
   2 "Ming"-class submarines
   1 "Golf"-class submarine
   1 "Han"-class (nuclear-powered) submarine
   7 Luta-class destroyers (with STYX SSM)
   4 Gorky-class destroyers (with STYX SSM)
   18 frigates
   19 patrol escorts
Air Forces
   90 TU–16 bombers
   300 IL–28 bombers
   3,700 MiG–17s and MiG–19s (in fighter units)
   80 MiG–21s (in fighter units)
   Some F–9s (in fighter units)
   500 MiG–15s and F–9s (in fighter-bomber service)
   350 helicopters (all types)
Nuclear Forces
   2 CSS–3 (limited-range ICBM, 3,500 miles)
   30–40 IRBM
   30–40 MRBM

Source: *International Institute for Strategic Studies, The
Military Balance, 1979–1980, London, 1979.*
Angus M. Fraser, *"Military Modernization in China,"* Problems of Communism, *xxviii (September–December 1979), 38.*

permanent basis. For instance, troops for the Shenyang Military Region are stationed almost permanently in the northeast and are responsible for the defense of the northeastern provinces of Jilin, Liaoning, and Heilongjiang—each of the three is a military district by itself. In addition, the most heavily populated city in the northeast—Shenyang—is a garrison command, which is in charge of all ground, air, and naval forces in the area. The Shenyang Garrison Command reports directly to the Shengyang Military Region. The autonomous region of Inner Mongolia, like Xizang and Xinjiang, is a military region. Because of the tension and open clashes along the Ussuri and Amur Rivers on the Sino-Soviet border, the Inner Mongolian Military Region is now under the direct jurisdiction of the Beijing Garrison Command. Increased importance has been attached to the Inner Mongolian Military Region at Urumqi for the defense and security of western and northwestern China. So long as Sino-Soviet border disputes remain unresolved, and so long as Muslim unrest in Xinjiang continues,[3] the Inner Mongolian Military Region and the Sheng-yang Military region will remain crucial in China's national defense and security.

Each military region has a regional military commander and at least a political commissar (see Table 6.3). Sometimes the military commander for the region simultaneously holds the post of political commissar. Regional military commanders and commissars can be shifted from region to region or can be promoted up to the central headquarters in Beijing. Provincial military district commanders report to their respective regional commands, which in turn delegate responsibilities for local administrative, logistical, recruitment, and mobilization matters to the districts. In addition, the military commands in the provinces and garrison commands in large cities are responsible for maintaining law and order, as was so vividly demonstrated during the Cultural Revolution.

A close relationship between the regional military commands and the civil authorities in the provinces dates back to the days of the civil war against the Guomindang, when the armies operated in a specific region of the country. During the guerrilla days, the field armies were divided into five major groupings to provide civil and military administration for the regions they occupied: the First Field Army under the command of Marshal Peng Dehuai in the northwest region, the Second Field Army under Marshal Liu Bocheng in the southwest region, the Third Field Army under Marshal Chen Yi in east China, the Fourth Field Army under Marshal Lin Biao in the central and southern regions, and the Fifth Field Army under Marshal Nie Rongzhen in the north and northeast regions.[4]

The close link between the military and civil authorities in the provinces was cemented by the use of the military control commission.[5] The military control commission was a device used to take over administrative functions from the defeated Guomindang government during the gradual transition from civil war to normalcy. Each liberated town, county, and city was placed under a military control commission, established by the commanders of the newly arrived field army units. The ranking military officer for a particular locality held concurrently the leading position in the military control commission and the top political administrative post for the local government. Local administrative machinery, schools, factories, economic enterprises, and communications were placed under the jurisdiction of the military control commission. On the regional level, congruent with the six major administrative regions, were the six military regions under the control of the field armies. The highest organ of government in these regions was the regional military control commission. The chairperson of the regional military control commission was the senior military officer in charge of the military region and the field army headquarters.

While dissolution of military control began in 1953 and was completed in 1954, the close link between the military and the regional, provincial, and local authorities continued. To a large extent, these field army units remained stationed mostly in these areas, although after the Lin Biao affair in 1973, there was a reshuffling of some officers. Following the Korean War, most units sent to the front were reassigned to the regions from which they had been recruited.[6] Today local military commands still maintain local ties and concerns which have been established through the years and which are shared by the local civil authorities.

The field army system has been seen by some scholars as a partial explanation for factionalism in the military. They see the elite field army systems competing with each other for power and for representation of their regions.[7] Other scholars have found very little evidence, within the field army system, of political powerplays or of competition for assignments to the various military regions.[8] At any event, it must be kept in mind that the Military Affairs Committee directly controls a main or central force, as distinct from regional forces, of about sixteen army corps. These units can be employed under direct orders from the central authorities in Beijing.

THE PEOPLE'S MILITIA

The militia was founded during the Jiangxi soviet days as an elitist organization to augment the Red Army and guerrilla units. During the civil war period, the militia's strength was not more than 8 or 10 percent of the total population under communist control. The people's militia have undergone six distinct stages of development since the establishment of the People's Republic in 1949.[9]

After liberation and during the Korean War, the activities of the militia were expanded to include maintenance of law and order, participation in joint defense measures with the PLA forces in border areas, and the spearheading of land reform activities.[10] This expansion of militia activities in no way altered its basic character as an elite force subordinated to the PLA command and discipline.

The people's militia acquired a new role with increased status when the people's commune and the Great Leap Forward programs were launched during 1958–59. The militia became a nationwide mass movement: It was integrated into the structure of the communes in the countryside and grew enormously to approximately 220 million by 1959. Under the concept of "everyone a soldier," members of the communes simultaneously engaged in agriculture, industry, trade, and military work. The militia became the vehicle for mass mobilization for collective action as military organizational techniques and discipline were incorporated into the communes.[11] During this period the PLA had at first to share, and then gradually to relinquish, its authority and control over the militia to the communes and the party leadership within the communes. Simultaneously, the militia's status was elevated to a position coequal with that of the PLA in defending the countryside against possible enemy attack. These power shifts signaled the party's dissatisfaction with the army's desire to seek modernization in the midst of radicalized crash programs, and generated resentment and hostility within the PLA. At this stage of development, the notion of the militia as a countervailing force to the regular army had not yet surfaced.

In early 1960, following the failure of the Great Leap, substantial changes were made in the militia's role.[12] The militia's priorities were reordered to place productive tasks before military training. To ensure responsible behavior of the militia and its cadres and to curb its wide-ranging activities, overall control of the militia's structure and training was returned to the PLA provincial and district commands. From 1960 to 1961, the militia was under tight political control and both its size and its activities were curtailed.[13]

On the eve of the Cultural Revolution, efforts were made to strengthen the political education of the militia so that it could become an instrument for political struggle. In 1967, during the midst of the Cultural Revolution, the army journal—then under the control of the radicals—defined the militia not only as "a partner and assistant to the PLA" but as "an important instrument for the dictatorship of the proletariat and a revolutionary weapon of the masses." The militia was asked to work with the regular army and the public security forces to suppress and smash the reactionaries and revisionists who wanted to restore capitalism.[14] The nature of the militia's participation in the Cultural Revolution, however, was largely dependent upon the stand taken by the local party authority and the PLA units in a given locality. In most rural areas, the local militia functioned as an integral part of the established party apparatus. When the authority of the party became disrupted as a result of the upheaval, the militia organization also became disrupted, or simply vanished. In other instances the local militia organization and personnel, which had established close ties with the county or municipal party committees, gave support to the established authorities in a showdown. We have well-documented case studies of the role played by the military and the militia in the provinces and cities, illustrating local armed resistance against the central authority during the Cultural Revolution.[15]

The Sino-Soviet border clashes in 1969 served as the primary reason to reactivate and strengthen the militia.[16] The campaign for war preparedness also revived charges against Liu Shaoqi and Peng Dehuai for their alleged inattention to the building up of the militia and for their overemphasis on development of a professional and modernized army. Many work conferences were held during 1969–70. A constant theme at these conferences, as laid down by Chairman Mao, was that organizational control of the militia must be placed under the local party committees because they had a better grasp of the role of the militia in a "people's war."[17] To ensure the party's control over the militia, party committee members at the local level were designated to serve as leading cadres of the militia. Only party members could serve as commanders of the militia. Since the role of the militia was to assist the regular armed forces in defending against foreign incursion, the PLA Chief of Staff Office was responsible for developing a system that would utilize and manage militia weapons.[18]

The urban militia, as mentioned briefly in Chapter 1, was formed in 1973 by the radicals for the ostensible purpose of providing auxiliary service in case of foreign aggression. It soon became apparent that the real purpose of the urban militia was to provide the radicals with an "armed force"—a politically reliable instrument among the industrial workers in urban centers—for use in the political struggle for power.[19] Since the radical leaders, such as Zhang Chunqiao and Wang Hongwen, did not trust the political reliability of the regular PLA armed forces, an independent command structure was set up to direct the activities of the urban militia. In Shanghai, Beijing, Guangzhou, and Tianjin, the command headquarters of the workers' militia were headed by leaders identified with the trade union federations in those cities. Both the urban militia and the trade union federations were under the control of the municipal party committees, which were bastions of the radicals. The Shanghai urban militia was singled out by the radical-controlled mass media as a model for others to emulate. Although the alleged coup plan of the Shanghai radicals who opposed Hua Guofeng's appointment as successor to Mao never materialized in the crucial weeks of late September 1976, there can be no doubt about the radicals' intention to use the urban militia as a political instrument in any contest for power.[20]

The command structure and work of the militia as a whole was reorganized following the arrest of the Gang of Four. Its overall role as an auxiliary to the regular armed forces in the event of a war has once again been revived.[21] The current command of the militia is exercised by the PLA General Staff Office through the People's Armed Forces units at the provincial military district level. The party shares the responsibility of providing direction for the militia within PLA units.[22] As a result of the use of urban militia units by the radicals during the contest for political power in 1976, the militia today operates essentially in rural areas.[23] References in the 1978 state constitution to militia building were deleted from the 1982 state constitution. The role of the rural militia was curtailed and limited to auxiliary functions in the event of a people's war.[24] Public security functions, once entrusted to the urban militia by the radicals, are no longer assigned to the militia. Militia units in rural areas are still expected to engage in production, and military training is conducted under the supervision of the regular PLA. China has not abandoned completely the concept of a people's war. Marshal Nie Rongzhen reemphasized that China must not only have a powerful regular army but also must organize the militia to fit the Maoist doctrine of "everyone a soldier."[25] Deng Xiaoping also spoke of the militia's role in civil air defense.[26] Thus, the militia, now reorganized and supervised by the regular PLA, remains an important component of China's national defense.

THE MILITARY IN CHINESE POLITICS

Militarism, as one of the major problems facing the Chinese, at least in the first half of this century, continues to play an important—if not decisive—role in Chinese politics. The presence of militarism, its relation to social and political organizations, and its effect upon the process of social and political transformation in Chinese communist society can be a useful framework for analyzing the military's role in politics. Martin Wilbur defined militarism in Chinese political development as a "system of organizing political power in which force is the normal arbiter in the distribution of power and in the establishment of policy."[27] Modern Chinese political development is, to a large extent, influenced by the power of armies, on one hand, and by the techniques involved in the use of armies and in military organization, on the other.

For decades prior to the unification effort undertaken by the Chinese Nationalists in 1926, a system of regional military separatism dominated the political scene in China. Under the system independent military-political groupings, each occupying one or more provinces, functioned as separate political entities and engaged in internecine warfare in order to preserve their own separate regions and to prevent their rivals from establishing a unified and centralized political system. To say that contemporary China has been plagued by the problem of control of armies is really an understatement. It is largely by military means and through military organization and technique that the Chinese Nationalists tried, and the Chinese communists succeeded, in reestablishing a "unified hierarchical and centralized political system."[28] The military thus constitutes a dominant group in society, and the military institution has played a dominant role in political development.[29] The military has always occupied a special position in Chinese communist society. As mentioned in Chapter 3, the Chinese Communist Party, for a long time, was the army. Party membership grew from the 40,000 Long March survivors in 1936 to over 1.2 million members in 1945. Over 1 million of the total membership in 1945 constituted the military supply system.[30] These people were regular members of either the army or the party, working without salary and under a military type of discipline. Robert Tucker has labeled this unique system of militarizing the party as military communism, to distinguish it from all other forms of communism.[31] It became evident in recent years that party leadership has depended upon party members in the army to carry on political work, to restore order, and to use the army as a coercive instrument in the contest for political power and succession.

The PLA's Political Role
from 1949 to 1966

As we have noted, during the years right after the new regime came to power, the PLA continued to govern the provinces under the military control commission.[32] Before the dissolution of military government in the provinces during 1953 and 1954, China became involved in the Korean War. The war made the military leaders painfully aware of the need to modernize the armed forces with the most up-to-date weaponry and combat skills. Figuring prominently in the issue of modernizing the military was the pressing policy question of whether to develop a nuclear strategy to confront the United States in the Pacific.[33] These concerns of the military were the basis for Marshal Peng Dehuai's criticism of Mao and the Great Leap programs. Peng's strategy for modernization was defeated at the Lushan party conference in the summer of

1959, and he was purged for daring to disagree with Mao's policies on mass mobilization and the communes.

Lin Biao, who succeeded Peng as defense minister, launched a two-fold ideological campaign under the Socialist Education Campaign.[34] The first part of the campaign was aimed at tendencies toward professionalism, reliance on technical skills and weaponry, and elitism within the PLA. Party cells, or committees, were formed at the company level to supervise the work of the professionally trained military officers. Simultaneously, an intensive study of Mao's thought on politics and revolutionary military strategy was required of all PLA officers and soldiers. A massive printing of millions of copies of the "little red book," *Quotations from Chairman Mao Zedong,* was distributed first to the PLA ranks and later to the general public under the second part of the campaign: emulation of the PLA by the whole nation. The PLA was to be a model, a paradigm, of the new communist life. Under the direction of the military, political and ideological verbal symbols, or abbreviated slogans, were disseminated throughout the nation to reshape societal values and attitudes. PLA heroes and their diaries became key material in the campaign. The symbols, such as "self-sacrifice," "determination will prevail," and "primacy of politics," were closely related to Mao's policies for developing China.[35]

In 1965 politicization of the military reached its peak with the abolition of ranks and insignia for the PLA. This symbolized the PLA's return to its guerrilla image of a "proletarian army" of the masses waging class struggle under the firm control of the Mao-Lin faction of the party. The political and ideological work in the military was emphasized as the only way for the party to control governmental bureaucracies. Military officers increasingly were assigned positions of importance in the administrative agencies of the party and government.[36] These developments made it fairly clear to the rest of Chinese society that it was the military, not the regular party under Liu Shaoqi and others opposed to Mao's concepts of reliance on politics, that was in control. It was also clear that Mao and Lin's strategy of "people's war," with its emphasis on reliance on the human factor and guerrilla tactics, was to be used in any possible confrontation with the United States in Indo-China. The strategy had been elaborated to include a plan for China's survival in the event of nuclear war.[37] The acceptance of the strategy for people's war served as the basis for purging those senior PLA officers who advocated military professionalism and modernization. The stage was set for Mao, then a minority voice within the party, to mount a concerted attack against the bureaucratic party establishment, in the form of the Cultural Revolution.

The PLA in the Cultural Revolution, 1967–69

During the initial stage of the Cultural Revolution—from April to December, 1966—it was not the leaders' intention to directly involve the military. The major actors at the center invoked the military's power, prestige, and authority only to provide powerful backing for the radicalized students against the established party apparatus. The initial role of the military was essentially to present guidelines and to identify targets for the attack. In this initial phase, the military's own newspaper, *The Liberation Army Daily,* became the authoritative source of messages concerning the course of the upheaval. The military also provided, at this initial phase, the logistical support for the students who were moving en masse all over China to gain revolutionary experience by rebelling against the party apparatus. The logistical support included the use of military vehicles for transportation and army barracks for lodging.

The occasion for the PLA to intervene in the Cultural Revolution came in the early part of 1967, when the widespread breakdown of party and state authority resulted in bloodshed and disorder. Thus, in January, the Cultural Revolution was transformed into a gigantic onslaught on the party's machinery. The call for the PLA to intervene in the Cultural Revolution resulted primarily from rising resistance to the seizure of established party and government apparatus by revolutionary rebel groups. In many instances the struggle for power involved rival groups and contending factions within the ranks of the revolutionary masses. The intervention of the PLA thus served two interrelated purposes: to restore law and order and to throw the army's weight behind the Maoist radicals. In essence, the latter meant the PLA's entry into a factional struggle within the party. Once the local PLA commander decided to intervene, in the form of armed suppression, the action of the PLA was swift and decisive. Incidents of brutal suppression of the Red Guard groups became common, and February to May, 1967, was a time of bloody armed struggle in all parts of China.

PLA and the Red Guards.   From the time it intervened in the Cultural Revolution, the PLA acted too swiftly and alienated a large segment of the Red Guard groups. The PLA commands in many localities certainly exhibited strength as well as a large amount of arrogance in carrying out their role. The tough attitude of the PLA gave the various contending factions a pretext for organized resistance. Less than a week after the general order was given for the PLA to intervene in the local power struggle, the Military Affairs Committee, on January 28, 1967, had to issue orders to restrain the assertiveness and initiative of the PLA. The Military Affairs Committee urged the troops to support resolutely the "genuine" revolutionary rebel groups—the Red Guards—without giving specific instructions as to how to identify a genuine revolutionary rebel group. It warned the troops not to arrest anyone without specific orders, and not to confiscate properties or mete out physical punishment indiscriminately. The Military Affairs Committee directive also revealed the existence of open attacks by the Red Guard groups upon PLA units.[38] These attacks on military organizations and public security agencies were widespread in February and March, 1967.[39] In many of these incidents, the PLA—in the name of law and order—opened fire on the unruly groups and made arrests. In Jinan the PLA declared that some ten Red Guard organizations made up of workers were counterrevolutionary, and thus disbanded them. When the workers who belonged to these organizations resisted, they were arrested or were beaten up by the PLA troops. Thousands more were imprisoned in buildings commandeered by the PLA in many cities.[40]

A large part of the PLA's problem with the Red Guard groups stemmed from the inability of the PLA commands in these local situations to tell which faction was the genuine revolutionary group. The moment the PLA recognized one faction in the power seizure, it was immediately attacked by the other faction or factions. In self-defense the PLA in many of these situations used force to suppress other factions.

As a result of complaints and criticisms concerning PLA intervention, orders were issued on April 6 by the Military Affairs Committee for the military in the provinces to curb the use of force in restoring order. Violent behavior of the contending Red Guard groups reached such an uncontrollable state, abetted by the restrictive April 6 order, that a new order had to be issued on June 6 to restore law and order in the provinces. The June 6 order, issued jointly by the Military Affairs Committee, the State Council, and the Cultural Revolution Group, revealed the extent of the chaos throughout the country. PLA troops stationed in the provinces were authorized (1) to arrest and punish, according to law, any individual or group that committed actions of looting, pillaging, or destroying of public documents or property; and (2) to prevent any unauthorized arrests and assaults. Nowhere in the text of the directive was the PLA specifically given authority to use force to compel violators to comply with the directive.[41]

The June 6 order placed the PLA in an extremely vulnerable position. On one hand, there was the nationwide appeal for "struggle by reason and persuasion," reinforced by the April 6 order which restricted PLA action in cases of in-fighting between and among the factions. On the other hand, armed clashes and other disorderly conduct had to be controlled, if not suppressed by force. The responsibility for restoring order and maintaining discipline among the Red Guard groups rested on the PLA's shoulders, the only effective coercive instrument available. Any action taken by the PLA for the explicit purpose of carrying out the June 6 directives would have required force, which would instantly arouse hostility and resentment among the groups being suppressed. Many PLA commands simply refused to take any action under these circumstances for fear of being criticized and reprimanded. The PLA's failure to act in maintaining law and order led to an upsurge in lawlessness carried on by the various contending factions of Red Guard groups. These anarchical activities included seizing arms and equipment from PLA troops and arsenals. In many of these incidents, the PLA troops simply remained passive.[42] Confronted with contradictory directives, some PLA commands acted on their own, guided by their respective regional predilections. The July 20 Wuhan incident was a good case in point.

The Wuhan Incident, July 1967. Two competing factional organizations were formed to seize power in the city of Wuhan.[43] One, the General Headquarters for Proletarian Revolution in the Wuhan area, was made up largely of university students and steel workers. The other, the One Million Heroes, was composed mainly of regular government and party cadres, elements of the militia, and factory workers; this group had the support of the

Wuhan Military District Command under Chen Jaidao, and the Wuhan party apparatus. The One Million Heroes was under the leadership of cadres from the public security agencies, who had a close working relationship with the PLA stationed in Wuhan city. The One Million Heroes dominated power-seizure activities in the Wuhan area not only because of its numerical strength but also because of the support it received from the military command and the party apparatus. It frequently employed force to suppress the opposing Red Guard groups in the area. In the first few days of July, the One Million Heroes forcefully occupied the staging centers of its rival group and thus nullified the latter's activities altogether. Beijing then appealed to the Wuhan Regional Military Command for cessation of these suppressive activities, to no avail. On July 14 two emissaries, Xi Fuzhi and Wang Li of the Central Cultural Revolution Group, were flown to Wuhan with specific instructions from Premier Zhou to settle the factional struggle on the spot. On July 19 the Wuhan Regional Military Command called a meeting, attended by representatives of the two rival mass organizations. There Wang Li presented Zhou Enlai's directive for an investigation of the Wuhan Military District Command's mistaken activities in its support of the Left, and for restoration of the good reputation of the steel workers' union.

On the evening of July 20, elements of the PLA local command, with the aid of the One Million Heroes, put the two emissaries from Beijing under house arrest. Beijing's response was to mobilize swiftly available army and naval units of the centrally controlled main force mentioned earlier, for a showdown. The result was the release of the two emissaries and the disbanding of the One Million Heroes. The regional PLA commander in Wuhan, Chen Jaidao, and the political commissar were relieved of their commands and were flow to Beijing for reeducation (Chen, too, has been rehabilitated recently).

The Wuhan incident represented an open revolt led by a powerful regional PLA commander in defiance of the Cultural Revolution and its leaders in Beijing. It also reflected, in retrospect, two basic difficulties in the PLA's intervention: the problem of identifying "genuine" revolutionary factions among the feuding Red Guards, and the close identification of provincial and district military commanders with the established local party structure. The incident also marked the beginning of the intensive use of the main force, controlled by Beijing, to restore order in the localities where the regional forces failed to perform.

China Under Military Control

By September 1967 the central authorities finally realized that chaos and violence in the country could be halted only by placing the nation under military control. Besides providing the needed coercive force, military control would enable provincial party apparatuses to be reorganized and transformed into the new revolutionary committees.

The Military Affairs Committee was responsible for supervising the PLA main force once it had taken control of a city or a province. Initially this included (1) maintaining revolutionary discipline and protecting proletarian revolutionary groups; (2) supporting revolutionary factions within the public security bureau; and (3) purging the established public security bureau of anti-revolutionary elements. Party newspapers and all broadcasting facilities were placed under PLA supervision, and the PLA was given the responsibility of supervising economic, financial, and relief activities. Nationally, military control was imposed on the country's communication and transportation systems. There was evidence that PLA officers were assigned to a number of ministries in the State Council at the government level. Senior PLA officers with managerial expertise were identified as directors or deputy directors in the State Planning Commission and in the ministries of finance, commerce, food supply, and foreign trade.[44]

By May 1968, with the active support of the PLA, twenty-four out of twenty-eight provinces and autonomous regions had established revolutionary committees based on the principle of the Three-Way Alliance in place of the old party apparatus. Special PLA units—elements of the main force, under the exclusive direction of the Military Affairs Committee at the Central Committee level—were formed with specific instructions to help the localities complete the formation of the new revolutionary committees.

Authority for these special units was contained in a directive: The central forces were to act as the "representative in full authority" of the Military Affairs Committee, and, as such, they were given power to supervise the local PLA units in implementing the directives of Beijing. Any resistance on the part of local PLA units to the orders, or refusal to cooperate with the special PLA units, could mean the arrest of their commanders and the disarming of their units as fighting forces. The directive was also very explicit as to the authority given to the special PLA units in dealing with the revolutionary mass organizations to curb further armed struggle: Arrest and punish those leaders of the contending factions who resist the return of seized weapons and ammunition, punish severely those who continue to incite armed bloodshed, return fire on those who continue to incite the masses to attack the PLA, bring the conflicting leaders together for negotiation in order to achieve "Great Unity," and finally, perform educational and propaganda work among these Red Guard groups.[45]

Ostensibly, the primary purpose of the special PLA units of the main force was to consolidate and accelerate the formation of the revolutionary committees in the provinces and the autonomous regions. Their major objective was to serve notice to the local military commanders to cut their local ties and regional predilections by lending their support to the revolutionary groups. Beijing had by now realized that in-fighting among the contending factions often was triggered by the alliance between the local PLA commands and the conservative party apparatus. The momentum for the speedy establishment of unity among all revolutionary groups was retarded by the incessant fighting. Dispatching special PLA units into the regional and provincial military districts would also provide protection to the already hardpressed groups loyal to Beijing. The immediate consequence of dispatching the special PLA units was the speedy establishment of the revolutionary committees in the remaining provinces of Yunnan, Fujian, and the autonomous regions of Xizang and Guangxi.

MILITARY POLITICS
SINCE THE CULTURAL REVOLUTION

By the spring of 1969, when the Ninth Party Congress met, the military had been thrust by the Cultural Revolution into a dominant position in the provincial and municipal revolutionary committees. As we pointed out in Chapter 1, the revolutionary committees were temporary power structures established to reflect the alliance of the military, rehabilitated veteran party cadres, and the mass organizations, such as the Red Guard groups. The dominant position of the military is illustrated in Table 6.2. Of the twenty-nine chairpersons for the provincial, autonomous regions and three centrally administered munici-

TABLE 6.2   Military Dominance in Provincial Party Committees, 1968–75

	Number Affiliated With							
	PLA		Party		Mass		Total	
Position Held	No.	%	No.	%	No.	%	No.	%
	1968–69							
Chairperson of Provincial Revolutionary Committees	20	68%	9	32%	—	—	29	100%
Vice-Chairperson	63	34%	52	29%	66	36%	181	100%
	1970–71							
Secretary of Provincial Party Committees	95	60%	53	34%	10	6%	158	100%
	1974–75							
Secretary of Provincial Party Committees	74	47%	68	43%	16	10%	158	100%

Sources: For 1968–69 the tabulation is based on James C. F. Wang, "The PLA in Communist China's Political Development" (unpublished doctoral dissertation, University of Hawaii, 1971).

For 1970–71 the tabulation is based on Parris Chang, "The Decentralization of Political Power in China since the Cultural Revolution," paper presented at the Second Sino-American Conference on Mainland China, June 1972, pp. 6–7.

For 1974–75 the tabulation is based on Robert A. Scalapino, "The CCP's Provincial Secretaries," Problems of Communism, *vol. xxv, no. 4 (July–August 1976), 27.*

pal revolutionary committees, twenty (68 percent) were affiliated with the PLA as either commanders or political commissars for provincial or regional military districts. Only nine (32 percent) of these chairpersons were party cadres, representing the old guard party bureaucratic power. Despite repeated pleas from Beijing that the Red Guard groups not be discriminated against, not a single Red Guard leader was ever appointed as chairperson of a provincial-level revolutionary committee. Leaders of the Red Guard groups made a better showing in the vice-chairperson distribution. Of the 181 known vice-chairpersons for these twenty-nine revolutionary committees, sixty-six (36 percent) were leaders of Red Guard groups. Sixty-three (34 percent) were PLA commanders and political commissars, and fifty-two (29 percent) were veteran party cadres. Again, the combined strength of the PLA and the veteran party cadres occupying the position of vice-chairperson in the revolutionary committees for the provinces overwhelmed those who represented the Red Guard groups. One other fact pointed out vividly the influence of the PLA in the provincial revolutionary committees; eight of thirteen PLA regional commanders (military regions of Guangzhou, Fuzhou, Shengyang, Nanjing, Wuhan, Xinjiang, Xizang, and Inner Mongolia) were concurrently serving as chairpersons of the provincial revolutionary committees under their military jurisdictions. This alone demonstrated the ascendency of the regional military's influence in Communist China's political development.

The dominant position of the military in the provinces continued in the 1970–71 period of party rebuilding. Table 6.2 shows that of some 158 party secretaries of various ranks in provincial party committees in 1971, about 60 percent were military officers from regional and provincial commands, 34 percent were veteran party cadres, and only 6 percent were leaders from the ranks of mass organizations.

The rapid expansion of military power in the provinces, and the continued dominance of the PLA in Chinese politics in general (following the conclusion of the Ninth Party Congress) became a major factor in the Lin Biao affair, which came to a head in September 1971.[46] The key question raised in the Lin Biao affair was who should have control of the political system in China: a civilian party under Mao, or the military under Lin Biao. The purge of Lin was a direct consequence of the tensions which developed between the civilian party and the military as it expanded its power, and the tensions which had developed between the central military command and the regional military power base in the provinces. In the end, the powerful regional commanders opposed Lin and contributed significantly to his purge.[47] The Lin Biao affair was an important benchmark in party-army relations. It also meant that the rapid expansion of the military's role under Lin Biao had constituted a threat to the power and authority of Mao and Zhou Enlai. Events of the post-Lin Biao period (from 1971 to 1974) largely centered on restoring the party's control over the military under Mao's 1929 dictum that "the party must command the gun." These events can be summarized as follows:

First, a massive purge was undertaken at the central command structure level, which had been the main base of Lin's support. In addition to the disappearance of some nine senior military leaders—including the chief of staff and the commanders of general logistics, the air force, and the navy—more than forty other ranking officers associated with the Lin group were purged.

Second, a movement was launched to reduce the involvement and role of the military in politics. A January 4, 1973, announcement issued by the State Council, headed by Zhou Enlai, and by the party's Military Affairs Committee, headed by Zhou's close ally Marshal Ye Jianying, directed PLA units in all regions and provinces to observe strictly the policies of the party. They stressed that the PLA's role was primarily military, rather than political. Public media stressed the need to observe military discipline and to concentrate on military affairs. Visitors to China now found fewer military representatives on school and university campuses and in factories. Coincident with the campaign to play down the role of the military in Chinese society was the reappearance of many party veterans who had been vilified during the Cultural Revolution.

Third, some analysts of Chinese politics suggest that there was also a deliberate attempt by Mao and Zhou Enlai to reduce the influence of the military in the decision-making process at both the national level and the regional and provincial levels.[48] As shown in Table 6.2, members of the military serving as party secretaries in the provinces declined from ninety-five (60 percent) in the 1970–71 period to seventy-four (47 percent) in the 1974–75 period. The most dramatic decline in military participation in the political process came at the powerful Politburo level. In 1969 the twenty-five member Politburo included thirteen PLA senior officers, or 52 percent of the membership. In 1973 the twenty-one member Politburo included only seven PLA senior officers, or 33 percent of the membership. Military representation on the Central Committee declined less drastically, from 43 percent of the full members on the Ninth Central Committee in 1969 to approximately 32 percent on the Tenth and Eleventh Central Committees. Interestingly, while PLA regional or provincial commanders holding concurrently the post of provincial party secretary decreased from fourteen to eight during the post-Lin period, their representation on the Central Committee remained fairly stable, as shown in Table 6.3. The continued high participation rate in the Central Committee by the military commanders and political commissars for the regional and provincial commands apparently reflects their continuing importance in the Chinese political power structure.

The Tenth Party Congress of August 1973 not only officially disposed of the Lin Biao affair but approved the formation of a new power structure. The latter was based on the coalition of the forces under Premier Zhou and those following the party ideologues Jiang Qing, Zhang Chunqiao, Yao Wenyuan, and the new rising star, Wang Hongwen, who was elected vice-chairperson of the CCP. The new power structure clearly revealed the ascendency of Zhou and his veteran party cadres, who in the aftermath of the dominance exercised by Lin Biao had received support from the majority of regional and provincial military commanders and political commissars. For the first time in decades, the new coalition was in a position in 1974 to make shifts in the

TABLE 6.3   PLA Regional and Provincial Commanders and Political Commissars on the Tenth Through Twelfth Central Committees by Military Regions

	Number of Full Members on Central Committees					
	PLA Commanders			PLA Commissars		
Military Regions	Tenth	Eleventh	Twelfth	Tenth	Eleventh	Twelfth
1. Guangzhou	2	1	1	2	5	1
2. Chengdu	1	1	1	3	1	—
3. Fuzhou	1	—	1	1	3	1
4. Kumming	3	2	1	1	2	1
5. Lanzhou	1	1	—	3	5	—
6. Shen yang	2	3	2	3	2	3
7. Nanjing	2	2	1	5	5	—
8. Beijing	1	1	2	3	7	—
9. Wuhan	1	1	1	3	3	—
10. Xinjiang	1	2	—	1	2	1
11. Xizang	—	—	—	1	2	—
12. Inner Mongolia	1	1	2	1	—	2
13. Jinan	1	1	1	—	2	1
	17	16	13	27	39	10

Source: For the Tenth and Eleventh Central Committees, see Peking Review, *14 (April 4, 1969), 9;* Peking Review, *35 (August 26, 1977), 14–16; and* Peking Review, *36 (September 7, 1973), 9–10.*

For the Twelfth Central Committee, see Issues and Studies, *vol. xviii, no. 11 (November 1982), 26–38.*

personnel at the regional and provincial military commands: Seven of the eleven commanders of the military regions were transferred or swapped posts. Ellis Joffe has pointed out several significant inferences that can be drawn from the reshuffling of the regional military commanders, many of whom held concurrently the position of first party secretary for a province. First, the removal of these military commanders from their bases of operations, some held since the early 1950s, strengthened immeasurably the center's control over the provinces. Second, the successful removal of the officers revealed their military discipline and their commitment to the center.[49]

The coalition formed in 1973 proved to be temporary and in many ways illusory. The heart of the new power structure was the veteran party administrators, reinforced by the key military figures brought to the center by Zhou. The weakest element of the coalition was the party's radical ideologues, the Gang of Four, who had tried unsuccessfully to organize the urban militia as a countervailing force to the PLA.

This brief study of the Chinese military's role in politics clearly shows that the PLA emerged as a major force in the party and government between 1969 and 1977. Approximately 31 percent of the regular members on the Eleventh Central Committee of the party, elected in 1977, were representatives of the PLA. Of the sixty-two PLA representatives on the Eleventh Central Committee, fifty-five, or 27 percent, were active PLA commanders and political commissars from the regional military commands. When this 27-percent representation of PLA members stationed in the provinces was added to the 40 percent representing provincial party secretaries of various ranks, it became evident that the provinces retained a formidable voice in the nation's highest decision-making council. Although the military's representation on the full membership of the Twelfth Central Committee (1982) declined in comparison to that on the Eleventh Central Committee (1977), it still represented 22 percent of the total. This, together with the representation of party and government administrators/technocrats, accounted for more than 74 percent of the total full membership of 210 on the Twelfth Central Committee.

MILITARY REFORM
UNDER DENG

Nothing has really changed with regard to Mao's old dictum: Political power grows out of the gun barrel, and the party must command the gun. Since Mao's death the man in the party in command of the gun has been none other than Deng Xiaoping. In 1974, when Deng was reinstated after being purged during the Cultural Revolution, one of the pivotal positions he held was that of chief of staff for the PLA. Because of Deng's many years of close association with the military—both as political commissar and as the party's general secretary—he was the only person in the top hierarchy after Mao's death who could command respect and support from most PLA officers. Later, when Deng returned for the second time in 1977, he was not only the PLA's chief of staff but also the vice-chairperson of the MAC—the de facto political supervisor of the armed forces.

One of Deng's first goals was to consolidate his control over the central command structure of the armed forces. He accomplished the task in two carefully mapped out moves. One was to reshuffle the commanders and commissars for the military regions so as to ensure the retention of only those who supported his policies. By the spring of 1980, Deng was able to appoint ten of the eleven commanders for the eleven military regions. The only regional military commander who retained his appointment (uninterrupted since 1969) was Li Desheng of the Shengyang Military Region for the northeast provinces facing the Soviet border. An extensive reshuffling and purge also were carried out in the provincial military districts.

Deng's second move was to staff key military positions at the central command headquarters with his trusted associates. On the eve of the Twelfth Party Congress in September 1982, it was clear that Deng had established firm control over the central command structure. Deng was elected chairman of the MAC, a position comparable to supreme commander in chief for the armed forces. Yang Shangkun, his associate and a Politburo member, was made the permanent vice-chairman and general secretary for the MAC. Deng packed the standing committee of the MAC with his supporters. He promoted Yang

Dezhi, the commander of the Chinese forces in the 1979 border war with Vietnam, to the position of chief of staff for the PLA. By 1981 all senior officers for the general logistics, rear services, and all commanders of the Chinese air force and navy were considered Deng's supporters.

Deng's next objective was to implement reforms in the command structure and in personnel. He recommended the following three reforms: (1) Streamline the military command structure below the MAC level. (2) Modernize officer training. (3) Upgrade the competence of military officers. The PLA organizational structure was fragmented in such a way that there were separate commands for the air force, navy, artillery, armored units (tank corps), antichemical units, railway corps, engineering corps, and regional and provincial military districts. The thirty-eight army corps stationed in the military regions generally received their operational orders from their PLA general headquarters at the center.[50] Similarly, the air force, the navy, and the artillery in the military regions received their orders directly from their own headquarters at Beijing. Deng felt that it would be more efficient to have the forces and services all placed under the direct command of the military regions. For instance, the artillery corps would not be placed under "the dual command" of the military regions and the artillery's own headquarters.[51]

Deng also thought that reform was needed in the military officer corps training. Deng and his senior military associates believed that modern warfare requires knowledge and understanding about science and technology and that special skills in modern warfare must be developed among the military officer corps through curriculum improvement in the military academies. The course content at the military academies seemed outdated in terms of tactics and strategies, and a large portion of the curriculum remained devoted to Mao's guerrilla strategy of a people's war.[52]

Third, Deng felt the need to replace the large number of aging officers who clung to their posts but who had limited education and outdated concepts. These officers had little knowledge or understanding about modern science and technique. While they remained in their positions, artificial barriers had been erected between the armed forces and the service academies, preventing able young academy officers from receiving actual command posts.[53] Thus, Deng proposed a concerted campaign to elevate younger service academy officers with knowledge of modern science and with the needed vigorous physical strength to command posts.[54]

By the summer of 1983, some measures had been introduced to support Deng's proposed reforms. One guaranteed aged officers a retirement pension equivalent to their full salary. In addition, a special bonus would be granted to every retired officer for each year of service. This meant that a military officer who served fifty years would receive an additional fifty yuan per month.[55] Housing allowance and a car would be added as special inducements for early retirement of high-ranking officers. For example, a political commissar could receive as much as 120,000 yuan in housing allowance and retirement.[56] Simultaneously, age limits were imposed on the commanders at various levels. The following age limits have been reported: corps commanders, 55; divisional commanders, 45; regimental commanders, 35; battalion commanders, 30; and company commanders, 25.[57] Finally, a system of rapid promotion for younger officers in the military was instituted to provide youthfulness and competence.

But some of the policies for military reform have aroused strong dissent within the military. Since the military has traditionally stood for Mao's ideological purity, the reassessment of Mao's role in party history generated some resentment within PLA ranks. The assessment of Mao as a man who made mistakes in his later years might be regarded as a political compromise to placate old guard military leaders who still view Mao as infallible. Deng's lengthy lecture at the 1978 All-Army Political Conference praising Mao and his three rules of discipline and eight points of attention, formulated in the guerrilla days during the 1930s, might also be viewed as a concession to the PLA old guard.

The campaign for "socialist spiritual civilization," articulated by Deng and Hu Yaobang, also caused controversy among the military.[58] This campaign reemphasized moral standards, education, culture, science, literature and arts, and a general knowledge of humankind.[59] Deng was reported to have summarized the "socialist spiritual civilization" campaign by coining the phrase: "To possess ideals, moral standards, civilization, and discipline."[60] When Deng instructed the military to emphasize culture and general knowledge as well as politics, some of the old guard military leaders protested. It was said that Wei Guoqing, then the director of the PLA general political department in charge of education and propaganda, did not share Deng's view on the importance of cultural emphasis in military training.[61] Yang Shangkun, the MAC's general secretary, rebuked Wei by pointing out that both science and culture were equally important in military training.[62] Subsequently, Wei was replaced by Yu Quili, also a Politburo member. The removal of Wei Guoqin indicated the continued presence of dissent in the military.

Deng Xiaoping was caught in another controversy with the military. A veteran army writer, Bai Hua, wrote a screenplay, "Bitter Love," which was an angry film about the death of an artist persecuted during the Cultural Revolution. The play cast a poor image of the party and denigrated Mao by symbolism. The PLA condemned the writer for writing the play. On the other hand, the play coincided with Deng's attempts to reassess Mao and the mistakes he made during the Cultural Revolution. In this case Deng sought a compromise solution that would placate the dissenters in the military. Evidently, in order to forestall a direct attack on the author and indirectly on Deng, Hu Yaobang pressured Bai Hua to make self-criticism confessing his "ideological errors."

Another area of friction between Deng and the military was the low priority Deng gave to defense spending. China's defense outlay in 1979 was 22.2 billion yuan. It was reduced to 19.3 billion yuan in 1980 and in 1981 was further reduced to 16.8 billion yuan.[63] Thus, the 1981 defense expenditure was down 5.4 billion yuan, or almost 25 percent, from the 1979 level. This huge reduction in military spending aroused the PLA's concern and criticism.

The level of defense expenditure was increased by 1 billion yuan to an estimated 17.8 billion yuan in 1982, and was held at that level for 1983. In terms of China's total national expenditures, defense spending represented only about 15 percent in 1982 and 14 percent in 1983. One of the first consequences of the defense cuts was the demobilization of some 400,000 soldiers in 1980.[64] The ultimate goal was eventually to reduce the total PLA strength of about 4 million soldiers by as much as a third. The central government was faced with the burden of finding suitable employment for the large number of demobilized soldiers. A number of them were placed in various public security positions.[65] Some participated in protest demonstrations as a way of expressing their resentment.[66] Reductions in military spending also meant the curtailment of benefits and privileges for the officers and soldiers.

An indirect cause of friction between the pragmatic leaders and the military was generated by the new agricultural policies for the communes. Peasant families have always provided the major source of recruitment for the PLA. The new liberal agricultural policies of fixing output quota at household level and of permitting sideline production have brought general prosperity to rural peasants—so much so that those who stay on the farm are earning more than military recruits.[67] This has led to low morale in the military. Many soldiers are thinking of getting out of military service and returning to the rural communes. Aware of the morale problem within the military, Deng sought ways to boost spirits. One measure he suggested was to restore the rank and insignia which had been abolished in 1965 by Mao in his desire to make the army more egalitarian. The reinstitution of military rank for the officers and soldiers would mean more prestige, if not more pay. An avid bridge player, Deng's trump card for luring PLA support for his policies and programs was his pledge to modernize the military and to promote military professionalism.

MILITARY MODERNIZATION

There has always been a demand for military professionalism and modernization. China's decision to develop a nuclear bomb in the early 1960s, the purge of Peng Dehuai, and the debate over Mao's military strategy all revolved around the question of military modernization and professionalism. This demand most likely became more urgent after 1969, as Sino-Soviet relations deteriorated and border incidents increased. After almost twenty years of debate and neglect, the new Chinese leadership has come out squarely on the side of military modernization. In an all-army political works conference, Hua Guofeng stated that "our army must speed the improvement of its weapons and equipment and raise its tactical and technical level."[68] By this, Hua meant the acquisition of modern arms and equipment, including missiles and nuclear weapons. Marshal Ye Jianying pointed out at the same conference that "a modern war will be more ruthless and more intense than past wars," and that the Chinese military establishment must devote its efforts to "more proficient techniques and tactics, military skills, and commandership."[69]

The theme of military modernization has been stressed continuously by Deng and Hu Yaobang. Politburo member Yang Shangkun, Deng's most valued supporter in the party's MAC, articulated the thesis that it was essential for the military to acquire modern "scientific, cultural, and technical knowledge." He made it abundantly clear that strength in war was more than a matter of the army's size—it must be seen "in the degree of modernization of equipment and the people's ability to use such equipment."[70] Yang Dezhi, the PLA chief of staff, also spoke of the urgent need to upgrade the technical level of military personnel through advanced training and education.[71] One Western military expert indicated that the Chinese military probably was fifteen years behind the U.S. military in technological training.[72]

The Chinese realize that the basic requirement for military modernization is the rapid development of heavy industries, as well as research in science and technology, which takes time. To fill the large deficiences which exist in their technology, the Chinese at first thought they could embark on a program of weapons purchase from abroad. Chinese military missions, headed by senior military officers, most of whom were vilified for advocating military professionalism during the Cultural Revolution, shopped around in England, France, and West Germany with an eye toward the possible purchase of the latest weapons: tanks, antitank missiles, fighter planes, and helicopters. While the United States remained opposed to sales of sophisticated modern weapons to the Chinese, it had tacitly given approval to its allies in Western Europe to sell such weapons to China.[73] In 1978 an agreement was signed between China and West Germany, under which China was reportedly to have purchased 600 antitank missiles.[74] Then China and Italy reached an agreement for a missile guidance system and helicopters.[75] China's interest in the purchase of modern arms was also given a boost by a change in United States policy under the Carter administration. In January 1980 former Secretary of Defense Harold Brown paid a visit to China. He indicated to the Chinese that the United States was willing to sell, on a case-by-case basis, certain kinds of equipment, including trucks, communication gears, and possibly early warning radar systems. In 1980 the Pentagon also approved sales of battlefield radar and computers, helicopters, and transport planes.[76] In July 1980 the Chinese signed an agreement with France to purchase fifty helicopters worth about $57 million.[77] There were reports that the Chinese were interested in purchasing French Mirage F-1 fighter planes and heavy duty helicopters.[78] In 1981 Canada offered to sell the Chinese certain defensive weapons (mostly aircraft and radar equipment).[79] Chinese agents also concluded an agreement with the United Kingdom for the purchase of Rolls-Royce supersonic jet engines.[80] The Chinese strategy may involve studying the mechanisms of the sophisticated modern weaponry purchased in limited quantities from the West, as a means of acquiring the needed weapon-making technology. This would be more beneficial for military modernization from a long-term point of view, and it would be less costly than massive purchases of the available modern weapons.

When we discuss the complex issue of Chinese military modernization, we need to keep in mind that there is a running debate among Chinese leaders on the priority of this issue, or a conflict between the need to develop and modernize basic industries as opposed to developing the military. The conflict has usually been resolved by placing military modernization second to the need for economic development.[81] In fact, the Chinese have always stressed the importance of economic development as basic to all progress. One of the reasons for the late Marshal Peng Dehuai's criticism of Mao's 1958 Great Leap policy was the former's concern over the delay in modernizing China's military—a criticism which brought on Mao's wrath and led to Peng's eventual purge. Peng's concern stemmed from his experience in commanding Chinese forces in Korea during the early 1950s. Peng argued that a strong industrial base was the foundation for military modernization. Mao's view prevailed, and the concept of a revolutionary army with stress on the human element, not on sophisticated weapons, remained a basic military doctrine. After that, the "people's war" concept dominated Chinese military thinking. Not until 1975, when the late premier Zhou Enlai proposed a ten-year modernization plan, was the issue of military modernization placed on a par with modernization of agriculture, industry, and science and technology. In fact, modernization of defense was not openly discussed by the Chinese leaders until 1977, when Mao had passed away and the Gang of Four had been arrested. Even in 1977 Marshal Ye insisted that modernization of China's basic industries was essential and necessary for its national defense.[82] (This view was not shared by one special interest group, the National Defense Industry Office within the Chinese defense establishment, which argued that modernization of defense industries would place new demands on other industries and thus motivate the progress of the economy as a whole.)[83]

The relegation of military modernization to a lower priority than the modernization of industry and agriculture is perhaps more understandable when one looks at the cost factor involved. The Rand Corporation estimated that China would have to spend between $41 billion and $63 billion in order to completely modernize her conventional fighting forces.[84] This estimate is for 3,000 to 8,000 new medium tanks, 8,000 to 10,000 armed personnel carriers, more than 20,000 heavy duty trucks, 6,000 air-to-air missiles, and 200 to 300 fighter-bombers.[85] Closely linked to an enormous price tag of $41 billion to $63 billion was the lack of available foreign exchange needed to pay for the weapons. Western analysts speculated that one means of paying for the arms modernization would be to step up, as has already been done, exports from China of strategic metals, such as titanium, tantalum, and vanadium—all lightweight and heat resistant metals used in aircraft.[86]

The inability and unwillingness of China to commit huge financial resources to large-scale purchases of modern, sophisticated weapons from abroad has forced China to develop several alternative military strategies for defense.[87] One is the development of nuclear weapons, on the ideological grounds that the nuclear monopoly by the superpowers must be broken. While China's nuclear capability will be discussed in Chapter 10, suffice it to say here that China has detonated a hydrogen bomb from the air and has developed a creditable delivery system of tactical weapons with nuclear warheads. China also launched three new satellites in 1981 to ensure an early warning system against possible Soviet nuclear attack. In May 1980 China launched its first long-range ICBM, with a range of 6,000 miles, over the Pacific and missed the intended target by only twenty-seven miles. As mentioned earlier, China has not abandoned entirely the strategy of people's war. Many Chinese military officers still believe that a war would be fought under Chinese conditions. The editor of the *Beijing Review,* on the occasion of the 1982 army day celebration, said: "It is still fundamentally true that it is men, not materials, that decide the outcome of war. If a war breaks out, we will mobilize the masses of people to swamp the enemy in the ocean of people's war."[88] The PLA chief of staff, Yang Dezhi, while stressing the need for technical training of officers, also insisted that "in fighting a people's war today, the decisive factor is still a fighter's courage, consciousness and the mental preparation to sacrifice one's life."[89] The military action in the Falklands in 1982 certainly has forced many nations, including China, to reflect on the statement that "war remains first and foremost a human encounter."[90]

While the long-range goal is a modernized military, the Chinese military leaders recognize that the old military doctrine of people's war, or guerrilla warfare, must remain a basic ingredient in their war preparedness plans for some time to come.[91] But China's month-long military action in Vietnam in the spring of 1979 may alter that military approach, for the pace of China's invasion was rather slow, and casualties were high—20,000 killed and wounded. China's invasion of Vietnam showed that its military lacked mobility, which was the result of not having enough armored vehicles for combat purposes.[92] Thus, the Chinese military will have to compete with other industries in China for priority in modernization.

NOTES

1. Hu Sheng, "On the Revision of the Constitution," *Beijing Review,* 18 (May 13, 1982), 16.

2. *Ta Kung Pao Weekly Supplement* (Hong Kong), September 16, 1982, p. 5.

3. See Donald H. McMillen, "The Urumqi Military Region: Defense and Security in China's West," *Asian Survey,* vol. xxii, no. 8 (August 1982), 705–31; and Raphael Israeli, "The Muslim Minority in the People's Republic of China," *Asian Survey,* vol. xxi, no. 8 (August 1981), 901–19.

4. See William Whitson, "The Field Army in Chinese Communist Military Politics," *The China Quarterly,* 37 (January–March 1969), 1–30; and Jurgen Domes, *The Internal Politics of China, 1949–1972* (New York: Holt, Rinehart & Winston, 1973), pp. 21–26.

5. John Gittings, *The Role of the Chinese Army* (London: Oxford University Press, 1967).

6. Whitson, "The Field Army in Chinese Communist Military Politics," p. 7.

7. Ibid., pp. 2–26. Also see Y. C. Chang, *Factionalism and Coalition Politics in China: The Cultural Revolution and Its Aftermath,* (New York, Praeger Publishers, 1976), p. 77.

8. William L. Parish, Jr., "Factions in Chinese Military Politics," *The China Quarterly,* 56 (October–December 1973), 667–99; and Harvey W. Nelson, "Military Forces in the Cultural Revolution," *The China Quarterly,* 51 (July–September 1972), 444–74.

9. See James C. F. Wang, "The Urban Militia as a Political Instrument in the Power Contest in China in 1976," 541–45.

10. Gittings, *The Role of the Chinese Army,* pp. 201–24.

11. Ibid.

12. Ibid.

13. Ibid.

14. *Renmin Ribao,* March 17, 1969, p. 1.

15. Philip Bridgham, "Mao's Cultural Revolution: The Struggle to Consolidate Power," *The China Quarterly,* 41 (January–March 1970), 1; Parris Chang, "Changing Patterns of Military Roles in Chinese Politics," in *The Military and Political Power in China in the 1970s,* ed. William Whitson, (New York: Holt, Rinehart & Winston, 1972), pp. 47–70; Jurgen Domes, "The Cultural Revolution and the Army," *Asian Survey,* vol. viii, no. 5 (May 1968), 349–63; John Gittings, "Reversing the PLA Verdicts," *Far Eastern Economic Review,* 30 (July 25, 1968), 191–93; Ellis Joffe, "The Chinese Army in the Cultural Revolution: The Politics of Intervention," *Current Scene,* vol. viii, no. 18 (December 7, 1970), 1–25; Ellis Joffee, "The Chinese Army after the Cultural Revolution: The Effects of Intervention," *The China Quarterly,* 55 (July–September, 1973), 450–77; Thomas Jay Matthews, "The Cultural Revolution in Szechwan," in *The Cultural Revolution in the Provinces,* Harvard East Asian Monographs, no. 42 (Cambridge, Mass.: Harvard University Press, 1971), pp. 94–146; Margie Sargent, "The Cultural Revolution in Heilungkiang," ibid., pp. 16–65; Vivienne B. Shue, "Shanghai After the January Storm," ibid., pp. 66–93; Harvey Nelsen, "Military Forces in the Cultural Revolution," *The China Quarterly,* 51 (July–September, 1972), 448–50; Ralph Powell, "The Party, the Government, and the Gun," *Asian Survey,* vol. x, no. 6 (June 1970), 441–71; William Whitson, *The Chinese Communist High Command: A History of Military Politics, 1927–69* (New York: Holt, Rinehart & Winston, 1971).

16. *Renmin Ribao,* March 29, 1969, p. 2.

17. Chiang Ye-shang, "Military Affairs for 1970," *The China Monthly,* 82 (January 1971), 11–12.

18. Based on monitored provincial broadcast. See *Chung-kung yen-chiu (Studies on Chinese Communism),* vol. 6, no. 1 (January 1973), 40–41.

19. See "Failure of 'Gang of Four's' Scheme to Set Up a 'Second Armed Forces,' " *Peking Review,* 13 (March 25, 1977), 10–12; and " 'Gang of Four's' Abortive Counter-Revolutionary Coup," *Peking Review,* 25 (June 17, 1977), 22–25. Also see Wang, "The Urban Militia as a Political Instrument," pp. 545–59.

20. Failure of 'Gang of Four's' Scheme to Set Up a 'Second Armed Forces,' " pp. 10–12; " 'Gang of Four's' Abortive Counter-Revolutionary Coup," pp. 22–25; and Wang, "The Urban Military as a Political Instrument," pp. 545–59.

21. Nieh Jung-chen, "The Militia's Role in a Future War," *Peking Review,* 35 (September 1, 1978), 16–19.

22. See June T. Dreyer, "The Chinese People's Militia: Transformation and Strategic Role," paper presented at the 32nd annual meeting of the Association of Asian Studies, March 21, 1980.

23. See "Regulation on Militia Work," *Issues and Studies,* vol. xvi, no. 2 (February 1980), 76.

24. "The Concept of People's War," *Beijing Review,* 31 (August 2, 1982), 3.

25. See Nieh Jung-chen "The Militia's Role in a Future War," p. 19.

26. " 'August 1' Army Day," *Peking Review,* 31 (August 4, 1978), 3.

27. Martin Wilbur, "Military Separatism and the Process of Reunification under the Nationalist Regime, 1922–1937," in *China in Crisis,* vol. 1, no. 1, eds. Ho Pi-ting and Tang Tsou (Chicago: University of Chicago, 1968), p. 203.

28. Ibid.

29. Ibid.

30. Treadgold, *Soviet and Chinese Communism: Similarities and Differences,* p. 25.

31. Robert C. Tucker, "On the Contemporary Study of Communism," *World Politics,* vol. xix, no. 2 (January 1967), 242–57.

32. Parris Chang, "Changing Patterns of Military Roles in Chinese Politics," in *The Military and Political Power in China in the 1970s,* ed. William Whitson (New York: Holt, Rinehart & Winston, 1972), p. 48.

33. See Alice Langley Hsieh, *Communist China's Strategy in the Nuclear Era* (Englewood Cliffs, N.J.: Prentice-Hall, 1962).

34. See Chalmers Johnson, "Lin Piao's Army and Its Role in Chinese Society," *Current Scene,* vol. iv, no. 13 (July 1, 1966), 1–10, and no. 14 (July 15, 1966), 1–11. Also see Ralph L. Powell, "The Increasing Power of Lin Piao and the Party-Soldiers, 1959–1966," *The China Quar-*

terly, 34 (April–June, 1968), 38–65; and Ellis Joffe, "The Chinese Army Under Lin Piao: Prelude to Political Intervention," in *China: Management of a Revolutionary Society*, ed. John M. H. Lindbeck (Seattle, Wash. and London: University of Washington Press, 1971), pp. 343–74.

35. See Mary Sheridan, "The Emulation of Heroes," *The China Quarterly*, 33 (January–March 1965), 47–72; and James C. F. Wang, "Values of the Cultural Revolution," *Journal of Communication*, vol. 27, no. 3 (Summer 1977), 41–46.

36. Powell, "The Increasing Power of Lin Piao and the Party-Soldiers, 1959–1966," pp. 38–65.

37. See Lin Biao, "Long Live the Victory of People's War," *Peking Review*, 32 (August 4, 1967), 14–39.

38. Military Order Defines PLA Activities in the Cultural Revolution," *Samples of Red Guard Publications*, vol. II (U.S. Department of Commerce, Joint Publications Research, August 8, 1967).

39. Ibid.

40. "Comrade Hsieh Fu-chih's Speech on April 20 to the Peking Revolutionary Committee," *Hongqi (The Red Flag)*, 61 (May 6, 1967), 19–20.

41. "Immediately Cease Physical Violence," *Renmin Ribao* editorial, May 22, 1967, p. 1.

42. See summary of Chiang Ching's speech on September 5 to representatives from Anhwei Province in *Renmin Ribao*, September 17, 1967, p. 1.

43. See Thomas W. Robinson, "The Wuhan Incident: Local Strife and Provincial Rebellion during the Cultural Revolution," *The China Quarterly*, 47 (July–September 1971), 413–38; and Deborah S. Davis, "The Cultural Revolution in Wuhan," in *The Cultural Revolution in the Provinces*, pp. 147–70.

44. *Renmin Ribao*, September 3, 1967, p. 1.

45. "Directive of the Central Committee, the State Council, Military Affairs Committee, and the Cultural Revolutionary Group Concerning the Dispatch of Central Support for the Left Units to Regional and Provincial Military Districts," *Studies on Chinese Communism*, vol. ii, no. 8 (August 31, 1968), 109–17; and *Renmin Ribao*, September 7, 1968, pp. 1–4.

46. See Y. M. Kau, *The Lin Piao Affair: Power Politics and Military Coup* (White Plains, N.Y.: International Arts and Sciences Press, 1975), pp. *xxxi–xxviii;* Ellis Joffe, "The Chinese Army after the Cultural Revolution," pp. 468–77; and Parris Chang, "The Changing Patterns of Military Participation in Chinese Politics," *ORBIS*, vol. xvi, no. 3 (Fall 1972), 797–800.

47. Ellis Joffe, "The Chinese Army after the Cultural Revolution," pp. 450–77. For the account of Lin Piao's crash, see Cheng Huan, "The Killing of Comrade Lin Piao," *Far Eastern Economic Review* (July 22, 1972), 11–12; *The New York Times*, July 23, 1972, pp. 1, 16. For the official version, see Chou En-lai, "Report to the Tenth National Congress of the Communist Party of China," *Peking Review*, 35–36 (September 7, 1973), 18. Also see Philip Bridgham, "The Fall of Lin Piao," in *The China Quarterly*, 55 (July–September, 1973), 427–49; Ying-mao Kau and Pierre M. Perrolle, "The Politics of Lin Piao's Abortive Military Coup," *Asian Survey*, vol. xiv, no. 6 (June 1974), 558–77; and Ying-mao Kau, *The Lin Piao Affair*, pp. xix–li.

48. See Parris Chang, "China's Military," *Current History*, vol. 67, no. 397 (September 1974), 101–5; Ellis Joffe, "The PLA in Internal Politics," *Problems of Communism*, vol. xxiv, no. 6 (November–December 1975), 1–12.

49. Ellis Joffe, "The PLA in Internal Politics," p. 12.

50. Harvey W. Nelson, *The Chinese Military System: An Organizational Study of the PLA* (Boulder, Colo.: Westview Press, 1977), p. 10.

51. See Lo Bing, "Inside Story About PLA Reform," *Zhengming* (Hong Kong), 66 (April 1983), 8.

52. William R. Heaton, Jr., "Professional Military Education in China: A Visit to the Military Academy of the PLA," *The China Quarterly*, 81 (March 1980), 122–28.

53. *Ming Pao* (Hong Kong), March 6, 1983, p. 1.

54. See *Beijing Review*, 31 (August 4, 1978), 3–4. Also see *Ming Pao* (Hong Kong), March 6, 1983, p. 1.

55. *Ming Pao* (Hong Kong), March 24, 1982, p. 1.

56. Ibid.

57. *Zhengming* (Hong Kong), 66 (April 1983), 9.

58. On socialist spiritual civilization, see the following: *Beijing Review*, 45 (November 8, 1982), 13; *Beijing Review*, 37 (September 13, 1982), 21–26; *Beijing Review*, 47 (November 22,

1982), 3. Also see *Hongqi,* 15 (August 1, 1982), *Zhengming* (Hong Kong), 61 (November 1982), 8–9.

59. *Zhengming* (Hong Kong), 61 (November 1982), 8.

60. Ibid.

61. Ibid; and *Zhengming* (Hong Kong), 62 (December 1982), 9–10.

62. *Hongqi,* 15 (August 1, 1982), 8–9. Also see *Zhengming* (Hong Kong), 61 (November 1982), 9.

63. Wang Bingqian, "Report on Financial Work," *Beijing Review,* 39 (September 29, 1980), 17; "Report on the Final State Account for 1980 and Implementation of the Financial Estimates for 1981," *Beijing Review,* 2 (January 11, 1982), 16; and "Report on the Implementation of the State Budget for 1982 and the Draft Budget for 1983," *Beijing Review,* 3 (January 13, 1983), 16.

64. *Far Eastern Economic Review* (September 25, 1981), 55.

65. Ibid.

66. *Ming Pao* (Hong Kong), July 6, 1981, p. 1.

67. *Far Eastern Economic Review* (September 25, 1981), 55. Also see Lo Din, "Candid View of a PLA Divisional Cadre," *Zhengming* (Hong Kong), 65 (March 1983), 17.

68. "Chairman Hua's Speech at All-Army Political Work Conference," *Peking Review,* 24 (June 16, 1978), 10.

69. "Vice-Chairman Yeh Chien-ying's Speech," *Peking Review,* 25 (June 23, 1978), 12; Also, *Peking Review,* 32 (August 5, 1977), 14.

70. " 'August 1' Army Day," *Beijing Review,* 32 (August 9, 1982), 6.

71. *Ta Kung Pao Weekly Supplement,* August 5, 1982, p. 3.

72. See Drew Middleton, "Supplying Weapons to China," New York Times Service, as reprinted in *Honolulu Star-Bulletin,* April 16, 1981, A–14.

73. *The New York Times,* May 18, 1978, A–6.

74. See Leo Y. Y. Liu, "The Modernization of the Chinese Military," *Current History* (September 1980), 11.

75. *Far Eastern Economic Review* (November 16, 1979), 21–22; and "Premier Hua Visits Italy: Building a Bridge of Friendship," *Beijing Review,* 45 (November 9, 1979), 13–14.

76. See *The New York Times,* May 30, 1980, p. 1; *Honolulu Advertiser,* May 30, 1980, A–1. Also see Christopher F. Chuba, "U.S. Military Support Equipment Sales to PRC," *Asian Survey,* vol. xxi, no. 4 (April 1981), 469–84. Also see Michael Gelter, "U.S. Willing to Sell Military Equipment to the Chinese," Washington Post Service, as reprinted in *Honolulu Advertiser,* January 25, 1981, A–20.

77. *Ming Pao* (Hong Kong), August 28, 1982, p. 1.

78. *Ming Pao* (Hong Kong), August 28, 1982, p. 1.

79. *Honolulu Advertiser,* August 21, 1981, B–1.

80. See Jonathan Pollack, *Defense Modernization in the PRC,* The Rand Corporation, N–1214-1-AP, 1979.

81. See Christopher F. Chuba, "U.S. Military Support Equipment Sales to the PRC," p. 483; Francis J. Romance, "Modernization of China's Armed Forces," *Asian Survey,* vol. xx, no. 3 (March 1980), 304–5; and Harlan W. Jencks, "Defending China in 1982," *Current History,* 476 (September 1982), 249.

82. *Peking Review* 21 (May 10, 1977) 18.

83. *Guangming Daily,* January 20, 1977, p. 5.

84. *The New York Times,* January 4, 1980, A–3.

85. Middleton, "Supplying Weapons to China"; and Pollack, *Defense Modernization in the PRC.* Also see Angus M. Fraser, "Military Modernization in China," *Problems of Communism* (September–December 1979), 34–49. For an earlier estimate see Edward N. Lutwak," Problems of Military Modernization for Mainland China," *Issues and Studies,* vol. xiv, no. 7 (July 1978), 58.

86. Drew Middleton, "Sales of Rare Metals May Pay for China's Armed Buildup," New York Times Service, as reprinted in *Honolulu Star-Bulletin,* December 31, 1981, A–34. Also see Chuba, "U.S. Military Support Equipment Sales to the PRC," pp. 460–84; and Douglas T. Stuart and William T. Tow, "Chinese Military Modernization: The Western Arms Connection," *The China Quarterly,* 90 (June 1982), 262.

87. See Thomas W. Robinson, "Chinese Military Modernization in the 1980s," *The China Quarterly,* 90 (June 1982), 231–51.

88. "The Concept of People's War," p. 3.

89. *Ta Kung Pao Weekly Supplement,* July 29, 1982.

90. Jeffrey Record, "Men, Not Hardware, Still Decisive on Battlefield," Washington Post Service, as reprinted in *Honolulu Advertiser,* December 15, 1982, A-23.

91. Hsu Hsiang-chen, "Heighten Our Vigilance and Get Prepared to Fight a War," *Peking Review,* 32 (August 11, 1978), 8-11.

92. For an assessment of the Chinese military invasion of Vietnam, see Drew Middleton, "China's Lack of Mobility," New York Times News Service feature, reprinted in *Honolulu Star Bulletin,* March 9, 1979, A-17.

Mass Participation and Political Action— Chinese Style

One of the most dramatic and sometimes frightening aspects of the contemporary Chinese political scene is the participation of millions of people in mass campaigns waged periodically by the regime for a variety of purposes—from the eradication of pests, to land reform, to socialist education, and finally to the Cultural Revolution. There were more than seventy-four mass campaigns waged on the national level from 1950 to 1978, and perhaps a third of that number waged locally over the same period. The average length of these mass campaigns has been between seventeen and eighteen months.[1] In addition to these campaigns, which generally engulf the entire populace, rural peasants and urban residents have been required to participate regularly in some sort of conscious political activity—usually as participating members of "small groups,"[2] the organizational devices used to assure active participation by ordinary citizens in political action. The basic purpose of the extraordinary stress upon active mass participation and periodic mass campaigns has been to inculcate new values and to induce correct attitudinal and behavioral patterns essential for making political, social, and economic changes necessary in building a socialist society.

Before we take up such pertinent topics as the extent and manner of mass participation and the style, techniques, and significance of mass campaigns, a few words must be said about the Chinese masses. The Chinese population was estimated at 800 million in the mid-1960s, with a projected 2 percent per annum growth rate.[3] This translates into an annual increase of approximately 16 million people to the already enormous population. Based on this projection, there is no question that by the 1980s China's total population will have reached 1 billion. The State Statistical Bureau announced in June 1979 a population of 975 million. In July 1982 China conducted its third census—the world's largest—assisted by more than 5 million interviewers, computers made in the United States, and United Nations experts. The State Council's Statistical Bureau announced that China's population was 1,031,882,511, including the populations of Taiwan, Hong Kong, and Macao.[4] Since only a small percentage of this total population are party members or cadres, the term *masses* refers to more than 90 percent of the people. Roughly 80 percent of the masses live in the countryside as toiling peasants, and the remaining 20 percent reside in the cities. Although China has a land area as large as that of the United States (about 3.7 million square miles), most of China's huge population is concentrated along the valleys of the two major river basins, the Huanghe and the Changjiang, and their tributaries. About 85 percent of the land area is hilly or mountainous and is sparsely populated.

Great strides have been made since 1949 in raising the literacy rate in China. At present, the literacy rate for adults is more than 65 percent, with a higher rate for those who live in urban areas.[5] Adult education, with political education as its main content, has contributed to the gradual reduction of illiteracy among the adults in China over the past three decades. While local dialects were a serious barrier to effective political communication before 1949, adults below the age of forty-five today can converse effectively in the standard spoken language known as "Putonghua." It is a common sight for visitors to China to see the simplified Chinese written characters alongside the romanization, for standard uniform pronunciation in schools in various regions of China. The Chinese masses, both rural and urban, are constantly being exposed to the networks of the political communication system: controlled mass media in the form of newspapers, radio broadcasts, and wall posters; the organizational units to which the masses in one way or another become attached; and the "small group," or "xiaozu," into which the masses have been organized and through which mass mobilization efforts are achieved. Aspects of the political communication system and the impact on mass participation and mobilization will be discussed later in this chapter.

In Chapter 2 we discussed in detail the meaning and significance of mass line in the thought of Mao. We may summarize the concept of Mao's mass line as a process by which the leaders (cadres) and the people (masses) establish a close relationship: The cadres attempt to seek willing compliance from the masses. In essence, the mass line concept, as applied in practice, is a process of "mutual education of leaders and led," by which unity among the masses is achieved on a given issue, and through which the masses can lend their overwhelming support by participating in the implementation of the decision.[6] Thus, participation in Chinese politics involves three sets of actors—the top leadership at the Politburo level, the cadres at the middle level, and the masses at the bottom—and a host of actions, which include listening, learning, reacting, summing up, interpreting or reinterpreting changing attitudes, and decision making.

It must be obvious by now that unlike political participation in the United States, where there is a wide variation in the degree of political involvement by the American people at various socioeconomic levels,[7] a vast majority of Chinese citizens must engage, often forcefully, in mandatory activities. But discretionary participation such as writing letters to the editors or contacting cadres is low. It is somewhat erroneous to assume that the vast majority of Chinese who participate in formal and legal political activities are automatically classified as activists. Chairman Mao once said that more than 60 percent of the populace must be considered fence-sitting middle-of-the-roaders, and only about 20 percent as progressives or activists.[8] One recent study, based on responses of refugees from mainland China, on frequency of political participation by mode indicated that although a majority of Chinese do participate in various forms of political activities, their sincerity in participation varies with the mode: The more formal the mode of participation, the less sincerity there is on the part of the participants.[9] Still, the regime's institutionalization of mass participation in politics and in decision making has been highly successful, especially when one considers the enormous size of China's population. Let us now turn to the fundamental question: In what ways do the Chinese masses participate in politics?

FORMS OF PARTICIPATION
IN CHINA

There are a variety of ways the Chinese masses participate in the "democratic management" of their political life. Mao's concept of mass line was enshrined in the 1982 state constitution, promulgated by the Fifth National People's Congress. That constitution states: "All state organs and functionaries must rely on the support of the people, keep close touch with them, heed their opinions and suggestions, accept their supervision and work hard to serve them."[10]

Elections and Voting

While voting in elections may be the single most important act of citizen participation in Western democracies, it is only one form of legally approved political action for the people of China. The election process in China also differs from that in Western democracies in several crucial respects.

First, the CCP manages the electoral process at all levels. Most important is CCP control of the election committees, which prepare approved slates of candidates for all elective offices, from the national to the basic level. Before 1980 these slates presented only one candidate for each office and thus determined the outcome of the election. Briefly in 1979–80 some local county elections for people's congresses allowed campaign rallies with speeches by candidates. The election law enacted in 1981–82 prohibited campaign rallies. The new election process is used primarily as a vehicle to arouse interest and heighten political consciousness among the people. In late 1979 deputies to the county people's congress were elected directly from a slate of candidates by secret ballot by the eligible voters. (The 1980 election of deputies from Hunan Teachers College in Changsha attracted worldwide attention when students in Changsha demonstrated at the provincial party headquarters to protest school authorities' decision to add another candidate to the final list of nominees in an effort to head off the election of one of the candidates, Liang Heng, who had declared that he did not believe in Marxism.[11]) By 1981 it was reported that 95 percent of the 2,756 local governments at the county level had been elected by people's congresses.[12]

Second, as we have noted, all elections above the basic level are indirect. At the basic level, the people elect directly the people's congresses, according to Article 97. Basic-level congresses elect the county-level congresses, which in turn elect the provincial congresses. The provincial congresses then elect the National People's Congress. There is no breakdown of how many national deputies each provincial people's congress can elect, even though the total number of deputies who met in March 1978 for the Fifth National People's Congress to adopt the new state constitution was 3,497. In compiling the number of deputies to the provincial people's congresses, as reported in the government controlled media, we arrive at a total of 28,709 deputies for the provinces and autonomous regions. Based on the reports of twenty-five provinces and autonomous regions, there were an average of 1,148 deputies for each province.[13]

Third, while the frequency of elections is prescribed by law, the legal schedule seldom has been followed in practice. There have been seven local elections since the founding of the People's Republic: 1953–54, 1956–57, 1958, 1961, 1963, 1966, and 1979–81. Both the 1953–54 and the 1956 elections had a respectable 86 percent voter turnout, somewhat below the usual turnout of over 90 percent for most communist countries.[14] Unfortunately, we have little information about the local elections after 1956.[15] But based on published accounts by the Chinese for the 1980 county-level elections, the typical local election process seemed to involve the following procedures.[16] The first step was the establishment of electoral districts for a county. Election districts were designated as follows: communes, if they had populations between 5,000 and 20,000; production brigades, if they had populations between 5,000 and 8,000; and industrial units, with requisite populations within the county. The local county and township governments decided their own ratios of population per deputy. For instance, in the local election for Tongxiang county in Zhejiang province in east China, it was established that there would be one rural county deputy for every 1,600 people, and one township deputy for every 400 people.[17]

A second step in the local election process was to publicize the election laws, particularly reforms introduced in 1979, such as direct election at the county level and below, secret ballot, the requirement that a 50 percent majority is needed to win, and the mandate that there be more candidates than the number of elective offices on the ballot. Publicity about the election laws was carried out by "agiprop" teams dispatched to the villages and towns, by radio and wall posters, and by small study groups. A third step involved the registration of eligible voters. Article 34 of the 1982 constitution stipulates that anyone who is a citizen and who is at least eighteen years old has the right to vote or to be a candidate for election, except for those deprived of political rights by law.

The fourth step in the election process was the nomination of candidates. The CCP, other minor democratic parties, and the mass organizations were permitted to nominate candidates for election. A voter or a deputy could nominate candidates if seconded by three other persons. At this stage the list of candidates was announced and circulated publicly, and "consultations" were held among the voters' groups within the electoral districts. The purpose of "consultations" was to allow the various groups, including the CCP, to screen out candidates and narrow the list to manageable proportions, so that only the preferred candidates could be presented for final balloting. In the case of Tongxiang county's 1980 election, there were more than 6,000 nominations for 500 deputy's seats in the preliminary round.[18] The list was finally narrowed down to a number between 750 and 1,000.[19] At this stage a voter could raise objections to anyone on the list. Of course, most nominees on the list doubtless were CCP members.

Now the actual campaign for votes was initiated by the candidates and the voting groups who nominated them. Information about candidates was printed and distributed among the various voter groups and was also disseminated through posters on public bulletin boards and on the radio. Finally, balloting was held on election day, within the various electoral districts. Election day in China usually has been a festive day accompanied by fireworks and the beating of gongs. After the ballots were counted, the newly elected deputies made speeches at meetings called by the elections committee, which certified the final vote count. The institutionalization of direct election at the county level, expected to be extended to the provinces and the nation in the future, may in the long run provide a much healthier means through which popular energy can be channeled than the negative mass campaigns to which China had been accustomed for so long.

It should be noted that direct election of team leaders at the production-team level, the lowest accounting and administrative unit in a rural commune, is more meaningful. At this level voting takes place at regular intervals to elect cadres for the production team. Even though the slate of cadres to be elected by the team members must be approved by the brigade, the very process of election provides the team members with a significant opportunity to participate in selecting their leaders and, on some occasions, in articulating the resolution of issues.[20]

Mass Organizations

In China literally thousands if not millions of people daily participate in politics as members of a myriad of "mass organizations." These mass organizations have been described as the "organizational matrix" of the party's rule over the masses.[21] They serve not only as institutions for political education but also as what Lenin termed the "transmission belt" for party policy. They are used as vehicles to gain support for policies and to mobilize the masses for implementing policies. The enormous membership and widespread extension of the networks from these mass organizations assure participation in political action by millions of adults and youths. All these mass organizations are formed on the basis of special interest or occupation and serve as "bridges and links" between the party and the masses.[22] The four largest and most active mass organizations—the Communist Youth League, the All-China Federation of Trade Unions, the All-China Women's Federation, and the peasants' associations—have been reactivated, following disruption during the Cultural Revolution. All held national congresses in the fall of 1978.[23]

The Communist Youth League (CYL) of China reported a membership of over 48 million in 1978 under a new leadership approved by the party. About 26 million, or 54 percent, of the CYL membership were recruited between 1978 and 1982.[24] With the disbanding of the Red Guard organizations for secondary school students in November 1978, the CYL can be expected to increase in size and importance. For instance, 2.7 million CYL members recruited between 1978 and 1982 were admitted into the CCP.[25] In the past the CYL has served as a vast reservoir for new party members and has provided political and ideological education for China's youth. Many of the party's leaders have come up from the ranks of the CYL. Hu Yaobang, the party's general secretary, was the head of the CYL for many years. Hu Qiaomu, a newly elected Politburo member and director of the party's research department, was also at one time a key figure in the youth league. So was Hu Qili, now director of the Central Committee's General Office. Many secondary school students will consider it necessary to join the CYL in order to ensure entrance to universities. Every other day the CYL publishes a journal, *China Youth,* which generally reflects the party's views on youth and their problems.[26]

The All-China Federation of Trade Unions, an important mass organization in industrial centers, was most active prior to the Cultural Revolution. The upheaval disrupted the functioning of this workers' mass organization to such an extent that by January 1967 it was dissolved at both the national and the local levels. Many of the union leaders were purged by the Red Guards and were charged with being followers of the Liu Shaoqi line, with being opposed to the class struggle, and with emphasizing expertise in production.[27] From 1967 to 1973, workers were organized into revolutionary workers' congresses, dominated at the national level by radicals, such as Wang Hongwen and Ni Zhifu. The latter later lent his support to Hua Guofeng. During the period from 1973 to the arrest of the Gang of Four in October 1976, trade union committees in factories functioned as adjuncts of the factory revolutionary committees. These trade union committees were primarily responsible for political education of the workers and supervision of social insurance, welfare, and factory safety measures.[28] Whatever the current organizational structure, workers in factories frequently meet and actively participate in mass action, particularly with regard to production efficiency: "to lower costs, to raise productivity, to stimulate innovation and new design, to develop aspects of decision making, to improve proletarian work style."[29] In an address to the Ninth National Trade Union Congress in October 1978, Politburo members Deng Xiaoping and Ni Zhifu urged the delegates to support the party's program for modernization and labor discipline and to observe the return to the system of decision making by the factory managers.[30]

The All-China Women's Federation once had a membership of close to 100 million. However, it ceased to function as a mass organization in 1967, during the Cultural Revolution. The women's federation's basic function has been to mobilize women in support of the various programs initiated by the party. Since women "shouldered half the sky," as the Chinese are fond of saying, this mass organization played an important role in the past in helping to obtain support for party programs and policies and in providing political education for its vast membership. The reactivated All-China Women's Federation selected the following items for its new program: promoting equal pay for equal work, with proper attention to conditions peculiar to women, such as pregnancies and maternity leaves; turning "petty housekeeping" into productive work and providing more time for rest and recreation; developing better educational care for the children, and supporting family planning and planned population growth; and developing friendly contacts with women of other countries.[31]

The peasants' association is another important mass organization. Inactive during the 1950s, the peasants' associations were reestablished in 1963 to serve as watchdog agencies to oversee the work performance and to monitor the behavior of the cadres, many of whom had engaged in antisocialist actions during the early 1960s, such as "eating too much or owning too much, extravagance and waste, nepotism, corruption, theft, and destruction of public property."[32] Under a June 1964 regulation, the peasants' associations were asked to participate in a host of governmental activities: public security surveillance over counterrevolutionary activities, propaganda and educational work among the people, and administrative consultation on commune policies prior to implementing any decisions by the cadres. Since the Cultural Revolution, the party branch at the basic levels of rural communes has controlled and manipulated the mass organizations, such as the peasants' associations, the All-China Women's Federation, and the Communist Youth League.

Urban residents are organized into neighborhood committees, the lowest level of mass organization for urban areas. As pointed out in Chapter 5, the resident group is made up of fifteen to forty households. A small group of household representatives discusses and resolves neighborhood problems such as housing, social welfare, sanitation, marriage, and birth control.[33] A primary function of the resident group is political education of members living in the area. Thus, the resident groups in urban areas serve as instruments both for participatory democracy and for mass mobilization. They are comparable to production teams or brigades in rural communes.

Small Study Groups

No discussion of mass participation in China is adequate without a close examination of the small group.[34] Across China cadres in offices, workers in factories, peasants in communes, students in schools, soldiers in the armed forces, and residents in neighborhood committees are organized in small groups, known as the xiaozu. Everyone in China is also identified and referred to by the units (danwei) to which they belong.[35] Whereas a "xiaozu" is a small group formed for a political study purpose, a "danwei" is a larger organizational unit such as an office or a factory or a workplace. Usually the small groups are formed from the members of the lowest organizational unit in factories, offices, and communes.[36] Frequently, an entire class in a school, even at the primary level, becomes a small group.[37] It is a common practice to have representatives of the mass organizations—such as the peasants' association, the trade union, or the Communist Youth League—work with the party committee at the lowest unit to organize these small groups.

The most important activity of the small groups is political study. In conversation with a small study group in a May Seventh cadre school near Beijing, where I visited in 1973, it was pointed out that political study for the group began with each member studying the works of Marx, Engels, and Mao on their own.[38] Sometimes they were asked to study an important editorial or special article in the *People's Daily*. A leader was generally assigned to the study group to answer questions about the reading content. Next, the group studied collectively, both engaging in group discussion and questioning each other's understanding of the reading material. Toward the end of the group's collective study, the group leader entered into the discussion by pointing out the important theoretical points and how they related to correct thinking and behavior, or simply the correct revolutionary line. After grasping the correct line, members of the group engaged in self-criticism for the purpose of making the necessary changes in their thinking and behavioral patterns. The author has been told that during the self-criticism stage, unity is reached by all members of the group on the meaning of the readings for their daily lives. In addition to political studies, small groups engage in problem solving for work units. Empirical studies, using refugees as informants, have indicated problems in the execution of small group dynamics and have raised questions about the quality and sincerity of members' participation.[39] Boredom, disinterest, and deliberate reticence during group discussions are common in many office and factory units and in production brigades in the communes.

What can be said about the effects of small groups as an organizational technique in terms of implementing Mao's concept of mass line? First, there is no question, as James Townsend concluded, that the small group has permitted personal participation in politics and has thus made it real and meaningful.[40] Second, it is a very effective device for social control. Whyte employs a term, the "encapsulation" of the people, to describe how deviant behavior can be identified and corrected through mutual self-criticism and peer pressure.[41] The control that the regime exercises over its disciplined populace on the whole must be attributed to the workings of the small group. Third, it is a vehicle through which the party's directives and policies can be effectively communicated to the masses and can receive the necessary support for implementation. Fourth, it is through discussion, self-criticism, and self-evaluation that Chinese masses are becoming increasingly analytical, not only about their own affairs but about politics in general.

Mass Campaigns

A mass campaign in China can be defined as a movement, conceived at the top, which encourages and promotes active participation by the masses in collective action, for the purpose of mobilizing support for or against a particular policy or program. Rarely has an important policy or program been launched without a mass campaign to support it. It is generally easy to detect the launching of a mass campaign. Since all mass campaigns require the active participation of the masses, the signal, or message, for the start of the campaign must be conveyed either in heavily couched ideological language or in "coded names" form, as Lucian Pye has pointed out.[42] The signal is sent through newspaper editorials or in statements made by key party leaders and displayed in newspaper headlines. First, an important speech—made by a key leader and accompanied by an editorial highlighting the major themes—is disseminated. Soon slogans embodying the key ideas of the campaign, as outlined in the published speech or editorial, appear in the masthead of newspapers, on walls, and on banners in communes and factories. These articles and editorials become basic source material for small group discussion and study. During the Cultural Revolution, activists in universities and high schools displayed their wall posters (dazibao) to pinpoint a particular theme or target to be struggled against in a campaign. Photographic displays or exhibits illustrating key leaders' ideas also appear in prominent locations. It has become a standard practice, for instance, for the government-owned and controlled printing corporation, the Xinhua Bookstore, to display photo exhibits outside the walls of its branch stores all over China.

Next, massive public rallies and demonstrations are staged. The rally in Tian An Men Square (October 24, 1976) for the campaign to criticize the Gang of Four drew a million people. In these campaign kickoffs, leading national, provincial, and local party and government cadres make repetitious speeches, outlining the purpose and targets for the campaign and exhorting the masses to participate and demonstrate their enthusiastic support.

Public rallies and demonstrations are followed by intensive study in small groups. The intensity of small group study varies from one basic unit to another. For instance, it is not unusual for some factories to require daily political study by small groups for half an hour to one hour during the evening. Such was the case at the beginning of the anti-Lin Biao campaign in 1972.[43] Generally speaking, small group meetings tend to become more numerous during a mass campaign. As the campaign intensifies, the small group study in various basic units also becomes tense, particularly when the stage of criticism and self-criticism is reached. In the early days, when the land reform program was launched, and at the time of the Cultural Revolution, struggle or accusation meetings took place when campaign procedure called for attacks, mostly verbal but sometimes physical, against the "enemy." Some campaigns may call for the masses to make a sacrifice for the collective good. Sometimes the deeds of a model hero are used as examples, as in the early phases of the Cultural Revolution, when such PLA heroes as Lei Feng were used as models for emulation.[44]

From an organizational point of view, the key to the success of any mass campaign is in the cadres dispatched from the national and provincial party committees to the basic units in factories and production brigades in the communes. Work teams of these cadres were originally used during the Socialist Education Campaign in 1963–65 to conduct on-the-spot investigations of charges made against corrupt cadres in the rural areas. Once the charges were substantiated through the team's firsthand investigation among the peasants, the members of the work teams were responsible for preparing and executing mass criticism to clean up corrupt practices within the cadre ranks. Finally, the work team was to recommend punitive measures for the wrongdoers and to institute necessary changes. During the Cultural Revolution, Mao's-thought propaganda teams were recruited among the PLA units and workers, primarily to mobilize the masses through discussion and study of Mao's teachings. Members of the work team in a mass campaign are campaign supervisors, whose main task is to see that the masses participate in the movement through meetings and study sessions. Millions of cadres must have been recruited in urban areas to form these work teams during the campaign to criticize the Gang of Four.

Mass campaigns have been institutionalized and have become an indispensable part of contemporary political life. The fact that there have been more than seventy campaigns waged at the national level since the founding of the republic in 1949 testifies to the frequency of their occurrence—an average of two per year. Charles Cell has classified mass campaigns into three basic groupings:[45] (1) campaigns waged on politics and economic development programs, frequently aimed at instituting basic changes; (2) ideological campaigns waged primarily to make social reforms or to induce new social values among the populace; and (3) campaigns waged to weaken or eliminate groups or individuals considered enemies of the people, such as landlords, counter-revolutionaries, and rightist elements. Some major mass campaigns, however, cannot readily be classified into any of these categories because of the multiplicity of themes. The Great Proletarian Cultural Revolution of 1966–68 is such a campaign. However, the pragmatic leaders now in power have indicated that large-scale mass campaigns cannot be undertaken in the future. They argued that the large-scale class struggles after 1953 were wrong and were in fact harmful to China's socialist system.

Wall Posters

Wall posters, a form of political communication closely associated with mass campaigns, have been common in major urban centers in China since the Cultural Revolution. Political messages written by hand on paper of various sizes and colors have been posted on walls and sidewalks in China as a form of protest since the days of the emperors. During imperial times this form of petition to redress wrongs was considered a right of the people, but of course the petitioner risked the consequences of arrest or physical abuse by authorities.

During the guerrilla days, the Chinese communist movement made wall posters a channel through which party members could voice their criticisms or complaints about inner party affairs. Wall posters were institutionalized in the 1950s, when numerous mass campaigns were waged—for example, the 1957 antirightist mass campaign. Initially the 1957 campaign called for free criticism of the regime under the slogan "letting a hundred flowers bloom." But when the intellectuals finally responded to the call by pointing out ills and defects in the Chinese communist system, they became the target for attack.

They were called "rightists" and "counterrevolutionary" and were subjected to purges and vilification. The behavior and thinking of the intellectuals were exposed in wall posters. It was then fashionable for anyone to put up a character poster on a wall or bulletin board of a workplace for the purpose of exposing a colleague or superior for his or her wrong political views, bad personal behavior, or even private life. Public exposure via wall posters reached its height during the Cultural Revolution, when party leaders were attacked by wall posters containing information deliberately provided by the radical leaders close to Mao. Libelous and malicious charges were made frequently, and the attackers were not required to reveal their identities. This practice of making malicious statements against others via wall posters gave the authors license to slander.

Too often the contents of these big-character posters were unsubstantiated rumors or sheer hearsay, but once posted, they caused irreparable damage to the persons under attack. Since China is a closed society, wall postering served a useful purpose, frequently giving insights into policy debates or pending inner party struggles among the top leaders. A large portion of what we learned about the early phase of the Cultural Revolution came from wall posters tacked up by the feuding Red Guards. Occasionally, wall posters—if they were spontaneous expressions—serve as a barometer for reading public opinion. The 1976 Tian An Men demonstration probably fell into this category: Poems posted and read orally on that spring Sunday morning conveyed the public's respect for the departed premier and support for the purged Deng Xiaoping. This event is now viewed as something very positive, presaging the eventual downfall of the Gang of Four.[46]

In the final analysis, all wall poster campaigns, like all mass campaigns of the past, can be abruptly terminated when the authorities call for a halt, even though Article 45 of the 1978 constitution stipulated that Chinese citizens "have a right to speak out freely, air their views fully, hold great debates, and write big-character posters." The flurry of free expression exhibited on the Democracy Walls in Beijing was abruptly halted in March 1979 by the authorities on the grounds that it was too excessive in criticizing the leaders and the system.

MASS CAMPAIGNS SINCE THE CULTURAL REVOLUTION, 1971–78

There have been at least seven major and two minor mass campaigns waged since the conclusion of the Cultural Revolution. Table 7.1 presents a summary of the general nature and duration of these recent mass movements. The first six major campaigns—anti-Lin Biao, anti-Confucius, *Water Margin,* study of the dictatorship of the proletariat, anti-capitalist roaders, and anti–Gang of Four—were rectification campaigns aimed at the problem of leadership tension and crisis. The modernization campaign launched in 1978 was for both

TABLE 7.1   Mass Campaigns Since 1969

	Time Period	Type of Campaign	Targets And Goals
1. Anti–Lin Biao	1971–73	rectification	Lin Biao, and his supporters in party, government, and PLA
2. Anti–Confucius	1974–75	ideological/ rectification	Zhou Enlai and moderates in party and government
3. *Water Margin*	1975–76	ideological/ rectification	Zhou Enlai, Deng Xiaoping, and possibly Hua Guofeng
4. Study the Dictatorship of the Proletariat	1975	ideological/ rectification	Zhou Enlai, Deng Xiaoping, and 4th NPC programs
5. Campaigns against Capitalist Roaders	Spring 1976	ideological	Deng Xiaoping
6. Anti–Gang of Four Campaign	1976–78	rectification	the radical elements of the party
7. Emulation Campaign in Railroads	March 1977	economic/ rectification	railway efficiency, security, and discipline
8. Nationwide Sanitation Campaign	1978	attitudinal	sanitation and public health
9. The Four Modernization Campaign	1978	economic/ attitudinal	economic development

economic and attitudinal purposes. The remaining two minor campaigns were directed at specific goals—railway reform and improved sanitation. Let us examine these recent campaigns in some detail.

Anti–Lin Biao Campaign, 1971–73

The anti–Lin Biao campaign began soon after Lin's demise in September 1971, but his name was not mentioned in the mass media until after the convening of the Tenth Party Congress in August 1973. Thus, for roughly the first two years of the campaign, the general populace was quite confused about the theme and target of the campaign. For one thing, the political views of Lin Biao had been very close to those of Mao Zedong, particularly during the days of the Cultural Revolution. As a campaign with ideological content, it was difficult at the beginning to pinpoint exactly the main divergent view of Lin Biao. Part of the campaign focused initially more on Lin's "personal foibles than on errors of line."[47] As the campaign progressed, Lin Biao's alleged plot against Mao became the dominant theme of the campaign, to illustrate Lin's antiparty activities. During this campaign an extensive purge was undertaken at the national, regional, and provincial levels to eliminate the remnants of Lin's supporters in the party, government, and PLA. On the whole, the first stage of the anti–Lin Biao campaign from 1971–73 was weak in ideological content and explanation but strong in rectification and the purge of

Lin's supporters and sympathizers. In comparison with previous mass campaigns, including those essentially of a rectifying nature, the anti–Lin Biao campaign aroused limited mass enthusiasm. Perhaps there were more secret meetings held by the party units at all levels to explain events that had taken place two years earlier, but there was evidently less open discussion than usual by the masses and the cadres.[48]

Anti-Confucius and Anti–Lin Biao Campaign, 1973–74

At first the anti-Confucius campaign sounded like an academic debate. It began when a noted Chinese historian and scholar, Guo Moruo, published an article on ancient Chinese history in the party's theoretical journal.[49] Guo dated the transition from "slave" to "feudal" society at about 206 B.C. This began a debate among China's historians, at least on the surface, on the subject of periodization. Soon the scholars' debate veered from the question of periodization to whether Confucius was a conservative reactionary. With the public disclosure at the Tenth Party Congress in August 1973 of Lin Biao's alleged plot against the party and Chairman Mao, a link was established between Confucius and Lin Biao: Lin was castigated as a convert to Confucian teachings.[50] While Confucius advocated the restoration of the rule of the slave-owning society of the Western Zhou dynasty (1066–771 B.C.), Lin wanted to restore revisionist tendencies to denigrate the gains of the Cultural Revolution. The general tenor of the articles that proliferated to criticize Lin Biao and Confucius gave the appearance of a militant mass campaign comparable to a mini–Cultural Revolution. There was some upsurge in the campaign, with participation by the masses, during most of the spring of 1974.[51] By midsummer the targets had enlarged to include problems that had surfaced with respect to a number of Cultural Revolution reforms, such as illegal entry into the universities by the "back door," the reluctance of urban youth to work in the countryside, and the failure of cadres to participate in manual labor. Between the upsurges of the mass campaign, there was a period of cautious retreat into militancy.

Even in the midst of the campaign to criticize Lin Biao and Confucius, there was confusion, particularly outside of China, about the real intended target and the authority actually directing the campaign. Some observers in the West interpreted the campaign as a movement directed by Premier Zhou against the radicals and the remnants of the Lin Biao clique.[52] Others viewed the campaign as an attack directed by the radicals against Premier Zhou and his attempts to return to the pre–Cultural Revolution programs, which included the return of Deng Xiaoping to power.[53] One observer, Parris Chang, divided the campaign into two different phases, with two different leadership factions directing it: the radicals in control of the campaign from 1972–73, with the joint conservative forces of the central leadership and the provincial military as its target; and Zhou Enlai's pragmatic group in control in 1974, with Lin Biao as a target, in order to downgrade the ideological impact of the radicals' attack on the conservatives.[54]

In 1977 the *Beijing Review* reported that during 1974 the Gang of Four attempted to manipulate the anti-Confucius and anti–Lin Biao campaign. At a series of meetings in January 1974, they developed material for dissemination, including tapes, which criticized those who obtained admittance to the army and the universities by the "back door," or by using private connections. At these meetings the radicals, led by Jiang Qing, evidently decided to direct the campaign against the PLA, the leaders of the party's Military Affairs Commission, and Zhou Enlai. Immediately subsequent to the January meetings, the name of the eleventh-century B.C. Duke of Zhou, implying Premier Zhou Enlai, was added to the targets in the mass media.[55] The anti–Lin Biao and anti-Confucius campaign faded away during the early months of 1975 and was replaced by two offshoots, the movement to study the dictatorship of the proletariat, and the *Water Margin* campaign—both waged by the radicals to attack Zhou Enlai and his pragmatic programs.

Dictatorship of the Proletariat Campaign, 1975

While this new campaign was personally launched by Mao on the heels of the Fourth National People's Congress in January 1975, it was managed by the radicals. The purpose of the campaign was to bring out into the open disagreement with Zhou Enlai over policies and the rehabilitation of many leaders vilified during the Cultural Revolution. In this campaign the radicals hoped to generate the mass participation and militancy that the anti-Confucius and anti–Lin Biao campaigns had lacked. In typical fashion the campaign began with an outpouring of theoretical articles in the mass media, mostly written by a group of radical propagandists under the name of the "mass criticism group of Beijing and Qinghua Universities."[56] At the heart of the campaign was the radicals' concern over the pragmatic policies in the economic sector: continuation of private plots and sideline enterprises of the peasants in the communes, and reliance on managers and specialists in industrial production. Zhou Enlai had advocated a modernization program in his report to the Fourth National People's Congress. The implementation of Zhou's long-range modernization plan meant major changes in the economic sphere, coupled with educational reforms, to upgrade China's scientific and technological development. The arguments of the radicals focused on these areas of economic modernization, which inevitably would entail emphasis of material incentives and the creation of a new "bourgeois class" of industrial managers and specialists.

In the midst of this new campaign, labor unrest, protesting the unequal distribution of wages which placed the lower ranks of workers at a disadvantage, was reported in the industrial regions of east China.[57] Troops had to be dispatched to quell riots in Hangzhou, the capital of Zhejiang, caused by workers demonstrating for reform of the wage differential system and for wage increases.[58] When, in the summer of 1975, it became evident that the campaign for the study of the dictatorship of the proletariat lacked mass support, a new attack was mounted in August against Zhou Enlai, which was based on criticism of a popular novel about a peasant rebellion.

Campaign to Criticize *Water Margin,* August-November 1975

The campaign to criticize the popular novel *Water Margin* was an attack against Premier Zhou by innuendo. The radicals, in their desperation to curb "bourgeois tendencies," may have felt that an emotional appeal—coupled with the vehicle of a familiar heroic folk tale—would succeed in gaining the attention of the masses where the intellectual approach had failed.

Water Margin relates how a group of 108 peasants and government officers, under the able leadership of Sung Jiang, mounted a successful rebellion against corrupt officials during the Sung Dynasty in the twelfth century. The popular novel, which was abridged in the late Ming Dynasty, ends here. The original novel went on to relate how Sung Jiang accepted a pardon from the emperor and then served the emperor in suppressing other rebellions. The Shanghai radicals criticized the ending of the popular novel, and quoted Mao as saying that Sung Jiang was a reactionary because he capitulated to the emperor and practiced revisionism.[59] By innuendo, the radicals' campaign literature called Premier Zhou Enlai and his supporters, who advocated more pragmatic programs, "present day Sung Jiangs" who practiced capitulation and revisionism.[60] The campaign lasted only about three months; its sudden disappearance from the political scene may be attributed to its ineffectiveness.

Campaign Against Capitalist Roaders, January-September 1976

This rather short-lived campaign, instigated by the radicals, was aimed at Deng Xiaoping, the vice-premier of the State Council and a possible successor to the ailing Zhou Enlai. The campaign began with wall posters posted in Beijing by radical students from Beijing and Qinghua Universities.[61] As the posters began to appear, attacking him as a "capitalist roader," Deng disappeared from the political scene. Other rehabilitated veteran cadres who had been reinstated in the government and party were called "right deviationists." When the Tian An Men incident occurred in April, Deng Xiaoping was charged with instigating this mass demonstration to disrupt the political order. As pointed out in Chapter 1, the Tian An Men incident apparently was a spontaneous demonstration in support of Zhou Enlai and Deng against the radicals. Following the Tian An Men incident, Deng was formally removed from office and the campaign began to criticize him for attempting to reverse the "correct verdict of the Cultural Revolution," particularly in the field of education. Deng's plans to develop science and technology and to revitalize industry were attacked by the radical press.[62] Like the mass campaigns waged by the radicals in 1974 and 1975, this campaign against Deng Xiaoping not only failed to arouse popular enthusiasm but created confusion among the masses. The campaign was terminated with the arrest of the four radical leaders in early October, following Mao's death.

Campaign to Criticize the Gang of Four, December 1976 to 1978

This campaign was launched officially at the Second National Conference on Agriculture in December 1976. Hua Guofeng outlined the two-step development of the campaign: (1) to expose the radicals' plot to take over the party and state and (2) to reveal and criticize their past "criminal" and "counterrevolutionary" activities.[63] The conduct of this campaign closely followed the pattern of past campaigns which had the sanction of the leaders in control of the party. Party committees at all levels were used as focal centers for implementation. Work teams from urban areas in each province were dispatched to the countryside to help the communes prepare and organize meetings and study sessions. It has been reported that for the first several months of 1977, some 400,000 cadres assigned to these work teams were sent to the countryside in Anhui, Fujian, Henan, Shanxi, and Sichuan provinces alone.[64] The campaign was conducted both in public meetings and in small study groups. The mass media presented a daily diet of criticism of the "nation's scourge" (the misdeeds of the Gang of Four), and big-character posters proliferated. In official briefings in factories and communes, foreign visitors were told that production had increased since the downfall of the Gang of Four.

Exposés of various organizational units' struggles against the Gang of Four when they were in power gave a fairly good idea of how the radical leaders "interfered" in the work of every sector of society. They shed light on the conflicts over key issues between the radicals and the Zhou Enlai group. The theoretical group of the prestigious Chinese Academy of Sciences charged that the radicals considered scientific inquiry and pure research as "bourgeois in nature."[65] The mass criticism group of the State Planning Commission revealed that the Gang of Four was opposed to centralized planning, rational industrial management, training of skilled technicians, and importation of advanced technology from abroad.[66] The theoretical study group of the Ministry of Foreign Affairs criticized Jiang Qing for "issuing statements to foreigners without authorization" and for "divulging classified information of the party and the state," as well as for creating confusion in China's foreign trade.[67]

This mass outpouring of criticism against the radical leaders was, of course, also being used to mobilize public opinion in favor of the pragmatic policies and programs of Hua Guofeng and Deng Xiaoping, which were basically those endorsed by Zhou Enlai. The exposure of the wrongdoings of the radical leaders was to help explain the sweeping reversal of the Cultural Revolution policies of the past decade. The campaign was also intended to create a favorable climate for the new leaders to exercise control over their opposition. From September 1976 to the spring of 1977, there were reports of unrest and disorder in many parts of the country.[68] The intensive mass campaign allowed the new leaders to carry on the necessary purge within the party and governmental apparatus in order to consolidate their power. Hua's political report to the CCP Eleventh Party Congress in August 1977 made it very clear that the mass campaign would eradicate the Gang of Four's "pernicious influence in every field."[69] The purge was to extend to all individuals who were involved in the "conspiratory" activities of the Gang of Four.

The campaign to criticize the Gang of Four was also accompanied by two minor mass movements: the emulation campaign in railway administration and the nationwide sanitation campaign. The first, primarily aimed at the railway workers, was intended to improve the efficiency of the railways. The second was a crash program to improve China's sanitation, and was reminiscent of the mass campaigns to eradicate pests in the early 1950s.

DEMOCRACY WALL
MOVEMENT 1978–79[70]

For more than a year, between November 1978 and December 1979, worldwide attention was focused on the daily posting of handwritten messages on a brick wall, 12 feet in height and about 120 feet long, located at Changan Avenue near the Xidan crossing in the western district of downtown Beijing. Later, this wall came to be known as the Democracy Wall. Initially the appearance of the wall posters at the Xidan crossing may have had the blessing of the leadership faction, following the practice established during the early days of the Cultural Revolution. Some of the contents may have been leaked deliberately to the activists, who then aired them in the posters.

In March 1978 the first series of wall posters, in the form of poems, appeared on the Xidan Democracy Wall. Wu De, then the mayor of Beijing and the Politburo member who read the riot act to the 1976 demonstrators on Tian An Men, was attacked by name in the wall posters by the participants in the 1976 demonstration. This seemed to have signaled the events to come. The first officially approved act was the publication of a demand for a reversal of the verdict on the 1976 Tian An Men demonstration in the CYL periodical. By October 11, 1978, Wu De was forced to resign as mayor of Beijing, and shortly thereafter hundreds of participants arrested in the 1976 Tian An Men riot were released and exonerated. During late October and early November, a sudden release of pent-up feelings increased the output of posters dramatically. This seemingly spontaneous outpouring of wall posters on Democracy Wall might have coincided with the convening of the party's central work conference, which was planning the Third Plenum of the Eleventh Central Committee. During this period the pragmatic leaders under Deng had locked horns with the "Whatever" faction on issues such as the new ideological line of "seeking truth from fact," the reversal of the 1976 Tian An Men demonstration, the rehabilitation and exoneration of purged leaders of the Cultural Revolution and, most important of all, the assessment of Mao and his role in the Cultural Revolution.

A study of the wall posters for that period revealed three main trends: the condemnation of political persecution authorized by Mao; petitions for the redress of personal grievances inflicted upon those who were persecuted during the Cultural Revolution; and the advocacy of democracy, justice, and human rights.[71] The proliferation of wall posters provided Deng Xiaoping with public support in his contest for power against the "Whatever" faction at the party's Third Plenum. As if by mere coincidence, decisions adopted by the party were identical to the concerns expressed by the posters on the Democracy Wall. For instance, the Third Plenum corrected the "erroneous conclusions" on veteran party leaders such as Peng Dehuai, Bo Yibo, and Yang Shangkun by exonerating and rehabilitating them.[72] The plenum also declared that the Tian An Men events of 1976 were "revolutionary actions."[73] It adopted the ideological line that "practice is the sole criterion for testing truth."[74] It was also decided to establish a discipline inspection commission within the party to enforce and investigate violation of party rules and regulations. While the plenum did not yet make an assessment of Mao's role in the Cultural Revolution, it hinted strongly that Mao, as a Marxist revolutionary leader, could not possibly be free of "shortcomings and errors."[75] It became evident that Deng Xiaoping had encouraged the wall posters when he told both a group of Japanese visitors and then Robert Novak, an American syndicated columnist, that the wall posters were officially tolerated.[76]

The Democracy Wall movement entered its second phase early in December 1978. In addition to candid expressions in support of sexual freedom and human rights, some criticisms of Deng Xiaoping now appeared. Deng had shifted his earlier stand and now expressed disapproval of the posters' criticism of the socialist system. There may have been other reasons for Deng's change of mind. It is possible that Deng had been subjected to criticism within the party for not having taken a stronger stand to curb the expressions of dissent at the Democracy Wall—members of the "Whatever" faction still sat on the Politburo even though they were criticized for their past role in the Cultural Revolution. Perhaps genuine concern about restoring stability and unity led to curbing the freewheeling activities at the wall. It was also very possible that Deng and his intimate colleagues were really apprehensive about the close contacts established by the participants with the foreign reporters who had been invited into the dissenters' homes to talk about democracy and human rights.[77]

During December 1978 activists associated with the Democracy Wall movement became dissatisfied with the success of their poster campaign and looked for ways to expand the campaign for democracy and human rights. They formed dissident organizations and study groups with names such as Enlightenment Society, China Human Rights Alliance, and the Thaw Society. Each published its own underground journals and offered them for sale at the Democracy Wall. Most publications were poorly produced with primitive mimeograph machines. Nevertheless, some of the underground publications soon attracted worldwide attention as American, British, Canadian, and French reporters were given copies for overseas consumption. Excerpts from underground journals, such as *Beijing Spring,* obviously inspired by the 1968 "Prague Spring" of the Soviet invasion of Czechoslovakia; *April Fifth Forum,* derived from the demonstration at the Tian An Men on April 5, 1976; and *Tansuo (Exploration),*[78] were translated and published in foreign papers all over the world. The appearance of these underground journals and the topics they discussed (freedom of speech, democracy, law and justice, human rights, and modernization of science and technology) were reminiscent of the May Fourth movement sixty years earlier. The new movement spread to many provinces and cities in China. It also tried to forge an alliance with the many protest groups formed by demobilized soldiers and peasants who came to Beijing in increasing numbers. Then China launched its border war with Vietnam. Pressures now mounted for Deng Xiaoping to curb the dissident movement.

It was reported on March 16, 1979, that Deng informed the senior cadres of central government departments that a ban would be imposed on activities at the Democracy Wall.[79] When news of Deng's decision leaked out, Wei Jingsheng, an articulate editor, published an attack on Deng in a special issue of his underground journal, *Tansuo (Exploration).* Deng did not at first place an immediate ban on dissident activities at the Democracy Wall. Instead, he outlined "Four Fundamental Principles," which held that officials could accept wall poster dissent if it upheld the socialist road, the dictatorship of the proletariat, the leadership of the party, and Marxism-Leninism and Mao's thought.[80] Wei's editorials had slandered Marxism-Leninism and Mao's thought and had advocated the abandonment of the socialist system. Wei was arrested on March 29 along with thirty other dissidents. Simultaneously, the government-controlled mass media strongly criticized activities at the Democracy Wall. While the dissidents were under arrest, wall posters were allowed on the Democracy Wall, including ones which accused two leaders of the "Whatever" faction (Wang Dongxing and Chen Xilian) of alleged financial irregularities and misconduct. These wall posters were believed to have been sanctioned by the Deng group in its move to oust Politburo members who were key figures in the "Whatever" faction.[81]

Wei was not brought to trial until October 16; in a one-day trial he was sentenced to fifteen years imprisonment for having supplied military intelligence to Western reporters (including names of commanders and troop numbers in China's war with Vietnam), for slandering Marxism-Leninism, and for encouraging the overthrow of the socialist system.[82] Wei subsequently appealed to the Beijing Municipal Higher Court, but his plea was rejected.[83] Meanwhile, on the recommendation of the Standing Committee of the National People's Congress, the Beijing Municipal Revolutionary Committee issued an order on December 6, 1979, which (1) prohibited wall posters on the Democracy Wall at Xidan but allowed such activities to take place at the Moon Altar Park, an area removed from downtown Beijing; (2) required registration of all those who wanted to display wall posters at the new site; (3) declared unlawful any disclosure of "state secrets" and false information; and (4) imposed punishments on those who created disturbances or riots at the new site.[84] On the night of December 7, a cleaning crew whitewashed the remaining posters still glued to the Democracy Wall at Xidan and thus ended a movement that had attracted worldwide attention.

The final phase of the Democracy Wall movement came in February 1980, when the Fifth Plenum of the Eleventh Central Committee decided to rehabilitate Liu Shaoqi, to remove the "Whatever" factional leaders from the Politburo, and to install Deng's close supporters Hu Yaobang and Zhao Ziyang to membership of the Politburo's Standing Committee.[85] With the removal of the "Whatever" faction from the Politburo, Deng proceeded to remove the last vestige of the Cultural Revolution: Article 45 of the 1978 state constitution, known as the "Sida" or the "four big rights"—*daming* ("speak out freely"), *dafang* ("air views fully"), *dabianlun* ("hold great debate"), and *dazibao* ("put up big-character posters"). In Deng's view the four big rights "had never played a positive role in safeguarding the people's democratic rights."[86] Instead, Deng now argued that they had become weapons and tools employed by ultra-Leftists like Lin Biao and the Gang of Four to advance their aims.[87] It was now the party's view that the very use of these rights had caused chaos during the Cultural Revolution decade. The wall posters, it was now charged, tended to incite "anarchism" and "factionalism."[88] Thus, Article 45 needed to be stricken from the 1978 constitution if political unity and stability were to be preserved.[89] The National People's Congress in its third session endorsed the party's stand, amending the 1978 constitution by deleting the "Sida" rights.[90] The removal of Article 45 ended China's youthful dissenters' brief flirtation with democracy and human rights. Having been encouraged initially by the forces under Deng to exercise the "Sida" rights, particularly the use of wall posters, to discredit Deng's opponents on the Politburo, the young dissenters were then "betrayed" by Deng as he gained power and control in the party and government. However, it might also be argued that to Deng and his close colleagues, victims of the Cultural Revolution, any appearance of anarchy and chaos, reinforced by the pent-up energy and frustration of the young, constituted a serious threat to China's political stability. Deng and his supporters believed that the energy of the people must be directed toward modernization, not toward dissent. It could also be true, as many Western reporters and diplomats believe, that Deng had to crack down on the movement as a "tradeoff" for support from other leaders, in his maneuvers to consolidate his power.[91]

The mass campaign, as we have seen in this section, is a unique form of participation for the people of China. These movements have been employed for a variety of purposes: instilling ideological conformity, developing popular acceptance of economic programs, and resolving intraparty conflicts among leaders at the top. These mass movements also have been used to combat inertia of the masses and the cadres in implementing new economic programs, as well as to restrain cadre corruption by means of mass criticism. The mass campaigns launched in the post–Cultural Revolution era of the 1970s were mainly for rectification, to resolve conflicts among the top elites. In these mass campaigns, the shifting ideological pitch and targets for attack certainly created confusion and uncertainty for the populace as a whole. But, as Alan Liu has pointed out, the integrative effect of these mass campaigns for the Chinese nation has been valuable and lasting in terms of uniformity of language in political expression and the acquisition of the organization skills demanded by mass campaigns.[92] The Chinese, through those mass campaigns, have indeed become "organization people" in a society which traditionally has been full of centrifugal tendencies.

SUMMARY

We have discussed the many ways in which the masses in China participate in political life. Like citizens in many other countries of the world, where popular elections for public or political offices are permitted, the Chinese do participate in elections at the local, or basic, level. But unlike most countries that hold elections, the Chinese participate in politics far more extensively and through many modes of participation—voluntary or pressured, in mass organizations, in small study groups, and in periodic mass campaigns. This participation has had a number of effects. Most important has been the political socialization—the formation of political beliefs and values—of the vast population. This socialization process allowed drastic social reform to take root in the communist Chinese experience. It also awakened a population that was formerly unaware, unconcerned, and unmotivated about government to participate in politics in a very personal way.[93]

With the major proponents of mass campaigns—Mao and the Gang of Four—removed from the political scene, what can we expect of mass campaigns in the future? The pragmatic leadership has indicated that certain modifications will have to be introduced to make the participatory process practical as well as meaningful. Deng Xiaoping warned his colleagues at the Eleventh Party Congress in 1977 that the mere incantation of slogans and the enormous amount of time spent on empty talk must be eliminated. Although no one in China has said that political studies are no longer important in schools, a basic agent for socialization, it has been made clear that an excessive number of hours ought not to be devoted to political and ideological studies at the expense of hard learning. Intellectuals and scientists have been told to return to their laboratories for more research activities. They have also been reminded of the importance of raising their political consciousness through studies and self-criticism during their spare time. Thus, political study and mass campaigns, somewhat curtailed, will continue to be an essential part of political life in China. The campaign for re-registration of CCP members for the three year period from 1983 to 1986, for the purpose of weeding out the incompetent must be viewed in this light.

NOTES

1. Charles P. Cell, *Revolution At Work: Mobilization Campaigns In China* (New York: Academic Press, 1977).

2. Martin King Whyte, *Small Groups and Political Rituals in China* (Berkeley, Calif.: University of California Press, 1974).

3. John S. Aird, "Population Growth and Distribution in Mainland China, and Recent Provincial Population Figures," *The China Quarterly,* 73 (March 1978), 35–38, 44.

4. "The World's Biggest Census," *Beijing Review,* 32 (August 9, 1982), 16–25; and "The 1982 Census Results," *Beijing Review,* 45 (November 8, 1982), 20–21. For the twenty-nine provinces, municipalities, and autonomous regions, the population is 1,008,175,288.

5. See Charles S. Taylor and Michael C. Hudson, *World Handbook of Political and Social Indicators* (New Haven, Conn.: Yale University Press, 1972), p. 232.

6. See Jack Gray and Patrick Cavendish, *Chinese Communism in Crisis: Maoism and the Cultural Revolution* (New York: Holt, Rinehart & Winston, 1968); and Lewis, *Leadership in Communist China,* p. 70.

7. See Kenneth Prewitt and Sidney Verba, *Principles of American Government,* 2nd ed. (New York: Harper and Row, Pub., 1977), p.p. 65–67.

8. See "Speech at the Lushan Conference, 23 July 1959," in *Chairman Mao Talks to the People,* pp. 134–39.

9. V.C. Falkenheim, "Political Participation in the People's Republic of China" (unpublished paper presented at the 1978 annual meeting of the Association for Asian Studies, Chicago, March 31–April 2, 1978). Permission from author to make this reference.

10. See Article 27 of the 1982 constitution, in Appendix A.

11. See Butterfield, *China: Alive In the Bitter Sea,* pp. 421–22. Laing Heng subsequently left China for the U.S. with his wife Judy Shapiro. Together they wrote a biography, *Son of the Revolution* (New York: Alfred A. Knopf, 1983). Also see *The New York Times,* October 15, 1980; and Shan Zi, "Election in Changsha," *The Asia Record,* vol. 3, no. 3 (June 1982), 26.

12. "Election at the County Level," *Beijing Review,* 5 (February 1, 1982), 18. For a detailed study of the 1979 election law reform and county-level elections in 1980, see Brantly Womack, "The 1980 County-Level Elections in China: Experiment in Democratic Modernization," *Asian Survey,* vol. xxii, no. 3 (March 1982), 261–77.

13. *Renmin Ribao,* December 10, 1977, p. 1; December 14, 1977, p. 1; December 15, 1977, p. 1; December 20, 1977, p. 1; December 23, 1977, p. 1; December 24, 1977, p. 1; December 27, 1977, p. 1; December 29, 1977, p. 1; January 4, 1978, p. 1; January 6, 1978, p. 1; January 9, 1978, p. 1; January 10, 1978, p. 1.

14. See James Townsend, *Political Participation in Communist China* (Berkeley Calif.: University of California Press, 1969), p. 119. The figure of 86 percent turnout that Townsend used was based on Chinese reports compiled by the Union Research Service, Hong Kong. For a comparative voter turnout in different countries, see Gabriel A. Almond, *Comparative Politics Today: A World View* (Boston: Little, Brown and Co., 1974), p. 60.

15. There are few statistics for local elections except for the 1953–54 election. See Townsend, *Political Participation in Communist China,* pp. 115–36.

16. For Chinese coverage of recent elections, see "Election of Deputies to a County People's Congress," *Beijing Review,* 8 (February 25, 1980), 11–19; *Beijing Review,* 18 (May 4, 1981), 5; and *Beijing Review,* 5 (February 1, 1982), 13–19. Also see Womack, "The 1980 County-Level Elections in China," pp. 266–70.

17. "Election of Deputies to a County People's Congress," p. 14.

18. Ibid., pp. 16–17.

19. Ibid.

20. John P. Burns, "The Election of Production Team Cadres in Rural China: 1958–74," *The China Quarterly,* 74 (June 1978), 273–96. For election of shop leaders in a factory, see Zhi Exiang, "The Election of Shop Heads," *China Reconstructs,* vol. xxviii, no. 5 (May 1979), 6–8.

21. Doak Barnett, *Communist China: The Early Years, 1949–55* (New York: Holt, Rinehart & Winston, 1964), p. 30.

22. "The PRC's New Labor Organization and Management Policy," *Current Scene,* vol. xv, nos. 11 and 12 (November–December 1977), 18–23; and Ni Chih-fu, "Basic Principle for Trade Union Work in the New Period," *Peking Review,* 44 (November 3, 1978), 7–13, 24.

23. "Mass Organizations Reactivated," *Peking Review,* 20 (May 19, 1978), 10–13; "Women's Movement in China: Guiding Concepts and New Tasks," *Peking Review,* 39 (September 29, 1978), 5–11. See also Ni Chih-fu, "Basic Principle for Trade Union Work in the New Period," p. 24.

24. "Communist Youth League Congress Opens," *Beijing Review,* 52 (December 27, 1982), 4.

25. Ibid.

26. See Butterfield, *China: Alive in the Bitter Sea,* pp. 142–43; Bernstein, *From the Center of the Earth,* pp. 172–73; and Garside, *Coming Alive: China After Mao,* pp. 322–24, 210.

27. See *Peking Review,* 4 (January 26, 1968), 7. Also, see "China's Trade Unions—An Interview with Chen Yu, Vice-Chairman of All China Federation of Trade Unions," *China Reconstructs,* vol. xxviii, no. 5 (May 1979), 9–12.

28. See Charles Hoffmann, "Worker Participation in Chinese Factories," *Modern China: An International Quarterly,* vol. 3, no. 3 (July 1977), 296.

29. Ibid., p. 308.

30. "Greeting the Great Task," *Peking Review,* 42 (October 20, 1978), 5–8; and Ni Chih-fu, "Basic Principle for Trade Union Work," pp. 10–13.

31. Kang Ke-ching, "Women's Movement in China: Guiding Concepts and New Tasks," *Peking Review,* 39 (September 29, 1978), 8–11. Also see "The Women's Movement in China—An Interview with Lou Qiong," *China Reconstructs,* vol. xxviii, no. 3 (March 1979), 33–36. Butterfield, *China: Alive in the Bitter Sea,* pp. 166–72; and David Bonavia, *The Chinese* (New York: Lippincott & Crowell, Pub., 1980), p. 165.

32. CCP Central Committee 23-Point Regulation on Cadres Policy, 1965. For details see Richard Baum, *Prelude to Revolution: Mao, the Party, and the Peasant Question, 1962–66* (New York: Columbia University Press, 1975), pp. 76–82.

33. "The Neighborhood Revolutionary Committee," in *China Reconstructs,* vol. xxii, no. 8 (August 1973), 2–3.

34. For an in-depth study of small groups, see Whyte, *Small Groups and Political Rituals in China.* Also see Townsend, *Political Participation in Communist China,* pp. 174–76.

35. For a more recent account of the small groups, see Butterfield, *China: Alive in the Bitter Sea,* pp. 40–42; and Bonavia, *The Chinese,* pp. 45–46.

36. Whyte, *Small Groups and Political Rituals in China,* p. 172; and Butterfield, *China: Alive in the Bitter Sea,* pp. 40–42, 323–26.

37. Whyte, *Small Groups and Political Rituals in China,* p. 105.

38. See James C. F. Wang, "May 7th Cadre School for Eastern Peking," 524–25.

39. Whyte, *Small Groups and Political Rituals,* pp. 212–13; and Falkenheim, "Political Participation in the People's Republic of China." Permission to use the summary findings of the paper has been given by the author.

40. Townsend, *Political Participation in Communist China,* p. 176.

41. Whyte, *Small Groups and Political Rituals,* pp. 15–16, 233.

42. Pye, "Communications and Chinese Political Culture," *Asian Survey,* vol. xviii, no. 3 (March 1978), 228–30.

43. Conversation with Fred Engst, an American who worked in a factory in China from 1960–76.

44. See Mary Sheridan, "The Emulation of Heros," *The China Quarterly,* 33 (January–March 1968), 47–72; and James C. F. Wang, "Values of the Cultural Revolution," *Journal of Communication,* vol. 27, no. 3 (Summer 1977), 41–46.

45. See Charles P. Cell, "Making the Revolution Work: Mass Mobilization Campaigns in the People's Republic of China" (unpublished doctoral dissertation, University of Michigan, 1973), pp. 26–28.

46. "T'ien An Men Incident: Completely Revolutionary Action," *Peking Review,* 47 (November 24, 1978), 6. For examples of the poems posted at T'ien An Men, see David S. Zweig, "The Peita Debate on Education and the Fall of Teng Hsiao-p'ing," *The China Quarterly,* 74 (March 1978), 155–57. For a recent version of the T'ien An Men incident, see "The Truth about the T'ien An Men Incident," *Peking Review,* 45 (December 1, 1978), 6–17.

47. John Bryan Starr, "China in 1974: 'Weeding Through the Old to Bring Forth the New,' " *Asian Survey,* vol. xv, no. 1 (January 1975), 6.

48. *The New York Times,* October 12, 1972, sec. 1, p. 1; also see Thomas W. Robinson, "China in 1972: Socio-Economic Progress Amidst Political Uncertainty," *Asian Survey,* vol. xiii, no. 1 (January 1973), 8. The same experience was shared by many American visitors, like myself, who visited China in 1972 and 1973.

49. For a detailed account of the scholarly debate on the anti-Confucius campaign and its link with the anti-Lin Biao campaign, see the following articles: Peter R. Moody, Jr., "The New Anti-Confucius Campaign in China: the First Round," *Asian Survey,* vol. xiv, no. 4 (April 1974), pp. 307–25; Starr, "China in 1974," p. 6; Parris Chang, "The Anti-Lin Biao and Confucius Campaign: Its Meaning and Purposes," *Asian Survey,* vol. xiv, no. 10 (October 1974), 871–86;

and Merle Goldman, "China's Anti-Confucius Campaign, 1973–74," *The China Quarterly,* 63 (September 1975), 435–62.

50. Lin Biao and the Doctrine of Confucius and Mencius: by the Mass Criticism Group of Peking and Tsinghua University," *Peking Review,* 7 (February 15, 1974), 6–12.

51. "Workers, Peasants, and Soldiers Are the Main Force in Criticizing Lin Biao and Confucius," *Peking Review,* 7 (February 15, 1974), 12–15.

52. See Merle Goldman, "China's Anti-Confucius Campaign, 1973–74," p. 435; and Leo Goodstadt, "Back to the 'Four Cleans,' " *Far Eastern Economic Review,* January 14, 1974, 14.

53. John Bryan Starr, "China in 1975: 'The Wind in the Bell Tower,' " *Asian Survey,* vol. xvi, no. 1 (January 1976), 43–48; and Parris Chang, "The Anti-Lin Biao and Confucius Campaign: Its Meaning and Purposes," pp. 874–77.

54. Chang, "The Anti-Lin Biao and Confucius Campaign," pp. 880–84.

55. "A Factual Report—'Gang of Four's' Plots in the Movement to Criticize Lin Biao and Confucius," *Peking Review,* 16 (April 15, 1977), 27–29.

56. "Such Was This 'Writing Group,' " *Peking Review,* 50 (December 9, 1977), 16–17; and "Who is Liang Hsiao," *Peking Review,* 43 (October 21, 1977), 22–24.

57. Saikowski, "China's Industrial Push and New Hope," *Christian Science Monitor* (Boston), July 10, 1975, p. 8.

58. Ibid.

59. "Unfold Criticism of 'Water Margin,' " *Peking Review,* 37 (September 12, 1975), 7–8. Also, see Chu Fung-ming, "Criticism of 'Water Margin,' " *Peking Review,* 9 (February 27, 1976), 7–11.

60. See "Unfold Criticism of 'Water Margin' ": pp. 7–8.

61. See "Tsinghua University: Mass Debate Brings Changes," *Peking Review,* 7 (February 13, 1976), 7–9; and "Tsinghua University: The Great Proletarian Cultural Revolution Continues and Deepens," *Peking Review,* 12 (March 19, 1976), 9–11.

62. See "Grasp the Crucial Point and Deepen the Criticism of Teng Hsiao-p'ing," *Peking Review,* 35 (August 27, 1976), 5–6; and Kao Lu and Chang Ko, "Comments on Teng Hsiao-p'ing's Economic Ideas of the Comprador Bourgeoisie," *Peking Review,* 35 (August 27, 1976), 6–9.

63. See "Speech at the Second National Conference on Learning from Tachai in Agriculture," *Peking Review,* 1 (January 1, 1977), 37.

64. "Marching to New Victories," *Peking Review,* 10 (March 4, 1977), 13.

65. "A Serious Struggle in Scientific and Technical Circles," *Peking Review,* 16 (April 15, 1976), 24–27.

66. "Why Did the 'Gang of Four' Attack 'The Twenty Points'?" *Peking Review,* 42 (October 14, 1977), 5–13.

67. "Premier Chou Creatively Carried Out Chairman Mao's Revolutionary Line in Foreign Affairs," *Peking Review,* 5 (January 28, 1977), 6–15.

68. See Jurgen Domes, "China in 1977: Reversal of Verdicts," *Asian Survey,* vol. xviii, no. 1 (January 1978), 3–9; and "The 'Gang of Four' and Hua Kuo-feng: Analysis of Political Events in 1975–76," *The China Quarterly,* 71 (September 1977), 492.

69. "Political Report to the Eleventh National Congress of the Communist Party of China, August 12, 1977," *Peking Review,* 35 (August 26, 1977), 44–45.

70. For the coverage of the Democracy Hall movement by Western reporters stationed in China, see Garside, *Coming Alive: China After Mao,* pp. 212–39; Bonavia, *The Chinese,* pp. 246–56; Butterfield, *China Alive in the Bitter Sea,* pp. 406–34; Bernstein, *From the Center of the Earth,* pp. 215–42, 246–56; and John Fraser, *The Chinese: Portrait of a People* (New York: Summit Books, 1980), pp. 203–71. Also see Jay Mathews, "Dissident's Sentence Stirs Sharp Criticism," Washington Post Service, as reprinted in *Honolulu Advertiser,* October 26, 1979, and *Newsweek,* December 11, 1978, pp. 41–43. For an analysis of the movement as a whole, see Kjeld Erik Brodsguard, "The Democracy Movement in China, 1978–1979: Opposition Movements, Wall Posters Campaign, and Underground Journals," *Asian Survey,* vol. xx, no. 7 (July 1981), 747–74. For Chinese coverage in the *Beijing Review,* see the following issues: 8 (February 23, 1979), 6; 49 (December 7, 1979), 3–4; 50 (December 14, 1979), 6–7; 10 (March 10, 1980), 10; 17 (April 28, 1980), 3–5; 40 (October 6, 1980), 22–28; 45 (November 9, 1979), 17–20. For a collection of translation of the writings by the Chinese on human rights, see James D. Seymour, edited, *The Fifth Modernization: China's Human Rights-Movement, 1978–1979* (Stanfordville, N.Y.: Earl

McColeman Enterprises, Inc., 1980). Also see Philip Short, *The Dragon and the Bear: China and Russia In the Eighties* (William Morrow and Company, Inc., 1982), pp. 252-264.

71. See Brodsguard, "The Democracy Movement in China, 1978-1979," pp. 759-61; and Garside, *Coming Alive: China After Mao*, pp. 213-22.

72. "Communiqué of the Third Plenary Session of the Eleventh Central Committee of the CCP," *Beijing Review*, 52 (December 29, 1978), 6.

73. Ibid., p. 13.

74. Ibid., p. 15.

75. Ibid.

76. Garside, *Coming Alive: China After Mao*, pp. 223-26. Also see Bonavia, *The Chinese*, p. 245.

77. Garside, *Coming Alive: China After Mao*, pp. 264-98.

78. See Brodsguard, "The Democracy Movement in China; 1978-1979," pp. 747-74. Also see "China's Dissidents," Washington Post Service, as reprinted in *Honolulu Advertiser*, September 15, 1979, A-17; and Melinda Liu, "Wei and the Fifth Modernization," *Far Eastern Economic Review* (November 27, 1979), 22-23.

79. Garside, *Coming Alive: China After Mao*, p. 256.

80. See *Hongqi*, 5 (May 4, 1979), 11-15. Also see David Bonavia, "The Flight From Freedom," *Far Eastern Economic Review* (October 26, 1979), 9-10.

81. *The New York Times*, July 1, 1979, p. 6.

82. "Wei Jingsheng Sentenced," *Beijing Review*, 43 (October 26, 1979), 6-7.

83. "The People's Verdict," *Beijing Review*, 46 (November 6, 1979), 15-16.

84. See *Beijing Review*, 50 (December 14, 1979), 6; *The New York Times*, December 9, 1979, p. 3; *Christian Science Monitor*, December 11, 1979, p. 7; and *Ming Pao* (Hong Kong), December 9, 1979, p. 1.

85. "Communiqué of the Fifth Plenary Session of the Eleventh Central Committee of the CCP," *Beijing Review*, 10 (March 10, 1980), 8-9.

86. Ibid., p. 10.

87. "The 'Dazibao': Its Rise and Fall," *Beijing Review*, 40 (October 6, 1980), 23-24.

88. "Big Character Posters Not Equivalent to Democracy," *Beijing Review*, 17 (April 28, 1980), 4.

89. "Communiqué of the Fifth Plenary Session," p. 10.

90. "National People's Congress Ends Session," *Beijing Review*, 37 (September 15, 1980), 3.

91. See *Far Eastern Economic Review* (October 26, 1979), 9, and (October 19, 1979), 38-40.

92. *Communications and National Integration in Communist China* (Berkeley, Calif.: University of California Press, 1971), pp. 115-16.

93. See Whyte, *Small Groups and Political Rituals in China*, pp. 16, 234; and Townsend, *Political Participation in Communist China*, p. 176.

The Politics

of Modernization:

Economic

Development,

Trade, and the

Management System

8

In short, in the next 20 years we must keep a firm hold on agriculture, energy, transport, education and science as the basic links, the strategic priorities in China's economic growth. Effective solution of these problems on the basis of an overall balance in the national economy will lead to a fairly swift rise in the production of consumer goods, stimulate the development of industry as a whole and of production and construction in other fields and ensure a betterment of living standards. . . . The general objective of China's economic construction for the two decades between 1981 and the end of this century is . . . to quadruple the gross annual value of industrial and agricultural production. This will place China in the front ranks of the countries of the world. . . .[1]

> Hu Yaobang
> September 1, 1982

In the five years from 1981 to 1985, we plan to increase the gross value of our industrial and agricultural production by 21.7 per cent, an average annual increase of 4 per cent. . . The Sixth Five-Year Plan is a plan for steady development in the course of readjustment, for promotion of China's modernization and for continued improvement in the people's living standards. Fulfillment of this plan is vital to the future of our whole modernization programme and to the interests of the people of all our nationalities.[2]

> Zhao Ziyang
> November 30, 1982

The above quotations are from statements by China's two new leaders, Hu Yaobang (general secretary of the CCP) and Zhao Ziyang (premier of the State Council). In a nutshell, the goal of China's modernization program is to improve the living standards of the people, as well as the strengthening of national defense. While Hu emphasizes the "strategic priorities" of developing agriculture, energy, transport, education, and science over the long run, Zhao outlines the short-run task of the Sixth Five-Year Plan (1981–85), which would provide a modest annual growth rate in industry and agriculture.

Let us begin our examination of this subject with a brief review of economic development policies in China from 1953–75.

ECONOMIC DEVELOPMENT

Overview of Economic Development Policies and Rate of Growth, 1953–75

The development of the Chinese economy has not been what one might describe as a smooth operation. On the contrary, it has been erratic and volatile. In the initial years, 1949–52, the regime's priority was to seek as rapidly as possible economic recovery and rehabilitation in the aftermath of a long period of war and the dislocation of the country's productive capacity. In 1953 the regime embarked on long-range planning of its economic development, employing the Stalinist model of centralized planning with emphasis on development of heavy industries. As was indicated in Chapter 1, the First Five-Year Plan was followed by a shift in development strategy in 1958, which placed emphasis on mass mobilization and intensive use of human labor under the Great Leap. While rapid economic recovery followed the failure of the Great Leap, this recovery was disrupted by the Cultural Revolution in the mid-1960s. The post–Cultural Revolution period, 1969–75, witnessed the development of mixed emphases, both on local economic self-reliance and self-sufficiency and on continued selective centralized management of a number of heavy industries, transport, banking, and foreign trade. No major economic policy was formulated until 1975, when Zhou Enlai consolidated his political power in the aftermath of the Lin Biao affair.

Between 1953 and 1975, covered by the economic development policies discussed above, the rate of economic growth in China was approximately 6 percent. This was quite an impressive record when compared with other developing nations,[3] particularly in view of the size and density of China's population and the interruptions that occurred during the Great Leap and the Cultural Revolution.

Emergence of Pragmatic Development Policies

The reversal from a mass-mobilization-oriented strategy to a comprehensive and orderly planning strategy for modernization occurred at the beginning of 1975, when the Fourth National People's Congress convened to revise the 1954 constitution. Premier Zhou proposed a two-stage development for China's national economy: a comprehensive industrial system by 1980, and a comprehensive modernization program in agriculture, industry, national defense, and science and technology by the year 2000.[4] While preliminary discussions were held within the State Council's various functional ministries in regard to the guidelines for implementing comprehensive plans to step up the economy, the radicals were set to attack any action that would reverse the gains made by the Cultural Revolution or restore "bourgeois rights." Yao Wenyuan, the radical's theoretical spokesperson, authored an article in the party's theoretical journal, *Hongqi* (*Red Flag*), in which he raised at least four major points of disagreement with Zhou on the development of the economy.[5] First, Yao argued that a gap existed between the workers and peasants, between town and country, and between mental and manual labor, and that these differences must be removed or polarization and inequality would inevitably result. A comprehensive program for national economic development eventually would place the elite technocrats in a position of power and prestige and, thus, widen these gaps in society. Second, Yao argued that once the technocrats were in power, they would "restore capitalism in the superstructure" and would redistribute capital and power according to mental power and skills, rather than on the basis of to "each according to his work." Third, Yao attacked the plan for reintroducing material incentives to induce workers and peasants to produce more in the name of modernization. Wage incentives to "lure the workers" represented to Yao the corrupt practice of the bourgeois right. Fourth, Yao labeled the rationale for increasing agricultural and industrial production—the fact that the peasants "lacked food and clothing"— as nothing but a scheme to "undermine the socialist collective economy." Zhou and his supporters believed that raising the living conditions of the peasants would result in greater production, and that the only way to encourage the peasants to produce more is to provide them with incentives such as the private plot and free markets. The radicals believed that introducing material incentives in order to spur production would alter the nature of the commune system, which was based on "the socialist collective economy."

The pragmatic planners under Premier Zhou ignored the radicals' attacks and continued to prepare comprehensive plans for modernization. Deng Xiaoping was brought back to the party and the State Council to initiate a series of planning conferences within the central government, which also involved members of China's scientific elite from the Chinese Academy of Sciences. These planning conferences produced three documents: a set of guidelines for the party and the nation for the modernization program, a twenty-point outline for the acceleration of industry, and a plan for the development of science and technology.[6] The radicals labeled these documents Deng Xiaoping's "three poisonous weeds." Deng, who was purged for the second time after the Tian An Men incident in April 1976, was charged with restoring centralized power in the administration of economic affairs to the state Council's functional ministries, with placing managers of enterprises in control in industrial plants, and with instituting rules and regulations in industrial plants for the purpose of restoring labor discipline.[7] Echoing the demand made by Zhang Chunqiao for the exercise of total dictatorship over the bourgeoisie, the mass criticism group of China's two leading universities— Beijing and Qinghua—argued that scientific research institutions, which were dominated by the bourgeois intellectuals before the Cultural Revolution, must be in the hands of the masses. Scientific research must be carried on in an "open door" manner so that workers are integrated with the educated elite and so that theory is integrated with practice. The radicals at these universities argued that class struggle must continue and that "nonprofessionals can lead professionals."[8]

After the arrest of the Gang of Four, Hua Guofeng reintroduced Zhou Enlai's comprehensive plan for modernization and brought Deng Xiaoping back to revive his guidelines for accelerated industrial and scientific development. Hua pledged his support to these economic plans at the Eleventh Party Congress in August 1977, when he declared

> We must build an independent and fairly comprehensive industrial and economic system in our country by 1980. By then farming must be basically mechanized, considerable increases in production must be made in agriculture, forestry, an-

imal husbandry, side-line production and fishery, and the collective economy of the people's communes must be further consolidated and developed.

Scientific research ought to anticipate economic construction, but it now lags behind, owing to grave sabotage by the "Gang of Four." This question has a vital bearing on socialist construction as a whole and must be tackled in earnest.[9]

Hua presented a detailed set of development plans to the Fifth National People's Congress in March 1978. The plan consisted of two interrelated plans, comparable to Premier Zhou's 1975 two-stage development plan: a ten-year, short-term development plan, and a twenty-three-year, long-term, comprehensive plan. The short-term plan called for 400 million metric tons of grain production, a 60 million ton capacity for steel production, and an overall 10 percent per year increase in industrial production by 1985.[10] The ten-year plan also called for at least "85 percent mechanization in all major processes of farmwork" in the communes. The ten-year plan is to be followed by a series of five-year plans to push China "into the front ranks of the world economy."[11] Figure 8.1 presents the types and range of the capital construction projects planned in 1978. These huge projects included large opencast coal mines, oil field pipelines, modern iron and steel complexes, chemical fertilizer plants, farm machinery plants, and railway construction.

READJUST, RESTRUCTURE, CONSOLIDATE, AND REFORM, 1978–81

The modernization plan launched in 1978 was an ambitious one. It called for production of 60 million metric tons of steel by the year 2000, the mechanization of 85 percent of agriculture, and completion of 120 large-scale capital construction projects involving an investment of $360 billion. To the pragmatic leaders like Deng Xiaoping and Chen Yun, not only were the 1978 targets unrealistic, but the plan for implementing the program was unworkable and reminiscent of the 1958 "crash program." The 1978 plan laid undue emphasis on the development of heavy industry at the expense of consumer goods and light industries. The focal point of debate among the top leaders was once again the question of priorities. The debate, as in 1958, was inextricably intertwined with ideology. Hua Guofeng, as mentioned in Chapter 1, was blamed for the "Leftist tendency" in the 1978 program that resulted in imbalance and a national financial deficit. By the spring of 1979, it became obvious that the 1978 modernization plan needed revision. To understand China's economic readjustment from 1979 to 1981, we need to take a brief look at the economic problems that surfaced soon after the 1978 modernization plan was launched.[12]

First, there was the key issue of industry versus agriculture. The orthodox Stalinist strategy of economic development, with emphasis on heavy industry, invariably placed a hardship on the agricultural sector. A leading Chinese economist pointed out that between 1949 and 1978, investment in heavy industry increased more than 90 percent, as compared to a mere 2.4

percent increase in agriculture.[13] The immediate consequence of a slow growth rate in agricultural output was China's dependence on grain purchases from abroad. Second, there was the issue of heavy versus light industries. Because of the emphasis on investment in heavy industry, investment in light and consumer industries was insufficient to allow this sector to produce enough goods to meet the people's daily needs. In other words, "market supplies for the main light industrial goods have all along fallen short of needs."[14]

Third, the Chinese experience had shown that in the development of heavy industry, excessive stress was placed on the development of metallurgical, machine-building, and processing industries. In the process, energy resources development (coal and electric power) and transport facilities were neglected. This resulted eventually in a critical energy shortage, and transportation and communications services remained backward. This problem was illustrated by the situation at the Baoshan steel complex.[15] When the giant Baoshan steel complex was almost completed in 1979, the Chinese discovered that there was not enough power available to turn the rolling steel mills, and that a new port was needed to handle the ores imported from Brazil and Australia. Fourth, heavy industrial development required large-scale investment in capital construction projects, as shown in Figure 8.1. Too often these projects' requirements far exceeded the available personnel, machinery, finances, and material resources. For example, the Baoshan steel complex near Shanghai was constructed with Japanese, West German, and American know-how at a cost of about $27 billion—or an amount equal to about 40 percent of China's national budget for 1981.

The numerous projects under development during 1978–79, shown in Figure 8.1, almost exhausted China's financial resources. The shopping spree for modern equipment and contracts for capital construction projects resulted in a $6 billion deficit in China's national budget and consumed about $8 billion of China's foreign reserves. Finally, there was the need to upgrade the efficiency of management in Chinese enterprises. Most Chinese factories were either overequipped with machines or overstaffed. Most of the plants were not operating at full capacity.

In April 1979 a central work conference was convened to discuss corrections and readjustments in the 1978 modernization program. Simultaneously, the Chinese central government was forced to revise, postpone, or cancel many contracts signed with foreign concerns, particularly Japanese firms. The NPC at its second session in June 1979 approved a series of urgent measures to readjust the modernization program by retrenchment.[16] First, it decided to readjust the priorities. Light and consumer industries were to be given equal, if not greater, emphasis as compared to heavy industry. The overambitious plan for 60 million metric tons of steel by 1985 was revised downward to 45 million metric tons. Energy and power industries were scheduled to be developed and expanded more rapidly. Capital construction projects for heavy industries were to be curtailed, so that a large amount of investment funds would be freed. Second, it reached the conclusion that the structure for economic management had to be overhauled. Enterprises were to be given the real de-

FIGURE 8.1:   Capital Construction Projects of 1978

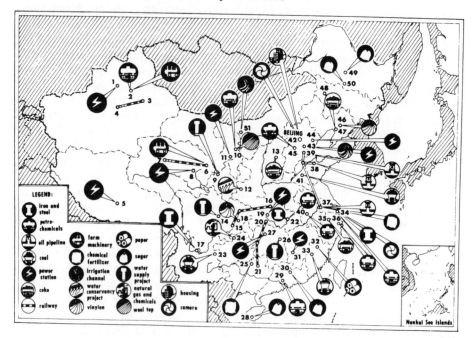

More than 1,000 major projects were started in 1978. A third has been completed or partially completed. The map shows a few of them.

1. Manas River Hydropower Station
2. Xinjiang Petrochemical Works
3. Turpan (Southern Xinjiang Railway)
4. Korla (Southern Xinjiang Railway)
5. Yangbajain Geothermal-Power Station
6. Xining (Qinghai-Xizang Railway)
7. Golmud (Qinghai-Xizang Railway)
8. Longyangxia Hydropower Station
9. Lanzhou water supply project
10. Wool top mill and oil refinery in Yinchuan
11. Qingtongxia water control project
12. Fengjiashan Reservoir
13. Coking plant of the Taiyuan Iron and Steel Company
14. Chengdu water supply project
15. Chongqing (Xiangfan-Chongqing Railway)
16. Xiangfan (Xiangfan-Chongqing Railway)
17. Panzhihua Iron and Steel Company
18. Sichuan Vinylon Mill
19. Gezhouba Hydropower Station
20. Zhicheng (Zhicheng-Liuzhou Railway)
21. Liuzhou (Zhicheng-Liuzhou Railway)
22. Wuhan Iron and Steel Company's 1.7-metre rolling mill and Wuhan Petrochemical Works
23. Housuo Coal-Dressing Plant
24. Chishui Natural Gas and Chemical Plant
25. Hechi Nitrogenous Fertilizer Plant
26. Changsha water supply project
27. Fengtan Hydropower Station

28. Yanglan Sugar Refinery
29. Guangzhou Petrochemical Works
30. Wengyuan Sugar Refinery
31. Wanan Hydropower Station
32. Nanping Paper Mill
33. Yongan Coal Mine
34. Baoshan Iron and Steel Complex, Shanghai Petrochemical Complex and Shanghai Camera Factory
35. Sintering plant of the Hangzhou Iron and Steel Works
36. Zhejiang Oil Refinery
37. Qixiashan Chemical Fertilizer Plant and Luning oil pipeline, Nanjing
38. Dongying (oil pipeline)
39. Cangzhou (oil pipeline)
40. Anqing Petrochemical Works
41. Yanzhou coal base
42. Housing construction and camera factory, Beijing.
43. Beidagang Power Plant and Tianjin Petrochemical and Chemical Fibre Complex
44. Douhe Power Plant, Tangshan
45. Renqiu Oilfield
46. Liaoyang Petrochemical and Chemical Fibre Complex
47. Coking plant of the Anshan Iron and Steel Company
48. Huolinhe Coal Mine
49. Anda Sugar Refinery
50. Zhaoyuan Sugar Refinery
51. Ancillary project of the Huanghe River irrigation area.

Source: Beijing Review, *12 (March 23, 1979).*

cision-making power and initiative. The old concept of "egalitarian tendency" had to be discarded; those who had demonstrated success would now be given authority and reward. Provinces and localities were to be given increased power in planning, financing, and foreign trade. Third, it decided that factory managers must be given power in the operation of the plants, in order to spur production. Managers were permitted to set prices for their own products; and they were required to apply to the banks to borrow operating funds and pay interest. Fourth, it mandated that all enterprises must produce quality products.

This austere readjustment program was to span the three-year period from 1979 to 1981. Reform measures in the economy would slow down China's growth rate from 12 percent in 1978 to about 7 percent in 1979 and to just over 5 percent in 1980.[17] These scaled-down goals represented the admission that the country had gone ahead too fast and was forced to apply the brakes.[18]

Nevertheless, the economic reforms introduced by the pragmatic leaders under Deng did not produce the desired results. Total state investment for capital construction in 1980 remained high, and more projects were initiated than were canceled. This occurred mainly because of the policy to permit local officials and plant managers more autonomy and initiative, which resulted in "expanding welfare related projects, building clubs, cultural halls, hospitals, housing, and other facilities."[19] In addition, a number of new local enterprises began operations, and existing enterprises expanded. Thus, the state was forced to spend more on investment than it actually had. By 1980–81 Deng and his colleagues had second thoughts about their reforms for the industrial system. They now imposed budget reductions on capital construction and military spending. During 1981–82 China returned to a more centralized control policy mixed with some individualized market practices. Further expansion of both central and local enterprises was curtailed. Enterprises were no longer permitted to earn general profits on all manufactured goods and state farm produce—the state attempted to dry up sources of funds for their expansion. China began to experience inflation. The official annual rate of inflation was put at 7 percent, but more likely it reached between 10 and 12 percent for consumer prices in most urban areas.[20] Industrial wages were frozen as another anti-inflationary measure. Approval by the State Planning Commission was required for all funds for capital construction. Expansion in agriculture and in light and consumer industries was allowed to continue, with increased funds allotted by the state. Capital construction funds for heavy industry were reduced in 1981 from $37 billion to $22 billion, or a reduction of 40 percent.[21] This meant that many large industrial projects valued at about $65 billion had to be either postponed or canceled.[22] Many of these industrial projects were under contract with foreign concerns from Japan, West Germany, and the United States. Contracts were for both machinery and the construction of plants in large- and medium-scale industries, such as steel, petrochemicals, and oil drilling.

The 1979 economic reforms were intended to correct two basic problems: the overemphasis on the investment in and accumulation of heavy industries, discussed earlier, and the need for incentives to spur production. China's leading economists, and planners such as Chen Yun (a Politburo member and former director of state planning) and Xue Muqiao (now an advisor for state planning), argued that the "scale of economic construction must be commensurate with the nation's capabilities"; The state should make a substantial investment in capital construction in heavy industries only when the people's livelihood had made marked improvement.[23] Chen Yun was quoted as saying that the distribution of the limited supply of raw materials should be given first to those industries "that ensure the production of people's daily necessities."[24] To proceed otherwise would be "Leftist thinking." It would be a "Leftist" error if the percentage of accumulation in national income—that is, the amount of money and material resources channeled into construction of large-scale heavy industrial projects as fixed assets and inventories—was disproportionately high. Figure 8.1 provides a vivid picture of investment in heavy industrial construction projects originally planned in 1978, when the slogan was "taking steel as the key link." The accumulation ratio of fixed assets and inventories channeled into the building of heavy industrial projects was 36 percent of the national income.[25] When this imbalance occurred, Chen Yun was the most influencial voice arguing for a reduction in capital construction investment and an increase in consumer goods industries.

The development strategy shift from heavy to light industries, in terms of state investment in the two sectors, was made not only because of the need to provide consumer goods for the exploding population but also for more expedient reasons. Heavy industries tend to consume an enormous quantity of energy resources. Light industries, on the other hand, require less energy, and also provide more jobs. It has been pointed out that in China a 1 percent shift in the ratio from heavy to light industries saves 6 million tons of coal.[26] In addition, light industries produce China's export goods, which earn needed foreign exchange.

It seems clear from this summary that China has been experimenting with "remedial measures."[27] Nevertheless, there has been no fundamental alteration of its socialist economic system.

THE ECONOMIC PLANNING PROCESS[28]

Approval of an economic plan by the Fifth National People's Congress is the final step in a three-stage planning process involving governmental agencies and party committees at all levels.[29] This process is diagramed in Figure 8.2.

During the first stage, the State Council prepares a preliminary draft of the plan, with proposed quotas and targets, as a basis for nationwide consultation. Two important central agencies under the State Council play a vital role in drafting the preliminary plan: the State Planning Commission and the State Statistical Bureau. In addition, the functional ministries of the State Council are also involved in the initial planning.

Since the Cultural Revolution, the provincial revolutionary committees,

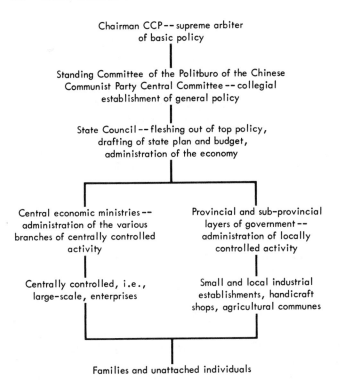

FIGURE 8.2: China's Economic Decision-making Structure

Source: Arthur G. Ashbrook, Jr., "China: Economic Overview, 1975" in China: A Reassessment of the Economy, *Joint Economic Committee, Congress of the United States (Washington, D.C.: Government Printing Office, July 10, 1975), p. 48.*

now the provincial people's government, have participated in the planning process at the second stage. With the emphasis on decentralization, many of the governmental agencies below the provincial level have also participated in the formulation of economic plans. All these agencies engage in planning activities, which include setting quotas and determining the resources needed to meet the various targets in terms of investment, transport, revenues, labor, and social welfare. This second stage, which is a departure from the Soviet planning model, allows the provincial agencies, in consultation with planning units in the enterprises and communes, to develop realistic, detailed proposals, based upon the national preliminary plan and proposed targets and quotas. At this stage the tentative plan with detailed proposals is scrutinized by the masses, workers, peasants, staffs of enterprises, and party committees of the productive units. They can offer suggestions or recommendations on the tentative plan. Thus, opportunities are provided for negotiation on the specific production proposals between the enterprises or communes and the planning officials from the center.

The final draft of the development plan is prepared by the planning officials at the various ministries in joint sessions and is then forwarded to the State Council, which in turn submits it to the party's Central Committee for endorsement. It is this final draft plan, as approved by the Central Committee, which Zhao Ziyang, in his capacity as the premier, submitted to the November 1982 session of the National People's Congress for final approval. It should be noted that only after approval by the National People's Congress does the tentative plan become the official development plan. Any major readjustment of or revision to the plan must also have the final approval of the NPC. The State Council then transmits the details of the plan downward to the provinces, municipalities, counties, communes, and production units for implementation.

PLANNED ECONOMY, MARKET SOCIALISM, AND THE SIXTH FIVE–YEAR PLAN (1981–85)

Since 1979 a familiar sight in many Chinese cities has been individual vendors, hawkers, and shopkeepers selling their goods and services—activities long prohibited by the government. When urban authorities began granting licenses to private entrepreneurs in 1979 for business, Westerners were delighted to be able to purchase fresh produce from the countryside and eat a good meal in a small family restaurant without waiting in line. Some 300,000 small private enterprises were reported to be operating in cities in 1979, with over 810,000 in existence at the end of 1980, and 2.6 million in 1983.[30]

The rationale for this new policy was that "individual economy," or private enterprises, should no longer be considered "capitalistic," and that it must be allowed to play a role in supporting the socialist economy.[31] Apparently, there was some resistance to the new policy: For example, the *People's Daily* accused the state commercial agencies of hanging on to the old practice of "monopoly economy."[32] Still, before 1966 there were at least 2 million small individual producers providing goods and services to meet the market demands that the state-owned economy failed to deliver.[33] These individual producers disappeared during the Cultural Revolution and were not revived until 1979, when economic readjustment and reform became necessary. The leadership hoped that the incentives provided by the "individual economy" would help spur production and fill gaps in the system once again. In addition, it was realized that the "individual economy" would open up jobs for the urban unemployed.

The existence of individual enterprises alongside the socialist collective enterprises raises serious questions, since the two are seemingly incompatible. It must be remembered that within the Soviet model of a centralized planned economy, China has had a pattern of alternating policy approaches on the extent to which market forces should play a role in the economy. These policies, as pointed out in Chapter 1, became the focus of debate and dissension among the top leaders. The fiasco of the 1958 Great Leap crash program paved the way for the economic readjustment and recovery in the 1960s, when there was a relaxation in the strict control over market forces. The Cultural Revolution, with its excessive emphasis on the role of ideology, destroyed the gains made during the early 1960s, and with them went the permissible free markets for peasants and the profit-and-loss principle for industrial management. Now China once again returned to the pre-1966 policy of relaxing the state's control over market forces in the midst of a planned economy.

Under the 1979 adjustment, not only were market forces allowed in the "individual economy," but they were introduced into state enterprises as part of a series of reforms to motivate growth. Many of the reforms had emerged from experiments conducted by Zhao Ziyang in enterprises selected as pilot projects in the province of Sichuan. During 1980–81 thousands of state enterprises were subjected to "market socialism" experiments through the introduction of the following reform measures:[34] (1) State-owned factories were allowed to produce for market demand as long as they fulfilled the assigned state quota. (2) State-owned enterprises were given the freedom to purchase needed raw material through the market, rather than remaining dependent on central allocation. (3) Prices for the products were to be set by the supply and demand mechanism. In other words, for these concerns microeconomic decisions on production would be governed by market forces, not by the state plan. All state-owned enterprises were to be respononsible for their own profit and loss.

To some observers it seems, this view certainly is not widely accepted. What emerged in the early 1980s in China might be a variant of the Yugoslav and Hungarian market socialism that coexisted with the centralized planned economy.[35] The approach was best explained by Chen Yun, the architect of the current economic development strategy. Chen Yun pointed out that "the planned economy is to play the major role and market regulation the supplementary role."[36] He decried the idea that planning should be abandoned once the incentive system has been introduced in enterprises and agriculture. Chen Yun then illustrated the relative roles of planning and the market mechanism in this way: "We must have plans in running enterprises. In running socialist enterprises, we should take into consideration the following factors: whether there is a market for the products, where the raw materials come from and how enterprises are managed."[37] Chen Yun's approach was to let both the planned and the market economy coexist. Xue Muqiao, China's leading economist today, argued that merchandise should be produced by the enterprises in accordance with market demands. He condemned the old practice of state monopoly, which tended to choke market demands to death.[38] Xue advocated self-regulation of consumer goods by market demands, free markets for the peasants to sell their sideline products in the cities, and local autonomy for those provinces which were more adaptable to foreign trade.[39] Xue, however, insisted that basic items such as steel and petroleum be regulated under centralized planning. Premier Zhao told the NPC delegates that the proper relationship between the planned economy and market regulation was that "enterprises in the key branches of the economy or products vital to the economy must be organized mandatorily in accordance with the state plan; only those numerous small enterprises or individual producers whose products accounted were either 'inconvenient' or 'impossible' to enforce unified planning were permitted, within limits of the state plan, to produce items in accordance with changing market conditions."[40]

Thus, it was under the strategy of planned economy with market regulation that China launched its Sixth Five-Year Plan (1981–85) in November 1982.[41] As can be seen from Table 8.1, the plan was a modest one, calling for steady but slow economic growth. The Sixth Five-Year Plan had been delayed for two years to allow readjustment and reform to take place, so that policy errors and imbalances could be corrected. Key features of the Sixth Five-Year Plan were as follows:[42] First, gross value of agricultural and industrial production was set at about 871 billion yuan for 1985, or a 21.8 percent increase over 1980, which gave China an annual rate of growth of about 4 percent over the five-year period. (There was every expectation that the growth rate would be exceeded before 1985.) Second, by 1985 grain production was targeted for 360 million metric tons, a 12 percent increase over the 1980 figure, or an average annual growth rate of slightly over 2 percent. However, the annual increase in all agricultural output under the plan was set at over 4 percent, a slightly higher annual rate than the 3.4 percent increase that China experienced over the twenty-eight-year period between 1953 and 1980. Third, 1985 steel production, the key to heavy industry, was set for 39 million metric tons, a mere 5 percent increase over 1980. Fourth, significant increases were targeted for energy development in coal mining, inland oil extraction, hydroelectric

TABLE 8.1   China's Sixth Five-Year Plan, 1981–85

	1980	1985	% increase
Grain (million tons)	320.0	360.0	12.3
Cotton (million tons)	2.7	3.6	33.0
Yarn (million tons)	2.9	3.5	22.8
Sugar (million tons)	2.5	4.3	67.3
Coal (million tons)	620.1	700.0	12.9
Steel (million tons)	37.1	39.0	5.0
Electricity (million kw)	300.6	362.0	20.4
Import (million yuan)	29.1	45.3	55.6
Export (million yuan)	27.2	40.2	48.1
Total Import and Export (million yuan)	56.3	85.5	52.0
Education/Science/Technology (million yuan)	57.5	96.7	68.0
Gross value of Industrial and Agricultural products (million yuan)	715,900.0	871,000.0	21.8

a yuan = $0.60

Source: Zhao Ziyang, "Report on the Sixth Five-Year Plan," Beijing Review, 51 (December 20, 1982), 11.

power, and thermo power stations. Fifth, total investment allocated for capital construction for the five-year period was about 230 billion yuan ($115 billion), with about one-fifth of the amount allocated for energy resource development and improvement in China's transport and communications system. Sixth, China was to expand her exports and imports by 52 percent by 1985. Lastly, the average income for China's peasants would rise from 191 yuan ($95.50) in 1980 to 255 yuan ($127.50) by 1985.[43]

For the foreseeable future, China would have to maintain this modest rate of growth and operate under austerity budgets. The finance minister reported in December 1982 that the spending curb would have to be continued until the end of 1985, since China was expected to have an official annual deficit of 3 billion yuan ($1.5 billion) for the next three years.[44]

AGRICULTURAL REFORM: THE RESPONSIBILITY (INCENTIVE) SYSTEM

The single most important change in recent years for the people's commune has been the introduction of the responsibility system for the peasants. It is, in essence, an incentive system. The system—introduced in 1978 but put into effect in 1980—is a modification of Liu Shaoqi's "Three Freedoms and One Guarantee," which was introduced in the early 1960s as a part of the economic recovery program after the failure of the Great Leap. Both Liu and his policy were attacked by the radicals during the Cultural Revolution as "revisionist" and "capitalist." Liu's policy included (1) free markets, (2) private plots, and (3) peasant responsibility for managing their own farms on the basis of contracts for fixed output quotas for each household. In 1978, at the Third Plenum of the Eleventh Central Committee, the party under the leadership of Deng Xiaoping revived the main features of the old Liu policy as a way to step up agricultural production.

The 1978 party resolution on agricultural reform urged that remuneration for work in the communes be based on the principle of "to each according to his work" by stressing quality of work. In addition, the party resolution directed that private plots and sideline production were now "necessary adjuncts of the socialist economy and must not be interfered with."[45] Central Committee Document No. 75, issued in November 1980, outlined a number of approved methods for use of the "responsibility system."[46] These methods were all based on contracts issued by the production teams to the peasants for specific quotas of output or work accomplished. Under all methods pay was to be based on the level of production or work accomplished. The contracts, depending on local conditions and tradition, could be issued to individuals, to households, or to work teams. One type, "Baochan Daohu" ("To fix farm output quota for each household") permitted a commune to make land available to each household, usually a family, in accordance with its labor capacity. The production team and the household signed a contract fixing the quota the household was obligated to fulfill. This quota included a portion for the team's quota for the state and a portion to meet commune expenses.

Another type of rural responsibility system was the concept of full responsibility to the household, "Baogan Daohu." Under this method the household signed a contract with the production team to assume all responsibility for work on the land and to bear the entire responsibility for their own profit and loss.

Under this arrangement land was contracted to the household on a per capita basis by the production team. In addition, farm implements and draft animals were permanently assigned to the household under contract. The household not only had to meet the state procurement requirements, but it had to assume full responsibility for managing the land and fulfilling all its obligations to the collective—in this case the production team. After deduction of the various cost items for the state and the collective, the remainder of the earnings went to the household.

Unique advantages of the job responsibility system described above were (1) encouraging peasants to work harder in order to receive more income, (2) allowing the peasants to manage their own production under the most favorable local conditions, rather than under the "commandism" of rural cadres— thus permitting the peasants to have more initiative and autonomy; and (3) avoiding the problem of constant complaints by peasants about unfair distribution of earnings. The advantages of the responsibility system, combined with the policy of private plots and free markets, gave a tremendous boost to peasant morale and resulted in increased output and work enthusiasm.

By 1981 the rural responsibility system had been adopted in all the provinces. By mid-1982 official figures reported that 90 percent of the production teams in the communes had adopted some form of the responsibility system.[47] While there were differences in the methods or arrangements adopted, depending on type of produce and locale, on the whole the income of the peasants increased significantly under the responsibility (incentive) system.[48]

The introduction of the responsibility system for agricultural production was not without criticism. Some felt that China was about to abolish the collective commune system. Others cried out that the new agricultural policy was a "bourgeois policy."[49] Defenders of the new policy countered by arguing that under the new incentive system, peasants could expect increased income and general overall prosperity. Premier Zhao pointed out, when he introduced the agricultural reform experiment in Sichuan, that any innovation must be considered socialist as long as the means of production are publicly owned and as long as the Marxist principle of "to each according to his work" is observed.[50] One Western scholar noted: "In Guangdong, at least, it seems not to have weakened the commitment to a collective economy."[51] As a final note, the new reform in agricultural production eventually may remove some of the glaring shortcomings of the collective commune system in China; Premier Zhao pointedly told the NPC in December 1982:

Many places report that, with the introduction of the responsibility system, production has gone up, the relationship between cadres and peasants has markedly improved and bureaucraticism, arbitrary orders, corruption, waste, and other obnoxious practices have declined sharply.[52]

PROBLEMS IN
INDUSTRIAL PRODUCTION
AND MANAGEMENT

The average annual rate of growth for industrial production from 1953 to 1974 has been estimated at a very respectable rate of about 11 percent. The performance from 1975 to 1977 has been placed at a slightly lower rate, between 9 and 10 percent per year.[53] The official Chinese estimate put the annual growth rate from 1966 to 1977 at 12 percent.[54] In his presentation of the Sixth Five-Year Plan to the NPC, Premier Zhao proposed a lower growth rate for industrial production than had existed during the previous twenty-eight years.[55] He pointed out candidly that although the growth rate for industrial output was not low in the past, the economic results—meaning quality, variety, and design of industrial products—had been "very poor." In the Sixth Five-Year Plan, he demanded better economic results. Before we discuss recent attempts to introduce reforms into the industrial system, it will be necessary to review very briefly some of the features of China's industrial system that made it possible for the nation to achieve a 10 to 11 percent average annual increase.

What were the key features of the Chinese industrial system? One obvious factor was the nationalization of basic industries. State ownership of all large enterprises since 1956 had enabled the state not only to establish a centralized budget process but also to reinvest a sizable share of earnings in new plants and equipment for further increases in production. One specialist on the Chinese economy pointed out that by the end of the First Five-Year Plan, 75 percent of state revenues came from the earnings of state-owned enterprises and that state revenues constituted one-third of China's national income.[56] Closely related to the capacity for reinvestment was the policy of keeping industrial wages at low levels; income not distributed to the workers could be reinvested.

Another key factor was the initial strategy of placing emphasis on the development of heavy industries, particularly machine tool factories and iron and steel plants. Iron and steel production remains the key to future growth of China's industries.[57] Steel plants are located strategically in eight major centers, with the largest at Anshan in the northeast, producing about 25 percent of the total national output. During the 1980s a new steel plant, the Baoshan complex, will be added to the Shanghai industrial region (with loans from Japan) as well as the Wuhan steel complex in central China. China needs new mines for both coal and iron to feed the steel furnaces (see Figure 8.1). In addition, efficient coal- and iron-mining equipment will have to be imported from abroad in order to boost production. Modern large-scale blast furnaces are needed. Most of the furnaces in use in 1978 were built by the Soviets in the 1950s.

Finally, emphasis on the development of a large number of medium- and small-scale, labor-intensive industries has been a major factor in the rapid gains in industrial production. These decentralized, relatively small enterprises take advantage of the abundance of labor in rural areas, using a minimum of capital goods, and thus freeing investment for heavy industry. The policy of "walking on two legs" therefore develops simultaneously heavy industry, which is capital-intensive and centralized, and medium to small industry, which is labor-intensive and decentralized. The small industries, with employment ranging from 15 to 600, are owned either by the state, the county or the communes.[58] Many of the small- and medium-sized industries, such as cement, brick, fertilizer, and farm machinery plants, are linked to agricultural production. The importance of small-scale industries in rural communes can be illustrated by the following cycle of development: Annual rainfall must be caught by dams and reservoirs, which are constructed with cement; with the availability of water for irrigation of the fields, more chemical fertilizer is needed to produce a higher yield of crops; with the prospect of a higher yield, agricultural machinery, such as tractors, harvesters, and water pumps, is needed. In one year 54 percent of China's synthetic ammonia was produced by about 1,000 small fertilizer plants.[59] The United States' delegation on small-scale industry, which visited China in 1975, pointed out that these small-scale industries save time in construction, solve the problem of limited transport facilities for rural areas, and allow for the exploitation of available local resources.[60] These small-scale industries in rural areas also have the ideological justification of removing the urban-rural dichotomy.

As of 1980–81 China had 348,000 industrial enterprises. Of these, about 84,000 were state owned, and employed 74.5 million workers. The remaining 264,000 were collectively owned enterprises, employing about 21 million workers.[61] Included in these are the small-scale industries which are found in urban areas in the form of neighborhood enterprises managed by the neighborhood committees. In the early 1970s, visitors to China were frequently led to such street enterprises in the midst of a residential area for the workers. Housewives of the neighborhood were employed in a small factory, making small items such as bulbs for flashlights or transistors for radios. Charles Bettelheim suggested that the housewives who worked in the neighborhood small-scale enterprises were not motivated by economic need to augment the family's income but rather by the ideological call to contribute to production.[62] Bettelheim's suggestion was no longer valid when China permitted the development of individualized private enterprises for profit in 1978. At that time cities like Shanghai were faced with serious unemployment problems as millions of China's urban youth entered the labor market. In order to ease the plight of the jobless millions in the cities, as mentioned earlier, neighborhood committees organized small business enterprises in handicrafts, commerce, and services. At the end of 1980, there were as many as 810,000 such private enterprises, and the figure soared to 2.6 million in 1983.

Like every other aspect of China's economic and political development, the management of industrial enterprises has been subject to policy alterations. The party's control over the management of enterprises waxed and waned as the development strategy vacillated from reliance on technical expertise to mass participation from 1953 to the Cultural Revolution.[63] The Cultural Revolution placed so much emphasis on the participatory aspect of "politics-in-command" that industrial workers took over the plants and managed them through committees. For over a decade there was confusion and laxity in industrial management. Instead of "relying on experts to run the factories," groups of workers, revolutionary rabble-rousers, managed them. This mass movement in industry was exemplified by the Anshan steel and iron factory and was therefore called the Anshan Charter.[64] The essence of the Anshan Charter was to make the workers masters of socialist industry.[65] At the height of the Cultural Revolution, workers discarded factory rules and regulations, often with some justification, since these regulations were voluminous and practically incomprehensible to ordinary workers. As the Cultural Revolution intensified, a state of anarchy existed in many factories. By 1969, when the Ninth Party Congress met, efforts were made to restore order and discipline in industrial plants. Workers participated cooperatively in enacting basic rules, which required punctuality, quality control, and safety measures. The Daqing oil fields became the national model for strict observance of rules and regulations by workers and staff. After their arrest in October 1976, two radical leaders, Yao Wenyuan and Zhang Chunqiao, were attacked for rejecting rules and regulations in factories.[66] In 1977 Hua Guofeng urged his compatriots to reverse the habit of laxity in industrial production and to follow the Daqing model, a "fine example of how a good job can be done in socialist industry."[67]

Recently a more determined effort was made to break the long-established practice of what Premier Zhao termed "giving everybody an iron rice bowl."[68] One reason for China's low labor productivity was the "iron rice bowl" system, under which there was no dismissal, suspension, or demotion of workers in state enterprises. The system guaranteed a worker's wage irrespective of the individual's work. As a recent *People's Daily* editorial commented, the system "places dependency on the state, encourages laziness and discourages hard work."[69] Premier Zhao insisted that the major aim of the current economic reform program is to apply "the principle of more pay for more work, less pay for less work and no pay for no work."[70] Enterprises now under the new policy must undergo reform for self-management. The responsibility system means that a factory can (1) develop its own production plan in order to fulfill the state plans and (2) turn out products for the consumer markets and sell them at fixed state prices. A factory can also produce goods for export and keep the foreign exchange earnings for improvement in its equipment and technology. Further, a factory can keep its profits for production expansion, workers' welfare improvement, or even for bonuses. The new policy stipulated that the plant or factory recruit its own workers according to ability and give rewards as well as punishment to workers.[71] It was reported that the experiment of granting more power to enterprises for self-management was applied to more than 6,000 state enterprises in 1980–81 and that there was increased value of output for a vast majority.[72]

A nagging problem in the industrial sector has been the remuneration system and the related question of material incentives.[73] For many years it was debated whether to have egalitarianism or disparity in income distribution. The pragmatic moderates, such as Zhou Enlai and Deng Xiaoping, argued that the incentive system, based on timework, piecework, and bonuses, was the only way to live up to the principle of "to each according to his work".[74] On the other hand, Yao Wenyuan and other radicals feared that continuing wide disparity of wages could lead only to an unequal distribution of "commodities and money."[75]

Carl Riskin pointed out that the Chinese industrial wage system is basically a bourgeois method of distribution.[76] Payment in factories is based primarily on timework, supplemented by piecework. Since 1977 the wage differential has included the level of a worker's skill and the employment of bonuses as production inducements. The 1977 wage policy allows for the elevation or promotion of workers with outstanding achievements without their climbing "the wage ladder rung by rung."[77] The present timework payment is governed by an eight-grade wage scale, from a minimum of 34 to a maximum of 110 yuan. A worker's grade within the scale is based on skill and training, length of service, and performance record. Technicians, engineers, and plant managers come under a separate wage system.

In October 1977 a wage increase was promulgated by the State Council for about 60 percent of China's industrial workers, the first major increase since 1963. The new wage increases moved some 46 percent of the workers, whose wages were at the lowest levels, up one grade in the scale. Workers who were receiving more than 90 yuan had no increase or adjustment. This action apparently was taken to raise workers' standards of living in line with greater prosperity and to alleviate dissatisfaction in the industrial centers.

This was followed by a supplementary wage increase of 5 yuan per month, or the equivalent of $3, for each worker, to compensate for the rise in food prices. Thus, the average monthly income for each worker was 68.8 yuan in 1981, a 26.4 percent increase since 1978, according to a survey conducted recently by the State Statistical Bureau for families in the cities of Beijing, Tianjin, and Shanghai.[78] These wage figures did not differentiate between workers from state-owned enterprises and those from urban cooperative enterprises, which employed mostly housewives and retirees—who, as a rule, received lower wages.[79] Another major wage reform was the introduction of a "floating" wage system, providing a flexible wage scale for workers according to the amount and the quality of the work performed. The old fixed wage system was said to encourage "inertia, laziness and living off socialism."[80] Under the fixed wage system, raises were given by the state according to a worker's seniority rather than for skill or capability. The "floating" wage system was part of the experiment to elicit more enterprise responsibility.[81] All these reform measures were designed to provide incentives in order to spur increased production.

In addition to wage increases for the Chinese industrial workers, a varied system of bonuses also was reintroduced into the state enterprises. Briefly, the bonus system, which is identical to the one that existed before the Cultural

Revolution, calls for the distribution of an additional income allowance, usually not more than 10 percent of the enterprise's total wage bill. This additional income allowance, as explained to the author by the cadres in a ball-bearing plant in Loyang in the summer of 1978, was given to an enterprise only if it fullfilled the assigned quota of production. This additional allowance is then distributed to the plant's various workshops or groups, including workers' congresses of the trade union federation in large enterprises, which decide how the bonus is to be awarded. The decision may be an across-the-board distribution to all or most workers in the plant, with each worker receiving only a few yuans. At other times the bonus consists of consumer items, such as clothing or food, for those who have been good workers and who observe work discipline. The bonus system is by no means uniform for all enterprises in China. Some enterprises adhere to the egalitarian concept of distributing bonuses to all workers regardless of the quality and quantity of individual work performed. This across-the-board distribution of bonuses to all workers in a plant has been subject to criticism, as revealed in the mass media in 1979. A recent experiment in bonus distribution is based on "group overfulfillment of quota."[82] Under the experiment bonuses are given to those units or groups within a factory which overfilled their quota. The bonuses are distributed among group members who overfulfilled the individual quota. Those group members who fail to overfulfill the quota are penalized. The result is increased productivity and more efficiency. Recently, the Guangdong provincial party committee established some guidelines on bonus distribution: (1) Bonuses should be given only as a reward for extra work. (2) Those who produce more should be given more bonuses. (3) The rate of increase in bonuses should not be lower than the rate of increase in productivity.[83] These guidelines were introduced because the bonus system initially had produced abuses, inefficiency, and waste.[84] Since 1981 enterprise managers also have been asked to refrain from indiscriminate use of bonuses for production increase—this is in order to check price inflation in urban areas.

CAN THE GOALS
OF MODERNIZATION
BE ACHIEVED?

In this chapter we have tried to present a picture of China's efforts to modernize after 1949, with emphasis on the post-Mao era. Modernization means industrialization and economic growth, supported and strengthened by a formula of universal education which emphasizes the learning of modern science and technology. The politics of modernization in China since 1949 has focused primarily, although not exclusively, on how China can be transformed into an industrialized nation, equal to other nations who are in the forefront of technological development. Because of the lack of unity among the leaders in answering this question, policies and programs for modernization have vacillated between the revolutionary mass mobilization model and the professional and orderly development model. The continuous conflict and ambivalence toward these strategies for modernization dominated the flow of Chinese politics during the past several decades. Beneath the struggle, however, is the pervasive feeling in Chinese society and among peoples of all developing nations that they want a better way of life in terms of both moral and material well-being; and that this can come about only through the continuous acquisition of knowledge in science and technology.

Will China be able to achieve its goal of modernization? The answer rests on a number of factors. One is the ability of the leaders to maintain unity and some degree of cohesiveness so as to provide the needed political stability and climate for orderly development. Another is China's ability to develop its energy resources and transportation facilities. Equally important is China's ability to curb its population growth in the next decade. China also needs to strengthen its educational system in order to pave the way for development in science and technology. Such development is also contingent upon China's willingness to keep her doors open to trade with other nations.

Let us examine briefly three important factors that could contribute to the successful implementation of China's modernization program before the year 2000: reform in the management system, energy resources development, and population control.

Reform in the Management System[85]

Managerial reform calls for the swift development of effective intermediate- and lower-level leadership to implement the plans of modernization. This factor will be influenced or shaped to a large extent by the unity and cohesiveness at the top levels of leadership. Closely related to the development of effective leadership is the urgent need to acquire managerial skills in the industrial and agricultural sectors. While the American business community is beginning to unlock the secrets of Japanese management success,[86] the Chinese economy is characterized by inefficiency, waste, and poor management. We have mentioned earlier that corrective measures were introduced in order to make the Chinese economic system more efficient and productive. But a great deal still needs to be done to improve management techniques at the enterprise level.

Several years ago Sir Yue-Kong Pao, a Hong Kong–based shipping tycoon, complained that when he cabled Beijing on business matters, it usually took three to five days to get someone to reply. When he made a long-distance telephone call to Beijing, he found that no one seemed to be responsible for making any decisions. The problem here is that the Chinese management executive does not behave as a businessperson normally behaves elsewhere in the world. A Chinese management executive typically acts like a bureaucrat. Management decisions are made vertically. Clearance is required in the bureaucratic hierarchy before a decision can be made. There is also a tendency in Chinese bureaucratic management to adhere to conformity.[87] The end result has been that no one wants to take a different approach or be innovative. Thus, the prevailing climate in Chinese organizations is one of "indifference or irrelevance."[88] Worse still, Chinese management executives make no decisions, nor do they take any risks at all.

A further problem is that workers in a Chinese factory are typically inexperienced and lack the skill required to do the job adequately.[89] This general lack of skill and experience extends to managers as well.[90] The concept of an unbroken "iron rice bowl" (job security) is so deeply implanted in the minds of Chinese workers that it is difficult to introduce any system of evaluation for job performance. Chinese economist Xue Muqiao urged that the state institute "a system of examination, appraisal and promotion and transfer" for the industrial workers as a basic management reform.[91] He also asked that incompetent workers be dismissed, a management right that most Chinese enterprises are very reluctant to exercise.

In 1980 the State Council issued a set of guidelines to allow enterprises to experiment with self-management. The guidelines, among other things, specified (1) that the type of merchandise produced must meet market demands; (2) that certain levels of profits must be retained for expansion and/ or improvement of plant facilities; and (3) that enterprises must recruit their own workers.[92] Effective implementation of these reform measures, however, depends on the adoption of modern management techniques and some fundamental changes in the existing personnel system. (Some provinces, such as Guangdong, have formed business management associations to study management skills, with a view toward improving provincial enterprise management.)[93] In short, managerial training for cadres in industry is urgently needed. In addition, China's pragmatic leaders must find ways to improve work efficiency by solving such problems as overstaffing, bureaucratic red tape, and endless meetings.

Development of Energy Resources[94]

Although China does have an abundance of untapped energy resources in the form of coal, oil, and water power, these resources have not been developed sufficiently to meet industrial demands. In fact, there has been a constant energy shortage in recent years, which has idled as much as 20 percent of China's industrial plants.[95] One cause of the shortage was relying on known coal and oil deposits and neglecting to explore potential new sources. This neglect was bolstered by the blind belief, reinforced by many years of radical propaganda, that the output of China's Daqing oil field could meet any increased industrial needs. However, the sudden, unprecedented expansion in capital construction projects under the modernization program of 1978 taxed China's energy capacity to its limit. For example, the Wuhan steel complex in central China, built with investment and technical aid from Japan and the West, consumed the entire electric power output of Hubei province at the time of its completion. Another major cause of the shortage was the use of inefficient and obsolete plants and equipment by most Chinese industries, which wasted large quantities of energy.

The energy shortage and the resultant loss of industrial output became a priority item in China's Sixth Five-Year Plan. According to the plan, a significant portion of the state's investment is to be allocated for energy and transportation development—over $10.3 billion, or about one-fifth of the total budget for capital construction. As can be seen in Table 8.1, China planned to increase coal output by almost 13 percent, from 620 million to 700 million metric tons, and electric power by over 20 percent, from 300 million to 362 million kilowatts by 1985. Oil production was to increase substantially in joint ventures with foreign concerns.

China has been blessed with large oil reserves. Much publicity has been given to the fact that China could become a strong oil exporter in the future. Even now China exports some oil. In 1982 China produced about 700 million barrels of oil, or about 2 million barrels per day. About half of this production was consumed domestically.[96] Trade figures show that China exported to the United States over $100 million in crude oil and gasoline products in 1980. How large, then, are China's total oil reserves? The Chinese have estimated their oil reserves at about 30 billion to 60 billion tons, with two-thirds onshore and one-third offshore.[97] This would be about three times the estimated reserves of Saudi Arabia.[98] An official U.S. government estimate has put China's onshore reserves at 39 billion barrels, and offshore recoverable reserves at 50 to 70 billion barrels.[99] A United Nations expert estimated that the Chinese could produce 8 million barrels per day by the year 2000.[100] Another expert, from Hawaii's East-West Center, cautioned that China might not even reach an output of 500 million barrels per year in the 1980s if joint international ventures in offshore exploration did not materialize.[101]

China has decided to explore its offshore oil reserves. It has been estimated that the offshore oil deposits are in the range of 10 to 20 billion tons, most of which lie on the continental shelf in the South China Sea and the Bohai Basin in the Yellow Sea off east China. A new China National Offshore Oil Corporation was formed to be responsible for the exploration, development, production, and marketing of the product. In February 1982 China promulgated a set of regulations on offshore oil exploration for joint ventures with foreign firms.[102] These regulations designated forty-three blocks for concessions, or leases, in the South China Sea and the Yellow Sea, to be put up for bids from foreign concerns.[103] By August 1982 thirteen groups, composed of thirty-three foreign oil firms, had submitted bid proposals to China. Foreign oil firms participating in the bidding included most American giant oil firms, such as Atlantic Richfield (ARCO), Chevron, Cities Services, Exxon, Getty Oil, Mobil, Philips Petroleum, Texaco, and Union Oil, as well as British, French, Canadian, and Japanese firms.[104] Exploration arrangements provided for preferential customs duties or complete exemption for imported oil-drilling machinery, and gave foreign operators the right to export oil from China. The joint ventures simultaneously solved several problems for the Chinese. Paramount was the tremendous expense of exploratory drilling, estimated at $200 million for each zone in the South China Sea.[105] The benefits of the joint ventures included (1) provision of capital for development; (2) transfer of advanced foreign technology to China; (3) provision of oil to fill China's power needs; and (4) creation of foreign exchange from oil exports.

China has also embarked on construction of its first nuclear plant, to be located on Hangzhou Bay not far from Shanghai. The nuclear power program is planned to supplement China's energy needs for the future.[106]

China has not signed the 1958 Nuclear Nonproliferation Treaty which requires signatory nations to submit to inspection of their nuclear power plants.[107] Thus, China first sought help from the French. When French president Mitterand visited China in May 1983, he signed a $2 billion trade agreement to build a nuclear reactor in the southern province of Guangdon.[108] China has been negotiating with the United States for some time for an agreement that would permit China to purchase American nuclear technology.[109] On Premier Zhao's January 1984 visit to the United States, a significant agreement was signed in which the United States government would provide the Chinese with peaceful nuclear technology—the sale of nuclear reactors and related equipment—over the next two decades. In order to meet the United States legal requirement that any nation which receives American nuclear technology must agree to safeguards and controls on its use, the Chinese premier declared that China would refrain from advocating nuclear proliferation or helping other nations develop nuclear weapons. For the present, China is hungry for energy, but it may become an "energy giant" in the foreseeable future.

Population Control[110]

As expected by many demographers, the July 1982 national census showed that China's total population was over one billion with an annual growth rate of 1.5 percent. Of the total, 51.5 percent were male, and 48.5 were female. The far ranging implication of this huge population on China's economic development is quite obvious. Premier Zhao told the 1982 NPC that "the execution of our national economic plan and the improvement of the people's living standards will be adversely affected" if population growth is not controlled.[111] This was certainly a most candid admission by a top Chinese leader that the Malthusian theory of population was valid, a theory that Mao Zedong never accepted as applicable to a socialist China. Premier Zhao directed that population growth be kept to below 1.3 percent per annum, so that China's total population would not exceed 1.06 billion by 1985.[112]

How can China's population explosion be controlled? During the 1970s the much-publicized measure for population control was delayed marriage for the young. In addition, clinics were permitted to provide abortion services. Some birth control devices were disseminated in factories. Then, in 1977, the target became one child per family. As the 1982 census demonstrated, these measures were not able to check the enormous population growth. A major factor was the persistence of the traditional preference among the rural population for male offspring. While female infanticide was still an accepted practice in some rural areas, Premier Zhao condemned the practice.[113] The difficulty in controlling population growth is aggravated by the fact that 62 percent of the population in 1982 was under thirty-five years of age. As the young people reach the age of marriage and childbearing, the total number of births can be expected to rise dramatically—unless strict control measures are imposed. So far, the one child per couple policy has been observed widely only in the urban areas. Under this policy the state imposes punitive measures, such as a 2 percent reduction in salary, on a couple refusing abortion of their second child. Following the birth of the second child, a flat 15 percent salary reduction is imposed on the parents until the child has reached the age of 7. In urban areas couples have been encouraged to sign a contract pledging a one-child family in order to receive better and more spacious housing.[114] Obtaining general acceptance of the one-child-per-family policy among the peasants in rural China remains a Herculean task involving education, persuasion, and strong pressure from the state. Such efforts must be made, however, if China is to defuse its population bomb.

NOTES

1. "Create a New Situation in All Fields of Socialist Modernization," 15.

2. "Report on the Sixth Five-Year Plan," *Beijing Review,* 51 (December 20, 1982), 11.

3. See Arthur G. Ashbrook, "China: Economic Overview, 1975," in *China: A Reassessment of the Economy,* Joint Economic Committee, U.S. Congress (Washington, D.C.: Government Printing Office, July 10, 1975), p. 24; and Jan S. Prybyla, "Some Economic Strengths and Weaknesses of the People's Republic of China," *Asian Survey,* vol. x, no. 12 (December 1977), 1122.

4. Chou En-lai, "Report on the Work of the Government," *Peking Review,* 4 (January 24, 1975), 23.

5. Yao Wen-yuan, "On the Social Basis of the Lin Biao Anti-Party Clique" *Hongqi, 3 (1975),* as translated in the *Peking Review,* 10 (March 7, 1975), 5–10.

6. For the full text of these three documents, see *Issues and Studies,* vol. xiii, no. 6 (June 1977), 107–15; no. 8 (August 1977), 77–99; no. 9 (September 1977), 63–70. For commentaries on the radicals' attack on Deng's three documents, see Chi Wei, "How the 'Gang of Four' Opposed Socialist Modernization," *Peking Review,* 11 (March 11, 1977), 6–9; Hsiang Chun, "An Attempt to Restore Capitalism Under the Signboard of Opposing Restoration," *Peking Review,* 34 (August 19, 1977), 29–32, 37; and Mass Criticism Group of State Planning Commission, "Why Did the 'Gang of Four' Attack 'The Twenty Points'," *Peking Review,* 42 (October 14, 1977), 5–13.

7. Chang Ch'un-ch'iao, "On Exercising All-Round Dictatorship Over the Bourgeoisie," *Hongqi, 4 (1975),* as translated in *Peking Review,* 14 (April 4, 1975), 5–11. Also see Kao Lu and Chang Ko, "Comments on Teng Hsiao-p'ing's Economic Ideas of the Comprador Bourgeoisie," *Peking Review,* 35 (August 27, 1976), 6–9.

8. Repulsing the Right Deviationist Wind in the Scientific and Technological Circles," *Peking Review,* 18 (April 30, 1976), 6–9.

9. Hua Kuo-feng, "Political Report to the Eleventh National Congress of the CCP," *Peking Review,* 35 (August 26, 1977), 50.

10. Hua Kuo-feng, "Report on the Work of the Government," *Peking Review,* 10 (March 10, 1978), 19.

11. Ibid.

12. "Readjusting the National Economy: Why and How?" *Beijing Review,* 26 (June 29, 1979), 13–22.

13. *China Trade Report,* April 1980, p. 9.

14. "Readjusting the National Economy: Why and How?" p. 14.

15. *Ming Pao* (Hong Kong), June 14, 1979, p. 1. Also see Martin Weil, "The Baothan Steel Mill: A Symbol of Change in China's Industrial Development Strategy," *China Under the Four Modernizations,* Part 1, Joint Economic Committee, Congress of the United States (Washington, D.C.: Government Printing Office, August 13, 1982), pp. 365-91.

16. "Report on the Work of the Government," *Beijing Review,* 27 (July 6, 1979), 12-20; and *Far Eastern Economic Review* (October 5, 1979), 78-80.

17. See Lowell Dittmer, "China in 1981: Reform, Readjustment, Rectification," *Asian Survey,* vol. xxii, no. 2 (January 1982), 35.

18. These were the words used by Huang Hua, then minister for foreign affairs, in an interview in Ottawa, Canada. See Peter Stursberg, "Restructuring China Policy in the Wake of Chairman Mao," *The Canadian Journal of World Affairs* (May/June, 1981), 5.

19. Dittmer, "China in 1981," p. 36.

20. See *Business Week,* January 19, 1981, p. 38; and *Asiaweek,* February 20, 1981, p. 34.

21. Stursberg, "Restructuring China Policy," p. 33.

22. *Asiaweek,* February 20, 1981, p. 33.

23. "Further Economic Readjustment: A Break with 'Leftist' Thinking," *Beijing Review,* 12 (March 23, 1981), 27. Also see Xue Muqiao, *Current Problems of the Chinese Economy* (Beijing: The People's Publishers, 1980).

24. "Further Economic Readjustment," p. 28.

25. See Nai-Ruenn Chen, "China's Capital Construction: Current Retrenchment and Prospects for Foreign Participation," *China Under the Four Modernizations,* Part 2, pp. 50-52; and Richard Y.C. Yin, "China's Socialist Economy in Action: An Insider's View," *Journal of Northeast Asian Studies,* vol. 1, no. 2 (June 1982), 97-98.

26. *Asiaweek,* February 20, 1981, p. 33.

27. Jan S. Prybyla, "Economic Problems of Communism: A Case Study of China," *Asian Survey,* vol. xxii, no. 12 (December 1982), 1226. Also see *China Trade Report,* February 1981, p. 10.

28. Thomas G. Rawski, "Chinese Economic Planning," *Current Scene,* vol. xiv, no. 4 (April 1976), 1-15; and Dwight Perkins, "China's Fourth Five-Year Plan," *Current Scene,* vol. xii, no. 9 (September 1974), 1-7. Also see E.L. Wheelwright and Bruce McFarlane, *The Chinese Road to Socialism: Economics of the Cultural Revolution* (New York and London: Monthly Review Press, 1970), pp. 129-42; Audrey Donnithorne, *China's Economic system* (London: George Allen and Unwin, 1967), pp. 457-95.

29. Rawski, "Chinese Economic Planning," p. 2.

30. Sidney Lens, "Private Enterprises in China," reprinted in *Honolulu Star Bulletin,* October 1, 1981, A-19. Also see Takashi Oda, "Private Enterprise in China Fills the Gap," *Christian Science Monitor,* February 2, 1983, p. 6; and Bradley K. Martin, "Capitalism with a Chinese Flavor," *Baltimore Sun,* as reprinted in *Honolulu Sunday Star Bulletin and Advertiser,* December 21, 1980, C-19. For 1983 figure see Robert Delfs, "Private Enterprise Without Capitalism Is China's Goal: An Incentive Socialism," *Far Eastern Economic Review* (April 28, 1983), 40. Also see *The New Yorker* (January 23, 1984), 43-85.

31. *People's Daily,* January 9, 1983, p. 1. Also see *Takung Pao* (Hong Kong), June 2, 1983, p. 1.

32. *People's Daily,* January 9, 1983.

33. *Ming Pao* (Hong Kong), August 17, 1980, p. 1.

34. See David Bonavia, "Peking Watch," in *China Trade Report,* August 1982, p. 2, and February 1, 1981, p. 10; Zhu Minzhi and Zou Siguo, "Chen Yun on Planned Economy," *Beijing Review,* 12 (March 12, 1982), 12.

35. *China Trade Report,* August 1982, p. 2, and February 1981, p. 10.

36. Zhu Minzhi and Zou Siguo, "Chen Yun on Planned Economy," p. 12.

37. Ibid., p. 17.

38. *Hongqi,* 8 (April 6, 1982), 32.

39. Ibid., pp. 32-33.

40. "Report on the Sixth Five-Year Plan," p. 26

41. Ibid., pp. 10-35.

42. Report on the Sixth Five-Year Plan," pp. 11-16.

43. *China Trade Report,* January 1983, p. 12.

44. Ibid.

45. "Communiqué of the Third Plenary Session of the Eleventh Central Committee," 12.

46. For the text of the document, see "Several Questions in Strengthening and Perfecting the Job Responsibility System for Agricultural Production," *Issues and Studies,* vol. xvii, no. 5 (May 1981), 77–82. Also see "Rural Contract," *Beijing Review,* 45 (November 10, 1980), 5–6.

47. "A Programme for Current Agricultural Work," *Beijing Review,* 24 (June 14, 1982), 21.

48. See Graham E. Johnson, "The Production Responsibility System in Chinese Agriculture: Some Examples from Guangdong," *Pacific Affairs,* vol. 55, no. 3 (Fall 1982), 430–51.

49. "Let Some Localities and Peasants Prosper First," *Beijing Review,* 3 (January 19, 1981), 19–22; "System of Responsibility in Agricultural Production," *Beijing Review,* 11 (March 16, 1981), 3–4; and "Small Plots for Private Use," Beijing Review, 26 (June 29, 1981), 3–4.

50. "System of Responsibility in Agricultural Production," p. 4.

51. Johnson, "The Production Responsibility System," p. 451.

52. "Report on the Sixth Five-Year Plan," p. 33.

53. See "PRC Economic Performance in 1975," *Current Scene,* vol. xiv, no. 6 (June 1976), 1–14; and "The PRC Economy in 1976," *Current Scene,* vol. xv, nos. 4 and 5 (April–May 1977), 1–10.

54. Hua Kuo-feng, "Report on the Work of Government," p. 20.

55. "Report on the Sixth Five-Year Plan," p. 12.

56. Robert F. Dernberger, "Past Performance and Present State of China's Economy," in *China's Future: Foreign Policy and Economic Development in the Post-Mao Era,* eds. Allen S. Whiting and Robert F. Dernberger (New York: McGraw-Hill, 1977), pp. 95, 140.

57. For information on China's steel production, see Alfred H. Usack, Jr., and James D. Egan, "China's Iron and Steel Industry," in *China: A Reassessment of the Economy,* pp. 264–88.

58. American Rural Small-Scale Industry Delegation, *Rural Small-Scale Industry in the People's Republic of China* (Berkeley, Calif.: University of California Press, 1977), p. 1. Also, for an article on the evolution of China's policy toward the development of small industries, see Carl Riskin, "Small Industry and the Chinese Model of Development," *The China Quarterly,* 46 (April–June 1971), 245–73; and Carl Riskin, "China's Rural Industries: Self-Reliant System or Independent Kingdom?" *The China Quarterly,* 73 (March 1978), 77–98.

59. Chaing Hung, "Small and Medium-sized Industries Play Big Role," *Peking Review,* 45 (November 7, 1975), 23–25.

60. See *Rural Small-Scale Industries in the People's Republic of China;* and "Small Enterprises," *Peking Review,* 46 (November 15, 1974), 22.

61. See Sidney Lens, "Private Enterprises in China." Also see *Ta Kung Pao Weekly Supplement,* January 13, 1983, p. 1.

62. Charles Bettelheim, *Cultural Revolution and Industrial Organization: Changes in Management and the Division of Labor* (New York and London: Monthly Review Press, 1974), p. 47.

63. See Stephen Andors, *China's Industrial Revolution: Politics, Planning, Management, 1949 to the Present* (New York: Pantheon, 1977); Eckstein, *China's Economic Revolution,* pp. 84–108; Barry M. Richman, *Industrial Society in Communist China* (New York: Vintage Books, 1969), pp. 671–720; and Joan Robinson, *Economic Management in China* (London: Anglo-Chinese Educational Institute, 1976).

64. China's Iron and Steel Industry Advances Rapidly Along Chairman Mao's proletarian Revolutionary Line," *Peking Review,* 40 (October 3, 1968), 32–34.

65. See three rather revealing articles on a state-owned watch factory in Shanghai, entitled "The Workers Are the Master," *Peking Review,* 26–28 (June 29, July 6, and July 13, 1973), 11–14, respectively.

66. Wang Che, "The 'Gang of Four' Pushed Anarchism," *Peking Review,* 14 (April 1, 1977), 23–26.

67. Hua Kuo-feng, "Report on the Work of Government," p. 20; and Li Hsien-nien, "Opening Speech at the National Conference on Learning from Teaching in Industry," *Peking Review,* 18 (April 29, 1977), 15–17.

68. "Report on the Sixth Five-Year Plan," p. 30.

69. *People's Daily,* December 29, 1982, p. 1.

70. "Report on the Sixth Five-Year Plan," p. 30.

71. "After the Enterprises Have the Right to Self-Management," *Beijing Review,* 6 (Feb-

ruary 9, 1981), 3; "More Authority for Enterprises Revive the Economy," *Beijing Review,* 14 (April 4, 1981), 21-29; "Individual Economy," *Beijing Review,* 33 (August 18, 1981), 3.

72. "More Authority for Enterprises Revive the Economy," p. 23.

73. See the following works for detailed information and analysis: Peter Schran, "Institutional Continuity and Motivational Change: The Chinese Industrial Wages System, 1950-1973," *Asian Survey,* vol. xiv, no. 11 (November 1974), 1014-32; Jan S. Prybyla, "A Note on Incomes and Prices in China," *Asian Survey,* vol. xv, no. 3 (March 1975), 262-78; and Riskin, "Workers' Incentives in Chinese Industry," in *China: Reassessment of the Economy,* pp. 199-224.

74. "Implementing the Socialist Principle 'To Each According to His Work,' " *Peking Review,* 33 (August 18, 1978), 11-19.

75. Ibid., p. 13; and "After Wages Went Up," *Peking Review,* 18 (May 5, 1978), 21.

76. Riskin, "Workers' Incentives in Chinese Industry," p. 199.

77. "Implementing the Socialist Principle," p. 16.

78. *Ta Kung Pao Weekly Supplement,* March 18, 1981, p. 6.

79. See Jan S. Prybyla, "Key Issues in the Chinese Economy," *Asian Survey,* vol. xxi, no. 9 (September 1981), p. 928.

80. *Ta Kung Pao Weekly Supplement,* January 20, 1983, p. 4.

81. Takashi Oka, "China's Economic Revolution: Experimenting with Incentives," *Christian Science Monitor,* March 31, 1983, pp. 1, 8. Also see *China Trade Report,* February 1981, p. 10.

82. *People's Daily,* May 15, 1981, p. 1.

83. *Nanfang Daily,* June 21, 1981, p. 1.

84. John Erik, "China's Bonus System is Backfiring," *The Asian Wall Street Journal Weekly,* May 4, 1981, p. 12.

85. See the following article for a discussion of China's management problems: Xue Muqiao, "On Reforming the Economic Management System, I, II, III," *Beijing Review,* 5 (February 4, 1980), 16-21; 12 (March 24, 1980), 21-25; and 14 (April 7, 1980), 20-26; Richard Y.C. Yin, "China's Socialist Economy in Action," *Journal of Northeast Asian Studies,* vol. 1, no. 2 (June 1982), 105-9; and James O'Toole, The Good Managers of Sichuan," *Harvard Business Review,* vol. 59, no. 3 (May-June 1981), 28-40.

86. See at least two of the more popular books on Japanese management theories: William Ouchi, *Theory Z: How American Business Can Meet the Japanese Challenge* (New York: Addison Wesley, 1980); and Richard T. Pascale and Anthony G. Athos, *The Art of Japanese Management: Applications for American Executives* (New York: Warner Books, 1982).

87. David A. Hayden, "The Art of Managing Chinese Ventures," *The Asian Wall Street Journal Weekly,* July 6, 1981, p. 12.

88. Ibid. p. 12.

89. Frank Ching, "Poor Management and Irresponsible Workers Frustrate Foreign Partners in Chinese Factory," *The Asian Wall Street Journaleekly,*   December 15, 1980, p. 2.

90. O'Toole, "The Good Managers of Sichuan," p. 38. Also see *Ta Kung Pao Weekly Supplement,* December 2, 1982, p. 11.

91. Xue Muqiao, "On Reforming the Economic Management System (I)," *Beijing Review,* 12 (March 12, 1980), p. 24.

92. "On Reforming the Economic Management System (I)," p. 25.

93. *Ta Kung Pao Weekly Supplement,* December 22, 1980, p. 6.

94. For China's energy prospects and development, see Kim Woodard, *The International Energy Relations of China* (Stanford, Calif.: Stanford University Press, 1980); "China's Energy Prospects," *Problems of Communism,* xxix (January-February 1980), 61-67; "China and Offshore Energy," *Problems of Communism,* xxx (November-December 1981), 32-45; Vaclay Smil, *China's Energy Achievements, Problems, Prospects* (New York: Praeger Publ., 1976); Selig S. Harrison, *China, Oil, and Asia: Conflict Ahead?* (New York: Columbia University Press, 1977); and Randall W. Hardy, *China's Oil Future: A Case of Modest Expectations* (Boulder, Colo.: Westview Press, 1978).

95. "The Keys to Industrial Development," *Beijing Review,* 5 (January 31, 1983), 16.

96. *Ta Kung Pao Weekly Supplement,* May 27, 1982, p. 15.

97. Story is told in Butterfield, *China: Alive in the Bitter Sea,* p. 262.

98. *China Trade Report,* October 15, 1982, p. 48. Also see *Ta Kung Pao Weekly Supplement,* April 15, 1982, p. 2.

99. *Ta Kung Pao Weekly Supplement*, May 27, 1982, p. 15.

100. See *Honolulu Star Bulletin*, May 19, 1982, A–3.

101. *China Trade Report*, May 1981, p. 10.

102. *China Trade Report*, March 1982, p. 6. Also see *Ta Kung Pao Weekly Supplement*, February 11, 1982, pp. 8–9.

103. *China Trade Report*, March 1983, pp. 8–10.

104. *China Trade Report*, October 15, 1982, pp. 48–52.

105. *China Trade Report*, May 1981, p. 10.

106. See *The New York Times*, September 19, 1982, p. 11; and Ted Chan, "China Goes it Alone on Nuclear Power," United Press International, as reprinted in *Honolulu Advertiser*, March 18, 1983, A–19.

107. *The New York Times*, September 19, 1982, p. 11.

108. See *Honolulu Advertiser*, May 5, 1983, A–23.

109. See editorial of the *Los Angeles Times*, as reprinted in *Honolulu Star Bulletin and Advertiser*, Sunday edition, July 30, 1983, A-8.

110. For China's 1982 population census, see "The World's Biggest Census," *Beijing Review*, 32 (August 9, 1982), 16; "The 1982 Census Results," *Beijing Review*, 45 (November 8, 1982), 20–21; and "Report on the Sixth Five-Year Plan," p. 18.

111. "The 1982 Census Results," p. 20; and "Report on the Sixth Five-Year Plan," p. 18.

112. "Report on the Sixth Five-Year Plan," p. 18.

113. Ibid.

114. See Michele Vink, "China's Draconian Birth Control Program Weighs Heavily on Its Women," *Asian Wall Street Journal Weekly*, November 23, 1981, pp. 1, 21.

The Politics

of Modernization:

Education,

Science/Technology,

and the

Intellectuals

9

Two important factors have influenced, if not dominated, Chinese educational policies since 1949. First, education has been used as an instrument for the inculcation of new values and beliefs to build a new socialist revolutionary society. Second, changes in the content and form of education invariably have been intertwined with the shifting policies and strategies of economic development. Although the basic goal of the regime has been to construct a socialist state, the implementation of this basic goal has involved periodic shifts in emphasis between "red" (politics) and "expert" (technology). Let us begin our discussion by examining the educational policies which governed the administration of schools and universities prior to the advent of the Cultural Revolution in 1966.

EDUCATIONAL POLICIES
BEFORE THE
CULTURAL REVOLUTION

The very first governmental decree on education, "Decision of the Reformation of the Education System," promulgated in October 1951, was intended to provide formal education stressing both technical training and the learning of the new socialist values.[1] Chinese educational reform in the early 1950s was modeled on the Soviet approach to education, which stressed technical training to develop specialized skills. This emphasis on technical training was in harmony with the need to develop adequate personnel to implement the First Five-Year Plan (1953 to 1957). There was a great increase in the number of special technical schools at the secondary and university levels to help produce skilled workers to fill the estimated 1 million positions that would be required by the industrial plants transferred from the Soviet Union.[2] In many instances the length of schooling at the secondary and university levels was increased to ensure the quality of technical training. In addition, spare-time educational opportunities were made available for workers and peasants who were to be trained as semiskilled workers.[3] Student enrollment in spare-time primary and middle schools increased from a combined total of less than 2 million in 1953 to about 9 million in 1957.[4] The Great Leap placed increased emphasis on the need to combine education and productive labor. With the introduction of communes in the countryside and the stress on self-sufficiency, local communities assumed the full responsibility for maintaining schools. A summary of the Chinese educational system on the eve of the Cultural Revolution follows.

Primary Schools

On the advice of Soviet advisors, the length of primary schooling was initially reduced by one year, to a term of five years, to extend the system and to produce more graduates. By 1953 the length of primary schooling had reverted back to six years. In rural areas the length of primary schooling was usually limited, perhaps to three or four years, with many of the schools on a half-study, half-work basis. Initially, primary school was neither compulsory nor universal. During the first ten years of the regime's rule, enrollment in primary schools increased from a little over 24 million in 1949 to 51 million in 1953 and to over 86 million in 1958.[5] Between 1953 and 1958, approximately 27.5 million adult peasants and workers enrolled in spare-time primary schools.[6] The curriculum for primary schools contained a heavy emphasis on political and ideological value formation as well as the usual subjects: Chinese language, arithmetic, and introduction to general science.

Secondary Schools

There were several types of secondary, or middle, schools prior to the Cultural Revolution. The first kind were the general, academically oriented secondary schools, which included three years at the junior level and three years at the senior level. These academically oriented schools were found exclusively in urban areas before 1958. Second were vocational schools, which emphasized practical training and teacher education. The length of attendance at these vocational secondary schools was usually three to four years. Third were specialized polytechnic schools that prepared students for work in industry, agriculture, public health, and commerce and trade. These specialized secondary schools emphasized little solid academic instruction and were almost exclusively found in urban areas before 1958. Most of the vocationally oriented and specialized schools were on a half-study, half-work basis. The Great Leap and the communization programs expanded the half-study, half-work vocational secondary schools into the communes, where agricultural production became the main content of instruction. There were enormous increases in enrollment in all types of secondary schools.[7] In 1953 enrollment in middle schools, including spare-time schools, was at 3.3 million; enrollment in secondary technical schools, including spare-time schools, was about 1.7 million. By 1958 enrollment for middle schools, including spare-time schools, was over 9 million; and enrollment in secondary technical schools, including spare-time schools, was 1.4 million. A large percentage of the middle school enrollment was in the countryside. By 1958 the educational thrust was to teach whatever was required by the communes to help agricultural production. In addition to a heavy emphasis on agricultural subjects, rural middle schools' curricula included political and ideological studies and arithmetic. Sparetime rural secondary specialized schools now began to teach machinery repair and tractor driving.

The mushrooming of secondary schools, and their tremendous increase in enrollment, soon presented problems as regarded the job situation in the urban areas. The First Five-Year Plan's economic acceleration had encouraged migration to the urban areas, but the number of jobs generated by the economy simply could not keep pace with the potential workers who flocked to the urban areas. Two basic changes in China's educational policy were made to meet this problem: First, the number of spare-time specialized secondary schools was reduced; and second, all graduates from primary and secondary schools who could neither find jobs in factories nor go on to technical colleges or universities were sent to the countryside to engage in agricultural production. This was the beginning of the youth rustication program, which will be discussed separately.

The problems of rapid growth of the urban population and the resultant unemployment in urban areas were solved in 1958 by the Great Leap, which called for mass mobilization and labor-intensive production in the countryside. Students were told to participate as farmers or workers after school. Expansion of half-study, half-work schools resumed in both urban and rural areas. In addition, political education became an even more essential part of the curriculum, to inculcate the values of being both "red" and "expert."[8]

Higher Education

Leo Orleans identified five different types of higher educational institutions in China prior to the Cultural Revolution:[9] There were comprehensive universities, comparable to American universities, with the traditional academic departments. These were four-year institutions of higher learning with full-time students. Then there were the polytechnic institutions, such as the famous Qinghua University, located in Beijing—a sort of Chinese M.I.T. Below these two types of universities were the new institutions of higher learning that proliferated during and after the Great Leap: (1) vocationally organized, specialized colleges; (2) enterprise-controlled spare- time industrial colleges for workers already employed by the industries; and (3) the low-quality and highly questionable institutions known as workers and peasants colleges, which mushroomed during the Great Leap. While comprehensive and polytechnic universities numbered between twenty and forty before 1966, the new institutions grew by the hundreds. Enrollment in institutions of higher education in 1949 was about 117,000. In 1959 the total figure had reached 810,000.[10]

Entrance to comprehensive and polytechnic universities was based on passing the entrance examination. A large percentage of students who were admitted to university work in the period under discussion were those who wanted to be engineers and scientists. The areas of specialization were determined according to the state plan and personnel needs in the scientific and technological fields. During the author's visits in 1973 to Beijing University, Qiaodung University in Xian, and Fudan University in Shanghai, it was pointed out by the faculties that before 1960, science instruction at the university level was under the influence of the Soviet Union, in terms of textbooks, laboratories, and equipment. Before the withdrawal of Soviet aid in June 1960, some 7,500 Chinese students had gone to the Soviet Union for either postgraduate work or specialized training. According to Leo Orleans, the total number of graduates from these institutions of higher learning from 1949 to 1966 was 1.7 million, with 34 percent in engineering, 27 percent in education, 11 percent in medicine, 8 percent in agriculture and forestry, 6 percent in natural sciences, and 5 percent in finance and economics.[11]

Before the Cultural Revolution, Chinese university education was modeled on the European system, with a great deal of formalism and rigidity. The role of the professor was to give formal lectures in class, with no opportunity for questions and answers or interaction between the instructor and the students. As doors of higher education opened to students of worker and peasant background (in 1957 about 36 percent of the university student body in China came from that social background), a serious problem of academic deficiency occurred among the students. Instructors were unwilling to provide remedial work for those who needed it, and were often contemptuous of those who were academically ill-prepared for university work.[12] Therefore, tension existed in the relationship between the students and their professors, coupled with feelings of resentment on the part of students who could not reach their instructors.[13] We will see later how this "feudal relationship" was corrected after the Cultural Revolution.

THE CULTURAL REVOLUTION AND EDUCATIONAL REFORM

The Cultural Revolution's greatest impact was in the area of education. Some far-reaching changes resulted from the revolutionary reforms introduced during the upheaval to overhaul the educational system at all levels. In the following pages, we will discuss some of the changes and innovations in Chinese education introduced during the Cultural Revolution and its aftermath.

It must be kept in mind that for at least two years, from 1966 to 1968, all schools and universities were closed because of the disruption caused by the students' participation in the Cultural Revolution. When the central government ordered the schools to reopen and students to return to their classes in late 1967 and early 1968, the normal combined length of attendance for both primary and middle schools was shortened from twelve years to nine years.[14] Most rural areas shortened the combined length of attendance in both primary and middle schools to a bare seven years. It was reasoned that by the time the youngsters completed their middle school education, they would be fifteen or sixteen, "a suitable age to begin taking part in farm work." Those who finished the shortened secondary education in urban areas were expected to work in factories to gain practical experience. Upon reaching the age of fifteen or sixteen, all youths who had completed secondary education were required to render at least three years of practical work or service before considering entrance to higher education. This requirement for three years of practical work experience relieved some of the pressure for entrance to colleges and universities. University education, particularly at technical colleges, was similarly shortened to three years or less.

Then, drastic changes were made in the curriculum in both schools and universities. Primary school instruction revolved around subjects on politics and ideology and rudimentary agriculture or industry. Language arts and arithmetic were barely squeezed in between these political and practical subjects. In the secondary schools, academic subjects, such as language arts, arithmetic, and history, were taught in conjunction with productive labor and political and military training. Mao's principle that "education must serve proletarian politics and be combined with productive labor" became the key factor in developing instructional content in all schools. Primary and secondary education was devoted mainly to the acquisition of knowledge which had immediate application to economic production. Many primary and secondary schools were structured on the half-study, half-work basis. Rural education was structured to cultivate pride in being peasants, appreciation of agricultural work, and a desire for "striking roots" in the countryside. The attitude developed by many rural students, that "the first year they are still country folks, the next year they become different, and the third year they look down on their parents," was condemned as revisionist.[15] University book learning which was impractical and irrelevant to problem solving was expanded to integrate theory and practice. To implement this integration, universities established factories on campus to manufacture marketable products. In addition, long-time factory workers who had practical experience were allowed to enroll in university classes in physics, chemistry, or mechanical engineering. Visitors to Chinese universities in the 1970s, as a rule, were shown the facilities on campus where experienced factory workers worked alongside young students on some aspect of science, such as solid state physics or transistor making. One of China's leading scientists and educators, Professor Zhou Peiyuan, then vice-president of the Chinese Academy of Science and president of Beijing University, said in 1973:

> Beijing University has shortened the period of schooling, enrolled students from among workers, peasants, and soldiers with practical experience, and changed the road and approach in conducting education. The faculty of sciences has established direct contact with factories, and the university has set up its own workshops. Teachers and students spend a certain amount of time in productive labour at factories where teaching and scientific research are done in combination with practice. . . . The university has seven factories and twenty-seven workshops, plus a farm, and has established regular contact with sixty-five industrial enterprises. This has effectively promoted changes in the system, contents, and method of teaching.[16]

The Cultural Revolution severely condemned the system of evaluating student performance by examination. Entrance examinations and the practice of holding students back a year for failure to pass the examinations were labeled as the "revisionist line of education." Entrance examinations for universities were abolished when these institutions were reopened in 1970. In their place a system of nominations and recommendations was adopted for all institutions of higher learning. The new system called for the following methods of nomination: (1) self-nomination by individual students; (2) nomination by the masses; and (3) recommendation by the party leadership. High school graduates thus nominated then had to be approved by the institutions. The purpose of the new system was to enable youngsters from a "revolutionary social background"—workers, poor and lower-middle peasants, members of the army, and youth who had gone down to live with the peasants—to have the opportunity to enter universities. Clearly, the new system was designed to meet complaints at the time that the universities, the road to one's future station in life, had become the preserve of the elites and tended to exclude those political activists who were endowed with revolutionary fervor. The new admissions policy was aimed not only at greatly increasing recruitment of youths from the proper "revolutionary social background," but it limited admissions to those who had acquired practical experience, either as workers in factories or in communes. In 1970 most universities required two or three years of practical experiences prior to entrance. Thus, under the new system—with its lack of entrance examinations—150,000 workers, peasants, and PLA members were admitted to universities from 1970 to 1973. With the admission of large numbers of students who did not have adequate preparation, academic standards had to be lowered and remedial classes organized.

The administration and management of education during the Cultural Revolution was taken out of the hands of the professional educators. Local revolutionary committees began taking control of the schools in October 1968 through the dispatch of worker and peasant Mao's Thought Propaganda Teams, with the active participation of PLA soldiers.[17] These teams ended strife among the students[18] and worked with the students and teachers to reorganize educational content, placing more stress on the study of Mao's thought and relating education to productive labor. In addition to the revolutionary committees that administered the schools and universities, there was a "Revolution in Education Committee" on campus to provide daily guidance in carrying out the reform measures in these institutions, particularly in higher education.[19] Members of these educational committees were cadres and teachers. At Fudan University in Shanghai, where the author visited in 1973, cadres who were workers in the revolutionary committee dominated the university's administration; the leading cadre who directed Fudan University was a skilled worker in a textile factory in Shanghai.

In rural areas primary schools were run by the production brigades, and secondary schools by the communes. This meant that the revolutionary committees on the communes were in full charge of education. Two reasons were generally given for the reform. One was purely ideological: "Since the fundamental question of revolution is political power" and the "fundamental question of revolution in education is also the question of power," proletarian education must be in the hands of the people in order to prevent the growth of the revisionist educational line. The second was more practical: "We (lower-middle peasants) can decide the teaching contents and, in a way we see fit, plan when classes take place."[20] Another important fact was that in brigade-run schools, teachers were members of the same commune, "eating the same kind of food and living in the same kind of housing as the poor and lower-middle peasants."[21] In urban areas primary schools were generally run by neighborhood revolutionary committees or street committees; secondary schools were run by neighborhood revolutionary committees and factories located in the area. The new revolutionary management of schools by local units reflected the Cultural Revolution's emphasis on decentralization. It also relieved the state from spending enormous amounts of money for primary and secondary education.

A number of radical educational experiments were undertaken during the Cultural Revolution and its aftermath, most notably in extension work at agricultural colleges and in short-term courses for workers in "July 21" workers' colleges. Many agricultural colleges extended their teaching to practical learning situations in the countryside. Traditionally, an agricultural college insisted that students learn from textbooks, in individual classes, arranged by stages in the curriculum: for instance, a basic course on botany, followed by a specialized course in plant physiology and crop cultivation. Under the reform, students were taught the rice seedlings process simultaneously with a basic course on plant physiology and a specialized course on crop cultivation.[22] Also, short extension courses were provided for older peasants to help them understand the scientific methods.[23] The first experiment with a workers' college was made by the Shanghai Machine Tools Plant, in response to Mao's directive of July 21, 1968, shortening the length of schooling and revolutionizing education.[24] These "July 21" workers' colleges selected experienced workers from the plant, and capable students from the middle school administered by the plant, to form a technical college with short-term instruction on instruments and their components. This training of semiskilled workers to become skilled technicians in a short period was comparable to the on-the-job or personnel retraining programs funded by the United States government in recent years. Typically, the curriculum at these workers' colleges consisted of political education, militia activities, mathematics, mechanical engineering, and related technical subjects. Encouragement was often given to the workers' college to design machinery for the plant. There was a phenomenal growth of workers' colleges in many provinces. In one year Liaoning Province claimed that the number of such colleges increased from 52 to 270, with a total student enrollment of 25,300. Heilongjiang had 333 such institutions, with an enrollment of 17,800, or 20 percent of all students in higher education in that province.[25] Both agricultural extension work and short-term on-the-job training were designed to raise the scientific capability of the peasants and workers, in the nation's quest for rapid scientific and technological development. As one participant in the workers' college explained: "We should . . . build a magnificent contingent of working-class intellectuals, with socialist culture and technical knowledge, and adept in production."[26]

REVERSAL OF THE
CULTURAL REVOLUTION
EDUCATIONAL POLICY

The reforms and innovations introduced during the Cultural Revolution and its aftermath created a host of problems. As Chinese leaders reviewed the educational field in the 1970s, they discovered that the quality of education had fallen and that the gap between China and the industrial nations in science and technology had widened rather than narrowed over the past decade.[27] The disappearance of a large number of scientific research institutes reflected the almost complete abandonment of basic research in science and technology.[28] The deterioration in educational quality was attributable to the inordinate amount of classroom time spent on ideological and political studies, the absence of examinations to measure students' performance, and the lack of discipline in schools.[29] The morale of the country's 9 million teachers and educational workers was at a low ebb.

Premier Zhou was the first leading party and government official to take action to arrest the declining state of education. In 1973 the State Council, under Zhou's direction, reinstated entrance examination requirements for universities and colleges. Zhou called for more research by both scientific institutions and universities. The premier asked that certain academically superior students be enrolled in universities directly after graduation from secondary school. All these measures were designed to improve the quality of education and to recruit potential young scientists. The radical ideologues, of course, waged a campaign of criticism against these educational policies, which reversed the reforms introduced by the Cultural Revolution. At first the attack focused on the question of entrance examinations to universities. In June 1973 a number of universities in several provinces began the cultural examination system, which required nominees to pass both an oral and a written test prior to admission. The oral portion of the test dealt with political studies and experience gained through labor; the written portion dealt with academic knowledge, with emphasis on mathematics, physics, and chemistry. The cultural examination became a public issue after a protest by a student who was sent to a commune in 1968. Following nomination to the university by his commune brigade in 1973, he took the entrance test but refused to answer questions in physics and chemistry. Instead, at the instigation of the radicals, he wrote a protest letter on his examination paper, stating that he had followed Chairman Mao's directive to go down to the countryside to engage in collective productive labor for almost five years. Since he had to work long hours as a captain of a production team in the commune, he had found no time to review the subjects learned five years earlier in secondary school. Following this protest, articles in the *People's Daily* and the *Red Flag,* the party's theoretical journal controlled by the radicals, criticized abuses in the administration of the cultural examinations.[30] They argued that this examination system failed to take into account the importance of a student's revolutionary fervor and the practical experience and that there had been cases of favoritism where cadres had wrangled admission for their children "through the back door." A week before the convening of the Tenth Party Congress, an editorial, reputedly written by Mao, appeared in the *People's Daily,* supporting the campaign against the unfair entrance examination system and urging everyone to "go against the tide"—a slogan reminiscent of the 1966 Cultural Revolution's "dare to rebel."[31]

Now the battle line had been drawn on educational policies. The initial skirmishes were won by the radicals, who attacked the minister of education during 1975 and 1976 and succeeded in removing him from that office. The radicals charged (1) that the revisionists had dominated China's education for seventeen years, from 1949 to 1966; and (2) that most teachers and students were so bourgeois as to be ranked as "the stinking ninth category of class enemy of socialism."[32]

THE NEW EDUCATIONAL POLICY AFTER MAO[33]

In a speech to the Chinese Scientific and Technical Congress in the spring of 1980, Hu Yaobang, the CCP general secretary, said China's young people must become the effective force and reserve in science and technology. He also indicated that education of China's youth was the key to building this reserve. In a major speech to the 1978 National Educational Work Conference, Deng Xiaoping outlined China's new educational policy, which was formulated to meet the needs of modernization.[34] First, Deng urged that educational quality be improved at the primary and secondary school levels— "We must fill out the courses in primary and secondary schools with advanced scientific knowledge"—by upgrading the curriculum content and reinstituting the examination system.[35] Then he called for a tightening of school discipline, with emphasis on elevating students' moral, intellectual, and physical levels. Third, Deng reiterated the important role education must play in China's modernization. Last, he asked for respect for the teachers and care for their well-being in terms of better working conditions and compensation. Let us now review briefly the changes that have taken place since the pragmatists came to power.

In primary schools major changes were made in the length of schooling and instructional content. In 1977 the 9.8 million primary schools, with a total enrollment of 146 million students, did not provide all youngsters with a five-year primary education. In fact, the goal announced in 1977 of guaranteeing eight years of schooling in rural areas and ten years in urban areas was simply a wish that was not possible to fulfill.

In 1981 many urban primary schools provided six years of schooling for children between the ages of seven and twelve, and rural schools offered four to five years of primary education. As compared to what existed during the Cultural Revolution, the length of primary schooling had been extended somewhat. However, leading educators spoke out at the June 1983 session of the Chinese People's Political Consultative Conference in favor of a compulsory six-year primary education for rural areas in order to eradicate illiteracy, which was estimated to affect 25 percent of the total population.

The new primary school curriculum is designed to give children "a sounder education," developing their moral, intellectual, and physical well-being.[36] Instructional content at the primary level, at least in urban areas such as Beijing and Shanghai, consists of Chinese language (children now are expected to master 2,000 characters), arithmetic, general science, and foreign language

(English, Russian, Japanese, or German in the third year). Urban primary schools add subjects such as music, art, ethics, and geography to the curriculum, to replace political-ideological studies. Primary schools in China have become more conventional and academically oriented. Also, more emphasis is given to moral education—including instruction on being "polite, honest, brave, industrious, modest and economical," helpful to others, and good in personal hygiene—as well as to love the "socialist motherland."[37] Many of these conventional moral instructions are incorporated in the rules of conduct for pupils.[38] Good students are now expected to be all-around persons, not only excelling in examinations but also to be sound "ideologically, intellectually and physically."[39]

Work-study programs are again instituted in many schools. On-campus factories or workshops in urban areas, and farm plots in rural areas, are provided so that youngsters can engage in practical work projects. It has been reported recently that 431,000 of China's 1 million primary and secondary schools instituted work-study programs in the form of small-scale factories, farms, and tree nurseries.[40] A basic purpose of these programs is to train students so that they would eventually become "workers with a socialist consciousness and culture."[41]

In 1979 there was a shift of emphasis in the role of secondary education in China. The pre-1965 policy of stressing vocational training was revived.[42] Secondary schools are now entrusted with the dual task of producing graduates for university work and good workers for society.[43] Vocational classes in secondary and middle schools are designed to equip students with marketable and productive skills. Many urban secondary schools offer training in tourism, foreign trade, commerce, electrical appliance repair, sewing, food preparation and service, and printing.[44] Emphasis is put on vocational education for several reasons. One reason is to redress the past overemphasis on general education. There is a shortage of skilled personnel at the entry and intermediate levels in factories and enterprises. In addition, millions of secondary school graduates simply cannot find jobs, because of their lack of technical training. Finally, institutions of higher learning in China can only absorb 3 to 4 percent of each year's secondary school graduates.[45]

Premier Zhao indicated that under the Sixth Five-Year Plan, (1981–85) China would produce a trained and skilled labor force large enough to meet rising demands in industries and enterprises.[46] The newly instituted policy for secondary schools includes the following reforms: (1) the addition of more vocational and technical courses in the secondary school curriculum; (2) conversion of some middle schools into vocational or agricultural schools which would take in junior middle school (junior high) graduates and provide them with three years of vocational training; and (3) new technical schools.[47] However, graduates of vocational schools would not be provided with jobs automatically. They must pass examinations before employment, with placement depending on skill and performance.[48] In 1982 some 630,000 new students reportedly were enrolled in vocational and secondary schools.[49] While the present policy for secondary education places emphasis on vocational and technical training, most urban areas also have embarked on the development of academically oriented secondary schools, known as "key schools." In the 1950s "key schools" devoted their efforts to producing quality education. They received special government funds and had the best-trained teachers and best facilities. Students selected for the "key schools" were generally the brightest and best qualified intellectually. The unique features of "key schools," once attacked by the radicals as "revisionist" and elitist, were revived in 1978 in many urban areas. A deputy director of education for the Shanghai municipality told a visiting group of American educators that the city was moving rapidly toward the establishment of a network of "key schools" with ample budgets and superior teachers for the brightest students.[50]

The most significant reform in higher education since 1976 has been the reintroduction of competitive examinations for university entrance. You may recall from Chapter 1 that between 1970 and 1974, the radicals had imposed a "recommendation model"[51] for university entrance, where graduates of secondary schools were able to apply for university entrance after two or three years of practical work. Applicants would be screened by their own work units on the basis of their work records as well as political factors. Final admission was based on review by provincial authorities and university administrations. For a brief period, between 1973 and 1974, Zhou Enlai experimented with combining recommendations with a "cultural examination" system. The experiment was abandoned after radicals mounted an attack on the examination system and on Zhou Enlai himself.[52]

In 1977 the government revived the examination system for university entrance. In the summer of that year, approximately 5.7 million young people took the entrance examinations, which were administered on a nationwide basis. The leading universities admitted over 1,100 successful candidates, with a large percentage coming from peasant and cadre family backgrounds.[53] But the total number of candidates admitted to colleges in 1977 reached 278,000. For the three-year period between 1977 and 1979, some 738,000 new students were admitted to the universities via competitive examinations, as follows: 278,000 in 1977, 290,000 in 1978, and 270,000 in 1979.[54] The total number of secondary school graduates or equivalents who took the examinations was 5.7 million in 1977, 5 million in 1978, and 4.6 million in 1979.[55] But the level of annual admissions to universities averaged less than 300,000. This meant that only a very small percentage of the millions of applicants were successful in gaining admittance each year. Even under the Sixth Five-Year Plan, not more than 400,000 will be accommodated in 1985.[56] The problem remains how to provide further education for the unsuccessful applicants who desire it.

To help fill the need for large numbers of skilled and technically competent personnel for modernization, the Chinese have devised alternative educational programs. One program uses television and radio for instruction in urban centers such as Beijing and Shanghai. For example, courses in mechanical engineering, electronics, chemistry, physics, and mathematics are offered as key components of a three-year program. Students who successfully complete the TV university program are given diplomas and recognized as bona fide college graduates by the state.[57] In 1979 the Central Broadcasting and Television University in Beijing granted graduation certificates to half a million students.[58] At that time 1.3 million enrolled college students were mainly factory workers, miners, teachers, and military personnel.[59]

Another innovation is the establishment of affiliated colleges by regular accredited institutions of higher learning on campuses of secondary schools. Students attending affiliated colleges are regular workers in factories, seeking advanced training in specialized skills.[60] Spare-time colleges are yet another way to provide further technical training for the young. Trade union federations organize classes for workers who were selected by competitive examination to enroll in these colleges to study economic law and management.[61] Finally, admittance of additional students to universities on a self-paying basis provides opportunities to secondary school graduates. A number of universities in Beijing open their doors to those who failed the entrance examinations but who could pay a tuition of 20 yuan (about $10) per term. These students are not allowed to stay in dormitories. Upon graduation, the self-paid students would receive a certificate and apply for jobs themselves instead of being assigned by the state.[62]

Recently a debate developed among China's educators on the question of whether development in higher education was moving at too slow a pace. Those who took this view argued that during the past thirty years, China had produced only 3 million university graduates. The minister of education, on the other hand, argued against a more rapid rate of growth; instead, he stressed improvement in quality of education. Some even argued that China's 8 percent average annual growth rate in the number of full-time university students over the past thirty-two years compared rather favorably with countries such as the United States—with an average annual growth rate of 5 percent over the past thirty years—and the Soviet Union, with an annual average growth rate of only 2.4 percent.[63]

The hard fact is that total student enrollment in Chinese universities is about 2 million, or 0.2 percent of China's total population, as compared to 12 million students in American colleges and universities, or about 5 percent of its total population. However, the most serious problem in education is not the annual growth rate but rather the problem of providing broader opportunities for millions of youths, especially in the urban areas, to acquire technical skills and specialized training so that they too can take part in the modernization plans. Chinese leaders must find satisfactory solutions to the "crisis of unfulfilled expectation" among the disillusioned urban youth.[64] Otherwise, the ugly ghost of the Cultural Revolution might reappear to haunt them. However the policy now is to produce only the number of university graduates as the existing limited facilities could permit.

Whatever the outcome of the current debate, one thing seems to be very clear. The pragmatic leaders must make a strong commitment to accelerate the expansion of education, particularly at higher educational levels. Premier Zhao explained this well when he told the NPC in December 1982 that upgrading "the educational, scientific, technological and cultural levels of the whole people is a major guarantee for building a modern material civilization and also a major aspect in building a socialist spiritual civilization."[65]

THE XIAFANG MOVEMENT
FOR URBAN YOUTH[66]

It has been estimated that over 20 million middle school graduates were sent down to the countryside to work in communes from the beginning of the Cultural Revolution, in 1966, to 1977. This massive transfer of urban secondary school graduates to rural areas and sparsely populated autonomous regions was designed to accomplish a number of objectives.[67] Ideologically, the transfer to the countryside was supposed to reduce the gap created by the differences in urban and rural living standards and to remove elitist tendencies prevalent among educated urban intellectuals who generally looked down on the peasants. Pragmatically, it was seen as a means of solving the urban unemployment problem; at the same time, it bolstered the rural economies where intensive labor was the strategy for development.

This annual migration of educated youths proved to be of benefit to rural development. First, their physical labor contributed to sorely needed food production. In addition, these youths frequently served as "agents of technological change." Many have become agricultural technicians or rural paramedics, "barefoot doctors" in public health and paramedical work.[68] Others gradually became leaders on production teams or brigades.

The tangible benefits of the program that transferred urban youths to the countryside often were marred by problems. The peasants frequently looked upon these urban youths as an additional burden.[69] Too often peasants felt that urban youths were not really suited to the hard labor in the fields, and they resented spending time teaching them how to do simple manual work. Young male and female students from the cities often found the work too hard and rural backwardness too difficult to endure over a lengthy period of time. These urban youths were reluctant to remain on the communes longer than was necessary, and they viewed their stay as only transitory. Some escaped the misery of their hard life on the communes by smuggling themselves back to the cities; without a job or food coupons, they soon became wanderers on the city streets or were sheltered by friends and relatives. By 1977–78 Chinese leaders admitted that these problems needed to be corrected.[70] There were reports of poor housing and inadequate diet for the inexperienced urban youths who were not able to earn the minimum number of work points to allow for an adequate standard of living.

Some changes were introduced into the xiafang movement after the pragmatic reformers began to consolidate their power in 1978. The new policy no longer required urban secondary school graduates to go to the countryside. They could continue their studies or work in the cities; they could elect to go to such frontier regions as the Inner Mongolia or Xinjiang autonomous regions; or they could simply opt for the countryside. Those who elected to go to the countryside were no longer required to stay with a production team in a commune. Instead, many urban youths were sent as contract workers to state farms or collectively owned farms set up especially for them. The new policy at first provided a rotation system between city jobs and farm work after two to three years. (Then it was abandoned because of sit-down strikes staged by the unhappy youths.)[71] While working in the countryside, youths would receive special technical training provided by urban factories and commercial enterprises.[72]

DISCONTENT
AMONG THE YOUTH

About 160 million young people who were between the ages of eight and eighteen at the time of the Cultural Revolution have been termed the "lost generation." These youths, who were in their mid-twenties to mid- thirties in 1980, had their education interrupted by the great upheaval. Among this group, at least 20 million secondary school graduates were sent down to the countryside under the xiafang movement, or "the downward transfer."

The bulk of the "lost generation" suffered widespread discontent and disillusionment.[73] Many of these young people faced a "crisis of confidence" in attitudes toward the CCP and China's socialist system. Those dissenters who formed the core of the 1978–79 Democracy Wall movement, discussed in Chapter 7, were drawn largely from this age group. Having wasted their time in the Cultural Revolution, many of them now possessed neither the education nor the necessary skills to be gainfully employed. Rural youth faired much better, in that they always knew there would be little opportunity for them to migrate to the cities and find jobs in the factories. Today, with the new incentive system in the countryside, more rural youngsters prefer to remain on the farm.

Urban unemployment for the young reached a critical point in the period between 1978 and 1981. With the introduction of individualized enterprises in the cities, many unemployed urban youths have gone into small businesses for themselves. Still, large numbers remain unemployed. Some have committed crimes in the cities. Others have even committed suicide because of failure to pass the annual university entrance examinations. Thus, the future outlook for China's youth seems rather bleak. If their pent-up energy is not channeled toward useful ends, if their disillusionment about the system is not alleviated, and if they are not made a useful part of the march toward modernization, then they will remain a potential source of unrest in the future.

THE ROLE OF SCIENCE
AND TECHNOLOGY
IN MODERNIZATION

A historic milestone was reached in the spring of 1978 when some 6,000 scientists and technicians gathered in Beijing to discuss and endorse the plans for China's development of modern science and technology. In his keynote address to the conference, Deng Xiaoping, by then vice-premier of the State Council, criticized the party for not providing adequate services, supplies, and working conditions for scientists.[74] This was certainly a far cry from the days when the intellectuals, scientists, and technicians were labeled, by Yao Wen-yuan, "an exploiting class" with strong bourgeois prejudices,[75] and when Deng himself was charged by the radicals with advocating the "poisonous weed" of advanced scientific development.

Since 1949 science policy has vacillated between professional orientation and mass mobilization, depending on China's development policies.[76] Whitson noted that during each alteration period, the leadership embraced a different set of approaches toward the identifiable issues of planning, the role of self-sufficiency, and the place of technology transfers from abroad.[77] During the First Five-Year Plan, professionals and technical bureaucrats held a position of dominance. Consequently, they emphasized centralized planning and control over the allocation of resources, importation of some 300 complete industrial plants from the Soviet Union, and scientific and technical training of Chinese in the Soviet Union. Following the withdrawal of Soviet aid in 1960, the Great Leap altered the basic approach from professionalism—with heavy reliance on technological transfers from abroad—to Mao's approach to self-reliance and "disdain" for foreign technology. The alternating pattern reappeared with some variations during the periods of economic recovery following the Great Leap and the Cultural Revolution.

The Cultural Revolution disrupted the scientific community in a number of ways. Scientists and technicians were criticized for their professional sins: their aloofness from and disinterest in politics, their privileged status and high salaries, and their theoretical research, unrelated to practical problems. Established in 1958 under the supervision of the State Council, the State Scientific and Technological Commission was supposed to provide direction for scientific research, administer scientific and technological programs, and approve funds for research. The organization's leading members, however, were subjected to Red Guard criticism and harassment for their elitist orientation. Many of the scientific cadres associated with the commission were sent to the countryside for rehabilitation through physical labor, and the commission disappeared as an organization.

The Academy of Sciences, which conducts reseach in the various physical and social sciences, both directly and though affiliate members, was subjected to criticism and purges. At the height of the upheaval, it was reported that thousands of its members had been sent to the factories and communes for physical labor.[78] The president of the academy, the late Guo Moruo, a noted historian, managed to survive by making self-criticism in which he repudiated all his previous writings. Typically, the academy's affairs were taken over by a revolutionary committee, with the PLA and the masses participating in decision making. Members were forced to spend long hours in political reeducation and ideological remolding.

Some members of the academy were sent to factories and communes to engage in applied research. Many of the research institutes of the academy decentralized their operations during the Cultural Revolution by establishing provincial and local branches, which proliferated and duplicated activities. Although Cultural Revolution strategy did not contribute to basic scientific research, some observers in the West viewed some of the reforms in science and technology as innovative from a developmental perspective. Genevieve Dean has argued that China's urgent need was for the application of innovative native technology to solve immediate problems of development, and that high-level research was too sophisticated to be of any use to the ordinary peasants and workers.[79] Oldham and Lee saw the prospect of mass participation in developing native technology, based on local initiative and resources, as enriching the economic life of the Chinese.[80] Oldham noted that mass training of ordinary workers as "amateur technicians" might be viewed as a beginning step toward the eventual formation of a "highly specialized corps of technicians."[81]

In contrast to Mao and the radicals, who questioned both the practicality and the ideological impact of modern science, Deng Xiaoping and his pragmatic colleagues see the "mastery of modern science and technology" as the key to modernization. They have admitted frankly that China lags behind some of the advanced countries, such as the United States, by as much as fifteen to twenty years in food production.[82] To catch up with the ever-expanding body of world knowledge, China plans to learn from the advanced nations and to develop her own scientific capabilities. Modernization, or "the mastery of modern science and technology," as Deng Xiaoping would phrase it, has involved at least a three-pronged approach since 1978: the recruitment of a "mammoth force" of scientific and technical personnel, the strengthening of China's scientific and technological institutions, and the acquisition of advanced technology from abroad.

Recruitment of Scientific and Technological Personnel

In 1978 Politburo member Fang Yi, then a vice-premier in the State Council, presented an outline of the national plan for science and technological development, in which he called for the recruitment of a force of 800,000 "professional scientific researchers" between 1978 and 1985.[83] It was obvious that there was a serious shortage of trained technical personnel. The government pointed out that in 1979 only 300,000 scientific and technological personnel were working in the 2,400 national research organizations and 600 universities.[84] Richard Suttmeier estimated that almost 41 percent of the 1.3 million university graduates for 1978–85 (or 553,500 to be exact) would need to be in science and engineering, and all must be engaged in research in order to meet the targeted personnel needs set by the national plan.[85] What was even more urgent was the need to provide a professional corps of what Suttmeier called "research S & T personnel capable of exercising scientific leadership and of conducting independent research."[86] S & T personnel would be much more highly trained than the present vast number of "scientific and technology workers'' in state enterprises and organizations. As shown in Table 9.1, a total of more than 5.7 million ''scientific and technological workers'' were employed by state enterprises in 1981.[87]

As urged by Politburo member Chen Yun, China must still recruit scientific and technological specialists as advisors in policymaking.[88] According to Suttmeier, there were ways that China could possibly overcome the huge gap in scientific leadership needs. One was to reinstitute postgraduate work for midcareer training.[89] In August 1981 the Chinese Academy of Sciences, the Academy of Social Sciences, and the Ministry of Education authorized

TABLE 9.1 Scientific and Technological Personnel in State Organs and Enterprises, 1981 (in thousands)

Personnel Departments	Total	Engineering and Technical	Agro-Technical	Health	Scientific Research	Teaching
Nation's Total	5,714	2,077	328	1,680	338	1,291
1. Industry and Construction	1,596	1,229	4	268	15	80
2. Prospecting and Designing	237	221	1	10	3	2
3. Agriculture, Forestry, Water Resources, and Meteorology	462	168	231	41	5	17
4. Transport, Post, and Telecommunications	174	152		19		3
5. Commerce, Foods, Services, and Materials Supply and Marketing	47	25	10	11	1	
6. Urban Public Utilities	25	19	1	4	1	
7. Scientific Research	346	35	3	13	293	2
8. Culture, Education, Health, and Social Welfare	2,534	45	2	1,286	16	1,185
9. Banking and Insurance	3	3				
10. Government Departments and Organizations	290	180	76	28	4	2

Source: Hu Ji, "Updating Science and Technology," Beijing Review, 7 (February 14, 1983), 16.

11,000 postgraduate students to sit for master's degree examinations, and 420 to sit for the doctoral degree.[90] Another way was to send postgraduate students abroad for advanced training in science and technology. As of 1983 there were about 10,000 Chinese students and scholars in the United States, a majority of them doing advanced studies in the sciences. Scientific training could also be obtained through exchanges with foreign countries. For instance, since the normalization of relations in January 1979, China's scientific contacts with the United States have expanded considerably. Under the Science and Technology Agreement, signed on January 31, 1979, during Deng's visit to the United States, numerous accords were concluded for cooperative exchanges. These included such subject areas as agriculture, space science, higher energy physics, information science, meteorology, atmospheric science, marine and fishery science, medicine, hydroelectric power, earthquake science, and environmental protection.[91] In May 1982 more agreements were reached on cooperative programs on transportation, nuclear research, and aeronautics. These were set up under the auspices of a U.S.-China Joint Commission on Cooperation in Science and Technology.[92] A typical pattern under these agreements was to bring Chinese scientists to the United States and send American scientists to China as advisors.

A related problem in expanding recruitment of scientific personnel was how to use their talent to the fullest, a point stressed clearly by Deng Xiaoping at a meeting with the leaders of the State Planning Commission.[93] Generally, since the scientists were also intellectuals, they were often despised by many. Deng hit hard on this point in 1978 when he talked to the first national science conference. He publicly rejected the radicals' assertion that scientists were not part of the productive forces, and instead contended that "brain workers who serve socialism" were part of the working people. At the 1978 national science conference, Deng clearly repudiated the treatment of intellectuals and technicians over the past decade:

> We cannot demand that scientists and technicians, or at any rate, the overwhelming majority of them, study a lot of political and theoretical books, participate in numerous social activities, and attend many meetings not related to their work.
>
> How can you label as "white" a man who studies hard to improve his knowledge and skills? Scientists and technicians who have flaws of one kind or another in their ideology or their style of work should not be called "white," if they are not against the party and socialism. How can our scientists and technicians be accused of being divorced from politics when they work diligently for socialist science?[94]

Deng went on to ask that the party stop interfering in the work of scientific and research institutions and restore the decision-making authority on technical matters to the directors and deputy directors of these agencies. The party committee's work in a scientific institution should be judged by the scientific results and the training of competent scientific personnel.[95]

The problem of the full utilization of scientific personnel remains a serious one today. Bo Yibo, a veteran economist and former vice-premier, was recently quoted as saying that there were a number of reasons why the talents of the scientific community were not fully exploited. He accused the leading cadres in state enterprises and government organs of failing to recognize the importance of science and technology, and thus failing to utilize persons with special expertise. Cadres also neglected to cultivate and promote scientific personnel in their units. In addition, specialist personnel were too often improperly assigned tasks for which they had no expertise.[96]

Strengthening Chinese Scientific and Technological Institutions

To supervise the development program in science, the Fifth National People's Congress reinstated the Scientific and Technology Commission and elevated it to ministerial status under the State Council. This commission is, in essence, an overall policy-making body. The commission and its counterparts in the provinces act as scientific advisors to the party committees and government on economic development projects. The commission also has sponsored a series of national conferences on science and technology. Together with the State Planning Commission and the State Economic Commission, they plan, coordinate, and implement scientific research. A key role in scientific research was given to the prestigious Chinese Academic of Sciences. The academy provides funds and direction for 117 research institutes with a combined staff totaling 75,000.[97] Until 1981 the leadership of the academy was in the hands of party committees within each of the research institutes; party committees in these institutes were then told that they must confine their work to political and ideological matters.[98,99] In 1978 a new Academy of Social Sciences was formed to facilitate research and studies in the social sciences. The first president of the academy was Hu Qiaomu, a close colleague of both Deng and Hu Yaobang. In the fall of 1982, he was elected to the Politburo, and the presidency of the academy was passed on to Ma Hung, an economist.

Under the Sixth Five-Year Plan, allocations for education, science, culture, and public health accounted for almost 16 percent of all state expenditures. Funds allocated for science and technology were earmarked for expanding both basic and applied research to meet economic development needs.[100] To what extent Marxist ideology would continue to play a role in research on social and natural sciences remained to be seen.[101] However, in a recent policy outline, the State Science and Technology Commission stated that it was important to establish "an atmosphere of seriousness and truth seeking," and that research conclusions should be based on facts and "objective law." The commission declared that the time had come "to put a stop to the evil trends of opportunism and falsification."[102] A problem that remains in Chinese politics is the bureaucratic maze that sooner or later may disrupt scientific and technological policies. Despite the institutional reforms, the formulation of major scientific policies are to be made jointly by no less than six state agencies under the State Council: the state Planning Commission, the Economic Commission, the Capital Construction Commission, the Agriculture Commission, the Energy Commission, and the Machine Building Industry Commission.[103] This bureaucratic decision-making will inevitably hamper China's progress in science and technological programs.

Acquisition and Transfer of Science and Technology

China's main strategy for technological transfer in the 1970s was purchase from abroad—frequently acquiring complete industrial plants. This strategy was called "turnkey," because the complete facility required the keys to open it for operations. Between 1972 and 1975, China imported some 170 complete industrial plants, valued at $2.6 billion, from eight European nations, Japan, the United States, and the Soviet Union.[104] Most of these plants were for basic industries, such as steel, electricity, petroleum, and chemical fertilizer. The Chinese could expand capital formation by copying a complete imported plant, which was a "carrier of new technology."[105] Former vice-premier Fang Yi made it very clear in 1978 that "an important way to develop science and technology at high speed is to utilize fully the latest achievements in the world in science and technology and absorb their quintessence." He said, "We should introduce selected techniques that play a key and pace-setting role."[106] During a brief spell of euphoria in 1977–78, proposed contracts for purchasing technology from abroad proliferated; however, financial realities forced a readjustment of priorities in 1979. The government then made efforts to address the questions of how to digest and absorb foreign technology and how to deal with the problem of financing. The purchase of complete sets of equipment was not always satisfactory. At times imported equipment was found to be unsuitable for the intended localities. In other cases there was too much equipment imported, or the technology imported was inappropriate. There was a failure generally "to study the equipment, and master and spread knowledge of its use."[107]

The present policy for scientific and technological purchases from abroad consists of the following guidelines:[108] (1) Purchases must be selective—"We should start by considering our national economic requirement, our technical base, etc., not just go after the newest and the most advanced." (2) Foreign technology "must be integrated with China's own research projects, otherwise there can be no true digestion and absorption," and (3) Scientists must study foreign scientific techniques through published journals, conferences, and exchanges. The new policy in science and technology calls for "buying techniques, software and samples of machinery." The Chinese are trying to restrict purchases of equipment to what will be the most useful for their technological development, or as the Chinese say, "To buy hens for them to lay eggs." Hu Yaobang told the 1982 party congress: "We must refrain from indiscriminate import of equipment, and particularly of consumer goods that can be manufactured and supplied at home."[109] It is interesting to note that recently the

Reagan administration granted China a "friendly but non-allied" status to permit it to purchase higher-level electronics and computers under some restrictive guidelines. The Chinese have also discovered three effective ways to acquire advanced foreign technology rapidly: joint ventures with foreign business concerns, countertrade factors, and special economic zones for trade and foreign investment.

Joint venture.[110]   The idea of cooperative business ventures between a communist nation and a capitalist one was pioneered by the Yugoslavs in 1967. In July 1979 the Fifth NPC at its second session adopted a joint venture law governing both Chinese and foreign investments.[111] The law contains three basic provisions:[112] protection by the Chinese government of investment by a foreign concern in a joint venture; pledge by the foreign concern that the technology or equipment contributed from abroad "shall be truly advanced and appropriate to Chinese needs"; and a guarantee for the retention by the foreign concern in the joint venture of the net profits after appropriate Chinese income taxes are paid.[113] The joint venture law serves as a framework allowing foreign investors to negotiate and enter into contracts with the Chinese government. While the law defines the role of foreign investment on Chinese soil, its emphasis is on the advanced technology a foreign investor or firm can share with the Chinese. A usual format in such arrangements is the 51/49 percent joint ownership agreement between the Chinese government and foreign firms. The Chinese provide land, labor, and the necessary infrastructure, and the foreign investor provides the investment capital and equipment.

As of 1982 there were approximately thirty-nine joint ventures, with a total investment in China of more than $200 million. Most investments came from Japan, the United States, France, West Germany, Australia, and Switzerland. A model of this type of investment was the China-Schindler joint venture, involving a Swiss manufacturer in partnership with Jardine Matheson of Hong Kong.[114] They formed a partnership to set up factories in China to produce lifts, or elevators. In its first year of operation (1980–81), this joint venture yielded about $3.5 million in profits. The latest such arrangement was the joint $51 million deal between China and American Motors Corporation to produce Jeeps and Jeep engines at Beijing Auto Works. According to the contract, AMC was to invest $8 million initially, with another $8 million in advanced technology, to assist in the modernization of the Beijing Auto Works. For AMC the advantage lay in cheap labor costs, enabling AMC Chinese-made Jeeps to compete favorably in the Southeast Asian market.[115]

Countertrade factors.   Countertrade factors is another technique for obtaining foreign investment and technology.[116] The following scenario illustrates the technique. Assume that China wishes to import advanced mining equipment, to develop its coal resources. Under countertrade factors payment for the equipment would be deferred until the coal mined with the equipment is sold to the exporter. This device enables China to acquire technology in exchange for the product the technology will produce. It preserves China's limited foreign exchange reserves. As of 1982 China's foreign exchange and gold reserves were estimated at 12.6 million troy ounces.[117] This technique provides a good way to reduce foreign trade deficits.

Specialized economic zones.[118]   Specialized economic zones are really free trade or tax-free zones that provide customs exemptions and preferential treatment to balance foreign trade. Since 1979 the Chinese government has established four such zones in southern China, all ports opening into the South China Sea: Zhuhai, facing the Portuguese colony of Macao; Shenzhen, near Xianggang (Hong Kong); and Shantou and Xiamen, in Fujian province. One of the main objectives was to have these specially designated zones serve as "bridges for introducing foreign capital, advanced technology and equipment and as classrooms for training personnel capable of mastering advanced technology."[119] Some of these zones, such as Shenzhen (near Hong Kong) and Zhuhai (near Macao), were multipurpose zones where a host of economic activities could take place: industry, commerce, housing, agriculture, and tourism. The other two zones would primarily process exports. Imports into all zones are tax free, except for cigarettes and alcohol, which have a reduced tariff. Workers in the zones are hired by contract under a basic wage scale, with a flexible floating wage system. Chinese currency at present is the only currency permitted in these zones. But eventually, foreign currencies will be permitted under special regulations. Most of the funds for investment in these special economic zones come from foreign investors.[120]

THE TREATMENT OF CHINESE INTELLECTUALS[121]

As of 1982 there were about 20 million intellectuals in China—that is, anyone who has had more than secondary education. Thus, a teacher, a university professor, a technician, a writer, or an engineer is defined as an intellectual. As a rule, a vast majority of them are not party members. In most societies this category of educated persons is treated with respect and valued as precious human assets. In China this was not the case between 1957 and 1978. In 1957 Chinese intellectuals were labeled "rightists"; they were to be suspected, put down, or despised. From 1957 through the decade of the Cultural Revolution (1966–76), Chinese intellectuals were not only labeled as "rightist" but as "the stinking ninth category" by the radicals. They were despised and persecuted merely because they possessed education, knowledge, and skills. The Cultural Revolution radicals did not consider them productive members of the socialist society. To the radical ideologues, it was better to be a peasant or a worker than a "stinking" intellectual.

When the pragmatic reformers came back to power in 1977, they set out to correct the negative attitude toward the intellectuals. The new leaders realized that China's modernization could not possibly proceed without the people who possessed the "brain power." In 1978 Deng quoted Marx and Lenin to prove that scientists and technological personnel were integral parts of the productive force. "Intellectuals," Deng cited Lenin as saying, "engage in scientific and technical work who themselves are not capitalists but scholars."[122] Deng went on to say that "brain workers who serve socialism are a part of the working people."[123] He argued further that so long as intellectuals were not opposed to the party or socialism, "we should, in line with the party's policy of uniting with, educating and remolding the intellectuals, bring out their specialized abilities, respect their labor and take interest in their progress, giving them a warm helping hand."[124]

However, "Leftist" attitudes toward intellectuals linger on into the era of the Sixth Five-Year Plan. The truth of the matter is that many intellectuals are not given full opportunities to apply their specialized knowledge and skill. In a recent article in *Hongqi,* Politburo member Nie Rongzhen made it clear that the middle-aged intellectuals—about 5 million men and women in their forties and fifties, serving as the backbone of China's modernization program—continued to receive low wages and to face many difficulties.[125] Marshal Nie, in the winter of 1982, urged that provisions be made to take good care of the middle-aged intellectuals who could provide enormous contributions to China's modernization. Nie indicated that in many government units, the intellectuals were still not being treated well and were not trusted.[126] There were frequent stories in the mass media about how some intellectuals were mistreated, demoted, and castigated by jealous local people. While most workers had received two wage increases since 1977, middle-aged intellectuals with twenty years of service received only one raise, a mere 7 yuan, or the equivalent of $3.50. They were also given cramped housing arrangements. During the author's visits to China, some middle-aged intellectuals spoke about "three heavies and two neglects"; namely, heavy family burden, heavy responsibility, and heavy pressure at work; and inadequate remuneration and meager living conditions.[127] Discrimination against the intellectuals continued mainly because of the lingering fear among the people of "bourgeois academic authority." For many intellectuals the memory of their persecution after 1957 was too vivid for them to be optimistic about the future. Unless the pragmatic leaders are successful in reversing the anti-intellectual climate, China's success in modernization will be very much in jeopardy.

NOTES

1. Hung-ti Chu, "Education in Mainland China," *Current History,* vol. 59, no. 349 (September 1970), 168–70; and Leo A. Orleans, "Communist China's Education: Policies, Problems, and Prospects," in *India and China: Studies in Comparative Development,* ed. Kuan-I Chen and Jogindar Uppal (New York: Free Press, 1971), pp. 276–77.

2. Joel Glassman, "Educational Reform and Manpower Policy in China: 1955–1958," *Modern China,* vol. iii, no. 3 (July 1977), 265–66.

3. Ibid., pp. 268–69.

4. Ibid., p. 272.

5. The figure for 1949 was taken from "Primary Schools in China," *Peking Review,* 36 (September 8, 1978), 15. Figures for 1953 and 1958 were taken from State Statistical Bureau

of 1960, as reprinted in Glassman, "Educational Reform and Manpower Policy in China," pp. 212, 281.

6. Glassman, "Educational Reform and Manpower Policy in China," pp. 212, 281.

7. Ibid., p. 268.

8. Ibid., p. 280; Hung-Ti Chu, "Education in Mainland China," p. 181; and Orleans, "Communist China's Education," p. 282.

9. Orleans, "Communist China's Education," pp. 282-83.

10. Hung-Ti Chu, "Education in Mainland China," p. 169; and Orleans, "Communist China's Education," p. 282.

11. Orleans, "Communist China's Education," p. 288.

12. Philip E. Ginsburg, "Development and Educational Process in China," *Current Scene,* vol. xiv, no. 3 (March 1976), 3-4. Also see *Survey of China Mainland Press* (SCMP), no. 784, pp. 22-23.

13. Ginsburg, "Development and Educational Process in China," p. 4.

14. "It is Essential to Rely on the Poor and Lower-Middle Peasants in the Educational Revolution in the Countryside," *Peking Review,* 39 (September 27, 1968), 21.

15. Ibid., p. 20; and "A New-Type School Where Theory Accords with Practice," *Peking Review,* 44 (November 1, 1968), 4-8.

16. *Hsinhua News Agency* (NCNA), a special for October 1, 1975, p. 22. My own notes in a briefing session given by Professor Zhou on the campus of Beijing University in January 1973 contained similar expressions.

17. See Ellen K. Ong, "Education in China since the Cultural Revolution," *Studies in Comparative Communism,* vol. iii, nos. 3 and 4 (July–August 1970), 158-75.

18. See William Hinton, *Hundred Day War: The Cultural Revolution at Tsinghua University* (New York and London: Monthly Review Press, 1972).

19. Robert McCormich, "Revolution in Education Committees," *The China Quarterly,* 57 (January–March 1974), 134-39.

20. "Power is the Fundamental Question of Revolution in Education," *Peking Review,* 51 (December 20, 1968), 8.

21. Ibid., p. 8.

22. "An Agricultural College in the Countryside," *Peking Review,* 48 (September 29, 1974), 25-26; and "Peasants-College Graduates-Peasants," *Peking Review,* 7 (February 14, 1975), 13-15.

23. "Peasants-College Graduates-Peasants," p. 13.

24. " 'July 21' Workers' Colleges," *Peking Review,* 26 (June 25, 1975), pp. 16-20; and "A Worker after Graduating College," *Peking Review,* 37 (September 12, 1975), 16-19, 21-22.

25. "A Worker after Graduating College," p. 12.

26. "Shifts in Higher Education Policy," *Current Scene,* vol. xiii, no. 9 (September 1975), 26.

27. See Hua Guofeng, "Report on the Work of Government," p. 27; and Fang Yi, "On the Situation in China's Science and Education," *Peking Review,* 2 (January 13, 1978), 15.

28. Deng Xiaoping, "Speech at the National Educational Work Conference," *Peking Review,* 18 (May 5, 1978), 7-8.

29. Fang Yi, "On the Situation in China's Science and Education," p. 15.

30. *Renmin Ribao,* February 2, 1974, p. 1.

31. *Renmin Ribao,* August 13, 1973, p. 1.

32. "A Great Debate on the Educational Front: Repudiating the Gang of Four's 'Two Estimates,' " *Peking Review,* 51 (December 16, 1977), 4-9.

33. For facts and figures about Chinese education since 1978 from the *Beijing Review,* see the following issues: 37 (September 14, 1981), 7-8; 6 (February 6, 1982), 28; 42 (October 18, 1982), 23; and 47 (November 22, 1982), 27. Also see Michael W. Kirst, "Reflections on Education in China," *Phi Kapan,* vol. 60, no. 2 (October 1978), 124-25; Ralph W. Tyler, "Chinese Education," *Phi Kapan,* vol. 60, no. 1 (September 1978), 26-29; "A Glimpse at Chinese Education," *Today's Education* (September/October 1979), 48-50; H. William Koch, "People and Publishing in China," *Physics Today,* vol. 32, no. 8 (August 1979), 32-37; Frank F. Wong, "Education and Work in China: What Can We Learn from China's Experience?" *Change: The Magazine of Higher Learning* (November/December 1980), 24-58; A. Tom Grunfeld, "Innovations in Post-Secondary Education in China," *The China Quarterly,* 90 (June 1980), 281-85; John J. Cogan, "China's Fifth Modernization: Education," *Phi Kapan,* vol. 62, no. 4 (December 1980), 268-72;

Jonathan Unger, "The Chinese Controversy Over Higher Education," *Pacific Affairs,* vol. 53, no. 1 (September 1980), 29–47; Ann Kent, "Red and Expert: The Revolution in Education at Shanghai Teachers' University, 1975–76," *The China Quarterly,* 86 (June 1981), 304–21; Zhang Suchu, "Rice Paddy Educations for China's Elite," Los Angeles Times Service, as reprinted in *Honolulu Advertiser,* July 19, 1982, A-7; Takashi Oka, China Schools: Less Rote, More Ideology," *Christian Science Monitor,* August 3, 1981, p. 3; Suzanne Pepper, "China's Schools Turning an Old Leaf," *Asian Wall Street Journal Weekly,* September 21, 1981, p. 11; "China's Nagging Educational Dilemma," *Asian Wall Street Journal Weekly,* December 28, 1981, p. 11; Edward J. Kormondy, "The PRC: Revitalizing an Educational System," *Change: The Magazine of Higher Learning,* vol. 14, no. 5 (July/August 1982), 33–35.

34. Deng Xiaoping, "Speech at the National Education Work Conference," pp. 6–12.

35. Ibid., p. 7.

36. "Six-Year Curriculum Restored in Primary Schools," *Beijing Review,* 49 (December 8, 1980), 6.

37. "Moral Education in the Schools," *Beijing Review,* (December 7, 1981), 21.

38. "Good Marks Are Not Everything," *Beijing Review,* 16 (April 19, 1982), 8–9.

39. Ibid., p. 9.

40. "Work-Study Programmes in Primary and Middle Schools," *Beijing Review,* 45 (November 8, 1982), 21.

41. Ibid., p. 21.

42. For discussion on vocational training at secondary schools, see the following issues of *Beijing Review:* 28 (July 13, 1979), 7–8; 35 (September 1, 1980), 5–6; 46 (November 17, 1980), 7–8; and 25 (June 21, 1982), 8–9.

43. "Reforming Middle School Education," *Beijing Review,* 35 (September 1, 1980), 5.

44. "Vocational and Technical Education," *Beijing Review,* 25 (June 21, 1982), 8.

45. Statistical data came from the following issues of *Beijing Review:* 28 (July 13, 1979), 7, and 46 (November 17, 1980), 7.

46. See Premier Zhao's report in *Beijing Review,* 51 (December 20, 1982), 16.

47. "Reforming Middle School Education," p. 6.

48. "Vocational and Technical Education," *Beijing Review,* 25 (June 21, 1982), 8.

49. Ibid. p. 8.

50. "Education: Apex and Base of a Pyramid," *Beijing Review,* 20 (May 18, 1979), 6. Information about Shanghai "key schools" program was based on notes taken by the author at the group interview, August 6, 1979.

51. See Unger, "The Chinese Controversy Over Higher Education," pp. 29–47; also see Dale Bratton, "University Admission Politics in China, 1970–1978," *Asian Survey,* vol. xix, no. 10 (October 1979), 1008–22.

52. See Unger, "The Chinese Controversy Over Higher Education," pp. 36–38; and *Ming Pao* (Hong Kong), April 30, 1977.

53. "New College Student," *Peking Review,* 16 (April 21, 1978), 11.

54. "Affiliated Colleges Set Up," *Beijing Review,* 3 (January 19, 1979), 31; and 41 (October 12, 1979), 6.

55. "New College Student," *Beijing Review,* 41 (October 12, 1979), 6.

56. "Report on the Sixth Five-Year Plan," 15.

57. "TV University," *Beijing Review,* 7 (February 16, 1979), 7; and 1 (January 5, 1981), 8.

58. "China's TV Universities," *Beijing Review,* 1 (January 5, 1981), 8.

59. "TV University," p. 7. Also see Edward J. Kormonly, "The PRC: Revitalizing An Educational System," *Change: The Magazine of Higher Education,* vol. 14, no. 5 (July/August, 1982), 34–35.

60. "Affiliated Colleges Set Up," p. 31.

61. "Spare-Time College for Beijing's Staff and Workers," *Beijing Review,* 11 (March 16, 1981), 31.

62. "Open More Avenues for Education," *Beijing Review,* 30 (July 28, 1980), 19; and 39 (September 29, 1980), 6.

63. "Is China's Higher Education Developing Too Slowly?" *Beijing Review,* 6 (February 8, 1982), 28.

64. Unger, "The Chinese Controversy Over Higher Education," p. 46.

65. "Report on the Sixth Five-Year Plan," p. 15.

66. See Thomas P. Bernstein, *Up to the Mountains and Down to the Villages: The Transfer of Youth from Urban to Rural China* (New Haven, Conn.: Yale University Press, 1977).

67. The following works on the youth to the countryside movement may be of interest to readers: Bernstein, *Up to the Mountains and Down to the Countryside: The Transfer of Youth from Urban to Rural China,* and "Urban Youth in the Countryside: Problems of Adaptation and Remedies," *The China Quarterly,* 69 (March 1977), 75-108; D. Gordon White, "The Politics of Hsia-Hsiang Youth," *The China Quarterly,* 59 (July-September 1974), 491-517; Laurence J. C. Ma, "Counterurbanization and Rural Development: The Strategy of Hsia-hsiang," *Current Scene,* vol. xv, nos. 8 and 9 (August-September 1977), 1-12; "1975 Down-to-the-Countryside Program," *Current Scene,* vol. xiv, no. 2 (February 1976), 16-18.

68. Laurence J.C. Ma, "Counterurbanization and Rural Development," p. 8.

69. Bernstein, "Urban Youth in the Countryside," pp. 85-86.

70. Hua Guofeng, "Report on the Work of Government," p. 30.

71. Jay Mathews, "Chinese Youth: No," Washington Post Service, as reprinted in *Honolulu Advertiser,* February 18, 1980, A-9.

72. *Ta Kung Pao Weekly Supplement,* December 11, 1980, p. 7.

73. Thomas B. Gold, "Alienated Youth Cloud China's Future," *Asian Wall Street Journal Weekly,* May 18, 1981, p. 13; John Roderick, "China's Youth Problem," Associated Press, as reprinted in *Honolulu Star Bulletin,* September 15, 1980, A-21; and Richard Critchfield, "Youth Turnout Dogma, Turn on Radios," *Christian Science Monitor,* August 1, 1980, p. 13. Also see Mary-Louise O'Callaghan, "A Streak of Individualism in China's Youth," *Christian Science Monitor,* July 22, 1983, p. 3.

74. Teng Hsiao-p'ing, "Speech at Opening Ceremony of National Science Conference, March 18, 1978," *Peking Review,* 12 (March 24, 1978), 17.

75. Theoretical Group of the Chinese Academy of Sciences, "A Serious Struggle in Scientific and Technical Circles," *Peking Review,* 16 (April 15, 1977), 24-27.

76. Richard Suttmeier, "Science Policy Shifts, Organizational Change and China's Development," *The China Quarterly,* 62 (June 1975), 207-41. Also see William W. Whitson, "China's Quest for Technology," *Problems of Communism,* xii (July-August 1973), 16-30.

77. Whitson, "China's Quest for Technology," pp. 17-18.

78. Bruce J. Esposito, "The Cultural Revolution and China's Scientific Establishment," *Current Scene,* vol. xii, no. 4 (April 1974), 2-3.

79. Genevieve Dean, "China's Technological Development," *New Scientist* (May 18, 1972), 371-73.

80. C.H.G. Oldham, "Technology in China: Science for the Masses?" *Far Eastern Economic Review* (May 16, 1968), 353-55; and Rensselaer W. Lee, III, "The Politics of Technology in Communist China," in *Ideology and Politics in Contemporary China,* ed. Chalmers Johnson (Seattle, Wash. and London: University of Washington Press, 1973), pp. 301-25; Jonathan Unger, "Mao's Million Amateur Technicians," *Far Eastern Economic Review* (April 3, 1971), 115-18; and *China: Science Walks on Two Legs* (New York: Avon Books, 1974).

81. Oldham, "Science and Technological Policies," in *China's Developmental Experience,* ed. Michael Oksenberg (New York, Washington, and London: Praeger Publishers, 1973), pp. 80-94.

82. Teng Hsiao-p'ing, "Speech at Opening Ceremony of National Science Conference," p. 10; and Hua Kuo-feng, "Raise the Scientific and Cultural Level of the Entire Chinese Nations," *Peking Review,* 13 (March 31, 1978), 6-14.

83. "Outline National Plan for Development of Science and Technology, Relevant Policies and Measures," *Beijing Review,* 14 (April 7, 1978), 7.

84. "30th Anniversary of Chinese Academy of Sciences," *Beijing Review,* 46 (November 16, 1979), 3.

85. Richard Suttmeier, "Politics, Modernization and Science," *Problems of Communism,* vol. xxx, no. 1 (January-February 1981), 30.

86. Ibid., p. 30.

87. "Updating Science and Technology," *Beijing Review,* 7 (February 14, 1983), 16.

88. See "Outline Report on Policy Governing the Development of Our National Science and Technology by the State Science and Technology Commission, February 23, 1981," in *Issues and Studies,* vol. xviii, no. 5 (May 1982), 88-101.

89. Suttmeier "Politics, Modernization and Science," p. 31.

90. See *Ming Pao* (Hong Kong), February 20, 1982, p. 1; and *Ta Kung Pao Weekly Supplement,* August 6, 1981, p. 4.

91. See *GIST,* Bureau of Public Affairs, Department of State, March 1981.

92. *Honolulu Advertiser,* May 11, 1983, H-1.

93. *Ta Kung Pao Weekly Supplement,* December 2, 1982, p. 1.

94. Teng Hsiao-p'ing, "Speech at Opening Ceremony of National Science Conference," p. 15.

95. Ibid., p. 17.

96. *Ming Pao* (Hong Kong), February 25, 1982, p. 1.

97. *Ta Kung Pao Weekly Supplement,* May 14, 1981, p. 1.

98. Ibid., p. 1; and issue of May 21, 1981, p. 3.

99. Teng Hsiao-p'ing, "Speech at Opening Ceremony of National Science Conference," p. 17.

100. "Report on the Sixth Five-Year Plan," p. 16.

101. See James Reardon-Anderson, "Science and Technology in Post-Mao China," *Contemporary China,* vol. 2, no. 4 (Winter 1978), 42–43.

102. "Outline Report on Policy Governing the Development of Our National Science and Technology," p. 99.

103. Ibid., p. 94.

104. See Dave L. Denny, "International Finance in the People's Republic of China," in *China: A Reassessment of the Economy,* pp. 701–2. Also see Kent Morrison, "Domestic Politics and Industrialization in China: The Foreign Trade Factor," *Asian Survey,* vol. xviii, no. 7 (July 1978), 690–98.

105. Shannon Brown, "Foreign Technology and Economic Growth," *Problems of Communism,* xxvi (July–August 1977), 30–32.

106. "Outline Report on Policy Governing the Development of Our National Science and Technology," p. 93.

107. "On China's Economic Relations with Foreign Countries," *Beijing Review,* 22 (May 31, 1982), 15.

108. "Outline Report on Policy Governing the Development of Our National Science and Technology," p. 93.

109. "Creating A New Situation in All Fields of Socialist Modernization," p. 20.

110. For joint venture projects and laws, see Peter Nehemkis and Alexis Nehemkis, "China's Law on Joint Ventures," *California Management Review,* vol. xxii, no. 4 (Summer 1980), 37–46; *Law of the PRC on Joint Ventures Using Chinese & Foreign Investment,* Wen Wei Po (Hong Kong), July 1979; James Roselle, "Local Lenders May Aid China Venture," *Asian Wall Street Journal Weekly,* September 7, 1981, p. 12; Frank Ching, "China Is Adopting Cautious Approach to Joint Ventures," *Asian Wall Street Journal Weekly,* July 27, 1981, p. 4; Phijit Chong, "More Clues to a Taxing Puzzle," *Far Eastern Economic Review* (March 21, 1980), 99; *Joint Venture Agreements in the People's Republic of China,* U.S. Department of Commerce, 1982; and David C. Brown, "Sino-Foreign Joint Ventures: Contemporary Developments and Historical Perspective," *Journal of Northeast Asian Studies,* vol. 1, no. 4 (December 1982), 25–55.

111. Nehemkis and Nehemkis, "China's Law on Joint Ventures," pp. 37–46.

112. "The Law of PRC on Joint Ventures Using Chinese and Foreign Investment," *Beijing Review,* 29 (July 20, 1979), 24–26.

113. Ibid., p. 24.

114. *China Trade Report,* October 1981, p. 8.

115. *Newsweek,* May 16, 1983, pp. 75–76.

116. See Robert D. Dennis, "The Countertrade Factor in China's Modernization Plan," *The Columbia Journal of World Business,* vol. xvii, no. 1 (Spring 1982), 67–75.

117. *Ta Kung Pao Weekly Supplement,* March 11, 1982, p. 6.

118. See "New SEZ Regulations Made Public," *Ta Kung Pao Weekly Supplement,* December 24, 1981, pp. 1, 3; *China Trade Report,* April 1982, p. 10, and April 1983, p. 6. Also see a special article in *Beijing Review,* 50 (December 14, 1981), 14–21; John J. Putman, "Special Economic Zones: China's Opening Door," *National Geographic,* vol. 164, no. 1 (July 1982), 64–83.

119. Xu Dixin, "China's Special Economic Zones," *Beijing Review,* 50 (December 14, 1981), 14–17.

120. See *China Trade Report,* April 1982, p. 10, and April 1983, p. 6; *Ta Kung Pao Weekly Supplement,* August 20, 1981, p. 1, and December 24, 1981, p. 1.

121. For more discussion about the Chinese intellectuals, see Jerome B. Grieder, *Intellectuals and the State in Modern China: A Narrative History* (New York: Free Press, 1981); Merle Goldman, *China's Intellectuals: Advise and Dissent* (Cambridge, Mass.: Harvard University Press, 1981); Richard C. Kraus, "Intellectuals and the State in China," *Problems of Communism,* vol. xxxi, no. 6 (November–December 1982), 81–84; Takashi Oka, "China Tries to Use Once-Scorned Intellectuals for Modernizing," *Christian Science Monitor,* February 4, 1983, pp. 1, 6; Fox Butterfield, "China's Persecution of Intellectuals," New York Times Service, reprinted in *Honolulu Star Bulletin,* December 10, 1981, A–2, and *China: Alive in the Bitter Sea,* pp. 416–19; *Hongqi,* 24 (December 16, 1982), 4–12; and Gerald Chen, "The Middle-aged Intellectuals," *Ta Kung Pao Weekly Supplement,* September 23, 1982, p. 14.

122. Teng Hsiao-p'ing, "Speech at Opening Ceremony of National Science Conference," *Peking Review,* p. 11.

123. Ibid., p. 12.

124. Ibid., p. 15.

125. *Hongqi,* 24 (December 16, 1982), 10.

126. Ibid.

127. Notes taken on author's visits in 1978 and 1979. Also see *Ming Pao* (Hong Kong), March 6, 1983, p. 1; and *Beijing Review,* 49 (December 6, 1982), 3–4

China's Role

in

World Politics

STAGES OF EVOLUTION
IN CHINESE FOREIGN POLICY

This chapter will focus on current themes and issues in China's foreign policy. It is necessary at the very outset, however, to sketch briefly the evolution of present-day Chinese foreign policy, so that we may better understand China's role in world politics. We need to point out that China's foreign policy is invariably shaped by a number of factors; among the most important are her geography, history, political ideology, the flow and ebb in her internal politics, and the exertion of international pressures at any given moment. An examination of the development of China's foreign relations since 1950 reveals four distinct stages of evolution: (1) the concern for border settlement and security, 1950–53; (2) the pattern of oscillation between militancy and peaceful coexistence, 1954–65; (3) China's self-imposed isolation during the Cultural Revolution, 1966–68; and (4) China's return to conventional diplomacy under international pressure, and her increased tempo of international contacts after 1969.

Concern for Border Settlement
and Security, 1950–53

Much of China's external activity during the years of consolidation was devoted to securing her frontiers and attempting to regain her lost territories, such as Xizang (Tibet) and Taiwan. China also wanted to eliminate foreign influence in neighboring countries which shared borders. In pursuing these objectives, the Chinese employed force during the early 1950s. The successful landing of General MacArthur's United Nations forces at Inchon in September 1950 cut the North Korean forces in half and paved the way for a rapid advance of UN forces deep into the territory of North Korea and up to the Yalu River, which separated China and North Korea. The Chinese watched the deteriorating situation in Korea with fear and apprehension. The fear that the United States forces, under the United Nations command, would cross the Yalu into Manchuria finally prompted the Chinese to intervene in the Korean conflict in October 1950.[1] Before the Chinese intervention in the Korean War, China sought to regain the island of Taiwan by force. The attempt was met by United States determination to protect the Nationalist-held island in the Formosa Strait. Similarly, Chinese forces marched into Xizang in October 1950, despite protests from India. During much of this period, China was viewed by the rest of the world as a revolutionary nation that was both belligerent and determined to employ armed struggle for the purpose of securing her frontier and regaining lost territories. Because of China's belligerent behavior and seemingly expansionist mood, as evidenced by her action in Xizang, a containment policy was imposed on China by the United States, which in essence extended the United States defense perimeter to the Pacific coast of China from Japan, to Okinawa, to Formosa, to the Philippines. Later, the containment policy was bolstered by the formation of the Southeast Asian

Treaty Organization to provide a defense perimeter on the land mass bordering China's southwest provinces.

Influence of Domestic Politics
on the Oscillation Pattern
of China's Foreign Policy, 1954-65

The record of Chinese foreign policy from 1954 to 1965 reveals a striking pattern of oscillation between militancy and peaceful coexistence. These alternating periods of tension and relaxation in China's relations with other nations were closely related to changes in her internal politics. They reflected both the style of leadership and the developmental strategy for achieving socialism and the goals of industrialization. Thus, when China entered the arena of world politics at the Geneva Conference of 1954 and the Bandung Conference of 1955—the golden age of Chinese diplomacy—her policy and behavior reflected the confidence of the regime and the cohesion of its leaders in launching the orderly and pragmatic developmental program of the First Five-Year Plan at home.

The Geneva Conference of 1954 was convened by the foreign ministers of France, the Soviet Union, the United Kingdom, and the United States for the purpose of settling the problems of Indochina (Cambodia, Laos, and the Vietnams), as well as the unification problem of Korea, following cessation of hostility and the signing of the Korean armistice agreement in the summer of 1953. A French victory in the Indochina war waged against the Viet Minh forces was already very doubtful. A political settlement aimed at preventing an armed takeover by the forces of Ho Chih-min in Indochina was the basic motivation for the Geneva Conference of 1954. The conference did produce a declaration prohibiting foreign military bases or forces in the three states of Vietnam, Laos, and Cambodia. In addition, separate agreements were signed for the eventual independence of the three Indochina states through elections to be supervised by an International Control Commission. The conference failed to provide any political settlement for the unification of Korea. The Geneva Conference marked China's debut in conventional international diplomacy. It gave the outside world an opportunity to see the affable Zhou Enlai confront John Foster Dulles of the United States and Anthony Eden of Great Britian in the intricate games of international diplomacy.

In the spring of 1955, Zhou Enlai and Nehru played a dominant role at the first Bandung Conference, which brought together for the first time the nonaligned nations of Asia and Africa as a third world force. The Bandung Conference produced the famous five principles—mutual respect for sovereignty and territorial integrity, mutual nonaggression, noninterference in each others' internal affairs, equality and mutual benefit, and peaceful coexistence—as the guide for relations among the nations participating in the conference.

When dissension over developmental strategy surfaced among China's leaders, as was the case during the Great Leap (from 1958 to 1961), the posture of China's foreign relations became militant, calling for worldwide revolutionary struggle. Tension mounted in the Formosa Strait during the summer of 1958, as the Chinese bombarded the Nationalist-held offshore islands of Mazu and Jinmen, only twelve miles away from the Chinese mainland. When the Chinese realized the United States' firm intention to back up the Nationalists by using the Seventh Fleet to escort ships to the offshore islands, and Krushchev's policy not to provoke the United States into a war in the Far East, they reverted to a conciliatory attitude, resumed ambassadorial talks with the United States, and temporarily stopped bombardment of the offshore islands. The Chinese later resumed bombardment on odd-numbered days only.

When moderation in economic development was resumed during 1962, after the fiasco of the Great Leap and the related crash programs, interaction with other countries increased at a fantastic rate. Between late 1963 and early 1965, Premier Zhou visited fourteen countries in Asia, Africa, and Europe. Liu Shaoqi, as the chief of state for the People's Republic of China, paid state visits to countries in South and Southeast Asia in 1963. These expanded diplomatic activities were designed to win friends among the Third World countries of Asia and Africa, most of whom were not aligned with either of the two superpowers. By June 1960 the rift between China and the Soviet Union began to be noticed by the outside world. It was evidenced by the arguments they hurled at each other and the zeal exhibited by the Chinese in trying to win friends in the underdeveloped Third World—at the expense and discomfort of the Soviet Union.

Chinese Foreign Policy during the Cultural Revolution, 1966–68

In many ways the Cultural Revolution represented the lowest point in the regime's foreign relations. During this period there were almost no major pronouncements in foreign policy, and contact with other nations consisted mainly of visits from friendly nations and occasional state receptions for visiting dignitaries. In the midst of the upheaval, more than forty of China's envoys were recalled from abroad, with no replacement sent to many countries with which China had established diplomatic relations. Extreme militancy was evident in the treatment of foreigners in Beijing during the early stages of the Cultural Revolution.

For a brief period, the Cultural Revolution evidently paralyzed China's very instrument for conducting foreign relations, the Ministry of Foreign Affairs. China's foreign minister, Chen Yi, was under attack by the radicalized Red Guards, who actually seized the ministry in the summer of 1967. Liu Shaoqi, for a time a leading foreign policy maker in the early 1960s, was purged. Red Guard attacks on Liu Shaoqi and on the Ministry of Foreign Affairs practically immobilized senior foreign policy personnel.[2] Recent disclosures revealed that during the Cultural Revolution, the radicals not only attempted "to meddle in foreign affairs work" but tried to "seize the diplomatic power of the central leading organs."[3] With this in-fighting and turmoil, it is little wonder that Chinese foreign policy during the Cultural Revolution was directionless. Some observers concluded that the issues debated among the dissenting top leaders in China during the upheaval had been triggered by the United States' escalation of the war in Vietnam. For example, Robert Scalapino argued in 1968 that the Cultural Revolution was a victory for Mao and his supporters, brought on by the need to readopt guerrilla strategy to fight an imminent invasion of China by the United States forces in Southeast Asia.[4] Similarly, Donald Zagoria argued that the United States involvement in Vietnam in 1965 was a "catalyst" that brought about open disagreement among top Chinese leaders on the policy most suitable to meet the threat poised to China's southwest border—a debate that eventually engulfed the whole nation in an unprecedented upheaval.[5]

The spillover of Cultural Revolution demonstrations and riots into neighboring countries, such as those in Hong Kong and Burma in 1967, led some observers to conclude that the export of Mao's revolutionary thought and the Chinese revolutionary experience had become the main objective of China's foreign policy.[6] Recent disclosures by Chinese officials on these incidents abroad, as well as the antiforeign campaign conducted inside China during the early stages of the Cultural Revolution, have raised doubts about this. For a short period, Zhou Enlai apparently lost control over the direction of foreign policy.[7] In a speech the deputy chief for the Hong Kong branch of the New China News Agency revealed that the 1967 campaign waged in Hong Kong and Macao, under the banner "opposing British, resisting brutality," was carried out by Lin Biao in opposition to both Mao and Zhou's policies.[8] The statement implied that Zhou Enlai, who was responsible for China's foreign affairs, was unable to prevent these occurrences. Thus, the Chinese are now saying that the export of China's revolutionary model during the Cultural Revolution was not a part of the legitimate Chinese foreign policy design.

China's Return to Conventional Diplomacy, 1969-76

From the post–Cultural Revolution period to Mao's death in 1976, Chinese foreign policy contained fewer ideological polemics and was more conventional and pragmatic. Admittedly, there were differences among the leaders with respect to a number of domestic problems emanating from the Cultural Revolution, but these differences on domestic policies had little impact on China's foreign policy. The armed clashes along the Sino-Soviet frontier in the spring of 1969 had awakened the Chinese to the stark reality that China stood completely isolated and vulnerable to the Soviet military power amassed along the border. It seemed possible to the Chinese that the Soviet Union might very well try to repeat its 1968 military invasion of Czechoslovakia by attacking China. Doak Barnett called this China's "military-security concerns."[9] The breakdown in China's relations with the rest of the world during the Cultural Revolution had to be repaired to check the Soviets. This could be done by a well-executed, pragmatic foreign policy designed to strengthen China's international position in general and to restore the power balance in Asia. Gestures toward peaceful coexistence became pronounced in China's post–Cultural Revolution foreign policy, including moves toward rapprochement with the United States. The signing of the Shanghai communiqué in February 1972 by President Nixon and Premier Zhou Enlai represented an unprecedented diplomatic victory for Zhou; it provided China with the needed leverage to check the threat posed by the Soviet Union. Coupled with this major thrust in China's new foreign policy was a desire to reestablish or cement her friendship with fraternal communist nations in Eastern Europe, North Korea, and North Vietnam. Chinese diplomatic efforts even penetrated into Western Europe, where China supported Britain's entry into the Common Market. At the same time, Chinese propaganda depicted the Soviet Union as one of the two superpowers bent on "imperialist" domination of the world.

All mention of exporting the Chinese revolutionary model, a primary theme of the Cultural Revolution, disappeared from the media and from official pronouncements during the 1970s. When the Paris Peace Agreement was signed in 1973 to terminate the United States involvement in the Vietnam War, China supported it. At the same time, China indicated that she would now welcome United States presence in Asia by deliberately refraining from her usual criticism of the security arrangement between the United States and Japan and of United States bases in the Pacific. Meanwhile, diplomatic overtures were made by the Chinese to woo former members of the Southeast Asian Treaty group, such as the Philippines and Thailand. The shape of the new Chinese foreign policy was clearly outlined by Premier Zhou in his reports on the government to the Tenth CCP Congress in August 1973 and to the Fourth National People's Congress in January 1975. These two important speeches revealed the dominance of Zhou Enlai in the formulation of a new conciliatory pragmatic foreign policy. It is in this regard that we need to review briefly Zhou's perception of the international situation and China's relation to it.

The main concern expressed by Premier Zhou in these speeches was the possibility of a "surprise attack on our country by Soviet revisionist social-imperialism."[10] Zhou complained that in 1975 the Soviets had refused to sign an agreement with China to prevent armed conflict on the border and to disengage the two nations' armed forces in the disputed area along the Ussuri River.[11] Despite the long-standing differences between the two countries, Zhou was rather conciliatory when he directed his remarks to the Soviet leadership. Zhou noted that these differences should not have obstructed "the maintenance of normal state relations" between the two countries. With deterioration of relations, Zhou became even more concerned about talk of détente or "collusion" between the two superpowers, the United States and the Soviet Union. Zhou saw the collusion of the two nuclear powers as only temporary, because in the long run, the two must contend for global hegemony, the cause of tension in the world. Zhou pointed out that the Soviet Union had stepped up its competition with the United States not only in the Third World but in Western Europe as well. Based on Zhou's new concept of world politics, China appealed to the rest of the world to form a united front to resist Soviet Union–United States détente, a disguised form of superpower hegemonism that eventually would lead to war:

> Their fierce contention is bound to lead to world war some day. The people of all countries must get prepared. Détente and peace are being talked about everywhere in the world; it is precisely this that shows there is no détente, let alone lasting peace, in this world.[12]

China's foreign policy, as Zhou pointed out in 1973 and 1975, was to support not only the countries of the Third World against this new form of imperialism or hegemonism but also those in the West, and Japan. In this process of forming a united front with other nations against superpower hegemonism, China would, however, continue to improve her relations with the United States and, at the same time, do all she could to isolate the Soviet Union in the Asian power balance. It is this strategy, as outlined by Zhou Enlai in 1973 and 1975, that constitutes the foundation of China's present-day foreign policy.

China's Independent Foreign Policy, 1982

In the midst of expanded contacts with the United States and the reopened negotiations with the Soviet Union (between 1978 and 1983), the new leaders began to articulate the need for "an independent foreign policy." In a banquet given in April 1982 in honor of Joao Bernardo Vieira, president of Guinea-Bissau, Premier Zhao said that China must follow "an independent foreign policy."[13] Then, at the 1982 September party congress, party chief Hu Yaobang elaborated on what was meant by that suggestion. Hu said that since 1949 "we have shown the world by deeds that China never attaches itself to any big power or group of powers, and never yields to pressure from any big powers."[14] It has always been China's long-term strategy, Hu reminded the party delegates, not to be "swayed by expediency or by anybody's instigation or provocation."[15] Hu's remarks were preceded by Deng Xiaoping's opening statement, in which he warned: "No foreign country can expect China to be its vassal or expect it to swallow any bitter fruit detrimental to its interest."[16] Later, identical expressions were made by a senior advisor to the Chinese Academy of Social Sciences.[17]

Finally, the concept of an independent foreign policy is enshrined in the preamble to the 1982 constitution (see Appendix A). Seemingly, an independent foreign policy means a number of things. One obvious intention is that China not align itself with either of the two superpowers. Perhaps this is China's way of saying that it is not interested in being someone else's "China card" in the triumvirate's diplomatic games. One could also infer that China is not going to make concessions to either of the superpowers in return for tacit alignment in a fluid international situation. Chinese leaders seemed to be saying that it would be wise for China to declare an independent foreign policy that would continue to be acceptable to the Third

World of nonaligned nations. Perhaps Premier Zhao's trip to ten African nations in December 1982 was designed to cement China's continued tie to the Third World. One might also interpret China's declaration of an independent foreign policy as a warning to the United States; strained relations existed between the two countries, caused by American arms sales to Taiwan and the imposition of quotas on Chinese textile exports to the American market. Finally, China may simply have decided to reexamine its foreign policy strategy, which has basically been anti-Soviet and pro-United States. There were reports that Deng's pro-American policies were now being reexamined and criticized as Sino-American relations deteriorated.[18]

MAJOR THEMES IN CHINESE FOREIGN POLICY

After they ascended to leadership, Hu Yaobang and Zhao Ziyang made several extensive trips abroad to deliver some well-articulated speeches on international affairs. In reviewing four recent key official documents on China's foreign policy, we can identify three major themes in China's foreign policy for the 1980s and beyond:[19] Mao's theory of three worlds; anti-superpower hegemonism; and anti-détente, Strategic Arms Limitation Treaty (SALT), and China's nuclear capability.

Mao's Theory of Three Worlds

The Chinese generally attributed the origin of the "three worlds" concept to a quotation from Mao, from his talk in February 1974 with either Kaunda of Zambia or Boumediene of Algeria:

> In my view, the United States and the Soviet Union form the first world. Japan, Europe, and Canada, the middle section, belong to the second world. We are the third world. . . . The third world has a huge population. With the exception of Japan, Asia belongs to the third world. The whole of Africa belongs to the third world, and Latin America, too."[20]

Actually, the concept was formed back in 1955 by Zhou Enlai, Nehru, and Tito at the Bandung Conference, when they called for unity against imperialism and nonalignment. Deng Xiaoping officially announced China's concept of three different worlds to the international community at the Sixth Special Session of the United Nation's General Assembly in April 1974.[21]

In his report to the 1982 party congress, Hu Yaobang reaffirmed China's tie to the Third World: "Socialist China belongs to the third world. China has experienced the same sufferings as most other third world countries. China regards it as her sacred international duty to struggle resolutely against imperialism, hegemonism and colonials, together with the other third world countries."[22] In talks with Joao Vieira of Guinea-Bissau, Zhao promised that China would support the Third World's just demands for political independence and a change in the international economic order.[23] At an official luncheon in Algiers on December 2, 1982, the visiting Premier Zhao told his African friends that equality and mutual benefit were the basic principles behind China's economic and technological cooperation with the Third World nations.[24] In his welcoming speech to inaugurate the Beijing South-South Conference in December 1982, Zhao called for the removal of the "unjust and inadequate old international economic order" as a condition for attaining the Third World goal of economic development.[25] In an interview in Morocco in December 1982, Zhao praised the contributions made by the nonaligned nations in safeguarding the interests of the Third World nations.[26] In reassuring visitors from Africa that China had neither repudiated Mao totally nor his foreign policy of opposing superpower hegemonism, the offical Chinese position was that "China will always be a member of the Third World. We will carry on the foreign policy Chairman Mao formulated during his last years."[27]

What is the significance of China's concept of the three worlds? First, the Chinese have seen the world realistically in terms of the widening disparity between the vast majority of the world's people—who live in developing countries—and the affluent people, who live in the developed countries. Deng Xiaoping, speaking in 1974 at the Sixth Special Session of the United Nations Assembly on the question of world distribution of wealth and raw materials, stated that the superpowers continue to exploit the peoples of the Third World by paying low prices for the raw materials from the developing countries and raising the export prices of the manufactured products sold to them. This was the main concern of practically all Asian, African, and Latin American countries at that special United Nations conference. Second, a three-fold, differentiated world, with contradictions between the parts, fits well into the Chinese communist traditional ideological framework. The struggle between the First World and the Third World (the poor nations), with the support of the Second World (Japan, Canada, and Western Europe), is looked upon by the Chinese as present-day class struggle on a world scale.[28] Third, the Chinese policy to support the Third World allows her to develop a broad coalition to alienate the Soviet Union from the developing nations. The Soviet Union's interference in Angola and elsewhere in Africa was seen as an example of social-imperialism that the developing nations must guard against. In a general debate in the United Nations Assembly, Huang Hua, then Chinese foreign minister, stated:

> To further its aggression and expansion, social-imperialism is trying to fool people by flaunting the signboard of "a natural ally of the developing countries" who "supports the national-liberation movements." Besides, it is doing its utmost to sow discord among the third world countries. It confers on you the title "progressive" on one day, but labels you "reactionary" the next. Now supporting one against another, now the other way round, it stops at nothing in creating dissension and undermining the unity of the third world countries.[29]

Fourth, the theory of the Third World represents a clear departure from the Cultural Revolution stance of China as a revolutionary model to be emulated by others. Hua Guofeng made it very clear at the Eleventh Party Congress in

August 1977 that "revolution cannot be exported."[30] Instead, China's new orientation in world politics is, first of all, to identify "the main revolutionary forces, the chief enemies, and the middle forces that can be won over and united" to form an international coalition. This new orientation in China's foreign policy of a united front implies a realignment in the existing international relations, which included China's moves to establish relations with the European Common Market countries and Tito's Yugoslavia.

Anti-superpower Hegemony

The concept that no nation should exercise its preponderant influence over another was one of the principles the United States and China agreed on in the Shanghai communiqué of February 28, 1972, signed by President Nixon and Premier Zhou Enlai: "Neither should seek hegemony in the Asia-Pacific region and each is opposed to efforts by any other country or group of countries to establish such hegemony."[31] Antihegemonism has become a major objective in Chinese foreign policy; one communiqué after another, signed by China and various friendly nations, has contained this expression in varying degrees of intensity.[32] While the United States is one of the two superpowers indicted, the Chinese seem to focus their attack on the Soviet Union and her social imperialism. Hu Yaobang placed blame on the Soviet Union's hegemonist policies for the deterioration of Sino-Soviet relations.[33] Zhao Ziyang told Joao Vieira of Guinea-Bissau that "the cause of the current tension and turbulence in the world lies in the scramble between two superpowers."[34] Hu cited the massing of Soviet troops along the Chinese border over a twenty-year period, Soviet support of Vietnam's invasion of Kampuchea (Cambodia), and Russia's occupation of Afghanistan as proof of the threat of Soviet hegemonism.[35] Superpower hegemonism, intoned Hu Yaobang, was the main source of instability and turmoil in the world and therefore, to safeguard world peace, "the most important task for the people of the world today is to oppose hegemonism."[36] China vowed that it would neither seek the status of a superpower nor commit aggression abroad.[37] The United States is viewed by the Chinese as the superpower which is striving to preserve its vested interests" and which is thus less dangerous than the Soviet Union, which is "trying hard to extend its sphere of influence."[38] The Chinese have made a point of cataloging the Soviet Union's penetration into Europe, Africa, the Middle East, the Persian Gulf region, and the Asian-Pacific basin in recent years, to prove that "social imperialism is the more aggressive and adventurous of the two superpowers and is the major threat to world peace and security."[39] While the Chinese deny that they consider the Soviet Union the more dangerous superpower because it occupied the disputed areas along the Sino-Soviet frontier, the military might of the Soviet Union, and her war-making capability, is a major consideration in China's perceptions. The Chinese perceive that the entire Soviet economy has been placed on a "military footing," and they are keenly aware that there are Soviet troops stationed in foreign countries, particularly in Czechoslovakia, which "is completely under prolonged (actually indefinite) military occupation."[40]

Some time ago Deng Xiaoping stated that a superpower "is an imperialist country which everywhere subjects other countries to its aggression, interference, control, subversion, or plunder, and strives for world hegemony."[41] The Chinese believe that a number of local wars have begun through the interference of the two superpowers in the affairs of Third World countries, and that more local wars may result from the Soviet Union's strategic deployment around the world in competition with the United States. The Chinese seem to believe that the competition between the two superpowers will inevitably lead to world war. The Chinese formula for averting the outbreak of war was outlined by her foreign minister in a recent speech at the United Nations: (1) Make third world countries aware of the "growing danger of war" and be prepared for such an eventuality. (2) Frustrate the superpowers' expansion and aggression. (3) Make no compromises or actions of appeasement in dealing with the superpowers.[42] In addition, the Chinese feel that the struggle against hegemonism can be waged on the economic front by the Third World. Since the superpowers, as the Chinese perceive them, are becoming more dependent upon the supplies of raw materials from the Third World, a united effort must be formed to establish "a new international economic order," defending not only the economic rights and interests of the Third World countries but also the price for the raw materials from them.[43] This new international economic order calls for stabilizing the prices of primary commodities such as coffee, cocoa, and sugar through negotiations at the United Nations, reducing or canceling debts incurred by the poor Third World countries, providing more funds for development, and easing credit conditions and restraints on the transfer of technology and scientific knowledge.[44] All these measures proposed by the Chinese are aimed at winning the support of the Third World countries, which in the past have demanded the enactment of these programs to relieve their economic plight.

Premier Zhao told the delegates to the Beijing South-South Conference in April 1983 that the Third World nations must struggle to expand their economies and change the inequitable international economic order. But he warned that the task was an arduous one because "the superpowers either stubbornly reject the idea of restructuring the old international economic order or take an indifferent attitude towards it."[45] Zhao pledged that China would join the Third World nations in carrying on "the unremitting struggle" for the establishment of a new international economic order. He argued that the poor Third World nations must select development stategies suitable to their own conditions; they should not be forced to make domestic reforms as a precondition for the establishment of a new international economic order."[46]

Détente, SALT Talks, Disarmament, and China's Nuclear Capability

The time was late November 1974; the places were Ulan Bator in the People's Republic of Mongolia and a conference room in the Great Hall of the People on Tian An Men Square in Beijing. While attending an anniversary celebration in Ulan Bator, Mongolia, Soviet Party Chief Leonid Brezhnev announced that he had rejected the Chinese proposal for the withdrawal of troops along the disputed Sino-Soviet frontier as a precondition for establishing normal relations between the two countries. In Beijing, meanwhile, Secretary of State Henry Kissinger was trading jokes with Deng Xiaoping, the Chinese deputy premier, before briefing the Chinese on the Ford-Brezhnev nuclear arms agreement reached at the Vladivostok summit conference. Kissinger flew directly to Beijing after the summit in order to assure the Chinese that there were no secret protocols reached between the United States and the Soviet Union which might be construed by the Chinese as unfriendly toward China. This extraordinary mission by Secretary of State Kissinger was undertaken with the full realization that the Chinese were opposed to any accord on the strategic limitation of nuclear and other sophisticated weapons between the two superpowers. In 1972, at the United Nations, the Chinese made known to the world their opposition to the policy of détente and efforts to relax the nuclear arms race. As the Chinese chief delegate to the United Nations said recently: "How can we afford to relax and to sleep when a superpower has deployed a million troops along our border?"[47]

The Chinese wasted no time in castigating the theme of détente at the conclusion of the Helsinki summit in the fall of 1975, when some progress was made in the Strategic Arms Limitation Talks (SALT) between the United States and the Soviet Union. This time the Chinese called the talk of détente by Moscow a fraud to mask Soviet expansion in other parts of the world, as demonstrated by its intervention in Angola.[48] To the Chinese, détente is synonymous with nuclear arms expansion: "Therefore, in the interest of 'détente' it is necessary to feverishly step up manufacturing even more 'weapons of mass destruction.' "[49] The Chinese view the SALT talks as a veil for intensifying the nuclear arms race between the two superpowers, and the negotiations on SALT as "a form of struggle by which each side tries to restrict the other's expansion and build up its own strength."[50] The Chinese also see détente between the two superpowers and the SALT talks as a design by the Soviet Union to create a false sense of security for many nations in Western Europe and, thus, as an opportunity to greatly strengthen their relative military position and nuclear capability vis-à-vis Western Europe. The Chinese think that the countries of Western Europe must bolster their national defenses: To accept détente and disarmament is to appease Soviet expansionism.[51] One might add that it is probable that détente had made it increasingly difficult for China to isolate the Soviet Union; therefore she was vehemently opposed to détente, even at the risk of jeopardizing her rapprochement with the United States.

The Chinese were relieved to see the end of détente when the Soviet Union invaded Afghanistan in 1979. To China, Soviet occupation of Afghanistan showed that détente was a "fraud" and a "smokescreen" to mask Moscow's aggressive expansionism.[52] The invasion also vindicated China's long-held belief that the Soviet Union was a "socialist imperialist nation." China believed that détente was part of a Soviet grand global strategy to gain time in the military and economic contest against the United States, a "cover" to camouflage Soviet intentions to weaken the West in order "to win without a war."[53]

In the special session of the United Nations General Assembly on disarmament, the Chinese seemed to take three positions with respect to universal disarmament.[54] First, the Chinese held that general disarmament must begin with the Soviet Union and the United States, the two superpowers. China resented Soviet Foreign Minister Gromyko's appeal to all other members of the United Nations to take steps to halt the armament race. The Chinese argued that medium and small countries must strengthen their defenses in order to protect themselves against the threat posed by the military might of the superpowers. Second, the Chinese objected to the Soviet view that the real threat to world peace lies in nuclear armaments, since the superpowers have accumulated an enormous arsenal of conventional weapons in preparation for a possible conventional war. The Chinese position, therefore, was that genuine disarmament must involve both nuclear and conventional weapons. Third, the Chinese also objected to the Soviet proposal for an international convention for guaranteeing the security of nonnuclear states. To the Chinese, the purpose of this proposal was "to bind, hand and foot, the numerous small and medium-sized countries and deprive them of their capabilities for self-defense" by restricting the possession of nuclear armaments to the superpowers alone.[55] The Chinese counterproposal was that a superpower like the Soviet Union should be the first to declare the nonuse of nuclear weapons "under whatever conditions against the nonnuclear countries, instead of playing tricks of one kind or another."[56]

At the UN's special session on disarmament, held in June 1982, Huang Hua, then the Chinese foreign minister, proposed a three-step measure to bring about an immediate end to the arms race. First, all powers should reach an agreement not to use nuclear weapons. While such an agreement is pending, nuclear free zones should be established. Second, the superpowers—the Soviet Union and the United States—should stop all testing and manufacturing of nuclear weapons and agree to a 50 percent reduction in their nuclear arsenals, to be followed by all other nuclear states. Third, this should be followed by conventional weapons disarmament and pledges by all nations not to use conventional arms to intervene in the affairs of any other nation.[57] Huang Hua also specified China's need for an extended period of international peace in order to complete her goals of modernization.[58] In addition to the above proposal, China urged the prohibition of chemical weapons and the establishment of a verification group, made up of representatives of all the nuclear-and nonnuclear-weapon states, to carry out an effective verification program on the disarmament agreements.[59]

China's Nuclear Capability

In 1957 China decided to undertake a costly program for nuclear development, in terms of both atomic devices and missiles. This followed prolonged debate within the party and the military hierarchy.[60] It was a hard decision, both because of the cost involved, and because of the realization that a nuclear weapons program had to be developed without Soviet aid or advice. Since then, the Chinese have considered the nuclear program a supreme example of self-reliance and determination. China had her first nuclear test in October 1964, her first thermonuclear test of about 200 kilotons in May 1966, and her first atmospheric test of several megatons in November 1971. During the fourteen years from 1964 to 1978, at least thirty-six nuclear tests were conducted in the Xinjiang and Inner Mongolian desert areas. China also developed a system of about 20 intermediate ballistic missiles with a range of up to 1,000 miles, as well as 100 medium-range ballistic missiles with a range of 500 to 750 miles. Both systems are capable of carrying nuclear warheads. In April 1970 China put her first satellite into orbit around the world. Since then, China has launched twelve more satellites. In May 1980 it also launched an intercontinental ballistic missile (ICBM), with a range of about 6,000 miles, which landed 27 miles east of its target in the South Pacific. In September 1981 three new satellites in a single rocket were launched to orbit above the earth as an early warning system to protect against possible Soviet nuclear missile attacks. At that time China was said to have possessed 30 to 40 ICBMs and 30 to 40 Intermediate Range Ballistic Missiles (IRBMs).[61] She has two ICBMs with a range of 3,000 to 6,000 miles.[62] Although China lags behind in other aspects of scientific and technological development, her nuclear and space programs are progressing steadily, and she must be regarded as a nuclear power.

Even though she has become a member of the exclusive "nuclear club," China has consistently opposed the test ban and the nonproliferation treaties, based on the contention that (1) the test ban treaty was designed by the superpowers to prevent the less developed nations from acquiring nuclear weapons, and (2) China's nuclear program was purely for defensive purposes. Zhou Enlai once declared for the Chinese government that unless there was total disarmament, including the destruction of all nuclear weapons by all powers and the dismantling of foreign military bases, China would continue to develop her own nuclear weapons for defensive purposes.[63] Certainly, China's nuclear capability was one of the several factors which compelled the United States to seek rapprochement with China in 1971. The growth of China's nuclear capability not only altered the power balance in Asia but also made the world realize that any arms control program, such as the SALT talks or President Reagan's strategic arms reduction talks (START), would be meaningless in the long run without China's participation. The Chinese view these strategic arms talks with skepticism, seeing them as leading inevitably to "a new round of the arms race, not disarmament," because both superpowers continue to develop and improve their nuclear arsenals.[64]

SINO-SOVIET CONFLICT
AND THE BORDER DISPUTE

At the time of the founding of the People's Republic of China, in 1949, the Soviet Union was China's only ally. The alliance was cemented in a thirty-year Sino-Soviet treaty of peace and friendship, ratified in April 1950, after months of hard negotiation by the Chinese. Although the treaty provided an automatic extension for five additional years, the Chinese decided in April 1979 to terminate the treaty when it expired in April 1980. This decision by the Chinese not to renew the treaty represented a benchmark in the two nations' turbulent relations over the past three decades.

The first signs of the rupture in the Sino-Soviet alliance appeared in 1953–54. At the conclusion of the Korean War, China was eager to obtain a commitment from the Soviet Union for support in confronting the containment policy imposed by the United States in Asia. The Soviet Union's stance at that time was to move toward a global policy of peaceful coexistence. As the United States extended its protection to Taiwan, concluding a mutual defense treaty with the Chinese Nationalists in 1954, Chinese uneasiness was demonstrated in her militancy toward the Taiwan issue. The situation reached crisis proportions in 1958. In the face of a nuclear threat from the United States, the Chinese sought a commitment from the Soviet Union for nuclear protection. When Khrushchev refused the Chinese request, the rupture in Sino-Soviet relations became enlarged and at times quite explosive. Thus, 1958 was a turning point in Sino-Soviet relations. Not only did a serious difference develop in the two nations' approach toward the Asian power balance situation vis-à-vis the United States containment policy, but at that critical juncture, the Chinese decided to switch their economic development strategy from centralized planning with emphasis on heavy industry and heavy dependence on Soviet aid, to mass mobilization of the Great Leap and the commune programs. It was, then, a combination of differences over both the changing Asian situation and the appropriate economic development model that provided the fuel for the ongoing ideological dispute as to which system was more purely Marxist-Leninist. The Soviet Union's decision to withdraw economic development aid from China in 1960 added more bitterness to the already rapidly deteriorating relationship. From 1960 until the Cultural Revolution, the Sino-Soviet conflict was manifested in several forms. First, both countries engaged in a continuous verbal duel in the form of polemics (arguments) heavily couched in ideological terms. For instance, Mao's ninth polemic in 1964 charged that the brand of communism practiced by the Soviet Union under Khrushchev was "phony" and deviationist. Second, by the mid-1950s, China had decided to compete with the Soviet Union for influence in the Third World. The major role played by China at the 1955 Bandung Conference of neutral and nonaligned nations of Asia and Africa was indicative of China's changing policy approach. After Bandung Chinese economic and technical aid became an important instrument for wooing countries of the Third World to the Chinese side, in competition with the Soviet Union and the Chinese Nationalists. Third, China seized every opportunity to engage in propaganda warfare against the Soviet Union on issues of revolutionary war, superpower hegemony, détente, and disarmament. Fourth, the Sino-Soviet conflict and competition became more intense and acute when it involved influence over fraternal communist countries bordering China, such as North Korea and North Vietnam. The 1979 Sino-Vietnam conflict must be viewed in this light. The chain of events which prompted

China to take "punitive" military action against Vietnam in the spring of 1979 was triggered by the Vietnamese moving away from Chinese influence to Soviet influence, as seen in the Soviet-Vietnamese treaty of alliance, signed in November 1978. The Chinese could not take lightly this Soviet alliance with an Asian nation bordering her territory. As incidents along the unmarked border increased, and as successive expulsions of overseas Chinese from Vietnam occurred, the Chinese became more impatient. When, in January 1979, the Chinese-backed Cambodian regime of Pol Pot collapsed under the pressure of the invading Vietnamese army, the Chinese leaders—possibly with some dissenting voices in the inner council—decided to take military action. The action, according to Deng Xiaoping, was taken to "teach the Vietnamese a lesson." One might add that this action was directed at Moscow as well as at Hanoi.

At the heart of Sino-Soviet relations is the question of the disputed borders along their common frontiers. Specifically, the disputed areas are north of the Amur River, east of the Ussuri River on China's northeast border, and the part of the Ili Valley on China's northwest Xinjiang region, as shown in Figure 10.1. The Chinese claimed that 12,700 square miles of territory north of the Amur River were Chinese but were ceded to Czarist Russia under pres-

FIGURE 10.1   Disputed Border Along the Sino-Soviet Frontier (Indicated by heavy lines)

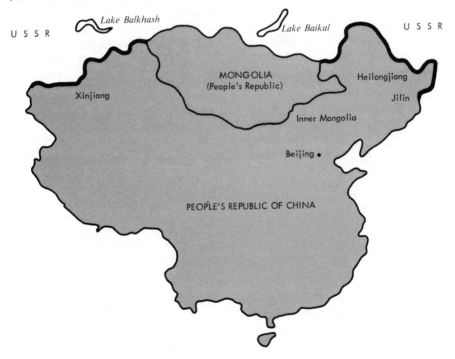

sure in 1860.[65] The Ili Valley was taken by Russian troops in 1867 when the Muslims in Xingjiang rebelled against Chinese rule.

When the first Sino-Soviet boundary negotiations began in 1964, the Chinese government indicated that it "would not demand the return of the approximately 1.5 million square kilometers of land annexed by Czarist Russia under unequal treaties.[66] The territory included 600,000 square kilometers of land north of the Heilong River, taken by Russia under the Treaty of Aigun (1858); 400,000 square kilometers of land east of the Ussuri River, taken under the Treaty of Peking (1860); and 440,000 square kilometers of land east and south of Lake Balkhash, plus 70,000 square kilometers of land west of the Ili Valey in the Pamirs, taken under the Treaty of Peking and the Treaty of St. Petersburg (1881).[67] China did claim from the Soviet Union land in the Ili Valley in the Pamir mountain range which borders China and Afghanistan. In refuting the claim, the Soviet Union argued that the boundary of the Pamir in the Ili Valley was established in a series of diplomatic notes in 1894. The Chinese countered this by introducing documents to prove that the disputed Pamirs boundary remains unsettled and that both governments had agreed to maintain a temporary status quo.[68] The Chinese based their case on the 1884 protocol to the Treaty of St. Petersburg, which provided a status quo agreement on the disputed boundary.[69] The Soviet government, as late as 1979, appeared ready to make some concessions to China on the Pamirs dispute.[70] But the invasion of Afghanistan in December 1979 made it difficult for the Soviet government to make concessions. The Afghan invasion also increased Chinese concern over the disputed Pamirs area.

China perceived the Soviet invasion of Afghanistan as part of a grand strategy to expand Soviet influence and hegemonism. The occupation of Afghanistan allowed the Soviet Union a land passage into Iran and Pakistan and the Indian Ocean, a strategic sea lane that leads to the Persian Gulf through the Hormuz Strait.[71] The Chinese also were alarmed at the Soviet's ability to mobilize a large force on short notice for a sudden surprise attack.[72] In addition, Soviet forces were also using Afghanistan to test their weapons and tactics. But more important was Soviet annexation of the Wakhan corridor of the Pamirs, which in effect sealed off local routes into both Pakistan and China (see Figure 10.2). The Soviets used the Wakhan corridor as a supply depot for its troops because it was safe from guerrilla harrassment.[73] As can be seen from Figure 10.2, the Soviet Union could now influence relations between China, India, and Pakistan. The invasion of Afghanistan made the Pamirs boundary dispute less likely to be settled. Neither China nor the Soviet Union would be willing to make any concessions so long as Afghanistan continued to be occupied by Soviet troops and China continued to promote the anti-Soviet front by supplying aid to the Afghan guerrillas.[74]

The border dispute between China and the Soviet Union did not surface openly until 1963–64. From March to September, 1963, a spate of mass-media editorials and open letters raised the question of the unsettled frontier north of the Ili Valley in the Xinjiang autonomous region.[75] In the fall of 1963, the Soviet Union responded by presenting an account of Chinese violations of the

FIGURE 10.2 Geopolitics of the Wakhan Corridor

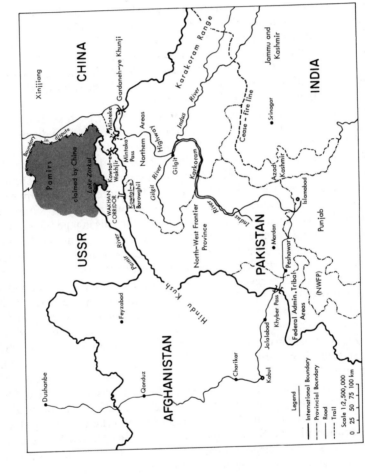

Source: Yaacov Vertzberger, "Afghanistan in China's Policy," *Problems of Communism*, xxxi (May–June 1982), 11. Reprinted by permission of the publisher.

border from 1960 to 1963. According to the Soviet account, there were over 5,000 border violations committed by the Chinese in 1962 alone.[76] It was said that dozens of incidents along the 4,000-mile frontier occurred each day, including smuggling and other illegal entries into China. In 1964, amidst charges and countercharges, negotiations were begun to demarcate the border and to fix navigation lines on the boundary rivers of Amur and Ussuri. While these negotiations made little progress toward a mutual agreement on the disputed border, there were no serious flare-ups along the frontier until March 1969. For a two-week period—from March 2 to March 15, 1969—Chinese and Soviet troops clashed over the ownership of an island named "Chenpaotao" by the Chinese and "Damansky" by the Soviets (see Figure 10.3). These clashes, or deliberate ambushes of each other's border patrols, resulted in some casualties on both sides. The immediate consequence of these March 1969 border clashes, irrespective of motives or linkage to domestic politics,[77] was the intensified fortification of military installations on both sides of the frontier. This led to further tension in Sino-Soviet relations.

Curiously, the 1969 border clashes also brought both sides much closer to an agreement on means for reducing tension and for settling disputed areas. We now know that in September 1969 top-level negotiations were conducted in Beijing, which produced the so-called September 11 Agreement of Understanding between Soviet Premier Aleksei Kosygin and Premier Zhou Enlai. The Chinese claimed that the Soviet Union had agreed to a framework for further negotiation toward reducing tension between the two countries: (1) "The armed forces of the Chinese and Soviet sides disengage by withdrawing from, or refraining from entering, all the disputed areas along the Sino-Soviet border;" and (2) "both sides reach an agreement on the provisional measures for maintaining the status quo of the border."[78] In 1973 Premier Zhou indicated to C.L. Sulzberger of *The New York Times* that Kosygin had agreed to these two provisions but that the Soviet Union had done nothing since to move toward the implementation of any of the points agreed upon.[79] What Zhou did not point out to Sulzberger was that the Soviet Union had, in January 1971, proposed to the Chinese a treaty on the nonuse of force by both sides in settling their border disputes.[80] By the summer of 1971, not only had Chinese attitudes toward the conciliatory moves by the Soviet Union stiffened, but a basic policy change toward the United States was also in the offing. The signing of the Shanghai communiqué in February 28, 1972, marked both a major turning point in Sino-American relations and the beginning of a period of deterioration in Sino-Soviet relations. The China-United States agreement not to seek superpower hegemony in Asia and the Pacific and to oppose other nations that establish such hegemony was aimed at the Soviet Union.

As a countermeasure to the gradual rapprochement between the United States and China, the Soviet Union, in 1973, offered to the Chinese a draft treaty of mutual nonaggression, which contained a provision that read: "Each party to the treaty pledges itself not to invade the other party on land, sea, or air with any types of arms or threaten it with such invasion."[81] The Chinese rebuffed the Soviet offer and argued instead for the implementation of the

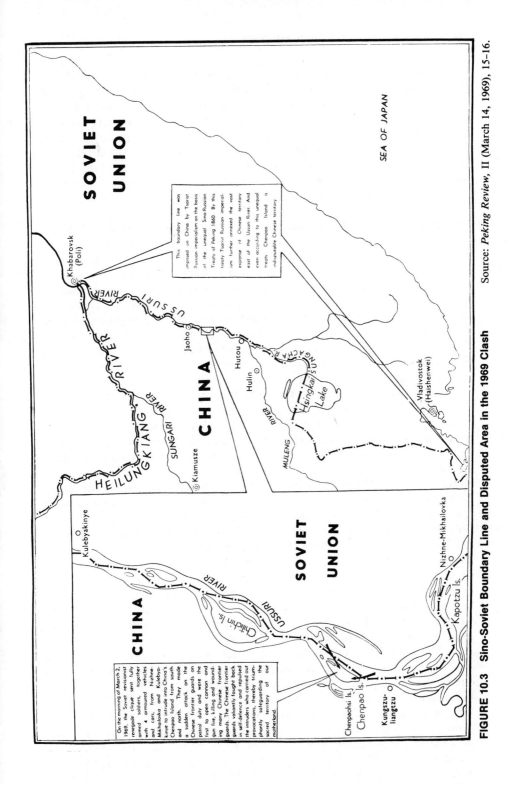

FIGURE 10.3 Sino-Soviet Boundary Line and Disputed Area in the 1969 Clash

Source: *Peking Review*, II (March 14, 1969), 15–16.

September 11, 1969, Agreement of Understanding between Kosygin and Zhou, which called for the withdrawal of armed forces from the disputed areas. From 1973 to 1976, Sino-Soviet negotiation toward the settlement of the border disputes was at a standstill, accompanied, nevertheless, by verbal barrages hurled at each other. When Mao Zedong died in September 1976, the Soviet Union thought at first that this was an opportunity to improve Sino-Soviet relations. Not only did Brezhnev send the fraternal party's condolences on Mao's death, but all media criticism of China was halted for several months. In addition, Ambassador Illichev returned to Beijing after more than a year's absence. But if the Soviet Union expected improved Sino-Soviet relations with the new leadership in China, which their gestures after Mao's death certainly indicated, the illusion was soon shattered by Hua Guofeng's harsh words at the Eleventh Party Congress in August 1977. Hua charged that "the Soviet leading clique has betrayed Marxism-Leninism" and that it wanted to exert its hegemony everywhere in the world.[82] Hua blamed the Soviet Union for the impasse in Sino-Soviet border negotiations over the previous eight years. He challenged the Soviet leaders by saying: "If it really has any desire to improve the state relations between the two countries, this clique should prove it by concrete deeds."[83] Undaunted by Chinese intransigence, the Presidium of the U.S.S.R. Supreme Soviet sent a conciliatory letter in February 1978 to the Standing Committee of the Chinese National People's Congress, on the eve of the convocation of its Fifth Congress. The letter proposed a joint statement by both countries that their relations be based on the five principles of peaceful coexistence advocated by Zhou Enlai: equality, mutual respect for sovereignty, territorial integrity, noninterference in internal affairs, and nonuse of force in the settlement of disputes (see Appendix D). The Chinese responded by charging that such a joint statement on the five principles of peaceful coexistence would be only a "hollow statement" at best. The Chinese wanted the Soviet Union to admit that it had agreed to the September 11, 1969, Agreement of Understanding. The Chinese then made a counterproposal which provided not only for the disengagement of the armed forces on both sides in the disputed border areas but also called for the withdrawal of Soviet forces now stationed along the Sino-Soviet border and in the People's Republic of Mongolia as well. Thus, the Chinese insisted that the Soviet Union must accept a precondition before negotiations to normalize relations could proceed: "When you have a million troops deployed on the Sino-Soviet border, how can you expect the Chinese people to believe that you have a genuine and sincere desire to improve the relations between our two countries?"[84]

The subsequent border incursion, which occurred two months after the exchange of notes between the parliaments of the two countries, seems to strengthen the argument presented by the Chinese side for the withdrawal of Soviet armed forces from the disputed border areas. On May 9 a Soviet army helicopter violated China's air space by crossing the border river and penetrating four kilometers (about two and a half miles) into the production center of a commune in Heilongjiang province in the northeast. The Chinese protested and charged that thirty Soviet paratroopers landed in Chinese territory, firing on and seizing the inhabitants.[85] On May 12 the Soviet Ministry of

Foreign Affairs apologized to the Chinese and stated that the intrusion had occurred in order to arrest an armed criminal. In spite of the Soviet admission of the intrusion and the apology for the incident, the Chinese oral statement to the Soviet Ambassador to China, V.S. Tolstikov, was hostile. To the Chinese, the border intrusion was not "a case of inadvertent trespass into the Chinese territory" but was simply a deliberate "military provocation organized by the Soviet side, a bloody incident created by Soviet troops."[86]

There had also been some slight movement on both sides of the Sino-Soviet dispute toward a rapprochement: In February 1978 the Soviets sent a conciliatory note to the Chinese for renewed negotiations of their differences; and the Soviet Union cautiously refrained from taking military action along the Sino-Soviet border during the Chinese military incursion into Vietnam in March 1979. Meanwhile, in April 1979 the Chinese proposed negotiations "for the solution of outstanding issues and the improvement of relations between the two countries," even while announcing their intention not to renew the peace and friendship treaty when it expired in 1980.

By the summer of 1979, both sides felt there was a need to hold fresh negotiations on questions affecting Sino-Soviet relations. On September 23 a Chinese delegation led by a vice–foreign minister left Beijing for Moscow. In the first round of talks, the first in fifteen years, the Soviet delegation proposed that both sides pledge not to use nuclear or conventional weapons and both sign a joint statement not to seek hegemony in Asia or elsewhere in the world. The Chinese, it was reported, refused even to discuss any aspect of the Soviet proposal until certain preconditions were accepted by the Soviets: the reduction of forces along the Chinese border, the withdrawal of Soviet troops from the People's Republic of Mongolia, and the ending of Soviet aid to Vietnam.[87] The Soviet Union was reported to have offered the Chinese a joint declaration endorsing the principles of peaceful coexistence. This agreement would replace the thirty-year treaty of friendship which was due to expire in April 1980.[88] When the invasion of Afghanistan by the Soviet Union began in December 1979, Sino-Soviet talks were abruptly halted. Later the Chinese explained: "It is apparently inappropriate to continue Sino-Soviet negotiations and consultation."[89] A media campaign was mounted in China which severely criticized the Soviet invasion of Afghanistan.[90] At a banquet honoring visiting Egyptian vice-president Mubarak,[91] Deng Xiaoping demanded the withdrawal of Soviet troops from Afghanistan. Li Xiannian, then vice-premier, later president of the PRC, proposed three principles for resolving the Afghan crisis: unconditional withdrawal of Soviet troops, self-determination by the Afghan people, and world support for the Afghan people against Soviet aggression.[92]

As Sino-Soviet talks on the border dispute became frozen, the Chinese began to make overtures to the United States for a closer alliance. In January 1980 Harold Brown, President Carter's defense secretary, made a trip to China.[93] Then, on October 5, 1980, tension along the border increased again when the Chinese government protested the intrusion of four Soviet armed personnel into Chinese territory in the Inner Mongolia region.[94] Amidst speculation as to the possibility of a closer Sino-American military arrangement, the pressure was now on the Soviet government to make moves to reopen the Sino-Soviet talks. The most conciliatory gesture to that end was made by Leonid Brezhnev on March 24, 1982, when he gave a speech in the central Asian city of Tashkent. Brezhnev reaffirmed the Soviet Union's support for China's claim of Taiwan and pledged that the Soviet Union had no territorial claims on China: "We are prepared to come to terms, without preconditions, on terms acceptable to both sides to improve Soviet-China relations on the basis of mutual respect for each other's interests, noninterference in each other's affairs, certainly not to the detriment of third countries."[95]

The Chinese responded by insisting that the Soviet Union demonstrate its desire for improved relations with China by "actual deeds."[96] Hu Yaobang told the September 1982 party congress that all the Soviet Union had to do to improve Sino-Soviet relations was to "take practical steps to lift their threat to the security of our country" and that "deeds, rather than words, are important."[97] By deeds, the Chinese now included the issues of Afghanistan and Kampuchea, in addition to the stationing of Soviet troops along the Chinese border.[98] But Brezhnev repeated his desire to seek reconciliation with China by declaring that both nations were moving closer to a resumption of the talks abruptly halted in 1979.[99] Finally, in early October 1982, Soviet Deputy Foreign Minister Ilyichev unexpectedly arrived in Beijing to begin the negotiations. The talks lasted through the end of October, with China insisting on Soviet acceptance of the preconditions proposed earlier. In March 1983 the talks resumed in Moscow with hopeful signs of possible agreement on the border disputes. One tangible sign of Soviet sincerity was its decision to conduct less frequent military exercises in the border areas. During the talks the Soviets proposed that discussions not include "problems concerning third countries," as a way to avoid Chinese demands for withdrawal of Soviet troops from Afghanistan, reduction of forces in Mongolia, and aid to Vietnam.[100]

While the boundary disputes were still being negotiated, the two sides took a number of steps to reduce tension and improve relations. In February 1982 a transportation agreement was signed which provided transshipments of containerized cargo between ports of the two countries. In March 1983 a Sino-Soviet goods exchange and payment agreement was signed under which there would be further expansion in trade between the two countries. The trade agreement would provide China with Soviet steel, plate glass, chemical products, and machinery, and China would export mineral products, meat, cotton, silk, textiles, tea, and light industries to the Soviet Union.[101] Sino-Soviet trade in 1982 was valued at $302 million, and under the 1983 trade agreement it would grow to $1 billion. Sino-Soviet cultural and sports exchange programs also resumed. An important agreement was also made by the Sino-Soviet joint commission concerning navigation on the boundary rivers of Amur and Ussuri. In 1982 there was a marked deterioration in Sino-American relations, caused mainly by the Reagan administration's decision to sell arms to Taiwan. The strained Sino-American relationship seemed to have prompted the Soviet Union to move closer to China. Thus, one witnessed a "bidding game" in the triangular relations of the three countries.[102]

dal. The Chinese were also preoccupied with their own internal struggle as the radicals mounted an assault against Zhou Enlai and his pragmatic policies under the anti-Confucius campaign. Zhou Enlai's reference to Sino-American relations in his report to the Fifth National People's Congress in January 1975 was vague. He noted that improvements had been made in the past three years and that he believed the relations would continue to improve "as long as the principles of the Sino-American Shanghai communiqué are carried out in earnest."[104] In contrast, Zhou devoted more time to outlining the impasse in Sino-Soviet relations and appealed to the Soviet leaders to "sit down and negotiate honestly."

When President Ford arrived in Beijing on December 2, 1975, he was the second American president to sit down with the aging but still alert Mao Zedong. Zhou Enlai was already dying of cancer. The Chinese leader with whom Ford and Kissinger negotiated was Deng Xiaoping, a man about to be purged for the second time by the radicals and their supporters. Because of the conclusion of the Helsinki agreement at the SALT talks in the fall of 1975, the Chinese saw détente between the two superpowers as a major concern. Deng opened his speech at the welcoming banquet by mentioning the agreement between China and the United States in the 1972 Shanghai communiqué not to seek hegemony—he called this an "outstanding common point." While Deng did not mention the stumbling block of the Taiwan question, he stated that "so long as the principles of the Shanghai communiqué are earnestly observed," normalization of relations "will eventually be realized through the joint efforts of our two sides." He went on to say: "At present, a more important question confronts the Chinese and American people—that of the international situation." He discussed the intensified competition for world hegemony, which would lead to war: "Rhetoric about 'détente' cannot cover up the stark reality of the growing danger of war."[105] After two days of lengthy sessions with the Chinese, each lasting more than two and a half hours, no new ground was broken in the bilateral relationship. At the farewell banquet hosted by the Americans, President Ford tried to reassure the Chinese: "I reaffirmed that the United States is committed to complete the normalization of relations with the People's Republic of China on the basis of the Shanghai communiqué."[106] At the end of the five-day visit, there was no joint communiqué as there had been at the end of the Nixon visit in 1972. What specific agreement, if any, was reached by President Ford and the Chinese became a subject for speculation. Had either Kissinger or Ford secretly promised the Chinese that the United States would sever diplomatic relations with Taiwan after the presidential election in 1976, in order to facilitate the normalization of relations with Beijing? Deng Xiaoping was quoted in the fall of 1977 as remarking that President Ford had indeed promised that he would break off relations with Taiwan upon his reelection in 1976. Former President Ford has since denied that such a promise was made to the Chinese during his visit. The fact remains, leaving aside the question of the alleged verbal promise by Ford, that Deng Xiaoping's remark indicated the strain in the Sino-American relations during the mid-1970s.

With the change in the administration in Washington following the 1976 presidential election, the Chinese waited patiently for the Carter administration to make a move. The succession struggle after the deaths of Zhou Enlai and Mao in 1976 had prevented the Chinese from being overly concerned about the normalization of relations. With the arrest of the Gang of Four and the emergence of a new leadership in China, the focus in Sino-American relations was placed once again on the question of Taiwan, the obstacle to the normalization of relations.

In his keynote address to the Eleventh Party Congress on August 18, 1977, Hua Guofeng proposed a formula for ending the impasse in Sino-American relations. The formula contained three specific actions to be taken by the United States: (1) Break diplomatic relations with Taiwan. (2) Withdraw all United States forces and military installations from the island and from the Taiwan Strait. (3) Repeal the 1954 Mutual Defense Treaty signed by the United States and the Taiwan government.[107] Perhaps Hua was responding to a signal sent by President Carter in June, when Carter said that he was looking for "a formula which can bridge some of the difficulties that still separate us."[108] Secretary of State Cyrus Vance was sent to Beijing on August 22 to try to break the deadlock and to initiate exploratory talks on Hua's three-point formula. While Vance spent four days in Beijing discussing the formula proposed by Hua Guofeng, there was little official indication from either side as to what had been discussed or what agreement, if any, had been reached. Then, within ten days after Vance's departure from China, Vice Premier Deng Xiaoping revealed some of the substance of the consultation with Vance in an interview with a delegation of executives from the Associated Press.[109] Deng confided that the Vance visit represented a setback in Sino-American relations, since the secretary of state had failed to sever diplomatic relations with Taiwan after the 1976 election, as Deng claimed President Ford had promised during his December 1975 trip to China. Deng also revealed that China had rejected Vance's offer of full diplomatic relations with Beijing coupled with changing the United States embassy in Taiwan to a liaison office. It was obvious that the Chinese were not satisfied with the United States response to Hua Guofeng's formula for the settlement of the Taiwan question. The Carter administration was then deeply involved in the negotiation of the Panama treaty and was actively seeking a solution to the Mideast problem. Normalization of relations with China was a basic objective of the administration's foreign policy but was certainly not a top priority at that time. The Chinese seemed to have stood firmly on the three-point formula and the Shanghai communiqué, which recognized Taiwan as an integral part of China. Hua Guofeng said, in 1977, that to tell China what she should do about Taiwan, and in what manner, was in itself an infringement on China's domestic affairs.

China experts in the American academic community offered a number of proposals intended to enable the United States to break the deadlock on the Taiwan question. These experts, both inside and outside the government, agreed that United States relations with China must be normalized on a basis similar to her relations with the Soviet Union, and that normalized relations with China were crucial to stabilization in Asia, a basic objective in the overall United States foreign policy. Curiously, it was primarily because of United States concern over the stability of Asia immediately after the Korean War that the Mutual Defense Treaty was consummated with the Chinese Nationalists in Taiwan. Now this very defense treaty impeded normalization of relations with the People's Republic of China. Focusing on the problem of the Mutual Defense Treaty of 1954, Jerome Cohen of Harvard University suggested that some sort of guarantee be given to ensure the peaceful settlement of the Taiwan issue at the time when the United States and China established full relations with each other. Such a guarantee could be made either unilaterally or bilaterally.[110] For instance, the Chinese could unilaterally declare that China has the right to claim Taiwan by force but elects not to do so and has no intention of doing so. The United States could unilaterally declare her determination to maintain peace and security in the Pacific. Similarly, both countries could declare jointly that the Taiwan Strait is a demilitarized zone. Doak Barnett of the Brookings Institution, on the other hand, suggested that the United States must impress upon the Chinese that they should set aside the Taiwan question for the present and deal with the United States on other problems. For example, China and the United States might cooperate in the area of military security. It would be in the interest of both countries to cooperate in improving China's defense capabilities in the face of the Soviet military threat on her border.[111] In many respects the strategy outlined by Doak Barnett seemed to have been followed for a while by President Carter's national security advisor, Zbigniew Brzezinski. In his visit to Beijing during May 1978, Brzezinski assured the Chinese that the United States also was concerned and apprehensive about the Soviet Union's interference around the world and about the Soviet threat to the Chinese. He told the Chinese: "The United States does not view its relationship with China as a tactical expedient. We recognize—and share—China's resolve to resist the effort of any nation which seeks to establish global or regional hegemony."[112] Then he expanded by saying that the Sino-American friendship was based on three beliefs: A Sino-American relationship would be beneficial to world peace; a secure and strong China was in America's interest; and a strong and powerful United States was in China's interest.[113] Brzezinski's remarks certainly pleased the Chinese, in view of the May 1978 Soviet incursion into Chinese territory on the Ussuri River. These remarks, however, were certainly anti-Soviet and bear-baiting. Brzezinski also continued the practice established by Kissinger of briefing the Chinese on the United States position on the SALT talks with the Soviet Union. He perhaps went a step further than Kissinger by disclosing the secret thinking of the United States on security and strategic goals.[114] Brzezinski's trip to China did not provide any immediate breakthrough in the negotiations for normalizing relations between the two countries. There was also a rising vocal opposition in the United States to immediate normalization of relations with China at the expense of Taiwan.[115]

A breakthrough finally did occur in the fall of 1978. At a meeting with the head of the Chinese liaison office in Washington in September 1978, the

Carter administration proposed that the United States immediately would recognize the government of the People's Republic of China if the Chinese would waive their insistence on the simultaneous repeal of the United States 1954 Mutual Defense Treaty with Taiwan. From then on, the Chinese began to hint to visitors from abroad that the "Japan formula" would break the deadlock with the United States over the question of normalizing relations. These hints were also given to Japanese reporters by Vice-Premier Deng Xiaoping on his trip to Japan to sign the Sino-Japanese Peace Treaty in October 1978. The "Japan formula" meant that China would not object to continued United States economic, trade, and cultural relations with Taiwan once the United States finally recognized the People's Republic. These diplomatic gestures led to a series of intensive secret negotiations between Beijing and Washington, which ultimately produced the joint communiqué of December 15, 1978, calling for the establishment of normal diplomatic relations on January 1, 1979 (see Appendix F).

The joint communiqué stated that while the United States would recognize the government of the People's Republic as the sole and legal government of China on January 1, 1979, it nevertheless would continue to maintain "cultural, commercial, and other unofficial relations with the people of Taiwan." In addition, both sides reaffirmed the principles contained in the Shanghai communiqué of 1972: the antihegemony provision, recognition of Taiwan as an integral part of China, and the pledge to reduce international military conflicts in Asia. An exchange of ambassadors and the establishment of embassies between Beijing and Washington were to commence on March 1, 1979.

The joint communiqué, as a formal diplomatic instrument, did not reveal all the concessions made by each side that led to the final agreement for normalization of relations. The areas or points of concession were to be found mainly in other statements. The joint communiqué did indicate clearly that one point of the three-point formula laid down by Hua Guofeng in 1977— the severance of United States diplomatic relations with Taiwan—was met. The United States agreement on the other two points was revealed in a separate United States statement (see Appendix F-4) announcing that (1) the United States would notify Taiwan of her intention to repeal the 1954 Mutual Defense Treaty on January 1, 1980, giving a year's notification for cancelation of the treaty obligations, as prescribed by the treaty itself; and (2) the United States would withdraw the remainder of its military personnel, about 750 people, from Taiwan by April 1979.

What concessions did the United States obtain from China? First, the United States made a unilateral declaration (see Appendix F-4) that she desired a peaceful settlement of the Taiwan issue. The official United States statement said

> The United States is confident that the people of Taiwan face a peaceful and prosperous future. The United States continues to have an interest in the peaceful resolution of the Taiwan issue and expects that the Taiwan issue will be settled peacefully by the Chinese themselves.

In his nationwide broadcast on the normalization of relations, on December 15, 1978, President Carter declared:

> As the United States asserted in the Shanghai communiqué in 1972, we will continue to have an interest in the peaceful resolution of the Taiwan issue.
> I have paid special attention to insuring that normalization of relations between the United States and the People's Republic will not jeopardize the well-being of the people of Taiwan.

Neither of the above statements, nor the United States' clear intention to continue "cultural, commercial, and other unofficial relations with the people of Taiwan," has been contradicted or challenged by the Chinese.

Furthermore, the United States evidently told the Chinese during the negotiations for normalization of relations that it intended to sell to Taiwan selective defensive weapons after the termination of the Mutual Defense Treaty with Taiwan in 1980. In an interview with MacNeil and Lehrer on December 18, Dr. Brzezinski—the president's national security advisor—said that such a sale of arms to Taiwan would be authorized, "if in fact such requests are needed," as governed by the presence or absence of any future "tension, hostility, and conflicts" in the area. Discussing possible future United States arms sales to Taiwan, Huo Guofeng—chairperson of the CCP—said in a Chinese television interview that the Chinese, at the time of the negotiations, "absolutely would not agree to this" after the abrogation of the Mutual Defense Treaty. Then Hua also revealed: "Nevertheless, we reached an agreement on the joint communiqué." That the issue of arms sales to Taiwan by the United States did not become a stumbling block to normalization of relations certainly was a major concession on the part of the Chinese. Possible arms sales to Taiwan and the continued patrolling of the Formosan Strait by the United States Seventh Fleet could be considered a reasonable substitute for the abrogated Mutual Defense Treaty of 1954. It seemed to be the judgment of the United States, based on "the implicit understanding with the Chinese," as indicated by Dr. Brzezinski in the MacNeil and Lehrer interview, that there would be no violent resolution of the Taiwan issue and that there would be expanded close cooperation and friendship between China and the United States in the changing international strategic situation on a global scale. Both President Carter and Dr. Brzezinski emphasized that from a purely military point of view, it would not only be costly but would also be very risky for the Chinese to launch an invasion of Taiwan. An invasion of that scope would require air and naval superiority across a hundred miles of water, an unobtainable position for China for some time to come.

The recognition by the United States of the People's Republic of China in January 1979 ended thirty years of ill feeling and conflict between the two countries. However the rapprochement was basically an "awkward compromise,"[116] despite the europhia that had been generated initially from the normalization activities. The single most influential factor in the normalization of relations was, and still is, "the grand obsession of Soviet threat," as Strobe Talbott calls it, or strategic considerations in the face of Soviet military pressure. At the foundation of Sino-American relations is the desire to provide a check on Soviet military expansion, an approach described by Richard Solomon (a participant in the Sino-American rapprochement in the 1970s) as "a negative or reactive approach" in building lasting relations.[117] The immediate consequence of this anti-Soviet-based Sino-American normalization was the emergence of a realignment of the power relations between China, the Soviet Union, and the United States—the "triangular politics." In the 1970s Sino-American rapprochement made both the Chinese and the Soviet Union move closer to the United States but "farther away from each other."[118] By the time the Soviets invaded Afghanistan in December 1979, strategic considerations had become even more dominant in Sino-American relations.[119] This made it possible for China and the United States to discuss possibilities of "limited forms of military cooperation." This poses a dilemma for the United States in the 1980s. Let us pause here for a brief look at the Sino-American strategic moves for cooperation which are motivated by Soviet military expansion— particularly the Afghan invasion.

It was obvious that the Chinese were pushing the United States to take some sort of action that would block Soviet military actions in Afghanistan. Upon arrival in Beijing in January 1980, Harold Brown, President Carter's secretary of defense, was told by Deng Xiaoping that concrete action was needed "to defend world peace against Soviet hegemonism."[120] Brown responded by saying that the United States would consider providing China— on a case-by-case basis—with nonlethal but "dual-use technology," such as radar and communications equipment.[121] As mentioned in Chapter 6, the United States also said it would not object to Chinese purchases of modern military hardware from those European countries who were America's allies. Brown agreed to a program of periodic discussion and consultation with the Chinese on military policies.[122] Six months later, when President Carter and Hua Guofeng met in a Tokyo hotel, their conversation focused on the strategic threat posed by the Soviet's support of the Vietnamese invasion of Kampuchea, and the Soviet invasion of Afghanistan.

The 1980 presidential election made the Chinese very uneasy about future strategic cooperation, in view of candidate Reagan's campaign pledges to upgrade Taiwan's official status. But they soon relaxed when in March 1981 President Reagan gave personal assurances to the PRC envoy that he would observe the Sino-American normalization agreement.[123] Furthermore, President Reagan seemed more than willing to embrace an approach that would block Soviet military expansion anywhere in the world. In so doing, he was said to have authorized the continuation of a joint China-United States military intelligence operation in northwestern China that monitored Soviet missile tests.[124]

But Sino-American strategic cooperation became snarled when the issue of arms sales to Taiwan surfaced in 1980–81. In June 1981, on his visit to China, Secretary of State Alexander Haig said that the United States would remove some restrictions on the purchase of sophisticated arms by the Chinese; but he also indicated to the Chinese that the United States planned to continue arms sales to Taiwan as provided by the Taiwan Relations Act. The Taiwan Relations Act (passed by a vote of 90 to 6 in the Senate and 345 to 55 in the House in April 1979) was formulated in reaction to President Carter's unilateral declaration in December 1978 abrogating the 1955 Mutual Defense Treaty with Taiwan. That action was challenged later by twenty-five conservatives, led by Senator Barry Goldwater, in a U.S. district court suit which ruled against the president. Upon appeal by President Carter, the appeals court overturned the district court ruling by upholding the president's authority to abrogate the treaty. When Carter's Taiwan Relations Act came to Congress for approval, a host of amendments were introduced which stipulated that the president, with Congress, would determine what "defense articles" would be made available to Taiwan for its defensive needs. In its final form, Section 2(b)(5) of Public Law 98–8 (the Taiwan Relations Act) stated that it was proper for the United States "to provide Taiwan with arms of a defensive character." On the basis of that unilateral authorization, the Reagan administration decided to offer a "package deal" by providing both Chinas the arms they wanted. For Taiwan, the arms sales involved contracts for F-5Es (equipped with Sidewinder missile rockets) and the production of spare parts under joint production in Taiwan by Northrop for the island's fleet of F-100s.[125]

Chinese reaction was swift and unequivocal. They argued on legal grounds that since the Shanghai communiqué of 1972 recognized Taiwan as a part of China, the arms sales authorized by the Taiwan Relations Act was an interference in China's internal affairs. China hinted strongly of a possible reversal of relations with the United States. Now the American administration was confronted with a dilemma: to continue arms sales to Taiwan as authorized by the Taiwan Relations Act, or to face a downgrading of relations with the PRC. Related to this dilemma was the question of how far the United States must go in honoring agreements regarding Sino-American security cooperation and the sale of modern sophisticated weapons to the PRC. In January 1981 the Reagan administration announced that the United States would not sell Taiwan the more advanced fighter planes such as the 5Gs or FXs, but America was ready to sell Taiwan more F-5E fighter planes and spare parts. This move was said to have been influenced by conservative elements among Reagan supporters and by the aircraft industry represented by Northrop.[126] At the same time, as a way of resolving the dilemma, a series of consultations with the PRC on the issue of arms sales to Taiwan were initiated in November 1981. On August 17, 1982, after almost ten months of negotiation, the two sides agreed in a joint communiqué (see Appendix G) to conditions on arms sales to Taiwan: The Chinese made a strong statement that its fundamental policy toward Taiwan was for "peaceful reunification" with mainland China—Chinese officials reiterated their proposal—made to Taiwan on September 30, 1981—for reunification as evidence of that intention. The United States, reacting to China's pledge, indicated that it "does not seek to carry out a long-term policy of arms sales to Taiwan" and promised a gradual reduction of such sales "for over a period of time to a final solution." The interesting part of the joint communiqué was that the United States did not set a timetable for the gradual reduction of arms sales to Taiwan, or the termination date for ending such sales. In a notification which went through "appropriate channels," the United States informed Taiwan of these facts.[127] In fact, the United States indicated to Taiwan that it would not seek prior consultation with Beijing on arms sales for Taiwan, nor would it want to revise the Taiwan Relations Act, as suggested by Beijing.[128] While official Chinese reaction was cautious, it warned that any interpretation designed to link the August 17 communiqué on arms sales to Taiwan with the Taiwan Relations Act was unacceptable,[129] obviously referring to the statement made by John Holdridge, the assistant secretary of state, that "the administration would live up to the commitment to Taiwan under the Taiwan Relations Act."[130]

The August 17 communiqué on arms sales to Taiwan gave the Chinese only a vague assurance that such sales would be gradually reduced, and then terminated altogether, someday in the future. The United States had maintained its flexibility and freedom by providing neither a definite timetable for reduction nor a termination date for its arms sales to Taiwan, as mentioned earlier. In retrospect the Taiwan arms sales issue might have provided the impetus for Chinese leaders to formulate an independent foreign policy by not relying too much on the United States. Deng Xiaoping certainly did not mince any words in his remarks to the 1982 party congress: "No foreign country can expect China to be its vassal or expect it to swallow any bitter fruit detrimental to its own interest."[131]

The long-term arms sales to Beijing have not yet materialized. There were a number of reasons given by Chinese officials to explain why no large-scale arms purchases were made. As was mentioned in Chapter 6, large-scale purchases of sophisticated modern weapons are quite costly. In their march to modernization, the Chinese felt that the top priority should be given to industrial and agricultural development. Beyond the question of cost, China had to consider the effect it would have on American arms sales to Taiwan. It can be argued that the sale of sophisticated modern weapons to Beijing would provide the excuse for pro-Taiwan elements in America to demand an increase in sales of arms to Taiwan. The Chinese also may view the unpredictability of American policies as a shaky basis for close cooperation.

In addition, the United States has had reservations about arms sales to China. For instance, it was feared that large-scale arms sales to Beijing might provoke a Soviet reaction—perhaps an increase in its military pressure along the Chinese border or in Asia generally. Although the United States should not permit Soviet "paranoia and protests"[132] to dictate the extent and level of Sino-American security cooperation, the wisdom of a policy requiring larger arms sales to China in response to Soviet misbehavior is questionable.[133] Richard Solomon proposed that a limited sale to China of lethal defensive military equipment, such as antitank rockets or air-to-air missiles, would be permissible in the face of "highly threatening Soviet initiative,"[134] but he also cautioned that American security should not rely on the "instability of the strategic triangle" or "the uncertain future of the Moscow-Beijing feud."[135] There seemed to be some agreement among a number of experts that Sino-American policy should not become "a hostage to the vicissitudes of the Sino-Soviet tensions."[136]

China experts also argued that a much sounder basis on which to build a lasting Sino-American relationship lay in cementing a tie between the two nations based on trade and educational, cultural, and technological contacts and exchanges. The basic objective for both China and the United States is to see a politically stable and militarily strong China which, in turn, rests on the success of China's modernization program. Thus, it was argued, the United States could make some impact on the speed and orientation of China's modernization by actively "participating" in its modernization so as to ensure it from political instability and economic chaos in the future.[137]

The total two-way trade between China and United States was $2.3 billion in 1979, $4.8 billion in 1980, over $5.5 billion in 1981, and $5.1 billion in 1982. A $5.2 billion trade turnover was expected for 1982. Since 1979 America has sold more to China than it has purchased, thereby deriving a trade surplus. More than half of American exports to China consisted not of machinery or technology transfers but rather of agricultural products such as wheat, soybeans, and fibers.[138] Chinese exports to this country in recent years consisted mainly of petroleum products and wool-cotton fabrics. Sino-American trade relations have been strained because the United States has insisted on the imposition of textile quotas. (The two nations failed to reach an agreement early in 1983 on which categories, rates, and rules should apply to Chinese textiles). The United States insisted that China be subject to import quotas in the same way as were the other Asian textile export countries, such as Hong Kong, Korea, and Taiwan. China argued, on the other hand, that textile exports to the United States constituted 35 percent of her total trade with the United States and was thus a major foreign exchange earner for China. It also argued that because the United States has had a surplus in the bilateral trade arrangements since 1979, it would only be fair to give China preferential treatment.[139] In August 1983 the United States and China initialed a five-year agreement on textiles by raising slightly the Chinese import quota. This agreement removed an irritant in the bilateral relations between the two nations.

On the educational-cultural-technological exchange front, the overall picture was very encouraging, though marred occasionally by minor irritations. The rapid growth in exchanges is highlighted in the following statistics: In 1980 more than 70,000 Americans visited China and about 10,000 Chinese came to the United States; and Chinese commercial and scientific delegations to the United States averaged nearly 130 per month by late 1980.[140] By the end of 1982, there were some 9,000 Chinese students and scholars working in research centers in every part of the United States.[141] While the Chinese placed 2,100 officially sponsored scholars in American universities, over 100 American scholars were placed in Chinese institutions for study in science and the humanities. As of 1981 fourteen scientific and technological exchange programs were in operation, ranging from agriculture and basic sciences to space technology. In the private sector, numerous educational and cultural exchanges have taken place between the two countries; these are in such areas as press and publications, performing arts, exhibits, sister cities and states (operating in twenty-two states), and sports.

The only setback to the ever-expanding educational-cultural-technological exchanges was the defection of and granting of political asylum to a nineteen-year-old Chinese tennis star, Hu Na. The American grant of political asylum to Hu Na provoked strong Chinese reaction and was viewed as evidence of "hegemonist behavior" on the part of the United States.[142]

Despite the Reagan administration's insistence to sell arms to Taiwan and to continue implementation of the Taiwan Relations Act, Sino-American relations reached a new level of cooperation in January 1984 when Chinese premier Zhao Ziyang paid an official visit to Washington at the invitation of President Reagan, who paid a return visit to China in April 1984. Zhao's visit to Washington was highlighted by the signing of several agreements in Sino-American technical and economic cooperation. One of the agreements signed, as mentioned in Chapter 8, was the United States pledge to provide the Chinese with nuclear technology and equipment for the next two decades. At a breakfast meeting on January 12 Reagan and Zhao signed another accord which extended the science and technology exchanges between the two countries for five years or to 1989. They also signed an agreement under which the United States would provide financial arrangements and studies for new industrial projects for China. However Reagan's surprising succession of Sino-American cooperation still must be viewed in the perspective of their common strategic interests to checkmate the Soviet Union.

THE SINO-JAPANESE PEACE TREATY AND TRADE RELATIONS

Although most nations view Japan as a modernized and westernized nation because of her technological and industrial capacity, the Chinese see Japan as a member of the Second World in their three-world perception. Hua Guofeng said at the Eleventh Party Congress in 1977 that China would support Second World countries, European nations and Japan, "in their struggle against control, intimidation and bullying by the superpowers."[143] The countries of the Second World, according to the Chinese, are no longer the main force that dominate and oppress the Third World countries. Instead, the countries of the Second World are subject to "interference" and "bullying" by the superpowers. China would like to form a united front with the Second World countries against this superpower hegemony. Japan, naturally, has figured prominently in China's strategy for a united front with the Second World.

Improving Sino-Japanese relations may have become the top priority in China's new independent foreign policy. In a meeting with Japanese premier Zenko Suzuki on September 28, 1982, Deng Xiaoping pointed out that Sino-Japanese relations was the first item discussed by Hu Yaobang in his report to the 1982 party congress.[144] The normalization of relations between China and Japan, from the Chinese point of view, was a "protracted struggle." In the 1950s and 1960s, Japan's official contact with China was restricted by the United States containment policy and concerns for the security of the Pacific. Furthermore, Japan politically and economically supported the Chinese Nationalists in Taiwan. The Chinese, on the other hand, used trade to lure Japanese business interests into increased contacts. Special trade agreements were awarded to selected Japanese firms on a nongovernmental basis. By the late 1950s, trade between China and Japan exceeded $100 million per year. By 1960 some 200 Japanese firms, such as Toyota Motors, Tokyo Electric, and Anzai Fertilizer Co., had a large volume of trade with China under the "friendly firms" arrangement. Under this arrangement the Chinese permitted trade only with those Japanese firms that were sympathetic to China and that accepted the principles of no hostility toward China, no support for the "two-China" policy, and no hindrance to normal relations. The Chinese limited contracts for "friendly firms" to only one year, making long-term planning impossible for the Japanese. The desire of these private "friendly firms" for long-term contracts led to the signing of the Liao-Takasaki Agreement in November 1962. Under the agreement the "friendly firms" were to receive a five-year contract, provided they adhered to the political principles mentioned above. Trade between China and Japan then soared, reaching over $300 million a year for the next several years. Then, to accelerate the trade relations, the Chinese supplemented the Liao-Takasaki Agreement with other short-term arrangements, usually one-year contracts, known as "memorandum trade."

By 1971 trade had reached $820 million a year, and pressure began to build within Japan's ruling Liberal Democratic Party for a change in Japan's policy toward China, particularly in Japan's adherence to United States policy. Visits to China by Japanese trade missions and political delegations became more frequent. Within the Liberal Democratic Party, there was increasing criticism of Japan's support for a "two-China" policy and of its loyalty to Taiwan. The Chinese intensified their drive for normalized relations with Japan. Persuasive pressure was applied on every Japanese delegation visiting China for changes in Japan's China policy. When President Nixon announced, in July 1971, that he would visit China soon (the "Nixon shock"), and the United States resolution for a two-China policy failed in the United Nations, Japan's two-China policy—advocated by Prime Minister Eisaku Sato of the ruling Liberal Democratic Party—began to collapse. At this time the Chinese mounted a propaganda campaign against the buildup of Japan's military capability. Zhou Enlai, in his lengthy interview with James Reston of *The New York Times,* expressed his concern about the development of militarism in Japan.[145] On the eve of Nixon's departure for China, the Chinese Ministry of Foreign Affairs issued a strongly worded statement criticizing the reversion of Okinawa to Japan as a fraud, because the reversion agreement included several islands claimed by China. A Chinese statement on the inclusion of the islands belonging to China in the reversion agreement revealed their feelings: "Japanese militarism and U.S. imperialism are colluding in speeding up implementation of the scheme to annex China's territory."[146] The Shanghai communiqué, which declared that Taiwan was an integral part of China and that the United States would ultimately withdraw its military complex from the island, forced the Sato government to abandon its China policy, as Gene Hsiao has pointed out.[147]

Sato's successor, Prime Minister Tanaka, lost no time in recovering from the "Nixon shock" by accepting an invitation from China to move speedily toward normalization of relations. Tanaka arrived in Beijing on September 25, 1972, and five days later a joint statement was issued which contained a nine-point agreement for terminating "the abnormal state of affairs" between the two countries. Specifically, Japan recognized the People's Republic of China as the "sole legal government of China" and Taiwan as "an inalienable part of China." Both countries agreed to the immediate establishment of full diplomatic relations and pledged not to seek hegemony in the Asia-Pacific region. The agreement also provided for conclusion of a peace treaty and negotiations for agreements on trade, navigation, aviation, and fisheries.[148] It will be recalled that the People's Republic of China was not a party to the San Francisco peace treaty, which ended the allied occupation of Japan in 1954.

One interesting development occurred soon after the signing of the Tanaka-Zhou agreement for the normalization of relations in 1972—the emergence of the "Japan formula" for continuing Japan's economic ties with Taiwan. When diplomatic relations with Taiwan were terminated, Japan's investment in the island was over $500 million and the volume of trade was at an $800 million-a-year level.[149] This economic relationship was maintained between Japan and Taiwan by a nongovernmental arrangement: The Japanese embassy and consular services in Taiwan were replaced by the Japan Interchange Association, a semiprivate, incorporated entity for coordinating economic and trade relations. The Chinese Nationalists formed the East-Asia Relations Association in Japan to conduct trade relations between the two countries. Beijing raised no objection to these arrangements. By the mid-1970s, trade between Japan and Taiwan exceeded $2.9 billion a year.[150] Trade between China and Japan also flourished after the 1972 normalization agreement, reaching $3.2 billion by 1974.[151] Hong Kim indicated that the two major factors responsible for the increased trade with China were Japan's willingness to extend the necessary credit to China, and China's need for steel, machinery, and technology.[152]

While a direct consequence of the Tanaka-Zhou agreement on normalization of relations was a flourishing trade, China and Japan remained deadlocked for almost six years over the conclusion of a treaty of friendship and peace. The slow progress in negotiations for a peace treaty was attributable to the emergence of the Soviet Union as an issue. Japan had resisted Chinese insistence that an antihegemony clause, which was essentially aimed against the Soviet Union, be included in the treaty. During this time Japan was having difficulty in her negotiations with the Soviet Union over the important issue of fishery rights, one of the many delicate problems facing the two countries. Japan was not very comfortable when China's propaganda criticized the Soviet Union for behaving like an overlord and intimidating the Japanese in the fishery negotiations over the boundaries of the 200-mile economic zone, formulated at the United Nations Law of the Seas Conference.[153] Nor was the stand taken by the Chinese, that the Soviet Union return the four northern islands off Hokkaido in the Kuril Islands to the Japanese, diplomatically welcomed. The Soviet Union had warned Japan that they opposed the antihegemony clause and had offered to have Japan join in its new "Asian security system." The deadlock over a Sino-Japanese peace treaty was broken after Japan concluded an agreement on fishery rights with the Soviet Union. To overcome Chinese insistence on and the Soviet Union's opposition to the antihegemony clause, the Japanese finally persuaded the Chinese to accept an additional clause in the treaty which would read: "The present treaty shall not affect the position of either contracting party regarding its relations with third countries." With the inclusion of this additional clause, the Japanese could tell the Soviet Union that the antihegemony clause should not be considered as anti-Soviet Union. The peace treaty between China and Japan was finally signed in Beijing on August 12, 1978 (see Appendix E). The treaty was to remain in force for ten years, during which time both countries pledged to adhere to the five principles of peaceful coexistence (respect for sovereignty and territorial integrity, mutual nonaggression, noninterference in international affairs, equal and mutual benefit, and mutual respect), to seek no hegemony in the Asia-Pacific region, to promote cultural and economic relations, and to promote the exchange of peoples.

What were the implications of the Sino-Japanese peace treaty? First, it officially ended the longstanding animosity between the two countries and opened a new chapter of equal relations between China and Japan. Second, the antihegemony clause aimed at the Soviet Union was a victory for the Chinese. With this peace treaty and the Shanghai communiqué, which also contained an antihegemony clause, China felt perhaps less isolated in a new Asian balance of power. Third, the Chinese could look forward to expanded long-term trade agreements with Japan. This was particularly important for China's long-term program of modernization, since Japan could supply a large portion of China's requirements for machinery and technology.[154] Similarly, Japan could count on China to supply needed raw materials and even light industrial goods, which were more expensive for her to produce. Fourth, conclusion of the Sino-Japanese peace treaty showed that neither the Taiwan problem nor the United States Security Treaty, originally aimed at containing possible Chinese communist expansion in Asia, was a barrier to permanent relationships based on friendship and mutual respect. Finally, Chinese flexibility and accommodation on the antihegemony issue in the peace treaty with Japan may have provided clues for strategies to normalize relations between China and the United States.[155]

During the decade following diplomatic normalization in 1972, Sino-Japanese relations have proved beneficial to both nations. For some time Japan has been China's leading trade partner. The bilateral trade between China and Japan was about $10 billion in 1981, twice the Sino-American trade in the same year. In 1982 trade declined in value to $8.8 billion.[156] Sino-Japanese trade patterns showed that China was the chief supplier of Japan's "basic clothing." Half of China's crude oil, about 8 million tons annually, also went to Japan. Under the 1978 trade agreement, China was supposed to have delivered 15 million tons annually, a target the Chinese failed to fulfill because of inefficient management of the onshore and offshore operations.[157] As mentioned in Chapter 9, China utilized the "countertrade factor"—that is, the stipulation that imported equipment and technology would be paid for by China when it sold its crude oil to Japan. In fact, Japan had been China's major supplier of the machinery and technology needed for modernization. Major projects such as the Baoshan steel complex near Shanghai, offshore oil drilling in the Yellow and South China Seas, assembly lines for auto-making, and production of television sets were all undertaken with Japan's assistance and know-how.

Japan was also one of China's major creditors. In September 1982 China and Japan signed a loan agreement of $260 million for harbor construction and railroad development.[158] In 1981 Japan extended $1.3 billion in credit to help China finance the modernization of its plants and equipment. Part of the loan would be used for completing the Baoshan steel complex and the Daqing petrochemical project.

To further cement close relations, Chinese Premier Zhao Ziyang visited Japan in June 1982. This was followed by former Japanese Premier Suzuki's trip to China in the fall to mark the tenth anniversary of the normalization of Sino-Japanese relations. While in Japan, Zhao proposed a set of principles to promote economic ties between the two countries: continued peaceful and friendly relations, equality and mutual benefit, and a lasting and stable friendship, "from generation to generation, impervious to international storms."[159] Cabinet officials of the two countries have held periodic conferences to review progress made in their relations. In their second conference, held in Tokyo in mid-December 1981, both sides agreed to seek expanded trade in oil and coal and exploration of offshore energy resources.[160] These regularized conferences served to provide channels of information exchange and trouble shooting in Sino-Japanese relations. The provisions for consultation by government officials of cabinet rank from both countries may have been prompted by China's abrupt policy shift in 1978–81, resulting in the cancelation or postponement of contractual arrangements made by Japanese firms with the Chinese. With the regularized consultations, Japan is now in a better position to be forewarned of any major changes in an otherwise not-so-stable China.

The Japanese were rather apprehensive about economic conditions in China. Many Japanese businesspeople were caught off guard in 1978–79 and were annoyed by China's unilateral decision to cancel contracts. However, their anger was abated somewhat in 1981 after China decided to compensate them for voided contracts and to make payment for supplies already delivered. (Mitsubishi Heavy Industries, which headed the group of Japanese companies that built the Baoshan steel complex, was compensated more than $40 million).[161] In their business transactions, the Chinese seemed to have struck a hard bargain with Japanese business interests. For instance, China's willingness to provide compensation for the canceled contracts was conditioned on Japan's promise to extend a credit loan that would enable it to complete its heavy industrial projects, such as the Baoshan steel complex and Daqing petrochemical plants.[162] Between 1979 and 1981, Japanese businesspersons and government officials were not so sure what China really wanted in its ambitious economic development and had doubts about China's technical skills in achieving its goals.[163] Another strain put on Sino-Japanese relations was China's fear of a possible revival of Japanese militarism. Paradoxically, China had argued earlier that Japan should rearm itself in view of the threat of Soviet military expansion in the Pacific. Hua Guofeng made a strong case to Yasushiro Nakasone, then Japan's director general for defense, that Japan must be able to defend itself.[164] Hua's press interview on his visit to Japan in June 1980 stressed Japan's right to rearm and defend itself.[165] Similar expressions were repeated by China's new foreign minister, Wu Xueqian, in a series of talks with Susumu Nikaido, special envoy of Premier Nakasone. Wu added that Japan's armed forces should be defense-oriented against external threats and that a rearmed Japan "would not constitute a threat to its friendly neighbors."[166]

Yet, in the summer of 1982, China—like many other Asian countries—complained about the intent of Japan's educational ministry to rewrite its 1983 school textbook on its World War II military invasion of China. A blistering media attack was mounted against the Japanese government for plans to downplay Japanese military atrocities in China. In protest, China postponed the planned visit of the Japanese education minister in August. Cries of Japanese military revival reverberated throughout the Chinese media. The acrimonious dispute was finally resolved after Japan promised not to revise the textbooks before 1985. Japanese school teachers were instructed by the government to refer to the 1937 attack on China as an invasion, not as an "advance."

Basically, China has supported American-Japanese security arrangements, including the rearming of Japan as a major military partner of the United States to maintain regional security. As a leading trade partner and major supplier of technology for China's modernization, Japan actively participates in China's economic development. In the long run, this may serve as the foundation for a secure and stable China and for a peaceful East Asia.[167]

In conclusion, China's perception of three worlds, its fear of the Soviet Union, the normalization in Sino-American relations, and the ratification of the peace treaty with Japan all seem to point to the development of a new international pattern in Asia and the Pacific. The region is no longer dominated by one or two powers. Now there is a new, but delicate, power balance based on four power centers: Beijing, Moscow, Tokyo, and Washington. China, because of her geographic location and large population, will hold one of the keys to the balance and future stability of the region. But, in the final analysis, the futures of both China and Japan are closely linked to their cooperation with the United States.

NOTES

1. See Allan Whiting, *China Crosses the Yalu* (Stanford, Calif.: University Press, 1960); and Trumbull Higgins, *Korea and the Fall of MacArthur* (Cambridge: Oxford University Press, 1960).

2. Daniel Tretiak, "The Chinese Cultural Revolution and Foreign Policy," *Current Scene,* vol. viii, no. 7 (April 1, 1970), 1–26; and Melvin Gurtov, "The Foreign Ministry and Foreign Affairs in the Cultural Revolution," *The China Quarterly,* 40 (October–December 1969), 65–102.

3. The Theoretical Study Group of the Ministry of Foreign Affairs, "Premier Chou Creatively Carried Out Chairman Mao's Revolutionary Line in Foreign Affairs," *Peking Review,* 5 (January 28, 1977), 15.

4. "The Cultural Revolution and the Chinese Foreign Policy," *Current Scene,* vol. vi, no. 13 (August 1, 1968), 1–15.

5. *Vietnam Triangle: Moscow, Peking, Hanoi* (New York: Pegasus, 1967).

6. Peter Van Ness, *Revolution and Chinese Foreign Policy* (Berkeley, Calif.: University of California, 1970), pp. 232–36.

7. "Premier Chou Creatively Carried Out Chairman Mao's Revolutionary Line in Foreign Affairs," p. 15.

8. *Ming Pao* (Hong Kong), September 7, 1978, p. 8.

9. "Peking and the Asian Power Balance," *Problems of Communism,* xxi (July–August 1976), 36–40.

10. Chou En-lai, "Report to the Tenth National Congress of the Communist Party of China," *Peking Review,* 35–36 (September 7, 1973), 24.

11. Chou En-lai, "Report on the Work of the Government," *Peking Review,* 4 (January 24, 1975), 24.

12. Ibid.

13. "Zhao Ziyang on China's Foreign Policy," *Beijing Review,* 18 (May 13, 1982), 6.

14. "Create a New Situation in All Fields of Socialist Modernization," pp. 29–33.

15. Ibid., p. 29.

16. "Adhere to Independent Foreign Policy," *Beijing Review,* 46 (November 15, 1982), 21.

17. Ibid., pp. 21–23.

18. See Michael Parks, "Deng's U.S. Policy Under Attack: Chinese Call for Much Harder Line," Los Angeles Times Service, as reprinted in *Honolulu Advertiser,* May 23, 1983, B-1. Also see Harry Harding, "Change and Continuity in Chinese Foreign Policy," *Problems of Communism,* xxxii (March–April 1983), 8–16 and Allan S. Whiting, "Assertive Nationalism in Chinese Foreign Policy," *Asian Survey,* 8 (August 1983), 913–931.

19. Foreign policy themes and issues are culled from the following official documents: Hu Yaobang, "Creating a New Situation in All Fields of Socialist Modernization"; "Zhao Ziyang on China's Foreign Policy"; Theoretical Group of the Ministry of Foreign Affairs, "Premier Chou Creatively Carried out Chairman Mao's Revolutionary Line in Foreign Affairs," pp. 6–15; and Huang Hua, "The International Situation and China's Foreign Policies," *Peking Review,* 40 (October 10, 1978), 12–17, 35.

20. Editorial Department of *Remin Ribao,* "Chairman Mao's Theory of the Differentiation of the Three Worlds Is a Major Contribution to Marxism-Leninism," *Peking Review,* 45 (November 4, 1977), 11.

21. "Speech By Teng Hsiao-p'ing, Chairman of Delegation of People's Republic of China," Supplement to *Peking Review,* 15 (April 12, 1974), i–ii.

22. "Create a New Situation in All Fields of Socialist Modernization," p. 31.

23. "Zhao Ziyang on China's Foreign Policy," p. 6.

24. "Premier Zhao Visits 10 African Countries," *Beijing Review,* 1 (January 3, 1983), 6–7.

25. "Premier Zhao Ziyang's Speech at Beijing South-South Conference," *Beijing Review,* 16 (April 18, 1983), i.

26. "South-South Cooperation," *Beijing Review,* 2 (January 10, 1983), 20.

27. Shen Yi, "China Belongs Forever to the Third World," *Beijing Review,* 39 (September 29, 1981), 23–25.

28. "Chairman Mao's Theory of the Differentiation of the Three Worlds," p. 11; and Hua Kuo-feng, "Political Report to the Eleventh Party Congress," p. 41.

29. Huang Hua, "The International Situation and China's Foreign Policies," *Peking Review,* 40 (October 10, 1978), 14.

30. "Political Report to the Eleventh National Congress," p. 42.

31. "Joint Communiqué," *Peking Review,* 9 (March 3, 1972), 5.

32. See Joachim Glaubitz, "Anti-Hegemony Formulas in Chinese Foreign Policy," *Asian Survey,* vol. xvi, no. 3 (March 1976), 205–15.

33. "Creating a New Situation in All Fields of Socialist Modernization," p. 31.

34. "Zhao Ziyang on China's Foreign Policy," p. 6.

35. "Creating a New Situation in All Fields of Socialist Modernization," p. 31.

36. Ibid.

37. "China Will Never Seek Hegemony," *Beijing Review,* 6 (February 7, 1983), 17.

38. Huang Hua, "The International Situation and China's Foreign Policy," p. 12.

39. Ibid., pp. 12–13; and Hua Kuo-feng, "Unite and Strive to Build a Modern, Powerful Socialist Country," pp. 40–41.

40. "Chairman Mao's Theory of the Differentiation of the Three Worlds," pp. 21, 23. Also see "History Has a Lesson to Teach," *Peking Review,* 34 (August 25, 1978), 21–22.

41. "Speech by Teng Hsiao-p'ing," p. v.

42. Huang Hua "The International Situation and China's Foreign Policy," p. 13.

43. "Third World Countries Unite Against Hegemony in Economic Sphere," *Peking Review,* 47 (November 18, 1977), 23–25.

44. Huang Hua "The International Situation and China's Foreign Policy," p. 17.

45. "Premier Zhao Ziyang's Speech at Beijing South-South Conference," p. 1.

46. "For a New International Economic Order," *Beijing Review,* 44 (November 2, 1981), 14–15.

47. Huang Hua, "Superpower Disarmament Fraud Exposed," *Peking Review,* 22 (June 2, 1978), 9.

48. Soviet Détente Fraud Exposed," *Peking Review,* 3 (January 14, 1977), 31–32.

49. Ibid., p. 32.

50. "Soviet-U.S. Nuclear Talks: An Analysis," *Peking Review,* 51 (December 16, 1977), 22. Also see "What Do Moscow-Vaunted 'Détente' and 'Disarmament' Add Up to?", *Peking Review,* 50 (December 9, 1977), 22–24.

51. "France and Germany: Voices Against Appeasement," *Peking Review,* 6 (February 10, 1978), 23–25; and "Soviet Détente Exposed," p. 32.

52. "Moscow's Dumb-Bell Strategy," *Beijing Review,* 8 (February 25, 1980), 8; and "Why the Soviet 'Détente' Smokescreen," *Beijing Review* 10 (March 10, 1980), 24–25.

53. "Expanionist Soviet Global Strategy," *Beijing Review,* 25 (June 21, 1981), 22–25; and "Some Observations on Soviet Détente," *Beijing Review,* 42 (October 18, 1982), 16–22.

54. See "Who Should Disarm First?" *Peking Review,* 24 (June 16, 1978), 25–26; "Nuclear and Conventional Armaments Must Be Reduced Simultaneously," *Peking Review,* 25 (June 23, 1978), 27–29; Huang Hua, "The International Situation and China's Foreign Policies," pp. 15–16.

55. Huang Hua, "The International Situation and China's Foreign Policies," p. 16.

56. Ibid.

57. "China's Position on Disarmament," *Beijing Review,* 25 (June 21, 1982), 15–18; and 28 (July 12, 1982), p. 11.

58. Ibid., p. 18.

59. "The UN: China's Disarmament Proposal," *Beijing Review,* 28 (July 12, 1982), 11.

60. See Alice Langley Hsieh, *Communist China's Strategy in the Nuclear Era* (Englewood Cliffs, N.J.: Prentice-Hall, Inc., 1962). Also see E. Ted Gladue, Jr., *China's Perception of Global Politics* (Washington, D.C.: University Press of America, Inc., 1982); Agatha S.Y. Wong-Fraser, "China's Nuclear Deterrent," *Current History,* vol. 80, no. 467 (September 1981), 245–49, 275; Harlan W. Jencks, "Defending China in 1982," *Current History,* vol. 81, no. 476 (September 1982), 246–50, 274; and Agnus M. Fraser, "Military Modernization in China," *Problems of Communism,* xxviii (September–December 1979), 34–49.

61. Gladue, *China's Perception of Global Politics,* pp. 65–66.

62. Ibid., and Wong-Fraser "China's Nuclear Deterrent," p. 248.

63. *Peking Review,* 42 (October 16, 1964), 2–4.

64. "Soviet-U.S. Disarmament Talks Lead Nowhere," *Beijing Review,* 48 (November 29, 1982), 11–12.

65. The figure is based on the actual Chinese claim of about 33,000 square kilometers of territory ceded under the treaties of 1860. Since 1 square kilometer equals about 0.386 square mile, it came to 12,738 square miles, or to round off, 12,700 square miles. This has been the figure the Chinese indicated to the Western and the Japanese press. All UP, UPI, and *New York Times* correspondents used the figure of 12,700 square miles in their dispatches.

66. "The Crux of the Sino-Soviet Boundary Question (1)," *Beijing Review,* 30 (July 28, 1981), 12.

67. See "The Crux of the Sino-Soviet Boundary Question (2)," *Beijing Review,* 37 (September 14, 1981), 21–23.

68. "China-USSR: The Disputed Area of the Pamirs," *Beijing Review,* 37 (September 14, 1981), 21–23.

69. See John W. Garver, "The Sino-Soviet Territorial Dispute in the Pamir Mountains Region," *The China Quarterly,* 85 (March 1981), 107–118.

70. Ibid., p. 118.

71. Ibid. Also see *Beijing Review,* 4 (January 28, 1980), 9; and Yaacov Vertzberger, "Afghanistan in China's Policy," *Problems of Communism,* xxxi (May–June, 1982), 8.

72. Vertzberger, "Afghanistan in China's Policy," p. 8.

73. Ibid., p. 10.

74. Garver, "The Sino-Soviet Territorial Dispute in the Pamir Mountains Region," p. 118.

75. "Letter of the Central Committee of the CCP of February 29, 1964, to the Central Committee of CPSU," *Peking Review,* 19 (May 8, 1964), 12–18.

76. Ibid.

77. See Thomas Robinson, "The Sino-Soviet Dispute," *The American Political Science Review,* vol. xvi, no. 4 (December 1972), 1175–1202; and Neville Maxwell, "Why the Russians Lifted the Blockade at Bear Island," *Foreign Affairs,* vol. 57, no. 1 (Fall 1978), 138–45.

78. The text of the agreement of understanding is to be found in "Real Deeds, Yes; Hollow Statements, No!", *Peking Review,* 13 (March 31, 1978), 15. Also see an interview by C.L. Sulzberger of *The New York Times* with Chou En-lai, "Chou Attacks the Soviet for Delaying Border Pact," *The New York Times,* October 29, 1973, pp. 1, 8.

79. *The New York Times,* October 29, 1973, p. 8.

80. "Real Deeds, Yes; Hollow Statements, No!", p. 14.

81. Ibid., p. 15.

82. "Political Report to the Eleventh National Congress of CCP," pp. 42–43.

83. Ibid., p. 43.

84. "Chinese Foreign Ministry's Note to the Soviet Embassy in China," *Peking Review,* 13 (March 31, 1978), 18.

85. "Protest against Soviet Military Provocation," *Peking Review,* 20 (May 19, 1978), 3–4; and "Chinese Foreign Ministry's Oral Statement to the Soviet Ambassador," *Peking Review,* 21 (May 26, 1978), 20–21.

86. "Chinese Foreign Ministry's Oral Statement," p. 21.

87. See James Reston, "Wintry Winds in Moscow," New York Times Service, as reprinted in *Honolulu Star Bulletin,* November 29, 1979, A–19. Also see Eric Bourne, "Sino-Soviet Talks Reach Impasse," *Christian Science Monitor,* as reprinted in *Honolulu Advertiser,* November 16, 1979, A–27.

88. *The New York Times,* December 12, 1979, C–7.

89. "Afghanistan: What's Moscow After," *Beijing Review,* 4 (January 28, 1980), 9.

90. See the following issues of the *Beijing Review:* 1 (January 7, 1980), 3; 4 (January 28, 1980), 9; 10 (March 10, 1980), 25; 16 (April 21, 1980), 11.

91. "Soviet Armed Forces Must Withdraw from Afghanistan," *Beijing Review,* (January 14, 1980), 8.

92. "Three Principles for Solution to Afghan Issue," *Beijing Review,* 11 (March 17, 1980), 3; and *Beijing Review,* 50 (December 12, 1982), 6–7.

93. See the following reports: Norman Kempster, "USSR Spurs U.S.-China Accord," Los Angeles Times Service, as reprinted in *Honolulu Advertiser,* January 15, 1980, A–10; Takashi Oka, "U.S.-China Ganging up Against Soviet Union," *Christian Science Monitor,* January 10, 1980, p. 1; and Jay Mathew, "U.S.-China To Aid Countries Near Afghanistan," Washington Post Service, as reprinted in *Honolulu Advertiser,* January 10, 1980, A–18.

94. "Protest Against Intrusion by Soviet Armed Personnel," *Beijing Review,* 41 (October 13, 1980), 7.

95. *The New York Times,* March 25, 1982, p. A-8.

96. "Chinese Spokesman on Brezhnev's Remarks," *Beijing Review,* 14 (April 5, 1982), 7.

97. "Creating a New Situation in All Fields of Socialist Modernization," p. 31.

98. "Sino-Soviet Relations," *Beijing Review,* 29 (July 19, 1982), 3.

99. See *The New York Times,* September 27, 1982, p. 3, and October 5, 1982, A-9; and *Christian Science Monitor,* October 4, 1982, p. 6. Also see *Time Magazine,* October 11, 1982, p. 76.

100. "Attitude on Sino-Soviet Talks," *Beijing Review,* 12 (March 21, 1983), 11-12; and *Ta Kung Pao Weekly Supplement,* April 22, 1982, p. 5.

101. "Attitude on Sino-Soviet Talks," p. 11.

102. See Stanley Karnow, "Triangular Diplomacy's Danger," Register and Tribune Syndicate, as reprinted in *Honolulu Advertiser,* December 4, 1980, A-24; Joseph Kraft, "U.S. Should Join 'Bidding Game,' " Los Angeles Syndicate, as reprinted in *Honolulu Advertiser,* November 29, 1982, A-8; and *Far Eastern Economic Review* (March 12, 1982), 36. Also see David Bonavia, "Sino-Soviet Relations: Old Game, New Moves," *Far Eastern Economic Review,* June 9, 1983, 14-15 and "Sino-Soviet Relations: A Threat From Peking," *Far Eastern Economic Review,* June 23, 1983, 13-14. For further background studies on Sino-Soviet relations, see the following books on the subject: Richard Wich, *Sino-Soviet Crisis Politics: A Study of Political Change and Communication* (Cambridge, Mass. and London: Council on East Asian Studies, Harvard University Press, 1980); Herbert J. Ellison, editor, *The Sino-Soviet Conflict: A Global Perspective* (Seattle and London: University of Washington Press, 1982); and C.G. Jacobsen, *Sino-Soviet Relations Since Mao: The Chairman's Legacy* (New York: Praeger, 1981).

103. For the text of the Joint Communiqué, see Appendix C, which is derived from *Peking Review,* 9 (March 3, 1972), 4-5.

104. Chou En-Lai, "Report on the Work of the Government," p. 24.

105. "Vice Premier Teng Hsiao-p'ing's Toast at Banquet Honoring President Ford," *Peking Review,* 49 (December 5, 1975), 8.

106. "President Ford's Toast at Farewell Banquet by President Ford," *Peking Review,* 50 (December 12, 1975), 6.

107. "Political Report to the Eleventh National Congress of the Communist Party of China," p. 42.

108. *Department of State Bulletin,* June 13, 1977, p. 625.

109. See Louis D. Boccardi, "China Says Vance's Visit Was a Setback," Associated Press release, as reprinted in *Honolulu Star-Bulletin,* September 6, 1977, A-1. Also see *Ming Pao Daily News,* (Hong Kong), September 9, 1977, p. 1; and *The New York Times,* September 9, 1977, sec. 1, p. 1.

110. "A China Policy for the Next Administration," *Foreign Affairs,* vol. 55, no. 1 (October 1976), 34-35.

111. "Military-Security Relations between China and the United States," *Foreign Affairs,* vol. 55, no. 2 (April 1977), 584-97; and *A New U.S. Policy Toward China* (Washington, D.C.: Brookings Institution, 1971), pp. 68-69.

112. "Dr. Brzezinski in Peking," *Peking Review,* 21 (May 26, 1978), 5.

113. Ibid.

114. *The New York Times,* May 28, 1978, sec. 1, pp. 1, 6.

115. "Military-Security Relations between China and the United States," pp. 584-97. Richard H. Solomon, "Thinking Through the China Problem," *Foreign Affairs,* vol. 56, no. 2 (January 1978), 341. Solomon, a former member and China expert on Kissinger's national security staff, analyzed all the major arguments in the United States that were opposed to the normalization.

116. Strobe Talbott, "The Strategic Dimension of the Sino-American Relationship," in *The China Factor: Sino-American Relations and The Global Scene,* ed. Richard Solomon (Englewood, N.J.: Prentice-Hall, 1981), p. 82.

117. Richard Solomon, "The China Factor in America's Foreign Relations: Perceptions and Policy Choices," in *The China Factor,* p. 21.

118. Talbott, "The Strategic Dimension of the Sino-American Relationship," p. 84. The strategic consideration in Sino-American normalization is clearly documented in the following: Zbigniew Brzezinski, *Power and Principle: Memoirs of the National Security Adviser, 1977-1981*

(New York: Farrar, Straus & Giroux, 1983), pp. 196–233; "President Carter's Instructions to Zbigniew Brzezinski for His Mission to China, May 17, 1978" in *Power and Principle,* Annex I, pp. 1–5; and Jimmy Carter, *Keeping Faith: Memoirs of a President* (Toronto and New York: Bantam Books, 1982), pp. 186–211.

119. Solomon, "The China Factor in America's Foreign Relations," p. 22.

120. "U.S.-China Security Relationship," in *GIST,* Bureau of Public Affairs, Department of State, July 1980.

121. See Murray Marder, "Soviets and Taiwan Tangle U.S.-China Ties," Washington Post Service, as reprinted in *Sunday Honolulu Star Bulletin and Advertiser,* June 7, 1981, B-1; and Kempster, "USSR Spurs U.S.-China Accord," A-10.

122. Kempster, "USSR Spurs US-China Accord," p. A-10.

123. *Honolulu Advertiser,* March 23, 1981, A-1.

124. Talbott, "The Strategic Dimension of the Sino-American Relationship," p. 92.

125. See Robert Sutter, "U.S. Arms Sales to Taiwan: Implications for American Interests," *Journal of Northeast Asian Studies,* vol. 1, no. 3 (September 1982), 29. Also see Doak Barnett, *U.S. Arms Sales: The China-Taiwan Tangle* (Washington, D.C.: Brookings Institution, 1980).

126. Sutter, "U.S. Arms Sales to Taiwan," pp. 33, 38.

127. Statement made by John Holdridge, Assistant Secretary of State for East Asia and Pacific Affairs, before the House Foreign Affairs Committee on August 18, 1982, is to be found in Current Policy No. 413, Bureau of Public Affairs, Department of State, August 1982, p. 4. Also see *The New York Times,* August 17, 1982, A-1, A-8.

128. *The New York Times,* August 18, 1982, A-13.

129. "The U.S. Should Strictly Observe Agreement," *Beijing Review,* 35 (August 30, 1982), 25–26.

130. *The New York Times,* August 17, 1982, A-8.

131. "Adhere to Independent Foreign Policy," p. 21.

132. Talbott, "The Strategic Dimension of the Sino-American Relationship," p. 95.

133. Ibid., p. 98.

134. Ibid., p. 98.

135. Solomon, "The China Factor in America's Foreign Relations," p. 25.

136. Talbott, "The Strategic Dimension of the Sino-American Relationship," p. 110; and Solomon, "The China Factor in America's Foreign Relations," p. 25.

137. Solomon, "The China Factor in America's Foreign Relations," p. 28. Also see John Bryant Starr, *The Future of U.S.-China Relations* (New York and London: New York University Press, 1981).

138. *China Trade Report,* September 1982, p. 7. Also see Henry J. Groen, "U.S. Firms in the PRC Trade," *China Under the Four Modernizations,* Part 2, pp. 329–67.

139. *Asiaweek,* February 25, 1983, p. 25.

140. "U.S.-PRC Exchanges," *GIST,* Bureau of Public Affairs, Department of State, March 1981.

141. See "Phenomena, Comments and Notes," *Smithsonian,* vol. 13, no. 11 (February 1983), 30.

142. See Fox Butterfield, "China Athlete Defects-The Ball's on Our Court," *The New York Times,* as reprinted in *Honolulu Star Bulletin,* March 25, 1983, B-1.

143. "Political Report to the Eleventh National Congress," p. 42.

144. *Ta Kung Pao Weekly Supplement,* September 30, 1982, p. 3.

145. "Official Transcript of Reston's Conversation with the Chinese Premier in Peking," *The New York Times,* August 10, 1971, C-14.

146. "Statement of the Ministry of Foreign Affairs of the PRC," and "Tiaoyu and Other Islands Have Been China's Territory since Ancient Times," *Peking Review,* 1 (January 7, 1972), 12–14.

147. "The Sino-Japanese Rapprochement: A Relationship of Ambivalence," in *Sino-American Détente and Its Policy Implications,* ed. Gene Hsiao (New York: Holt, Rinehart & Winston, 1974), p. 165.

148. "Joint Statement of the Government of PRC and the Government of Japan," *Peking Review,* 40 (October 6, 1972), 1–13.

149. See Hsiao, "The Sino-Japanese Rapprochement," p. 175.

150. Hong N. Kim, "Sino-Japanese Relations since the Rapprochement," *Asian Survey,* vol. xv, no. 7 (July 1975), 561.

151. Ibid., p. 561.

152. Ibid., p. 561. Also see S.H. Chou, "China's Foreign Trade," *Current History,* vol. 71, no. 419 (September 1976), 85–87.

153. "Japan-U.S.S.R. Fishery Talks: Hegemonism Goes against the Will of the People," *Peking Review,* 17 (April 22, 1977), 46, 48; "Support Japanese People's Just Struggle," *Peking Review,* 20 (May 13, 1977), 17–18; "Why Are the Fishery Overlords Satisfied?" *Peking Review,* 34 (August 19, 1977), 43–44.

154. See "Vice Premier Teng at Tokyo Press Conference: New Upsurge in Friendly Relations between China and Japan," *Peking Review,* 44 (November 3, 1978), 15.

155. During President Ford's visit to China in December 1975, the Chinese had suggested the "Japan Model" to the U.S. as an acceptable means to normalize Sino-U.S. relations. See Ron Nessen, *It Sure Looks Different from the Inside* (New York: Playboy, 1978), p. 139.

156. *Asiaweek,* February 25, 1983, p. 24. Also see Richard K. Nanto, "Sino-Japanese Economic Relations," *China Under the Four Modernizations,* Part 3, pp. 109–27.

157. *Asian Wall Street Journal Weekly,* March 2, 1981, p. 6.

158. *Ta Kung Pao Weekly Supplement,* September 30, 1982, p. 3.

159. "Three Principles for Sino-Japanese Economic Relations," *Beijing Review,* 24 (June 14, 1982), 6.

160. "Joint Press Communiqué on the Second Conference of Sino-Japanese Government Officials," *Beijing Review,* 52 (December 28, 1981), 16.

161. *Asian Wall Street Journal Weekly,* September 28, 1981, p. 10.

162. *Asian Wall Street Journal Weekly,* August 24, 1981, p. 8.

163. See Raphael Pura and Nobuko Hashimoto, "Japan Reassesses China Trade Ties," *The Asian Wall Street Journal Weekly,* June 27, 1981, p. 10.

164. Linda Mathews, "Rearm, China Tells Japan," Los Angeles Times Service, as reprinted in *Honolulu Advertiser,* May 26, 1980, A-9.

165. "Premier Hua Gives Press Conference in Tokyo," *Beijing Review,* 23 (June 9, 1980), 12.

166. "Japanese Special Envoy's Visit," *Beijing Review,* 9 (February 28, 1983), 8. For a detailed discussion on Sino-Japanese security cooperation, see William T. Tow, "Sino-Japanese Security Cooperation: Evolution and Prospects," *Pacific Affairs,* 56, 1 (January 1983), 51–83.

167. See William T. Tow, "Sino-Japanese Security Cooperation: Evolution and Prospects," *Pacific Affairs,* vol. 56, no. 1 (Spring 1983), 51–83.

The Constitution of the People's Republic of China (1982)

TABLE OF CONTENTS*

PREAMBLE

China is one of the countries with the longest histories in the world. The people of all nationalities in China have jointly created a splendid culture and have a glorious revolutionary tradition.

Feudal China was gradually reduced after 1840 to a semi-colonial and semi-feudal country. The Chinese people waged wave upon wave of heroic struggles for national independence and liberation and for democracy and freedom.

Great and earth-shaking historical changes have taken place in China in the 20th century.

The Revolution of 1911, led by Dr. Sun Yat-sen, abolished the feudal monarchy and gave birth to the Republic of China. But the Chinese people had yet to fulfill their historical task of overthrowing imperialism and feudalism.

After waging hard, protracted and tortuous struggles, armed and otherwise, the Chinese people of all nationalities led by the Communist Party of China with Chairman Mao Zedong as its leader ultimately, in 1949, overthrew the rule of imperialism, feudalism and bureaucrat-capitalism, won the great victory of the new-democratic revolution and founded the People's Republic of China. Thereupon the Chinese people took state power into their own hands and became masters of the country.

After the founding of the People's Republic, the transition of Chinese society from a new-democratic to a socialist society was effected step by step. The socialist transformation of the private ownership of the means of production was completed, the system of exploitation of man by man eliminated and the socialist system established. The people's democratic dictatorship led by the working class and based on the alliance of workers and peasants, which is in essence the dictatorship of the proletariat,

Beijing Review, 52 (December 27, 1982), 10–52. (Adopted on December 4, 1982, by the Fifth National People's Congress of the People's Republic of China at its fifth session.)

has been consolidated and developed. The Chinese people and the Chinese People's Liberation Army have thwarted aggression, sabotage and armed provocations by imperialists and hegemonists, safeguarded China's national independence and security and strengthened its national defence. Major successes have been achieved in economic development. An independent and fairly comprehensive socialist system of industry has in the main been established. There has been a marked increase in agricultural production. Significant progress has been made in educational, scientific, cultural and other undertakings, and socialist ideological education has yielded noteworthy results. The living standards of the people have improved considerably.

Both the victory of China's new-democratic revolution and the successes of its socialist cause have been achieved by the Chinese people of all nationalities under the leadership of the Communist Party of China and the guidance of Marxism-Leninism and Mao Zedong Thought, and by upholding truth, correcting errors and overcoming numerous difficulties and hardships. The basic task of the nation in the years to come is to concentrate its effort on socialist modernization. Under the leadership of the Communist Party of China and the guidance of Marxism-Leninism and Mao Zedong Thought, the Chinese people of all nationalities will continue to adhere to the people's democratic dictatorship and follow the socialist road, steadily improve socialist institutions, develop socialist democracy, improve the socialist legal system and work hard and self-reliantly to modernize industry, agriculture, national defence and science and technology step by step to turn China into a socialist country with a high level of culture and democracy.

The exploiting classes as such have been eliminated in our country. However, class struggle will continue to exist within certain limits for a long time to come. The Chinese people must fight against those forces and elements, both at home and abroad, that are hostile to China's socialist system and try to undermine it.

Taiwan is part of the sacred territory of the People's Republic of China. It is the lofty duty of the entire Chinese people, including our compatriots in Taiwan, to accomplish the great task of reunifying the motherland.

In building socialism it is imperative to rely on the workers, peasants and intellectuals and unite with all the forces that can be united. In the long years of revolution and construction, there has been formed under the leadership of the Communist Party of China a broad patriotic united front that is composed of democratic parties and people's organizations and embraces all socialist working people, all patriots who support socialism and all patriots who stand for reunification of the motherland. This united front will continue to be consolidated and developed. The Chinese People's Political Consultative Conference is a broadly representative organization of the united front, which has played a significant historical role and will continue to do so in the political and social life of the country, in promoting friendship with the people of other countries and in the strugle for socialist modernization and for the reunification and unity of the country.

The People's Republic of China is a unitary multinational state built up jointly by the people of all its nationalities. Socialist relations of equality, unity and mutual assistance have been established among them and will continue to be strengthened. In the struggle to safeguard the unity of the nationalities, it is necessary to combat big-nation chauvinism, mainly Han chauvinism, and also necessary to combat local-national chauvinism. The state does its utmost to promote the common prosperity of all nationalities in the country.

China's achievements in revolution and construction are inseparable from support by the people of the world. The future of China is closely linked with that of the whole world. China adheres to an independent foreign policy as well as to the five principles of mutual respect for sovereignty and territorial integrity, mutual non-aggression, non-interference in each other's internal affairs, equality and mutual benefit, and peaceful coexistence in developing diplomatic relations and economic and cultural exchanges with other countries; China consistently opposes imperialism, hegemonism and colonialism, works to strengthen unity with the people of other countries, supports the oppressed nations and the developing countries in their just struggle to win and preserve national independence and develop their national economies, and strives to safeguard world peace and promote the cause of human progress.

This Constitution affirms the achievements of the struggles of the Chinese people of all nationalities and defines the basic system and basic tasks of the state in legal form; it is the fundamental law of the state and has supreme legal authority. The people of all nationalities, all state organs, the armed forces, all political parties and public organizations and all enterprises and undertakings in the country must take the Constitution as the basic norm of conduct, and they have the duty to uphold the dignity of the Constitution and ensure its implementation.

CHAPTER ONE
GENERAL PRINCIPLES

Article 1   The People's Republic of China is a socialist state under the people's democratic dictatorship led by the working class and based on the alliance of workers and peasants.

The socialist system is the basic system of the People's Republic of China. Sabotage of the socialist system by any organization or individual is prohibited.

Article 2   All power in the People's Republic of China belongs to the people.

The organs through which the people exercise state power are the National People's Congress and the local people's congresses at different levels.

The people administer state affairs and manage economic, cultural and social affairs through various channels and in various ways in accordance with the law.

Article 3   The state organs of the People's Republic of China apply the principle of democratic centralism.

The National People's Congress and the local people's congresses at different levels are instituted through democratic election. They are responsible to the people and subject to their supervision.

All administrative, judicial and procuratorial organs of the state are created by the people's congresses to which they are responsible and under whose supervision they operate.

The division of functions and powers between the central and local state organs is guided by the principle of giving full play to the initiative and enthusiasm of the local authorities under the unified leadership of the central authorities.

Article 4   All nationalities in the People's Republic of China are equal. The state protects the lawful rights and interests of the minority nationalities and upholds and develops the relationship of equality, unity and mutual assistance among all of China's nationalities. Discrimination against and oppression of any nationality are prohibited; any acts that undermine the unity of the nationalities or instigate their secession are prohibited.

The state helps the areas inhabited by minority nationalities speed up their economic and cultural development in accordance with the peculiarities and needs of the different minority nationalities.

Regional autonomy is practised in areas where people of minority nationalities live in compact communities; in these areas organs of self-government are established for the exercise of the right of autonomy. All the national autonomous areas are inalienable parts of the People's Republic of China.

The people of all nationalities have the freedom to use and develop their own spoken and written languages, and to preserve or reform their own ways and customs.

Article 5   The state upholds the uniformity and dignity of the socialist legal system.

No law or administrative or local rules and regulations shall contravene the Constitution.

All state organs, the armed forces, all political parties and public organizations and all enterprises and undertakings must abide by the Constitution and the law. All acts in violation of the Constitution and the law must be looked into.

No organization or individual may enjoy the privilege of being above the Constitution and the law.

Article 6   The basis of the socialist economic system of the People's Republic of China is socialist public ownership of the means of production, namely, ownership by the whole people and collective ownership by the working people.

The system of socialist public ownership supersedes the system of exploitation of man by man; it applies the principle of "from each according to his ability, to each according to his work."

Article 7   The state economy is the sector of socialist economy under ownership by the whole people; it is the leading force in the national economy. The state ensures the consolidation and growth of the state economy.

Article 8   Rural people's communes, agricultural producers' co-operatives, and other forms of co-operative economy such as producers', supply and marketing, credit and consumers' co-operatives, belong to the sector of socialist economy under collective ownership by the working people. Working people who are members of rural economic collectives have the right, within the limits prescribed by law, to farm private plots of cropland and hilly land, engage in household sideline production and raise privately owned livestock.

The various forms of co-operative economy in the cities and towns, such as those in the handicraft, industrial, building, transport, commercial and service trades, all belong to the sector of socialist economy under collective ownership by the working people.

The state protects the lawful rights and interests of the urban and rural economic collectives and encourages, guides and helps the growth of the collective economy.

Article 9   Mineral resources, waters, forests, mountains, grassland, unreclaimed land, beaches and other natural resources are owned by the state, that is, by the whole people, with the exception of the forests, mountains, grassland, unreclaimed land and beaches that are owned by collectives in accordance with the law.

The state ensures the rational use of natural resources and protects rare animals and plants. The appropriation or damage of natural resources by any organization or individual by whatever means is prohibited.

Article 10   Land in the cities is owned by the state.

Land in the rural and suburban areas is owned by collectives except for those portions which belong to the state in accordance with the law; house sites and private plots of cropland and hilly land are also owned by collectives.

The state may in the public interest take over land for its use in accordance with the law.

No organization or individual may appropriate, buy, sell or lease land, or unlawfully transfer land in other ways.

All organizations and individuals who use land must make rational use of the land.

Article 11 The individual economy of urban and rural working people, operated within the limits prescribed by law, is a complement to the socialist public economy. The state protects the lawful rights and interests of the individual economy.

The state guides, helps and supervises the individual economy by exercising administrative control.

Article 12 Socialist public property is sacred and inviolable.

The state protects socialist public property. Appropriation or damage of state or collective property by any organization or individual by whatever means is prohibited.

Article 13 The state protects the right of citizens to own lawfully earned income, savings, houses and other lawful property.

The state protects by law the right of citizens to inherit private property.

Article 14 The state continuously raises labour productivity, improves economic results and develops the productive forces by enhancing the enthusiasm of the working people, raising the level of their technical skill, disseminating advanced science and technology, improving the systems of economic administration and enterprise operation and management, instituting the socialist system of responsibility in various forms and improving organization of work.

The state practises strict economy and combats waste.

The state properly apportions accumulation and consumption, pays attention to the interests of the collective and the individual as well as of the state and, on the basis of expanded production, gradually improves the material and cultural life of the people.

Article 15 The state practises economic planning on the basis of socialist public ownership. It ensures the proportionate and co-ordinated growth of the national economy through overall balancing by economic planning and the supplementary role of regulation by the market.

Disturbance of the orderly functioning of the social economy or disruption of the state economic plan by any organization or individual is prohibited.

Article 16 State enterprises have decision-making power in operation and management within the limits prescribed by law, on condition that they submit to unified leadership by the state and fulfil all their obligations under the state plan.

State enterprises practise democratic management through congresses of workers and staff and in other ways in accordance with the law.

Article 17 Collective economic organizations have decision-making power in conducting independent economic activities, on condition that they accept the guidance of the state plan and abide by the relevant laws.

Collective economic organizations practise democratic management in accordance with the law, with the entire body of their workers electing or removing their managerial personnel and deciding on major issues concerning operation and management.

Article 18   The People's Republic of China permits foreign enterprises, other foreign economic organizations and individual foreigners to invest in China and to enter into various forms of economic co-operation with Chinese enterprises and other economic organizations in accordance with the law of the People's Republic of China.

All foreign enterprises and other foreign economic organizations in China, as well as joint ventures with Chinese and foreign investment located in China, shall abide by the law of the People's Republic of China. Their lawful rights and interests are protected by the law of the People's Republic of China.

Article 19   The state develops socialist educational undertakings and works to raise the scientific and cultural level of the whole nation.

The state runs schools of various types, makes primary education compulsory and universal, develops secondary, vocational and higher education and promotes pre-school education.

The state develops educational facilities of various types in order to wipe out illiteracy and provide political, cultural, scientific, technical and professional education for workers, peasants, state functionaries and other working people. It encourages people to become educated through self-study.

The state encourages the collective economic organizations, state enterprises and undertakings and other social forces to set up educational institutions of various types in accordance with the law.

The state promotes the nationwide use of *Putonghua* (Common Speech based on Beijing pronunciation).

Article 20   The state promotes the development of the natural and social sciences, disseminates scientific and technical knowledge, and commends and rewards achievements in scientific research as well as technological discoveries and inventions.

Article 21   The state develops medical and health services, promotes modern medicine and traditional Chinese medicine, encourages and supports the setting up of various medical and health facilities by the rural economic collectives, state enterprises and undertakings and neighbourhood organizations, and promotes sanitation activities of a mass character, all to protect the people's health.

The state develops physical culture and promotes mass sports activities to build up the people's physique.

Article 22   The state promotes the development of literature and art, the press, broadcasting and television undertakings, publishing and distribution services, libraries, museums, cultural centres and other cultural undertakings, that serve the people and socialism, and sponsors mass cultural activities.

The state protects places of scenic and historical interest, valuable cultural monuments and relics and other important items of China's historical and cultural heritage.

Article 23   The state trains specialized personnel in all fields who serve socialism, increases the number of intellectuals and creates conditions to give full scope to their role in socialist modernization.

Article 24   The state strengthens the building of socialist spiritual civilization through spreading education in high ideals and morality, general education and education in discipline and the legal system, and through promoting the formulation and observance of rules of conduct and common pledges by different sections of the people in urban and rural areas.

The state advocates the civic virtues of love for the motherland, for the people, for labour, for science and for socialism; it educates the people in patriotism, collectivism, internationalism and communism and in dialectical and historical materialism; it combats capitalist, feudalist and other decadent ideas.

Article 25   The state promotes family planning so that population growth may fit the plans for economic and social development.

Article 26   The state protects and improves the living environment and the ecological environment, and prevents and remedies pollution and other public hazards.

The state organizes and encourages afforestation and the protection of forests.

Article 27   All state organs carry out the principle of simple and efficient administration, the system of responsibility for work and the system of training functionaries and appraising their work in order to constantly improve quality of work and efficiency and combat bureaucratism.

All state organs and functionaries must rely on the support of the people, keep in close touch with them, heed their opinions and suggestions, accept their supervision and work hard to serve them.

Article 28   The state maintains public order and suppresses treasonable and other counter-revolutionary activities; it penalizes actions that endanger public security and disrupt the socialist economy and other criminal activities, and punishes and reforms criminals.

Article 29   The armed forces of the People's Republic of China belong to the people. Their tasks are to strengthen national defence, resist aggression, defend the motherland, safeguard the people's peaceful labour, participate in national reconstruction, and work hard to serve the people.

The state strengthens the revolutionization, modernization and regularization of the armed forces in order to increase the national defence capability.

Article 30   The administrative division of the People's Republic of China is as follows:

(1)   The country is divided into provinces, autonomous regions and municipalities directly under the Central Government;

(2)   Provinces and autonomous regions are divided into autonomous prefectures, counties, autonomous counties and cities;

(3)   Counties and autonomous counties are divided into townships, nationality townships and towns.

Municipalities directly under the Central Government and other large cities are divided into districts and counties. Autonomous prefectures are divided into counties, autonomous counties, and cities.

All autonomous regions, autonomous prefectures and autonomous counties are national autonomous areas.

Article 31   The state may establish special administrative regions when necessary. The systems to be instituted in special administrative regions shall be prescribed by law enacted by the National People's Congress in the light of the specific conditions.

Article 32   The People's Republic of China protects the lawful rights and interests of foreigners within Chinese territory, and while on Chinese territory foreigners must abide by the law of the People's Republic of China.

The People's Republic of China may grant asylum to foreigners who request it for political reasons.

CHAPTER TWO
THE FUNDAMENTAL RIGHTS
AND DUTIES OF CITIZENS

Article 33   All persons holding the nationality of the People's Republic of China are citizens of the People's Republic of China.

All citizens of the People's Republic of China are equal before the law.

Every citizen enjoys the rights and at the same time must perform the duties prescribed by the Constitution and the law.

Article 34   All citizens of the People's Republic of China who have reached the age of 18 have the right to vote and stand for election, regardless of nationality, race, sex, occupation, family background, religious belief, education, property status, or length of residence, except persons deprived of political rights according to law.

Article 35   Citizens of the People's Republic of China enjoy freedom of speech, of the press, of assembly, of association, of procession, and of demonstration.

Article 36   Citizens of the People's Republic of China enjoy freedom of religious belief.

No state organ, public organization or individual may compel citizens to believe in, or not to believe in, any religion; nor may they discriminate against citizens who believe in, or do not believe in, any religion.

The state protects normal religious activities. No one may make use of religion to engage in activities that disrupt public order, impair the health of citizens or interfere with the educational system of the state.

Religious bodies and religious affairs are not subject to any foreign domination.

Article 37   The freedom of person of citizens of the People's Republic of China is inviolable.

No citizen may be arrested except with the approval or by decision of a people's procuratorate or by decision of a people's court, and arrests must be made by a public security organ.

Unlawful deprivation or restriction of citizens' freedom of person by detention or other means is prohibited; and unlawful search of the person of citizens is prohibited.

Article 38   The personal dignity of citizens of the People's Republic of China is inviolable. Insult, libel, false charge or frame-up directed against citizens by any means is prohibited.

Article 39   The home of citizens of the People's Republic of China is inviolable. Unlawful search of, or intrusion into, a citizen's home is prohibited.

Article 40   The freedom and privacy of correspondence of citizens of the People's Republic of China are protected by law. No organization or individual may, on any ground, infringe upon the freedom and privacy of citizens' correspondence except in cases where, to meet the needs of state security or of investigation into criminal offences, public security or procuratorial organs are permitted to censor correspondence in accordance with procedures prescribed by law.

Article 41   Citizens of the People's Republic of China have the right to criticize and make suggestions to any state organ or functionary. Citizens have the right to make to relevant state organs complaints and charges against, or exposures of, violation of the law or dereliction of duty by any state organ or functionary; but fabrication or distortion of facts with the intention of libel or frame-up is prohibited.

In case of complaints, charges or exposures made by citizens, the state organ concerned must deal with them in a responsible manner after ascertaining the facts. No one may suppress such complaints, charges and exposures, or retaliate against the citizens making them.

Citizens who have suffered losses through infringement of their civic rights by any state organ or functionary have the right to compensation in accordance with the law.

Article 42   Citizens of the People's Republic of China have the right as well as the duty to work.

Using various channels, the state creates conditions for employment, strengthens labour protection, improves working conditions and, on the basis of expanded production, increases remuneration for work and social benefits.

Work is the glorious duty of every able-bodied citizen. All working people in state enterprises and in urban and rural economic collectives should perform their tasks with an attitude consonant with their status as masters of the country. The state promotes socialist labour emulation, and commends and rewards model and advanced workers. The state encourages citizens to take part in voluntary labour.

The state provides necessary vocational training to citizens before they are employed.

Article 43   Working people in the People's Republic of China have the right to rest.

The state expands facilities for rest and recuperation of working people, and prescribes working hours and vacations for workers and staff.

Article 44   The state prescribes by law the system of retirement for workers and staff in enterprises and undertakings and for functionaries of organs of state. The livelihood of retired personnel is ensured by the state and society.

Article 45   Citizens of the People's Republic of China have the right to material assistance from the state and society when they are old, ill or disabled. The state develops the social insurance, social relief and medical and health services that are required to enable citizens to enjoy this right.

The state and society ensure the livelihood of disabled members of the armed forces, provide pensions to the families of martyrs and give preferential treatment to the families of military personnel.

The state and society help make arrangements for the work, livelihood and education of the blind, deaf-mute and other handicapped citizens.

Article 46   Citizens of the People's Republic of China have the duty as well as the right to receive education.

The state promotes the all-round moral, intellectual and physical development of children and young people.

Article 47   Citizens of the People's Republic of China have the freedom to engage in scientific research, literary and artistic creation and other cultural pursuits. The state encourages and assists creative endeavours conducive to the interests of the people that are made by citizens engaged in education, science, technology, literature, art and other cultural work.

Article 48   Women in the People's Republic of China enjoy equal rights with men in all spheres of life, political, economic, cultural and social, including family life.

The state protects the rights and interests of women, applies the principle of equal pay for equal work for men and women alike and trains and selects cadres from among women.

Article 49   Marriage, the family and mother and child are protected by the state.

Both husband and wife have the duty to practise family planning.

Parents have the duty to rear and educate their minor children, and children who have come of age have the duty to support and assist their parents.

Violation of the freedom of marriage is prohibited. Maltreatment of old people, women and children is prohibited.

Article 50   The People's Republic of China protects the legitimate rights and interests of Chinese nationals residing abroad and protects the lawful rights and interests of returned overseas Chinese and of the family members of Chinese nationals residing abroad.

Article 51   The exercise by citizens of the People's Republic of China of their freedoms and rights may not infringe upon the interests of the state, of society and of the collective, or upon the lawful freedoms and rights of other citizens.

Article 52   It is the duty of citizens of the People's Republic of China to safeguard the unity of the country and the unity of all its nationalities.

Article 53   Citizens of the People's Republic of China must abide by the Constitution and the law, keep state secrets, protect public property and observe labour discipline and public order and respect social ethics.

Article 54   It is the duty of citizens of the People's Republic of China to safeguard the security, honour and interests of the motherland; they must not commit acts detrimental to the security, honour and interests of the motherland.

Article 55   It is the sacred obligation of every citizen of the People's Republic of China to defend the motherland and resist aggression.

It is the honourable duty of citizens of the People's Republic of China to perform military service and join the militia in accordance with the law.

Article 56   It is the duty of citizens of the People's Republic of China to pay taxes in accordance with the law.

CHAPTER THREE
THE STRUCTURE
OF THE STATE

Section I
The National People's
Congress

Article 57   The National People's Congress of the People's Republic of China is the highest organ of state power. Its permanent body is the Standing Committee of the National People's Congress.

Article 58 The National People's Congress and its Standing Committee exercise the legislative power of the state.

Article 59 The National People's Congress is composed of deputies elected by the provinces, autonomous regions and municipalities directly under the Central Government, and by the armed forces. All the minority nationalities are entitled to appropriate representation.

Election of deputies to the National People's Congress is conducted by the Standing Committee of the National People's Congress.

The number of deputies to the National People's Congress and the manner of their election are prescribed by law.

Article 60 The National People's Congress is elected for a term of five years.

Two months before the expiration of the term of office of a National People's Congress, its Standing Committee must ensure that the election of deputies to the succeeding National People's Congress is completed. Should exceptional circumstances prevent such an election, it may be postponed by decision of a majority vote of more than two-thirds of all those on the Standing Committee of the incumbent National People's Congress, and the term of office of the incumbent National People's Congress may be extended. The election of deputies to the succeeding National People's Congress must be completed within one year after the termination of such exceptional circumstances.

Article 61 The National People's Congress meets in session once a year and is convened by its Standing Committee. A session of the National People's Congress may be convened at any time the Standing Committee deems this necessary, or when more than one-fifth of the deputies to the National People's Congress so propose.

When the National People's Congress meets, it elects a presidium to conduct its session.

Article 62 The National People's Congress exercises the following functions and powers:

(1) to amend the Constitution;

(2) to supervise the enforcement of the Constitution;

(3) to enact and amend basic statutes concerning criminal offences, civil affairs, the state organs and other matters;

(4) to elect the President and the Vice-President of the People's Republic of China;*

(5) to decide on the choice of the Premier of the State Council upon nomination by the President of the People's Republic of China, and to decide on the choice of the Vice-Premiers, State Councillors, Ministers in charge of ministries or commissions and the Auditor-General and the Secretary-General of the State Council upon nomination by the Premier;

(6) to elect the Chairman of the Central Military Commission and, upon his nomination, to decide on the choice of all the others on the Central Military Commission;

(7) to elect the President of the Supreme People's Court;

(8) to elect the Procurator-General of the Supreme People's Procuratorate;

(9) to examine and approve the plan for national economic and social development and the reports on its implementation;

---

*Previously translated as Chairman and Vice-Chairman of the People's Republic of China .—*Tr.*

(10) to examine and approve the state budget and the report on its implementation;

(11) to alter or annul inappropriate decisions of the Standing Committee of the National People's Congress;

(12) to approve the establishment of provinces, autonomous regions, and municipalities directly under the Central Government;

(13) to decide on the establishment of special administrative regions and the systems to be instituted there;

(14) to decide on questions of war and peace; and

(15) to exercise such other functions and powers as the highest organ of state power should exercise.

Article 63 The National People's Congress has the power to recall or remove from office the following persons:

(1) the President and the Vice-President of the People's Republic of China;

(2) the Premier, Vice-Premiers, State Councillors, Ministers in charge of ministries or commissions and the Auditor-General and the Secretary-General of the State Council;

(3) the Chairman of the Central Military Commission; and others on the Commission;

(4) the President of the Supreme People's Court; and

(5) the Procurator-General of the Supreme People's Procuratorate.

Article 64 Amendments to the Constitution are to be proposed by the Standing Committee of the National People's Congress or by more than one-fifth of the deputies to the National People's Congress and adopted by a majority vote of more than two-thirds of all the deputies to the Congress.

Statutes and resolutions are adopted by a majority vote of more than one half of all the deputies to the National People's Congress.

Article 65 The Standing Committee of the National People's Congress is composed of the following:

the Chairman;

the Vice-Chairmen;

the Secretary-General; and

members.

Minority nationalities are entitled to appropriate representation on the Standing Committee of the National People's Congress.

The National People's Congress elects, and has the power to recall, all those on its Standing Committee.

No one on the Standing Committee of the National People's Congress shall hold any post in any of the administrative, judicial or procuratorial organs of the state.

Article 66 The Standing Committee of the National People's Congress is elected for the same term as the National People's Congress; it exercises its functions and powers until a new Standing Committee is elected by the succeeding National People's Congress.

The Chairman and Vice-Chairmen of the Standing Committee shall serve no more than two consecutive terms.

Article 67 The Standing Committee of the National People's Congress exercises the following functions and powers:

(1)   to interpret the Constitution and supervise its enforcement;

(2)   to enact and amend statutes with the exception of those which should be enacted by the National People's Congress;

(3)   to enact, when the National People's Congress is not in session, partial supplements and amendments to statutes enacted by the National People's Congress provided that they do not contravene the basic principles of these statutes;

(4)   to interpret statutes;

(5)   to examine and approve, when the National People's Congress is not in session, partial adjustments to the plan for national economic and social development and to the state budget that prove necessary in the course of their implementation;

(6)   to supervise the work of the State Council, the Central Military Commission, the Supreme People's Court and the Supreme People's Procuratorate;

(7)   to annul those administrative rules and regulations, decisions or orders of the State Council that contravene the Constitution or the statutes;

(8)   to annul those local regulations or decisions of the organs of state power of provinces, autonomous regions and municipalities directly under the Central Government that contravene the Constitution, the statutes or the administrative rules and regulations;

(9)   to decide, when the National People's Congress is not in session, on the choice of Ministers in charge of ministries or commissions or the Auditor-General and the Secretary-General of the State Council upon nomination by the Premier of the State Council;

(10)   to decide, upon nomination by the Chairman of the Central Military Commission, on the choice of others on the Commission, when the National People's Congress is not in session.

(11)   to appoint and remove the Vice-Presidents and judges of the Supreme People's Court, members of its Judicial Committee and the President of the Military Court at the suggestion of the President of the Supreme People's Court;

(12)   to appoint and remove the Deputy Procurators-General and procurators of the Supreme People's Procuratorate, members of its Procuratorial Committee and the Chief Procurator of the Military Procuratorate at the request of the Procurator-General of the Supreme People's Procuratorate, and to approve the appointment and removal of the chief procurators of the people's procuratorates of provinces, autonomous regions and municipalities directly under the Central Government;

(13)   to decide on the appointment and recall of plenipotentiary representatives abroad;

(14)   to decide on the ratification and abrogation of treaties and important agreements concluded with foreign states;

(15)   to institute systems of titles and ranks for military and diplomatic personnel and of other specific titles and ranks;

(16)   to institute state medals and titles of honour and decide on their conferment;

(17)   to decide on the granting of special pardons;

(18)   to decide, when the National People's Congress is not in session, on the proclamation of a state of war in the event of an armed attack on the country or in fulfillment of international treaty obligations concerning common defence against aggression;

(19)   to decide on general mobilization or partial mobilization;

(20)   to decide on the enforcement of martial law throughout the country or in particular provinces, autonomous regions or municipalities directly under the Central Government; and

(21)   to exercise such other functions and powers as the National People's Congress may assign to it.

Article 68　The Chairman of the Standing Committee of the National People's Congress presides over the work of the Standing Committee and convenes its meetings. The Vice-Chairmen and the Secretary-General assist the Chairman in his work.

Chairmanship meetings with the participation of the Chairman, Vice-Chairmen and Secretary-General handle the important day-to-day work of the Standing Committee of the National People's Congress.

Article 69　The Standing Committee of the National People's Congress is responsible to the National People's Congress and reports on its work to the Congress.

Article 70　The National People's Congress establishes a Nationalities Committee, a Law Committee, a Finance and Economic Committee, an Education, Science, Culture and Public Health Committee, a Foreign Affairs Committee, an Overseas Chinese Committee and such other special committees as are necessary. These special committees work under the direction of the Standing Committee of the National People's Congress when the Congress is not in session.

The special committees examine, discuss and draw up relevant bills and draft resolutions under the direction of the National People's Congress and its Standing Committee.

Article 71　The National People's Congress and its Standing Committee may, when they deem it necessary, appoint committees of inquiry into specific questions and adopt relevant resolutions in the light of their reports.

All organs of state, public organizations and citizens concerned are obliged to supply the necessary information to those committees of inquiry when they conduct investigations.

Article 72　Deputies to the National People's Congress and all those on its Standing Committee have the right, in accordance with procedures prescribed by law, to submit bills and proposals within the scope of the respective functions and powers of the National People's Congress and its Standing Committee.

Article 73　Deputies to the National People's Congress during its sessions, and all those on its Standing Committee during its meetings, have the right to address questions, in accordance with procedures prescribed by law, to the State Council or the ministries and commissions under the State Council, which must answer the questions in a responsible manner.

Article 74　No deputy to the National People's Congress may be arrested or placed on criminal trial without the consent of the Presidium of the current session of the National People's Congress or, when the National People's Congress is not in session, without the consent of its Standing Committee.

Article 75　Deputies to the National People's Congress may not be called to legal account for their speeches or votes at its meetings.

Article 76　Deputies to the National People's Congress must play an exemplary role in abiding by the Constitution and the law and keeping state secrets and, in production and other work and their public activities, assist in the enforcement of the Constitution and the law.

Deputies to the National People's Congress should maintain close contact with the units which elected them and with the people, listen to and convey the opinions and demands of the people and work hard to serve them.

Article 77   Deputies to the National People's Congress are subject to the supervision of the units which elected them. The electoral units have the power, through procedures prescribed by law, to recall the deputies whom they elected.

Article 78   The organization and working procedures of the National People's Congress and its Standing Committee are prescribed by law.

Section II
The President of the People's
Republic Of China

Article 79   The President and Vice-President of the People's Republic of China are elected by the National People's Congress.

Citizens of the People's Republic of China who have the right to vote and to stand for election and who have reached the age of 45 are eligible for election as President or Vice-President of the People's Republic of China. The term of office of the President and Vice-President of the People's Republic of China is the same as that of the National People's Congress, and they shall serve no more than two consecutive terms.

Article 80   The President of the People's Republic of China, in pursuance of decisions of the National People's Congress and its Standing Committee, promulgates statutes; appoints and removes the Premier, Vice-Premiers, State Councillors, Ministers in charge of ministries or commissions, and the Auditor-General and the Secretary-General of the State Council; confers state medals and titles of honour; issues orders of special pardons; proclaims martial law; proclaims a state of war; and issues mobilization orders.

Article 81   The President of the People's Republic of China receives foreign diplomatic representatives on behalf of the People's Republic of China and, in pursuance of decisions of the Standing Committee of the National People's Congress, appoints and recalls plenipotentiary representatives abroad, and ratifies and abrogates treaties and important agreements concluded with foreign states.

Article 82   The Vice-President of the People's Republic of China assists the President in his work.

The Vice-President of the People's Republic of China may exercise such parts of the functions and powers of the President as the President may entrust to him.

Article 83   The President and Vice-President of the People's Republic of China exercise their functions and powers until the new President and Vice-President elected by the succeeding National People's Congress assume office.

Article 84   In case the office of the President of the People's Republic of China falls facant, the Vice-President succeeds to the office of President.

In case the office of the Vice-President of the People's Republic of China falls vacant, the National People's Congress shall elect a new Vice-President to fill the vacancy.

In the event that the offices of both the President and the Vice-President of the People's Republic of China fall vacant, the National People's Congress shall elect a new President and a new Vice-President. Prior to such election, the Chairman of the Standing Committee of the National People's Congress shall temporarily act as the President of the People's Republic of China.

Section III
The State Council

Article 85   The State Council, that is, the Central People's Government, of the People's Republic of China is the executive body of the highest organ of state power; it is the highest organ of state administration.

Article 86   The State Council is composed of the following:

the Premier;

the Vice-Premiers;

the State Councillors;

the Ministers in charge of ministries;

the Ministers in charge of commissions;

the Auditor-General; and

the Secretary-General.

The Premier has overall responsibility for the State Council. The ministers have overall responsibility for the respective ministries or commissions under their charge.

The organization of the State Council is prescribed by law.

Article 87   The term of office of the State Council is the same as that of the National People's Congress.

The Premier, Vice-Premiers and State Councillors shall serve no more than two consecutive terms.

Article 88   The Premier directs the work of the State Council. The Vice-Premiers and State Councillors assist the Premier in his work.

Executive meetings of the State Council are composed of the Premier, the Vice-Premiers, the State Councillors and the Secretary-General of the State Council.

The Premier convenes and presides over the executive meetings and plenary meetings of the State Council.

Article 89   The State Council exercises the following functions and powers:

(1)   to adopt administrative measures, enact administrative rules and regulations and issue decisions and orders in accordance with the Constitution and the statutes;

(2)   to submit proposals to the National People's Congress or its Standing Committee;

(3)   to lay down the tasks and responsibilities of the ministries and commissions of the State Council, to exercise unified leadership over the work of the ministries and commissions and to direct all other administrative work of a national character that does not fall within the jurisdiction of the ministries and commissions;

(4)   to exercise unified leadership over the work of local organs of state administration at different levels throughout the country, and to lay down the detailed division of functions and powers between the Central Government and the organs of state administration of provinces, autonomous regions and municipalities directly under the Central Government;

(5)   to draw up and implement the plan for national economic and social development and the state budget;

(6)   to direct and administer economic work and urban and rural development;

(7)   to direct and administer the work concerning education, science, culture, public health, physical culture and family planning;

(8)   to direct and administer the work concerning civil affairs, public security, judicial administration, supervision and other related matters;

(9)   to conduct foreign affairs and conclude treaties and agreements with foreign states;

(10)   to direct and administer the building of national defence;

(11)   to direct and administer affairs concerning the nationalities, and to safeguard the equal rights of minority nationalities and the right of autonomy of the national autonomous areas;

(12)   to protect the legitimate rights and interests of Chinese nationals residing abroad and protect the lawful rights and interests of returned overseas Chinese and of the family members of Chinese nationals residing abroad;

(13)   to alter or annul inappropriate orders, directives and regulations issued by the ministries or commissions;

(14)   to alter or annul inappropriate decisions and orders issued by local organs of state administration at different levels;

(15)   to approve the geographic division of provinces, autonomous regions and municipalities directly under the Central Government, and to approve the establishment and geographic division of autonomous prefectures, counties, autonomous counties and cities;

(16)   to decide on the enforcement of martial law in parts of provinces, autonomous regions and municipalities directly under the Central Government;

(17)   to examine and decide on the size of administrative organs and, in accordance with the law, to appoint, remove and train administrative officers, appraise their work and reward or punish them; and

(18)   to exercise such other functions and powers as the National People's Congress or its Standing Committee may assign it.

Article 90   The Ministers in charge of ministries or commissions of the State Council are responsible for the work of their respective departments and convene and preside over their ministerial meetings or commission meetings that discuss and decide on major issues in the work of their respective departments.

The ministries and commissions issue orders, directives and regulations within the jurisdiction of their respective departments and in accordance with the statutes and the administrative rules and regulations, decisions and orders issued by the State Council.

Article 91   The State Council establishes an auditing body to supervise through auditing the revenue and expenditure of all departments under the State Council and of the local governments at different levels, and those of the state financial and monetary organizatioins and of enterprises and undertakings.

Under the direction of the Premier of the State Council, the auditing body independently exercises its power to supervise through auditing in accordance with the law, subject to no interference by any other administrative organ or any public organization or individual.

Article 92   The State Council is responsible, and reports on its work, to the National People's Congress or, when the National People's Congress is not in session, to its Standing Committee.

Section IV
The Central Military Commission

Article 93   The Central Military Commission of the People's Republic of China directs the armed forces of the country.

The Central Military Commission, is composed of the following:

the Chairman;

the Vice-Chairmen; and

members.

The Chairman of the Central Military Commission has overall responsibility for the Commission.

The term of office of the Central Military Commission is the same as that of the National People's Congress.

Article 94   The Chairman of the Central Military Commission is responsible to the National People's Congress and its Standing Committee.

Section V
The Local People's Congresses
and the Local
People's Governments
at Different Levels

Article 95   People's congresses and people's governments are established in provinces, municipalities directly under the Central Government, counties, cities, municipal districts, townships, nationality townships and towns.

The organization of local people's congresses and local people's governments at different levels is prescribed by law.

Organs of self-government are established in autonomous regions, autonomous prefectures and autonomous counties. The organization and working procedures of organs of self-government are prescribed by law in accordance with the basic principles laid down in Sections V and VI of Chapter Three of the Constitution.

Article 96   Local people's congresses at different levels are local organs of state power.

Local people's congresses at and above the county level establish standing committees.

Article 97   Deputies to the people's congresses of provinces, municipalities directly under the Central Government, and cities divided into districts are elected by the people's congresses at the next lower level; deputies to the people's congresses of counties, cities not divided into districts, municipal districts, townships, nationality townships and towns are elected directly by their constituencies.

The number of deputies to local people's congresses at different levels and the manner of their election are prescribed by law.

Article 98   The term of office of the people's congresses of provinces, municipalities directly under the Central Government and cities divided into districts is five years. The term of office of the people's congresses of counties, cities not divided into districts, municipal districts, townships, nationality townships and towns is three years.

Article 99   Local people's congresses at different levels ensure the observance and implementation of the Constitution, the statutes and the administrative rules and regulations in their respective administrative areas. Within the limits of their authority as prescribed by law, they adopt and issue resolutions and examine and decide on plans for local economic and cultural development and for the development of public services.

Local people's congresses at and above the county level examine and approve the plans for economic and social development and the budgets of their respective administrative areas, and examine and approve reports on their implementation. They have the power to alter or annul inappropriate decisions of their own standing committees.

The people's congresses of nationality townships may, within the limits of their authority as prescribed by law, take specific measures suited to the peculiarities of the nationalities concerned.

Article 100   The people's congresses of provinces and municipalities directly under the Central Government, and their standing committees, may adopt local regulations, which must not contravene the Constitution, the statutes and the administrative rules and regulations, and they shall report such local regulations to the Standing Committee of the National People's Congress for the record.

Article 101   At their respective levels, local people's congresses elect, and have the power to recall, governors and deputy governors, or mayors and deputy mayors, or heads and deputy heads of counties, districts, townships and towns.

Local people's congresses at and above the county level elect, and have the power to recall, presidents of people's courts and chief procurators of people's procuratorates at the corresponding level. The election or recall of chief procurators of people's procuratorates shall be reported to the chief procurators of the people's procuratorates at the next higher level for submission to the standing committees of the people's congresses at the corresponding level for approval.

Article 102   Deputies to the people's congresses of provinces, municipalities directly under the Central Government and cities divided into districts are subject to supervision by the units which elected them; deputies to the people's congresses of counties, cities not divided into districts, municipal districts, townships, nationality townships and towns are subject to supervision by their constituencies.

The electoral units and constituencies which elect deputies to local people's congresses at different levels have the power, according to procedures prescribed by law, to recall deputies whom they elected.

Article 103   The standing committee of a local people's congress at and above the county level is composed of a chairman, vice-chairmen and members, and is responsible, and reports on its work, to the people's congress at the corresponding level.

The local people's congress at and above the county level elects, and has the power to recall, anyone on the standing committee of the people's congress at the corresponding level.

No one on the standing committee of a local people's congress at and above the county level shall hold any post in state administrative, judicial and procuratorial organs.

Article 104   The standing committee of a local people's congress at and above the county level discusses and decides on major issues in all fields of work in its administrative area; supervises the work of the people's government, people's court and people's procuratorate at the corresponding level; annuls inappropriate decisions and orders of the people's government at the corresponding level; annuls inappropriate resolutions of the people's congress at the next lower level; decides on the appointment and removal of functionaries of state organs within its jurisdiction as prescribed by law; and, when the people's congress at the corresponding level is not in session, recalls individual deputies to the people's congress at the next higher level and elects individual deputies to fill vacancies in that people's congress.

Article 105   Local people's governments at different levels are the executive bodies of local organs of state power as well as the local organs of state administration at the corresponding level.

Local people's governments at different levels practise the system of overall responsibility by governors, mayors, county heads, district heads, township heads and town heads.

Article 106   The term of office of local people's governments at different levels is the same as that of the people's congresses at the corresponding level.

Article 107   Local people's governments at and above the county level, within the limits of their authority as prescribed by law, conduct the administrative work concerning the economy, education, science, culture, public health, physical culture, urban and rural development, finance, civil affairs, public security, nationalities affairs, judicial administration, supervision and family planning in their respective administrative areas; issue decisions and orders; appoint, remove and train administrative functionaries, appraise their work and reward or punish them.

People's governments of townships, nationality townships and towns carry out the resolutions of the people's congress at the corresponding level as well as the decisions and orders of the state administrative organs at the next higher level and conduct administrative work in their respective administrative areas.

People's governments of provinces and municipalities directly under the Central Government decide on the establishment and geographic division of townships, nationality townships and towns.

Article 108   Local people's governments at and above the county level direct the work of their subordinate departments and of people's governments at lower levels, and have the power to alter or annul inappropriate decisions of their subordinate departments and people's governments at lower levels.

Article 109   Auditing bodies are established by local people's governments at and above the county level. Local auditing bodies at different levels independently exercise their power to supervise through auditing in accordance with the law and are responsible to the people's government at the corresponding level and to the auditing body at the next higher level.

Article 110   Local people's governments at different levels are responsible, and report on their work, to people's congresses at the corresponding level. Local people's governments at and above the county level are responsible, and report on their work, to the standing committee of the people's congress at the corresponding level when the congress is not in session.

Local people's governments at different levels are responsible, and report on their work, to the state administrative organs at the next higher level. Local people's governments at different levels throughout the country are state administrative organs under the unified leadership of the State Council and are subordinate to it.

Article 111   The residents' committees and villagers' committees established among urban and rural residents on the basis of their place of residence are mass organizations of self-management at the grass-roots level. The chairman, vice-chairmen and members of each residents' or villagers' committee are elected by the residents.

The relationship between the residents' and villagers' committees and the grass-roots organs of state power is prescribed by law.

The residents' and villagers' committees establish committees for people's mediation, public security, public health and other matters in order to manage public affairs and social services in their areas, mediate civil disputes, help maintain public order and convey residents' opinions and demands and make suggestions to the people's government:

Section VI
The Organs of Self-Government
of National Autonomous Areas

Article 112   The organs of self-government of national autonomous areas are the people's congresses and people's governments of autonomous regions, autonomous prefectures and autonomous counties.

Article 113   In the people's congress of an autonomous region, prefecture or county, in addition to the deputies of the nationality or nationalities exercising regional autonomy in the administrative area, the other nationalities inhabiting the area are also entitled to appropriate representation.

The chairmanship and vice-chairmanships of the standing committee of the people's congress of an autonomous region, prefecture or county shall include a citizen or citizens of the nationality or nationalities exercising regional autonomy in the area concerned.

Article 114   The administrative head of an autonomous region, prefecture or county shall be a citizen of the nationality, or of one of the nationalities, exercising regional autonomy in the area concerned.

Article 115   The organs of self-government of autonomous regions, prefectures and counties exercise the functions and powers of local organs of state as specified in Section V of Chapter Three of the Constitution. At the same time, they exercise the right of autonomy within the limits of their authority as prescribed by the Constitution, the law of regional national autonomy and other laws, and implement the laws and policies of the state in the light of the existing local situation.

Article 116   People's congresses of national autonomous areas have the power to enact autonomy regulations and specific regulations in the light of the political, economic and cultural characteristics of the nationality or nationalities in the areas concerned. The autonomy regulations and specific regulations of autonomous regions shall be submitted to the Standing Committee of the National People's Congress for approval before they go into effect. Those of autonomous prefectures and counties shall be submitted to the standing committees of the people's congresses of provinces or autonomous regions for approval before they go into effect, and they shall be reported to the Standing Committee of the National People's Congress for the record.

Article 117   The organs of self-government of the national autonomous areas have the power of autonomy in administering the finances of their areas. All revenues accruing to the national autonomous areas under the financial system of the state shall be managed and used by the organs of self-government of those areas on their own.

Article 118   The organs of self-government of the national autonomous areas independently arrange for and administer local economic development under the guidance of state plans.

In exploiting natural resources and building enterprises in the national autonomous areas, the state shall give due consideration to the interests of those areas.

Article 119   The organs of self-government of the national autonomous areas independently administer educational, scientific, cultural, public health and physical culture affairs in their respective areas, protect and cull through the cultural heritage of the nationalities and work for the development and prosperity of their cultures.

Article 120   The organs of self-government of the national autonomous areas may, in accordance with the military system of the state and concrete local needs and with the approval of the State Council, organize local public security forces for the maintenance of public order.

Article 121   In performing their functions, the organs of self-government of the national autonomous areas, in accordance with the autonomy regulations of the respective areas, employ the spoken and written language or languages in common use in the locality.

Article 122   The state gives financial, material and technical assistance to the minority nationalities to accelerate their economic and cultural development.

The state helps the national autonomous areas train large numbers of cadres at different levels and specialized personnel and skilled workers of different professions and trades from among the nationality or nationalities in those areas.

Section VII
The People's Courts
and the People's Procuratorates

Article 123   The people's courts in the People's Republic of China are the judicial organs of the state.

Article 124   The People's Republic of China establishes the Supreme People's Court and the local people's courts at different levels, military courts and other special people's courts.

The term of office of the President of the Supreme People's Court is the same as that of the National People's Congress; he shall serve no more than two consecutive terms.

The organization of people's courts is prescribed by law.

Article 125   All cases handled by the people's courts, except for those involving special circumstances as specified by law, shall be heard in public. The accused has the right of defence.

Article 126   The people's courts shall, in accordance with the law, exercise judicial power independently and are not subject to interference by administrative organs, public organizations or individuals.

Article 127 The Supreme People's Court is the highest judicial organ.

The Supreme People's Court supervises the administration of justice by the local people's courts at different levels and by the special people's courts; people's courts at higher levels supervise the administration of justice by those at lower levels.

Article 128 The Supreme People's Court is responsible to the National People's Congress and its Standing Committee. Local people's courts at different levels are responsible to the organs of state power which created them.

Article 129 The people's procuratorates of the People's Republic of China are state organs for legal supervision.

Article 130 The People's Republic of China establishes the Supreme People's Procuratorate and the local people's procuratorates at different levels, military procuratorates and other special people's procuratorates.

The term of office of the Procurator-General of the Supreme People's Procuratorate is the same as that of the National People's Congress; he shall serve no more than two consecutive terms.

The organization of people's procuratorates is prescribed by law.

Article 131 People's procuratorates shall, in accordance with the law, exercise procuratorial power independently and are not subject to interference by administrative organs, public organizations or individuals.

Article 132 The Supreme People's Procuratorate is the highest procuratorial organ.

The Supreme People's Procuratorate directs the work of the local people's procuratorates at different levels and of the special people's procuratorates; people's procuratorates at higher levels direct the work of those at lower levels.

Article 133 The Supreme People's Procuratorate is responsible to the National People's Congress and its Standing Committee. Local people's procuratorates at different levels are responsible to the organs of state power at the corresponding levels which created them and to the people's procuratorates at the higher level.

Article 134 Citizens of all nationalities have the right to use the spoken and written languages of their own nationalities in court proceedings. The people's courts and people's procuratorates should provide translation for any party to the court proceedings who is not familiar with the spoken or written languages in common use in the locality.

In an area where people of a minority nationality live in a compact community or where a number of nationalities live together, hearings should be conducted in the language or languages in common use in the locality; indictments, judgments, notices and other documents should be written, according to actual needs, in the language or languages in common use in the locality.

Article 135 The people's courts, people's procuratorates and public security organs shall, in handling criminal cases, divide their functions, each taking responsibility for its own work, and they shall co-ordinate their efforts and check each other to ensure correct and effective enforcement of law.

CHAPTER FOUR
THE NATIONAL FLAG,
THE NATIONAL EMBLEM
AND THE CAPITAL

Article 136   The national flag of the People's Republic of China is a red flag with five stars.

Article 137   The national emblem of the People's Republic of China is Tian An Men in the centre illuminated by five stars and encircled by ears of grain and a cogwheel.

Article 138   The capital of the People's Republic of China is Beijing.

The Constitution

of the

Communist Party

of China (1982)

Appendix B

General Programme

The Communist Party of China is the vanguard of the Chinese working class, the faithful representative of the interests of the people of all nationalities in China, and the force at the core leading China's cause of socialism. The Party's ultimate goal is the creation of a communist social system.

The Communist Party of China takes Marxism-Leninism and Mao Zedong Thought as its guide to action.

Applying dialectical materialism and historical materialism, Marx and Engels analysed the laws of development of capitalist society and founded the theory of scientific socialism. According to this theory, with the victory of the proletariat in its revolutionary struggle, the dictatorship of the bourgeoisie is inevitably replaced by the dictatorship of the proletariat, and capitalist society is inevitably transformed into socialist society in which the means of production are publicly owned, exploitation is abolished and the principle "from each according to his ability and to each according to his work" is applied; with tremendous growth of the productive forces and tremendous progress in the ideological, political and cultural fields, socialist society ultimately and inevitably advances into communist society in which the principle "from each according to his ability and to each according to his needs" is applied. Early in the 20th century, Lenin pointed out that capitalism had developed to the stage of imperialism, that the liberation struggle of the proletariat was bound to unite with that of the oppressed nations of the world, and that it was possible for socialist revolution to win victory first in countries that were the weak links of imperialist rule. The course of world history during the past half century and more, and especially the establishment and development of the socialist system in a number of countries, has borne out the correctness of the theory of scientific socialism.

The development and improvement of the socialist system is a long historical process. Fundamentally speaking, the socialist system is incomparably superior to the capitalist system, having eliminated the contradictions inherent in the capitalist system, which the latter itself is incapable of overcoming. Socialism enables the people truly to become masters of the country, gradually to shed the old ideas and ways formed under the system of exploitation and private ownership of the means of production, and steadily to raise their communist consciousness and foster common ideals, common ethics and a common discipline in their own ranks. Socialism can give full scope to the initiative and creativeness of the people, develop the productive forces rapidly, proportionately and in a planned way, and meet the growing material and cultural needs of the members of society. The cause of socialism is advancing and is bound gradually to triumph throughout the world along paths that are suited to the specific conditions of each country and are chosen by its people of their own free will.

The Chinese Communists, with Comrade Mao Zedong as their chief representative, created Mao Zedong Thought by integrating the universal principles of Marxism-Leninism with the concrete practice of the Chinese revolution. Mao Zedong Thought is Marxism-Leninism applied and developed in China; it consists of a body of theoretical principles concerning the revolution and construction in China and a summary of experience therein, both of which have been proved correct by practice; it represents the crystallized, collective wisdom of the Communist Party of China.

The Communist Party of China led the people of all nationalities in waging their prolonged revolutionary struggle against imperialism, feudalism and bureaucrat-capitalism, winning victory in the new-democratic revolution and establishing the People's Republic of China—a people's democratic dictatorship. After the founding of the People's Republic, it led them in smoothly carrying out socialist transformation, com-

*Beijing Review, 38 (September 20, 1982), 8–21. (Adopted by the Twelfth National Congress of the Communist Party of China on September 6, 1982.)

pleting the transition from New Democracy to socialism, establishing the socialist system, and developing socialism in its economic, political and cultural aspects.

After the elimination of the exploiting classes as such, most of the contradictions in Chinese society do not have the nature of class struggle, and class struggle is no longer the principal contradiction. However, owing to domestic circumstances and foreign influences, class struggle will continue to exist within certain limits for a long time, and may even sharpen under certain conditions. The principal contradiction in Chinese society is that between the people's growing material and cultural needs and the backward level of our social production. The other contradictions should be resolved in the course of resolving this principal one. It is essential to strictly distinguish and correctly handle the two different types of contradictions—the contradictions between the enemy and ourselves and those among the people.

The general task of the Communist Party of China at the present stage is to unite the people of all nationalities in working hard and self-reliantly to achieve, step by step, the modernization of our industry, agriculture, national defence and science and technology and make China a culturally advanced and highly democratic socialist country.

The focus of the work of the Communist Party of China is to lead the people of all nationalities in accomplishing the socialist modernization of our economy. It is necessary vigorously to expand the productive forces and gradually perfect socialist relations of production, in keeping with the actual level of the productive forces and as required for their expansion. It is necessary to strive for the gradual improvement of the standards of material and cultural life of the urban and rural population, based on the growth of production and social wealth.

The Communist Party of China leads the people, as they work for a high level of material civilization, in building a high level of socialist spiritual civilization. Major efforts should be made to promote education, science and culture, imbue the Party members and the masses of the people with communist ideology, combat and overcome decadent bourgeois ideas, remnant feudal ideas and other non-proletarian ideas, and encourage the Chinese people to have lofty ideals, moral integrity, education and a sense of discipline.

The Communist Party of China leads the people in promoting socialist democracy, perfecting the socialist legal system, and consolidating the people's democratic dictatorship. Effective measures should be taken to protect the people's right to run the affairs of the state and of society, and to manage economic and cultural undertakings; and to strike firmly at hostile elements who deliberately sabotage the socialist system, and those who seriously breach or jeopardize public security. Great efforts should be made to strengthen the People's Liberation Army and national defence so that the country is prepared at all times to resist and wipe out any invaders.

The Communist Party of China upholds and promotes relations of equality, unity and mutual assistance among all nationalities in the country, persists in the policy of regional autonomy of minority nationalities, aids the areas inhabited by minority nationalities in their economic and cultural development, and actively trains and promotes cadres from among the minority nationalities.

The Communist Party of China unites with all workers, peasants and intellectuals, and with all the democratic parties, non-party democrats and the patriotic forces of all the nationalities in China in further expanding and fortifying the broadest possible patriotic united front embracing all socialist working people and all patriots who support socialism or who support the reunification of the motherland. We should work together with the people throughout the country, including our compatriots in Taiwan, Xianggang (Hongkong) and Aomen (Macao) and Chinese nationals residing abroad, to accomplish the great task of reunifying the motherland.

In international affairs, the Communist Party of China takes the following basic stand: It adheres to proletarian internationalism and firmly unites with the workers of all lands, with the oppressed nations and oppressed peoples and with all peace-loving and justice-upholding organizations and personages in the common struggle against imperialism, hegemonism and colonialism and for the defence of world peace and promotion of human progress. It stands for the development of state relations between China and other countries on the basis of the five principles of mutual respect for sovereignty and territorial integrity, mutual non-aggression, non-interference in each other's internal affairs, equality and mutual benefit, and peaceful co-existence. It develops relations with Communist Parties and working-class parties in other countries on the basis of Marxism and the principles of independence, complete equality, mutual respect and non-interference in each other's internal affairs.

In order to lead China's people of all nationalities in attaining the great goal of socialist modernization, the Communist Party of China must strengthen itself, carry forward its fine traditions, enhance its fighting capacity and resolutely achieve the following three essential requirements:

First, a high degree of ideological and political unity. The Communist Party of China makes the realization of communism its maximum programme, to which all its members must devote their entire lives. At the present stage, the political basis for the solidarity and unity of the whole Party consists in adherence to the socialist road, to the people's democratic dictatorship, to the leadership of the Party, and to Marxism-Leninism and Mao Zedong Thought and in the concentration of our efforts on socialist modernization. The Party's ideological line is to proceed from reality in all things, to integrate theory with practice, to seek truth from facts, and to verify and develop the truth through practice. In accordance with this ideological line, the whole Party must scientifically sum up historical experience, investigate and study actual conditions, solve new problems in domestic and international affairs, and oppose all erroneous deviations, whether "Left" or Right.

Second, wholehearted service to the people. The Party has no special interests of its own apart from the interests of the working class and the broadest masses of the people. The programme and policies of the Party are precisely the scientific expressions of the fundamental interests of the working class and the broadest masses of the people. Throughout the process of leading the masses in struggle to realize the ideal of communism, the Party always shares weal and woe with the people, keeps in closest contact with them, and does not allow any member to become divorced from the masses or place himself above them. The Party persists in educating the masses in communist ideas and follows the mass line in its work, doing everything for the masses, relying on them in every task, and turning its correct views into conscious action by the masses.

Third, adherence to democratic centralism. Within the Party, democracy is given full play, a high degree of centralism is practised on the basis of democracy and a sense of organization and discipline is strengthened, so as to ensure unity of action throughout its ranks and the prompt and effective implementation of its decisions. In its internal political life, the Party conducts criticism and self-criticism in the correct way, waging ideological struggles over matters of principle, upholding truth and rectifying mistakes. Applying the principle that all members are equally subject to Party discipline, the Party duly criticizes or punishes those members who violate it and expels those who persist in opposing and harming the Party.

Party leadership consists mainly in political, ideological and organizational leadership. The Party must formulate and implement correct lines, principles and policies, do its organizational, propaganda and educational work well and make sure that all Party members play their exemplary vanguard role in every sphere of work and every aspect of social life. The Party must conduct its activities within the limits permitted by the Constitution and the laws of the state. It must see to it that the legislative, judicial and administrative organs of the state and the economic, cultural and people's organizations work actively and with initiative, independently, responsibly and in harmony. The Party must strengthen its leadership over the trade unions, the Communist

Youth League, the Women's Federation and other mass organizations, and give full scope to their roles. The Party members are a minority in the whole population, and they must work in close co-operation with the masses of non-Party people in the common effort to make our socialist motherland ever stronger and more prosperous, until the ultimate realization of communism.

CHAPTER 1
MEMBERSHIP

Article 1   Any Chinese worker, peasant, member of the armed forces, intellectual or any other revolutionary who has reached the age of 18 and who accepts the Party's programme and Constitution and is willing to join and work actively in one of the Party organizations, carry out the Party's decisions and pay membership dues regularly may apply for membership of the Communist Party of China.

Article 2   Members of the Communist Party of China are vanguard fighters of the Chinese working class imbued with communist consciousness.

Members of the Communist Party of China must serve the people wholeheartedly, dedicate their whole lives to the realization of communism, and be ready to make any personal sacrifices.

Members of the Communist Party of China are at all times ordinary members of the working people. Communist Party members must not seek personal gain or privileges, although they are allowed personal benefits and job functions and powers as provided for by the relevant regulations and policies.

Article 3   Party members must fulfill the following duties:

(1)   To conscientiously study Marxism-Leninism and Mao Zedong Thought, essential knowledge concerning the Party, and the Party's line, principles, policies and decisions; and acquire general, scientific and professional knowledge.

(2)   To adhere to the principle that the interests of the Party and the people stand above everything, subordinate their personal interests to the interests of the Party and the people, be the first to bear hardships and the last to enjoy comforts, work selflessly for the public interest, and absolutely never use public office for personal gain or benefit themselves at the expense of the public.

(3)   To execute the Party's decisions perseveringly, accept any job and fulfill actively any task assigned them by the Party, conscientiously observe Party discipline and the laws of the state, rigorously guard Party and state secrets and staunchly defend the interests of the Party and the state.

(4)   To uphold the Party's solidarity and unity, to firmly oppose factionalism and all factional organizations and small-group activities, and to oppose double-dealing and scheming of any kind.

(5)   To be loyal to and honest with the Party, to match words with deeds and not to conceal their political views or distort facts; to earnestly practise criticism and self-criticism, to be bold in exposing and correcting shortcomings and mistakes in work, backing good people and good deeds and fighting against bad people and bad deeds.

(6)   To maintain close ties with the masses, propagate the Party's views among them, consult with them when problems arise, listen to their views and demands with an open mind and keep the Party informed of these in good time, help them raise their political consciousness, and defend their legitimate rights and interests.

(7)   To play an exemplary vanguard role in production and other work, study and social activities, take the lead in maintaining public order, promote new socialist ways and customs and advocate communist ethics.

(8)   As required by the defence of the motherland and the interests of the peo-

ple, to step forward and fight bravely in times of difficulty and danger, fearing neither hardship nor death.

Article 4   Party members enjoy the following rights:

(1)   To attend pertinent Party meetings and read pertinent Party documents, and to benefit from the Party's education and training.

(2)   To participate in the discussion, at Party meetings and in Party newspapers and journals, of questions concerning the Party's policies.

(3)   To make suggestions and proposals regarding the work of the Party.

(4)   To make well-grounded criticism of any Party organization or member at Party meetings; to present information or charges against any Party organization or member concerning violations of discipline and of the law to the Party in a responsible way, and to demand disciplinary measures against such a member, or to demand the dismissal or replacement of any cadre who is incompetent.

(5)   To vote, elect and stand for election.

(6)   To attend, with the right of self-defence, discussions held by Party organizations to decide on disciplinary measures to be taken against themselves or to appraise their work and behaviour, while other Party members may also bear witness or argue on their behalf.

(7)   In case of disagreement with a Party decision or policy, to make reservations and present their views to Party organizations at higher levels up to and including the Central Committee, provided that they resolutely carry out the decision or policy while it is in force.

(8)   To put forward any request, appeal or complaint to higher Party organizations up to and including the Central Committee and ask the organizations concerned for a responsible reply.

No Party organization, up to and including the Central Committee, has the right to deprive any Party member of the above-mentioned rights.

Article 5   New Party members must be admitted through a Party branch, and the principle of individual admission must be adhered to. It is impermissible to drag into the Party by any means those who are not qualified for membership, or to exclude those who are qualified.

An applicant for Party membership must fill in an application form and must be recommended by two full Party members. The application must be accepted by a general membership meeting of the Party branch concerned and approved by the next higher Party organization, and the applicant should undergo observation for a probationary period before being transferred to full membership.

Party members who recommend an applicant must make genuine efforts to acquaint themselves with the latter's ideology, character and personal history, to explain to each applicant the Party's programme and Constitution, qualifications for membership and the duties and rights of members, and must make a responsible report to the Party organization on the matter.

The Party branch committee must canvass the opinions of persons concerned, inside and outside the Party, about an applicant for Party membership and, after establishing the latter's qualifications following a rigorous examination, submit the application to a general membership meeting for discussion.

Before approving the admission of applicants for Party membership, the next higher Party organization concerned must appoint people to talk with them, so as to get to know them better and help deepen their understanding of the Party.

In special circumstances, the Central Committee of the Party or the Party committee of a province, an autonomous region or a municipality directly under the Central Government has the power to admit new Party members directly.

Article 6 A probationary Party member must take an admission oath in front of the Party flag. The oath reads: "It is my will to join the Communist Party of China, uphold the Party's programme, observe the provisions of the Party Constitution, fulfill a Party member's duties, carry out the Party's decisions, strictly observe Party discipline, guard Party secrets, be loyal to the Party, work hard, fight for communism throughout my life, be ready at all times to sacrifice my all for the Party and the people, and never betray the Party."

Article 7 The probationary period of a probationary member is one year. The Party organization should make serious efforts to educate and observe the probationary members.

Probationary members have the same duties as full members. They enjoy the rights of full members except those of voting, electing or standing for election.

When the probationary period of a probationary member has expired, the Party branch concerned should promptly discuss whether he is qualified to be transferred to full membership. A probationary member who conscientiously performs his duties and is qualified for membership should be transferred to full membership as scheduled; if continued observation and education are needed, the probationary period may be prolonged, but by no more than one year; if a probationary member fails to perform his duties and is found to be really unqualified for membership, his probationary membership shall be annulled. Any decision to transfer a probationary member to full membership, prolong a probationary period, or annul a probationary membership must be made through discussion by the general membership meeting of the Party branch concerned and approved by the next higher Party organization.

The probationary period of a probationary member begins from the day the general membership meeting of the Party branch admits him as a probationary member. The Party standing of a member begins from the day he is transferred to full membership on the expiration of the probationary period.

Article 8 Every Party member, irrespective of position, must be organized into a branch, cell or other specific unit of the Party to participate in the regular activities of the Party organization and accept supervision by the masses inside and outside the Party. There shall be no privileged Party members who do not participate in the regular activities of the Party organization and do not accept supervision by the masses inside and outside the Party.

Article 9 Party members are free to withdraw from the Party. When a Party member asks to withdraw, the Party branch concerned shall, after discussion by its general membership meeting, remove his name from the Party rolls, make the removal publicly known and report it to the next higher Party organization for the record.

A Party member who lacks revolutionary will, fails to fulfill the duties of a Party member, is not qualified for membership and remains incorrigible after repeated education should be persuaded to withdraw from the Party. The case shall be discussed and decided by the general membership meeting of the Party branch concerned and submitted to the next higher Party organization for approval. If the Party member being persuaded to withdraw refuses to do so, the case shall be submitted to the general membership meeting of the Party branch concerned for discussion and decision on a time limit by which the member must correct his mistakes or on the removal of his name from the Party rolls, and the decision shall be submitted to the next higher Party organization for approval.

A Party member who fails to take part in regular Party activities, pay membership dues or do work assigned by the Party for six successive months without proper reason is regarded as having given up membership. The general membership meeting of the Party branch concerned shall decide on the removal of such a person's name from the Party rolls and report the removal to the next higher Party organization for approval.

CHAPTER II
ORGANIZATIONAL SYSTEM
OF THE PARTY

Article 10   The Party is an integral body organized under its programme and Constitution, on the principle of democratic centralism. It practices a high degree of centralism on the basis of a high degree of democracy. The basic principles of democratic centralism as practised by the Party are as follows:

(1)   Individual Party members are subordinate to the Party organization, the minority is subordinate to the majority, the lower Party organizations are subordinate to the higher Party organizations, and all the constituent organizations and members of the Party are subordinate to the National Congress and the Central Committee of the Party.

(2)   The Party's leading bodies of all levels are elected except for the representative organs dispatched by them and the leading Party members' groups in non-Party organizations.

(3)   The highest leading body of the Party is the National Congress and the Central Committee elected by it. The leading bodies of local Party organizations are the Party congresses at their respective levels and the Party committees elected by them. Party committees are responsible, and report their work, to the Party congresses at their respective levels.

(4)   Higher Party organizations shall pay constant attention to the views of the lower organizations and the rank-and-file Party members, and solve in good time the problems they raise. Lower Party organizations shall report on their work to, and request instructions from, higher Party organizations; at the same time, they shall handle, independently and in a responsible manner, matters within their jurisdiction. Higher and lower Party organizations should exchange information and support and supervise each other.

(5)   Party committees at all levels function on the principle of combining collective leadership with individual responsibility based on division of labour. All major issues shall be decided upon by the Party committees after democratic discussion.

(6)   The Party forbids all forms of personality cult. It is necessary to ensure that the activities of the Party leaders be subject to supervision by the Party and the people, while at the same time to uphold the prestige of all leaders who represent the interests of the Party and the people.

Article 11   The election of delegates to Party congresses and of members of Party committees at all levels should reflect the will of the voters. Elections shall be held by secret ballot. The lists of candidates shall be submitted to the Party organizations and voters for full deliberation and discussion. There may be a preliminary election in order to draw up a list of candidates for the formal election. Or there may be no preliminary election, in which case the number of candidates shall be greater than that of the persons to be elected. The voters have the right to inquire into the candidates, demand a change or reject one in favour of another. No organization or individual shall in any way compel voters to elect or not to elect any candidate.

If any violation of the Party Constitution occurs in the election of delegates to a local Party congress, the Party committee at the next higher level shall, after investigation and verification, decide to invalidate the election and take appropriate measures. The decision shall be reported to the Party committee at the next higher level for checking and approval before it is formally announced and implemented.

Article 12 When necessary, Party committees of and above the county level may convene conferences of delegates to discuss and decide on major problems that require timely solution. The number of delegates to such conferences and the procedure governing their election shall be determined by the Party committees convening them.

Article 13 The formation of a new Party organization or the dissolution of an existing one shall be decided upon by the higher Party organizations.

Party committees of and above the county level may send out their representative organs.

When the congress of a local Party organization at any level is not in session, the next higher Party organization may, when it deems it necessary, transfer or appoint responsible members of that organization.

Article 14 When making decisions on important questions affecting the lower organizations, the leading bodies of the Party at all levels should, in ordinary circumstances, solicit the opinions of the lower organizations. Measures should be taken to ensure that the lower organizations can exercise their functions and powers normally. Except in special circumstances, higher leading bodies should not interfere with matters that ought to be handled by lower organizations.

Article 15 Only the Central Committee of the Party has the power to make decisions on major policies of a nationwide character. Party organizations of various departments and localities may make suggestions with regard to such policies to the Central Committee, but shall not make any decisions or publicize their views outside the Party without authorization.

Lower Party organizations must firmly implement the decisions of higher Party organizations. If lower organizations consider that any decisions of higher organizations do not suit actual conditions in their localities or departments, they may request modification. If the higher organizations insist on their original decisions, the lower organizations must carry out such decisions and refrain from publicly voicing their differences, but have the right to report to the next higher Party organization.

Newspapers and journals and other means of publicity run by Party organizations at all levels must propagate the line, principles, policies and decisions of the Party.

Article 16 Party organizations must keep to the principle of subordination of the minority to the majority in discussing and making decisions on any matter. Serious consideration should be given to the differing views of a minority. In case of controversy over major issues in which supporters of the two opposing views are nearly equal in number, except in emergencies where action must be taken in accordance with the majority view, the decision should be put off to allow for further investigation, study and exchange of opinions followed by another discussion. If still no decision can be made, the controversy should be reported to the next higher Party organization for ruling.

When on behalf of the Party organization, an individual Party member is to express views on major issues beyond the scope of existing Party decisions, the content must be referred to the Party organization for prior discussion and decision, or referred to the next higher Party organization for instructions. No Party member, whatever his position, is allowed to make decisions on major issues on his own. In an emergency, when a decision by an individual is unavoidable, the matter must be reported to the

Party organization immediately afterwards. No leader is allowed to decide matters arbitrarily on his own or to place himself above the Party organization.

Article 17   The central, local and primary organizations of the Party must all pay great attention to Party building. They shall regularly discuss and check up on the Party's work in propaganda education, organization and discipline inspection, its mass work and united front work. They must carefully study ideological and political developments inside and outside the Party.

CHAPTER III
CENTRAL ORGANIZATIONS
OF THE PARTY

Article 18   The National Congress of the Party is held once every five years and convened by the Central Committee. It may be convened before the due date if the Central Committee deems it necessary or if more than one-third of the organizations at the provincial level so request. Except under extraordinary circumstances, the congress may not be postponed.

The number of delegates to the National Congress of the Party and the procedure governing their election shall be determined by the Central Committee.

Article 19   The functions and powers of the National Congress of the Party are as follows:

(1)   To hear and examine the reports of the Central Committee;

(2)   To hear and examine the reports of the Central Advisory Commission and the Central Commission for Discipline Inspection;

(3)   To discuss and decide on major questions concerning the Party;

(4)   To revise the Constitution of the Party;

(5)   To elect the Central Committee; and

(6)   To elect the Central Advisory Commission and the Central Commission for the Discipline Inspection.

Article 20   The Central Commission of the Party is elected for a term of five years. However, when the next National Congress is convened before or after its due date, the term shall be correspondingly shortened or extended. Members and alternate members of the Central Committee must have a Party standing of five years or more. The number of members and alternate members of the Central Committee shall be determined by the National Congress. Vacancies on the Central Committee shall be filled by its alternate members in the order of the number of votes by which they were elected.

The Central Committee of the Party meets in plenary session at least once a year, and such sessions are convened by its Political Bureau.

When the National Congress is not in session, the Central Committee carries out its decisions, directs the entire work of the Party and represents the Communist Party of China in its external relations.

Article 21   The Political Bureau, the Standing Committee of the Political Bureau, the Secretariat and the General Secretary of the Central Committee of the Party are elected by the Central Committee in plenary session. The General Secretary of the Central Committee must be a member of the Standing Committee of the Political Bureau.

When the Central Committee is not in session, the Political Bureau and its Standing Committee exercise the functions and powers of the Central Committee.

The Secretariat attends to the day-to-day work of the Central Committee under the direction of the Political Bureau and its Standing Committee.

The General Secretary of the Central Committee is responsible for convening the meetings of the Political Bureau and its Standing Committee and presides over the work of the Secretariat.

The members of the Military Commission of the Central Committee are decided on by the Central Committee. The Chairman of the Military Commission must be a member of the Standing Committee of the Political Bureau.

The central leading bodies and leaders elected by each Central Committee shall, when the next National Congress is in session, continue to preside over the Party's day-to-day work until the new central leading bodies and leaders are elected by the next Central Committee.

Article 22 The Party's Central Advisory Commission acts as political assistant and consultant to the Central Committee. Members of the Central Advisory Commission must have a Party standing of 40 years or more, have rendered considerable service to the Party, have fairly rich experience in leadership and enjoy fairly high prestige inside and outside the Party.

The Central Advisory Commission is elected for a term of the same duration as that of the Central Committee. It elects, at its plenary meeting, its Standing Committee and its Chairman and Vice-Chairmen, and reports the results to the Central Committee for approval. The Chairman of the Central Advisory Commission must be a member of the Standing Committee of the Political Bureau. Members of the Central Advisory Commission may attend plenary sessions of the Central Committee as non-voting participants. The Vice-Chairmen of the Central Advisory Commission may attend plenary meetings of the Political Bureau as non-voting participants and, when the Political Bureau deems it necessary, other members of the Standing Committee of the Central Advisory Commission may do the same.

Working under the leadership of the Central Committee of the Party, the Central Advisory Commission puts forward recommendations on the formulation and implementation of the Party's principles and policies and gives advice upon request, assists the Central Committee in investigating and handling certain important questions, propagates the Party's major principles and policies inside and outside the Party, and undertakes such other tasks as may be entrusted to it by the Central Committee.

Article 23 Party organizations in the Chinese People's Liberation Army carry on their work in accordance with the instructions of the Central Committee. The General Political Department of the Chinese People's Liberation Army is the political-work organ of the Military Commission; it directs Party and political work in the army. The organizational system and organs of the Party in the armed forces will be prescribed by the Military Commission.

CHAPTER IV
LOCAL ORGANIZATIONS
OF THE PARTY

Article 24 A Party congress of a province, autonomous region, municipality directly under the Central Government, city divided into districts, or autonomous prefecture is held once every five years.

A Party congress of a county (banner), autonomous county, city not divided into districts, or municipal district is held once every three years.

Local Party congresses are convened by the Party committees at the corresponding levels. Under extraordinary circumstances, they may be held before or after their due dates upon approval by the next higher Party committees.

The number of delegates to the local Party congresses, at any level and the procedure governing their election are determined by the Party committees at the corresponding levels and should be reported to the next higher Party committees for approval.

Article 25   The functions and powers of the local Party congresses at all levels are as follows:

(1)   To hear and examine the reports of the Party committees at the corresponding levels;

(2)   To hear and examine the reports of the commissions for discipline inspection at the corresponding levels;

(3)   To discuss and decide on major issues in the given areas; and

(4)   To elect the Party committees and commissions for discipline inspection at the corresponding levels and delegates to the Party congresses at their respective next higher levels.

The Party congress of a province, autonomous region, or municipality directly under the Central Government elects the Party advisory committee at the corresponding level and hears and examines its reports.

Article 26   The Party committee of a province, autonomous region, municipality directly under the Central Government, city divided into districts, or autonomous prefecture is elected for a term of five years. The members and alternate members of such a committee must have a Party standing of five years or more.

The Party committee of a county (banner), autonomous county, city not divided into districts, or municipal district is elected for a term of three years. The members and alternate members of such a committee must have a Party standing of three years or more.

When local Party congresses at various levels are convened before or after their due dates, the terms of the committees elected by the previous congresses shall be correspondingly shortened or extended.

The number of members and alternate members of the local Party committees at various levels shall be determined by the next higher committees. Vacancies on the local Party committees at various levels shall be filled by their alternate members in the order of the number of votes by which they were elected.

The local Party committees at various levels meet in plenary session at least once a year.

Local Party committees at various levels shall, when the Party congresses of the given areas are not in session, carry out the directives of the next higher Party organizations and the decisions of the Party congresses at the corresponding levels, direct work in their own areas and report on it to the next higher Party committees at regular intervals.

Article 27   Local Party committees at various levels elect, at their plenary sessions, their standing committees, secretaries and deputy secretaries and report the results to the higher Party committees for approval. The standing committees at various levels exercise the powers and functions of local Party committees when the latter are not in session. They continue to handle the day-to-day work when the next Party congresses at their levels are in session, until the new standing committees are elected.

Article 28 The Party advisory committee of a province, autonomous region or municipality directly under the Central Government acts as political assistant and consultant to the Party committee at the corresponding level. It works under the leadership of the Party committee at the corresponding level and in the light of the relevant provisions of Article 22 of the present Constitution. The qualifications of its members shall be specified by the Party committee at the corresponding level in the light of the relevant provisions of Article 22 of the present Constitution and the actual conditions in the locality concerned. It serves a term of the same duration as the Party committee at the corresponding level.

The advisory committee of a province, autonomous region or municipality directly under the Central Government elects, at its plenary meeting, its standing committee and its chairman and vice-chairmen, and the results are subject to endorsement by the Party committee at the corresponding level and should be reported to the Central Committee for approval. Its members may attend plenary sessions of the Party committee at the corresponding level as non-voting participants, and its chairman and vice-chairmen may attend meetings of the standing committee of the Party committee at the corresponding level as non-voting participants.

Article 29 A prefectural Party committee, or an organization analogous to it, is the representative organ dispatched by a provincial or an autonomous regional Party committee to a prefecture embracing several counties, autonomous counties or cities. It exercises leadership over the work in the given region as authorized by the provincial or autonomous regional Party committee.

CHAPTER V
PRIMARY ORGANIZATIONS
OF THE PARTY

Article 30 Primary Party organizations are formed in factories, shops, schools, offices, city neighbourhoods, people's communes, co-operatives, farms, townships, towns, companies of the People's Liberation Army and other basic units, where there are three or more full Party members.

In primary Party organizations, the primary Party committees, and committees of general Party branches or Party branches, are set up respectively as the work requires and according to the number of Party members, subject to approval by the higher Party organizations. A primary Party committee is elected by a general membership meeting or a delegate meeting. The committee of a general Party branch or a Party branch is elected by a general membership meeting.

Article 31 In ordinary circumstances, a primary Party organization which has set up its own committee convenes a general membership meeting or delegate meeting once a year; a general Party branch holds a general membership meeting twice a year; a Party branch holds a general membership meeting once in every three months.

A primary Party committee is elected for a term of three years, while a general Party branch committee or a Party branch committee is elected for a term of two years. Results of the election of a secretary and deputy secretaries by a primary Party committee, general branch committee or branch committee shall be reported to the higher Party organizations for approval.

Article 32 The primary Party organizations are militant bastions of the Party in the basic units of society. Their main tasks are:

(1)   To propagate and carry out the Party's line, principles and policies, the decisions of the Central Committee of the Party and other higher Party organizations, and their own decisions; to give full play to the exemplary vanguard role of Party members, and to unite and organize the cadres and the rank and file inside and outside the Party in fulfilling the tasks of their own units.

(2)   To organize Party members to conscientiously study Marxism-Leninism and Mao Zedong Thought, study essential knowledge concerning the Party, and the Party's line, principles and policies, and acquire general, scientific and professional knowledge.

(3)   To educate and supervise Party members, ensure their regular participation in the activities of the Party organization, see that Party members truly fulfill their duties and observe discipline, and protect their rights from encroachment.

(4)   To maintain close ties with the masses, constantly seek their criticisms and opinions regarding Party members and the Party's work, value the knowledge and rationalization proposals of the masses and experts, safeguard the legitimate rights and interests of the masses, show concern for their material and cultural life and help them improve it, do effective ideological and political work among them, and enhance their political consciousness. They must correct, by proper methods, the erroneous ideas and unhealthy ways and customs that may exist among the masses, and properly handle the contradictions in their midst.

(5)   To give full scope to the initiative and creativeness of Party members and the masses, discover advanced elements and talented people needed for the socialist cause, encourage them to improve their work and come up with innovations and inventions, and support them in these efforts.

(6)   To admit new Party members, collect membership dues, examine and appraise the work and behaviour of Party members, commend exemplary deeds performed by them, and maintain and enforce Party discipline.

(7)   To promote criticism and self-criticism, and expose and overcome shortcomings and mistakes in work. To educate Party and non-Party cadres; see to it that they strictly observe the law and administrative discipline and the financial and economic discipline and personnel regulations of the state; see to it that none of them infringe the interests of the state, the collective and the masses; and see to it that the financial workers including accountants and other professionals who are charged with enforcing laws and regulations in their own units do not themselves violate the laws and regulations, while at the same time ensuring and protecting their right to exercise their functions and powers independently in accordance with the law and guarding them against any reprisals for so doing.

(8)   To educate Party members and the masses to raise their revolutionary vigilance and wage resolute struggles against the criminal activities of counter-revolutionaries and other saboteurs.

Article 33   In an enterprise or institution, the primary Party committee or the general branch committee or branch committee, where there is no primary Party committee, gives leadership in the work of its own unit. Such a primary Party organization discusses and decides on major questions of principle and at the same time ensures that the administrative leaders fully exercise their functions and powers, but refrains from substituting itself for, or trying to take over from; the administrative leaders. Except in special circumstances, the general branch committees and branch committees under the leadership of a primary Party committee only play a guarantory and supervisory role to see that the production targets or operational tasks assigned to their own units are properly fulfilled.

In Party or government offices at all levels, the primary Party organizations shall not lead the work of these offices. Their task here is to exercise supervision over all Party members, including the heads of these offices who are Party members, with regard to their implementation of the Party's line, principles and policies, their observance of discipline and the law, their contact with the masses, and their ideology, work style and moral character; and to assist the office heads to improve work, raise efficiency and overcome bureaucratic ways, keep them informed of the shortcomings and problems discovered in the work of these offices, or report such shortcomings and problems to the higher Party organizations.

CHAPTER VI
PARTY CADRES

Article 34   Party cadres are the backbone of the Party's cause and public servants of the people. The Party selects its cadres according to the principle that they should possess both political integrity and professional competence, persists in the practice of appointing people on their merits and opposes favouritism; it calls for genuine efforts to make the ranks of the cadres more revolutionary, younger in average age, better educated and more professionally competent.

Party cadres are obliged to accept training by the Party as well as examination and assessment of their work by the Party.

The Party should attach importance to the training and promotion of women cadres and cadres from among the minority nationalities.

Article 35   Leading Party cadres at all levels must perform in an exemplary way their duties as Party members prescribed in Article 3 of this Constitution and must meet the following basic requirements:

(1)   Have a fair grasp of the theories of Marxism-Leninism and Mao Zedong Thought and the policies based on them, and be able to adhere to the socialist road, fight against the hostile forces disrupting socialism and combat all erroneous tendencies inside and outside the Party.

(2)   In their work as leaders, conduct earnest investigations and study, persistently proceed from reality and properly carry out the line, principles and policies of the Party.

(3)   Be fervently dedicated to the revolutionary cause and imbued with a strong sense of political responsibility, and be qualified for their leading posts in organizational ability, general education and vocational knowledge.

(4)   Have a democratic work style, maintain close ties with the masses, correctly implement the Party's mass line, conscientiously accept criticism and supervision by the Party and the masses, and combat bureaucratism.

(5)   Exercise their functions and powers in the proper way, observe and uphold the rules and regulations of the Party and the state, and combat all acts of abusing power and seeking personal gain.

(6)   Be good at uniting and working with a large number of comrades, including those who hold differing opinions, while upholding the Party's principles.

Article 36   Party cadres should be able to co-operate with non-Party cadres, respect them and learn open-mindedly from their strong points.

Party organizations at all levels must be good at discovering and recommending talented and knowledgeable non-Party cadres for leading posts, and ensure that the latter enjoy authority commensurate with their posts and can play their roles to the full.

Article 37   Leading Party cadres at all levels, whether elected through democratic procedure or appointed by a leading body, are not entitled to lifelong tenure, and they can be transferred from or relieved of their posts.

Cadres no longer fit to continue working due to old age or poor health should retire according to the regulations of the state.

CHAPTER VII
PARTY DISCIPLINE

Article 38   A Communist Party member must consciously act within the bounds of Party discipline.

Party organizations shall criticize, educate or take disciplinary measures against members who violate Party discipline, depending on the nature and seriousness of their mistakes and in the spirit of "learning from past mistakes to avoid future ones, and curing the sickness to save the patient."

Party members who violate the law and administrative discipline shall be subject to administrative disciplinary action or legal action instituted by administrative or judicial organs. Those who have seriously violated criminal law shall be expelled from the Party.

Article 39   There are five measures of Party discipline: warning, serious warning, removal from Party posts and proposals for their removal from non-Party posts to the organizations concerned, placing on probation within the Party, and expulsion from the Party.

The period for which a Party member is placed on probation shall not exceed two years. During this period, the Party member concerned has no right to vote, elect or stand for election. A Party member who during this time proves to have corrected his mistake shall have his rights as a Party member restored. Party members who refuse to mend their ways shall be expelled from the Party.

Expulsion is the ultimate Party disciplinary measure. In deciding on or approving an expulsion, Party organizations at all levels should study all the relevant facts and opinions and exercise extreme caution.

It is strictly forbidden, within the Party, to take any measures against a member that contravene the Party Constitution or the laws of the state, or to retaliate against or frame up comrades. Any offending organization or individual must be dealt with according to Party discipline or the laws of the state.

Article 40   Any disciplinary measure against a Party member must be discussed and decided on at a general membership meeting of the Party branch concerned, and reported to the primary Party committee concerned for approval. If the case is relatively important or complicated, or involves the expulsion of a member, it shall be reported, on the merit of that case, to a Party commission for discipline inspection at or above the county level for examination and approval. Under special circumstances, a Party committee or a commission for discipline inspection at or above the county level has the authority to decide directly on disciplinary measures against a Party member.

Any decision to remove a member or alternate member of the Central Committee or a local committee at any level from posts within the Party, to place such a person on probation within the Party or to expel him from the Party must be taken by a two-thirds majority vote at a plenary meeting of the Party committee to which he belongs. Such a disciplinary measure against a member or alternate member of a local Party committee is subject to approval by the higher Party committees.

Members and alternate members of the Central Committee who have seriously violated criminal law shall be expelled from the Party on decision by the Political Bureau of the Central Committee; members and alternate members of local Party committees who have seriously violated criminal law shall be expelled from the Party on decision by the standing committees of the Party committees at the corresponding levels.

Article 41   When a Party organization decides on a disciplinary measure against a Party member, it should investigate and verify the facts in an objective way. The Party member in question must be informed of the decision to be made and of the facts on which it is based. He must be given a chance to account for himself and speak in his own defence. If the member does not accept the decision, he can appeal, and the Party organization concerned must promptly deal with or forward his appeal, and must not withhold or suppress it. Those who cling to erroneous views and unjustifiable demands shall be educated by criticism.

Article 42   It is an important duty of every Party organization to firmly uphold Party discipline. Failure of a Party organization to uphold Party discipline must be investigated.

In case a Party organization seriously violates Party discipline and is unable to rectify the mistake on its own, the next higher Party committee should, after verifying the facts and considering the seriousness of the case, decide on the reorganization or dissolution of the organization, report the decision to the Party committee further above for examination and approval, and then formally announce and carry out the decision.

CHAPTER VIII
PARTY ORGANS FOR
DISCIPLINE INSPECTION

Article 43   The Party's Central Commission for Discipline Inspection functions under the leadership of the Central Committee of the Party. Local commissions for discipline inspection at all levels function under the dual leadership of the Party committees at the corresponding levels and the next higher commissions for discipline inspection.

The Party's central and local commissions for discipline inspection serve a term of the same duration as the Party committees at the corresponding levels.

The Central Commission for Discipline Inspection elects, in plenary session, its standing committee and secretary and deputy secretaries and reports the results to the Central Committee for approval. Local commissions for discipline inspection at all levels elect, at their plenary sessions, their respective standing committees and secretaries and deputy secretaries. The results of the elections are subject to endorsement by the Party committees at the corresponding levels and should be reported to the higher Party committees for approval. The First Secretary of the Central Commission for Discipline Inspection must be a member of the Standing Committee of the Political Bureau. The question of whether a primary Party committee should set up a commission for discipline inspection or simply appoint a discipline inspection commissioner shall be determined by the next higher Party organization in the light of the specific circumstances. The committees of general Party branches and Party branches shall have discipline inspection commissioners.

The Party's Central Commission for Discipline Inspection shall, when its work so requires, accredit discipline inspection groups or commissioners to Party or state organs at the central level. Leaders of the discipline inspection groups or discipline inspection commissioners may attend relevant meetings of the leading Party organizations in the said organs as non-voting participants. The leading Party organizations in the organs concerned must give support to their work.

Article 44   The main tasks of the central and local commissions for discipline inspection are as follows: to uphold the Constitution and the other important rules and regulations of the Party, to assist the respective Party committees in rectifying Party style, and to check up on the implementation of the line, principles, policies and decisions of the Party.

The central and local commissions for discipline inspection shall carry out constant education among Party members on their duty to observe Party discipline; they shall adopt decisions for the upholding of Party discipline, examine and deal with relatively important or complicated cases of violation of the Constitution and discipline of the party or the laws and decrees of the state by Party organizations or Party members; decide on or cancel disciplinary measures against Party members involved in such cases; and deal with complaints and appeals made by Party members.

The central and local commissions for discipline inspection should report to the Party committees at the corresponding levels on the results of their handling of cases of special importance or complexity, as well as on the problems encountered. Local commissions for discipline inspection should also present such reports to the higher commissions.

If the Central Commission for Discipline Inspection discovers any violation of Party discipline by any member of the Central Committee, it may report such an offence to the Central Committee, and the Central Committee must deal with the case promptly.

Article 45   Higher commissions for discipline inspection have the power to check up on the work of the lower commissions and to approve or modify their decisions on any case. If decisions so modified have already been ratified by the Party committee at the corresponding level, the modification must be approved by the next higher Party committee.

If a local commission for discipline inspection does not agree with a decision made by the Party committee at the corresponding level in dealing with a case, it may request the commission at the next higher level to re-examine the case; if a local commission discovers cases of violation of Party discipline or the laws and decrees of the state by the Party committee at the corresponding level or by its members, and if that Party committee fails to deal with them properly or at all, it has the right to appeal to the higher commissions for assistance in dealing with such cases.

CHAPTER IX
LEADING PARTY
MEMBERS' GROUPS

Article 46   A leading Party members' group shall be formed in the leading body of a central or local state organ, people's organization, economic or cultural institution or other non-Party unit. The main tasks of such a group are: to see to it that the Party's principles and policies are implemented, to unite with the non-Party cadres and masses in fulfilling the tasks assigned by the Party and the state, and to guide the work of the Party organization of the unit.

Article 47   The members of a leading Party members' group are appointed by the Party committee that approves its establishment. The group shall have a secretary and deputy secretaries.

A leading Party members' group must accept the leadership of the Party committee that approves its establishment.

Article 48   The Central Committee of the Party shall determine specifically the functions, powers and tasks of the leading Party members' groups in those government departments which need to exercise highly centralized and unified leadership over subordinate units; it shall also determine whether such groups should be replaced by Party committees.

CHAPTER X
RELATIONSHIP BETWEEN
THE PARTY
AND THE COMMUNIST
YOUTH LEAGUE

Article 49   The Communist Youth League of China is a mass organization of advanced young people under the leadership of the Communist Party of China; it is a school where large numbers of young people will learn about communism through practice; it is the Party's assistant and reserve force. The Central Committee of the Communist Youth League functions under the leadership of the Central Committee of the Party. The local organizations of the Communist Youth League are under the leadership of the Party committees at the corresponding levels and of the higher organizations of the League itself.

Article 50   Party committees at all levels must strengthen their leadership over the Communist Youth League organizations and pay attention to the selection and training of League cadres. The Party must firmly support the Communist Youth League in the lively and creative performance of its work to suit the characteristics and needs of young people, and give full play to the League's role as a shock force and as a bridge linking the Party with the broad masses of young people.

Those secretaries of League committees, at or below the county level or in enterprises and institutions, who are Party members may attend meetings of Party committees at the corresponding levels and of their standing committees as non-voting participants.

Joint Communiqué

by China

and the United States[*]

Appendix C

Peking Review, 9 (March 3, 1972), 4–5.

(The Chinese and American sides reached agreement on a joint communiqué on February 27 in Shanghai. Full text of the communiqué is as follows.)

President Richard Nixon of the United States of America visited the People's Republic of China at the invitation of Premier Chou En-lai of the People's Republic of China from February 21 to February 28, 1972. Accompanying the President were Mrs. Nixon, U.S. Secretary of State William Rogers, Assistant to the President Dr. Henry Kissinger, and other American officials.

President Nixon met with Chairman Mao Tsetung of the Communist Party of China on February 21. The two leaders had a serious and frank exchange of views on Sino-U.S. relations and world affairs.

During the visit, extensive, earnest and frank discussions were held between President Nixon and Premier Chou En-lai on the normalization of relations between the United States of America and the People's Republic of China, as well as on other matters of interest to both sides. In addition, Secretary of State William Rogers and Foreign Minister Chi Peng-fei held talks in the same spirit.

President Nixon and his party visited Peking and viewed cultural, industrial, and agricultural sites, and they also toured Hangchow and Shanghai where, continuing discussions with Chinese leaders, they viewed similar places of interest.

The leaders of the People's Republic of China and the United States of America found it beneficial to have this opportunity, after so many years without contact, to present candidly to one another their views on a variety of issues. They reviewed the international situation in which important changes and great upheavals are taking place and expounded their respective positions and attitudes.

The Chinese side stated: Wherever there is oppression, there is resistance. Countries want independence, nations want liberation and the people want revolution—this has become the irresistible trend of history. All nations, big or small, should be equal; big nations should not bully the small and strong nations should not bully the weak. China will never be a superpower and it opposes hegemony and power politics of any kind. The Chinese side stated that it firmly supports the struggles of all the oppressed people and nations for freedom and liberation and that the people of all countries have the right to choose their social systems according to their own wishes and the right to safeguard the independence, sovereignty, and territorial integrity of their own countries and oppose foreign aggression, interference, control, and subversion. All foreign troops should be withdrawn to their own countries. The Chinese side expressed its firm support to the peoples of Vietnam, Laos, and Cambodia in their efforts for the attainment of their goal and its firm support to the seven-point proposal of the Provisional Revolutionary Government of the Republic of South Vietnam and the elaboration of February this year on the two key problems in the proposal, and to the Joint Declaration of the Summit Conference of the Indochinese Peoples. It firmly supports the eight-point program for the peaceful unification of Korea put forward by the government of the Democratic people's Republic of Korea on April 12, 1971, and the stand for the abolition of the UN Commission for the Unification and Rehabilitation of Korea. It firmly opposes the revival and outward expansion of Japanese militarism, and firmly supports the Japanese people's desire to build an independent, democratic, peaceful, and neutral Japan. It firmly maintains that India and Pakistan should, in accordance with the United Nations resolutions on the India-Pakistan question, immediately withdraw all their forces to their respective territories and to their own sides of the ceasefire line in Jammu and Kashmir, and firmly supports the Pakistan Government and people in their struggle to preserve their independence and sovereignty and the people of Jammu and Kashmir in their struggle for the right of self-determination.

The U.S. side stated: Peace in Asia and peace in the world requires efforts both to reduce immediate tensions and to eliminate the basic causes of conflict. The United

States will work for a just and secure peace: just, because it fulfills the aspirations of peoples and nations for freedom and progress; secure, because it removes the danger of foreign aggression. The United States supports individual freedom and social progress for all the peoples of the world, free of outside pressure or intervention. The United States believes that the effort to reduce tensions is served by improving communication between countries that have different ideologies so as to lessen the risks of confrontation through accident, miscalculation, or misunderstanding. Countries should treat each other with mutual respect and be willing to compete peacefully, letting performances be the ultimate judge. No country should claim infallibility and each country should be prepared to reexamine its own attitudes for the common good. The United States stressed that the peoples of Indochina should be allowed to determine their destiny without outside intervention; its constant primary objective has been a negotiated solution; the eight-point proposal put forward by the Republic of Vietnam and the United States on January 27, 1972 represents a basis for the attainment of that objective; in the absence of a negotiated settlement, the United States envisages the ultimate withdrawal of all U.S. forces from the region, consistent with the aim of self-determination for each country of Indochina. The United States will maintain its close ties with and support for the Republic of Korea; the United States will support efforts of the Republic of Korea to seek a relaxation of tension and increased communication in the Korean peninsula. The United States places the highest value on its friendly relations with Japan; it will continue to develop the existing close bonds. Consistent with the United Nations Security Council Resolution of December 21, 1971, the United States favors the continuation of the ceasefire between India and Pakistan and the withdrawal of all military forces to within their own territories and to their sides of the ceasefire line in Jammu and Kashmir; the United States supports the right of the people of South Asia to shape their own future in peace, free of military threat, and without having the area become the subject of great power rivalry.

There are essential differences between China and the United States in their social systems and foreign policies. However, the two sides agreed that countries, regardless of their social systems, should conduct their relations on the principles of respect for the sovereignty and territorial integrity of all states, nonaggression against other states, noninterference in the internal affairs of other states, equality and mutual benefit, and peaceful coexistence. International disputes should be settled on this basis, without resorting to the use or threat of force. The United States and the People's Republic of China are prepared to apply these principles to their mutual relations.

With these principles of international relations in mind, the two sides stated that:

— progress toward the normalization of relations between China and the United States is in the interests of all countries;

— both wish to reduce the danger of international military conflict;

— neither should seek hegemony in the Asia-Pacific region and each is opposed to efforts by any other country or group of countries to establish such hegemony; and

— neither is prepared to negotiate on behalf of any third party or to enter into agreements or understandings with the other directed at other states.

Both sides are of the view that it would be against the interests of the peoples of the world for any major country to collude with another against other countries, or for major countries to divide up the world into spheres of interest.

The two sides reviewed the long-standing serious disputes between China and the United States. The Chinese side reaffirmed its position: The Taiwan question is the crucial question obstructing the normalization of relations between China and the United States; the government of the People's Republic of China is the sole legal government of China; Taiwan is a province of China which has long been returned to the motherland; the liberation of Taiwan is China's internal affair in which no other country has the right to interfere; and all U.S. forces and military installations must be withdrawn from Taiwan. The Chinese government firmly opposes any activities which aim at the creation of "one China, one Taiwan," "one China, two governments," "two Chinas," and "independent Taiwan," or advocate that the "status of Taiwan remains to be determined."

The U.S. side declared: The United States acknowledges that all Chinese on either side of the Taiwan Strait maintain that there is but one China and that Taiwan is a part of China. The United States Government does not challenge that position. It reaffirms its interest in a peaceful settlement of the Taiwan question by the Chinese themselves. With this prospect in mind, it affirms the ultimate objective of the withdrawal of all U.S. forces and military installations from Taiwan. In the meantime, it will progressively reduce its forces and military installations on Taiwan as the tension in the area diminishes.

The two sides agreed that it is desirable to broaden the understanding between the two peoples. To this end, they discussed specific areas in such fields as science, technology, culture, sports, and journalism, in which people-to-people contacts and exchanges would be mutually beneficial. Each side undertakes to facilitate the further development of such contacts and exchanges.

Both sides view bilateral trade as another area from which mutual benefit can be derived, and agreed that economic relations based on equality and mutual benefit are in the interest of the peoples of the two countries. They agree to facilitate the progressive development of trade between their two countries.

The two sides agreed that they will stay in contact through various channels, including the sending of a senior U.S. representative to Peking from time to time for concrete consultations to further the normalization of relations between the two countries and continue to exchange views on issues of common interest.

The two sides expressed the hope that the gains achieved during this visit would open up new prospects for the relations between the two countries. They believe that the normalization of relations between the two countries is not only in the interest of the Chinese and American people but also contributes to the relaxation of tension in Asia and the world.

President Nixon, Mrs. Nixon, and the American party expressed their appreciation for the gracious hospitality shown them by the government and people of the People's Republic of China.

Feburary 28, 1972

The Chinese Foreign Ministry's Note to the Soviet Embassy in China*

Appendix D

*Peking Review, 13 (March 31, 1978), 17–18.

(Yu Chan, vice-minister of the Chinese Foreign Ministry, entrusted by the Standing Committee of the Chinese National People's Congress, on March 9 delivered to the Soviet Ambassador to China, Vasily S. Tolstikov, a note of the Chinese Foreign Ministry to the Soviet Embassy in Beijing. The note was a reply to the suggestion of the Soviet side that the two countries issue a joint statement on the principles of mutual relations and that a meeting of representatives of both sides be held for this purpose.

The Soviet suggestion was stated in a letter from the Presidium of the Supreme Soviet of the U.S.S.R. to the Standing Committee of the Chinese N.P.C. The letter was delivered by Viktor F. Maltsev, Soviet first vice-foreign minister, to Tien Tseng-pei, charge d'affaires ad interim of the Chinese Embassy in Moscow, on February 24 this year. A copy of it was delivered by Ambassador Tolstikov to the Chinese Foreign Ministry on February 27.

On March 20 TASS released to the public the text of the letter of the Presidium of the Supreme Soviet. Following is the full text of the Chinese Foreign Ministry's note to the Soviet Embassy in Peking, with that of the Soviet letter as an appendix, which has been published in the Chinese newspapers.)

THE SOVIET EMBASSY IN THE PEOPLE'S REPUBLIC OF CHINA

The Ministry of Foreign Affairs of the People's Republic of China is entrusted by the Standing Committee of the National People's Congress to reply to the letter of February 24, 1978 from the Presidium of the Supreme Soviet of the U.S.S.R. as follows:

China and the Soviet Union used to be friendly neighboring countries, and our two peoples have forged a profound friendship in their long revolutionary struggles. Responsibility for the deterioration of the relations between our two countries to what they are today does not lie with the Chinese side; China is the victim.

It is known to all that there exist differences of principle between China and the Soviet Union. The debate over these differences will go on for a long time. However, proceeding from the fundamental interests of the Chinese and Soviet peoples, the Chinese side has always held that the differences of principle should not impede the maintenance of normal state relations between the two countries on the basis of the Five Principles of Peaceful Coexistence. And to this end it has made unremitting efforts.

In September 1969, the Chinese premier and the Soviet chairman of the Council of Ministers held talks in Peking and reached an understanding on the normalization of relations between the two countries. The Chinese side has ever since abided by this understanding, and for its full implementation has earnestly and patiently held boundary negotiations with the Soviet side for as long as eight years. However, the Soviet side not only is unwilling to implement the understanding reached by the heads of government of the two countries, it even denies the existence of the understanding itself. As a result, the boundary negotiations remain fruitless to this day. In the meantime, the Soviet Union has unceasingly increased its armed forces on the Sino-Soviet border and in the People's Republic of Mongolia, and there is not the slightest change in the Soviet policy of hostility to China. In these circumstances, the Presidium of the Supreme Soviet of the U.S.S.R. has proposed in its letter that the two countries issue a hollow statement on principles guiding mutual relations, a statement which does not solve any practical problem. Its purpose in so doing is obviously not to improve Sino-Soviet relations, but lies elsewhere.

If the Soviet side really desires to improve Sino-Soviet relations, it should take concrete actions that solve practical problems. First of all, it should sign, in accordance with the 1969 understanding between the premiers of the two countries, an agreement on the maintenance of the status quo on the border, averting armed clashes and disengaging the armed forces of the two sides in the disputed border areas, and then proceed to settle through negotiations the boundary questions; and it should withdraw its armed forces from the People's Republic of Mongolia and from the Sino-Soviet border so that the situation there will revert to what it was in the early 60s. When you refuse to take such minimum actions as maintenance of the status quo on the border, averting armed clashes, and disengaging the armed forces of the two sides in the disputed border areas, what practical purpose would it serve to issue a worthless "statement of principles guiding mutual relations" except to deceive the Chinese and Soviet peoples and the world public! When you have a million troops deployed on the Sino-Soviet border, how can you expect the Chinese people to believe that you have a genuine and sincere desire to improve the relations between our two countries? Isn't it fully reasonable to ask you to withdraw your armed forces from the Sino-Soviet border and restore the situation that prevailed in the early 60s?

The normalization of relations between China and the Soviet Union is the common desire of our two peoples and it accords with their fundamental interests and those of the people of the world. For its part, the Chinese side will, as always, make efforts toward the end. What the Chinese side likes to see is real deeds and not hollow statements.

The Ministry of Foreign Affairs avails itself of this opportunity to renew to the Embassy the assurances of its high considerations.

Ministry of Foreign Affairs
of the People's Republic of China

Peking, March 9, 1978

Letter from the Presidium of the U.S.S.R. Supreme Soviet to the Standing Committee of the Chinese N.P.C.

The Standing Committee of the Chinese National People's Congress: Soviet-Chinese relations assumed over the recent years a nature that cannot but cause serious concern. The existing state of affairs leads to the creation of the atmosphere of mutual distrust, to the heightening of tensions in interstate relations. The vital interests of the Soviet and Chinese peoples require adoption of definite practical measures aimed at normalizing Soviet-Chinese relations in accordance with the aspirations and hopes of the peoples of the Soviet Union and the People's Republic of China.

The Soviet government repeatedly advanced concrete proposals aimed at bringing the relations between the U.S.S.R. and the PRC back to the road of good neighborliness, and expressed the U.S.S.R.'s readiness to normalize relations with China on the principles of peaceful coexistence. The government of the People's Republic of China for its part had officially stated that the PRC could build relations with the U.S.S.R. on the principles of peaceful coexistence. The Soviet people sincerely wish to see China a friendly prosperous power.

The Presidium of the U.S.S.R. Supreme Soviet, expressing the will and aspirations of the Soviet people, is once again stating its readiness to put an end to the present abnormal situation in the relations between the U.S.S.R. and the PRC and to stop the dangerous process of further aggravation of relations which may lead to serious negative consequences for our countries and peoples, for the destinies of peace in the Far East, in Asia, and throughout the world.

In order to materialize the desire expressed by the two sides to base their relations on the principles of peaceful co-existence and embody it in a tangible international act, the Presidium of the U.S.S.R. Supreme Soviet is suggesting that our countries come forward with a joint statement on the principles of mutual relations between the Union of Soviet Socialist Republics and the People's Republic of China. It is believed in the Soviet Union that a joint statement that the sides will build their relations on the basis of peaceful coexistence, firmly adhering to the principles of equality, mutual respect for sovereignty and territorial integrity, noninterference in the internal affairs of each other, and nonuse of force could advance the cause of normalization of our relations.

We suggest that, if the very idea of making such a statement is acceptable for the Chinese side, a meeting of representatives of both sides should be held at a sufficiently high level to agree on a mutually acceptable text of the statement in the shortest possible time.

The Soviet Union is prepared to receive representatives of the People's Republic of China. If the Chinese side deems it expedient that Soviet representatives should arrive for the aforementioned purpose in Peking, we agree to this. On our part, we are prepared to consider proposals of the PRC aimed at normalization of Soviet-Chinese relations.

The Presidium of the U.S.S.R.
Supreme Soviet

February 24, 1978

Treaty of Peace and Friendship Between the People's Republic of China and Japan*

Appendix E

*Peking Review, 33 (August 18, 1978), 7–8.

The People's Republic of China and Japan,

Recalling with satisfaction that since the government of the People's Republic of China and the government of Japan issued a joint statement in Peking on September 29, 1972, the friendly relations between the two governments and the peoples of the two countries have developed greatly on a new basis,

Confirming that the abovementioned joint statement constitutes the basis of the relations of peace and friendship between the two countries and that the principles enunciated in the joint statement should be strictly observed.

Confirming that the principles of the charter of the United Nations should be fully respected,

Hoping to contribute to peace and stability in Asia and in the world,

For the purpose of solidifying and developing the relations of peace and friendship between the two countries.

Have resolved to conclude a treaty of peace and friendship and for that purpose have appointed as their plenipotentiaries:

The People's Republic of China: Huang Hua, Minister of Foreign Affairs
Japan: Sunao Sonoda, Minister for Foreign Affairs

Who, having communicated to each other their full powers, found to be in good and due form, have agreed as follows:

Article I   1. The contracting parties shall develop durable relations of peace and friendship between the two countries on the basis of the principles of mutual respect for sovereignty and territorial integrity, mutual nonaggression, noninterference in each other's internal affairs, equality and mutual benefit, and peaceful co-existence.

2. In keeping with the foregoing principles and the principles of the United Nations Charter, the contracting parties affirm that in their mutual relations, all disputes shall be settled by peaceful means without resorting to the use or threat of force.

Article II   The contracting parties declare that neither of them should seek hegemony in the Asia-Pacific region or in any other region and that each is opposed to efforts by any other country or group of countries to establish such hegemony.

Article III   The contracting parties shall, in a good-neighborly and friendly spirit and in conformity with the principles of equality and mutual benefit and noninterference in each other's internal affairs, endeavor to further develop economic and cultural relations between the two countries and to promote exchanges between the peoples of the two countries.

Article IV   The present treaty shall not affect the position of either contracting party regarding its relations with third countries.

Article V   1. The present treaty shall be ratified and shall enter into force on the date of the exchange of instruments of ratification which shall take place at Tokyo. The present treaty shall remain in force for ten years and thereafter shall continue to be in force until terminated in accordance with the provisions of Paragraph 2 of this Article.

2. Either contracting party may, by giving one year's written notice to the other contracting party, terminate the present treaty at the end of the initial ten-year period or at any time thereafter.

In witness whereof the respective plenipotentiaries have signed the present treaty and have affixed thereto their seals.

Done in duplicate in the Chinese and Japanese languages, both texts being equally authentic, at Peking, this twelfth day of August 1978.

For the People's Republic   For Japan:
of China:
Huang Hua   Sunao Sonoda
(Signed)   (Signed)

Establishment of Diplomatic Relations between the People's Republic of China and the U.S.A.

Appendix

1. Joint Communiqué on the Establishment of Diplomatic Relations between the People's Republic of China and the United States of America[1]

The People's Republic of China and the United States of America have agreed to recognize each other and to establish diplomatic relations as of January 1, 1979.

The United States of America recognizes the government of the People's Republic of China as the sole legal government of China. Within this context, the people of the United States will maintain cultural, commercial, and other unofficial relations with the people of Taiwan.

The People's Republic of China and the United States of America reaffirm the principles agreed on by the two sides in the Shanghai communiqué and emphasize once again that:

— Both wish to reduce the danger of international military confict.

— Neither should seek hegemony in the Asia-Pacific region or in any other region of the world and each is opposed to efforts by any other country or group of countries to establish such hegemony.

— Neither is prepared to negotiate on behalf of any third party or to enter into agreements or understandings with the other directed at other states.

— The government of the United States of America acknowledges the Chinese position that there is but one China and Taiwan is part of China.

— Both believe that normalization of Sino-American relations is not only in the interest of the Chinese and American peoples, but also contributes to the cause of peace in Asia and the world.

The People's Republic of China and the United States of America will exchange ambassadors and establish embassies on March 1, 1979.

2. Statement of the Government of the People's Republic of China[2]

The government of the People's Republic of China on December 16 issued a statement on the establishment of diplomatic relations between China and the United States. The full text of the statement reads as follows:

As of January 1, 1979, the People's Republic of China and the United States of America recognize each other and establish diplomatic relations, thereby ending the prolonged abnormal relationship between them. This is a historic event in Sino-U.S. relations.

As is known to all, the government of the People's Republic of China is the sole legal government of China and Taiwan is a part of China. The question of Taiwan was the crucial issue obstructing the normalization of relations between China and the United States. It has now been resolved between the two countries in the spirit of the Shanghai communiqué and through their joint efforts, thus enabling the normalization of relations so ardently desired by the people of the two countries. As for the way of bringing Taiwan back to the embrace of the motherland and reunifying the country, it is entirely China's internal affair.

[1]*Peking Review,* 51 (December 22, 1978), 8.
[2]*Peking Review,* 51 (December 22, 1978), 8.

At the invitation of the U.S. government, Deng Xiaoping, vice premier of the State Council of the People's Republic of China, will pay an official visit to the United States in January 1979, with a view to further promoting the friendship between the two peoples and good relations between the two countries.

3. President Carter's Address to the Nation, Announcing Establishment of Diplomatic Relations between the United States and the People's Republic of China, December 15, 1978[3]

I would like to read a joint comminiqué which is being issued simultaneously in Peking at this moment by the leaders of the People's Republic of China:

"Joint comminiqué on the establishment of diplomatic relations between the United States of America and the People's Republic of China, January 1, 1979.

"The United States of America and the People's Republic of China have agreed to recognize each other and to establish diplomatic relations as of January 1, 1979.

"The United States of America recognizes the government of the People's Republic of China as the sole legal government of China. Within this context, the people of the United States will maintain cultural, commercial, and other unofficial relations with the people of Taiwan.

"The United States of America and the People's Republic of China reaffirm the principles agreed on by the two sides in the Shanghai communiqué and emphasize once again that:

"Both wish to reduce the danger of international military conflict.

"Neither should seek hegemony in the Asia-Pacific region or in any other region of the world and each is opposed to efforts by any other country or group of countries to establish such hegemony.

"Neither is prepared to negotiate on behalf of any third party or to enter into agreements or understanding with the other directed at other states.

"The United States of America acknowledges the Chinese position that there is but one China and Taiwan is part of China.

"Both believe that normalization of Sino-American relations is not only in the interest of the Chinese and American peoples but also contributes to the cause of peace in Asia and in the world.

"The United States of America and the People's Republic of China will exchange ambassadors and establish embassies on March 1, 1979."

Yesterday, the United States of America and the People's Republic of China reached this final historic agreement.

On January 1, 1979, our two governments will implement full normalization of diplomatic relations.

As a nation of gifted people who comprise one-fourth of the population of the earth, China plays an important role in world affairs—a role that can only grow more important in the years ahead.

We do not undertake this important step for transient tactical or expedient reasons. In recognizing that the government of the People's Republic is the single gov-

---

[3]*U.S. Policy Toward China: July 15, 1971—January 15, 1979,* Selected Documents, No. 9. Bureau of Public Affairs, The Department of State, Washington, D.C., January 1979, pp. 45–46.

ernment of China, we are recognizing simple reality. But far more is involved in this decision than a recognition of reality.

Before the estrangement of recent decades, the American and Chinese people had a long history of friendship. We have already begun to rebuild some of those previous ties. Now, our rapidly expanding relationship requires the kind of structures that diplomatic relations will make possible.

The change I am announcing tonight will be of long-term benefit to the people of both the United States and China—and I believe, to all the peoples of the world.

Normalization—and the expanded commercial and cultural relations it will bring with it—will contribute to the well-being of our own nation and will enhance stability in Asia.

These more positive relations with China can beneficially affect the world in which we and our children will live.

We have already begun to inform our allies and the Congress of the details of our intended action. But I wish also to convey a special message to the people of Taiwan, with whom the American people have had and will have extensive close and friendly relations.

As the United States asserted in the Shanghai communiqué in 1972, we will continue to have an interest in the peaceful resolution of the Taiwan issue.

I have paid special attention to insuring that normalization of relations between the United States and the People's Republic will not jeopardize the well-being of the people of Taiwan.

The people of the United States will maintain our current commercial, cultural, and other relations with Taiwan through nongovernmental means. Many other countries are already successfully doing this.

These decisions and actions open a new and important chapter in world affairs.

To strengthen and to expedite the benefits of this new relationship between the People's Republic of China and the United States, I am pleased to announce that Vice Premier Deng has accepted my invitation to visit Washington at the end of January. His visit will give our governments the opportunity to consult with each other on global issues and to begin working together to enhance the cause of world peace.

These events are the result of long and serious negotiations begun by President Nixon in 1972, and continued by President Ford. The results bear witness to the steady, determined bipartisan effort of our own country to build a world in which peace will be the goal and responsibility of all countries.

The normalization of relations between the United States and China has no other purpose than this: the advance of peace.

It is in this spirit, at this season of peace, that I take special pride in sharing this news with you tonight.

4. Text of U.S. Statement, December 15, 1978[4]

As of January 1, 1979, the United States of America recognizes the People's Republic of China as the sole legal government of China. On the same date, the People's Republic of China accords similar recognition to the United States of America. The United States thereby establishes diplomatic relations with the People's Republic of China.

On the same date, January 1, 1979, the United States of America will notify

---

[4]*U.S. Policy Toward China: July 15, 1971—January 15, 1979,* Selected Documents No. 9, Bureau of Public Affairs, The Department of State, Washington, D.C., January 1979, p. 48.

Taiwan that it is terminating diplomatic relations and that the Mutual Defense Treaty between the United States and the Republic of China is being terminated in accordance with the provisions of the treaty. The United States also states that it will be withdrawing its remaining military personnel from Taiwan within four months.

In the future, the American people and the people of Taiwan will maintain commercial, cultural, and other relations without official government representation and without diplomatic relations.

The administration will seek adjustment to our laws and regulations to permit the maintenance of commercial, cultural, and other nongovernmental relations in the new circumstances that will exist after normalization.

The United States is confident that the people of Taiwan face a peaceful and prosperous future. The United States continues to have an interest in the peaceful resolution of the Taiwan issue and expects that the Taiwan issue will be settled peacefully by the Chinese themselves.

The United States believes that the establishment of diplomatic relations with the People's Republic will contribute to the welfare of the American people, to the stability of Asia where the United States has major security and economic interest, and to the peace of the entire world.

U.S.-China Joint

Communiqué,

August 17, 1982*

Appendix G

*Current Policy No. 413, August 1982. U.S. Department of State, Bureau of Public Affairs, Washington, D.C.

1. In the Joint Communiqué on the Establishment of Diplomatic Relations on January 1, 1979, issued by the Government of the United States of America and the Government of the People's Republic of China, the United States of America recognized the Government of the people's Republic of China as the sole legal government of China, and it acknowledged the Chinese position that there is but one China and Taiwan is part of China. Within that context, the two sides agreed that the people of the United States would continue to maintain cultural, commercial, and other unofficial relations with the people of Taiwan. On this basis, relations between the United States and China were normalized.

2. The question of United States arms sales to Taiwan was not settled in the course of negotiations between the two countries on establishing diplomatic relations. The two sides held differing positions, and the Chinese side stated that it would raise the issue again following normalization. Recognizing that this issue would seriously hamper the development of the United States-China relations, they have held further discussions on it, during and since the meetings between President Ronald Reagan and Premier Zhao Ziyang and between Secretary of State Alexander M. Haig, Jr., and Vice Premier and Foreign Minister Huang Hua in October, 1981.

3. Respect for each other's sovereignty and territorial integrity and non-interference in each other's internal affairs constitute the fundamental principles guiding United States-China relations. These principles were confirmed in the Shanghai Communiqué of February 28, 1972 and reaffirmed in the Joint Communiqué on the Establishment of Diplomatic Relations which came into effect on Janaury 1, 1979. Both sides emphatically state that these principles continue to govern all aspects of their relations.

4. The Chinese Government reiterates that the question of Taiwan is China's internal affair. The Message to Compatriots in Taiwan issued by China on January 1, 1979 promulgated a fundamental policy of striving for peaceful reunification of the Motherland. The Nine-Point Proposal put forward by China on September 30, 1981 represented a further major effort under this fundamental policy to strive for a peaceful solution to the Taiwan question.

5. The United States Government attaches great importance to its relations with China, and reiterates that it has no intention of infringing on Chinese sovereignty and territorial integrity, or interfering in China's internal affairs, or pursuing a policy of "two Chinas" or "one China, one Taiwan." The United States Government understands and appreciates the Chinese policy of striving for a peaceful resolution of the Taiwan question as indicated in China's Message to Compatriots in Taiwan issued on January 1, 1979 and the Nine-Point proposal put forward by China on September 30, 1981. The new situation which has emerged with regard to the Taiwan question also provides favorable conditions for the settlement of United States-China differences over the question of United States arms sales to Taiwan.

6. Having in mind the foregoing statements of both sides, the United States Government states that it does not seek to carry out a long-term policy of arms sales to Taiwan, that its arms sales to Taiwan will not exceed, either in qualitative or in quantitative terms, the level of those supplied in recent years since the establishment of diplomatic relations between the United States and China, and that it intends to reduce gradually its sales of arms to Taiwan, leading over a period of time to a final resolution. In so stating, the United States acknowledges China's consistent position regarding the thorough settlement of this issue.

7. In order to bring about, over a period of time, a final settlement of the question of United States arms sales to Taiwan, which is an issue rooted in history, the two governments will make every effort to adopt measures and create conditions conducive to the thorough settlement of this issue.

8. The development of United States-China relations is not only in the interests

of the two peoples but also conducive to peace and stability in the world. The two sides are determined, on the principle of equality and mutual benefit, to strengthen their ties in the economic, cultural, educational, scientific, technological and other fields and make strong, joint efforts for the continued development of relations between the governments and peoples of the United States and China.

9. In order to bring about the healthy development of United States-China relations, maintain world peace and oppose aggression and expansion, the two governments reaffirm the principles agreed on by the two sides in the Shanghai Communiqué and the Joint Communiqué on the Establishment of Diplomatic Relations. The two sides will maintain contact and hold appropriate consultations on bilateral and international issues of common interest.

Index